Fire and Sword in the Sudan

Rudolph C. Slatin Pasha

Fire and Sword in the Sudan
Personal Recollections of Both Fighting
and Serving the Mahdists During the Later
19th Century

Rudolf C. Slatin Pasha
Translated by F. R. Wingate

Fire and Sword in the Sudan
Personal Recollections of Both Fighting and Serving the Mahdists During the Later 19th Century
by Rudolf C. Slatin Pasha
Translated by F. R. Wingate

First published under the title
Fire and Sword in the Sudan

Leonaur is an imprint of Oakpast Ltd
Copyright in this form © 2013 Oakpast Ltd

ISBN: 978-1-78282-114-4 (hardcover)
ISBN: 978-1-78282-115-1 (softcover)

http://www.leonaur.com

Publisher's Notes

The views expressed in this book are not necessarily those of the publisher.

Contents

Preface	9
Notes	11
My First Journey to the Sudan	15
Residence in Darfur, and Early History of the Province	39
The Government of Darfur	89
The Khalifa's Personal Account of the Rise of the Mahdi	117
Spread of the Revolt in Southern Darfur	138
The Siege and Fall of El Obeid	157
Vain Efforts to Stem the Tide of Mahdism in Darfur	165
Hicks Pasha's Expedition	205
The Fall of Darfur	220
The Siege and Fall of Khartum	248
Early Rule of Khalifa Abdullahi	326
Events in Various Parts of the Sudan	354
The Abyssinian Campaign	380
Mahdist Occupation of the Southern Provinces	405
Dissension and Discord	414
Miscellaneous Remarks	443
Miscellaneous Remarks (Continued)	468

Plans for Escape	495
My Flight	507
Conclusion	533

To
Her Most Gracious Majesty
The Queen of Great Britain and Ireland
And
Empress of India
Who Has Ever Shown Deep Solicitude for and Gracious
Sympathy With the European Prisoners
In the Sudan
This Record of His Life in Captivity
Is by Permission Humbly Dedicated by Her Majesty's
Most Devoted and Grateful

Rudolf C. Slatin

Preface

Prompted by the earnest entreaties of my friends rather than by any wish of my own to relate my experiences, I have written these chapters.

The few months which have elapsed since my escape have been so much occupied in resuming my official duties, compiling reports, and satisfying the kindly interest displayed by a large number of people in my strange fate, that any attempt at quiet and steady literary work has been almost impossible.

During my captivity I was unable to make any notes or keep any diaries; in writing, therefore, the following pages, I have been dependent entirely on my memory, whilst the whirl of the busy European world and the constant interruptions to which I have alluded, have given me little time to collect my scattered thoughts.

When, therefore, after having been debarred for so many years from intercourse with outside affairs, and entirely out of practice in writing down my ideas, I find myself urged to lose no time in publishing an account of my adventures, I must beg my readers to excuse the many defects they may notice.

My experiences have no pretence to being of any literary or scientific value, and the personal episodes I have described can lay claim to little importance; I have merely attempted to give to those interested in Sudan affairs a true and faithful account of my life whilst fighting and serving the Mahdists.

Rudolf Slatin.

London, October, 1895.

Notes

INTRODUCTORY NOTE
By Father Don Joseph Ohrwalder,

Late priest of the Austrian Mission Station at Delen, in Kordofan, and for ten years a captive in the Mahdi's Camp.

The joy at meeting my dear friend and former comrade in captivity, Slatin Pasha, in Cairo, after his miraculous escape, was indeed great; and it is with extreme gratification that I comply with the wishes of those friends who are interested in his experiences, to preface them with a few remarks.

To have been a fellow-sufferer with him for many years, during which the closest friendship existed between us,—a friendship which, owing to the circumstances of our captivity, was necessarily of a surreptitious nature, but which, interrupted as it was, mutually helped to alleviate our sad lot,—is I think a sufficiently good reason for my friends to urge that I should comply with their wishes.

Apart, however, from these purely personal motives, I need only refer to the fact that the small scraps of information which from time to time reached the outside world regarding Slatin Pasha, excited the deepest sympathy for his sad fate; what wonder, then, that there should have been a genuine outburst of rejoicing when he at length escaped from the clutches of the tyrannical *khalifa*, and emerged safely from the dark Sudan?

It is most natural that all those interested in the weal and woe of Africa should await with deep interest all that Slatin Pasha can tell them of affairs in the former Egyptian Sudan, which only a few short years ago was considered the starting point for the civilisation of the Dark Continent, and which now, fallen, alas! under the despotic rule of a barbarous tyrant, forms the chief impediment to the civilising influences so vigorously at work in all other parts of Africa.

Slatin Pasha pleads with perfect justice that, deprived all these years of intellectual intercourse, he cannot do justice to the subject; nevertheless, I consider that it is his bounden duty to describe without delay his strange experiences, and I do not doubt that—whatever literary defects there may be in his work—the story of his life cannot fail to be both of interest and of value in helping those concerned in the future of this vast country to realise accurately its present situation.

It should be remembered that Slatin Pasha held high posts in the Sudan, he has travelled throughout the length and breadth of the country and—a perfect master of the language—he has had opportunities which few others have had to accurately describe affairs such as they were in the last days of the Egyptian Administration; whilst his experiences during his cruel captivity place him in a perfectly unique position as the highest authority on the rise, progress, and wane of that great religious movement which wrenched the country from its conquerors, and dragged it back into an almost indescribable condition of religious and moral decadence.

Thrown into contact with the principal leaders of the revolt, unwillingly forced to appear and live as one of them, he has been in the position of following in the closest manner every step taken by the *Mahdi* and his successor, the *khalifa*, in the administration of their newly founded empire.

Sad fate, it is true, threw me also into the swirl of this great movement; but I was merely a captive missionary, whose very existence was almost forgotten by the rulers of the country, whilst Slatin Pasha was in the vortex itself of this mighty whirlpool which swamped one by one the Egyptian garrisons, and spread far and wide over the entire Sudan.

If, therefore, there should be any discrepancies between the account published some three years ago of my captivity and the present work, the reader may safely accept Slatin Pasha's conclusions as more correct and accurate than my own; the opinions I expressed of the *khalifa's* motives and intentions, and of the principal events which occurred, are rather those of an outsider when compared to the intimate knowledge which Slatin Pasha was enabled to acquire, by reason of his position in continuous and close proximity to Abdullahi.

In concluding, therefore, these remarks, I will add an earnest hope that this book will arouse a deep and wide-spread interest in the fate of the unhappy Sudan, and will help those concerned to come to a right and just decision as to the steps which should be taken to restore to civilisation this once happy and prosperous country.

That the return of Slatin Pasha from, so to speak, a living grave should bring about this restoration, is the fervent prayer of his old comrade in captivity and devoted friend,

Don Joseph Ohrwalder.

Suakin, *June, 1895.*

Translator's Note.

In preparing the edition in English of Slatin Pasha's experiences in the Sudan, I have followed the system adopted in Father Ohrwalder's *Ten Years' Captivity in the Mahdi's Camp.*

F. R. Wingate.

London, October, 1895.

CHAPTER 1

My First Journey to the Sudan

In July, 1878, when serving as lieutenant in H. I. H. the Crown Prince Rudolph's regiment, the 19th Foot, on the Bosnian frontier, I received a letter from General Gordon, inviting me to come to the Sudan and take service with the Egyptian Government, under his direction.

I had previously, in 1874, undertaken a journey to the Sudan, travelling by Assuan, Korosko, and Berber, and had reached Khartum in the month of October of that year; thence I had visited the Nuba mountains, and had remained a short time at Delen, where a station of the Austrian Roman Catholic Mission had just been established. From here I explored the Golfan Naïma and Kadero mountains, and would have made a longer stay in these interesting districts, but the revolt of the Hawazma Arabs broke out, and, being merely a traveller, I received a summons to return forthwith to El Obeid, the chief town of Kordofan. The Arab revolt, which had arisen over the collection of the excessively high taxes imposed by the government, was soon suppressed; but, under the circumstances, I did not think it worthwhile returning to the Nuba districts, and therefore decided to travel in Darfur.

At that time the Governor-General of the Sudan, Ismail Pasha Ayub, was staying at El Fasher, the capital of Darfur; and on reaching Kaga and Katul, I found, to my great disappointment, that an order had just been issued prohibiting strangers from entering the country, as it had been only recently subjugated, and was considered unsafe for travellers. I returned therefore, without further delay, to Khartum; where I made the acquaintance of Emin Pasha (then Dr. Emin), who had arrived a few days previously from Egypt in company with a certain Karl von Grimm.

At that time General Gordon was Governor-General of the Equatorial Provinces, and was residing at Lado; so to him we wrote asking for instructions. Two months afterwards the reply came inviting us to visit Lado; but in the meantime letters had reached me from my family in Vienna urging me to return to Europe. I had been suffering considerably from fever, and besides I was under the obligation of completing my military service the following year. I therefore decided to comply with the wishes of my family.

Dr. Emin, however, accepted Gordon's invitation, and he started soon afterwards for the south, while I left for the north. Before parting, I begged Emin to recommend me to General Gordon, which he did; and this introduction eventually resulted in my receiving the letter to which I have already referred, three years later.

Emin, it will be remembered, was, soon after his arrival at Lado, granted the rank of *Bey*, and appointed Governor of Lado; and on Gordon's departure he was nominated Governor-General of Equatoria, in which position he remained until relieved by Mr. Stanley, in 1889.

I returned to Egypt by the Bayuda Desert, Dongola, and Wadi Haifa, and reached Austria towards the close of 1875.

Gordon's letter, received in the midst of the Bosnian campaign, delighted me; I longed to return to the Sudan in some official capacity; but it was not till December, 1878, when the campaign was over and my battalion had gone into quarters at Pressburg, that I received permission, as an officer of the Reserve, to set out once more for Africa.

My brother Henry was still in Herzegovina; so, remaining only eight days in Vienna, to bid the rest of my family farewell, I left for Trieste on 21st December, 1878, little dreaming that nearly seventeen years would elapse, and that I should experience such strange and terrible adventures, before I should see my home again. I was then twenty-two years of age.

On arrival in Cairo, I received a telegram from Giegler Pasha, from Suez; he had just been appointed Inspector-General of Sudan Telegraphs, and was on his way to Massawa, to inspect the line between that place and Khartum; he invited me to travel with him as far as Suakin, and I gladly availed myself of his kind offer. We parted at Suakin, he proceeding by steamer to Massawa, while I made preparations to cross the desert to Berber on camels. I received every assistance from Ala ed Din Pasha, who was then governor, and who subsequently, as Governor-General of the Sudan, accompanied Hicks Pasha, and was killed with him when the entire Egyptian force was annihilated at Shekan, in November, 1883.

On reaching Berber, I found a *dahabia* awaiting me there by General Gordon's orders, and, embarking immediately, I arrived at Khartum on 15th January, 1879. Here I was shown every kindness and consideration; Gordon placed at my disposal a house situated not far from the palace, and a certain Ali Effendi was directed to attend to all my wants. In the course of our daily meetings, General Gordon used often to talk of the Austrian officers whom he had met at *Tultcha*, when on the Danube Commission, and for whom he entertained a genuine friendship. I remember his saying to me that he thought it was such a mistake to have changed our smart white jackets for the blue uniform we now wear.

Early in February, Gordon appointed me Financial Inspector, and I was instructed to travel about the country and examine into the complaints of the Sudanese who objected to the payment of the taxes, which were not considered unreasonably heavy. In compliance with these orders, I proceeded *via* Mesallamia to Sennar and Fazogl, whence I visited the mountain districts of Kukeli, Regreg, and Kashankero, in the neighbourhood of Beni Shangul; and then I submitted my report to General Gordon.

In this report I pointed out that, in my opinion, the distribution of taxes was unjust, and resulted in the bulk of taxation falling on the poorer landed proprietors, whilst those who were better off had no difficulty in bribing the tax-gatherers, for a comparatively small sum, to secure exemption. Thus enormous quantities of land and property entirely escaped taxation, whilst the poorer classes were mercilessly ground down, in order to make up the heavy deficit which was the result of this most nefarious system.

I further pointed out that much of the present discontent was due to the oppressive and tyrannical methods of the tax-gatherers, who were for the most part soldiers, Bashi-Bozuks, and Shaigias. These unscrupulous officials thought only of how to enrich themselves as quickly as possible at the expense of the unfortunate populations, over whom they exercised a cruel and brutal authority.

In the course of my journey, I frequently observed that the property of the Sudan officials—for the most part Shaigias and Turks—was almost invariably exempted from taxation; and, on inquiry, I was always told that this privilege had been procured, owing to the special services they had rendered the government. When I remarked that they received pay for their services, they appeared greatly offended and annoyed. However, on my arresting some of the principal delinquents, they admitted that their taxes were justly due. In Mesallamia, which is a large town situated between the Blue and White Niles, and a considerable trade centre, I found an immense collection of young women, the property of the wealthiest and most respected merchants, who had procured them and sold them for immoral purposes, at high prices. This was evidently a most lucrative trade; but how were the establishments of these merchants to be taxed, and what action was I to take? I confess that ideas and experience on this point quite failed me; and feeling my utter inability under these circumstances to effect any reform, and having at the same time little or no financial experience, I felt it was useless to continue, and therefore sent in my resignation.

Meanwhile, Gordon had gone off to Darfur, with the object of inquiring into the circumstances connected with the campaign against Suleiman, the son of Zubeir Pasha; but before leaving he had promoted Giegler to the rank of *pasha*, intrusting him with the position of acting governor-general during his absence. I therefore took the occasion to send him my report and resignation by the same post, and soon afterwards received a telegram from Gordon, approving my resignation of the position of Financial Inspector.

It was an immense relief to me to be free from this hateful task; I had no qualms of conscience, for I felt my utter inability to cope with the situation, such as I found it,—radically wrong, and corrupt through and through.

A few days later, I received a telegram from Gordon, appointing me Mudir of Dara, comprising the southwestern districts of Darfur, and ordering me to start at once, as I was required to conduct military operations against Sultan Harun, the son of a former *sultan*, and who was bent on endeavouring to wrest back his country from its Egyptian conquerors. Gordon further instructed me to meet him, on his return journey, somewhere between El Obeid and Tura el Hadra, on the White Nile. Having despatched my camels to this spot, where Gordon's steamer was waiting for him, I embarked without further delay, and on landing at Tura el Hadra, I proceeded west, and after two hours' ride reached the telegraph station of Abu Garad, where I learnt that Gordon was only four or five hours distant, and was on his way to the Nile.

I therefore started off again, and in a few hours found him halted under a large tree. He was evidently very tired and exhausted after his long ride, and was suffering from sores on his legs. I had fortunately brought some brandy with me from the stock on board his own steamer, and he was soon sufficiently revived to continue his journey. He asked me to come back with him to Tura el Hadra, to discuss the Darfur situation with him, and to give me the necessary instructions. He also introduced me to two members of his suite, Hassan Pasha Helmi el Juwaizer, formerly Governor-General of Kordofan and Darfur, and to Yusef Pasha esh Shellali, who was the last to join Gessi in his campaign against Suleiman Zubeir and the slave hunters. We were soon in the saddle; but Gordon shot far ahead of us, and we found it impossible to keep up with his rapid pace. We soon reached Tura el Hadra, where the baggage camels, which had previously been sent on ahead, had already arrived.

As the steamers were anchored in midstream, we were rowed out in a boat. I found myself sitting in the stern, next Yusef Pasha esh Shellali, and, as a drinking-cup was near him and I was thirsty, I begged him to dip it into the river, and give me a drink. Gordon, noticing this, turned to me, smiling, and said, in French, "Are you not aware that Yusef Pasha, in spite of his black face, is very much your senior in rank? You are only the Mudir of Dara, and you should not have asked him to give you a drink." I at once apologised in Arabic to Yusef Pasha, adding that I had asked him for the water in a moment of forgetfulness; to which he replied that he was only too pleased to oblige me or anyone else to whom he could be of service.

On reaching the steamers, Gordon and I went on board the *Ismaïlia*, while Yusef Pasha and Hassan Pasha went on the *Bordein*. Gordon explained to me in the fullest detail the state of Darfur, saying that he hoped most sincerely the campaign against Sultan Harun would be brought to a successful close, for the country for years past had been the scene of continuous fighting and bloodshed, and was sorely in need of rest. He also told me that he believed Gessi's campaign against Suleiman Zubeir would soon be over; before long, he must be finally defeated or killed, for he had lost most of his Bazinger troops (rifle-bearing blacks), and it was impossible for him to sustain the continual losses which Gessi had inflicted on him. It was past ten o'clock when he bade me "Goodbye." He had previously ordered the fires to be lighted, as he was starting that night for Khartum, and, as I stepped over the side, he said, in French, "Goodbye, my dear Slatin, and God bless you; I am sure you will do your best under any circumstances. Perhaps I am going back to England, and if so, I hope we may meet there."

These were the last words I ever heard him utter; but who could have imagined the fate that was in store for both of us? I thanked him heartily for his great kindness and help, and on reaching the riverbank, I stopped there for an hour, waiting for the steamer to start. Then I heard the shrill whistle, and the anchor being weighed, and in a few minutes Gordon was out of sight—gone forever!

On the following morning, mounted on the pony which Gordon had given me, and which carried me continuously for upwards of four years, I started off for Abu Garad, and, travelling thence by Abu Shoka and Khussi, reached El Obeid, where I found Dr. Zurbuchen, the Sanitary Inspector. He was about to start for Darfur, and we agreed to keep each other company as far as Dara. We hired baggage camels through the assistance of Ali Bey Sherif, the Governor of Kordofan; and just as we were about to set out, he handed me a telegram which had been sent from Foga, situated on the eastern frontier of Darfur; it was from Gessi, announcing that Suleiman Zubeir had fallen at Gara on 15th July, 1879: thus was Gordon's prediction verified that Suleiman must soon submit or fall.

It may not be out of place here to give a brief account of this campaign; its principal features are probably well known, but it is possible I may be able to throw fresh light on some details which, though almost twenty years have now elapsed, still possess an interest, inasmuch as it was this campaign which was the means of bringing to the front a man whose strange exploits in the far west of Africa are now exercising the various European Powers who are pressing in from the west coast, towards the Lake Chad regions. I refer to Rabeh, or, as I find he is now called, Rabeh Zubeir.

After the conquest of Darfur, Zubeir, who had by this time been appointed Pasha, was instructed by the then Governor of the Sudan, Ismail Pasha, to reside in the Dara and Shakka districts. At this particular period relations between Ismail and Zubeir were strained; the latter had complained of the unnecessarily heavy taxation, and had begged the Khedive's permission to be allowed to come to Cairo to personally assure His Highness of his loyalty and devotion. Permission had been granted, and he had left for Cairo. Soon afterwards Ismail Pasha Ayub also left Darfur, and Hassan Pasha el Juwaizer succeeded him as governor; while Suleiman, the son of Zubeir, was nominated as his father's representative, and was instructed to proceed to Shakka. Gordon, it will be remembered, had also succeeded Ismail Ayub as Governor-General, and had paid a visit of inspection to Darfur with the object of quieting the country, and introducing, by his presence and supervision, a more stable form of government.

On 7th June, 1878, Gordon arrived at Foga, and from there sent instructions to Suleiman Zubeir to meet him at Dara. Previous to this, information had reached him that Suleiman was not satisfied with his position, and was much disturbed by the news that his father was detained in Cairo by order of the government.

It is said that Zubeir had sent letters to his son urging on him and his followers that, under any circumstances, they should be independent of the Egyptian Government; and as it was well known that Suleiman's object was to maintain his father's authority in the country, his discontent was a factor which it was not possible to ignore.

From Foga, Gordon proceeded by Om Shanga to El Fasher, where he inspected the district and gave instructions for a fort to be built; and after a few days' stay there he came on to Dara, where Suleiman, with upwards of four thousand well-armed Bazingers, had already arrived, and was encamped in the open plain lying to the south of the fort. Conflicting opinions prevailed in Suleiman's camp in regard to the order that they were to move to Shakka. Most of his men had taken part in the conquest of Darfur, and consequently imagined that they had a sort of prescriptive right to the country, and they did not at all fancy handing over these fertile districts to the Turkish and Egyptian officials; moreover, Suleiman and his own immediate household were incensed against what they considered the unjust detention of Zubeir Pasha in Cairo, and it was evident they were doing all in their power to secure his return.

It must also be borne in mind that most of Zubeir's chiefs were of his own tribe—the Jaalin—and had formerly been slave-hunters. By a combination of bravery and good luck they had succeeded in taking possession of immense tracts of land in the Bahr el Ghazal province, and here they had exercised an almost independent and arbitrary authority; nor was this a matter of surprise when the uncivilised condition of both the country and its inhabitants is taken into consideration. They had acquired their position by plundering and violence, and their authority was maintained by the same methods. When, therefore, they learnt that Gordon was coming, they discussed amongst themselves what line of action they should take. Some of the more turbulent members were for at once attacking Dara, which would have been a matter of no difficulty for them; others advised seizing Gordon and his escort, and then exchanging him for Zubeir:

should he resist and be killed in consequence, then so much the better. A few, however, counselled submission and compliance with the orders of the government.

In the midst of all this discussion and difference of opinion, Gordon, travelling by Keriut and Shieria, had halted at a spot about four hours' march from Dara, and, having instructed his escort to follow him as usual, he and his secretaries, Tohami and Busati Bey, started in advance on camels. Hearing of his approach, Suleiman had given instructions to his troops to deploy in three lines between the camp and the fort; and while this operation was being carried out, Gordon, coming from the rear of the troops, passed rapidly through the lines, riding at a smart trot, and, saluting the troops right and left, reached the fort.

The suddenness of Gordon's arrival left the leaders no time to make their plans. They therefore ordered the general salute; but even before the thunder of the guns was heard, Gordon had already sent orders to Suleiman and his chiefs to appear instantly before him. The first to comply with this peremptory summons was Nur Angara; he was quickly followed by Said Hussein and Suleiman. The latter was not slow to perceive that the favourable moment had passed, and, therefore, at the head of a number of his leaders, presented himself before the ubiquitous governor-general.

After the usual compliments, Gordon ordered cigarettes and coffee to be handed round, and he then inquired after their affairs, and promised that he would do all in his power to satisfy everyone; he then dismissed them, and told them to return to their men. But he motioned Suleiman to remain; and when alone, told him that he had heard there was some idea amongst his men of opposing the government: he therefore urged him not to listen to evil counsellors. He gave him clearly to understand that it would be infinitely more to his advantage to comply with the orders of government than to attempt offensive measures, which must eventually end in his ruin; and after some further conversation, in which Gordon to some extent excused the enormity of Suleiman's offence on account of his extreme youth, he forgave him, and allowed him to return to his troops, with the injunction that he should strictly obey all orders in the future.

Meanwhile the escort which had been following behind from El Fasher arrived at the fort, and Gordon, after a short rest, sent for one of Suleiman's leaders, Said Hussein, with whom he discussed the situation. The latter declared that his chief, in spite of pardon, was even then ready to fight in order to secure his father's return and to get back his own power and authority. Gordon now appointed Said Hussein Governor of Shakka, and ordered him to start the following day with the troops he required; but he asked him to say nothing about his nomination for a few hours.

No sooner had he left Gordon than Nur Angara was summoned; and on being upbraided for the want of loyalty that evidently existed amongst the men, he replied that Suleiman was surrounded by bad advisers, who were driving him to his ruin, and that whenever he ventured to express a contrary opinion, Suleiman took not the smallest heed of what he might say. Gordon, convinced of his loyalty, appointed him Governor of Sirga and Arebu, in western Darfur, and instructed him to start the following day with Said Hussein and to take any men he liked with him.

When it came to Suleiman's ears that his two chiefs had been made governors by Gordon, he reproached them bitterly, and called to their minds how they owed all they possessed to his father's generosity; to this they replied that had it not been for their faithful services to his father, he would never have become so celebrated and successful. With these mutual recriminations the two new governors quitted Suleiman, and started at daybreak the following morning for their destination.

When they had gone, Gordon again sent for Suleiman and his chiefs. He at first refused to come; but on the earnest entreaties of the others, who urged that further resistance to Gordon's orders was out of the question, he yielded with a bad grace, and once more found himself face to face with him. On this occasion Gordon treated him with the greatest consideration, pointing out that he had come expressly to advise Suleiman against the folly of thinking that he could attempt to thwart the government by trusting in the bravery and loyalty of his Bazingers; he assured him that loyal service under government would bring him into a position which could not fail to satisfy his ambitions, and, that, further he had no reason to be concerned about his father's detention in Cairo, that he was treated with the greatest respect and honour there, and that he had only to exercise a little patience. Finally Gordon instructed him to proceed to Shakka with his men, and await his arrival there.

The following morning Suleiman received orders that on his arrival at Shakka the new governor had been instructed to make all provision for the troops, and that therefore he should start without delay,—an order which he at once carried into effect. Thus had Gordon, by his amazing rapidity and quick grasp of the situation, arrived in two days at the settlement of a question which literally bristled with dangers and difficulties. Had Suleiman offered resistance at a time when Darfur was in a disturbed state, Gordon's position and the maintenance of Egyptian authority in these districts would have been precarious in the extreme.

Gordon then returned to El Fasher and Kebkebia; already the disturbances which had been so rife in the country showed signs of abatement, and by his personal influence he succeeded in still further quieting the districts and establishing a settled form of government. Leaving El Fasher in September, 1877, he again visited Dara and Shakka, where he found that Suleiman had quite accepted the situation and was prepared to act loyally; he therefore appointed him Governor of the Bahr el Ghazal province, which had been conquered by his father; he further gave him the rank of *Bey*, with which Suleiman appeared much gratified, and expressed great satisfaction at Gordon's confidence in him. A number of slaves, with their masters, who, when Suleiman was in disgrace at Dara, had deserted him, and had gone over to Said Hussein, now returned to him; and thus, with a considerable acquisition to his strength, he left for Dem Zubeir, the chief town of his new province, which had been founded by his father.

Arrived here, he issued circulars to all parts of the country to the effect that he had been appointed Governor; and at the same time he sent a summons to a certain Idris Bey Ebtar to present himself forthwith before him. This Idris Bey Ebtar had, on Zubeir Pasha's departure for Cairo, been appointed by him as his agent in the Bahr el Ghazal. He was a native of Dongola, and in this fact lies, I think, the secret of the subsequent deplorable events.

The Bahr el Ghazal province is inhabited by an immense variety of negro tribes, who were more or less independent of each other until the Danagla and Jaalin Arabs, advancing from the Nile valley in their slave-hunting expeditions, gradually settled in the country and took possession of it. The Jaalin trace their descent back to Abbas, the uncle of the Prophet. They are very proud of it, and look down with the greatest contempt and scorn on the Danagla, whom they regard as descended from the slave Dangal. According to tradition, this man, although a slave, rose to be the ruler of Nubia, though he paid tribute to Bahnesa, the Coptic Bishop of the entire district lying between the present Sarras and Debba. This Dangal founded a town after his own name, Dangala (Dongola), and gradually the inhabitants of the district were known as Danagla. They are, for the most part, of Arab descent, but, having mixed freely with the natives of the country, have somewhat lost caste. Of course they too insist on their Arab descent, but the Jaalin continually refer to their Dangal origin, and treat them with contempt and derision. The relations between these two tribes must be fully recognised in order to understand what follows.

The friends of Idris Ebtar, who were for the most part Danagla, strongly urged him to disobey Suleiman's summons; and, in consequence, a situation arose which was entirely after the slave-hunter's own heart. To play off one chief against another, and thereby serve his own interest and derive personal benefit, is the Arab's delight; and in this instance it was not long before Idris Ebtar's defiance of Suleiman's authority developed into terror of being taken prisoner, and he fled the country to Khartum.

Arrived here, he reported that Suleiman was now acting as if the country were entirely his own; that instead of performing his duties as a governor, he had usurped the position of his father, who was rather a king than a governor; that he had given the best positions to his own Jaalin followers, to the exclusion of all the other tribes, more especially the Danagla, who were being tyrannized over and oppressed in every possible way,—indeed, according to Idris Ebtar's story, Suleiman was about to declare himself an independent ruler; and in support of his statement he produced quantities of petitions, purporting to have been received from merchants, slave-dealers, and others in the Bahr el Ghazal, all urging the government to dismiss Suleiman at once, and replace him by another governor. Assisted by his numerous relatives, Idris Ebtar made such a good case of it to the Khartum authorities that they offered him the post of governor in succession to Suleiman, on condition that he would supply a regular annual revenue of ivory and india-rubber, and that he would also provide annually a contingent of Bazinger recruits, trained to the use of fire-arms, for incorporation in the Egyptian Army.

In order to give full effect to his new appointment, he was given an escort of two hundred regular troops under a certain Awad es Sid Effendi, to whom instructions were given to comply absolutely with his orders.

Idris, leaving Khartum, proceeded by steamer up the White Nile, and thence by the Bahr el Ghazal to Meshra er Rek, eventually reaching Ganda, whence he wrote to Suleiman informing him that he had been dismissed. The receipt of this document was naturally the signal for a general commotion. Suleiman instantly summoned his relatives and friends to his side, and informed them in the most resolute manner that he would utterly refuse to comply with such an unfair order, pointing out with a certain amount of justice that since his arrival in Bahr el Ghazal he had had practically no dealings with the government, and that it was very unjust of them to act on mere suspicion, without giving him a chance of defending himself. He urged, moreover, that government was not dealing fairly in discharging him from a position which was his by right. But here Suleiman was to a certain extent incorrect in claiming territory which, though conquered by his father, was now the actual property of the government.

The meeting over, he wrote a letter in the above sense to Idris Ebtar, protesting in the strongest terms against his interference, accusing him of base ingratitude, and of acting in defiance of every law of honour and justice in having recourse to such means to gratify his personal ambitions. He further reminded him of the assistance and support ever accorded to him by his absent father, Zubeir, who, on being obliged to leave Darfur, had appointed him his agent; and he finally upbraided him for having gone to Khartum as he did and intrigued to be made governor, instead of coming and seeing him as he had ordered, after Gordon had appointed him (Suleiman) governor; and he wound up his letter by an emphatic refusal to pay the smallest attention to Idris Bey's summons.

In answer to this letter, Idris sent Suleiman an ultimatum, calling on him to either submit instantly, or take the consequences of being proceeded against as a rebel; to which Suleiman replied that he was quite prepared to let the sword decide between them.

It was now clear that war must inevitably result, and the merchants began to be alarmed for their lives and property. The Jaalin, of course, wished Suleiman to remain their chief, whilst the other tribes, considerably in the minority, sided with Idris, who, on assuring himself that a resort to arms was inevitable, despatched his brother, Osman Ebtar, with two hundred regulars and a number of Bazingers under Awad es Sid Effendi, to garrison Ganda, whilst he himself, with a small party of Bazingers, proceeded to collect some followers, with a view to making a sudden onslaught on Suleiman. The latter, however, incited by the intense hatred of his tribe for their Danagla enemies, did not hesitate to risk arbitration by the sword. Secretly collecting a number of his followers at Dem Zubeir, he made a sudden attack on the *zariba* at Ganda; and although Osman Ebtar and his men made a gallant stand, the *zariba* was soon reduced to ashes, the houses and huts, in accordance with Suleiman's orders, being completely destroyed, and the dead and wounded thrown into the flames.

After this bloody encounter, all attempts at arriving at a peaceful settlement were out of the question; it was now war to the knife between Suleiman and Idris, and the latter, learning of the disaster at Ganda, lost no time in returning to Khartum and reporting that Suleiman had revolted in the Bahr el Ghazal, and had declared his independence, which was, in fact, the case. Indeed, no time was lost by Suleiman in informing the principal Bahr el Ghazal merchants, such as Genawi Abu Amuri, Zubeir Wad el Fahl, and others, that he had resolved to take up arms against the government, and he begged them to co-operate with him. It was thus quite clear that Suleiman did not doubt the government would not give up a province like Bahr el Ghazal without making a final effort to hold it. The Danagla also, knowing that they had no mercy to expect from the Jaalin, set to work to strengthen their own positions; but the principal merchants, such as Ali Amuri and Zubeir Wad el Fahl, who were very anxious to do nothing which would jeopardise their relations with the government, stood aloof.

Meanwhile the news came that Romolo Gessi had reached Khartum, and had been appointed commander of the expedition against Suleiman and the slave-hunters. Accompanied by Yusef Pasha esh Shellali and forty officers and men, he proceeded in the first instance to Fashoda, where he secured the services of two companies of troops and further reinforcements of regulars and irregulars from Lado and Makaraka. At Gaba Shamba he found a considerable store of Remington rifles and ammunition and a number of Bazingers, which raised his force to upwards of two thousand five hundred rifles.

It was now (July, 1878) the rainy season, and operations against Suleiman were for the moment impossible. Gessi, therefore, proceeded to Rumbek, and from thence sent a summons to Genawi and Wad el Fahl to join him. With this order they at once complied, bringing with them a further reinforcement of some two thousand five hundred men, while Gessi received continual additions to his strength from the smaller merchants and others, so that when the wet season was over he found himself at the head of upwards of seven thousand men, besides two guns and a number of rockets, with which he prepared to march to Ganda.

Meanwhile, doubts being entertained of Said Hussein's loyalty,

Gordon despatched Mustafa Bey Abu Kheiran to replace him; and on the arrival of the latter at Shakka, Said Hussein was sent to Khartum under escort. His arrest was the signal for all Zubeir Pasha's old chiefs, such as Osman Wad Tayalla, Musa Wad el Haj, and others, to join Suleiman, who had in the meantime been concentrating his troops, and had been joined by thousands of minor slave-hunters, mostly Rizighat and Habbania Arabs, who were ever ready to side with the winners, in the hope of plunder. Thus Suleiman's force was numerically far superior to that of Gessi Pasha, who by this time had reached Ganda.

Arrived here, he at once proceeded to construct a *zariba* and entrench himself. Yusef Pasha and the others who had no knowledge of fortification, laughed at Gessi's precautions; but it was not long before they were fully convinced of their efficacy. Suleiman advanced to attack Ganda, on 25th December, 1878; and after a terrific onslaught, in which both sides lost heavily, he was forced to retire. In spite of this heavy defeat, Suleiman, in the course of the next three months, made four other unsuccessful attacks on Ganda; and at length, in March, 1879, Gessi, having procured ammunition and reinforcements, prepared to take the offensive against Suleiman, who had by this time suffered heavily, and had lost many of his best leaders.

On 1st May an action was fought, which was, comparatively speaking, insignificant in regard to losses, but resulted in Suleiman being forced to beat a precipitate retreat from Dem Zubeir; the large stock of slaves and booty falling into the hands of Gessi's Danagla followers, who, apparently without his knowledge, shared the plunder amongst themselves.

Suleiman's power was thoroughly broken, and he had now to decide between unconditional surrender to government, or flight into the interior of Africa. The Danagla had become possessors of all his property, including his enormous harem of some eight hundred women, besides those of his various chiefs, whose respective households could not have numbered less than one hundred women each,—indeed, every Bazinger, who was practically a slave, was also the possessor of one or two wives; and now all this immense amount of human loot had fallen into the hands of his enemies. Moreover, his scattered forces, which were now roaming about the country in search of work, made no secret of the quantities of gold and silver treasure which Suleiman had amassed, and which were now, no doubt, in the hands of Gessi's men.

When it is remembered that Suleiman's treasury included the

masses of gold and silver jewellery captured by his father at Dara, at Manawashi,—where Sultan Ibrahim had ruled, and had fallen on the capture of Darfur,—at El Fasher, at Kebkebia, etc., it can be readily understood what riches must have fallen into the hands of the government levies, and—perhaps unknown to their commander, who was ignorant of the language—had been divided up amongst them.

Gessi now quartered the bulk of his troops in the entrenched camp vacated by Suleiman, and with a comparatively small force proceeded to follow him up in pursuit. In order to conceal his whereabouts, Suleiman had scattered his men throughout the western districts; but Gessi came across one of his armed bands, under Rabeh, and dispersed it without much difficulty. Rabeh, however, escaped, and just at this period Gessi received orders from Gordon to meet him in Darfur; he therefore collected all his troops in Dem Suleiman, where they rested after their fatiguing campaign, whilst he himself, accompanied by some of his officers, amongst whom was Yusef Pasha esh Shellali, proceeded to Et Toweisha, where the caravan routes from Om Shanga, El Obeid, and Dara join, and here he met Gordon.

In this his second visit to Darfur, Gordon had ascertained that the Sudanese merchants of El Obeid had been selling arms and powder to the rebel Suleiman, with whom they naturally sympathised for their own selfish purposes; this contraband of war had been secretly despatched to Bahr el Ghazal through the intermediary of the Gellabas (petty traders), who obtained enormous prices from Suleiman: for instance, six to eight slaves would be exchanged for a double-barrelled gun, and one or two slaves was the price of a box of caps. The officials at El Obeid made some attempt to check this trade, but the difficulties were great. The districts between Kordofan and Bahr el Ghazal were inhabited principally by nomad Arab tribes such as the Rizighat, Hawazma, Homr, and Messeiria; it was, moreover, an easy matter for small parties of Gellabas to traverse, without fear of detection, the almost uninhabited forests, with which the country abounds; and even if an Egyptian official came across them, he was, as a rule, quite amenable to a small bribe.

Gordon was fully cognisant of all this, and therefore gave the order that trade of every description was to be stopped between El Obeid and Bahr el Ghazal. The merchants were, in consequence, ordered to quit all districts lying to the south of the El Obeid, Et Toweisha, and Dara caravan road, and to confine their trade entirely to the northern and western countries, whilst active operations were going on in Bahr

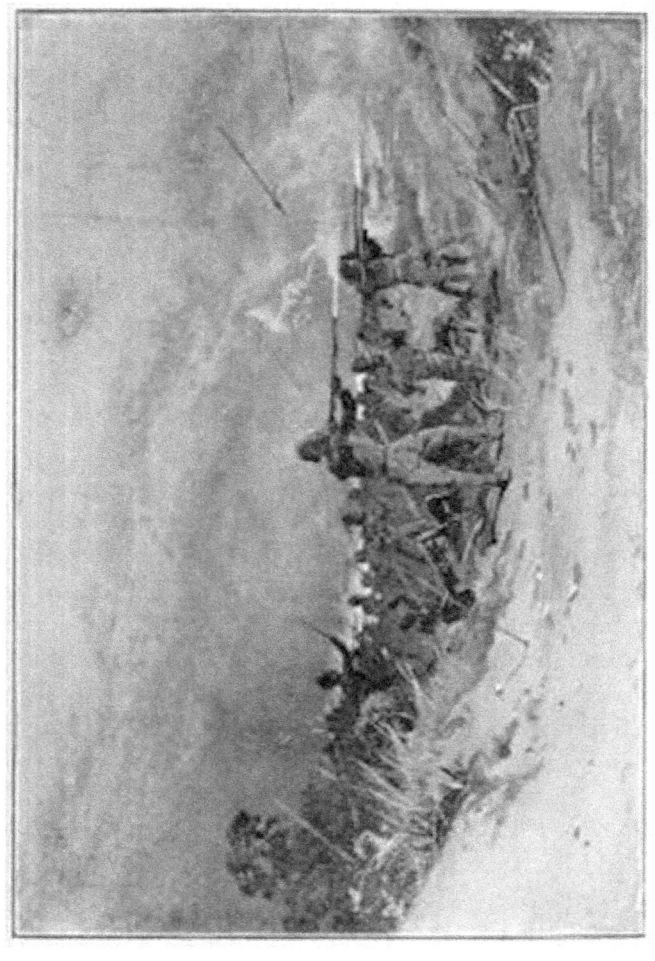

Gessi Pasha's Troops advancing to the attack on "Dem Suleiman."

el Ghazal. But, in spite of the strictness with which these orders were enforced, the chances of gain were so enormous and so enticing that the merchants grew almost insensible to the risk of discovery; and, in fact, the government had not at hand the means of checking the trade in an adequate manner,—indeed, in spite of the government restrictions, the trade rather increased than decreased.

Gordon, therefore, had to resort to very drastic measures. He ordered the *sheikhs* of the Arab tribes to seize all Gellabas in their districts, and forcibly drive them to Dara, Toweisha, Om Shanga, and El Obeid, and at the same time held them responsible for any Gellabas found in their countries, after a certain date. This order was welcomed by the greedy Arabs, who seized the occasion to pillage, not only the wandering traders, but even those who had been settled amongst them for years, and who had nothing to do with this illicit commerce; they gathered the wheat and the tares together, and cast out both indiscriminately, making considerable profit over the transaction. Gordon's order was now the signal for a wholesale campaign against the traders, who not only lost their goods, but almost every stitch of clothing they possessed, and were driven like wild animals in hundreds, almost naked, towards Dara, Toweisha, and Om Shanga. It was a terrible punishment for their unlawful communication with the enemies of the government.

Many of these traders had been residing amongst the Arabs for years. They had got wives, children, concubines, and considerable quantities of property, which in turn fell into the hands of the Arabs. The fates, indeed, wreaked all their fury on these wretched slave-hunters, and the retribution—merited as it undoubtedly was, on the principle of an eye for an eye, and a tooth for a tooth—was painful enough to witness, and had consequences which were more far-reaching; for it must be remembered that the majority of these petty traders were Jaalin from the Nile valley, and between them and their Arab oppressors there now arose the most implacable hatred, which has continued up to the present time, and which shows signs of increase rather than of diminution.

In point of humanity, this attack on the Gellabas may be open to question; but on closer investigation it will be apparent to all that it was not possible to deal with an anomalous situation, such as then existed, by political or philanthropic methods,—drastic and violent measures could alone be effective. The Arab himself says, "*Nar el ghaba yelzamha el harika*" (Against a prairie-fire, fire must be used); and the proverb was peculiarly applicable in this case.

Now, these traders being for the most part Jaalin, Shaigias and Danagla had, of course, relations and friends in the Nile valley; and, indeed, many of the latter were their intermediaries in the commercial and slave transactions which took place. Gordon's orders, therefore, were scarcely less unpopular amongst these Nile-dwellers, who could not understand why such severe measures were necessary, merely to prevent Gessi from being defeated in Bahr el Ghazal.

But to return to Gessi's movements. Having met Gordon at Toweisha, and explained the situation to him, he was instructed to proceed to Dara, while Gordon returned to Khartum, and with him Yusef Pasha Shellali, who during the entire campaign had served Gessi most loyally, but who had been told, by some of the numerous intriguers, that his chief was against him; he therefore begged Gordon to allow him to return with him to Khartum,—a request which was at once granted, while his services were further recognised by his promotion to the rank of *pasha*.

On his arrival at Dara, Gessi received information that Suleiman had quitted Bahr el Ghazal, and, having collected his forces, was somewhere in the southwest of Darfur. It was thought that he intended to unite with Sultan ben Seif ed Din, a direct descendant of the old Darfur kings, who was said to have collected a force with the object of opposing the government and driving out the foreigners. It is impossible to say whether this was really Suleiman's intention; but there is no doubt that Sultan Harun had never concluded an alliance with Suleiman, who, being the son of the conqueror of Darfur, by whom the dynasty had been destroyed, was hated by the Darfur people even more than were the Egyptians; the latter, in comparison with Zubeir's lawless gangs of Bazingers, had a slightly higher reputation, but both seemed to consider the Darfurians their legitimate prey, and both were guilty of acts of cruelty and oppression.

At this time the principal government official at Dara was Zogal Bey (Mohammed Bey Khaled); and Gessi, having left almost all his troops in Bahr el Ghazal, now begged him to place at his disposal two companies of regular troops, under the command of Saghkolaghasi Mansur Effendi Helmi; with these, and a certain Ismail Wad el Barnu,—an Egyptian born in Darfur, and well known for his bravery, and knowledge of the country,—Gessi set off for Kalaka, the headquarters of the Habbania Arabs. Here he was joined by Arifi Wad Ahmed, head Sheikh of the Habbania, and by Madibbo Bey, chief of the Rizighat, who was loyal to government, and could place several hundred horsemen in the field.

Suleiman's star was now declining. Abandoned by most of his own tribesmen, who had secretly made off through the forests to the Nile valley; deserted by the greater part of his trusted Bazingers, whom hunger, fatigue, and aimless wandering in pathless regions had hopelessly scattered; his footsteps dogged by Gessi, who was kept informed of his every movement,—he was, indeed, in sorry plight when Ismail Wad Barnu, despatched by Gessi with a summons to surrender, appeared before him at Gharra.

Ismail was well known to Suleiman, and had been instructed by Gessi to inform him that, should he submit, his life and the lives of his chiefs would be spared, and his women and children should not be touched, on condition that he handed over to him his Bazingers, with their arms, and made a solemn vow of loyalty to the Egyptian Government. Ismail pointed out to Suleiman that all hope of successful resistance was now at an end, and, as a native of the country, he gave it as his private opinion that Sultan Harun would never be induced to enter into alliance with him.

Suleiman now convened a meeting of his principal men to discuss the terms of peace offered by Gessi. Most of them were heartily tired of this constant fighting, in which they had been almost invariably defeated, but there were some who doubted the sincerity of the conditions proposed; Ismail, however, asserted in the strongest terms that he would guarantee the sincerity of Gessi, who himself longed to put an end to this useless bloodshed, and further stated that he had been authorised by him to take a solemn oath in his name that the conditions of surrender would be faithfully observed.

Suleiman and all his chiefs, with the exception of Rabeh, agreed to accept; but the latter pointed out, with a prescience, which subsequent events justified, that Suleiman had been warned, before he took up arms, of the danger he was incurring, and that once in the hands of his captors he could not hope for mercy. As regards himself, Rabeh declared that it would be pain and grief to him to separate from men who had been his companions in joy and sorrow all these years, but he gave them distinctly to understand that he would never place himself in the power of Gessi, whose success had been due to the Danagla, and who, though an European, was really in their hands. He begged his companions to remember the bitter animosity which existed between the Jaalin and Danagla, and recalled the merciless manner in which the former had treated the latter when Osman Ebtar had been defeated at Ganda.

He therefore had two proposals to make, *viz.*, to collect their entire force and march west into the Banda countries, which had hitherto been untouched by foreign intruders, and which could offer no resistance to the thousands of well-armed Bazingers they still had at their command. He then went on to say, that once the Black tribes had been subjugated, they could enter into relations with the kingdoms of Wadai, Baghirmi, and Bornu, and that it was most unlikely that Gessi and his men, who were tired of fighting, would follow them into distant and unknown regions, over which the government had no control, and from which it was not likely they could reap any benefit.

Should this proposal not meet with their approbation, then he would suggest that as they wished now to lead quiet lives with their fellow-tribesmen in the Nile valley, they should send a special deputation either to His Highness the Khedive or to Gordon Pasha, begging for pardon and peace; but that they should never do so through Gessi, whose only object was to secure their arms and Bazingers, and who, at the capture of Dem Suleiman, had unhesitatingly taken everything they possessed. If, therefore, they wished to save their lives and avoid the intrigues of the Danagla, all they had to do was to leave the Bazingers with their arms behind, and themselves proceed by Kalaka and Shakka and through the uninhabited forests of Dar Hamar to Foga, the western telegraph station on the Darfur frontier, whence they could wire their submission and ask for pardon, which would undoubtedly be granted.

Or they might, added Rabeh, proceed from Shakka through Dar Homr, and, skirting the northern Janghé country, reach El Obeid, where they could make their submission through the intermediary of the governor and their relative, Elias Pasha Wad Um Bereir. He concluded his speech by saying that should none of these proposals meet with approval, then he was prepared, with the greatest reluctance, to quit his lifelong friends, and, taking those who wished to join him, he would march west and take his chance; but, he added most emphatically, he would never place himself in the hands of Gessi and his Danagla.

These proposals were made by Rabeh to Suleiman and the others in the presence of Ismail Wad Barnu, who again urged that they should submit to Gessi, arguing that as the latter had been originally entrusted with the campaign, it would naturally be a point of honour with him to see to Suleiman's safety and to write favourably to government in regard to him; but, on the other hand, added Ismail, should Suleiman attempt to obtain pardon without Gessi's intermediary, then the latter would naturally be very angry, and would probably be the means of injuring him in the eyes of the government.

Musa Wad el Haj, one of Suleiman's best leaders, and who also had some influence with Gessi, now addressed Rabeh as follows: "You have made certain proposals in the hearing of Ismail Wad Barnu, who is Gessi's messenger. Should we concur with your proposals, what do you consider we should do with him?"

To this question Rabeh answered, "Ismail is our friend, and was trusted by Zubeir; far be it from me to wish him any harm. Should we decide on flight, then, in self-preservation, we must take him with us a certain distance and when we are out of reach of pursuit, let him go."

A long discussion now ensued, which resulted in a division of opinions: Suleiman, Hassan Wad Degeil (Zubeir's uncle), Musa Wad el Haj, Ibrahim Wad Hussein (the brother of Saleh Wad Hussein, the former Governor of Shakka, who had been arrested and sent to Khartum), Suleiman Wad Mohammed, Ahmed Wad Idris, Abdel Kader Wad el Imam, and Babakr Wad Mansur, all of the Gemiab section of the Jaalin tribe; also Arbab Mohammed Wad Diab of the Saadab section, agreed to accept Gessi's conditions and submit. But Rabeh, Abu el Kasim (of the Magazib section), Musa Wad el Jaali, Idris Wad es Sultan, and Mohammed Wad Fadlalla, of the Gemiab section, and Abdel Bayin, a former slave of Zubeir Pasha, decided not to submit under any circumstances, but to march west. Ismail, being of course most anxious to inform Gessi of Suleiman's submission, urged him to break up the meeting and to give him a written document that the conditions were acceptable. Suleiman complied, and with eight of his chiefs signed the compact and handed it to Ismail, who at once returned to Gessi at Kalaka with presents of several male and female slaves.

No sooner had he gone than Rabeh again came to Suleiman, and in the most earnest terms begged him to reconsider the matter; but Suleiman was obdurate, and Rabeh, therefore, retired heart-broken, beat his war-drums to collect his Bazingers and followers, sorrowfully bade his old companions farewell, and marched off in a southwesterly direction, to the sound of the *ombeÿa*, or elephant's tusk (the Sudan war-horn, which can be heard at an immense distance).

Several of Suleiman's men, seeing that Rabeh was determined not to submit, joined him, preferring the uncertainty of a life of adventure in the pathless forests to the risk of giving themselves up to the hated Danagla. But the five chiefs who had been his main supporters took the occasion to desert him at his first camping-station, intending to conceal themselves by the help of the Arab chiefs whom they knew, and eventually to make their way back to the Nile when all danger was over.

On receipt of Suleiman's letter of submission, Gessi set out with all speed for Gharra, accompanied by Ismail, who feared that Rabeh's counsels might after all prevail and that they had no time to lose; they took with them a considerable number of men, and were reinforced by contingents supplied by the Rizighat and Habbania chiefs. Arrived near Gharra, Gessi sent on Ismail to tell Suleiman that he had received the signed conditions, with which he was satisfied, and that he had come to personally accept his submission. In a short time Ismail returned, reporting Rabeh's flight with a considerable number of Bazingers and arms, and that Suleiman was quite prepared to surrender. Gessi therefore advanced to Gharra with his troops and met Suleiman, whose men had piled their arms. He verbally gave them the pardon for which they asked, and then ordered the Bazingers to be distributed between Sheikh Arifi and Madibbo Bey, while instructions were given to put the chiefs under a guard until the Government officials appointed to take charge of them should have been selected.

These orders were executed with great promptitude, and in two hours, out of the entire camp, only Suleiman and the chiefs, with their wives and families, remained, and over these a small guard was placed.

Now, as Rabeh had truly foretold, the intrigues of the Danagla against Suleiman began. They told Gessi that Suleiman's servants had reported that he already regretted having submitted, and that had he known that he was to be received in such a way, he would rather have died fighting. Gessi, although a man of an open and honourable disposition, was somewhat susceptible to such insinuations; he trusted his own men, and as they had risked their lives for him, he did not doubt their words. But he neither knew nor realised that his men were bent on Suleiman's destruction. The loot which they had taken in Dem Suleiman and in many other engagements was enormous, besides male and female slaves, gold and silver jewellery, and an immense amount of cash, all of which they had distributed amongst themselves, unknown to Gessi.

What they now feared was that Suleiman, being admitted to Gessi's favour, would inform him of what had occurred, and that he would enter a claim against the government. Moreover, it will be remembered how Idris Ebtar had by his intrigues given the authorities the impression that the Bahr el Ghazal revolt was entirely due to the Zubeir faction, while they showed themselves in the light of faithful adherents and martyrs to the government cause. They dreaded lest Suleiman might be sent to Khartum, whence he would probably obtain permission to visit his father in Cairo, and they knew that Zubeir possessed sufficient influence to institute claims against them for the seizure of his property, and would moreover do his utmost to show that Suleiman was not responsible for the revolt.

The Danagla, therefore, now resorted to the following base expedient: they informed Gessi that Suleiman had sent messengers to recall Rabeh, that he had given him instructions to make an attack on Gessi, who had only an insignificant force, and to whom they had surrendered under the impression that his force was much larger, but that Rabeh was sufficiently strong to easily overcome him, and thus completely turn the tables.

Mansur Effendi Helmi also came forward and corroborated these tales, adding that he was convinced Suleiman was just as hostile as before, and that on the smallest chance being given him he would not hesitate to revolt once more against the government.

Gessi was now fully convinced that their statements were true, and in consequence of their urgent declamations against Suleiman he went back on the promise he had made that their lives should be safe. In the course of the day he had Suleiman and the nine chiefs brought into his tent, and reproached them very severely for their traitorous conduct. To proud and uncivilised men these reproaches were unbearable, and they replied in an equally abrupt tone. Gessi, stung to anger, quitted the tent and ordered the Danagla, who were lurking about, to shoot them. In a moment the tent was pulled down over their heads, they were secured, their hands were tied behind their backs, and they were driven to the place of execution.

With the most bitter imprecations on their lips against the treacherous Danagla, they fell, shot through the back by the rifles of a firing party of Mansur Helmi's regulars, on the 15th July, 1879. Thus did fate overtake Suleiman and his friends. Death had come upon them treacherously, it is true; but they had abused the authority with which they had been vested, by their cruelty and ambition they had wrecked the provinces of Bahr el Ghazal and Darfur, and had reduced the inhabitants to an unparalleled state of misery and wretchedness.

Gessi lost no time in sending a telegram to the station at Foga reporting Suleiman's death and the conclusion of the campaign to Gordon. This news, as already related, reached me through Ali Bey Sherif the day I left El Obeid for Darfur.

Gessi now called on the Shaigias to hand over the Bazingers in their charge; but they reported that owing to an insufficient guard they had escaped; and as the story seemed credible, Gessi collected the remainder of his men, with the intention of proceeding to Bahr el Ghazal, where he wished to establish a settled form of government, in place of the constant warfare which had decimated this fertile province. Just before leaving, he received information that the five chiefs who had left Rabeh, *viz.*, Abdel Kasim, Musa Jaali, Idris Wad es Sultan, Mohammed Fadlalla, and Abdel Bayin; were in hiding amongst the Arabs; he therefore left orders for the Shaigia to search for them, and when found, to bring them for punishment before the Governor of El Fasher. Zogal Bey, the Governor of Shakka, was also ordered to do his utmost to catch these men, with the result that they were discovered without much difficulty, and brought, with *shebas* round their necks, to El Fasher, where Messedaglia Bey, without further ado, had them instantly shot. Thus, with the exception of Rabeh, the entire Zubeir gang was destroyed, and the power of the slave-hunters crippled.

The campaign had resulted in a considerable loss to government of arms and ammunition, and in a corresponding acquisition of strength to the great southern Arab tribes, such as the Baggara, Taisha, Habbania, and Rizighat, who both before and after the fall of Suleiman had captured numbers of Bazingers and immense quantities of loot; the subsequent effects of which were not long in showing themselves.

Chapter 2

Residence in Darfur, and Early History of the Province

I left El Obeid early in July, 1879, in company with Dr. Zurbuchen, the Sanitary Inspector-General, whom I had met in Cairo; our route took us through Foga, the telegraph terminus, and here I found a telegram from Gordon, telling me that he was proceeding on a mission to King John of Abyssinia.

We reached Om Shanga to find it crowded with Gellabas who had been turned out of the southern districts, and were really in a pitiable condition. Curiously enough, the news had spread far and wide that I was Gordon's nephew (I suppose on account of my blue eyes and shaven chin), and in consequence I was looked upon with some apprehension by these people, who considered him as the cause of all the troubles which they were now justly suffering. I was overwhelmed with petitions for support; but I told them that as Om Shanga was not in my district, I could do nothing for them,—and even if I could have spared them something from my private purse, I had neither the desire nor inclination to do so.

In one case, however, I confess to having broken the rule; but before relating this little episode, I should explain that my action must not be judged from the standpoint of purely Christian morality. In this case I admit to being guilty of even greater moral laxity in regard to the Moslem marriage law than is enjoined in the *Sharia*, or religious law; but when my readers have finished the story, I think they will perhaps share the feelings which prompted me to act as I did. Several of the merchants who had travelled from the Nile called upon me and begged me to interest myself in the case of an unfortunate youth, a native of Khartum and only nineteen years of age. They related that before quitting Khartum he had been betrothed to his beautiful but very poor young cousin; the parents had consented to the marriage, but he was to first take a journey and try to make some money.

On his arrival at Om Shanga a very rich old woman took a violent fancy to him. Whether the youth had been overcome by her riches, my informants did not say, but the old woman would have her way and had married him; and now, finding himself comparatively wealthy, he had no particular desire to give her up. The sad news had reached Khartum, the poor girl was distracted, and now I was asked to solve the difficulty. What was I to do? I called up the youth, who was unusually good-looking, and, taking him aside, I spoke to him with as serious a countenance as I could preserve; I pointed out how very wrong it was of him, a foreigner, to have married a strange old woman while his poor *fiancée* was crying her eyes out at home, and that even if his cousin's dowry was small, still, in honour bound, he should keep his promise. He hesitated for a long time, but at length decided to go before the *kadi* (judge of the religious law) and get a divorce.

I had previously seen the *kadi*, and had instructed him that should the youth seek a divorce, it was his duty to break the news as gently as he could to the old wife, as I was most anxious the separation should be carried out with as little commotion as possible; and, taking a guarantee from the young man's relatives that they would be responsible that he should go direct to Khartum, I warned the government official of Om Shanga that the youth was to be banished at two days' notice! I also told him that he might say what he liked about me to the old woman, and that I was quite ready to bear the blame, provided he could get her to give him some money for the journey.

Little did I imagine what a storm I had brought on my devoted head! It was about four o'clock in the afternoon, and I was lying on my *angareb* (native couch) in the little brick hut, when I heard the voice of an angry woman demanding to see me instantly. I guessed at once who it was, and, bracing my nerves for the fray, told the orderly to let her in. Dr. Zurbuchen, who was in the room with me, and whose knowledge of Arabic was very limited, was most desirous to leave me; but I was by no means anxious to be left alone with an angry woman, and at length persuaded him to stay.

No sooner was the divorced wife admitted than she rushed up angrily to Dr. Zurbuchen, whom she mistook for me, and shrieked in a tone of frantic excitement, "I shall never agree to a divorce. He is my husband, and I am his wife; he married me in accordance with the religious law, and I refuse to let him divorce me." Dr. Zurbuchen, thoroughly startled, muttered in broken Arabic that he had nothing to do with the case, and meekly pointed to me as the hard-hearted governor.

I could not help being amused at the extraordinary figure before me. She was a great strong woman, with evidently a will of her own; and so furious was she that she had quite disregarded all the rules which usually apply when Eastern ladies address the opposite sex. Her long white muslin veil had got twisted round and round her dress, exposing her parti-coloured silk headdress, which had fallen on her shoulders; she had a yellowish complexion, and her face was covered with wrinkles, while her cheeks were marked by the three tribal slits, about half an inch apart; in her nose she wore a piece of red coral, massive gold earrings in her ears, and her greasy hair was twisted into innumerable little ringlets, which were growing gray with advancing age. I thought I had never seen a more appalling looking old creature; but my contemplations were cut short by her screeching voice, which was now directed on me with renewed fury, and I was confronted with the same question she had addressed to the terrified doctor. Giving her time to recover her breath, I replied, "I quite understand what you say, but you must submit to the inevitable: your husband must leave; and as you are a native, I cannot permit you to go with him. You appear undesirous of having a divorce; but you must remember that, in accordance with the Moslem law, it is for the man to give the woman her divorce papers, and not the woman the man."

"Had you not interfered," she shrieked, "he would never have left me. Cursed be the day you came here!"

"I beg of you, do not say that," I answered; "you are a woman of means, and I should not think you would have any difficulty in securing another and perhaps older husband."

"I want no other," she literally screamed.

"Silence!" I said somewhat sharply. "The relatives of your former husband wish him to leave you; they complained that it was only your money which bound him to you; and now, whatever you may say, he is to leave tomorrow. Besides, do you not think it is outrageous that an old woman like you should have married a young lad who might have been your grandson?"

These last words drove her into a state of perfect frenzy; and, losing all control over herself, she threw up her hands, tore off her veil, and what else might have happened I know not, but my *kavass* (orderly), hearing the noise, rushed in and quietly but forcibly removed her from the room, cautioning her that her conduct was disgraceful, and that she had made a laughing-stock of herself. The following day her husband left, and I do not doubt her grief was considerable; but some years later I had the satisfaction of meeting the youth, married to his early *fiancée*, and already the father of a family; he thanked me profusely for having got him out of the clutches of the old woman and brought him to his present happy state. It is needless to relate that I slept soundly that night, convinced that I had done a good piece of work, and that it had cost me nothing.

Two days later we left Om Shanga, and halted for the night at Jebel el Hella, where we were met by Hassan Bey Om Kadok, the Sheikh of the northern Berti tribes, who had shown great loyalty and had been granted by Gordon the rank of *Bey*. He was a middle-aged man, very stout, with great broad shoulders and a round, smiling face; he might well have been called the Sudan "Falstaff." Some years later, when the tables were turned, and masters became servants, he and I found ourselves together as orderlies in the *khalifa's* body-guard, where his cheerful disposition and genial nature brightened an existence which at times was almost unbearable. His brother Ismail was exactly the opposite,—tall, thin, and serious; and the two brothers never by any chance agreed, except on one point, and that was their inveterate love of marissa (Sudan beer): to have each a large jar (made of pottery, and known in Darfur as the *Dulang asslia* or *Um bilbil*) of this *marissa*, and to vie with one another in emptying it first, was to them the greatest pleasure in life.

They invited us to sup with them, and for our evening meal an entire sheep, baked on charcoal, was served up, besides a quantity of roast fowls and a dish of *asida* (the latter is somewhat like the Italian *polenta*, and is eaten with all the courses); there were also several jars of *marissa*. We thoroughly enjoyed the food, leaving the *marissa* to our hosts, and substituting for it some of our own red wine. Hassan and Ismail, however, freely regaled themselves with wine as well as *marissa*; the effect on the former being to make him extremely talkative, while the latter became more and more silent. Hassan related many little incidents about Gordon, for whom he had the greatest admiration and regard. He was much grieved to hear he was going to Abyssinia. "Perhaps," said he, sadly, "he will go back to his own country, and never return to the Sudan again."

Curiously enough, he was partially correct. He then left the room and returned almost at once, carrying a magnificent saddle and sword. "Look," said he, "these are the last presents General Gordon gave me when I accompanied him to El Fasher; he was most kind and generous." Then Ismail showed us a rich gold embroidered robe which Gordon had presented to him. "Pride," said Hassan, "was unknown to Gordon."

One day, on our way to El Fasher, one of the attendants shot a bustard; and when we halted at noon, the cook at once boiled some water and threw the bird into the pot, so as to take off its feathers. Gordon, seeing this, went and sat himself down by the cook and began helping him to pull out the feathers. I at once rushed up and begged him to allow me to do this for him, but he answered, 'Why should I be ashamed of doing work? I am quite able to wait on myself, and certainly do not require a *Bey* to do my kitchen work for me.'"

Hassan continued chatting till a late hour. He related his experiences during Zubeir's conquest of Darfur, then of the subsequent revolts and the present situation, frequently reverting to Gordon, whom he held in great honour. "Once, travelling with Gordon," he remarked, "I fell ill, and Gordon came to see me in my tent. In the course of our conversation I told him that I was addicted to alcoholic drinks, and that I put down my present indisposition to being obliged to do without them for the last few days. This was really my indirect way of asking Gordon to give me something; but I was mightily disappointed, and, instead, received a very severe rebuke. 'You a Moslem,' said he, 'and forbidden by your religion to drink wines and spirits! I am indeed surprised. You should give up this habit altogether; every one should follow the precepts of his religion.' I replied, 'Having been accustomed to them all my life, if I now gave them up my health must suffer; but I will try and be more moderate in future.' Gordon seemed satisfied, got up, shook hands with me, and bade me goodbye. The following morning, before leaving, he sent me three bottles of brandy, with injunctions that I should use them in moderation."

Meanwhile Hassan's lanky brother sat in complete silence, leaning on his elbows and solemnly filling up and swallowing glass after glass of *marissa*, with an almost clockwork regularity. When we had stopped talking, he got up in a very deliberate manner, solemnly wiped his mouth with his hand, and said in a melancholy tone, "Yes, brandy is very good; it is not an alcoholic drink, it is medicine. Gordon is a great and benevolent man; we shall never see him again."

It was very late before our hosts left us, and, having ordered our baggage camels to start before daybreak, we had a few hours' sleep. The next morning at sunrise our riding camels were ready, and Dr. Zurbuchen and I looked about for our hosts to wish them goodbye. At length we saw Ismail hurrying towards us; his head was evidently suffering from the effects of the previous night. "Masters," he shouted, "we have always been told that in your country justice exists; I am sure that there guests never wrong their hosts. Last night, when your baggage camels started, your people carried off my best rug, which I had laid out for you to lie down on yesterday."

I made inquiries, and had no doubt that one of my men must have made off with the precious rug; so, ordering one of my *kavasses* to mount his camel and overtake the caravan, I patiently awaited his return. In due time he came back with the stolen rug, and, tied on behind him, one of my eight black soldiers who belonged to our escort. On being interrogated, the man said he had taken it by mistake; but as I had no doubt of his guilt I had him flogged and sent back a prisoner to the nearest military post at Om Shanga. I was much upset by the occurrence, for I knew that these people were apt to conclude that as the master is, so is the servant; and had I not acted with severity on this occasion I should probably have had a frequent recurrence of such thefts.

With profuse apologies to our hosts, we set off for El Fasher, and, passing through Brush, Abiat, and Ergud, reached there after five days' march.

For the last century El Fasher had been chosen as the capital of Darfur. It is built on two sandy hills running north and south, and separated by a valley some four hundred yards across, known as the Wadi Tendelti. The fort is situated on the western hill, and consists of a square mud-brick enclosure about three feet thick built on the slope, and surrounded with a ditch fifteen feet deep; at the corners were four small towers, manned with guns which fired from embrasures.

This enclosure embraces the government buildings, governor's house, officers' quarters, and men's barracks; but the quarters of the irregular cavalry are outside. The wells are down in the valley, about one hundred and fifty yards distant from the walls of the fort.

At this time Messedaglia Bey, an Italian, was Governor of El Fasher; he gave Dr. Zurbuchen and myself a cordial welcome, and allotted us quarters in the government buildings. We had both suffered somewhat from fever during our wet march, and therefore decided to rest here for a few days.

Darfur was formerly one of the line of ancient Central African kingdoms, stretching across the continent from west to east. Up to the early part of the seventeenth century the kings of Darfur had dominion over the country as far east as the Atbara; but the warlike Fungs, who at that time were one of the most powerful tribes of the Sudan, gradually drove the Darfurians back, and established their own authority up to the banks of the White Nile. In 1770 they wrested the province of Kordofan from the Darfur kings, but five years later it was retaken by the latter, and remained under their control until conquered in 1822 by Mohammed Bey Dafterdar, the brother-in-law of Ismail Pasha, who, it will be remembered, was burnt alive at Shendi. History has already described the heroic bravery of the Darfur troops led by Musallem, the Viceroy of Kordofan, who, with almost all his men, utterly ignorant of the effect of fire-arms, dashed up to the muzzles of the Turks' guns, and were annihilated almost to a man. Kordofan thus remained under Egyptian rule until, in 1883, it fell under the sway of the Mahdi.

Meanwhile, after the loss of Kordofan the Darfurians retired further to the west, and the kings now governed only a circumscribed area, of which Jebel Marra was the centre. The roads through these almost inaccessible mountains are few and very difficult, and in consequence the place is one of great strength. Many of the peaks are between six and seven thousand feet high, and separated from each other by deep and fertile valleys gradually descending to the plains below. During the rains the rivulets in these valleys become rushing torrents, and, flowing south into the main valleys of Wadi Asum and Wadi Ibra, convert them into two gigantic rivers, the latter emptying into the Bahr el Arab, which eventually joins the Bahr el Ghazal, and forms the main western tributary of the White Nile. The streams flowing north from Jebel Marra have a less rapid descent, and are quickly absorbed in the sandy soil of the desert.

In the valleys of Jebel Marra, barley, Turkish wheat, and *dukhn* are planted; but in the plains of Darfur only the latter can be grown, and it is therefore the ordinary food of the inhabitants. In the southern district it comes to maturity from ninety to a hundred days after being planted, but in some of the northern districts it ripens even twenty days earlier.

The original tribes of the country were the Furs and the Tago, the latter ruling for centuries over the entire district from their inaccessible strongholds in Jebel Marra. Tradition relates that about the fourteenth century, the Tungur Arabs, emigrating south from Tunis, scattered throughout Bornu and Wadai, and eventually reached Darfur, the first arrivals being two brothers, Ali and Ahmed, who, with their flocks, settled on the western slopes of Jebel Marra. Ali, who was older and better off than his brother, had recently married a beautiful young girl of his own tribe, and she, in turn, being constantly thrown with her brother-in-law, who was celebrated for his bravery, conceived a great fancy for him. One day, when her husband was away, she confessed her feelings to Ahmed, and implored him to help her out of her misery; but Ahmed's sentiments of right and honour in regard to his brother's wife could not be overcome by this appeal, though he promised that her secret should never be divulged.

The girl fell ill, and in her jealous love determined that her brother-in-law should never marry another; she therefore called her husband to her side and bade him swear, under a solemn oath, that he would never disclose what she was about to tell him, and then she whispered that his brother never ceased making love to her. Ali, horror-stricken at the thought of the deception of Ahmed, whom he dearly loved, and to whom he confided everything, was beside himself with grief; but he could not bring himself to believe entirely in his brother's perfidy, though the seeds of mistrust were sown. Meanwhile Ahmed, knowing that his sister-in-law's jealousy was aroused, did all he could by kindness and sympathy to pacify her and to treat her as if nothing had happened; the result, of course, being that Ali's suspicion grew into certainty, and he determined on revenge. He could not bear the thought of killing him, but wanted to inflict on him some lasting injury.

Two days later, he determined to move camp, and, sending on all his people with their flocks and herds, he remained behind with his brother, and began talking to him about ordinary matters. From this they got into a discussion on arms, and Ali, playfully drawing out his sword, in an unguarded moment struck Ahmed a blow on his right leg, severing the tendon Achilles; and then, making off as quickly as he could, he left his unfortunate brother weltering in his blood, who, too proud to cry out, calmly awaited death. This Ahmed el Makur (signifies one who is wounded, applying more especially to the sort of wound he received) was destined to become the founder of a new dynasty in Darfur, and this is how it came about.

Ali, whose love for his brother was not altogether extinguished, sent two of his slaves, Zayed and Birged (the forefathers of the great Zayedia and Birged tribes), with two camels, two she-camels, and a few necessaries, in search of Ahmed, but at the same time he told them that on no account were they to bring him back. He himself returned to the west, and, as the story goes, separated soon afterwards from his wife, as he could not bear the thought of his brother's supposed perfidy. The slaves, finding Ahmed unconscious from loss of blood, revived him, and at his request brought him to the nearest native settlement, where he was well received, and King Kor (the last of the Tago dynasty) was informed that a foreigner, who had been wounded in the leg by his brother, was in their village.

The king ordered Ahmed to be brought before him, in order to hear from his own lips the account of this strange event. Ahmed, however, refused to explain, and the matter remained a mystery; but he was taken care of and permitted to stay in the king's household. King Kor, like all his predecessors, was a heathen; he had become ruler by violence, was utterly ignorant of the outside world, and did not even know of the existence of any country outside his own immediate dominions; beyond making occasional raids from his mountain strongholds on the dwellers in the plains, he seldom left his hills. This savage old king took a fancy to the stranger, made him director of his household, and consulted him on all occasions. Gradually Ahmed rose to power. By judicious management he brought the unruly Tago chiefs into subjection, and portioned out the land amongst the poorer inhabitants, thus putting a stop to the constant internal raiding, and introducing a feeling of security and contentment hitherto quite unknown.

Ahmed during his long journey from Tunis had passed through many distant kingdoms, and, being a man of sense, he was able to apply his knowledge in introducing a number of reforms. One of those, still quoted, is the wonderful change he effected in the king's household. It had been the custom for centuries for any retainer to take his food at the time it pleased him, quite regardless of the wants of others. It therefore frequently happened that, "*first come, first served*," nothing remained for the later arrivals, who, in their anger, would fall on their comrades, and as often as not blood would be shed. Ahmed reformed all this by establishing a fixed hour for meals, at which all must be present, with the happy result that peace and tranquillity prevailed.

In this and a hundred other ways did Ahmed show his capacity, and became much beloved by the king, who, having no successors, gave him his favourite daughter as a wife, and before his death nominated him as his successor to the throne.

Almost all the inhabitants had a great respect for Ahmed, and on Kor's death they made him their king. The news spread far and wide, and on it becoming known to the Tungurs in Bornu and Wadai, they flocked into the country in such numbers as to partially displace the Tago; and now the only small settlements left of the former rulers are near Dara, where there is a Tago Sheikh, and also at Dar Sula, a long way to the west, where there is a semi-independent ruler called "Sultan Abu Risha et Tagawi," who is also known as "*El Jamus el asfar*," or the yellow buffalo.

Ahmed el Makur ruled happily for a long period, and a regular male succession was established. His great grandson was the celebrated Sultan "Dali," whose mother belonged to the Kera-Fur tribe, and thus consanguinity was established between the blacks and the Tungur dynasty. Dali was a very enlightened ruler; he travelled a great deal, and collected round him many men who could read and write; he divided the country into provinces and districts, and wrote the celebrated "*Kitab-Dali*," or penal code. The system of government inaugurated by Dali was carefully followed by his successors, and continued in use up to the middle of the present century.

One of the most noted of the Darfur rulers was Suleiman, who, being the son of an Arab mother, and having himself married an Arab woman, took the title of *Solong*, which is generally applied to those who consider themselves of Arab descent. It was through him that the country was definitely Moslemised; and his descendants, up to 1875, proudly boast of their Arab descent, and entirely ignore the Black element, which undoubtedly is there, and which may be said to show itself in the bitter hatred which has always existed between the ruling Darfur family and the nomad Arabs.

In accordance with Dali's code, the descent should devolve on the eldest son; but gradually the custom obtained of selecting one of the sons (provided he was in the direct line) who happened to be the most popular in the estimation of the court dignitaries, and especially in that of the "Abu Sheikh," the name given to the principal eunuch of the royal household. A rigorous exclusion was exercised over all sons who were addicted to alcohol or *marissa*.

Suleiman was succeeded by his son Musa, and the latter by his son Ahmed Bakr, who did all in his power to introduce foreigners into the country, as he hoped thereby to benefit his people. He was succeeded by his son Mohammed Dura, who is said to have had over a hundred brothers, of whom he caused fifty to be killed on coming to the throne; he is also credited with having killed his eldest son, whom he suspected of having pretensions to make himself king.

On his death his son Omar Leila succeeded, and he also was as unpopular as his father. He took command of the Darfur army which invaded Wadai, and was killed, being succeeded by his uncle, Abu el Kasem, who, with his brothers Mohammed Terab and Abderrahman, was amongst those who had escaped the slaughter when Mohammed Dura came to the throne. Abu el Kasem showed a great inclination to the Blacks, and incurred, in consequence, the hostility of his relations, who urged him to take the field against Wadai, and, having advanced, suddenly deserted him with the army, leaving him the Blacks only. It is said by some that he was at once killed in the battle which ensued, while others state that he remained for some time in Wadai, and then returned to attack his brother, Mohammed Terab, by whom he had been succeeded.

The latter proved himself a capable and energetic ruler, but towards the close of his reign he conceived the idea of enlarging his dominions and restoring the country to its early limits, which, it will be remembered, extended as far as the Atbara. He therefore issued a decree declaring war against the Fungs, and advanced with his brother Abderrahman and a mass of warriors, both horsemen and spearmen, in an easterly direction. Eventually they arrived at Omdurman, the present Dervish capital of the Sudan, and, to their surprise, found their further progress stopped by the Nile. The inhabitants had removed all the boats, so the construction of a bridge was attempted; but to cross a rapid river six hundred yards broad, was a task beyond the powers of the Darfur king, who remained stationary for months at Omdurman, vainly making attempt after attempt to overcome this impassable obstacle.

At length the chiefs, despairing of success, approached the king, and urged that the army should return to Kordofan and Darfur; but the latter, furious at his failure, threatened any one with death who should show any inclination to retreat. The leaders, however, were not to be baffled; secretly arranging with the king's favourite wife, Khadija, they convinced her that she would be performing a public service by poisoning her husband's food, which she did, nothing loath, and Abderrahman succeeded to the throne.

The stone walls erected by Sultan Mohammed Terab are to be seen to this day at the south end of Omdurman. His body was embalmed, taken to Bara, and conveyed thence to Tura, in Jebel Marra, some thirty-five miles west of El Fasher, the burial-place of the old Darfur sultans.

Abderrahman and the army returned to Darfur to find that Mohammed Terab's son, Ishaak, who had been appointed regent, refused to acknowledge his authority; with the result that a battle took place, in which Ishaak was killed.

Abderrahman's favourite wife was a certain Umbusa, of the Begu tribe. This tribe had emigrated from Bahr el Ghazal many years before, had settled in Darfur, and had been granted lands by the kings, on condition that they should annually supply a beautiful girl for the royal *harem*. The Begus are a purely African race, descended from the Monolké family, and Umbusa, besides being a great beauty, was endowed with exceptionally high qualities, which induced Abderrahman to raise her to the status of a legal wife; and in his advanced age she bore him a son, who was named Mohammed el Fadl.

It was during Abderrahman's reign that the traveller Browne visited Darfur, and it was this *sultan* who in 1799 sent an address of congratulation to Napoleon, then campaigning in Lower Egypt, and received from him in return a present of two thousand Black slaves. During his reign also the nominal capital of Kobbé was abandoned for El Fasher, which henceforth became the royal residence.

Abderrahman, before his death, placed his son in charge of the chief eunuch, Abu Sheikh Kura, who had originally been a slave, but had risen to a high position in the royal household; and at the age of thirteen, the youth succeeded to the throne. It is related that when Abderrahman died, Umbusa's father, Omar, was tending the flocks in Dar Begu, some fifty miles southwest of El Fasher, when suddenly a messenger was seen galloping a horse covered with foam, which fell dead before reaching him: the messenger, rushing forward, cried, "I bring you the glad tidings that the son of your noble daughter Umbusa was made Sultan of Darfur five days ago."

Without saying a word, Omar broke with his foot the wall of the *dabarek*,[1] and caused the water to flow over the sand, and then shouted, "No more shall the flocks of my family water at this well, for the great and merciful God has chosen my grandson to be ruler over Darfur;" and, saying this, he at once distributed his herds amongst those present, and then without delay proceeded to his grandson at El Fasher.

---

1. The *dabarek* is the circular pond usually made close to a well, into which the water when drawn up is poured, and which is then used as the drinking-trough for the flocks.

Mohammed el Fadl's first step as *sultan* was to declare his mother's tribe as free for ever, the annual tribute of a girl was no longer to be exacted, and buying and selling of Begus was made a crime punishable by death. For some four years the young king, under the guidance of Kura, ruled with energy and justice; but now intrigues crept in: it was whispered by some that Kura aimed at supreme power, while others asserted that the king was doing his utmost to deprive him of his authority; mutual mistrust, resulting in an open quarrel, prevailed, and in a fight which took place on the Rahad River, Kura was defeated, taken prisoner, and instantly executed.

After this, Mohammed el Fadl determined to coerce the proud Arab tribes who hesitated to comply with his orders and who frequently attempted to shake off the Darfurian yoke. His first step was to despatch the official in charge of Dara to the Beni Helba Arabs, who had refused to pay tribute. these were speedily coerced, and almost all their property confiscated; he then turned to the Ereikat tribe,—one of the most powerful in Darfur,—and these also were soon reduced to complete submission; but to subjugate the great Rizighat tribe was a more difficult matter. This was the most warlike and powerful tribe in the country. Several centuries ago an Arab from the far west named Ruzeik and his three sons, Mahmud, Maher, and Nueib, with their families, flocks, and herds, emigrated to the southern districts of Darfur; here in the vast forests they found abundance of food for themselves, and in these dense and pathless regions they were safe from intrusion.

As time went on their numbers rapidly increased, and, being joined by numerous smaller tribes, they became a power in the land, and the Sultans of Darfur were unable to gain their entire submission. Moreover, the districts they peopled were infested in winter by the *Um Bogone* (a kind of insect somewhat resembling the tsetse fly), which killed off the cattle.

Mohammed Fadl now decided that the only way to deal with the Rizighat was to completely surround them; by degrees their forests were encircled by myriads of Darfurians, and gradually the human chain closed in on the luckless tribesmen, who were slaughtered wholesale. At length some captives, being brought before the *sultan*, were asked where the main body of the Rizighat was to be found. "Sire," they answered, "we have all been separated and dispersed amongst your own army;" whereupon the *sultan* issued orders to his chiefs that all men of over thirty years of age wearing beards were to be slain; and after this order had been carried out, the survivors, who were all young men, and some thousands in number, were brought before him. These he classified according to their original families, and divided them into two sections: the first section were allowed to take back their captured wives and children and a proportion of their cattle, and were permitted to remain in their country; also to each widow whose husband had been killed in battle a milch-cow and an ox were given.

The second division, which was composed principally of the descendants of the families of Mohammed, Maher, and Nueib, were ordered to move into the northern districts of Darfur, and to occupy the lands formerly owned by the now almost exterminated Ereikat tribe. This section eventually developed into the powerful tribes now known as the Mahamid, Maheria, and Nueiba, who are, of course, the blood-relatives of the Rizighat, who are, in their turn, a division of the Baggara, or cattle-owning Arabs of the Western Sudan.

Mohammed el Fadl died early in 1838, and was succeeded by his son, Mohammed Hussein, who did his utmost to recover the popularity which his father had lost; about the year 1856, however, he became blind, and delegated most of his official work to his eldest sister, Iya Basi Zemzem,—it being an ancient Darfur custom that the eldest sister of the reigning *sultan* should receive the title of Iya Basi, and exercise a certain political influence. This worthy lady was both extravagant and immoral; the conduct of her court was notorious, and absorbed most of the state revenues. At this period the provinces of Bahr el Ghazal were subject to Darfur, and the Black tribes paid tribute of slaves and ivory to the *sultans*.

It often happened that the payment of this tribute was delayed, and this at once offered a pretext for a raid, in which the Darfurians invariably obtained large quantities of spoil. The ivory and many of the slaves were sold to the Egyptian merchants who travelled along the Arbaïn road between Assiut and Darfur, and for these, Turkish and European wares were exchanged. This trade was most lucrative on both sides, and gradually quantities of gold-brocaded stuffs, richly caparisoned saddles, silk embroideries, and other articles of luxury found their way into Darfur, besides quantities of jewellery as well as arms and ammunition.

And now we come to the period when the famous Zubeir Pasha enters on the scenes. A member of the Gemiab section of the Jaalin tribe, he quitted Khartum as a young man, and went south in search of a fortune. Already several merchants and slave-traders were established in the White Nile and Bahr el Ghazal districts, and the young Zubeir became the assistant of the well-known Ali Abu Amuri, so often mentioned by Sir Samuel Baker. Affairs prospered with him, and eventually he was able to set up an independent establishment, or *zariba*, of his own,—his labours lay, so to speak, in virgin soil; with well-armed bands of natives he gradually succeeded in annexing territories and amassing quantities of ivory and slaves, which he exchanged with the Nile merchants for arms and ammunition.

I do not think Zubeir Pasha was any worse or any better than the hundreds of other merchants occupied in a traffic which at that time was considered perfectly legitimate; but there is no doubt that he was a man of iron will, and of an energy and intelligence far above the average; and to these qualities may be attributed his ultimate success as an ivory and slave dealer. It is not my intention to describe the various steps by which he became practically ruler of the Bahr el Ghazal; it will be sufficient for my present purpose to say that at the time of which I write he had become one of the most powerful men in the Sudan, and it was not long before the tottering kingdom of Darfur fell bodily into his hands; and this is how it came about.

Zubeir, gradually extending his conquests into the northern districts of Bahr el Ghazal, began to encroach on those regions which were tributary to the Sultan of Darfur, and, anxious to avoid a quarrel, he wrote to Sultan Hussein to the effect that Blacks who had no masters, and were heathens, were, in accordance with the law of the Prophet, the fair spoil of the Moslems; to which Hussein replied that he, too, being a descendant of the ancient line, claimed similar rights to deal with black slaves and horse-dealers. By this latter epithet he referred to Zubeir, whom he classed amongst the other Jaalin known to the Darfurians as vendors of Dongola horses.

Zubeir, however, was not to be thwarted, and year by year his influence increased, until he had complete possession of all the Bahr el Ghazal districts which had paid tribute to Darfur. The effect of this on the luxury-loving Darfurians was painfully evident. They saw their main source of ivory and slave supplies cut off, and to meet the government expenditure increased taxation was enforced, which resulted in widespread discontent.

At this time there lived in Sultan Hussein's palace a certain Mohammed Belali of the Belala tribe, which is settled partly in Wadai and partly in Bornu. This man was a *fiki*, or religious teacher, and claimed

ZUBEIR PASHA.

noble descent, thereby ingratiating himself with Hussein, much to the annoyance of Iya Basi and the Vizir Ahmed Shata, who resented his interference, and eventually induced the *sultan* to drive him out of the country.

Breathing threats of vengeance, he proceeded to Khartum and informed the government of the immense riches and fertility of the province of Bahr el Ghazal and the Hofret en Nahas district, which no longer belonged to Darfur, and were now without a ruler. The astute Belali, whose sole object was to injure Sultan Hussein for having driven him out of the country, conceived this plot, which was destined to bring about a war with Darfur. Thoroughly trusted by the ignorant Khartum authorities, he was despatched, in company with Kutshuk Ali, who commanded some *bashi-bozuks* and two hundred regulars, to take possession of those supposed rulerless regions.

As may be imagined, Zubeir looked with no friendly eye on the intrigues of this upstart; but, with his far-seeing astuteness, he watched and waited patiently for the further development of his rival's plans. Meanwhile Kutshuk Ali died suddenly, and was replaced by Haj Ali Abu Nurein; and, at the instigation of the latter, Belali, emboldened by Zubeir's inaction, proceeded to seize some large stores of grain which he had prepared for his Bazingers. Zubeir did not hesitate to seize this chance, and, falling on him suddenly, drove him and his men off with some loss. Belali now collected as many men as he could, and made a determined attack on Zubeir's *zariba*, but was again repulsed. Severely wounded himself, he fled to Ganda, where he was pursued, captured by Zubeir's men, and taken back to the *zariba*, where he died.

Zubeir, however, was not slow to perceive that his action in this matter might have serious consequences. He therefore did all in his power to show that Belali was entirely to blame for what had occurred, and, by making valuable presents to Belali's men as well as to those in authority, he succeeded in having the matter reported to Khartum in its most favourable aspect, with the result that he received a full pardon, and was appointed Governor of Bahr el Ghazal.

Soon afterwards he confidentially pointed out to the governor-general that great discontent prevailed in the neighbouring State of Darfur, and that he had relations with some of the principal dignitaries who would gladly see the country annexed to Egypt; and he also volunteered to carry this out without further assistance from the government. After much deliberation his proposal was at length agreed to, and early in 1873 he made preparations to seize Shakka.

Let us turn now for a moment to the Rizighat. For years following on the terrible treatment they had received at the hands of the Darfur Sultan, they remained quiet and submissive, but gradually, as the governing power in Darfur grew weak, they recovered in proportion, and again assumed a semi-independent position between Darfur and Bahr el Ghazal.

Attempts were made to collect taxes from them, but they almost invariably drove off the tax-gatherers, and in one of these raids the Vizir Adam Tarbush, one of the principal Darfur commanders, lost his life,—curiously enough at the very spot where, some years later, I was destined to suffer a heavy defeat at the hands of the Dervishes.

On another occasion the Rizighat had fallen on a large caravan coming from the Nile and Kordofan to Bahr el Ghazal, with which were a number of Zubeir's relatives, almost all of whom were killed. Zubeir, rightly considering that the Rizighat owed allegiance to the Sultan of Darfur, called on the latter for compensation for the losses he had sustained; but the *sultan* either would not or could not give it, and Zubeir now openly gave out that, being unable to obtain satisfaction, he had determined to punish the Rizighat,—being well aware that this must lead to the fulfilment of the project to annex Darfur.

Meanwhile early in 1873 Sultan Hussein had died and had been succeeded by his son, who was nicknamed by the Darfurians Ibrahim Kuiko. I may here mention that some years later, when residing at El Fasher as governor, I made the acquaintance of the celebrated Fiki Mohammed el Heliki, who, though a Fellata by race, had been born there, and was infinitely the best authority on the former history of Darfur.

It greatly interested one to talk to this man, and I made a mass of notes which, with many other interesting records, fell subsequently into the hands of the Mahdists, and were burnt. I well remember Fiki Mohammed one day telling me the following story:

> Three years before the death of my master, Sultan Hussein,—may God give him peace,—I was talking to him about the present and future of the country. Bowing down his head and supporting it in his hand,—for the poor man had been blind for the last thirteen years,—he said, 'I feel that my country and the throne of my ancestors are about to be overthrown; God grant I may not live to see that day! Already I seem to hear the trumpets of the Turks and the distant sound of the *ombeÿa*

blown by the Bahhara.[2] May God have mercy on my son Ibrahim and on my unfortunate descendants!'

The *fiki* then went on to tell me that in spite of his old age and blindness, Sultan Hussein well knew the state of corruption of his country, and how impossible it was for him to check it; he realised the growing desire of the Egyptians to increase their conquests, and he instinctively knew that Zubeir and his Bazingers would be their instruments. He was a wise man, he said, and though God had deprived him of sight, He had sharpened his intellect.

Zubeir now lost no time in beginning operations. Quitting his fortified post of Dem Zubeir with a considerable force, he advanced towards Shakka, and on reaching the southern frontiers of Darfur he was joined by some of the principal chiefs of the Rizighat, such as Madibbo, Egeil Wad el Jangawi, and several of their men, who, being well acquainted with the districts, acted as his spies and scouts, and considerably facilitated his advance through their country, which was hostile.

Attacked incessantly by the Arabs, and suffering greatly from sickness and privations, Zubeir's force advanced steadily, and at length reached Abu Sigan, which is the centre of the Shakka district. There he learnt that Sultan Ibrahim had despatched a strong force against him, under his *vizir* (and father-in-law, Ahmed Shata, Ibrahim having married his daughter, Um Giddein). The latter, since the accession of his son-in-law, had grown discontented, and showed much reluctance in taking command of the expedition against Zubeir. He had told his friends he did not seek victory, but preferred to die honourably in the field rather than continue to live under the new rule. Zubeir meanwhile strengthened his position at Shakka, and made all preparations for the impending attack. He now received from the Rizighat a truly characteristic Arab message:

> The army of the Sultan of Darfur is advancing. You and they are our enemies. When you begin fighting, we shall remain neutral. If you are defeated, we shall harass you on your retreat, and shall kill you all. If you conquer, then shall we mount our swift horses, follow up the Darfurians, and share with you the booty.

Zubeir was quite satisfied with this arrangement, and patiently awaited events. In the early dawn his outposts saw in the far distance

---

2. The name given to the lords of the Bahr el Ghazal *zaribas* and their men.

the great Darfur army advancing, led by the warriors in coats of mail, wearing chain helmets, and mounted on richly caparisoned horses, whose gold and silver trappings glittered in the morning sun. In front of all, advanced the Vizir Ahmed Shata, as if seeking death. Zubeir withdrew all his men within the intrenchments, and when the Darfur host had approached sufficiently near, he opened a deadly fire on them. The *vizir's* horse was instantly shot; but, mounting another, he continued to advance until he fell, riddled with bullets; and with him many of his relations and members of his household, including Melek Sad en Nur and Melek en Nahas (the chief of the copper drums), whom the *sultan* had placed as his second in command.

Deprived of their leaders, the troops retired, and Zubeir seized the opportunity to make a counter attack on their flank, which broke up the army, and caused it to disperse in all directions. Instantly, from behind the trees, dashed clouds of Rizighat horsemen, who slaughtered the flying Darfurians, capturing immense quantities of valuable loot, and now they entirely threw in their lot with the conquerors, with the certainty that they would reap considerable benefit.

The few who succeeded in escaping the massacre fled to Dara, while Zubeir sent messages to El Obeid and Khartum, announcing the victory, and asking for the reinforcements of troops and guns which, in the event of his success, the authorities had agreed to place at his disposal. In due time these arrived, and he continued his advance towards Dara, his flank being covered by the advance of the governor-general from El Obeid to Om Shanga, at the head of three thousand regulars and a number of irregular horsemen.

With the exception of one small skirmish, Zubeir entered Dara unopposed, to find it completely deserted. Erecting a small fort on the sand-hill, he awaited the attack of Sultan Ibrahim's sons; but the latter, at the head of a considerable force, merely reconnoitred the position, and, returning to their father at El Fasher, urged him to lead his troops against Zubeir. Ibrahim now collected every available man; but large as were his hosts, there were few amongst them ready to lay down their lives for their ruler. At the head of his army, the *sultan* advanced to some houses which had belonged to the late *vizir*, and which were almost within range of the sand-hill, while Zubeir withdrew his troops into Dara, where he had made all preparations for a siege, and had collected a large store of grain.

Wishing to make a close inspection of Zubeir's position, Ibrahim, with a portion of his force, approached the town, and was met by a

A RIZIGHAT WARRIOR.

storm of bullets which killed several of his men, and forced him to retire. The remainder of his force, seeing what appeared to them to have been an attack by the *sultan* on Zubeir's position, which had failed, made some mocking remarks within his hearing. Burning with anger, he ordered some of his riflemen to advance and fire on his own troops, who were retiring on the camp, with the result that several were killed and wounded, and the remainder dispersed, while many of those within the camp took advantage of the confusion to desert to their homes.

Thus was Sultan Ibrahim the means of the destruction of his own army. And this incident subsequently lost him his kingdom and his life.

He now ordered what remained of his army to retire to Manawashi, making his chiefs believe that by this movement Zubeir would be drawn out of Dara, and he would be able to attack him in the open; but his men had now lost all confidence in him, and his army was still further reduced by numerous desertions. Zubeir, who had full information from his spies of what was going on in the *sultan's* camp, now followed him to Manawashi, and formed up in battle array, awaiting attack. His arrival was the signal for a general scuttle; men, women, and children fled in all directions; and Ibrahim, knowing that all was lost, determined to die an honourable death.

Donning his coat of mail and helmet, and accompanied by his sons, the *kadi*, and a few servants, all mounted on their magnificently trapped steeds, they sallied forth, and with drawn swords dashed at the enemy. Cutting his way through the first line of Bazingers, Ibrahim shouted, "*Fein sidkum ez Zubeir?*" (Where is your master, Zubeir?), and then made for the spot where Zubeir, dressed like his own men, was directing a gun against the assailants; but he had only gone forward a few steps when he and his little party fell, riddled with bullets. Thus perished the last of the long line of kings of Darfur, who had ruled this vast country and its millions of inhabitants uninterruptedly for centuries.

Zubeir ordered the dead *sultan* to be treated with the greatest respect. The *fikis* of Manawashi were directed to wash the body in accordance with the religious rites; and, wrapped in a costly shroud, it was buried with all honour in the mosque of the town.

He now lost no time in informing the governor-general, then at Om Shanga, of the victory; and the latter, anxious that the rich plunder of the province should not fall into Zubeir's hands, hurried forward without delay.

Meanwhile, Zubeir, advancing rapidly, arrived at El Fasher in two days, and took possession of the royal treasures, as well as quantities of silver-embossed saddles, arms, jewellery, and thousands of female slaves, whom he distributed amongst his men.

A few days afterwards, Ismail Pasha, the governor-general, arrived, but he was too late; the greater quantity of treasure had already been distributed, though Zubeir, by offering him costly presents, did all he could to secure his friendship. There is no doubt, however, that this episode was the commencement of the quarrel between the two men, which eventually developed into mutual deadly hatred.

The work of subduing the remainder of the country now began. Hasaballa, the old uncle of Sultan Ibrahim, had taken refuge in Jebel Marra, and Ismail Pasha ordered Zubeir to advance against him. It was not long before he succeeded in obtaining the submission of both him and the late *sultan's* brother, Abderrahman Shattut, both of whom were subsequently sent to Cairo,—and they died there; but their families are residing at the present time in Upper Egypt, and are in receipt of a liberal pension from the government. Several of their adherents, however, still held out in Jebel Marra, and, electing two younger brothers of Sultan Hussein, *viz.*, Bosh and Seif ed Din, as their leaders, they showed a determination to resist. Bosh's first step was to send a certain Gabralla, of the Fur tribe, as a spy to Zubeir's camp.

This man enjoyed the entire confidence of his chief, who had given him in marriage his beautiful daughter, Um Selima, in spite of the opposition of the family. Gabralla, on reaching Zubeir's camp, fell an easy prey to that astute warrior. The promise of pardon and a high position under the government were quite sufficient inducements to him to betray his father-in-law and give the fullest information as to his position and strength. He then returned to Bosh, whom he advised to remain where he was, as Zubeir's troops were suffering much from the cold and disease, and he had no intention to attack. Zubeir was, however, following in Gabralla's footsteps, and on a given signal, previously arranged between them, Bosh's camp was suddenly surprised, and easily fell into his hands, though Bosh and Seif ed Din succeeded in escaping to Kebkebia, where they again collected a force. Zubeir, however, followed them up, and in the pitched battle which ensued, both leaders were killed, and the last remnant of the Darfur force finally dispersed, leaving the country entirely in the hands of the Egyptian Government.

Zubeir, now promoted to the rank of *pasha*, returned to El Fasher, where Ismail Pasha was occupied in regulating the administration of the country and freely levying taxes; and it was not long before serious differences between the two men arose.

Zubeir, having conquered the country, was somewhat resentful that its government had not been confided to him, while Ismail, anxious to free himself from the incubus of Zubeir, ordered him to occupy Dara and Shakka with his troops; but the latter, angry at the treatment he had received, despatched a message from Dara, *via* El Obeid, to H. H. the Khedive, Ismail Pasha, begging to be allowed to come to Cairo. Permission was immediately accorded to him and any others who wished to proceed; and Zubeir, having appointed his son Suleiman as his agent, started without delay, taking with him numbers of male and female slaves and valuable presents. Travelling by Khartum and Korosko, he at length reached Cairo, where he was cordially received, and lost no time in laying before the *khedive* his grounds of complaint against Ismail Pasha Ayub. The latter was, in consequence, summoned to Egypt, and made several charges against Zubeir, with the result that both were kept in Cairo.

Meanwhile, Hassan Pasha Helmi el Juwaizer had been appointed the representative of the government in Darfur, and it was not long before the inhabitants began to settle down under the new system. They were tired of the arbitrary rule of the *sultans*, and longed for change; but they soon discovered that if their kings had chastised them with whips, their new rulers, in the shape of Zubeir's Bazingers and the crowds of irregular Shaigias and dishonest Egyptian officials, who swarmed into the country, chastised them with scorpions.

It was not long before the most bitter discontent prevailed throughout the country, and already there appeared signs of revolt. Electing Harun er Reshid, the son of Seif ed Din, as their *sultan*, they secretly planned the massacre of several of the small outlying garrisons, and in an incredibly short space of time the larger towns of Dara, El Fasher, Kebkebia, and Kulkul were closely invested. At El Fasher, the fort was twice almost successfully stormed, and on one occasion the governor, feeling that it must fall, had made all preparations to blow up the powder magazine and destroy himself and his garrison; but fortunately the troops, after a desperate encounter, succeeded in driving the enemy out of the position.

Meanwhile the Khartum authorities lost no time in sending a relieving force under Abd er Razzak Pasha, which, reinforced at El

Obeid, advanced to Darfur by forced marches, and at a place called Brush, midway between Om Shanga and El Fasher, they inflicted a heavy defeat on the rebels. Pushing on rapidly, El Fasher was relieved a few days later, reinforcements were sent to Kebkebia and Kulkul, and the country was once more made subject to the Egyptian Government.

On the recall of Ismail Pasha Ayub, Gordon was appointed Governor-General of the Sudan, and, as I have already related, he thought it expedient to visit Darfur without delay. In fact, when he reached El Fasher, Kebkebia, and Kulkul, the revolt was only partially suppressed; but, utterly fearless, he rode with only a small escort all over the country, and frequently placed himself in positions of extreme danger, from which his pluck and presence of mind alone saved him. From El Fasher he visited Dara, and by his kindness and sympathy with the people he succeeded in a large measure in quieting the districts; with a mere handful of men and the assistance of a few Rizighat Arabs he completely quelled the Mima and Khawabir Arabs, who were the most restless and independent tribes in the country, and gradually through his efforts peace was once more established throughout the land.

Sultan Harun with a few followers had taken refuge in the wilds of Jebel Marra, where they had been followed by Hassan Pasha Helmi, who twice defeated them at Murtal and Murtafal, and had pursued the survivors as far as Niurnia.

Gordon now turned his attention to the establishment of a government administration; his first step was to remit the greater part of the taxes, which, owing to the war, could not possibly have been paid, and he gave strict injunctions to the officials to deal leniently with the people, warning them that any disregard of his orders in this respect would be dealt with very severely. In order to equalise revenue and expenditure as far as possible, he reduced the Darfur garrison considerably, sending back to El Obeid and Khartum a large number of the regular infantry and cavalry who had been despatched to quell the late revolt. These economical measures, although undoubtedly very necessary in the interests of the new province, had subsequently a most disastrous effect.

Official business obliged him to return to Khartum, leaving Hassan Pasha Helmi as governor; and the latter, four months before my arrival, was relieved by Messedaglia Bey, who had been Governor of Dara for a few months.

Harun, meanwhile, had somewhat recovered himself, and established a species of independent rule in Niurnia, which had been in early times the capital of the Tago princes; from thence he would occasionally descend to the plains and raid the villages which had submitted to government, returning laden with booty to his stronghold.

Such was briefly the state of the province of Darfur when I arrived at El Fasher. The garrison of this town consisted of two battalions of regulars, two batteries of field artillery, and two hundred and fifty irregular Shaigia horsemen, under Omar Wad Darho; at Dara there was one battalion of regulars, one field battery, fifty irregular horsemen, and two hundred irregular riflemen, or Bazingers; while in Kebkebia and Kulkul there were six companies of regulars, four hundred Bazingers, and twenty-five horsemen.

After a few days' rest at El Fasher, Dr. Zurbuchen and I continued our journey to Dara, and were accompanied a short distance along the road by Messedaglia Bey, who told us that his wife was coming to Khartum, and that he was asking for leave of absence to go and meet her there and bring her to El Fasher. I suggested that it would be advisable to wait till Sultan Harun had been dealt with before bringing his wife so far; but Messedaglia replied there was not the least cause for fear, and that there were now quite sufficient troops in the country to suppress any local difficulties. I had heard, however, that Harun's influence was considerable, and that there was some apprehension that the now reduced government forces might be hard pressed. Having only just come to the country and having had no previous experience, it was of course impossible for me to judge; I therefore accepted Messedaglia's views on the situation, and, bidding him and Said Bey Guma, the commandant, farewell, we hurried on towards Dara, our road taking us through Keriut, Ras el Fil, and Shieria.

Zurbuchen was a very much older-looking man than myself, with a long black beard and spectacles, whilst I looked perhaps even younger than I was. The hair on my upper lip had scarcely begun to sprout, and altogether I had a most boyish face; consequently wherever we went he was invariably taken for the governor, and I for the doctor or apothecary. As we approached the end of our journey, the doctor, who was suffering from fever, had to ride slowly, and to save time for official work, I rode on slightly ahead, and happened to reach the village of Shieria (a day's march from Dara) a little before the appointed time.

I found the villagers busily preparing for our reception, the houses were being swept out, straw mats laid down, and the *kadi* and *sheikh* had spread out their carpets, on which the new governor was to repose. Making my camel kneel down, I got off, and to inquiries as to who I was, I answered, "One of the new governor's escort;" having previously warned the rest of my escort to say nothing. The inquisitive villagers now assailed me with innumerable questions. "What sort of man is the new governor?" said one.

"Oh," I replied, "I think he will do his best, and I believe he is inclined to be just and easy going."

"But is he brave and kind-hearted," said another.

This was rather a puzzling question to answer, so I replied guardedly, "He does not look as if he were afraid, but I haven't yet heard much about his courage; he has a manly appearance, and I believe he is kind-hearted; but of course it is impossible for him to satisfy everyone."

"Ah!" said another, "if we only had a governor like Gordon Pasha, then the country would indeed be contented; he never ceased to distribute money and presents, and never sent the poor and needy away without giving them something. I only once heard him say some harsh words, and that was when Suleiman Zubeir was at Dara, and when he turned to the *kadi*, saying that there were several bad characters amongst the Sudanese, and that it did not always do to treat them leniently."

"Yes," chimed in the *kadi*, "I heard him say so myself; but he referred only to the Gellabas and traders who came from the Nile, and who were implicated with Zubeir and his son in every description of unlawful trade by which they could benefit themselves."

"Gordon was indeed a brave man," said the *sheikh* of the village, who introduced himself as Muslem Wad Kabbashi, "I was one of his chiefs in the fight against the Mima and Khawabir Arabs: it was in the plain of Fafa and a very hot day. The enemy had charged us and had forced back the first line, and their spears were falling thick around us; one came within a hair's breadth of Gordon, but he did not seem to mind it at all, and the victory we won was entirely due to him and his reserve of one hundred men. When the fight was at its worst, he found time to light a cigarette. Never in my life did I see such a thing; and then the following day, when he divided the spoil, no one was forgotten, and he kept nothing for himself. He was very tender-hearted about women and children, and never allowed them to be distributed, as is our custom in war; but he fed and clothed them at his own expense, and had them sent to their homes as soon as the war was over.

One day, without letting him know, we put some women aside; but if he had found us out, we should have had a bad time of it."

After a short pause, I inquired about affairs in Dara and about the qualifications of the various officials; for I had already heard that they were very unreliable, and I was now told that they looked on my advent with no friendly eye.

Meanwhile Dr. Zurbuchen and the rest of the caravan had arrived, and at once the *sheikh*, *kadi*, and other village dignitaries lined up in a semi-circle to receive him, while I, concealing myself as much as possible, awaited with amusement to hear what Muslem Wad Kabbashi would say; he began with warm welcome to the new governor, praised his qualifications, and eloquently described the joy of all his people at his arrival. Poor Dr. Zurbuchen, whose comprehension of Arabic was very slight, became more and more perplexed. "Indeed I am not the governor," he urged, "I am only the Sanitary Inspector. The governor must have arrived long ago; but as he had only a few people with him, perhaps he has been mistaken for someone else."

I now thought it time to step forward, and laughingly thanked the villagers for their kind reception, assuring them that I would do all in my power to satisfy their wants, and that at the same time I looked to them to assist me in seeing my orders carried out. Of course they made the most profuse apologies for the mistake; but I assured them there was not the least necessity for their doing so. I was anxious, I said, to be on the most intimate and friendly terms with all of them, and I hoped they would allow the same friendly relations to continue. From that day forth, Sheikh Muslem Wad Kabbashi became one of my most faithful friends, and continued to be so, in times of joy and sorrow, until I left the country.

This little episode had given us all a hearty appetite, and we sat down to an excellent meal of roast mutton; and that over, we were again in the saddle, bivouacking for the night under a large tree about two hours' march from Dara. At sunrise the next morning I sent on a messenger to announce our approach, and on reaching the outskirts we were given a great military reception, the garrison was drawn up in line and a salute of seven guns fired, after which the troops filed off to their barracks, and, accompanied by Major Hassan Helmi, the commandant, Zogal Bey, the sub-governor, the *kadi*, and some of the principal merchants, we proceeded to the fort in which the government buildings are situated. The inspection lasted about half an hour, and I then went to my own quarters, in which I had ordered rooms to be prepared for Dr. Zurbuchen, who was to be my guest for a few days.

Dara, which is the capital of Southern Darfur, is built in the midst of a large plain of partly sand and partly clay soil, the fort itself being on the top of a low sand-hill,—in fact, on the same spot in which Zubeir Pasha had entrenched himself when invading the country. It was a rectangular stone enclosure twelve feet high, about five hundred yards long and three hundred yards broad, with flanking towers at each corner, and surrounded by a broad ditch twelve feet deep. The troops were quartered in huts built along the inside of the enclosure, and in the centre were the government buildings, consisting of the governor's house, divan, and the various offices and courts of justice, as well as the arms, grain-store, and prison. Some distance east of the fort was the old mosque built by Sultan Mohammed el Fadl, which the former governor had converted into a powder-magazine, but which Gordon had restored to the town for its proper purpose. Close to the southern gate were the houses of Zogal Bey, the *kadi*, and the commandant, built mostly of burnt brick and enclosed by walls.

The town of Dara, consisting chiefly of straw and mud huts, lay a few hundred yards to the east of the fort, while upwards of half a mile to the west was situated the village of Goz en Naam, and beyond it again the hamlet of Khummi.

Inclusive of the garrison, the population of Dara numbered between seven and eight thousand, most of whom belonged to the local tribes; but there were also a considerable number of Nile merchants and traders.

It being the month of *Ramadan*, which is the great fast, a meal of roasted meat, bread, dates, and lemonade had been prepared for us; but the officials sent a message to say they regretted they could not join us. I confess to being only too glad of this respite, for we were thoroughly tired. Our things unpacked, I now sat down to consider how to make myself as comfortable as I could.

At sunset, the gun boomed out the signal that one day more of Ramadan had gone; and now the hungry and thirsty inhabitants, their daily fast over, hurried to their evening meal. Zogal Bey, Hassan Effendi Rifki, Kadi el Beshir, and the chief merchant, Mohammed Ali, now came to see us, and asked us to dine with them; they were followed by a host of servants bearing roast mutton, fowls, milk, and rice,—which is usually eaten with hot melted butter and honey,—and dishes of *asida* (meat spread over with a thin layer of very fine *dukhn* flour, over which sauce is poured, and on the top of all is a thin layer of paste, sprinkled with sugar); this completed the menu. In a few minutes the ground just outside the house, which had been sprinkled with fine sand, was spread with carpets and palm mats, and on these the dishes were laid. Zogal Bey began distributing the viands amongst those who had come to welcome me, including the servants, but keeping, of course, the best dishes for the more select company.

We now sat down, and the tearing and rending of the roast sheep began with a vengeance; of course, knives and forks were out of the question. Scarcely had we settled down to the feast, when a great hubbub arose amongst the servants, who were evidently trying to prevent two men from pushing their way into our circle. I begged Zogal Bey to inquire what was the matter. Licking his greasy fingers, he got up, and returned in a few minutes, carrying a document which proved to be a letter from Ahmed Katong and Gabralla, the two chiefs of an irregular corps which garrisoned the station of Bir Gowi, some three days' march southwest of Dara: this was to say they had just received information that Sultan Harun was going to attack them, and that as they had only a small force, they proposed to evacuate their station, unless reinforcements could be sent at once; but they said that if they left the district, all the villages would be plundered.

There was no time to be lost, so I ordered Hassan Effendi Rifki to select two hundred regulars and twenty horsemen, to be ready to start with me at once for Bir Gowi. Zogal and Hassan both urged that it was unnecessary for me to go, as I wanted rest after the long journey; but I said that as my principal object in coming to Darfur was to fight Sultan Harun,—in accordance with Gordon Pasha's orders,—I intended to take the earliest possible opportunity of doing so. Seeing that I was not to be stopped, and secretly rejoicing that neither of them had been saddled with the responsibility of taking command, they now hurried on with the preparations.

The pony which Gordon had given me was too tired to be taken, so I asked if any one present could lend or sell me a good horse. Zogal happened to have just bought a large white Syrian horse, and at once sent for it; he was a strong, well-made animal, quite suitable for the fatigues of a campaign, and as he had formerly been owned by an officer, was used to the noise of firing. Seeing that I liked the look of the horse, Zogal immediately begged my acceptance of it by way of *diafa* (hospitality); but I went to some pains to explain to him that it was not customary in my country to accept such presents, and that here in the Sudan, he being my subordinate, I could not think of it. Unfortunately, I had previously mentioned Gordon's gift of a pony to me, and of course Zogal brought this up as a parallel case; but I replied that there was no objection to accepting a present from a high official given entirely by way of friendship. After considerable discussion, I at length succeeded in making him accept one hundred and eighty dollars; but he did so under great protest.

By midnight all was ready, and, bidding Dr. Zurbuchen goodbye, I started off for the southwest, saying that I hoped to see him again in four or five days.

I was young, strong, and keen to have some fighting experience, and I well remember my delight at the thought of a brush with Sultan Harun. The idea of difficulties and fatigue never crossed my mind; all I longed for was a chance of showing my men that I could lead them. At sunrise I halted my little party, which consisted of two hundred Blacks,—the officers also being Sudanese,—and the horsemen Turks and Egyptians, and addressed them in a short speech, saying that at present I was an entire stranger to them, but they should see I was ready to share fatigue and discomfort with them on all occasions, and that I hoped we should march rapidly forward with a good heart. Simple as my harangue undoubtedly was, I saw that it had made an impression, and when I had finished, they raised their rifles above their heads, in Sudanese fashion, and shouted that they were ready to conquer or die.

At noon we halted near a village, and I then carefully inspected the men. They were all well armed, and had a plentiful supply of ammunition; each man was also provided with a water-bottle made out of goat or gazelle skin, known as *"sen"* (pl. *siun*); but they had brought no rations with them. On inquiry, I was told, "Wherever you go in Darfur you will always find something to eat." I therefore made my way to the *sheikh* of the village, and asked him to supply some *dukhn*. This corn is generally soaked in water, then pressed, mixed with tamarind fruit, and eaten in this condition; the bitter-sweet water being an excellent thirst-quencher. This food Europeans usually find indigestible; but it is very nourishing, and is eaten almost exclusively by the Sudanese soldiers when campaigning.

I gradually got accustomed to it, taking it almost invariably when out on such expeditions; but I found that unless one was feeling very well, it generally brought on most painful indigestion. The *sheikh* now brought us the corn, and also a large dish of *asida*, which was divided amongst the men; and whilst they were having their meal, I asked the officers to share with me a tin of preserved meat, which they admitted was much superior to the *asida* and *dukhn*. I then called up my clerk, and told him to write out a receipt for the corn, which he was to give the *sheikh*, to be his voucher for the remission of taxation equivalent to the value of the *dukhn* supplied. But the good man, when he understood my orders, refused to accept the receipt, adding that it was not only his duty to give the corn, but that the rights of hospitality demanded it. I told him, however, that I was well aware the natives of Darfur were most generous; but to impose the feeding of two hundred men on him quite exceeded the bounds of hospitality, and that it was only just he should receive payment.

He at length agreed, and this conversation appeared to give him confidence; for he admitted that if this principle were always carried out, the natives would greatly appreciate it; but, unfortunately, it was the usual custom for troops arriving at a village to enter the houses, and take anything and everything they wanted, with the result that the inhabitants dreaded their approach, and at once tried to hide all they had. I thanked the *sheikh* for telling me this, and promised I would do all I could to rectify the evil. We moved on again at three o'clock, loaded with the blessings of this good man and his people, and after a quick march of four hours halted in a small plantation of trees. Our route had led us across a country overgrown with dense bush, and intersected by innumerable dry gullies; and here and there we passed a village buried amongst the trees.

From our halting-place I sent off two horsemen to Bir Gowi to announce our approach; and, after a refreshing rest of five hours under the wild fig-trees and tamarisks, we started off again, and marched almost uninterruptedly till noon the following day. We once or twice had to ask for corn, and always had the same difficulty in getting the *sheikhs* to accept the receipt; but as I insisted, they generally ended by gladly taking it. I was anxious, if possible, to reach Bir Gowi before dark, so pushed on; we passed on the way a large plantation of *deleb* palms, and had to be careful not to be struck by the heavy fruit, which, weighing from two to three pounds, and falling from a height of some forty feet, was a positive danger. Woe to the unfortunate traveller who thoughtlessly halts for the night in one of these palm-groves! The natives, however, are very careful, and generally warn the unsuspecting of the risk of sleeping anywhere near these trees when bearing fruit.

At sunset we reached Bir Gowi, which was situated in the centre of a large clearing; and to reach the station we had to pass between the stumps of trees, which considerably impeded the march. It was surrounded by a square *zariba*, each side of which measured about one hundred and eighty paces, and consisted of a thorn barricade about twelve feet thick and six feet high; on the inside, the ground was raised to enable the men to fire over it from a platform, and the whole was surrounded by a ditch nine feet wide, and about nine feet deep.

The garrison, consisting of some hundred and twenty men armed with rifles, was drawn up outside, with their officers, ready to salute. I halted the men, and, riding forward, saluted the garrison, and was welcomed by the vigorous beating of the *nahas* (copper war-drums) and *noggaras* (other drums, made from the hollow trunk of a tree, covered on both sides with skin), the blowing of bugles and antelope horns, and the rattling of dry skins filled with pebbles,—a very effective, but by no means melodious band, diversified by the occasional crack of rifles fired off in a promiscuous manner, and which could not exactly be compared to a *feu de joie*, though no doubt the intention was the same. After inspecting the garrison, I ordered my men to file into the fort. The interior of the *zariba* was filled with straw huts, those of the chiefs being surrounded by high straw enclosures; but there was sufficient room for us all, and I was given a good-sized hut, standing in almost the only open place visible.

The object of the Bir Gowi military post was to protect the surrounding villages from raids; but the strength of the garrison to take the offensive was insufficient, and it would probably have been of little use. Dismounting from my horse, I sat on an *angareb*, and sent for Ahmed Katong and Gabralla to discuss the situation, and obtain the latest news about Harun's movements. Katong soon arrived, hobbling along on a crutch. He belonged to the Fung tribe, his forefathers having been captured by the Furs, after the conquest of Kordofan, and he had been made Hakem Khot, or chief of the district; his duty being to collect taxes, and at the same time to be responsible for the security of the country. In reply to my question as to how he had become lame, he told me that some years before he had been struck in the knee by a bullet.

"Since that date," said Ahmed, "I always have a saddled horse near me. In the *zariba*, of course, it does not matter; but when travelling in these unsettled times, and when one is liable to be attacked at any moment, I lie down to sleep holding the bridle in my hand. Those with good legs can easily get away in case of danger; but with a stump like mine I cannot run, so I have taught myself to mount my horse quickly, with one leg."

I now begged them to give me the latest news about Harun. "Gabralla," said Ahmed, "sent out spies, who returned this afternoon, and who state that Harun has collected his men, but has not yet come down from the mountains;" and Gabralla, chiming in, said, "Yes, I did so, and have sent off others to watch his movements; if he comes here I don't think we shall run away now."

I could not help scanning this man with some curiosity. He was tall, and of the usual black complexion of the Fur tribe; he possessed also—which is very unusual—a well-shaped aquiline nose and a small mouth; he had a slight beard, was about forty years of age, and had a very pleasant expression. Yet this was the villain who had betrayed the father of his own beautiful wife! Was I to trust him, or not? He had certainly every inducement to be loyal, for should he fall into the hands of Harun, he would doubtless pay with his life for the death of his uncle and his father-in-law.

Naturally I gave him no occasion to discover my thoughts, and we chatted about former times, agreeing they were very different from the present; he then began to talk of himself, and told me how he was employed as a spy to bring the news of Harun's movements to Dara, and thence to El Fasher. He had between thirty and forty of his old slaves, who were armed, and whose duty it was to guard and serve him, whilst the older male servants and female slaves had to work in the fields and keep the household supplied with corn. Being in the pay of the government, he was quite content, but told me that he wanted to do something which would qualify him for the rank of *bey*. "Zogal, who is a friend of mine," he said, "is a *bey*."

By this time I was so thoroughly tired and sleepy after my long journey, followed by the two days' hard marching, that I went to bed; but my head ached, and the incessant beating of drums in my honour kept me awake all night, and the following morning I felt really unwell. Ahmed Katong came to see me, and I told him I had a bad headache. "We can easily cure that," said Ahmed, cheerfully. "I have a man here who can stop headaches at once; he is a much better man than the doctor at Dara,—indeed there is no doctor at Dara; he is really only an apothecary, with the courtesy title of doctor."

"All right," said I, "but how is he going to cure me?"

"Oh! it is very simple," he answered; "he places both his hands on your head, and repeats something; then you get perfectly well,—in fact, better than you were before."

"Then let him come at once," I cried. I was young and ignorant in those days, and I thought that possibly one of these wandering Arabs might have visited Europe and learned something of the magnetic cure, and had given up the pleasures of life in order to make himself useful to mankind. I confess to feeling a little mistrustful when I thought of what Ahmed had said; but then, after all, doctors in Europe speak, so why should not he? In a few minutes Ahmed ushered into my presence a tall dark man with a white beard, who appeared to be a native of Bornu, and introduced him as "the doctor who will cure your headache." Without a moment's hesitation, the doctor placed his hand on my head, pressed my temples with his thumb and forefinger, and, muttering a few words I could not understand, to my horror, spat in my face. In a moment I had jumped up and knocked him down; but Ahmed, who was standing by, leaning on his crutch, begged me not to take it in this way. "It was not really meant for rudeness," he said; "it is merely a part of the cure, and will do you much good."

But the poor doctor, whose confidence had been somewhat shaken, and was still standing at a distance, muttered, "Headache is the work of the devil, and I must drive it out; several passages from the *Koran* and the sayings of holy men direct that it should be chased away by spitting, and thus his evil work in your head will cease!" In spite of my annoyance, I could not help laughing.

"So I am supposed to be possessed of a devil," I said; "I trust he was only a little one, and that you have really driven him out." I did not, however, let him make a second experiment, and, giving him a dollar as compensation, I bade him goodbye, and he left me, calling down the blessings of Heaven on my poor head, which was still aching sadly.

All day we awaited news of Sultan Harun's movements, and as there was nothing to be done I kept to my bed. I was just dozing off, when my servant announced that Katong and Gabralla wished to see me. They were admitted, for I thought that no doubt they brought news of Harun; but it was only to say that it was the custom of the country, and one of the claims of hospitality, that, having only one horse, I should accept from each of them a fine country bred animal as a mark of their loyalty and respect. I replied to them much in the same terms as I had answered Zogal, adding that I had no doubt we should remain equally good friends without giving and taking presents, provided they continued to carry out their duties faithfully.

Although they appeared greatly distressed at my refusal to accept the horses, I have no doubt they went home rejoicing secretly that I had refused their gifts. However, before many minutes had passed, Gabralla came back and asked to say just a few words. He had been much pained, he said, by my refusal to take the horse, and now, as I was quite alone and very unwell, he took the liberty of offering me one of his maid-servants. "She is young and pretty," he said, "and has been well brought up in my house; she knows how to prepare native food, is good at housework, and is above all a good and careful nurse, and thoroughly understands all the ailments of the country." Again I was obliged to refuse this proffered kindness; so poor Gabralla went away somewhat downcast with his failure. But having already had a rather painful experience at the hands of the doctor, I was not particularly anxious to intrust myself to the tender mercies of even a dusky maiden, however proficient a nurse she might be.

The next morning I arose feeling quite myself again; and when I met Ahmed and told him that I had recovered, he at once answered, "Of course, I knew you would get quite well; Isa (the name of my doctor) has never yet put his hands on anyone and failed to cure him."

Another day passed, and still no news of Harun. Accompanied by Katong and Gabralla, I visited the market, which was about a hundred yards outside the *zariba*, and was held specially for the benefit of the surrounding villagers, who purchased here all they required. Sometimes the Beni Helba Arabs, who reside in this part of the country, are seen here. Women sitting on the ground expose palm mats for sale, as well as giraffe, antelope, and cow meat; salt is also an important commodity, besides a great variety of native vegetables which are used as ingredients in making sauces for the *asida* dish. Men are to be seen selling *takaki*, or native woven linen and cotton cloth, thread, *natron*, and sulphur, which the Arabs buy freely to grind, and mix with the grease with which they rub their heads. The women are usually the *marissa* vendors; and here and there a young female slave is exposed for sale. I thought I must buy something, so invested in a few palm mats.

On the following day, about noon, one of Gabralla's messengers returned with the news that Sultan Harun had collected his men, but still had not moved down from his summer resort in the hills. On the fourth day after our arrival at Bir Gowi, a second messenger came in and stated that when Sultan Harun heard from the natives that I had left Dara for Bir Gowi with the intention of fighting him, he had at once disbanded his men, who had dispersed over Jebel Marra.

Thoroughly disappointed with my first failure, I returned crestfallen to Dara, but before doing so visited the sulphur spring from which the station of Bir Gowi (or the strong well) is named. The warm water spouts up from the centre of a sandy depression, and is cooled by two small streams artificially led into it. Natives affected with rheumatism or diseases of the blood bathe in this spring, and are said to derive great benefit from its strengthening properties.

Nine days after leaving Dara I was back there again, and by that time Dr. Zurbuchen had gone, leaving behind him a letter in which he wished me all success. I also found that during my absence my unfortunate Arab clerk who had accompanied me when I was Financial Inspector, and had come with me to Dara, had become crazy: they had put him into a house next my own, and when I went to see him, he sprang forward to embrace me, crying out, "Thank God! Sultan Harun has done no harm to you; but Zogal Bey is a traitor, beware of him. I have ordered the fires in the engine to be lighted, in order that the train may take you to Europe, where you will be able to see your relations again. I shall come with you; but we must be careful about Zogal, he is a scoundrel!"

Evidently the poor man's mind was quite unhinged; nevertheless, crazy people sometimes speak the truth. I quieted the poor old man, and induced him to lie down till he heard the engine's whistle warning us to be off; and, commending him to the care of the servants, I went away. Five days later, the whistle had sounded, and the poor man had been carried off to his long home,—his death was, I suppose, due to a rush of blood to the brain.

I now busied myself with the administrative affairs of the province of Dara, which, exclusive of the districts of Kalaka and Shakka, comprised five divisions, or *kisms*, *viz.*, Toweisha, Kershu, Giga, Sirga, and Arebu, each of which was supposed to pay taxes at a fixed rate; but I found that the officials conducted affairs just as they pleased. It was thought impossible to take regular taxes from Arabs who had no settled places of abode, and whose wealth in cattle was continually increasing; a system had, therefore, been arrived at by which each tribe was assessed at a fixed sum, for the payment of which the head-*sheikh* was made responsible, and he, in turn, assessed the various sub-tribes by a mutual arrangement with which the government did not interfere.

I now ordered each district to forward lists to me showing the name and number of the villages and the names of the landowners and traders in every village. When these came in, it would be an easy matter to lay down definitely the rates to be paid by every individual. It was also my intention to make an inspection of every district, in order to see for myself the quality of soil, and assess the value locally; and at the same time my inspections would enable me to see for myself the strength of the Arab tribes, and thus acquire some real data for laying down the tribute which they should pay.

About a month after my return from Bir Gowi, I received a letter in French from Messedaglia, telling me that he had determined to put an end to the Harun trouble; and for this purpose he ordered me to move secretly *via* Manawashi and Kobbé, with a division of regular troops, towards Jebel Marra, and attack Niurnia, the Sultan's residence. At the same time, he wrote, he was despatching troops from El Fasher, *via* Tura, and from Kulkul, *via* Abu Haraz, to rendezvous at a certain spot and co-operate in the attack.

In compliance with this order, I left Dara with two hundred and twenty regulars and sixty Bazingers; but as the horses were unshod, and not used to hill work, I took only six of them. It was then the month of February, and extremely cold. We marched *via* Manawashi, where I visited the tomb of the last *sultan* of the Fur Dynasty, and on the following day we bivouacked near Kobbé, close to the defile which leads to Jebel Marra. Being now fairly near the enemy, I increased the outposts; but we passed the night without being disturbed. Early the next morning we began our march through the defile, carefully protecting the flanks by sending parties up the hills on both sides.

In an hour and a half we had traversed the valley and reached the village of Abdel Gelil, who was one of Harun's chiefs. He had quitted the village only the day before; and, dividing amongst the men the corn we found, we continued our march over most rugged country, alternate steep hills and deep valleys, and here and there a stony plain. My men, being unused to climbing of this description, got very tired. The country was completely forsaken; not a human being was to be seen. Occasionally, close to the track, we came across small deserted huts with stone walls and thatched roofs; and now and then were to be seen little patches of ground, either at the bottom of the valleys or on the slopes of the hills, planted with various sorts of wheat; and there were wild fig-trees in abundance.

That night we bivouacked on a small plateau; but, fearing to expose our position, we did not dare to light fires, though we could have procured plenty of wood from the huts. In spite of our warm clothing, the cold was bitter; but it was better to bear that than make ourselves a target for the enemy, who, armed with Remington rifles, were in all probability prowling about on the heights. At sunrise we marched on again, and halted in the afternoon on an open plain called by the natives *Dem es Sakat* (the cold camp); so named because Zubeir Pasha, in his Darfur campaign, had stayed here and had lost many men from the cold. The next day, although I had ordered a large fire to be lit, several of the men were reported to me as being unable to move, owing to the cold; but we mounted them on the donkeys and mules, and so brought them along with us.

At noon we reached the highest point of Jebel Marra, and had a magnificent view over the whole country; and far in the distance could be seen Niurnia, the objective of our expedition. This ancient capital of the Fur Sultans lay far down the valley, where it began to open out into the plain, and was almost buried in a mass of wild fig-trees. With my glasses I could just descry people apparently hurriedly quitting the village and leading their horses. We pushed on, but it took us four hours to climb down the mountain side; and it was not till sunset that, preceded by a line of skirmishers, we entered the town to find it completely evacuated.

Sultan Harun's mosque lay to the west of the town, and was enclosed by a stone wall four and a half feet high and a hundred yards square. The mosque itself was in the centre of the enclosure, and was a stone building about forty feet square, with a straw-thatch roof. Some three hundred yards from the mosque lay the houses of the *sultan*, built of mud and stone; and one of them was furnished with a second story. They were all surrounded by straw fences, and near them were the huts of the personal retainers and armed men. The open space between the mosque and house was divided by a silvery stream of beautifully clear water. The mosque being empty, I turned my men into it, as I thought it the safest place to be in in case of attack.

The same evening a mountaineer was caught creeping into the village; and on assuring him that I meant him no harm, he told me, through an interpreter (he did not speak Arabic), that Sultan Harun, with all his men, had left Niurnia that morning, and had gone west in the direction of Abu Haraz, but that he had sent all the young slaves and those not strong enough to march, to a safe place in the mountains, about an hour's distance from the town. As I had to wait for the troops from Kebkebia and Kulkul, which should have already arrived, it was impossible for me to pursue Harun. I therefore proposed to the spy, under promise of a good reward, that he should lead me to the hiding-place in the hills.

Accordingly, we started the next morning at an early hour, with one hundred men and a couple of horses, and had not been out more than half an hour when, from the direction from which we had just come, I heard some shots, and then a series of volleys. Was it possible Sultan Harun had suddenly returned and was attacking my men? I instantly turned back, and, galloping on in front, reached an open space, in which I saw soldiers firing at each other. My trumpeter, whom I had mounted behind me, now jumped down, and I shouted to him to sound the "Cease fire;" but for a few minutes I could not get them to take any notice. Still riding on, I came within range, and a bullet passed through the cloak I had thrown over my shoulders to keep out the cold, and my horse was slightly struck in the hind leg.

At last I managed to stop the firing, and summoned the officers to find out what had occurred. It now transpired that the troops advancing from El Fasher under Kasem Effendi and his assistant, Mohammed Bey Khalil, had been informed that Sultan Harun was in Niurnia. They had marched all night, and, concealing themselves behind the huts, had crept in unawares close to the big fire round which my men were sleeping, and had suddenly fired on them. The latter, alarmed, had jumped up and begun firing, believing that they were attacked by Harun's men.

My chief officer, Hassan Rifki (who was one of those who had been present at the death of Suleiman Zubeir), had done his utmost to check the firing by repeated bugle-signals; but the Fasher troops, who had been told that Sultan Harun also had buglers who wore the *fez*, could not be induced to stop. Curiously enough, during the late revolt several of the soldiers had deserted and joined Sultan Harun. It was only when I appeared on the scene that the contending parties realised what had happened. Both sides had suffered: three of my men had been killed and four wounded, while the Fasher troops had lost four killed and seven wounded. I had a small field dispensary, and dressed the wounds as best I could; and then ordered a statement of what had occurred to be taken down and sent to the authority concerned.

The horse which I had bought from Zogal, and which I had left at the mosque, was struck in the neck by a bullet, which had slightly penetrated, and he almost died from loss of blood; but fortunately the ball had not lodged in a vital part, and after some days he recovered.

We remained ten days at Niurnia, and still the troops coming from Kulkul had not arrived; while communication by letter-carriers between us and Dara and Fasher was interrupted by the mountaineers, who would not allow the messengers through.

During this waiting time I made a small expedition to the village of Abderrahman Kusa, one of Harun's principal men. But it was deserted, though I knew that the villagers were concealing themselves amongst the rocks and were watching our movements; they had always early information, and were able to make off in good time. During this march we came across some trees to which curious clay vessels had been attached, and which I learnt were beehives. On the advice of Sheikh Taher we did not go near the trees, as he said the bees would probably attack us, but halted some two miles away.

That evening Sheikh Taher, taking some wood and straw, smoked out one of the hives and brought us a quantity of excellent honey; but his servants, who accompanied him, carried in a dying Bazinger on a stretcher. He was one of my men; and when he saw the hives, he had fallen out of the ranks, and, tying some cloth round his hands and face, had attempted to procure some honey. The bees had attacked him, and he had fallen off the tree unconscious, where he lay until picked up by the others; and I do not think I ever saw a more terrible sight. His face was swollen beyond all recognition, and his tongue protruded to an enormous size from his widely distended mouth. The poor man never regained consciousness, and died in an hour or two.

We had to start off before sunrise the next morning, as the *sheikh* told us that when the sun was up the bees would probably attack us.

On our return to Niurnia I gave orders to start back the following day, marching *via* Dar Omongawi, Murtal, and Murtafal. On our way we passed through several villages and took the people entirely by surprise, for they had not expected us from the west. Most of the men had been collected by Sultan Harun, and those who could escape to the hills did so; but my men captured about thirty women, whom we took along with us for a short distance. In one village the people were so completely surprised that few of them had time to fly; and, seeing that they were only women, I sounded the halt, in order to give them a chance of getting away. I then formed up the men on the road, so as to prevent them scattering through the village, and in this formation we marched on.

One poor woman, I noticed, in her hurry to escape, had left her two children on a rock, while she herself fled like a gazelle up the mountain side. Going to the rock, I found two pretty little babies, quite naked, but with strings of coral round their waists and necks. They were as black as ravens, and probably twins about eighteen months old. Dismounting, I went up to them, and they began to cry and cling to each other; so, taking them in my arms, I told my servant to bring me some sugar from my travelling-bag. This pacified them at once; and, smiling through their tears, they munched what to them was probably the nicest thing they had ever tasted in their little lives. Then, taking two of the red handkerchiefs (a supply of which I generally carried about to offer as presents), I wrapped the babies up in them, laid them down on the rock again, and moved on some distance. Looking back, I saw a human being, evidently the mother, creeping down the rocks. Then, joyfully seizing her little ones, whom she thought perhaps she had lost forever, she fondled them most lovingly. She had got back her naked treasures clothed in lovely garments, and licking their little black lips all sticky with their feast of sugar.

After a three days' march we reached Murtafal; and from here I sent the Fasher troops back to their station, whilst we continued on to Dara. But before leaving, I had all the women whom we had picked up on the march to carry corn, collected together, and then set them free. I told them that next time I hoped their husbands would be more submissive, and in that case wives, husbands, and children need never be separated. A shriek of joy, a mutter of gratitude, and they were off like gazelles released from a cage.

I had now been away from Dara about three weeks, and had heard no news whatever. At the noon halt, the following day, my men brought before me some of the Beni Mansur tribe, who told me that Sultan Harun had attacked Dara, and, on being repulsed, had turned to Manawashi, which was about a day's march from where we were. They told me he had looted the place, and also burnt the village of Tanera, which belonged to Sheikh Maki el Mansuri, and was about six hours' march from us. This *sheikh*, whom I knew well, had lost everything, they said, and had barely escaped with his life.

Telling my informants to lose no time in bringing Sheikh Mansuri to me, I marched on at once towards Manawashi, and by the evening we had made good progress. I now ordered the halt for the night, and soon afterwards the *sheikh* arrived, in a very destitute condition. He had lost all his property, and had nothing left but the clothes in which he stood; and they were torn to shreds by thorns during his flight. Seating himself, he briefly related what had occurred. Sultan Harun, it appeared, on quitting Niurnia, had collected a considerable force, and had descended to the plains in the direction of Abu Haraz. Here he had a collision with the Kulkul troops, who had suffered slight loss, and had retired on Kebkebia; and that was the reason they had failed to come up to the rendezvous at Niurnia. Harun had advanced immediately on Dara, and the news of his approach had only reached the garrison two hours before he had made his night attack on the town, in which many of the inhabitants, including Khater, a brother of Vizir Ahmed Shata, had been killed, and several women captured.

Eventually driven out, he had retired to Manawashi, which he had partially destroyed; and detaching some of his men to Tanera, they had burnt the village and taken almost all the women. The unfortunate Sheikh Maki had been wounded in the leg, and had only escaped death by a miracle. It appeared that Harun was now in a position about four hours' march from me in a westerly direction, and was being followed up by Ahmed Katong and Gabralla, who, when Harun had passed through the Beni Helba country, had not been sufficiently strong to attack him, but were now doing their best to keep in touch with him, and send news of his movements to Dara and Fasher.

I at once despatched messengers with instructions to them to join me during the night, and to send spies to ascertain exactly where Harun was encamped. At dawn the following morning, Katong and Gabralla arrived, with about a hundred Bazingers. They reported that Harun had struck his camp, and was marching west with his entire force. A woman they brought with them, and who belonged to Sheikh Maki's village, also stated that Harun had collected all the women he had captured at Dara and Manawashi, and had addressed them as follows:

> I was not told that the unbeliever Slatin had liberated the women he had captured; but as I am a believer and the *sultan*, it is not fitting that I should keep you captive; you are therefore free; but my blood relatives I will keep with me, for I am the head of the family, and, therefore, their master.

The woman also stated that amongst those Harun had captured at Dara were some of the princesses of the royal house of Darfur, as well as Sheikh Maki's wife, who belonged to the late *sultan's* family. This sad news greatly distressed poor Sheikh Maki, whose cup of sorrow was indeed full to overflowing.

I now made preparations to march off at once in pursuit of Harun;

but my little expedition into Jebel Marra had considerably reduced my numbers. The cold had been fatal to many of the Blacks, and I remarked that those who were accustomed to eat meat and drink *marissa* stood the cold and hardships well; whilst those whose duties lay chiefly in tax-gathering amongst the nomad Arabs, and who consequently existed principally on milk, succumbed in large numbers.

Including Katong's and Gabralla's reinforcements, my little detachment consisted only of a hundred and seventy-five regulars and a hundred and forty Bazingers. The horses had all been lamed by the rough ground, except the gray which I rode. I had sent messengers to Dara to say that I was on my way back, and had arrived near Manawashi, where I wished the chiefs of the Beni Helba and Messeria Arabs to meet me, with their men; and starting off at a rapid pace, after a few hours' march, we reached the camp Sultan Harun had just quitted. It was completely deserted, and we made out from the tracks that the force had moved off at least nine or ten hours before; and, following them up, we found ourselves marching in a northwesterly direction towards El Fasher. From the tracks, we gathered that Harun's force numbered about four hundred rifles, some hundreds of sword and spear men, and about sixty horsemen. With so few, it would be impossible for him to attack Fasher. What, therefore, could be his intentions?

By sunset the troops were thoroughly exhausted, and darkness forced us to halt. Besides, there was no moon, and we could no longer make out the tracks. At the first streak of dawn, however, we continued our advance, and, to encourage the men, I walked the whole way. They had suffered considerably in Jebel Marra, and were thoroughly tired out; and had there been time, I would have relieved them by fresh troops from Dara. But there was not a moment to be lost; so we pushed on as best we could, making short halts every now and then. We had had no time to take in provisions, and, indeed, most of the corn in the villages had already been seized by Harun. My men were, therefore, getting famished; and when we reached Jebel Abu Haraz (about two days' march from El Fasher), I promised them that if we did not come up with the enemy on the following day, steps would then be taken to procure provisions at any cost.

At sunrise the next morning we reached the Abu Haraz wells, which we found deserted. We had had no water since the previous day; so we were obliged to halt for a short time, and we found a woman who had concealed herself, thinking we were the enemy. She reported that, the previous day, Harun had attacked Hillet Omar, the village of the Sultan of the Massabat (about four hours' march further on), which he had plundered, and killed a number of the inhabitants; but that she and other survivors had hidden in the forest, and so had escaped detection. Harun, she said, had moved on that morning, and could not be far off. She therefore offered to lead us along his tracks, which we had been obliged to leave the previous evening, owing to want of water. The news that before long we should come up with the enemy was hailed with delight, and, with the woman as our guide, we hurried forward, and were soon on their quite fresh tracks. Inspired with the prospect of a successful action, a speedy return to their wives and families, and a long rest, my men now moved on very cheerfully and at a good pace.

Our direction lay nearly due east, and about an hour before noon we came in sight of two small hills. Just then, some of Katong's and Gabralla's men, who were scouting out in front, brought in a wounded man, who stated that he had been taken prisoner at Hillet Omar, and had just escaped, having seen our red flag a long way off and knowing that he would be safe. Sultan Harun, he said, was halted a short distance beyond the small hills at Rahad en Nabak. We now increased the pace, and, galloping forward, I could see from the hills the position of the enemy. They were encamped on a grassy slope about two thousand five hundred yards away, and through my glass I could see the horses being saddled up, and much commotion, as if the camp were about to move on.

There was not a moment to be lost. Taking, therefore, a hundred and thirty regulars with me, I pushed straight on, my left flank being covered, at a distance of about half a mile, by forty-five regulars and forty Bazingers under Wad el Abbas, while Katong and Gabralla were ordered to remain as a reserve, concealed behind the rising ground.

The enemy had now discovered us. I therefore advanced at the double between the two hills, Wad el Abbas circling round the hill on the left; and once through, we deployed for attack. Half a mile further on, we came under a heavy rifle-fire; and my gray horse, which had only just recovered from his wound, got restive, and neither spurs nor whip were of any avail to make him move on. I therefore jumped off, and we continued advancing till within six hundred yards of Harun's line, when we halted and fired a volley. Then, ordering Wad el Abbas to double forward and wheel up to the right, we caught the enemy between a cross fire, under which they were soon forced to retire. I now lost no time in sending orders to the reserve to make a flank attack on the retreating enemy, which had the effect of turning Harun's retirement into a headlong flight, in which the *sultan's* horse was shot dead under him, and he himself only just eluded us.

If we had had cavalry, none could have escaped. As it was, our men pursued till nightfall, and inflicted great loss on the enemy. We halted that night at the Abu Haraz well, and collected our spoil, which consisted of a hundred and sixty rifles, four large copper war-drums, four flags, and two horses, the riders of which had both been killed. Our losses consisted of fourteen killed and twenty wounded. The women captured by Harun were all saved, and returned to their husbands.

Amongst our wounded was Babakr, the chief of Katong's Bazingers, who had personally attacked Harun, and was on the point of taking him prisoner, when he was shot by one of the *sultan's* guard. Some of the prisoners informed me that it had been Harun's intention to ally himself with the Mima Arabs, who had agreed to revolt against the government as soon as he could come to them; but he was now, after this defeat, forced to retire once more to Jebel Marra, whilst I and my exhausted troops marched back to Dara. On our way, we came across some four hundred Beni Helba and Messeria horsemen, who had come to join us, but were unfortunately too late for the fight.

At Dara, I found everything in the greatest confusion. When the enemy had attacked, the principal merchants, terrified of their lives, had fled to the fort, leaving their property at the mercy of Harun's men. The fort was still crowded with these people, who did not dare to return to their houses until the result of the fight between Harun and myself was known. My appearance on the scene was, therefore, the signal for general rejoicing, and the refugees now all returned to their own homes.

Meanwhile, Sultan Harun, who had recovered his defeat, again collected a force, and proceeded to Dar Gimmer, in the Kulkul district; and here he made a raid on the Arabs, captured their cattle and camels, and killed some merchants. On the news reaching Nur Bey Angara, the governor of the district, he advanced rapidly, covering the usual two days' march in twenty-six hours, and, early the following morning, he surprised Sultan Harun in his camp. In great haste, Harun's horse was saddled, but in mounting the stirrup-leather broke. Another horse was brought, and just as he was about to put his foot into the stirrup, a bullet hit him full in the chest, and he fell dead (March, 1880).

His fall was the signal for a wild flight, and Nur Angara took possession of his camp without any further difficulty. Sultan Harun's head was cut off and sent to El Fasher, and there was general rejoicing at his death. The few adherents, however, who had fled, now collected in Jebel Marra, and selected as their ruler Abdullahi Dudbenga, the son of Harun's uncle Abakir; but henceforth their raids became insignificant, and peace was once more restored to the country.

Three days after my return to Dara, I received a letter from Gessi Pasha, in Bahr el Ghazal, informing me that Dr. R. W. Felkin and the Rev. C. T. Wilson, of the English Church Missionary Society, were on their way from Uganda to Khartum, *via* Dara, and with them were some Waganda envoys sent by King Mtesa to Her Majesty the Queen of England. Gessi begged me to give them all help on their journey, and said that they were leaving for Dara on the date he was writing. I calculated, therefore, they would arrive in a few days, so I despatched mounted messengers to the Mamur and Sheikh of Kalaka, directing him to have the necessary food and provisions ready for them on their arrival, and to send them, with a strong escort, to Dara. It was not until fourteen days after the receipt of Gessi's letter that news reached me they had passed Kalaka, and were not far from Dara.

At the head of about forty horsemen I started off to welcome them, and met them, after a ride of two hours, in a small wood. Our meeting took place under a large tree, and the two travellers seemed to me to be very tired after their long journey. I had brought some breakfast with me, and, laying our rugs on the ground, we sat down and had a good meal. They had heard in the southern Kalaka district that I had gone off to fight Sultan Harun; and as the roads were considered unsafe, they had not ventured to come on, and that was the cause of the delay. Dr. Felkin, who had studied in Jena, spoke German well; but I had great difficulty in making myself intelligible in my broken English to the Rev. Mr. Wilson. After breakfast we rode on to Dara, where the garrison had turned out to welcome them. I then led them to the house prepared for their reception, where Zogal, the commandant, the *kadi* and chief merchant, came to pay their respects; and after the usual lemonade and talk, I told them that my guests were greatly in need of rest, on which they withdrew.

Having ascertained, through an interpreter, that Mtesa's envoys were fond of meat, I gave them a fattened ox, which they killed themselves, skinned, and then roasted on a wood fire; and with several draughts of *marissa*, to which beverage they had been introduced by an old *habitué*, they appeared to have had a thoroughly enjoyable feast. Indeed, so much did they relish this native drink that I was obliged to commission Zogal Bey to supply them daily with a considerable quantity.

Meanwhile our dinner-party consisted of the two travellers, Zogal and Rifki, and, as usual, we dined off roasted mutton; after dinner I gave our two native friends a hint to retire, and then Dr. Felkin and the Rev. Mr. Wilson began to relate their experiences in Uganda, as well as amongst the various tribes through which they had passed. I was immensely interested in all they told me, and could not help wishing I were at the great lakes instead of in Darfur. Outside, the singing and beating of drums was getting louder and more boisterous, and from curiosity we went out to look on. The company was a very cheerful one: men and women shouting and dancing round a big fire, on which huge pieces of meat were roasting, whilst close by stood the half-empty pitchers of beer.

We remained till late talking over our travels and the future of these countries. All they told me was of immense interest, and I, too, was able to give them the latest information from Europe, which, though months old, was news to them. At length, towards midnight we turned in, having come to the mutual conclusion that in the Sudan, as well as in Europe, matters seemed very unsettled.

Next morning we were up early, and had a two hours' ride, in which I showed my guests the surroundings of Dara, which were far from interesting; and on our return was told, much to my amusement, that the sight of a camel had caused Mtesa's envoys such alarm that they had fled. "Well," said I to Dr. Felkin, "as you have to make the rest of your journey on camel-back, it is advisable your men should get into the way of it; so if you will get them together I will send for a camel and put their courage to the test." He went off, and I sent for a camel belonging to one of the merchants, which was very big and fat.

By this time the envoys and others had arrived and the camel, appearing suddenly round a corner, caused almost a stampede. It was only the sight of the unconcern of Dr. Felkin and myself which kept them from bolting as hard as their legs could carry them. Dr. Felkin explained to them that the camel was a most patient and docile animal, on which they would have to make the remainder of their journey to Egypt, and that there was no cause for fear; still, they kept a respectful distance from the alarming beast, and when I told my *kavass* to mount and make it get up and sit down, their astonishment was boundless. At length one, more courageous than the rest, volunteered to mount; timorously approaching the animal, he was assisted into the saddle, and, having safely got through the operation of rising, with a beaming countenance he surveyed his friends from his lofty seat, and proceeded to make a speech to them on the pleasures of camel-riding.

Apparently he had invited them to share these pleasures with him, for suddenly, without a moment's warning, they rushed at the poor animal in a body, and began swarming up it. Some tried to mount by the neck, others by the tail, and half a dozen or so clung to the saddle trappings. For a moment the camel seemed stupefied by this sudden attack; but, recovering its presence of mind, it now lashed out in all directions, and in a moment had freed itself completely from every unfortunate Waganda who had been bold enough to approach it. I do not think I ever laughed so much in my life. These people evidently took the poor animal for a mountain; but the shocks they experienced when the mountain began to heave so terrified them that for long they would not come near it. However, first one and then another summoned up courage to mount, and by the time they left Dara they were all fairly proficient in the art of camel-riding.

I had in my household several young boys who had been taken from the slave-traders; and as Dr. Felkin had no servant to attend on him personally, I suggested he should take one of them. He accepted the offer gladly; so I handed over to him a bright little Fertit boy called Kapsun, whom he agreed to bring up in Europe. Two years and a half later, I received at El Fasher a letter written in English by little Kapsun, thanking me for allowing him to go with Dr. Felkin "to a country where everyone was so good and so kind," and saying that he had adopted the Christian religion, and was "the happiest boy in the world;" he also sent me his photograph in European clothes.

The time for the departure of my two friends came all too soon for me; but they were anxious to get on, and, mounted on their camels, they left for Khartum *via* Toweisha.

Sometime later I received a letter from Messedaglia telling me that he was leaving for Khartum to fetch his wife. No sooner had he reached that place than he got into some difficulty with the authorities and was discharged, and his place as Governor-General of Darfur was taken by Ali Bey Sherif, formerly Governor-General of Kordofan.

It was about the close of 1879 or early in 1880 that I received a letter from General Gordon, written in French some two months previously from near Debra Tabor, in Abyssinia. Although this letter was destroyed many years ago, I can remember almost the exact words, which were as follows:—

> Dear Slatin,—Having finished my mission to King John, I wanted to return the same way that I came; but when near Gallabat I was overtaken by some of Ras Adal's people, who forced me to go back, and I am to be taken under escort to Kassala and thence to Massawa. I have burnt all the compromising documents. King John will be disappointed when he finds he is not master of his own house.
>
> Your friend,
C. Gordon.

CHAPTER 3

The Government of Darfur

I now busied myself with the administrative affairs of the province of Dara. The returns which I had called for, showing the names and numbers of villages, their population, etc., were duly submitted to me, and I now resolved to travel over the entire district and personally inquire into the state of affairs.

There is very little money in cash in Darfur. The northern Arab tribes who act as camel-men, and who supply transport for the great caravan road between Assiut and Darfur, have a small amount of gold and silver coin; but in all other parts of the province payments are made principally in "*takia*," a sort of native-made cotton fabric, or in European gray cotton cloth, cut in various lengths; but it can be readily understood that such material, continually passing from hand to hand, greatly loses in value, and eventually will not even pass for its cost price.

Taxes were always paid in kind, such as corn, honey, camels, cows, sheep, and native-made cloth, and a certain fixed tariff being arranged, it became a simple matter to assess the taxation in Egyptian *piastres*. There were always merchants ready to purchase the various products and animals for which payment was generally made to government in corn, and in this latter commodity the salaries were paid to officers, soldiers, and officials. As the price of corn varied, it happened as often as not that the cash value of the salaries was in excess; but on the whole I think the system was not an unfair one.

My first tour of inspection took me to Toweisha and Dar el Khawabir, and back to Dara *via* Shieria. I then went to Shakka, *via* Kershu, and everywhere I assessed the exact amounts to be paid by all *sheikhs* and chiefs. At Shakka, Kalaka, and in Dar Beni Helba, by personal inspection and by inquiry, I did all I could to find out what the Arab tribes really possessed; and at the same time I was anxious to collect the Bazingers who had formed part of Suleiman Zubeir's army, but who were now scattered amongst the Rizighat, Habbania, and Taaisha Arabs. I therefore issued orders to all *sheikhs*, both great and small, to hand over the Bazingers to me; and though it was of course impossible to collect all, I nevertheless succeeded in getting some four hundred men capable of bearing arms, and these I at once sent under escort to Khartum. I was anxious also to increase the number of troops in my own district; but I hesitated somewhat to introduce into the ranks these Bazingers, who, accustomed to a life of liberty and freedom, might have a bad effect on the discipline of the men; and I also knew that if kept under very strict control they would be likely to desert, and, with their knowledge of the country and people, might prove an eventual source of danger.

On my return to Dara I learnt that General Gordon had left Abyssinia, had resigned his appointment as governor-general, and had been succeeded by Rauf Pasha, who was so well known in connection with Sir Samuel Baker's work in the Sudan.

The Gellabas and merchants whom Gordon had turned out of Kalaka and Shakka at the time of Suleiman Zubeir's revolt, now seized this opportunity to proceed to Khartum, and, relying on the ignorance of the new governor-general of the real state of affairs, they submitted petitions to the effect that the Arabs had plundered them of their wives, children, and property, and that they now sought the protection of the government. Rauf Pasha forwarded these petitions to me, with a covering letter to the effect that I was to deal justly with these people, restore to them their property, and do what I could to unite them with their families. Hundreds of Gellabas now came to Dara and submitted petitions of every description, enumerating, with the grossest exaggeration, the various articles for which they claimed compensation. I went to the trouble of having all these claims totalled up in one list,—ivory, ostrich feathers, gold and silver ornaments, etc., etc.; and I found that if all the property at present in the hands of the Arab tribes were confiscated and sold, it would not nearly cover the claims of the Gellabas.

I was obliged, however, to comply with my orders from Khartum; I therefore summoned the *sheikhs* of the various Arab tribes to Dara, and informed them of the claims of the merchants against them. Naturally they at once denied having taken anything whatever from them, and they told me privately that if government persisted in the payment of these claims, there would be no other course open to them than to emigrate to Wadai and Bornu. Some of them, however, agreed that if permitted they would endeavour to come to a mutual understanding with the merchants as regards the restoration of their wives and children; but they absolutely declined to do this if government interfered. These latter were about twenty in number; all the others, who had been turned out by General Gordon's orders, and who now amounted to some hundreds, I ordered back to Khartum, as it was quite impossible to come to any sort of arrangement which would satisfy them and the Arabs.

I reported fully the steps I had taken to Rauf Pasha, and urged him to pay no further heed to these claims. Soon after this, several of the Habbania Sheikhs came and informed me that the Gellabas whom I had ordered back to Khartum had—instead of going there—proceeded to Kalaka, where they had concluded a private arrangement with Ali Wad Fadlalla, the official tax-gatherer and a relative of Zogal Bey, to ignore my orders and, through his assistance, to force the Arabs to return the property, on condition that they (the Gellabas) and Fadlalla should share the proceeds between them.

As for various other reasons I wished to again inspect the southern districts, I took the *sheikhs* with me and set off for Kalaka, travelling *via* Nimr and Deain, where Madibbo Bey, head-*sheikh* of the Rizighat, resided. Here I promised Madibbo that on my way back I would endeavour to effect a reconciliation between him and Egeil Wad el Jangawi, with whom he was in continual dispute. Two days later, accompanied by forty horsemen, I reached Dawila, which is almost in the centre of the Kalaka district, and surprised my friend Fadlalla, who was quite ignorant of my approach. Questioned before the *sheikhs*, he could not deny that he had given orders for some of the property taken from the Gellabas to be returned to them; without delay I ordered the Arab *sheikhs* to bring before me all Gellabas in the district who had not special permits to trade, and in a few days one hundred and twenty-four of them were collected, and I found them to be the actual men whom I had ordered to Khartum.

When I asked them why they had disobeyed orders, they told me frankly that they had no intention of returning as poor men to their own country. I then told them to explain how, having no capital whatever, they proposed to enrich themselves,—especially as I had given orders that their claims, which were in the majority of cases utterly false, were not to be considered; and to my repeated questions they refused to give any answer. I therefore gave instructions to Fadlalla's assistant to take all the Gellabas as prisoners, under an escort of fifteen soldiers, to Hassan Agha, the Mamur of Shakka, to whom I gave orders to send them to El Obeid; and Fadlalla himself I placed under arrest, and gave instructions that he should be taken with me to Dara, to be tried for disobedience of orders.

Several of the merchants who were living with the Arabs came and thanked me for having helped them, saying the Arabs had voluntarily returned to them their concubines, children, and some of their property, and that they were living in peace and harmony with the natives of the country. I now appointed another *mamur* in place of Fadlalla, and, according to my promise, returned to Madibbo, who was expecting me.

As we were riding through the woods in the early morning we passed a place which smelt very strongly of the civet cat; and in reply to my question as to whether such animals were to be found there, the Habbania Sheikh replied, "Yes; but you surely do not want one, it will poison your whole house."

"Poison?" said I, in a tone of feigned surprise, for I well knew that the Arabs detest the civet cat.

"Yes," said he, "the civet of this cat has such a strong smell that you cannot get rid of it;" and he held his nose as we passed through the wood.

I answered, "Well, now, in my opinion sulphur has a much more disagreeable smell than civet."

"On the contrary," he replied, "sulphur is one of the choice perfumes of the country; we are used to it, and we enjoy it."

"Perhaps you are right," said I; "I have seen how mothers of the southern tribes mix together sulphur and fat and smear the bodies of their new-born children, as well as their own breasts, with it. Why should I wonder that you, who have lain on your mother's lap, drunk her milk, and gazed lovingly into her eyes, should think the sulphur smell pleasant? You have been bred and brought up in it, and so it happens that habit makes us used to everything."

The manners and customs of these wild Arabs always interested me, and the journey passed quickly enough in chatting with my companions. We frequently passed settlements of nomad Arabs, who always insisted on our partaking of their hospitality. The post which caught me up on the way brought me instructions from the governor-general that Dar Janghé, which up till recently had formed part of the province of Dara, was in future to be attached to Bahr el Ghazal, to which it really belonged. This new arrangement appeared to me to be a very satisfactory one, as the Janghé tribe were cattle-owners, and I had already a surplus of cattle tribute from the numerous Baggara tribes in Darfur, and was not at all desirous of adding to this stock, which fetched an exceptionally low price in the market. On the other hand, Gessi was delighted, for the Janghé were the only cattle-owners in his district, and the payment of taxes in kind suited his requirements, as it supplied meat for his troops.

After four days' march we reached Shakka, and halted at the station of Abu Segan, in which there was a small fort or enclosure surrounding a few mud-huts and *tukuls*, which served as quarters for the small garrison of between thirty and forty men and the *mamur*. Surrounding the fort, but at some distance from it, were the huts of the merchants who had immigrated from Darfur, and who practically formed the entire population. It was a well-known market for the district, the principal days being Friday and Monday, when numbers of Arabs came in to make their purchases.

I found Madibbo Bey here at the head of several hundred horsemen, and he informed me that Egeil Wad el Jangawi had gone to Khartum a month ago to make an official complaint about his discharge from the Sheikhdom. I therefore pushed on to Dara, and a few days after my return received a letter from Marcopoli Bey, Rauf Pasha's secretary, to the effect that Egeil had arrived in Khartum and had lodged a complaint against Madibbo Bey, whom he characterised as in league with me, and through whose intrigues he had been deprived of the office of Sheikh, and had even been threatened with death. The letter went on to say that every effort had been made to induce Egeil to return to Dara with a letter of recommendation to me, but he had refused to come, as he was convinced I was in Madibbo's hands.

In order, therefore, to get rid of the man, the case had been handed over to Ali Bey Sherif, acting Mudir of El Fasher, who had been instructed to settle it. In reply, I wrote that I had repeatedly written to Egeil ordering him to come to me, but that he had persistently refused, and that in consequence I must decline to employ any man as *sheikh* in my district who had objected to coming to see me when ordered to do so; and I added that as I had been suffering considerably from fever, and besides had several matters to place before the governor-general regarding the administration of the country, I requested permission to come to Khartum.

A few days later Ali Bey Sherif wrote from El Fasher that, having been charged to inquire into the Egeil matter, and being unable at present to come to Dara and examine into the case on the spot, he had in consequence delegated the Shaigia Sanjak, Omar Wad Darho, to represent him.

About a month after I had written for leave to go to Khartum, I received a reply approving, and two days before I started, Omar Wad Darho arrived, with an escort of one hundred horsemen. It was quite clear to me that as the country was perfectly tranquil, he had brought these men simply to plunder. He assured me that it was his intention to act in the matter under consideration entirely in accordance with my wishes; but I did not hesitate to tell him that it was his duty to inquire most carefully into the whole of the facts of the case, and to act justly in the interests of the government. At the same time he should not ignore the interests and wishes of the tribe in selecting as *sheikh* a man whom the tribe would accept, and who would at the same time have sufficient power to uphold the government authority. I then appointed Zogal Bey as my representative, and ordered him not to interfere in the conduct of the case, and to report the matter fully to Khartum.

I left Dara at the end of January, 1881, and, marching *via* Toweisha and Dar Homr, I reached El Obeid in nine days, and proceeded at once to the Mudiria to pay my respects to Mohammed Pasha Said, the governor. He gave me a very kind reception, and asked me to be his guest; but as I had previously known Ahmed Bey Dafalla, who had a horse ready to take me to the quarters he had specially prepared for me, I thanked the governor and proceeded to Dafalla's house, which was close to the gate. Here I found everything most comfortable. I was ushered into a large room hung with richly embroidered curtains, whilst laid out on two tables were all sorts of pleasant drinks and eatables, cigars, cigarettes, etc.; in fact, I could see that my host had done everything that was possible to make my stay pleasant.

Mohammed Pasha Said now came to return my call, and invited us both to dinner; and after he had gone I had visits from all the notables of the town. That evening at dinner he told me that he was coming to see me the following morning on official business. He duly arrived the next day, and, seeing my three black boys at the door, his first question was, "Are these boys free, or slaves?" I at once replied "free," and that they were in my service of their own free will and accord; they then showed him their manumission papers, which they kept in little brass boxes.

The *pasha* now turned to me and said, "My friend, you are a more careful man than I. I only wanted to take a rise out of you; but unfortunately you have turned the tables on me." This little episode brought us into a discussion on the slave question, and I remarked that in general terms I agreed with him that from the standpoint of morality no doubt the abolition of slavery was by all means to be recommended, but that in actually bringing these measures into effect we should do so with the greatest circumspection, and should not hurry matters, otherwise we should deprive the country of its means of obtaining labour, and we should also place the slave-owners in great difficulties by any sudden enforcement of the law. Gradual and resolute action was what was required. Mohammed Pasha Said quite concurred in these views, pointing out that everything should be done to improve the relations between the natives and the Egyptians and Turks, by whom they were governed, but that the sudden abolition of a system which had been a national custom from remotest times would most certainly lead to estrangement and difficulties.

I did not make a long stay in El Obeid, and the following morning I started off on camels, accompanied by two Maalia *sheikhs* who had caught me up on the road from Darfur. I had already telegraphed to Dr. Zurbuchen to get a room ready for me, and Said Pasha had officially reported my departure.

On the third day after leaving El Obeid we passed the station of Abu Garad, where I found a telegram from Zurbuchen begging me to be his guest; and the following day we crossed the Nile at Tura el Hadra at the spot where I had said goodbye to Gordon, and whose last words I remembered had been verified,—"I shall perhaps go to Europe."

The camel I was riding was a young one which Ahmed Dey Dafalla had bought for me, and they had forgotten to tell me that he should be ridden with both halter and nose-rein; consequently when we set off in the dark and I found he would not go on, I drove him, with the result that he set off at a gallop, and no amount of tugging at the nose-ring had the smallest effect in stopping him. He ran out of the track straight for some trees, and in an instant one of the branches, striking me in the chest, hurled me to the ground some yards away. I fell on my back with such a thump that it seemed to me as if two pillars of fire had shot out of my eyes up to the heavens, and for a few minutes I lost consciousness; but my *kavass*, who had rushed after me, picked me up, pulled at my joints, and turned my neck about, and in ten minutes I had come to and was able to mount the camel, which, when I had fallen, had patiently stood beside me. We rode till midnight; but the pain in my chest and spitting of blood obliged me to halt; after a few hours, however, I was able to move on again, and at length, bruised and sore, we reached Khartum seven days after leaving El Obeid.

Here I found Zurbuchen, who welcomed me heartily, and carried me off as his guest to a house near the Roman Catholic Mission, which had belonged to the late Latif Debono, a Maltese and a well-known slave-dealer.

The governor-general had sent his *kavass* to meet me with a message that I was to call on him during the afternoon; after a short rest, therefore, I presented myself at the palace, where I was well received by Rauf Pasha and his secretary, Marcopoli Bey, whom I had known before as Gordon's interpreter. I soon noticed that Rauf Pasha's cordiality had somewhat cooled down; and to my utter astonishment he announced that the leave of absence for which I had asked, in order to proceed to Cairo, had been granted me, and that Riaz Pasha had just telegraphed to that effect.

"But," said I, "I never wrote to Cairo for leave of absence."

"Then what does this telegram mean?" said he. "I think that you, as a soldier, should have known better than to have acted in this irregular manner. You should have applied for your leave through me, and not direct to Cairo; and now you say you never asked for any!" Marcopoli then read out the telegram, which ran as follows:

> To the Governor-General of the Sudan: Three months leave on full pay has been granted to R. Slatin, *mudir* of western Darfur.

I was at a complete loss to understand what had occurred, and all I could do was to repeat that I had not asked for leave. I could see perfectly well that Rauf Pasha felt insulted at my apparent disregard for his position, and in this I fully sympathised with him. The next day, however, light was thrown on the matter. Some time previously I had written home saying that I had been suffering lately from fever, and my dear mother, who is now dead, in her loving concern for her absent son, at once thought that I was concealing from her some terrible malady; she had, therefore, written to the authorities in Egypt, urging that I should be recalled to Cairo for medical treatment, and she was thus the innocent cause of this estrangement between Rauf Pasha and myself.

The matter explained, the governor-general at once apologised for having wrongfully accused me of irregularity, and was touched by my dear mother's love for me, saying that such affection can alone be returned by the deepest love and obedience on the part of the children. "I myself," said he, "love my mother with all my heart; though she is only a poor Abyssinian, and formerly a slave. At all times I am ready to ask her advice, and follow it in all matters relating to the family and home." Since this conversation I have often had occasion to notice the genuine love and affection which exists between parents and children of this race.

During my stay in Khartum I had frequent talks with Rauf Pasha on the state of my province, and I suggested that a more just and lenient form of taxation should be introduced in the Fasher and Kebkebia districts. I also asked him to allow me to order the Arab tribes to supply annually a certain number of young slaves, who should form a contingent from which the vacancies caused by sickness, deaths, and other casualties amongst the troops could be filled up; and I further proposed that the Arabs should be allowed to pay their tribute in slaves instead of cattle, as by this means I hoped to win back Suleiman Zubeir's Bazingers, who were scattered amongst the tribes, and whose knowledge of the use of fire-arms was, in my opinion, a continual source of danger to the government. Rauf Pasha concurred in all these suggestions, and gave me written orders to this effect.

When I arrived in Khartum, a certain Darfuri named Hassan Wad Saad en Nur, whose father had been killed with Vizir Ahmed Shata in Shakka, came to me, and begged me to intercede for him to be permitted to return to his country; meeting Rauf Pasha shortly afterwards, I begged him to allow this, and he gave instructions for his discharge to be at once made out. A few days later, however, he sent for me and explained that after further inquiry he had decided to cancel Nur's discharge. I explained that he had only acted like the rest during the revolt, and that now it was not possible for him to do any further harm. Rauf Pasha, however, remained resolute, and I, feeling annoyed, retorted that as I had given Nur my word that he should return with me, it remained for Rauf Pasha to decide whether he would let him go or whether he would discharge me, and, bidding him goodbye, I marched off.

Two days later he again sent for me, and said that I was wrong in having given Nur my word so quickly. I fully admitted the justice of this censure, and to my surprise he then said that he had reconsidered the matter, and had decided to let Nur go; and as regards myself he thought me a stubborn but capable official, and had in consequence requested His Highness the Khedive, Mohammed Tewfik Pasha, to appoint me Governor-General of Darfur, with the title of *bey*. I thanked him for his kind words, and assured him that I should do my utmost to justify his confidence in me.

Rauf Pasha now asked me to state in writing that I would be responsible for the future good behaviour of Nur; and this I did gladly, feeling convinced that after all my trouble on his behalf the man would prove loyal and faithful. On returning to my house I sent for Nur, who had spent two days of suspense, dreading that his discharge would be refused; and when I told him the good news, he fell at my feet and poured out his gratitude in the most voluble terms. I felt that he was a man of honour, and that I could trust him: little did I know that I had taken a snake into my bosom.

My short stay in Khartum passed rapidly in the company of my many friends. Bishop Comboni and Fathers Ohrwalder and Dichtl had arrived from Cairo towards the end of January, 1881, as well as Hassan Pasha, the chief of the Financial Department, Busati Bey, Consul Hansal, and others. Ohrwalder and Dichtl put up in my quarters; and many a long talk used we to have over our own beloved country.

On 25th January, 1881, Gessi arrived at Khartum very seriously ill. During his journey from Meshra er Rek he had been hemmed in by the "*suds*," or barriers of floating vegetation through which travellers must at times cut their way with axes. For three months and more he had struggled hopelessly to make his way through them, and the terrible sufferings undergone by him and his men through famine and sickness are almost indescribable. He lost the majority of his men and crew, and acts of cannibalism were of daily occurrence. He was at length rescued by Marno in the steamer *Bordein*, and brought to Khartum, where he was most carefully tended by the Mission sisters; but the shock to his system had been so great that he could not recover his strength, despite every effort made by Dr. Zurbuchen.

It was at length decided to try and send him to Egypt, and we made all arrangements to make his journey as comfortable as possible. He was particularly anxious to take with him his servant Almas, who happened to be a eunuch; but Rauf Pasha, fearing that it might create a scandal, and that strictures might be passed on his government of the Sudan, for a long time refused permission for him to go. Yielding, however, to the persistence of Zurbuchen and myself, he at length authorised it, and on 11th March we carried poor Gessi in a sort of litter to the governor's *dahabia*, in which he was towed to Berber, thence he was carried across to Suakin, where he arrived on 10th April, and, embarking a fortnight later, reached Suez on 28th, too weak almost to move. He was taken to the French hospital, where he expired two days later.

Meanwhile matters in Darfur had not been progressing very satisfactorily. Zogal Bey wrote that Omar Wad Darho had been conducting himself very badly at Shakka, and I showed the report to Rauf Pasha, who telegraphed that he was to return at once to El Fasher.

Having now thoroughly recovered, I decided to return and take up my new duties as soon as possible. Rauf Pasha placed a steamer at my disposal, and, accompanied by Bishop Comboni and Father Ohrwalder, whom I promised to mount on my camels as far as El Obeid, we quitted Khartum on 29th March. Consul Hansal, Marcopoli Bey, Zurbuchen, and Marquet travelled with us in the steamer as far as Tura el Hadra, and here we bade them goodbye. Little did I think that one only of that company should I ever meet again, and under what strange circumstances I was once more to return to the capital of the Sudan. I was very young, the heavy responsibilities of my new and important position occupied all my thoughts, and I was full of high hopes for the future, but fate had a strange and terrible destiny in store for me.

After five days' march we reached El Obeid, and from here the bishop made a tour through Jebel Nuba, while Father Ohrwalder remained at El Obeid, and was eventually sent to the mission station of Delen, in southern Kordofan. I stayed in El Obeid a few days only, and, having received telegraphic orders to proceed to Foga, I bid my two friends farewell. One of them—the good bishop—I was destined never to see again; he died in Khartum on 10th October, 1881. The other,—my dear friend Ohrwalder,—like myself, was soon to go through many strange and horrible experiences before we were again to meet as fellow-captives of the as yet unknown *Mahdi*, who was shortly to overthrow every vestige of government authority in the Sudan.

Two days later I quitted El Obeid, and, travelling *via* Abu Haraz and Shallota, reached Foga, where I found a telegram from His Highness the Khedive, officially appointing me Governor-General of Darfur, and directing me to proceed forthwith to El Fasher, to take over the duties from Ali Bey Sherif. I had some urgent business to do in

Dara, and several private letters to attend to; but I thought it advisable to proceed at once to El Fasher, where I arrived on 20th April. Here I found much intriguing going on, from the *mudir* down to the lowest clerk in the office; the *kadi* and his *employés* were all at variance, and even the clerks of the law-courts had sued each other for contempt. Several petitions had been filed against officials; there were all sorts of charges pending against false witnesses; cases regarding breaches of morality abounded; in fact, it would have required years to settle the mass of suits and petitions brought before me for decision. A few I managed to settle, but I regret to say that I had to leave the greater number pending.

The most important case was that against Nur Angara, his *sanjak*, and the Kulkul officials, who, with their complainants, had all been summoned to El Fasher, whence, after freely bribing the officials with money and slaves, they were sent back to Kulkul without any decision having been given. There was a large box full of correspondence on this subject, most of which was not worth the paper it was written on; I therefore sent instructions to Nur Angara, his officials, and the complainants, who were all living at Kulkul without work, to come to El Fasher; and, pending his arrival, I endeavoured to establish some sort of order in regard to tributes, taxation, etc. Several cases had also been filed against the late *mudir*, Said Bey Guma,—who was at the same time commander of the troops,—but it was impossible to prove them; and as it was imperative that I should have an assistant, I reinstated him as Mudir of El Fasher.

There was no doubt he was an intriguer; besides being excessively parsimonious, he was not liked by the officers, and was famed for his vocabulary of bad language; but at the same time he was a brave soldier in the field, and this quality,—especially amongst Egyptians,—was excessively rare in these distant regions. I therefore re-employed him, on condition that he would amend his ways; and I frankly told him that if he gave me the slightest trouble I should discharge him, and pack him off to Khartum. I knew this would be a terrible punishment; for, though an Egyptian, he had become greatly attached to Darfur.

Major Hassan Effendi Rifki, commanding at Dara, I transferred to the command of a battalion at El Fasher, under Ali Bey Sherif, as he was constantly drunk; but no sooner had he come under my observation than he appeared before me twice in a state of intoxication, and I was obliged to discharge him and send him to Khartum. Meanwhile, Nur Angara and the host of defendants and complainants duly arrived, and I very soon found out that the latter had been for the most part his friends, through whose help he had become *mudir*; but as he had abandoned them, they were anxious to revenge themselves by plotting against him. On the other hand, Nur Angara himself was a most resolute villain; without rhyme or reason, and often merely to satisfy his own brutal pleasure, he shed blood; and as for his views in regard to the property of his fellow creatures, they were beyond the conception of the most advanced Social Democrat in the world.

As he was a *bey*, and held the rank of colonel, I ordered the proper salute to be fired when he entered the fort, gave him a hearty welcome, and ordered his attendants to be lodged in one of Omar Wad Darho's houses, lying to the north of the town. He was a tall, beardless man, with a dark copper-coloured complexion, and the usual three slits on his cheeks; he had an energetic and wild look, but when talking he appeared to be a perfectly harmless individual. He was a Dongolawi, and had been brought up by the Shaigi, Melek Tumbal, who was formally a *sanjak*, and claimed descent from the Shaigia kings. When quite a boy he had come to Cairo, and, owing to his connection with Zubeir and his son, he had acquired to some extent the goodwill of the government. He had an old mother of about sixty years of age living in Dongola, and in spite of his wild character she had the same affection and care for her son which Rauf Pasha's mother had for him. It is said that when Gordon was in Dongola, an old woman asked to see him, and on entering, said: "I am Nur Angara's mother, and have come to seek your help."

"But," said Gordon, "you have a good-for-nothing son, who passes his time in riotous living instead of looking after his old mother."

"Ah!" said the old woman, "may he be always happy! I forgive him, but I want you to help me."

Gordon presented her with £50 from his own pocket, and she returned home heaping blessings on his head and on that of her undutiful son.

After speaking some time to Nur Angara about his province, I referred quite casually to his great case, saying that I had had no time to examine carefully into the matter, and that when he and his traducers had rested sufficiently, I proposed sending them on to El Obeid. The next day happened to be the first of *Ramadan*, and all the people were fasting except Nur Angara, who did little else but drink *araki* and *om bilbil*, and listen to the music of antelope-horns and *noggaras* played by his attendants, and every now and then he ordered the big war-drum to be beaten. So irritated was I by this constant noise that I sent orders to him to stop it, telling him at the same time that it was a matter of no concern to me whether he fasted or not; but I declined to allow him—a Moslem, and an Egyptian official—to cause public annoyance, and I told him he had no right to disregard public opinion.

"I shall comply with your orders," said he, "and stop my noisy amusements; but I never did care for Ramadan, and never shall. I shall continue to drink as much as I like, and I don't care a brass farthing what people say or think of me."

I could see that he was then under the influence of drink, so I ordered him to go to his house and prepare to leave. Two days later he quitted El Fasher for El Obeid, and on arrival there was at once discharged from the government service. Ali Bey Sherif also left when he had finally handed over the province to me, and I now proposed going on a tour of inspection through the entire country, with the administration of which I had been intrusted.

Just as I was making preparations to start, news arrived that a fight had occurred between the Maheria and Bedeyat Arabs at Bir el Malha; and a few days afterwards Hasaballa, the head-*sheikh* of the Maheria, with many of the chiefs, arrived to represent the case. It appeared that the Maheria Arabs had gone, as usual, to the *natron* fields at Bir el Malha on the Arbaïn road, ten days' march north of El Fasher, to procure *natron* to sell in Darfur; here they had been surprised and attacked by their deadly enemies, the Bedeyat, who lived in the northeast portion of Wadai, and who captured some fifteen hundred camels, and took upwards of one hundred and sixty men prisoners. These tribes had been at war with each other from remotest times, and men captured were generally ransomed at the rate of ten to fifteen camels a head. It was usually considered that the Bedeyat belonged to Darfur, though they never paid tribute; and that, I suppose, was the reason for the Maheria *sheikhs* coming to me to ask for the forcible return of the captured men and camels.

The road between Assiut and Darfur had been formerly much used by merchants, and large caravans used to pass along it; but it had been discovered that it was also used as a slave route, and several merchants had been caught in this traffic and had been exiled; consequently, the Egyptian Government had given orders for the road to be closed. From the first day I arrived in El Fasher, I had heard nothing but complaints about the stoppage of trade along this road, and I had already represented to the government that this was the direct trade route with Egypt, and would serve as an outlet for the ivory, feathers, skins, and tamarisk fruit with which the country abounded, instead of sending it in a roundabout way to Khartum, and thence down the Nile, involving the merchants in heavy transport expenses as well as long delays. Government now approved of my reopening trade by this road, but held me responsible that no slaves should be sent along it. No sooner had I received this permission than I ordered a caravan to be prepared, and, under the guarantee and guidance of Sheikh Mohammed Wad Idris, some eight hundred camels started for Egypt, and in less than seven weeks I received a telegram *via* Khartum announcing their safe arrival at Assiut.

As I was very anxious to inspect the northern and western frontiers of Darfur, the complaint of the Maheria afforded me a pretext for doing so, and for settling their affairs as well. I therefore ordered them to supply, without delay, one hundred and fifty baggage-camels, and one hundred "*suga*," or large water-skins made of bullock's hide; this they readily agreed to do, and we named the village of Melek Hagger (the chief of the Zaghawa Arabs), lying to the north of Kebkebia, as the rendezvous.

About the middle of December, 1881, I left El Fasher with two hundred infantry and some irregular Shaigia cavalry, under Omar Wad Darho. This individual, it will be remembered, had been sent by Ali Bey Sherif to settle the Madibbo-Egeil differences, and having found on my return to Darfur that he had acted unjustly, I had discharged him; but he had subsequently told me that he had been ordered by Ali Bey Sherif to collect a considerable sum of money for him, and that, therefore, he could not act otherwise. I pardoned and reinstated him; moreover, most of the Shaigia horsemen in El Fasher were his relatives, and he was the only man who appeared to be able to exercise any degree of authority over them.

The first night after leaving El Fasher we camped near the Migdob wells, about half way to Kobbé; and when it was dark, I happened to stroll towards the wells, accompanied by one of my attendants. I was dressed in much the same way as the soldiers, and it was too dark for me to be recognised; I therefore came close to the well, and watched the women drawing water. Some Shaigia now came up to water their horses, and asked the women for their buckets, which they refused to give. "We shall first fill our jars," they said, "and then you can use the buckets."

"Your words are as a punishment sent from God," replied one of the Shaigia; "this is the result of bringing liberty into the country. By *Allah!* were it not so, and were not Slatin with us, you and your vessels would very soon be our property."

"God grant him a long life!" was the retort; and I strolled quietly away, thoroughly pleased to have heard with my own ears an admission from the mouths of Sudanese that they were thankful to the Europeans for having released them from the oppression and violence which had hitherto characterised the system of government in this country.

At 11 a. m. the next day we reached Kobbé, the old trade capital of Darfur, which was now inhabited principally by Jaalin, whose fathers and grandfathers, immigrating from the Nile valley, had intermarried with the local people. The *mamur* of this place was a certain Emiliani dei Danziger, of a Venetian family of Austrian origin. He had been given this position by Gordon, and I now sent him to act as Mudir of Dara. The people seemed sorry to say goodbye to him; they said he was a good man, and when slaves and masters disagreed, and the former wanted to leave the latter, he had often been able, by quiet words, to effect a reconciliation. Fortunately, I was not called upon to give any immediate decisions here on the slave question, and the following morning, leaving Kobbé, we marched, *via* Sanied el Kebir and Bir el Gidar, to Kebkebia, where we arrived in two days. Kebkebia is situated on a rocky plateau, and just at the edge of a deep *khor.*

In the centre of the town was a square, loopholed enclosure about nine feet high, constructed of rough stones and mud, smeared with whitewash, in which were the huts of the officers and the small garrison. Formerly the *mudir* and troops were quartered at Kulkul, but had been transferred here about a year and a half before. The buildings had not been completed, and, in consequence, the houses of Nur Angara and the other officials were situated outside the enclosure. The *khor* contained some good gardens and some very high palm-trees, which gave the town a most picturesque appearance.

After inspecting the garrison under Major Adam Omar, I proceeded to my quarters in the fort; and scarcely had I arrived there when I heard a great noise and commotion, which I was told proceeded from the houses occupied by Nur Angara's women. The noise increased to such an extent that I sent for Nur Angara's brother Idris, and asked him what was the cause. He began by making excuses, saying that it was only a little domestic dispute; but when I pressed him, he admitted that all these women knew that I had sent their lord and master to

El Obeid, and they wished to attract my attention. I now sent my chief clerk, Ahmed Effendi Riad, the *kadi* of the Mudiria, and Idris to make a full inquiry, and report. They returned shortly, and stated that several of the women complained before Idris of being kept by force in the house, and a few of them said that they had not the necessary means of living. I now sent the same deputation back again, and instructed the *kadi* to give the legal wives and their slave-girls injunctions to remain in the house and await their master's orders; and at the same time he was to legally nominate someone to look after them, while Idris was ordered to deduct any expenses incurred in the maintenance of the family, from Nur Angara's pay.

A list was then to be made of the remaining women, who were ordered to be sent to their relatives or tribes against receipts; and I further instructed the delegates to remain quite neutral, and force no one to leave the house who did not wish to do so, or who wished to stay until their master's return; I added that I would be responsible that such as wished to remain should be provided for. It is needless for me to add that women's affairs take quite as long a time to settle in the Sudan as they do in Europe; I was not, therefore, surprised that my delegates remained absent two hours, and in the lists which they brought back I found the names of no less than sixty young girls who pleaded for liberty. They had all been captured in the various campaigns, and their tribes were now the loyal subjects of the government. Their detention by force was, therefore, quite illegal, and I ordered them to be at once sent back to their relatives. Of the remaining thirty, some, owing to family matters, and others for various reasons, expressed a wish to remain, and I gave instructions for them to be supplied with the necessary means for living. As for Idris, I told him that I held him responsible for his brother's household, and that he must either look after the women or release them.

I also found the Bazingers and their wives in this station very discontented, and I did what I could to place matters on a better footing. Several of the neighbouring *sheikhs* came to see me here, amongst them Hegam of the Dar Massalit, Sultan Idris of Dar Gimr, El Mahi of Dar Jebel, and Hamad Tor Jok of the Beni Hussein. I had a most interesting conversation with these men, especially with the Massalit *sheikh*, who was constantly at war with the tribes on the Wadai frontier. He told me it was their custom to go to battle with their wives and children, who always carried the *om bilbil*.

"This drink," said he, "encourages one for the fight; and as for our wives and children, why should we leave them for our enemies? We always go out to conquer or die." I told him that I had heard it was the custom in their tribe to use the skins of their slain enemies as waterskins, in their natural form, and that if he had some of these skins, I hoped he would give me a male and female as specimens. The *sheikh* at once denied it; but the other *sheikhs* said that it was so, and Hegam admitted that it had been a tribal custom long ago. I begged him to search among his old war-trophies, and he promised he would do so; but he evidently failed to procure one, for he never again mentioned the subject. These *sheikhs* afterwards asked to see me privately, and each of them in turn offered me a horse, which, they said, was the custom of their country; but I persistently refused to accept one, much to their chagrin.

After inspecting the books, I left Kebkebia, accompanied by Omar Wad Darho, and directed the infantry to follow us to the village of Melek Hagger, where we had arranged to meet the Maheria *sheikhs*. The road now became practically a desert; but as it was winter time, and we were mounted, the journey was not a trying one. About half a day's march beyond Kebkebia, we reached the Ogelli wells, where our horsemen filled their water-bottles, and we started on again at midnight, so as to get over the distance as quickly as possible. In the early morning we were overtaken by some mounted messengers, despatched by Adam Omar with a French cipher message from Marcopoli Bey, in the governor-general's name, which had been sent to Foga, whence it had been posted on to Kebkebia *via* El Fasher. It ran as follows:

"A Dervish named Mohammed Ahmed has, without just cause, attacked Rashed Bey near Gedir. Rashed Bey and his troops have been annihilated. This revolt is very serious. Take the necessary steps to prevent malcontents in your province from joining this Dervish." I sent an immediate answer, as follows: "Your message received. I shall take the necessary steps to comply with your orders."

Some time previously, I had been told privately that a religious *sheikh* had been causing difficulty to the government by calling on the natives to resist authority. As, however, I had heard nothing of the matter officially, I concluded it had been satisfactorily settled; but now this annihilation of the Mudir Rashed Bey and his troops was evidently a matter of grave import. The movement must have suddenly assumed large dimensions; but who would have dreamt the results would have been so terrible and so widespread!

Having started on this expedition, I could not now well give it up without exciting mistrust; but I determined to bring it to a successful issue with the least possible delay. That evening we came across a herd of giraffe, which abound in this desert. Catching sight of us, they at once scattered; and as I was mounted on the fast little pony Gordon had given me, I galloped after one, and in a few minutes caught it up, and could with ease have killed it; but I knew that to cut it up and distribute the flesh would have taken hours, and the thought of this alarming telegram induced me to let the animal go. That night we halted at an ostrich hunter's settlement, and lost no time in lighting a fire to keep ourselves warm. We found these great desert tracts bitterly cold, and the Shaigia were so numbed they could scarcely sit on their horses. These districts contain quantities of ostriches, which are hunted by the Arabs and Gellabas.

A party of them, taking a supply of water on camels sufficient to last them for weeks, usually settle in some spot in the desert frequented by ostriches, where they build little straw huts just large enough to contain one man; and in these they patiently wait, on the chance of a stray shot. Of course, if a man is fortunate enough to discover where an ostrich has laid eggs and buried them in the sand, he will patiently watch until the eggs are hatched, when he seizes the little birds, puts them in the cage he has ready, and takes them off to the nearest market, where he invariably gets a good price for them.

We marched the whole of the next day, and at eleven o'clock the following morning reached the village of Melek Hagger, and were welcomed by the great Zaghawa Sheikh, who begged us to come to his village; but I preferred to camp under an enormous *nabak*-tree which stood in the centre of the *khor*, and was large enough to accommodate a hundred people under its shade. Hasaballa, Sheikh of the Maheria, was also there, and told me that he had collected the water-skins, and a hundred and fifty camels which were grazing close by. Adjutant-Major Suleiman Basyuni, at the head of two hundred infantry, also marched in that evening; and, having procured from the village the quantity of corn required, as well as two oxen which were offered by the *sheikhs* and specially killed for the troops, we were able to continue our march the next morning.

Two days later we reached Kama, the market town of the district ruled by Melek Saleh Donkusa. This Donkusa's sister, Khadiga by name, when quite a young girl, had been presented by her parents to Sultan Hussein, and had eventually entered his *harem*, while her brother, who had also come to El Fasher, obtained, owing to his superior ability, a high position in the palace. Khadiga eventually bore Sultan Hussein a son, who died; and the latter had then liberated both Khadiga and Saleh, and had appointed him *emir* of the portion of the Zaghawa tribe to which he belonged. Now it happened that the mother of Saleh and Khadiga was a Bedeyat maiden, and the present Bedeyat rulers were their uncles. All this I knew beforehand, and had already taken steps to use Donkusa as an intermediary between the Maheria and the Bedeyat, in order to induce the latter to give up the stolen camels without being obliged to have recourse to force.

Saleh informed me that, in accordance with my instructions, he had already sent word to the Bedeyat chiefs, and that he expected them to arrive in a few days to make their submission to me. He therefore begged I would wait at his village. I was much gratified with this news, for I was most anxious to settle matters quickly and get back to El Fasher. I told Saleh to let the Bedeyat chiefs know that I did not intend to be very severe, and that if they were really anxious to avoid a conflict, they should come at once; but at the same time I told him to warn them that I was very strong, and would not be tampered with.

It is a strange fact that the Bedeyat, although completely surrounded by Moslem states and peoples, are almost the only tribe in this part of Central Africa who still adhere to their old heathen customs. If their chiefs are asked by Mohammedans to repeat the creed, they can say, "There is no God but God, and Mohammed is his Prophet." But beyond this they know nothing; they are utterly ignorant of the precepts of the *Koran*, and never pray as Moslems.

Under the wide spreading branches of an enormous *heglik*-tree, and on a spot kept beautifully clean and sprinkled with fine sand, the Bedeyat beseech an unknown god to direct them in their undertakings, and to protect them from danger. They have also religious feasts at uncertain dates, when they ascend the hills, and on the extreme summits, which are whitewashed, they offer sacrifices of animals. They are a fine, stalwart race, very dark in colour, with straight features, a thin nose and small mouth, and resemble Arabs more than Negroes. The women are famed for their long flowing hair, and there are some great beauties amongst them, as one often finds amongst the free Arab tribes. They generally wear skins of animals round their waists and loins; but the higher class and their women dress in long flowing robes made of white Darfur cotton cloth.

Their food is very plain. Corn does not grow in their country, and

BEDAYAT PRAYING TO THE SACRED TREE.

is almost unknown to them. They take the seeds of the wild pumpkin, which grows there in abundance, and they soak them in wooden vessels made from the bark of trees. After taking the outer shells off, they leave the seeds to steep until they lose their bitterness, and then, straining them off and mixing them with dates, they grind them into a sort of flour, which is cooked with meat, and forms the principal food of the country.

They have also most strange customs as regards inheritance and succession. The cemeteries are generally situated at some distance from the villages; and when a father dies, the body is taken by all the relatives to be buried. The ceremony over, on a given signal they all rush together at the top of their speed to the deceased's house; and he who arrives first and fixes his spear or arrow in it is considered the rightful heir, and not only becomes possessor of all the cattle, but also of his father's wives and other women, with the exception of his own mother. He is at perfect liberty to marry them if he wishes, or he can set them free. A man's female household is entirely regulated by his financial position. It is great or small according as the lord and master is rich or poor.

As I before remarked, most of the people still adhered to their pagan customs, and it amused me greatly when Saleh Donkusa, who was by way of being a good Moslem himself, denied to me, in the most emphatic manner, that such customs were still in vogue in his tribe. I asked him what the great *heglik*-tree was which I had passed the previous day when riding through the *khor*, and why the ground underneath was sprinkled with fine sand. The question surprised him, and for a moment, he was silent; he then answered that it was the usual meeting-place in which tribal matters were discussed.

"The Maheria Arabs," said I, "wanted to graze their cattle near the tree; but when I saw that it was dedicated for some special purpose, I prevented them from doing so." He thanked me most heartily, and I could see that, though a fanatical Moslem himself, he was determined to uphold the ancient manners and customs of his tribe, and so retain his hold over them. I subsequently learned that it was entirely through him that the holy tree was preserved; and as my work was not that of a missionary, I had no desire to interfere in their religious matters, and possibly bring about difficulties with the Bedeyat, who had never seen a white man before.

I was beginning to lose patience, owing to the delay of the chiefs in coming, when a certain Ali Wad el Abiad arrived; he had been

Sub-Kadi of Shakka, and had just been discharged by Emiliani, against whom he made the most bitter complaints, charging him with allowing the clerks to do exactly as they pleased, because he was so ignorant of the Arabic language. He then told me he had heard in Shakka that a *dervish* had been preaching a *Jehad* (religious war) against the Turks (Government), and had already fought several successful actions. I immediately wrote off to Emiliani, telling him of the *kadi's* complaint, and urging him to do all in his power to prevent the Arabs communicating with the rebels, and to endeavour to do his utmost to keep the country tranquil. I also told him to lose no time in reporting to me fully on the general state of affairs.

At length, after a stay of six days at Kamo, Saleh came to me with the satisfactory news that the Bedeyat chiefs would arrive the next day. In concert with him, I selected the *heglik*-tree as the place of meeting, which was to be held one hour after sunrise and in which he was to act as the intermediary between myself and the Bedeyat. I then ordered our tents to be moved to within less than half a mile of the tree, and early the next morning I had the troops drawn up in line ready to receive the Bedeyat chiefs, whose approach Saleh now announced. Standing with my officers and *sanjak*, Omar Wad Darho, about one hundred yards in front of the line, with our servants holding the horses, we prepared to receive our distinguished visitors, who, guided by Saleh, were now seen advancing, with their hands crossed on their chests and heads bowed low. They had brought an interpreter with them, and through him we exchanged mutual greeting. I then ordered carpets to be spread on the ground, and asked them to be seated, whilst I and my officers sat on small field chairs; and, having partaken of sugar and water and dates, we began our palaver.

The four Bedeyat Sheikhs were tall, fine-looking middle-aged men, with good features and dressed in long white robes which no doubt our friend Saleh had prepared for them; they also wore the usual straight Arab sword. Their names were Gar en Nebbi, Bosh, Omar, and Kurukuru; but I am not quite sure that these high-sounding Arab names were not assumed for the occasion. Their attendants, numbering between sixty and seventy men, dressed in shirts and skins, stood some way behind, while Saleh Donkusa seated himself close to the Sheikhs and the interpreter.

The spokesman, Gar en Nebbi, now addressed the interpreter with the words "*Kursi Sellem*," to which the latter answered "*Sellem*," indicating that he was ready to translate; and he then began: "We belong

SURRENDER OF THE BEDAYAT TO SLATIN.

to the Bedeyat tribe, and our fathers and grandfathers have paid tribute to the Sultans of Darfur every two or three years when an officer was sent to collect it. You Turks have now subdued the Furs and have conquered the country, and you have never before asked us to pay tribute. You (Slatin)—as our friend and brother Saleh Donkusa has informed us—are the ruler of this country, and in token of submission we have brought you ten horses, ten camels, and forty cows. Do you, therefore, fix the amount of tribute to be paid by us."

It was now my turn to speak; so, repeating the "*Kursi Sellem*," I began: "I thank you for your submission, and I am only going to demand a small tribute; but I have specially come here to call on you to return the camels you stole from the Maheria, and release the prisoners you captured."

Gar en Nebbi, after a short pause, replied: "Since the time of our forefathers we have been in constant feud with the various Arab tribes. If we fight and take prisoners, it is our custom to allow them to be ransomed. We have often before released Maheria captives."

I referred to Sheikh Hasaballa to ask if this was so, and he answered in the affirmative; and then I asked whether he had ever done so since the Egyptian Government had taken possession of the country, or whether he referred to the period in which they were ruled by the Darfur Sultans.

"Before you conquered the country," he answered, "but only two years ago, the Maheria invaded our country; we repulsed them and drove them out, so that they returned empty-handed." I looked at Hasaballa, and saw from his silence that the Bedeyat was telling the truth.

"That may be so," I answered, "but at that time I was not governing this country. I am well aware that in those days you did what you thought was right, and I do not in any way blame you for it; but as I am now your master, I wish you to act in accordance with my orders. You should, therefore, hand over your prisoners; but as the Maheria previously attacked you, then I order that instead of returning them all the camels you took, you can retain half, as a reward for your bravery in having prevented them from pillaging your country."

A long pause now took place, and the four *sheikhs* discussed the matter between themselves. Gar en Nebbi then answered, "We shall comply with your orders; but as it will take a long time to collect the camels, which are scattered throughout the country, it will be easier for us to release the captives."

"Then look sharp," said I, "and carry out these orders as soon as possible; and when you have done so, I will release you from the payment of this year's tribute. I can quite understand that it may cause you some difficulty to return the camels and pay your taxes as well."

This arrangement apparently quite satisfied them, and they thanked me profusely; so I asked them to stay with us till the following day, and Saleh would look after all their wants. Then, mounting our horses, I gave the command to the troops to fire three volleys, which terrified the poor Bedeyat, who had scarcely ever seen fire-arms. Telling Saleh to bring the *sheikhs* before me the next morning at the same hour, I galloped off with my escort to the camp.

During the day I busied myself in considering how best to get back to El Fasher without endangering the success of my present expedition; I could not wait until the Bedeyat had collected and handed over their captives; moreover, I was disturbed about the condition of the water-skins supplied by the Maheria, and blamed Hasaballa severely for furnishing such bad equipment. Next morning, when the *sheikhs* arrived, I asked them if they had yet despatched men to collect the prisoners and camels; and when they answered no, I replied in an irritated tone that I could not possibly wait to see my orders carried out.

To this Gar en Nebbi answered, "Master, we are here to carry out your orders; you can return, and we shall deliver over the men and animals to Saleh Donkusa and Hasaballa, who is remaining as his guest."

"I have another proposal to make," said I. "I do not doubt your sincerity and loyalty, but I am anxious to know you better personally; I wish, therefore, you and any others you may desire to bring with you should accompany me to El Fasher, and at the same time tell your representatives to collect the men and animals and hand them over to Hasaballa, who is staying with Donkusa. When I hear at El Fasher that this has been done, I shall then send you back to your country laden with rich presents. You have never visited El Fasher yet, and you will be interested to see the seat of government and understand its power, and I sincerely trust that you and Saleh will concur with my proposal; you will be so pleased with all you will see that in future I know you will always comply most readily with my orders."

Saleh at once answered that he thought the proposal a very good one, and that he was content to stay behind, as he had already seen El Fasher. I saw by the faces of the Bedeyat that the idea pleased them, and after a long palaver amongst themselves they made up their minds to accompany me. Knowing that the sooner they carried out my orders about the return of the captives and camels the sooner they would start, they lost no time in nominating good men as their representatives with the tribe, and, selecting six men as their attendants, they announced they were ready to leave; but before starting they wished to swear the oath of fidelity, in which, of course, I readily acquiesced.

The ceremony was performed as follows: A horse's saddle was brought and placed in the midst of the assembly, and on this was laid a large earthenware dish filled with burning charcoal; a lance was then fixed to the saddle, and the head-*sheikhs*, with their attendants, now came forward and, stretching out their hands over the lance and burning charcoal, they recited the following words with great solemnity, "May my leg never touch the saddle, may my body be smitten with the lance that kills, and may I be consumed by the burning fire, if I ever break the solemn oath of fidelity which I now make to you."

After this solemn declaration I had now no doubt of the loyalty and honesty of these people.

That afternoon I gave the order to start, and, accompanied by the four Bedeyat chiefs and their attendants, we left Kamo, having given Saleh and Hasaballa most strict injunctions to inform me without delay when the tribe had complied with my instructions. Anxious to reach El Fasher without further delay, I left the *sheikhs* in charge of the infantry, telling the officers to do all that was possible to make their journey comfortable; and then, accompanied by Omar Wad Darho and my Shaigia escort, I set off at a rapid pace.

The first information I received on arrival at El Fasher was the sad news of the sudden death of Emiliani at Shakka. He had been suffering from heart disease for years, and at last it had carried him off; his officials, who did not understand the suddenness of the disease, thought they might be suspected of poisoning him, and had at once brought his body on a camel to Dara, where the apothecary held a rough post-mortem examination, and certified that death had occurred from natural causes. His body was buried at Dara, and I afterwards had a stone erected to commemorate my poor countryman who had died in this distant land.

I next learnt that some trouble had arisen at Shakka which would oblige me to go to Dara for a few days. Disquieting rumours also reached us of the state of affairs in Kordofan and Khartum; however, it was generally thought in government circles that the revolt would be speedily crushed by the military expedition despatched for this purpose.

A few days later the troops with the Bedeyat Sheikhs arrived, and in order to impress them, I ordered out all the garrison, and in the evening we had a grand firework display in their honour. I intrusted the *mudir* with looking after the comfort of my guests, but unfortunately I was not able to stay long with them; as soon as the horses were sufficiently rested, I started off again for Dara, accompanied by Darho and his two hundred Shaigias, leaving Said Bey Guma as *commandant* and representative of the government during my absence.

Chapter 4

The Khalifa's Personal Account of the Rise of the Mahdi

The revolt raised by the so-called Dervish proved to be of a very serious nature.

This man, Mohammed Ahmed, was born near the Island of Argo, in Dongola, and was of a poor and obscure family, but who claimed to be "*Ashraf*," or descendants of the "Prophet." Their claims to this dignity, however, were not inquired into or acknowledged by any one. In general he was known as a Dongolawi. His father was an ordinary *fiki*, or religious teacher, and had given him his early instruction in reading the *Koran* and in writing, and when still a child had taken him to Khartum; but he himself had died on his journey, near Kerreri, and here his son subsequently erected a tomb to him, known as the "*Kubbet es Sayed Abdullah*i" (the dome of Sayed Abdullahi).

Young Mohammed Ahmed was now left entirely to his own resources. He studied assiduously, and, being of a deeply religious disposition, he became a great favourite with his master, who taught him to learn the *Koran* by heart, and gave him his early instruction in theology; he subsequently went to Berber, and became the pupil of the well-known Mohammed el Kheir (formerly Mohammed ed Dekkeir), who completed his religious education. He remained for several years in Berber continually studying, and his unassuming nature, intelligence, and religious zeal made him a great favourite with his instructors. When he arrived at manhood he quitted Berber and went to Khartum, where he became a disciple of the celebrated and highly revered Sheikh Mohammed Sherif, whose father, Nur ed Dayem, and grandfather, Et Tayeb, had been the principal exponents of the *Sammania Tarika,* or doctrine.

The meaning of the word "*tarika*" is literally "way"; hence "Sheikh et Tarika" signifies "the guide to the way." The duties of these holy personages consist in writing a certain number of prayers and texts of the Prophet, which the devotees are called upon to repeat a certain number of times, and thus facilitate the "way" to those heavenly mansions which are the goal of all true believers. The Sheikhs et Tarika are therefore exponents of various doctrines, and each one bears the name of the original founder of the order; such as the "*Khatmia*," the "*Khadria*," the "*Tegania*," the "*Sammania*," etc. They are held in high respect by their disciples, who are their most devoted and obedient adherents.

Mohammed Ahmed soon showed himself a most zealous and ardent supporter of the *Sammania Tarika*, and became very devoted to its head, Sheikh Mohammed Sherif. He now went to live on the Island of Abba, on the White Nile, near Kawa, surrounded by several devoted disciples. They earned a livelihood by cultivating the lands, and received frequent gifts from religious persons who passed up or down the Nile. Mohammed Ahmed's grand-uncle, Mohammed Sharfi, had resided on the island for some years, and the young zealot had married his daughter. His two brothers, Mohammed and Hamed, also lived there, drove a good trade in boat-building, and supported the young *fiki*, who had hollowed out for himself a cave in the mud bank, and lived here in almost entire seclusion, fasting often for days, and occasionally paying a visit to the head of the order to assure him of his devotion and obedience.

One day it fell out that Mohammed Sherif, as is the custom on such occasions, had gathered together his *sheikhs* and disciples to celebrate the feast of the circumcision of his sons; he had also given out that his guests might amuse themselves by singing and dancing as they liked, and that as such feasts were occasions of rejoicing, he would pardon, in God's name, any sins that might be committed during the festivities which were contrary to the religious law. But the godly *fiki*, Mohammed Ahmed, pointed out to his friends that singing, dancing, and playing were transgressions against the laws of God, and that no man, be he even Sheikh et Tarika, could forgive such sins.

These views reached the ears of Mohammed Sherif, who, entirely disagreeing with Mohammed Ahmed's arguments, and being withal very angry at this assumption on the part of his disciple, called on him to justify himself. Consequently Mohammed Ahmed, in the presence of all the inferior *sheikhs* and *fikis*, came in the most humble manner before Mohammed Sherif and besought his forgiveness. Sherif, however, abused him roundly, called him a traitor and a sedition-monger who had broken his vow of obedience and fidelity, and ignominiously struck him off the list of disciples of the *Sammania* order.

Thoroughly humbled and subdued, Mohammed Ahmed now went to one of his relatives and asked him to make a *sheba*;[1] and with this on his neck, and his head besprinkled with ashes, he again returned in deep repentance to Mohammed Sherif, begging his forgiveness. The latter, however, utterly refused to have anything further to say to him, and, in despair, Mohammed Ahmed returned to his family in Abba. He held the founders of the *Sammania* order, Sheikhs Nur ed Dayem and et Tayeb, in the greatest respect, and to be removed with ignominy from his beloved *tarika* was a disgrace too hard to be borne. Shortly afterwards Mohammed Sherif happened to be in the neighbourhood, and again Mohammed Ahmed appeared before him in the *sheba* and ashes, and once more implored forgiveness. "Be off, you traitor!" shouted Mohammed Sherif. "Get away, you wretched Dongolawi, who fears not God and opposes his master and teacher! You have verified the words of the saying, '*Ed Dongolawi Shaitan mugalled bigild el insan*' (The Dongolawi is the devil in the skin of a man). By your words you try to spread dissension amongst the people. Be off with you! I shall never forgive you!"

Kneeling in silence, his head bowed low, Mohammed Ahmed listened to these scathing words; then, rising, he went sadly away. Tears streamed down his cheeks; but they were not now tears of repentance. Rage and anger burned within him, and these feelings were heightened by the knowledge of his powerlessness to do anything by which to wipe out this disgrace and insult. Boiling over with indignation, he returned to his home and announced to his faithful disciples that he had been finally abandoned by Mohammed Sherif, and that he now intended to apply to Sheikh el Koreishi, who lived near Mesallamia, to receive him into his order. This *sheikh* had succeeded the holy Sheikh et Tayeb, the grandfather of Mohammed Sherif, and was one of those authorised to maintain and teach the Sammania doctrines as he considered right; and on this account there was considerable jealousy between him and Mohammed Sherif.

In due time Sheikh el Koreishi's reply was received, saying that he would accept him gladly. Mohammed Ahmed and his disciples

---

1. A *sheba* is a piece of forked wood which is fixed on the neck by way of punishment, and in this position is very painful.

now made all preparations to proceed to Mesallamia, and were on the point of starting, when a message was received from Mohammed Sherif, directing him to appear before him, when he would give him a full pardon, and permit him to resume his old functions; but to this Mohammed Ahmed sent back a dignified answer that he felt perfectly innocent of any crime, and sought no forgiveness from him; and that moreover he had no desire to lower him in the eyes of the world by bringing about a meeting between him and "a wretched Dongolawi."

Sheikh Koreishi now received him with open arms; and the incident between the godly but cunning Mohammed Ahmed and his late spiritual guide spread far and wide in the Sudan. That an inferior in a religious order should have refused the forgiveness of his superior was an unheard-of proceeding; but Mohammed Ahmed did not hesitate now to proclaim openly that he had left his late superior because he could no longer have any respect for a master who acted contrary to the religious law. And in this way he secured an immense amount of public sympathy, which brought his name prominently forward, and added considerably to his prestige. Even in distant Darfur the matter was the principal topic of conversation, and his refusal to accept forgiveness made him the hero of the hour.

He obtained Sheikh Koreishi's permission to return to Abba, where he received visitors from all parts, who sought the blessing of this holy man; and common people now crowded to the island, seeing in him a sympathetic leader who was bold enough to openly defy his superiors. He received quantities of gifts, and these he openly distributed amongst the poor, thus earning the epithet of "*Zahed*" (the renouncer, or one who has renounced the good things of this life). He then made a journey through Kordofan, where the towns and villages abound with religious *fikis* of the most ignorant and superstitious description. Amongst them he had an enormous success. He also wrote a pamphlet, which he distributed amongst his specially trusted adherents, summoning them as true believers to do all in their power to purify the religion, which was becoming debased and insulted by the corruption of the government and the utter disregard of the officials for the tenets of the true faith.

A few months later the Sheikh el Koreishi died, and Mohammed Ahmed and his disciples lost no time in going at once to Mesallamia, where they erected a tomb, or dome, to his memory.

It was while here that a certain Abdullahi bin Mohammed, of the

Taaisha section of the Baggara (cattle-owning) tribe of southwestern Darfur, presented himself to Mohammed Ahmed and sought permission to be admitted into the Sammania Tarika; his request was granted, and Abdullahi swore eternal fidelity to his new master. This man was the eldest of the four sons of Mohammed et Taki, of the Juberat division of the Taaisha tribe, which in its turn was descended from the "*Aulad um Sura.*" His three other brothers were Yakub, Yusef, and Sammani; he also had a sister named Fatma.

The father was on bad terms with his relatives, and determined to proceed on pilgrimage with his whole family to Mecca, where he resolved to settle, and end his days in close proximity to the birthplace of his Prophet. Those who knew Et Taki described him as a good man, scrupulous in his attendance to his religious duties, and capable of curing diseases and insanity by means of *heggabs*, or religious charms; he was also a teacher of the *Koran*. Of his sons, Abdullahi and Yusef were the most unmanageable, and the father had the greatest difficulty in making them learn by heart even the few passages from the *Koran* necessary for the ordinary prayers. Yakub and Sammani, on the other hand, had more of their father's quiet disposition, and, having learnt their verses and commentaries, were able to help him in his religious duties.

The family had, it appears, joined the Furs in combating Zubeir's entry to Darfur, and the latter relates how, during the fight at Shakka, he took Abdullahi prisoner, and was about to have him shot, when some of the Ulema craved pardon for him, which he granted. Abdullahi, in his gratitude, subsequently sought out Zubeir secretly, and announced to him that he had had a dream, in which it had been shown to him that he was the expected Mahdi, and that he (Abdullahi) was to be one of his faithful followers. "I told him," relates Zubeir, "that I was not the Mahdi; but that when I became aware of the wickedness of the Arabs, and how they blocked the roads, I came to open them and establish trade."

Et Taki and the family quitted their home when Zubeir had concluded peace, and, travelling *via* Kalaka to Shakka, they had remained there two years, and had proceeded thence *via* Dar Homr and El Obeid to Dar Gimr, where they remained the guests of the head-*sheikh* for some months, and where Et Taki died, and was buried by the head-*sheikh*, Asaker Abu Kalam, at Sherkéla. Before his death he urged on his eldest son, Abdullahi to take refuge with some religious *sheikh* on the Nile, then immigrate to Mecca, and never return again to their country.

Leaving his brothers and sister under the care of Sheikh Asaker Abu Kalam, in accordance with the dying wishes of his father, Abdullahi set out for the Nile valley; and when making inquiries along the road, he heard of the dissension between Mohammed Ahmed and his *sheikh*, Mohammed Sherif, and he resolved to go to the former and ask him to allow him to join the order. "It was a very troublesome journey," said Abdullahi bin Sayed Mohammed, Khalifat el Mahdi (his full name), to me some years later, when he first became ruler of the Sudan; for at that time he used to talk openly to me, and had not learnt to mistrust me, as he did latterly.

In those days, as I shall subsequently relate, he would send for me and chat with me alone by the hour, seated on his beautifully made *angareb*, over which a palm-mat was spread, whilst I sat beside him on the ground, with my legs tucked up under me. "Yes, indeed, it was a very troublesome journey," he repeated. "At that time my entire property consisted of one donkey, and he had a gall on his back, so that I could not ride him; but I made him carry my water-skin and a bag of corn, over which I spread my rough cotton garment, and drove him along in front of me. At that time I wore the wide cotton shirt, like the rest of my tribe. You remember it, do you not, Abdel Kader? For you have only recently come from my beautiful country (he always used to call me "Abdel Kader," unless there happened to be present another man of the same name, when he would call me "Abdel Kader Saladin," *i. e.*, Slatin). My clothes and my dialect at once marked me out as a stranger wherever I went; and when I crossed the Nile, I was frequently greeted with 'What do you want? Go back to your country; there is nothing to steal here.'

"The Nile people do not think well of us," he continued, "because the merchants going west to Zubeir, in Bahr el Ghazal and to our countries, were frequently maltreated by the Arabs; and when I asked them where the *Mahdi*, who was known as Mohammed Ahmed, lived, they gazed at me incredulously, saying, 'What are you going to him for? He would not soil his lips by even mentioning the name of your race.' Everyone, however, did not treat me in this way; some would take pity on me and direct me. Once, when passing through a village, the people wanted to take my donkey away, saying that it had been stolen from them the year before; and they would have succeeded, had not an elderly and God-fearing man interposed and allowed me to pursue my way. I was continually mocked and hooted at during my long journey; and had not a few people out of sheer pity occasionally given me some food, I must have starved.

"At length I reached Mesallamia, and here I found the *Mahdi* busily engaged in building the tomb of the late Sheikh el Koreishi. On seeing him I entirely forgot all the troubles I had suffered on my journey, and was content to simply look at him and listen to his teaching. For several hours I was too timid to dare to speak to him; but at length I plucked up courage, and in a few words told him my story, and about the sad condition of my brothers and sister, and I begged him, for the sake of God and His Prophet, to allow me to become one of his disciples. He did so, and gave me his hand, which I kissed most fervently, and I swore entire submission to him as long as I lived. This oath I kept most scrupulously until the angel of death overtook him; and some day he will overtake us, and therefore we should ever be ready to meet him."

Pausing for a moment, he gazed at me, and I at once said, "Yes, indeed, sire, you have faithfully kept your promise; and the Lord God Almighty has rewarded you; for you, who at one time were despised and rejected, have now become absolute lord and sovereign of this land. Those who insulted you at that time should indeed be thankful that you have not wreaked vengeance on their heads. A man capable of such restraint must indeed be the successor of the Prophet." Abdullahi, I knew, loved praise and flattery, and on this occasion I perhaps almost exceeded the limits; but I was most anxious that he should continue to tell me his story.

"When I had taken the oath," continued Abdullahi, "the *Mahdi* called one of his disciples, named Ali, and said to him, 'You are brethren from this day; give each other your mutual support, trust in God, and do you, Abdullahi, obey the orders of your brother.' Ali was very good to me; he was as poor as myself, but when the *Mahdi* sent him any food he always shared it fairly with me. During the day we carried bricks required for building the tomb, and at night we slept side by side. In a month the dome was complete. At this time the *Mahdi* received hundreds of visitors, and had little time to look at or think of me; still, I knew that I had found a place in his heart, and he appointed me one of his flag-bearers.[2] When we left Mesallamia, people flocked around us to gaze at the *Mahdi*, whom they at that time called only Mohammed Ahmed, and listen to his teachings and seek his blessing.

---

2. When religious *sheikhs* go out to preach, they are generally preceded by men bearing flags, on which texts from the *Koran* are inscribed.

"It was in this way that we marched to the Island of Abba. My sandals were worn out, and I had to give my donkey to a *mukaddum* (superior disciple) to carry a sick man; but at length we reached the *Mahdi's* house, and now I fell very ill with dysentery. My brother Ali took me to his little straw hut, which was scarcely large enough to hold two people, looked after my food, and, as I was in bed, he used to fetch water from the river to enable me to perform my '*wadu*' [religious ablution].

"One evening he went to fetch the water, but did not return; and the next day I was told that he had been attacked and killed by a crocodile,—*Allah yerhamu! Allah yeghfurlu!* (May God be merciful, may God forgive him his sins!) I repeated these words after the *khalifa*, adding, "Sire, how great is your patience! and therefore has God exalted you. Now may I ask you if, during your illness, the *Mahdi* paid any attention to you?"

"No," replied Khalifa Abdullahi, "the *Mahdi* wished to try me. It was not till after Ali's death, and when I lay helpless in the hut, that he was told I was ill. One evening he came to see me. I was too weak to get up, so he sat beside me, and gave me some warm *medida* (a sort of meal pap which, mixed with melted butter, is used as a stimulant) out of my pumpkin gourd, saying, 'Drink that, it will do you good; trust in God.' He then left me, and shortly afterwards some of the brethren arrived, and took me, by his order, to a cottage near his own hut. He himself lived in a simple *tukul* (straw hut). From the moment I had taken the *medida* which he had given me I felt better; he had said it would do me good, and the *Mahdi* always speaks the truth, and cannot lie."

"Yes, indeed," I interposed; "the *Mahdi* is faithful and true, and you as his successor have followed exactly in his footsteps."

"Once near him," continued the *khalifa*, "I recovered rapidly, for I saw the *Mahdi* daily; he was as the light of my eyes, and my mind was at rest. He used to ask about my family, and said they had better remain in Kordofan for the present. 'Trust in God' was always the last thing he said to me. He now used often to come and talk privately with me, and one day he intrusted me with the secret of his divine mission. He was appointed as *Mahdi* by God, he said, and had been taken by the Prophet into the presence of the apostles and saints. But long before he intrusted me with his secret—indeed from the first moment I beheld his face—I knew that he was the messenger of God,—*el Mahdi el Muntazer* (the expected guide). Yes, these were indeed happy days, and we had then no cares or troubles; and now, Abdel Kader, as it is getting late, you had better go to bed."

"May God grant you a long life, and may He strengthen you to lead the true believers into the right path," said I; and I quitted his presence with the usual salute.

In Abdullahi, the *Mahdi* had a ready instrument at hand for his great work. It is strange to think that this man might never have risen to any importance, had he not quarrelled with Mohammed Sherif; but now the reputation he had already gained amongst the inhabitants of the Gezira (the country lying between the Blue and White Niles) raised hopes in his mind that he was destined for a high position. He now began to secretly tell his special adherents that the time had come when religion must be purified, that this was to be his work, and that those of them who wished might join him in it. But he always called himself the slave of God, and made believe that he was acting entirely on inspiration from above.

Abdullahi was able to give him full information about the western tribes, who, he said, being powerful and courageous, would gladly seize an occasion to fight for the religion of God and his Prophet, and to conquer or die. To secure their adherence he advised Mohammed Ahmed to make a tour through Kordofan; and, setting out, they proceeded to Dar Gimr, where Abdullahi's family immediately joined them and became his faithful adherents. He told them, however, that the time had not yet come for them to leave their homes; for the present they would be more useful in inciting the local inhabitants.

From Dar Gimr he proceeded to El Obeid, where he visited all the principal chiefs and *sheikhs*, religious and other, and by inquiring carefully into their views and opinions, he gradually laid the foundations for his great design. In the strictest secrecy he told those of whose fidelity he was assured that he had a divine mission to cleanse and purify the religion, already polluted and debased by corrupt officials. In El Obeid his most trusted confidant was the Sayed el Mekki, the head of the religious *sheikhs*; but he advised that for the present no active steps should be taken, as the government was very powerful and the tribes were too split up and disunited to be able to raise a revolt. Mohammed Ahmed took a more sanguine view, and between them it was agreed that Mekki should observe absolute secrecy, and should take no steps until Mohammed Ahmed should begin the movement, when he promised him his entire support.

After leaving El Obeid, he proceeded to Tagalla, where he interviewed Mek Adam Um Daballo, the ruler of the district, who received him very kindly, but who, on the advice of his *kadi*, refused to make any promises of assistance. He now returned to Abba, *via* Sherkéla.

During this tour Mohammed Ahmed had full opportunities of seeing for himself the state of the country, and he was soon convinced that there was a spirit of the most bitter hostility against the authorities on the part of the poorer population, who, as I have already pointed out, were taxed out of all proportion to their property, and who suffered terrible oppression and tyranny at the hands of the self-seeking and unscrupulous tax-gatherers who infested the country. Amongst the latter, there were now a considerable number of Sudanese, who lost no opportunity of enriching themselves and of putting their relatives in positions of secondary importance, to help them to this end.

As a case in point, Gordon's nomination of the wealthy Sudanese merchant Elias as Pasha and Governor-General of Kordofan created an immense amount of ill-feeling in the country; and the same might be said of his assistant, Abderrahman ben Naga, also a wealthy Kordofan merchant. Both of them were capable men, and understood the management of the people; but they worked entirely for their interests and those of their relatives. Moreover, a spirit of jealousy became rampant amongst other Sudanese of high rank, who considered themselves quite as capable of filling high positions as those who had been selected in preference to them. Consequently, when Elias Pasha sent orders to Mek Adam to pay his taxes, he refused point blank, as he was of royal descent.

"I pay for goods I buy from merchants, but I do not pay tribute to them," said Mek Adam proudly to the officials who had been sent to him. At the same time he sent to El Obeid to inquire if all the Turks and other "Whites" had died, as the government had now given high positions to men who were merely merchants, instead of to persons of high descent. These were the reasons for the subsequent discharge of Elias Pasha and Abderrahman from their official positions, and their substitution by Turks and Egyptians.

As regards the Europeans, there were very few of us; but as a rule we were liked and respected, because the people trusted our word; but I do not doubt that we also gave them cause at times to be dissatisfied with us. With probably the best intentions in the world, we would issue rules and regulations entirely at variance with the manners, customs, and traditions of the Sudanese.

There is also no doubt that our attitude in regard to the slave question caused wide-spread discontent. The religion permitted slavery, and from time immemorial the ground had been cultivated and the cattle tended by slaves. That slave-hunting and slave-driving led to the perpetration of the most horrible cruelties and bloodshed, I do not for a moment hesitate to admit; but this was a matter of very little concern to the slave-buyers, who as a rule did not ill-treat their slaves. Now we, by our activity and energy, had not only made the export of slaves from the Black countries almost impossible, but we listened to the complaints of slaves against their masters, and invariably set them free.

Mohammed Ahmed cleverly seized the occasion of all this discontent to act; he was well aware that religion was the only possible means of uniting all these discordant elements and widely diversified tribes who were at continual feud with each other; he therefore declared himself the "*Mahdi el Muntazer*"; thus at once creating himself a personality which must be superior to all others, and hoping by this means to drive out of the country the hated Turks, Egyptians, and Europeans. But still he thought the time for an open declaration was not yet ripe; he therefore continued to increase the number of his trusted adherents, till at length the nature of his divine mission became an open secret.

Some time previous to this, Rauf Pasha, Governor-General at Khartum, had been secretly told by Mohammed Sherif of Mohammed Ahmed's intentions; but it was known that the early differences between the two religious *sheikhs* had greatly embittered Sherif, and consequently the authorities did not lay much store by his statements, and merely concluded that Mohammed Ahmed was a holy man who had obtained a certain hold over the people, owing to his superior sanctity.

But now the government learnt from quite another source that this man was a danger to the public peace, and therefore they determined to put an end to the matter, once and for all.

For this purpose Rauf Pasha sent for Mohammed Bey Abu es Saud, who was known to Mohammed Ahmed, and despatched him in a steamer to Abba with orders to bring the Sheikh to Khartum. Mohammed Ahmed's friends, however, gave him timely warning, and told him that if he came to Khartum he would in all likelihood be kept there, through the intrigues of Mohammed Sherif. When, therefore, Saud appeared at Abba, he was welcomed by Abdullahi and Mohammed Ahmed's brother, who conducted him to the *sheikh*. Abu

Saud now informed him of the reports—false he admitted—which had been circulated about him, and strongly advised him to come to Khartum and justify himself before his master, the governor-general. "What!" shouted Mohammed Ahmed, rising suddenly, and striking his chest with his hand, "by the grace of God and his Prophet I am the master of this country, and never shall I go to Khartum to justify myself."

Abu Saud drew back terrified; he then tried to calm him by soft words; but Mohammed Ahmed, who had previously planned this scene with Abdullahi and his brother, continued to talk vehemently, and urged Abu Saud to believe in the truth of what he said.

Abu Saud was now, however, much concerned about the safety of his own person, and as soon as he could beat a safe retreat, he did so, and returned to Khartum to inform the astonished governor-general of the failure of his mission.

Mohammed Ahmed now realised that there was no time to be lost; his future depended entirely on his own immediate exertions, and he did not hesitate to instantly write to his adherents throughout the length and breadth of the Sudan, stirring them up against the government, while he directed his own immediate followers to prepare forthwith for the *Jehad*.

In the meantime, Rauf Pasha was not idle; realising, after his interview with Abu Saud, that the matter was very serious, he resolved to despatch two companies, each under the command of an adjutant-major, to seize this fanatic; and thinking to create emulation between them, he promised that the officer who succeeded in capturing him should be promoted at once to the rank of major. But this plan only ended in creating discord, and the consequences were direful in the extreme.

The troops, under the chief command of Abu Saud, were embarked in the steamer, *Ismaïlia*, which had been armed with a gun, and, quitting Khartum early in August, 1881, they proceeded to Abba; but on the journey discussions arose between the two officers and Abu Saud.

Meanwhile Mohammed Ahmed, who had news of the despatch of the steamer, collected his people, and, obtaining help from the Degheim and Kenana tribes near him, whom he summoned to join in a *Jehad*, he made all preparations to offer resistance, stirring up religious enthusiasm by declaring that the Prophet had appeared to him and announced that all persons taking part in this religious war should earn the title of "*Sheikh Abdel Kader el Gilani*" and "*Emir el Aulia*,"[3] titles highly prized amongst Moslems. Now, however, that matters had become really serious, those who came forward and offered to give up their property and lay down their lives for the great cause were not numerous.

The steamers arrived off Abba at sunset, and, in spite of Abu Saud's appeals, the two officers determined to disembark at once. But the commander, into whose heart fear had entered when he heard Mohammed Ahmed declaring that he was "master of the land," remained on board with his gun, and anchored in midstream. Both officers, entirely ignorant of the locality, and each jealous of the other winning the tempting reward, advanced by different paths in the dead of night along the muddy banks towards Mohammed Ahmed's settlement.

The latter with his adherents had quitted the huts, and, armed with swords, lances, and clubs, had hidden themselves in the high grass, whilst the troops, arriving from opposite directions, now opened a hot fire on the empty village, with the result that each inflicted considerable loss on the other; and in the midst of this hopeless confusion the villagers leapt from their ambush and created terrible havoc amongst the already demoralised men, who fled in all directions. A few only succeeded in reaching the bank and swimming out to the steamer; and Abu Saud, now thoroughly terrified, wished to return instantly to Khartum, but was at last induced by the captain to stay till the following morning, in the hope of picking up fugitives. None, however, came, and at dawn he steamed back at full speed, with his direful news.

The effect of this success on Mohammed Ahmed and his adherents can be readily understood; they had suffered little or no loss, though he himself had been slightly wounded in the arm, and Abdullahi, who dressed the wound, counselled that this little accident should be kept secret from the rest. Still, the number of his followers was not largely increased, as the local people were convinced that government would take strong measures to suppress the revolt, and they would not risk the losses which they felt certain would ensue.

Mohammed Ahmed, strongly urged by Abdullahi and his brothers to increase the distance between himself and the Khartum authorities, now resolved to retreat to southern Kordofan; and to avoid this

---

3. Favourites of God. The expression occurs in the *Koran* in the following verse: "Are not the favourites of God those on whom no fear shall come, nor shall they be put to grief?" (*Surah* x. 63).

move being considered a flight, he announced to his adherents that he had received an inspiration to proceed to Jebel Masa,[4] and there await further Divine instructions. Before quitting Abba, he appointed, also in accordance with the Divine Will, his four *khalifas*. The first of these was Abdullahi, who (the precedent of the Prophet being adopted) represented the Khalifa Abu Bakr es Sadik; Ali Wad Helu, of the Degheim tribe (White Nile), was chosen to represent the Khalifa Omar ibn el Khattab; and the representative of the fourth Khalifa, Ali el Karrar, was Mohammed esh Sherif, one of Mohammed Ahmed's relatives, who was then only a boy. The chair of the third Khalifa, Osman ibn Affan, was not filled for the moment, but was subsequently offered to and refused by the great Sheikh Es Sennusi, of Northern Africa.

To move this large following across the river was now a matter of some difficulty, for the people who owned boats, fearing that they might be accused of complicity, at first refused; but at length all—including a large contingent of Degheim and Kenana Arabs, who joined at the last moment—were transferred to the west bank; and, advancing into the Dar Gimr country, Mohammed Ahmed summoned the inhabitants of the districts through which he passed to follow him to Jebel Masa. The greatest enthusiasm now prevailed amongst his followers, who lost no opportunity of telling the credulous and superstitious populations through which they passed, of the wonderful miracles performed by the *Mahdi*. On one occasion, quite ignorant of any danger, he halted with only a few followers in close proximity to the camp of a certain adjutant-major named Mohammed Guma, who, with a party of sixty soldiers, was collecting taxes.

The latter, fearing the responsibility he might incur by attacking him without orders, referred to El Obeid for instructions; but long before they arrived the *Mahdi* had rejoined the bulk of his people and had continued his march; so this golden opportunity was lost. Years afterwards I met the unfortunate Guma in a sad and miserable plight in Omdurman. "Ah!" said he, "if I had only known then that I should be reduced to walking about barefoot, and begging my bread, I should not have asked for instructions, and so allowed that wretched Dongolawi to escape; it would have been better to have been killed than to have endured the miseries of this wretched existence."

---

4. The *Mahdi* is supposed to come from Jebel Masa in North Africa; but the astute Mohammed Ahmed did not hesitate to call Jebel Gedir, which was to be his destination in Kordofan, by this name, and thus fulfil one of the principal conditions of a "*Mahdi.*"

Another excellent opportunity of capturing him was also lost. It happened that Giegler Pasha had been ordered to come to El Obeid to represent the governor-general in connection with a case of embezzlement by a district inspector and wealthy Sudan merchant named Abdel Hadi; hearing that the so-called *Mahdi* was in the neighbourhood, he despatched, towards the end of September, Mohammed Said Pasha with four companies to arrest him and bring him to El Obeid. But either by design or through carelessness the expedition failed in its object; the troops, apparently, halted during the day at the place in which the rebels had slept the previous night, and after thus uselessly wasting three days, they returned to El Obeid, the result being that they were discredited as being afraid to attack, and the *Mahdi's* prestige rose proportionately.

It had been Mohammed Ahmed's intention to stay for a time at Jebel Tagalla; but Mek Adam, learning of this, sent one of his sons to him with a gift of corn and sheep, bearing a message that he thought he had better retire further into the interior. He was therefore obliged to continue his journey, and after a long and troublesome march at length reached Jebel Gedir, where, in addition to the local inhabitants, a section of the Kenana tribe now resided.

At this time Rashed Bey was Governor of Fashoda; and, being fully informed of the *Mahdi's* movements, resolved to attack him before he became more powerful. A German named Berghof was also in Fashoda. He was formerly a photographer in Khartum, but Rauf Pasha had sent him up the river as an inspector for the suppression of slavery. Rashed now advanced, accompanied by Berghof and Kaiku Bey, king of the Shilluks, towards Gedir. Entirely underrating the enemy with whom he had to deal, he marched with no military precautions, fell into a carefully prepared ambush, and some fourteen hundred of his men were annihilated. So sudden was the attack that there was not even time to fire a rocket. Rashed and a few of his personal attendants made a gallant defence, but were soon overpowered by superior numbers and killed.

This defeat occurred on 9th December, and Mohammed Ahmed no longer hesitated to call himself the *Mahdi*. His prestige, especially in the eyes of the Arabs, rose enormously; nevertheless, his relations with his immediate neighbours were not of the best. Khalifa Abdullahi, in subsequent conversations with me in Omdurman, referred to this period, as far as I can recollect, in the following words:

We arrived at last at Gedir, thoroughly tired out after our long and troublesome journey. The *Mahdi* had only one horse, and that of the inferior Abyssinian breed, while I had to walk almost the whole distance; but God grants strength to those true believers who are ready to lay down their lives for the faith. My brothers, Yakub, Yusef, and Sammani had joined us with their families, also my stepmother, who was nursing my baby at her breast. My brother Harun, too, would not stay behind, so he also joined us. I was always greatly concerned about my wife, stepmother, and child, who is Osman Sheikh ed Din, whom you now see before you. It did not so much matter for us men; troubles and afflictions are sent us by God, and we bear them, only too thankful that we should be chosen by Him to raise the faith which had been trodden down to the dust, and to teach our brethren.

But, teaching won't bring us food for our women and children. People flocked to us in crowds, it is true; but most of them were even more destitute than ourselves, and came to us for support. Those who were well off shunned us,—riches are the curse of this world,—and those who have them will be deprived of the joys of Paradise. The people whose countries we crossed did not give us much help; but the little he got the *Mahdi* graciously offered to the pilgrims, whom he considered as his guests. When I heard the women and children weeping, I felt sometimes that my heart would break; but when I gazed at the *Mahdi's* face I trusted in God and became at rest. Patience, Abdel Kader, is the highest virtue. Practise that, and God will reward you.

The defeat of Rashed Bey awakened the government to a sense of the serious nature of the revolt, and an expedition was at once organised and placed under the command of Yusef Pasha Shellali, who had greatly distinguished himself in Gessi's campaign in Bahr el Ghazal, and was noted for his courage and resource. A reinforcement of a battalion of infantry and some volunteers, under the command of Abdalla Wad Dafalla (the brother of Ahmed Wad Dafalla), with Abd el Hadi and Sultan Dima, was also to be sent from Kordofan.

Meanwhile the *Mahdi* despatched letters in all directions, proclaiming his victories and his Divine mission. He summoned all to join the *Jehad*, giving the name of Ansar[5] to his followers, and promising them four-fifths of the booty taken in war (the remaining fifth he reserved

---

5. That is, the "Helpers,"—a term given by the Prophet Mohammed to the early converts of El Medina.

for himself), while to those who should fall fighting for God and His religion he held out the certainty of the fullest enjoyment of the pleasures of Paradise. Thus did he pander to the main characteristics of the Sudanese, *viz.*, fanaticism and greed.

Yusef Pasha Shellali's force, which numbered some four thousand men, was composed of regular infantry under Mohammed Bey Suleiman and Hassan Effendi Rifki, whom I had previously discharged; the irregular cavalry were placed under the courageous Shaigia Melek, Taha Abu Sidr, and leaving Khartum on 15th March, 1882, they proceeded to Kowa, where they awaited the reinforcements expected from El Obeid.

Abdalla Wad Dafalla, however, found it no easy matter to collect volunteers. There was a general feeling that it was wrong to fight against a man of piety, and, moreover, as the *Mahdi* and his followers were little else than beggars, there was no enticement of rich plunder to allure them. Besides all this, Elias Pasha, the richest merchant in Kordofan and the ex-governor, was the deadly enemy of the Dafalla family, and exercised all his influence, which was still considerable, in preventing men joining him. However, Abdalla had agreed with the authorities to proceed, and, including regulars, the force with which he left El Obeid numbered some two thousand men; and joining with the remainder at Kowa, the entire expedition of six thousand strong proceeded to Fashoda, which was reached in the middle of May.

After a short rest, Yusef Pasha advanced west, and camped, on the evening of 6th June, at Mesat, near Jebel Gedir, confident of success. Why should such men as Yusef Pasha, Mohammed Bey, and Abu Sidr fear a starving crowd of sickly, half-famished, and almost naked Arabs? Had they not won victories on the White Nile at Duffilé? Had they not conquered Bahr el Ghazal, and brought the proud Sultans of Darfur to submission? What could this ill-armed and ignorant *fiki* do? Abdalla Wad Dafalla alone raised a note of warning that they should not underrate the danger. He had had a fall from his horse when marching out of El Obeid, which is considered a bad omen in the Sudan; but who was going to listen to this preacher in the wilderness?

They did not even think it worthwhile to cut down a few thorn bushes to make a *zariba*, but merely picked up a little of the scrub lying close by, and formed a rough enclosure, utterly inadequate for defence; so the *Mahdi's* sickly, half-famished, and almost naked Arabs fell on Yusef Pasha's army in the early dawn of the 7th June. Dashing through the slight inclosure, they were on the sleeping soldiers in a moment, and made short work of them. Yusef Pasha and Abu Sidr were killed in their night-shirts at the doors of their tents, and in a few minutes there was scarcely a man left alive. Abu Sidr's concubine rushed at her master's murderers, and shot two of them with a revolver; but she fell prone over his body, stabbed to the heart. Abdalla Wad Dafalla, with a few of his attendants, alone made a short stand; but they soon shared the fate of their companions.

When anything unusual happens in uncivilised countries, it is always considered by the natives as supernatural; and this was exactly the effect of Yusef Pasha's disaster on the credulous and superstitious minds of the Sudanese. For sixty years the country had been governed by the Turks and Egyptians. If the tribes refused to pay their taxes, they were invariably punished; and no one dared to question for a moment the right of the authorities to do so. Now this holy *fiki*, Mohammed Ahmed, had suddenly appeared on the scene. With a crowd of ill-armed and undisciplined men he had inflicted several crushing defeats on the well-armed and well-equipped government troops. There could now be no doubt he was the "*Mahdi el Muntazer,*" the expected *Mahdi*!

The defeat of Yusef Pasha placed the whole of southern Kordofan in his hands, and now he was in a position to make good his deficiencies. He had gained money, arms, horses, and loot of all sorts; and these he distributed amongst the chiefs of tribes who now flocked to him. They believed most firmly that he was the true Mahdi, whose only intention was to uphold the faith, and who had no regard for wealth and property.

The news of the *Mahdi's* victories now spread far and wide; and, amongst an uneducated population such as that of Kordofan, the accounts were exaggerated to a quite ridiculous extent. Roused by the spirit of fanaticism, numbers of them quitted their homes, and marched to Jebel Gedir, which was now openly re-named Jebel Masa, while others, gathering round the local chiefs, prepared to fight against the various government posts and stations scattered throughout the country.

This condition of affairs was eminently favourable to the ruling passions of the nomad Arabs. Under the cloak of a religious war, which owed its existence to them, they massacred, plundered, and robbed the natives who, they said, were loyal to the hated Turks; and at the same time they shook themselves free from the taxation imposed on them by a government they detested.

The *Mahdi* now placed himself in communication with the merchants of El Obeid, who, through their wealth and connection with the people, virtually ruled the town and a considerable part of the country. They thoroughly understood the situation. None knew better the weakness and effeteness of the government, and many were prepared to side with the *Mahdi*. Elias Pasha was the chief amongst these malcontents, and detested Ahmed Bey Dafalla, who was a great friend of Mohammed Pasha Said. He was well aware that these two would, in the event of the defeat of the rebels, do him all the harm they could. Elias Pasha, therefore, employed himself actively in secretly collecting adherents for the *Mahdi*. Many of the less wealthy merchants anticipated better times should the government be overthrown, whilst there were not a few who, though disinclined to the *Mahdi*, were driven to espouse his cause by the fear that, should he prove successful, their wives and property would fall into the hands of his victorious followers.

As for the religious *sheikhs*, this movement was one which held out the highest prospects of promotion for them. They prided themselves that one of their number had successfully dared to proclaim himself a *Mahdi*, and they looked to the time when he or his sons should drive out the hated Turk, and rule the land. A few—only a very few—sensible people foresaw the danger which would threaten the country should the *Mahdi* prove successful, and these did all they could to prepare the government for the coming storm; but their numbers were too small to have any effect.

Elias Pasha now sent his son Omar to acquaint the *Mahdi* with the situation, and to beg him to come forthwith to El Obeid; while Mohammed Pasha Said, realising that this would undoubtedly be the next step, and deluded with the idea that the people would be prepared to stand a siege with him, began to dig an enormous ditch round the town, and, at the suggestion of Ahmed Bey Dafalla, he put the government buildings in a state of defence, and built a parapet around them. His parsimonious ideas, however, led him into a grave error. Instead of laying in large stores of corn, which the merchants, seeking only their own interests, were perfectly ready to provide, he refused to pay more than peace prices. It was, in consequence, rapidly bought up at a higher rate by those who were already beginning to feel the effects of the disturbed state of the country; and so he lost the favourable moment to buy.

Meanwhile, massacres in the districts were of almost daily occurrence. Tax-collectors, detached military posts, and government officials fell an easy prey to the bloodthirsty Arabs. The Bederia tribe attacked and almost annihilated the inhabitants of Abu Haraz, which was a day's march distant from El Obeid, and only a few men, women, and children succeeded in reaching the capital; the rest were all killed or taken prisoners during the flight along the waterless track. Young girls were, of course, looked upon as valuable booty, and were given water by their captors; but the older women suffered the most horrible mutilation. Arms and legs were ruthlessly cut off merely to gain possession of the bracelets and anklets they wore.

A few days later, the town of Ashaf, in northern Kordofan, was attacked and plundered by the Arabs, though a defence was made by Nur Angara, who was living there at the time, and who assisted Sanjak Mohammed Agha Japo, formerly one of Gordon's *kavasses*. They were, however, eventually forced to retire on Bara. This Japo was an old Kurdi, and during the retreat he performed prodigies of valour. Collecting all the women and young girls in the centre of his square, he bade them sing songs of victory, saying that such music drove fear out of all hearts; and, making constant counter-attacks, he succeeded in bringing almost all the fugitives in safety to Bara.

This town was now attacked, and the Arabs repulsed; but, collecting in greater numbers under Sheikh Rahma, they completely invested it, and cut off all supplies.

A mass of Arabs had also collected at Kashgeil; and against these Mohammed Pasha Said despatched a battalion of regulars, who succeeded in temporarily dispersing them; but, in doing so, the troops lost so heavily that virtually it was little short of defeat; and, collecting again, these Arabs attacked Birket, where the entire garrison of two thousand men was put to the sword. A similar disaster overtook the troops at Shatt, on the White Nile, where two hundred were massacred; but their subsequent attack on Duem was repulsed, with a loss of two thousand men.

Meanwhile, the emissaries sent by the Mahdi to the Gezira had not been idle. The Gehéna, Agaliyin, Hawazma, and Hammada Arabs, under Abu Rof, had attacked and invested Sennar; but the town had been subsequently relieved by Sanjak Saleh Wad el Mek, who had been despatched thence with a large force of Shaigia.

The town of Abu Haraz, on the Blue Nile, had been invested by Sherif Ahmed Taha; and Giegler Pasha, who was acting governor-general in place of Rauf Pasha, had arrived in the neighbourhood, and had directed Melek Yusef of the Shaigia to attack the rebels with an inferior force, which was defeated. Melek Yusef, disdaining flight had got off his horse, and, seating himself cross-legged on his farwa (sheepskin), had ordered one of his slaves to kill him. Giegler had at once proceeded to Khartum, and, procuring reinforcements, had returned and attacked Ahmed Taha, who had been killed, and his head sent to Khartum. He had then cleared the neighbourhood of Sennar of rebels without suffering any serious loss.

In spite, however, of these temporary successes, troubles increased, and the government daily received alarming accounts of the disasters which had overtaken troops and inhabitants in various parts of the country. In consequence, Abdel Kader Pasha had been despatched to the Sudan as governor-general. He had arrived at Khartum on 11th May, 1882, and had busily set to work to place the town in a state of defence. These measures had some effect on the natives, and it was evident to them that the government intended to act resolutely; but, at the same time, it was perfectly clear to them that these steps were not merely precautionary, but were rendered absolutely necessary by the very serious position of affairs. The arsenal and dockyard, ammunition stores, magazines, and government archives must be safeguarded against all eventualities. Besides, one of the first acts of the new governor-general was to withdraw to Khartum a portion of the garrisons of Gallabat, Senhit, and Gera, in which districts there was at present complete tranquillity.

Meanwhile, Mohammed Ahmed fully realised that to kindle the smouldering fire into a blazing flame his presence was absolutely necessary. He therefore accepted Elias Pasha's invitation to come to El Obeid, and, leaving his uncle, Mahmud Sherif, with a few followers, to look after his wives and children in Jebel Masa, he descended into the plains, and marched with his forces towards the wealthy capital of Kordofan.

CHAPTER 5

Spread of the Revolt in Southern Darfur

When I quitted El Fasher for Dara, early in 1882, I was accompanied by three hundred and fifty mounted men under Omar Wad Darho. This large escort was quite unnecessary, but I thought it advisable to show the Arabs that the government had plenty of troops at its disposal to suppress any trouble on their part.

On arrival at Dara I visited poor Emiliani's grave, and put up a stone to his memory. Zogal Bey was administering affairs here as acting-governor in his place, and the general aspect looked very troubled. The southern Arab tribes—the Rizighat, Habbania, and Maalia—were in revolt; they held constant meetings, in which it was declared that Dervishes were flocking to the standards of the Mahdi, who had been sent by God to raise the Faith, and remove the oppression and tyranny of the hated officials; it was said that, armed merely with sticks, they had gained victory after victory over the government troops. Emiliani, whom I had previously sent to Shakka to report on affairs there, had been driven to distraction by the constant quarrels between Madibbo and Egeil Wad el Jangawi of the Rizighat tribe, and had ended by discharging Madibbo and replacing him by Munzel, who had previously acted for many years as principal Sheikh. Madibbo, enraged at this insult, had joined his own section, the Aulad Mohammed, who had immigrated at that time towards the Bahr el Arab for pasture.

I now sent letters to both Madibbo and Egeil, ordering them to keep their Arabs well in hand and stop these meetings which were being held, and at the same time I instructed Madibbo to come and see me and talk over his personal and tribal affairs. Just at the time I was despatching these letters, news arrived that, owing to the disturbed state of Shakka, the forty soldiers previously sent by Emiliani to assist the *sheikh* in collecting the taxes had been obliged to turn back, and were now within two days' march of Dara. I therefore ordered Mansur Effendi Helmi to proceed at once to restore order with two hundred and fifty regulars and twenty-five horsemen, and instructed Ismail Wad Barnu, who, it will be remembered, had been the intermediary between Gessi and Suleiman Zubeir, to accompany him. At the same time I sent word to Abakr, Sultan of the Begu tribe, who was thoroughly loyal, and particularly well acquainted with the Rizighat country, to join the expedition.

My instructions to Mansur Helmi were to act leniently with the Arabs, but at the same time with such discretion that the interests of the government should not suffer. I gave him, however, full powers to put down disturbances by force if other means failed. He marched off *via* Kalaka, whilst I returned forthwith to El Fasher to collect the various detachments of troops which were out in the district gathering taxes, and prepare for all eventualities. Before leaving Dara, I had a long and serious interview with Zogal. I had known this man well when I had been governor here, and it had come to my ears that he and Omar Wad Darho had had several talks about the *Mahdi* and his doings, and had agreed that should he continue to be victorious they would join him.

These two men were the richest officials in Darfur, and exercised great influence in the country: their secession would have been very serious; I therefore thought my best plan was to show them great friendliness, and do all that was possible to avoid a breach occurring between us. In my conversation with him I therefore made no allusion to his meetings with Darho, but confined myself to pointing out that he, being a relative of the *Mahdi* and at the same time a high government official, it behoved him to support lawfully constituted authority to his utmost. I reminded him that he had been born in Darfur and had been only an ordinary merchant, but that government had recognised his capacity and had given him one position after another, which he certainly could not hope his cousin the *Mahdi* would be able to confer on him.

I urged him not to be deluded by the exaggerated rumours he heard of the *Mahdi*'s prestige, and above all begged him to put aside all idea of his being credited with a Divine mission. Sooner or later, I said, the government must be victorious, and all those who had failed to support it in times of difficulty must expect severe punishment. I urged him to think of his women and children, who, by an ill-considered and thoughtless step on his part, might be placed in great difficulties; and I wound up by saying that I did not speak to him now as his official superior, but as to a friend who had worked together with me for long, and whose true interests I had at heart.

I think Zogal was favourably impressed by what I said; he admitted that as a relative of the *Mahdi* he could not help being struck by all that was going on, but at the same time he was most grateful for the favours bestowed on him by government, and he would seize every opportunity to prove that he was truly loyal. When I asked him point blank whether he was in personal communication with the *Mahdi*, he denied it, but showed me letters which the *Mahdi* had written to several of the religious *sheikhs*, inciting them to revolt, which he had intercepted. On inquiry, I found that the bearer of these letters had confessed to the battalion commander that he had received them from the *Mahdi* for distribution; I therefore ordered him to be tried by court-martial (the country being now subject to martial law). He was condemned to be shot, and in the interests of discipline I ordered the sentence to be carried out.

In saying goodbye to the officers and officials, I pointed out the absolute necessity of strict attention to their duties, and told them I would return from El Fasher as soon as possible; and, leaving the mounted troops in Dara, I departed for the capital, where I arrived after three days' march. The first news received was that the telegraph-station at Foga had been destroyed by the Homr Arabs, that the entire country in the neighbourhood of Om Shanga was unsettled, and that several people who were out in these districts collecting wood had been captured and enslaved by the Arabs.

Om Shanga was an important trade centre between El Obeid and El Fasher; it had a garrison of only sixty men, and as it contained some wealth, the Arabs would in all likelihood attack it. I therefore ordered Major Hussein Effendi Maher to proceed thither with reinforcements of two hundred men and fortify the place, and I also instructed Omar Wad Darho to advance towards it with three hundred horsemen, but at the same time I particularly warned him that the object of this expedition was to chastise the Arabs, and that I considered their conduct sufficiently bad to warrant their being freely plundered. I thoroughly understood Darho's disposition, and I was most anxious to create hostility between him and his men and the Arabs, who were now the firm adherents of the *Mahdi*, and thus by every means in my power prevent a coalition between them, which was the principal danger I feared.

The postal system was now completely interrupted, and I was obliged to send any communications to El Obeid and Khartum concealed in hollowed-out lance-staves, between the soles of boots or sandals, or sewn into the bearer's clothing. The extra ammunition I had ordered when in Khartum had, owing to the negligence of the officials, been delayed; it had reached El Obeid late, and now, the roads being cut, it could be sent no further. The man despatched in charge of this ammunition was a certain Mohammed Pasha Wad el Imam, the wealthiest merchant in Darfur, whom Gordon had turned out of the country, together with his brothers, for malpractices; and no sooner did he arrive at El Obeid than he joined the *Mahdi*. Also of the four hundred cavalry, mostly Turks and Egyptians, under the command of Mohammed Agha Abu Bala, destined for Darfur, one hundred only had been sent on, and the remainder were retained at El Obeid. I had therefore to make up my mind to do the best I could with the forces originally at my disposal in Darfur.

From the beginning I had enforced very strict discipline, and in consequence was not popular amongst the officers; they were inclined to pay little attention to the training of their men, and much preferred being sent to collect taxes, which, for them, was a very lucrative employment. In garrison they occupied themselves principally in building their houses and laying out their gardens, for which work they utilised the men under their command. I had at once put a stop to all this, and they had in consequence sent a petition to Cairo, signed by almost all of them, complaining that I was in the habit of removing powder from the magazines, that I taxed their houses and gardens, and had appointed as police inspector a Turkish sergeant in place of the officer I had discharged. But when the reply came from Cairo to say that as Governor-General of Darfur I was responsible for all such matters, and had the authority to do what I thought just and right, they found they were powerless, and had to put as good a face as they could on what they were pleased to call my innovations.

Meanwhile Major Hussein Maher and Omar Wad Darho sent in messages that the rebels were collected near Om Shanga and I at once despatched orders to them to attack.

From Dara I learnt that Madibbo on receiving my letter had refused to come, and had gone off to the *Mahdi* at Gedir instead; Egeil, who was with his cattle on the Bahr el Arab, also refused to come. Moreover, a certain Thiran of the Rizighat tribe and a relative of Madibbo, who had formerly been employed as a government tax-collector, had murdered in cold blood two soldiers who happened to have gone to him; he had also attempted to seize by force some of Sultan Begu's cattle, but had been wounded in the fray, taken prisoner, and sent to El Fasher for trial. He was found guilty, and I ordered his execution in the public market-place.

There was now no doubt that all the southern tribes were in a state of active revolt, and had every intention of joining the *Mahdi*; I therefore thought my headquarters should now be at Dara; so, taking two hundred infantry and seventy-five of the newly arrived cavalry, I proceeded thither. On my arrival I heard some interesting details regarding the progress of Mansur Helmi's expedition. It appeared that on his way he had come across the Om Sureir section of the Rizighat tribe, who had been implicated in a number of raids, had stolen a quantity of cattle, and had shown themselves generally hostile to government. Mansur had seized the *sheikhs*; but the latter had offered him a large bribe, which he had unhesitatingly accepted, and in consequence had released them, and returned them the greater part of their cattle. On his arrival at Shakka he had been attacked by some Rizighat and Maalia Arabs, and though he had driven them off with ease, he had lost Ali Agha Kanké, Omar Wad Darho's uncle, a most courageous man. He now officially informed me that an extensive revolt on the part of the Arabs was out of the question, and they were quite ready to serve the government loyally, if they received a full pardon for past offences.

An incident, however, had occurred which, though in itself insignificant, led to very serious consequences. I previously mentioned that on my way to Khartum I had been met by Sheikh Ali Wad Hegeir, of the Maalia tribe, who had accompanied me there. He had proved loyal and faithful to the government, and I had appointed him chief of the southern Maalia Arabs. Hearing that a meeting of the Rizighat Arabs under Sheikh Belal Nagur, with a view to joining the *Mahdi*, was about to be held, he resolved to attend the meeting and arrest this sedition-monger. Accompanied by his father-in-law and a few of his friends, he presented himself at the meeting, and, seeing some of his own tribe amongst the number, he called on them to separate themselves from the rest and come to him.

His summons was left unheeded, and a disturbance took place, in which Hegeir and his friends, being far in the minority, were severely handled, and barely escaped with their lives. The news of the fray had, however, preceded them and had been distorted, so that on reaching their home Hegeir was greeted by his wife with the words, "*Rageli hidlim wa Abuyi Rabta; Safar yomein sawuhum fi Gabta*" (My husband is a male ostrich, and my father a female ostrich; they made a two days' journey in a moment). Belal Nagur, however, pursued the fugitives, and, joined by the Maalia, attacked Hegeir's house.

The latter was urged by his friends to flee for protection to Mansur at Shakka; but, smarting under his wife's sarcastic verses he refused, saying, "I shall never fly to save my life. Better is it to fall under the sword than to be laughed at by a woman." And, true to his word, he defended himself against fearful odds until a spear split his head in twain, and he sank down to die, repeating his creed with his last breath. His father-in-law fell dead close to him; and his wife, who was the cause of this sad catastrophe, and had thus lost husband and father, was captured and enslaved.

Mansur Helmi, being now anxious to conclude arrangements with the tribes, begged that I should come to Shakka, as, being the representative of government and well known to the Arabs, I would have greater weight with them; he also expressed his opinion that a strong fort should be made in Shakka, and manned with a couple of guns. As it was most important to conclude terms with the Arabs, I resolved to comply with his request, and, taking one hundred and fifty regulars, twenty-five horsemen, and one gun, I started for Shakka.

Meanwhile, I had received news from Major Hussein Maher at Om Shanga that the new fort was nearing completion; and he enclosed a report from Omar Wad Darho, in which the latter stated that he had attacked the Arabs collected at El Esefer, two days distant from Om Shanga, had defeated them after a hard fight, and had captured a few horses. The bearers of these letters, however, stated that he had captured a very large number; and this news gave me considerable satisfaction, for I knew that he would be now more anxious to fight against the rebels, since he had the prospect of taking possession of captured loot. I at once wrote back, congratulating him on his successful action, and telling him to do what he liked with the horses; but at the same time I gave him strict orders not to proceed further east than Serna, and further south than El Esefer, both of which places were within the Kordofan frontier. I also gave him permission to fill up any casualties amongst his men by fresh recruits, if he could get them, provided he could depend on their loyalty; and I told him that if he continued to perform his duties satisfactorily I should not fail to recommend him to government for reward.

On arrival at Kalaka I was met by Mohammed Bey Abu Salama, one of the northern Maalia Sheikhs, who had been given the title of *bey* by Gordon, and who was waiting to receive me with an escort of forty armed Bazingers. He gave me the fullest information regarding the state of affairs in various parts of the country, and I knew I could implicitly rely on the statements of this faithful government servant. The southern Maalia tribes are perhaps the most drunken and immoral people of those districts; they are held in the greatest contempt by the Rizighat, Habbania, Messeria, and Homr Arabs, who are exceptionally moral and abstemious, and who never touch intoxicating drinks. The following anecdote relating to Sheikh Salama will best describe the peculiarities of these Arabs: One day, happening to return home unexpectedly, he found his sister had admitted her lover to his *angareb*. He had her instantly put in chains; and when his friends expostulated with him for this treatment, which in their estimation was excessively harsh for so trivial an offence, he replied that he had no objection to his sister having a lover, but he protested against her making her brother's *angareb* the place of assignation, and thereby detract from his dignity as *sheikh*.

Abu Salama with his Bazingers and about fifty horsemen accompanied me as far as Dem Madibbo, which was this *sheikh's* usual summer resort; but it was now completely deserted, with the exception of a few slaves, who ran away at our approach. I camped within about a mile of this place, and made a *zariba*, having resolved to remain here until I received news from Mansur Helmi. I had not long to wait. He had told me that there was no prospect of trouble with the Arabs, but that was when Madibbo was absent; he had now returned from a visit to the *Mahdi* in Jebel Gedir, laden with trophies and proofs of the success of the new prophet. He had been present when Yusef Pasha Shellali had been annihilated, and he brought with him quantities of arms, ammunition, horses, and female slaves, with which the *Mahdi* had presented him; he had also received from him a flag, which he had been told was accompanied by invisible angels, who would lead him to victory wherever he went.

Besides this, he brought numbers of proclamations, which he distributed broadcast. His tribe had no longer the slightest doubt that the government troops had been defeated, and he now summoned them to join in the *Jehad*. Obedient to his call, the Rizighat tribes to the northeast and southeast of Shakka flocked to the holy standard. But

Egeil still stood aloof; he could not forgive his quarrel with his rival, and resolved to remain neutral.

In a few days Madibbo had collected a force sufficiently strong to attack Mansur. The latter had made a *zariba* at Murrai, about half a day's march from Shakka, and thither most of the merchants, with their wives and families, had fled for protection. Early one Friday morning Madibbo with his hosts approached the *zariba*, and Mansur, instead of waiting to be attacked, foolishly sent out Rashed Agha with one hundred and fifty regulars and two hundred of Ismail Wad Barnu's, Sultan Abakr's, and the merchants' Bazingers,—the whole under Abder Rasul Agha, who had just joined from Kalaka. He himself stayed behind in the *zariba* with the rest of the troops. Rashed Agha advanced boldly without any scouts to the place where Madibbo was supposed to be, and the latter, dividing his men into three sections, ordered them to conceal themselves in the depressions of the ground and in the thick grass. The luckless troops saw too late the trap that had been laid for them. On a given signal the enemy attacked them in flank; they had only time to fire one volley, and the Arabs were amongst them. A pitiless massacre ensued. Sultan Abakr and Abder Rasul alone escaped, through the fleetness of their horses, back to the *zariba*, and all the rest perished.

Mansur Helmi, terrified at this sudden disaster, now completely lost hope; but Wad Barnu and Abakr encouraged the troops not to despair, with the result that when the victorious Madibbo attacked the *zariba* he was driven off with considerable loss. A messenger despatched by Mansur under cover of darkness, brought me the sad news of the catastrophe. In his alarm he had greatly exaggerated Madibbo's strength, and, consulting two of my most trusted officers, we decided that the best plan would be to send one hundred and fifty men and the gun to Murrai, while the remainder of the troops should proceed to Salama Bey's settlement, whither reinforcements from Dara would be instantly despatched, and from which place an advance on Murrai could then be made.

Madibbo, who had originally a few hundred rifles, had now captured three hundred more, as well as a quantity of ammunition. I had at my disposal only one hundred and fifty regulars, and, despatching these with the gun and a further supply of ammunition loaded on twenty camels, to guard which I detailed forty men, I left myself with only one hundred and ten men. I wrote to Mansur, instructing him that on the arrival of these reinforcements he should strengthen his position at Murrai as much as possible, and await my arrival with the reinforcements ordered from Dara. I thought it very unlikely that, having had one unfortunate experience outside the *zariba*, he would again risk leaving it; besides, I knew he had sufficient corn for some days. In my letter to Zogal, ordering him to send more troops, I merely mentioned that Mansur had suffered a slight reverse, as I greatly feared the effect of this bad news in Dara; and I told him we were all well, and hoped to make a successful attack without delay.

While at my *zariba* at Deain, Sheikh Afifi Wad Ahmed of the Habbania, accompanied by Sheikhs Khamis Wad Nenya and Khudr Wad Girba, arrived with twenty horsemen, and gave me assurances of their loyalty to government. The subsequent exploits of Afifi proved how true he was to his word. He told me frankly that the whole country was unsettled, and that almost all the tribes in the Kalaka neighbourhood wished to join the *Mahdi*.

Madibbo's prestige was no doubt greatly increased by his success against Mansur; constant contact for years with the government had taught him a great deal and he was as capable as he was brave. Learning that I was encamped with only a small force at Deain, he very rightly decided to leave Mansur alone and turn on me.

One evening just before sunset, when my men were out collecting wood, we were suddenly attacked by Madibbo's horsemen, who were seen in hundreds some distance off galloping towards the *zariba*. Sheikh Afifi instantly saddled his horse, mounted, and, standing before me with poised spear, shouted, "*Arifni zen! ana thor et tokash, abu galb min adem, ana bidaur el mot!*" (You know me well! I am the pushing ox, the man who has a heart of bone. I seek death!) and with this he dashed out of the *zariba*, and, disappearing amongst the trees, returned in a few minutes, his spear dripping with blood, and leading after him a captured horse; the two other *sheikhs* and their men also had a slight skirmish, losing one horse and capturing another. In a few moments we heard some rifle shots, and fearing that Madibbo's main body had arrived, I called the mounted Arabs into the *zariba* and prepared for defence. However, I soon ascertained that a small party only had come, and had taken up a position in a clump of trees; I therefore sent fifty men to drive them out, and they retired, leaving behind them three killed.

As it was now sunset, I summoned the *sheikhs* and officers, and explained that it was impossible to retreat now, as the camels carrying the ammunition would probably get frightened if we were attacked in the dark, and we should run the risk of losing them. It was better, I said, to wait till daylight, when we should in all probability be attacked, and that in view of Madibbo's great superiority in numbers it was advisable for us to remain entirely on the defensive, and await a favourable opportunity to retire on Dara. "Under these circumstances," I said, "we shall not require the horses. Do you, therefore, Afifi, and your men leave us under cover of darkness, and return to your country, which you should be able to reach in safety. You will be more use to us there than cooped up in this *zariba*."

After a short pause, Afifi replied, "My life is in God's hands, and man cannot escape his destiny. If it is God's will that I should die here tomorrow, so be it; but this might equally happen on my way back, for God is almighty. I think it a shame to leave you, and I prefer death to a life of shame. This is my opinion, and I have spoken it."

No sooner had Afifi concluded, than the Habbania Arabs, in one voice, shouted that they were all of the same opinion; and such a noise did they make that I was obliged to tell them the enemy would probably hear them. Being quite unable to make them change their minds, I agreed that they should remain till the following day. I now ordered the ditch inside the *zariba* to be deepened, to give more cover from the bullets, and the men worked hard all night. At dawn the next morning, the outposts reported a man in the distance waving a white flag, and on giving orders that he should be allowed to approach, I found him to be Sheikh Ishak el Abd, of the Rizighat tribe, and I went outside the *zariba* to confer with him.

Saluting, he handed me a letter from Madibbo, which my Arabic clerk now read to me; it was very long and bombastic, but not unfriendly in tone. He summoned me to submit, gave a full account of the defeat and death of Yusef Pasha Shellali, of which he himself had been an eye-witness, and then told me how he had been victorious over Mansur Helmi. He urged me, on his word as a former official and my friend, to believe in the truth of what he said, and then declared that, having seen the *Mahdi* with his own eyes, he had now not the smallest doubt that he was a man sent from God, and that all who resisted him must perish miserably.

Turning to my old friend Ishak, I laughingly asked him what he thought about it. "Master," said he, "I have eaten bread and salt with you, and therefore I will not deceive you: the whole country is in revolt, and everyone says he is the true *Mahdi*. If you intend to submit to Madibbo, I can guarantee that you need have nothing to fear."

"Never!" was my short reply. "I shall never lay down my arms to an Arab. Go to Madibbo, and tell him that battle must decide between us!"

"Master," answered Ishak, "I will not deceive you; every word I have said is true. I, personally, shall not fight against you; but my tribe is no longer under control."

"It is all the same to me," I replied, "whether you fight against me or not; one man alone cannot make much difference one way or the other." I then shook hands with him, and bade him goodbye.

Pressing my hand, he said, "If one day I am forced to fight you, I will let you know," and, mounting his horse, he was in a few minutes out of sight.

Returning to the *zariba*, I now made all preparations for the impending struggle. Amongst the refugees with us was a Greek named Alexander, who had come to Shakka with two camel-loads of spirits and clothing, which he expected to sell at an enormous profit at Shakka: also a certain Ali Wad Fadlalla, with ten Bazingers, had joined us. He was a man I had long since discharged from the *manurship* of Kalaka; but he expected in this way to re-establish himself in my good graces. Seeing the plight we were in, these two worthies did nothing but bemoan the ill luck which had brought them to my *zariba*.

Scarcely two hours had elapsed since Ishak had left, when, through my field-glasses I saw the enemy advancing. I at once sounded the "alarm," and every one went to his post. The attack came from the northwest, where there was a small wood which gave considerable cover. In the centre of our zar*i*ba was a mound, on the top of which I placed an old bench found in one of Madibbo's huts, and which an Egyptian had turned into a chair. Seated in this position, I obtained a good view of the surrounding country, as well as of all that was going on in the *zariba*. The enemy now advanced within rifle-range, and the bullets began to whistle about our ears. Getting up from the chair to give some order and have a better view, a shot whizzed past and struck the back of the chair in which I had just been sitting, and shivered it to pieces.

After this, I thought it advisable to take up a less-exposed position. The enemy's fire now became very hot, but the men were well protected in the trenches, and our loss was trifling. The horses and camels, however, suffered severely; and feeling that if kept huddled up in the *zariba* we might lose them all, I selected fifty men and, making a sortie from the southern entrance, we turned west, and, opening suddenly on the enemy's flank, inflicted considerable loss on him by a murderous cross-fire, eventually driving him from the position. However, we did not secure this success without paying for it. As far as I can recollect, we lost twelve killed, including Fadlalla, and the Greek Alexander was amongst the wounded.

Discussing the situation with my officers, it was decided that if the enemy attacked us the following day and we succeeded in repulsing him, we should be prepared to act offensively. We had some suspicion, too, that Sheikh Abu Salama was inclined to revolt; his conduct had undoubtedly altered considerably of late.

The day's experience had the effect of making the men deepen their trenches and heighten their breastworks, thus affording better protection to themselves and the animals. By the evening, thoroughly tired out, most of them had dropped off to sleep, and we anticipated a quiet night. But at about eleven o'clock we were startled by a brisk rifle-fire. Fortunately it was a very dark night, and the fire was ill-directed. So I ordered the men not to reply, and in consequence it slackened, and eventually ceased altogether.

Summoning Sheikh Afifi, I now asked him to send out some of his men to discover Madibbo's position, promising them they would be well rewarded if they brought back reliable information. In about two hours they returned, and reported that Madibbo was in his village with his Bazingers, while the Arabs were encamped to the south and west of it. They were in considerable force, but had taken no precautions for defence, and our spies, who had crept up quite close to their camp-fires, had overheard them laughing and joking at our not having replied to their fire, saying we must have been too frightened to do so.

Waiting for half an hour, I called up seventy men, and told them, before the officers, I wanted them to surprise Madibbo's camp; that if we fought an action in the open against superior numbers, we should probably lose heavily; but we had now ascertained the Arabs were quite unprepared, and a sudden night attack might completely demoralise them, and give us a chance of returning to Dara for reinforcements. The plan was thoroughly approved, and all the officers at once volunteered to join; but this I could not permit. So, leaving behind two officers, four buglers, and seventy men, I quitted the *zariba*, accompanied by Afifi, who refused to leave me.

Suspecting that possibly some of Abu Salama's people might get out and betray us, I gave the officers who remained behind strict injunctions that during our absence no one should leave the *zariba*, and that a most careful lookout should be kept; and advancing cautiously, guided by the spies, in the space of about an hour we found ourselves close to the enemy's camp. Our spies proved thoroughly trusty; and, besides, I had previously travelled in these districts, and knew the country well. Dividing up, therefore, into two parties, I placed one under the command of a very brave officer named Mohammed Agha Suleiman, a native of Bornu, and leading the other party myself, we crept up to within six or seven hundred yards of the unsuspecting foe, when I ordered the bugler to sound "Commence firing."

The confusion in the enemy's camp was now indescribable. Madibbo's Bazingers, leaving their arms, fled. The horses, terrified by this sudden commotion in the dead of night, became restive, broke their ropes, and bolted in all directions, chased by the Arabs. In a few minutes every one of Madibbo's huts was deserted, and in the distance could be heard the sounds of the terrified crowds, fleeing from our little band of seventy men. We had been completely successful, and it took Madibbo some days before he could collect his men again. I burnt his village, and the blazing flames, shooting to the sky, lighted up the deserted camp. Only two of my men had been wounded by thrown spears. We captured a large number of saddles, which I ordered to be thrown into the flames, as well as a quantity of old guns and matchlocks; but we kept the forty Remington rifles taken, and now marched back to the *zariba*, where we had a most enthusiastic welcome from the others, who had been awaiting our return with great anxiety.

I gave the order to move at sunrise the next morning. The entire neighbourhood was deserted, and during our five hours' march to Bir Delwei we met no one. Here, however, we were caught up by some Rizighat horsemen, who had followed us with the evident intention of finding out if we were really quitting the district. Afifi, catching sight of them, was after them in a moment, and, severely wounding Madibbo's cousin, Isa Feisal, he captured his horse. We now continued to march forward as rapidly as possible, hoping soon to meet the reinforcements which should have started by this time from Dara for the relief of Mansur Helmi. At midnight we reached Kelekle, where I resolved to give the exhausted men a good rest.

Here, under the pretext of telling his tribe to drive their cattle out of the Rizighat districts towards the north, Sheikh Abu Salama left us; but as he did not return the next morning, and as it was reported by some men I had sent out after him that he and his family, taking all their property with them, had left for the south, I had no doubt he had gone to join the rebels. Having still no news from Dara, I did not deem it advisable to wait longer, so continued my march north, and reached that town by noon the following day. I found the reinforcements and ammunition all ready to leave, and as the men I had brought back were tired, I determined to change them also, and return with a completely fresh force to help Mansur Helmi; but to my surprise, at daybreak the next morning, I received a letter from Ismail Wad Barnu, saying that he and Mansur were on their way to Dara, and would arrive the following day. This was to me most unsatisfactory news, for it meant that my difficulties in re-occupying Shakka would be considerably increased.

The next morning they arrived, accompanied by a few slaves, who were ready to drop down with fatigue. Calling up Mansur before a council of officers, I asked him officially, in writing, why he quitted his post without orders, and he replied that he was too tired to answer. I then called on Ismail Wad Barnu for a full explanation, and he stated as follows: "Having despatched the messenger to you with the news of our disaster, we hourly expected you to arrive. When the messenger returned, reporting that you were retiring on Dara for reinforcements, and that Madibbo was on the point of attacking you, we gave way to despair. Our corn was finished, and we had no means of procuring any more supplies. We therefore made up our minds to take to flight."

"But," said I, "where are the camels carrying ammunition and rockets? and where are all the merchants and their families who came to you for protection? There were some hundreds of you; and now you are only fifteen."

"We loaded the ammunition and rockets on the camels," replied Mansur, nervously, "and they and the merchants started the same time as we did; but we got separated on the march."

"What!" said I, in a tone of wonder, "how could heavily laden camels become separated from horsemen? Only in one way: they move slowly, and you have deserted them in your terror. How long did you take to come here?" By this time Mansur had worked himself into such a state of nervous excitement that he had become incoherent. I therefore again called on Wad Barnu to complete this painful narrative.

"We left the *zariba* three days ago," said he.

"Three days!" I said. "And yet you say that the camels separated from you. It is a seven days' march between Murrai and Dara. You are a civil official, Ismail, and joined this expedition by my orders. You need not be afraid. Tell me now, truthfully, why you left the others?"

"Master," said Ismail, who had by this time regained confidence, "when we heard that you were waiting for reinforcements from Dara, we held a consultation, and decided that, as we had only a small quantity of supplies left, we should abandon the position and come here. Mansur Effendi, being our chief, gave the order to march three hours before sunset. We loaded up the camels, and, with the merchants, their wives and children, all left the *zariba* together. The marching of so many of us made a great noise; and fearing that the enemy would hear it, Mansur called me up, and suggested that we should go on ahead, and that Ali Agha Guma, who was in command of the fifty men escorting the ammunition, should follow on and catch us up.

"At dawn the next morning we halted for some time, and at length Abder Rasul Agha arrived, reporting that he too had got separated from the caravan during the night. Master, where is the heart without fear? As the merciful and almighty God had delivered us, so we believed He would deliver the others; therefore we hurried on. Master, make allowance for us. Remember that we lost relatives and slaves in the battle, and that I am married and the father of children!"

Mansur listened to this confession in silence. I frequently called upon him to say anything which would justify his conduct; but his only excuse was that the ammunition column did not arrive at the appointed rendezvous, and that as he himself had so few men, he did not think it wise to go in search of them, and had therefore continued his march. I now directed the senior officer present to take Mansur's sword from him, to keep him in close arrest at the headquarter guard, and to take down in writing a full deposition of what had occurred.

Meanwhile I sent off spies in all directions to discover the whereabouts of the column, and for the moment abandoned all idea of an expedition to Shakka. Seven days later I received the joyful news that the column had safely arrived at Toweisha with almost all the merchants and their families, and as, up to the present, no disturbances had taken place in that district, the latter had asked permission to remain there. Three days afterwards the column was reported to be within an hour's march of Dara. I therefore rode out at the head of the whole garrison to meet them, and marched them in with all honours. On their arrival they were publicly entertained, and I gave all the non-commissioned officers a step, and promoted fifteen of them, who were specially recommended by Ali Agha Guma, to the rank of officer. Ali Agha now related the following.

In accordance with Mansur Effendi's orders, we loaded up the camels and started; the merchants, with their women and children, who had not been informed, now made a great commotion, and insisted on coming with us; the poor people well knew that if they remained behind they could expect no mercy from the Arabs. Mansur Effendi, alarmed at the noise, and fearing that the enemy might come down on us, was chiefly concerned about the safety of his own person, and therefore started off, directing me to catch him up the following morning. Now, how was it possible for me in a bushy, trackless region, with heavily laden camels, to catch up a man flying on a horse? I hurriedly collected the soldiers and the merchants, and told them that I proposed to march towards Goz el Maalia, and in this roundabout way, please God, we should avoid the enemy and reach home safely.

I knew that the country round Goz el Maalia was open, and that if attacked we should be able to defend ourselves better than in the enclosed country through which we were now marching. I knew that we were quite strong enough to force our way through the Maalia tribe, and therefore, repeating the '*Fatha*' (the Moslem creed) and asking the Almighty to protect us, we marched in a northeasterly direction, camels and women in the centre. Thank God, the darkness of the night helped us to pass through the enemy's country unobserved, and by sunrise we had reached the southwestern boundary of the Maalia country. Here we made a short halt, but did not dare to stay long.

We made the merchants' wives act as camel-drivers, and those who were ill and the children we mounted on camel-back on the top of the ammunition-boxes; in this way we managed to have about one hundred men with rifles as escort. We had sufficient corn for three or four days, and instead of water we quenched our thirst with the juice of the water-melons, which grew in abundance. At noon we were attacked by some Rizighat horsemen who had been joined by some Maalia; but by God's help, who forsakes not those in distress and danger, we drove them off, killing a few horses and men.

Although utterly exhausted, we did not dare to halt till sunset;

and, surrounding ourselves with a light *zariba*, we passed a quiet night, and started off again at sunrise the next morning. The enemy, being joined by some revolted villagers, again attacked us; but God gave us strength and courage, and we drove them off, and at length, after eight days' hard marching, we reached Toweisha safe and sound. The merchants and their wives and children left us there full of gratitude, and we thank the merciful God who has brought us unhurt out of all these dangers.

"I also thank God," said I, "that you are safe; I was greatly concerned about you. But tell me how goes it at Toweisha? How is the chief of the district, Abo Bey el Bartawi?"

"He himself seems loyal to government," he replied, "but his people have begun to get disaffected, and sooner or later, if good news is not received from Kordofan, he will join the rebels; at present, however, the Om Shanga garrison keeps him quiet."

I now publicly thanked Ali Agha Guma for his valuable services and for his forethought and bravery, and ordered his promotion from second to first lieutenant, writing to Cairo for confirmation. This plucky officer was a native of the Tagalla mountains, and had been trained as a soldier in Cairo.

As there was no officer of Mansur Helmi's rank in Dara, I sent him under escort to Fasher, with instructions to Said Bey Guma to deal with his case in accordance with the written depositions; at the same time I told him to send me two hundred infantry, also some ammunition and lead.

Meanwhile, I ascertained that Madibbo had returned to Deain, rebuilt his village, and concluded an offensive and defensive alliance with Sheikh Abu Salama. On the day I arrived in Dara I sent back the faithful and brave Afifi to Kalaka. He was very anxious not to go; but I told him that should his tribe revolt, he had permission to bring his wife and children to Dara; in the meantime he had better be with his people.

In order to dissipate any idea on the part of the rebels that I intended to sit down quietly and watch events, I despatched Ali Effendi Esmet with one hundred and eighty regulars to Hashaba, two days' march south of Dara,—one of Abu Salama's villages,—with orders to wait there till I had collected my forces. The news from the Om Shanga district was satisfactory. Omar Wad Darho, with his four hundred horsemen, succeeded in keeping the Arabs under; he had several skirmishes, and once or twice some losses, but on the whole he was successful. The continual strides now made by the revolt in Kordofan made postal communication more difficult than ever; all I could do was to send short cipher messages, very few of which ever reached their destination. One of my principal objects in keeping Darho at Om Shanga was that, in the event of the troops in Kordofan being successful, he could advance east, and, combining with them, reopen the post-road.

Zogal Bey, who was with me in Dara at this period, was performing his duties in a satisfactory manner. He was opposed to my getting reinforcements from El Fasher, saying I need not be so mistrustful; however, there was no doubt he had received letters from his relative, the *Mahdi*, but I do not think he answered them in writing: in fact, affairs in Darfur were not altogether unsatisfactory, and he was now certainly more careful and attentive to his duties.

During my stay here I did my utmost to collect Bazingers, and by promises to the *gellabas* I succeeded in getting many of them to place their servants at the disposal of the government. I also utilised the services of an old officer named Abdel Kader Wad Asi, who had formerly commanded the irregular cavalry in Dara, to collect as many horses as he could; and in a few days he got together upwards of one hundred and fifty. Meanwhile I had written to Sultan Abakr el Begawi—head-Sheikh of Berket—and to the Messeria and other tribes, to get ready and follow me to Shakka. Some of these readily obeyed the call; and as to those who hesitated, I did all I could, by working up tribal jealousies, to increase the ill-feeling between them and our enemies. Abder Rasul Agha, who had fled from Murrai with Mansur Helmi, I had imprisoned; but as he had on previous occasions shown capacity, and as my available officers were getting scarce, I released him, and put him in command of the Bazingers who were to remain behind in Dara, and told him to do all he could to procure more.

Most of the arms in store at Dara were old double-barrelled guns, flintlocks, and a few damaged Remingtons; these I had roughly repaired, and distributed to the Bazinger recruits. I had not much ammunition, and urgently ordered more to be sent from El Fasher. About a fortnight later, one hundred regulars duly arrived under Said Bey el Fula, a brave Sudanese, who brought me letters from Said Bey Guma. In these, my representative at the capital informed me that he could not send the ammunition, as he had no camels, and if he took them by force from the people, he feared the result; as soon as he could procure camels he would send me the ammunition and the other hundred men.

In reply to this I wrote back somewhat shortly that the despatch of the ammunition was an urgent necessity, and that if he could not obtain the camels from the Arabs, he must get them from the officers and employés on payment; I told him that I had to do this in Dara, as there were no other camels available in southern Darfur. It was perfectly clear to me that orders sent to El Fasher were not carried out with expedition. It was useless to waste more time; I therefore quitted Dara,—leaving behind an adequate garrison,—and set off for Hashaba, where it had been arranged the various friendly tribes would meet me.

Chapter 6

The Siege and Fall of El Obeid

Inspired by his numerous victories, and encouraged by Elias Pasha's urgent appeal that he should proceed to El Obeid, the *Mahdi* left Gedir, and, joined by thousands upon thousands of fanatical Arabs and slave-hunters, he advanced to Kaba, a village on the outskirts of the town.

From here he despatched horsemen to reconnoitre and summon all those who were willing to join his banners. He also wrote to Mohammed Pasha Said, calling on him to submit. His letter was read out before the officers; and at the suggestion of Mohammed Bey Skander and the majority of the officers the bearers of the letters were sentenced to be shot. Said Pasha himself was averse to this decision, but eventually gave way and confirmed the sentence, which was immediately carried out.

The secret emissaries were more successful; they had an easier task amongst the local population many of whom really believed in the *Mahdi*, and those who did not, well knew the weakness of the government and the very critical state of affairs. Besides, as I have already related, the hostility of Elias Pasha to Said Pasha and Ahmed Bey Dafalla had the effect of bringing over to the rebels the majority of the civil officials and principal merchants,—consequently, in a few days the bulk of the population moved bodily out of the town and joined the *Mahdi*. The latter had previously written to them that they had only to shut up their houses and leave all their property as it was, and when he entered the town he would guarantee that nothing should be touched. These injunctions they obeyed implicitly, taking with them, or burying in the ground, their money only.

On Ahmed Bey's advice, Said Pasha had divided up the town in such a manner that the evacuation of a large part of it by the merchants and others would not seriously affect the question of its defence; and he at once ordered the soldiers to collect all the corn they could find in the houses and store it in the citadel,—an operation which was carried out with considerable alacrity, and full advantage was taken of the occasion to freely loot the dwellings of the trustful populace, who had counted somewhat prematurely on the *Mahdi's* protective powers. Minni, of the Gowama Arabs, also freely pillaged the deserted town.

Mohammed Ahmed now spared no effort to rouse the fanatical spirit of the masses by whom he was surrounded. He preached day and night to a rapt audience on the heavenly joys in store for all those who joined the *Jehad*, and on Friday morning, September the 8th, this seething mass of human beings, armed only with swords and spears, rolled like the waves of the sea towards the town. All the arms taken in Rashed's and Shellali's expeditions had been left behind at Jebel Gedir, and the rifle fire of the defenders soon began to play with deadly effect on the crowd, who, utterly undeterred, and seeking only for blood and plunder, continued their advance, swarming into the ditches and up the parapet, and entering the deserted town.

At this critical moment Major Nesim Effendi told his bugler to sound the advance; and the signal being taken up by the other buglers, the soldiers, clambering up on to the tops of the walls and houses, brought a murderous fire to bear on the assailants. Slowly the surging mass, under this hail of lead, was driven back, leaving behind them thousands of killed and wounded. Once more they rallied and attempted again to storm; but again were they driven back with still greater slaughter, till at length the survivors retired out of range, and the gallant garrison was completely victorious.

In this assault the *Mahdi's* brother Mohammed, Khalifa Abdullahi's brother Yusef, the Kadi, and a host of *emirs* were killed. The *Mahdi* himself, during the attack, took up a position out of range, behind a small house; and had Said Pasha taken Ahmed Bey Dafalla's advice to pursue after the Dervishes had been routed, in all probability he would have been taken, and the subsequent bloodshed and horrors thus avoided.

But Said Pasha contented himself with this temporary success, believing that the *Mahdi* was too crushed to again attempt an attack, and that this defeat would probably destroy his influence. The *Mahdi's* relatives and near friends also realised this, and on their advice he removed his camp to Gianzara, a hill lying beyond range to the northeast of the town; and in this position maintained an open investment, while awaiting the arrival of the arms and ammunition for which he had sent to Jebel Gedir.

The mission station at Delen, which had been founded some eight years before, and which was guarded by eighty men of the slave guard, had long been in a critical position. Whilst on his way to El Obeid, the *Mahdi* had sent one of his adherents, Mek Omar, with instructions either to capture or kill all persons found there. The missionary Fathers, Joseph Ohrwalder and Luigi Bonomi, had arranged to flee with the troops and all the mission to Fashoda; but their plan fell through, owing to the cowardice of the captain commanding the troops. They were eventually obliged to submit, were robbed of all they had, and were marched as prisoners to El Obeid. Here the *Mahdi* and Khalifa Abdullahi made every effort to convert them and the sisters who were with them; but they remained firm. The following day they were taken, accompanied by thousands of howling Dervishes, to an open space where a great review was held. After momentarily expecting death, they were at length told their lives were spared, and they were handed over to the care of a Syrian named George Stambuli, who had joined the Mahdi from El Obeid.

At this time a most wonderful comet appeared, which was taken by the Sudanese as a sign from Heaven that the government was about to be overthrown, and that the true *Mahdi* had appeared on earth.

An expedition sent under Ali Bey Lutfi to relieve Bara and El Obeid, when on the march and suffering from thirst, was attacked by the Gowama Arabs under Fiki Rahma, and of the two thousand men of which it was composed, two hundred only succeeded in escaping to Bara. Soon after this Tayara was attacked, and its little garrison, after resisting manfully, was obliged to submit at the end of September.

Bara fell next, after a long and well-sustained siege. The garrison had inflicted considerable loss on the rebels, but a fire had broken out and burnt up almost all the corn. Hunger and disease had done their work, and, hopeless of any succour, Surur Effendi, the commandant, Nur Angara, and Mohammed Agha Japo, at the urgent request of the garrison, were forced to submit early in January, 1883, to Abderrahman Wad en Nejumi, and were conducted by him to Gianzara. On arrival here they received the *Mahdi's* pardon, and Surur Effendi, who was an Abyssinian by birth, but a particularly religious Moslem, was allowed by the *Mahdi* to have back a portion of his confiscated property; Nur Angara, being a Dongolawi, was also well received; and Japo, whose exploits during the retreat from Ashaf had reached the *Mahdi's* ears, was given back one of his own horses. The troops, who were all blacks, were made over to Khalifa Abdullahi, who subsequently transferred them to Hamdan Abu Anga, who was made *emir* of the force.

The astute Japo was not slow to show devotion to his new master, and begged for his blessing and for permission to get married, as hitherto he had lived a single life. The *Mahdi*, flattered that an old and irreligious man like Japo should show such complete submissiveness to his will, at once granted his request. A few days later, however, Japo came before the *Mahdi* with a very sorrowful face, and told him that the money he had given him for his marriage had been spent to no purpose, as he had divorced his wife.

"What!" said the *Mahdi*, "why should you have done this? Is she not pretty, or has she a bad character?"

"No," said Japo, "she has a far more serious fault: when I tell her to say her prayers, she refuses to do so; and a wife who does not pray is an abomination to me."

So delighted was the *Mahdi* with his supposed conversion that he gave Japo a large sum of money to get married again, and presented him with sufficient means to keep him from want for a long time. Some years later, after the *Mahdi's* death, I met Mohammed Japo in Omdurman, and I laughingly reminded him of this story.

"Yes," said he, "in spite of all the harm and evil done by the *Mahdi*, he was not, after all, such a bad man,—one could get something out of him; but I pity the man who relies on Khalifa Abdullahi's benevolence." Japo was quite right.

The *Mahdi* celebrated the capture of Bara with a salute of one hundred guns, and the unfortunate garrison of El Obeid, hearing the sounds, thought that a relieving army was approaching; but when they learnt that Bara had fallen, they became greatly disheartened. For months they had been suffering all the horrors of famine; food had risen to fabulous prices; no steps had been taken to lay in a stock of provisions, and there was a great scarcity of corn. A month before the capitulation *dukhn* had risen to four hundred dollars the *ardeb*; only the most wealthy could supply themselves with a little meat. The price of a camel rose to fifteen hundred dollars, a chicken might be had for thirty or forty dollars, and an egg for a dollar to a dollar and a half.

But my comrades in captivity, Fathers Ohrwalder and Rosignoli, have already described the horrors of that long and terrible time, and I need not repeat them here; suffice it to say that after a five months' siege, during which the most terrible privations were endured, and in which a very large proportion of the remaining population and garrison died of starvation, Mohammed Pasha Said was at last forced to capitulate. He wished to blow up the powder magazine; but the officers begged that their wives and children might be spared, and he was obliged to give way. He therefore wrote to the *Mahdi* that he was prepared to surrender the town.

The *Mahdi* replied that he and his officers need have no fear, and the following morning sent a deputation of leading merchants, under Mohammed Wad el Areik to Said Pasha, with instructions that he, the superior officers of the garrison, and the chief merchants should present themselves before him. The deputation had brought with them *jibbas* (the patched shirt adopted as a uniform by the followers of the *Mahdi*), which had now to be worn, and, mounting on horses, the sad cavalcade, led by Said Pasha, filed out of the fort which they had defended so long and bravely. With him were Mohammed Bey Skander, the commandant, Major Nesim Effendi, Ahmed Bey Dafalla, Mohammed Bey Yasin, and several other officers.

Seated on his *angareb*, on which a goat's skin was spread, the *Mahdi* received them kindly, gave them his hand to be kissed, and pardoned them. He told them that he of course understood they had been deceived in regard to him, having doubted his Divine mission; but that he forgave them, and now required them to take the solemn oath of allegiance, and complete submission to him and the cause. This formality over, he gave them dates and water, and urged them to renounce the pleasures of this world, and think only of the world to come. Turning to Said Pasha, he then said: "I do not blame you as a Turk for having done all you could to defend the post confided to you; but you did not do well to kill my messengers, for it is not right that messengers should be punished."

Before Said Pasha could reply, Skander Bey quickly answered, "Master and *Mahdi*, Said Pasha did not do this, but it was I, in my capacity as commandant of the fort, who ordered the execution, as I considered them rebels, and in this I did not do well, as you truly say."

"I did not mean by my question to ask you to justify yourself," said the *Mahdi*. "My messengers have obtained what they most desired; when they took the letters from me they sought the death of martyrs, and their wish was fulfilled. The merciful God has granted them their hearts' desire, and now they are in the enjoyment of all the pleasures of Paradise. May God grant that we may follow in their footsteps."

During this conversation, according to a plan prepared beforehand, Abu Anga and his men had occupied the fort, powder-magazine, and government buildings, whilst the *emirs* installed themselves in the officers' quarters. The *Mahdi* now told Wad el Areik, who happened to be a personal friend of Said Pasha, to take him and his officers back to their houses; but on their return they found them occupied, and were given to understand that their property had now been confiscated. Soon afterwards the *Mahdi* himself entered the town to inspect it, and ordered the garrison to quit the entrenchments. The women and children, who had so patiently waited for relief, were now ordered out to the *Mahdi's* camp, and were allowed to take nothing with them. Even the women were searched to the skin, in a most revolting manner, and anything found was instantly taken off to the Beit el Mal (*Mahdi's* treasury), where the property was subsequently distributed amongst the *emirs* and other high personages. In searching for gold and treasure the most heart-rending scenes were enacted, and weeping and wailing was heard on all sides, as the unfortunates were flogged to make them disgorge.

Said Pasha himself was called upon by Ahmed Wad Suleiman, the Mahdi's Emin Beit el Mal (or treasurer), to hand over all his money; but he replied that he had none. It was well known that he was a very wealthy man, but he obstinately denied he had anything. When the *Mahdi* heard this, he instructed Wad Suleiman to make every inquiry of Said Pasha's servants; and while he was occupied in doing this, the Mahdi continued conversing with Said Pasha on the precepts of religion, and frequently asked him, before the assembled masses, why he refused to disclose the hiding-place of his treasure, and Said Pasha as persistently denied that he had any money whatever.

In this way some time passed, and at length Wad Suleiman, who had meanwhile succeeded in getting one of the female servants to admit that her master had concealed the treasure in the wall, returned to the *Mahdi*, and whispered in his ear that they had found it. The latter, beckoning him to sit down, continued to talk of the vanities of this world, and the great necessity of renouncing them; and then, turning suddenly to Said Pasha, he said, "You swore a most solemn oath of allegiance; why, then, do you refuse to say where your money is? Money is the root of all evil. Do you now expect to gather more riches?"

"Oh, sire," replied Said Pasha, "I have neither money made honestly, nor money made dishonestly; do with me what you like." "Do you take me for an ordinary man?" replied the *Mahdi*. "Do you not understand that I am truly the '*Mahdi el Muntazer*,' and that the Prophet has revealed to me the hiding-place of your treasure, which you have concealed in the wall of your house? Go, Ahmed Wad Suleiman, to his house. Enter his room, and on the left side, near the door, remove the plaster from the wall, and there you will find the Turk's treasure. Bring it here."

During Wad Suleiman's absence Said Pasha sat disconsolately, close to the *Mahdi*, frowning deeply. He knew his treasure had been discovered, but he was too proud to admit that he had told an untruth, and he refused to join in the conversation. In a few minutes Suleiman returned, dragging behind him a large tin box, which he placed before the *Mahdi*, who opened it, and found it full of gold, packed up in small bags. Over £7,000 was counted out. "Mohammed Said," said the *Mahdi*, "you have told a lie; but I will forgive you. Ahmed, take the money to the Beit el Mal, and distribute it amongst the poor and needy."

"You, who preach renunciation, have now got my money; do what you like with it," said Said Pasha, turning on his heel and marching off.

The *Mahdi*, frowning darkly, muttered, "*Di ma biyenfa maana*" (This man won't do for us).

Said Pasha turned to Ahmed Bey Dafalla, who had witnessed this scene, and the *Mahdi* then addressed the latter in the following words: "Do not follow in the footsteps of your old friend; he has an obstinate disposition. Be honest and true to me, and I will give you all you require. I secretly warned your brother Abdalla, but it was God's will he should be overthrown. He blindly espoused the cause of God's enemies, the Turks, and fought against me. The merciful God has destroyed them. They were blown like chaff before the wind, and are now suffering all the torments of hell-fire. Ahmed, save your soul while you may. Be faithful to me, and when this life is over you shall enjoy the everlasting pleasures of Paradise, and God will receive you into His heavenly kingdom."

"Oh, *Mahdi*," said Ahmed Wad Dafalla, "I shall certainly not enter the heaven in which my brother Abdalla is not." And with that he rose and left the meeting.

Not a word did the *Mahdi* say, but it seemed to be quite understood that his sentence had been pronounced. Signing to his followers that the meeting was over, the latter now lost no time in complying with their master's wishes, which, though unexpressed, they well understood. In a few minutes it was known far and wide that the cursed Turk, Mohammed Said, had refused to disclose the hiding-place of his treasure, but that the Prophet had revealed it to the *Mahdi*. For some days tongues never ceased talking of this wonderful miracle; and far and wide spread Mohammed Ahmed's repute as the true *Mahdi*, sent from heaven to destroy the hated Turk.

Directions were now given to supply Said Pasha, Ahmed Bey, Ali Sherif, and the other officers with their beds, cooking-pots, clothing, and some money, until the Prophet further revealed to the *Mahdi* what he should do with his prisoners.

Mohammed Ahmed now occupied himself in writing letters and proclamations to all parts of the Sudan, announcing the capture of El Obeid, and enjoining on all the necessity of activity and endurance in the great religious war which had now spread over the country. He called on the faithful to renounce the pomps and vanities of this world, and to think and work only for the joys to come. He also issued very stringent regulations against smoking and drinking, imposing terrible penalties on any one found wilfully disobeying. Special instructions were also issued regarding marriage ceremonies, dowries, etc., and every effort was made by the *Mahdi* to follow the example set by the Prophet in his early wars.

Chapter 7

Vain Efforts to Stem the Tide of Mahdism in Darfur

Having reached Hashaba, I now did my utmost to organise a force capable of operating successfully against Madibbo. I had succeeded in getting the Gellabas either to join me themselves or give me their Bazingers. I called on Zogal Bey and his brother for help, and between them they collected two hundred of their Bazingers. I myself had also collected a number of Blacks, some of whom I had freed, and others I employed at a regular rate of pay. I had re-engaged Sharaf ed Din, formerly major and commandant of Bazingers at Kulkul, but who had been discharged by Nur Angara, as well as a number of Jaalin officers who had previously served with Zubeir Pasha. And now the tribes I had summoned to aid the government had arrived, and my force consisted approximately of the following:—

Regulars, armed with Remingtons	550
Gellabas	200
Armed Bazingers under Sharaf ed Din, amongst whom, as leaders, were Abder Rasul, Sheikhs Khudr, Umbatti, Mungid Madani, Hassan Wad Sattarat, Sultan Begu, Suleiman Wad Farah, Muslem Wad Kabbashi, and others	1,300
Various	100
Total guns (of which about 600 were Remington rifles)	2,150

Also a muzzle-loading mountain gun and thirteen artillerymen

The friendly tribes consisted of contingents from the Begu, Berket, Zagawa (of southern Darfur), Messeria, Tagu, and some of the Maalia who were hostile to Sheikh Abu Salama; numbering in all some seven thousand spearmen and four hundred horses.

The garrison I had left behind at Dara consisted of four hundred regulars, seven guns and the gunners required for their service, thirty horses, and two hundred and fifty Bazingers; all under the command of Zogal Bey, who was carrying on the duties of acting-governor, in Emiliani's place. With him I had also left a certain Gottfried Rott, a Swiss, and begged him to keep me fully informed of all that occurred. This Rott had been a schoolmaster at Assiut, and had discovered, some years previously, a quantity of slaves who were being smuggled along the Arbaïn road, for sale in Egypt.

In consequence of this service, Mr. Gladstone had written him a complimentary letter. He had also received an expression of approbation from the Anti-Slavery Society, and had been appointed by the Egyptian Government an inspector for the suppression of the slave-trade. He had been sent to me in Darfur, with instructions to proceed to Shakka, which was to be his district; but he arrived just as the troubles began, and I was obliged to keep him in Dara; he thoroughly understood our position, and I had requested him to abandon for the moment his anti-slavery work, which if persisted in would certainly have increased our difficulties. He was a good Arabic scholar, and in a very confidential talk I had with him, I confided to him my suspicions about Zogal, and asked him to find out all he could from his relatives, and keep me fully informed.

At the end of October I moved south, from Hashaba, with my entire force. The Rizighat country, through which we advanced, was covered with dense bush and forests; and, being constantly exposed to attack, I had to march in such a way as to avoid confusion in the event of an ambush or surprise.

The Bazingers on the flanks were well provided with buglers, in order to give timely warning of an alarm. The rear guard I made stronger than the flank guards because the Arabs generally attack from the rear, and I considered that in case of a flank attack I should have ample time to reinforce from the main body in case of necessity. The rear guard had, of course, the most troublesome duty to perform, as they had to look after any camels that broke down, and keep a careful lookout for men who fell out or attempted to desert; I therefore gave orders that it should be relieved daily by the flank guards in rotation from the left: thus the left flank guard would become rear guard, the relieved rear guard would become the right flank guard, and the latter would become the left flank guard. I also relieved the three hundred Bazingers and sixty regulars daily from the main body.

In this manner I hoped to reach Shakka without any serious loss; and on arriving there it was my intention to build a fort where I should mount the gun, and, leaving a small garrison there, make expeditions in light marching order to the various disturbed districts, where my Arab spearmen, if fortunate, would have ample opportunities of capturing any quantity of Rizighat cattle.

On arrival at Deain, we found quantities of corn stored in the new village just built by Madibbo; the guard he had left behind made a slight resistance, but were soon put to flight, and we encamped on the site of our old *zariba*. We found that Ali Wad Fadlalla's grave had been opened, and a skull and some bones lying close by were evidently his. We had covered the grave with a heap of thorns, and it was evident the Arabs had committed this sacrilege; they had taken off the shroud in which the body had been wrapped, and the hyenas had devoured all but the skull and bones.

I distributed the corn found in Madibbo's village amongst the men, and they had now sufficient supplies to last them some days. It was my intention to march direct on Shakka; but as there was some doubt about the water on the roads and the whereabouts of Madibbo, I sent two Rizighat spies—who were on bad terms with the remainder of the tribe, and had immigrated to Dara—to obtain the information I required. The day after they left, our camp was reconnoitred by Arab horsemen, but they kept at a respectful distance. Three days later the men returned, reporting that there was sufficient water on the road, and that Madibbo had driven all his cattle south of Shakka, where his force was probably collected; but they said they could procure no more definite information.

We therefore marched off; the men and Arabs all in the best possible spirits, laughing, joking, and discussing amongst themselves how they intended distributing the plunder they expected to get, and how they proposed dividing amongst themselves the wives and households of Madibbo and his *sheikhs*, on exactly the same plan as that adopted by the *Mahdi*. I had little fear as to the eventual result of our operations, but at the same time I was anxious to get to Shakka before being attacked.

As I was suffering from a heavy bout of fever, I handed over the

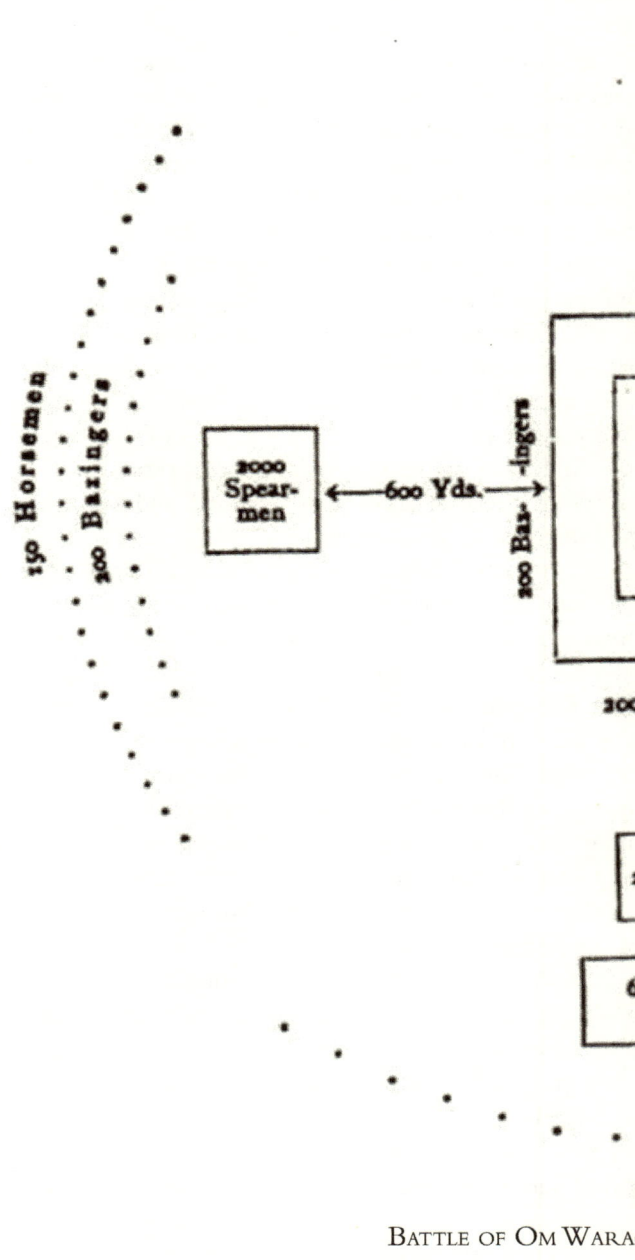

BATTLE OF OM WARAGAT-

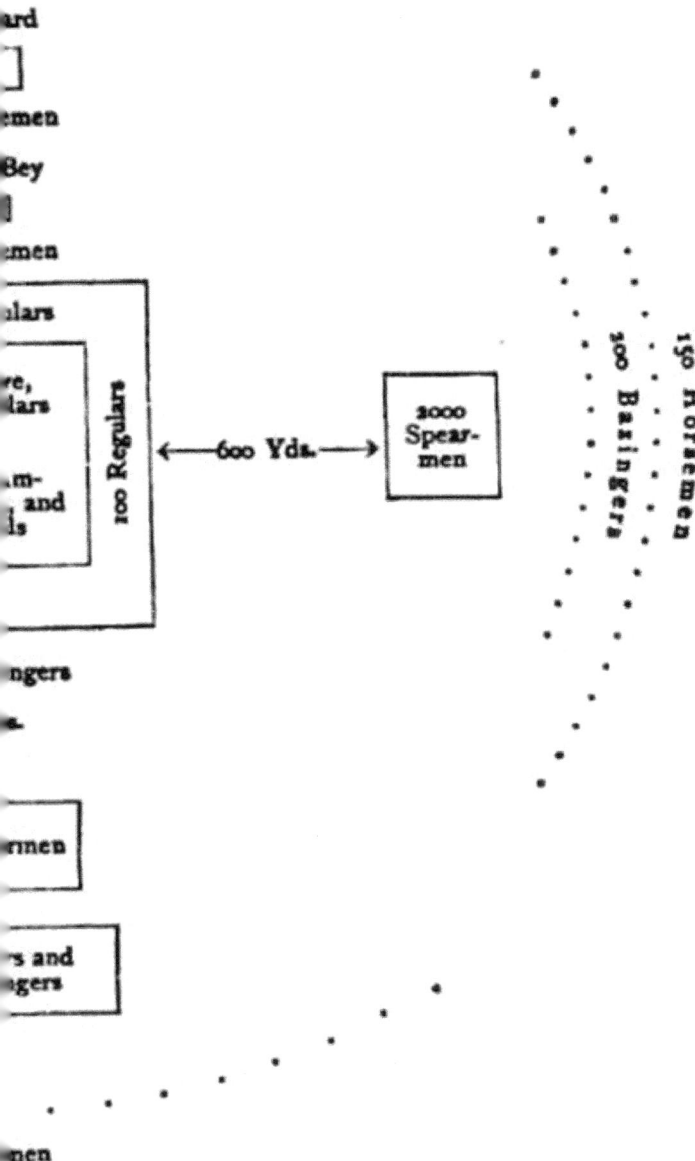

Disposition of Troops on the March to Shakka

command of the troops temporarily to Sharaf ed Din, but ordered him to remain close to me. The following day, having left the village of Kindiri on our flank, and having made a short halt, there was an alarm that horsemen were advancing to attack us. Immediately everyone was in his place, and, in spite of my fever, I joined the rear guard, whence the alarm had come; and from this position I could see numbers of horsemen—there might have been some hundreds, but owing to the intervening trees it was impossible to estimate accurately. Signalling to the flank guards to join me, I advanced with the cavalry and Arab horsemen, and a skirmish ensued amongst the trees, in which the enemy were driven back with some loss, and we captured six horses; our own losses were seven horses killed, two men missing, and several wounded. Having pursued for some distance, we returned, and as it was still early, the march was continued till nightfall, when we encamped at a place called Om Waragat.

Still suffering from fever, I told Sharaf ed Din to make exactly similar dispositions (see plan); and starting off the following morning, after a march of two hours we reached some more or less open but boggy moorland, at the southeast end of which were visible a few huts such as are erected by the Rizighat slaves who work in the fields. The vanguard had already cleared the soft ground; I had gone forward with it to examine the huts, whilst the men in the square were occupied in trying to help out the animals whose feet had sunk into the mire, when suddenly from the rear guard the alarm was sounded twice, followed almost immediately by some rifle-shots. Ordering the vanguard to hold the huts, I immediately galloped towards the left flank of the square, and, sounding for the reserve of ninety regulars, I proceeded towards the rear guard; but it was too late.

The Bazingers and regulars of the rear guard, having fired a volley, had no time to reload before the enemy was on them; and, overpowered by thousands of half-naked Arabs, they were being forced back on to the rear face of the square, the men composing which, fearing to fire on friend and foe alike, did nothing to stop the rush, and already several of the enemy had penetrated. Without a moment's hesitation, I ordered my bugler to sound "lie down" for those in the square, and, firing on the Arabs who had broken in, as well as on those still pushing on from behind, I checked the rush, and caused them to split up into two parties, who, trending off right and left, made for the flank guards already engaged with other parties of Arabs who were attacking them in front.

The confusion was now indescribable; within the square the Arabs who had already penetrated, although suffering heavily from the fire from my small party, were creating frightful havoc amongst the almost defenceless Bazingers, who, armed only with muzzle-loaders, could do nothing, whilst the regulars—so sudden had been the rush—had not even time to draw their bayonets; eventually, however, those who had entered were all killed. The flank guards, taken in front and rear, suffered even more heavily than the square, and, breaking up entirely, they fled in all directions, hundreds being killed by the Rizighat horsemen concealed in the forest.

The action had lasted only twenty minutes, but in that short space of time our losses were terrible. Fortunately, on the dispersion of the flanking parties the enemy had pursued them hotly. My fire, it is true, had driven them away from the square, but at what sacrifice! Amongst the regulars who had obeyed my signal to lie down, the losses had not been so severe; but the untrained Bazingers had suffered terribly, and many of our camels had also been killed.

In the midst of the confusion, I saw one of the enemy, who passed close to us, carrying off a red bag containing the fuses for the gun. He evidently thought he had some very special loot; and so indeed it was, as without the fuses our gun was useless. "Kir," said I to my young black attendant, who seldom left me, "let me see if you are as brave as you always say you are; go and fetch the red bag,—here is my horse;" and, jumping off, I gave it to him. He mounted, and taking only a spear in his hand, dashed off, returning in a few minutes with the red bag and a still redder spear.

The last horseman had disappeared in the distance, and I now sounded the "assembly." Only a few hundred responded to the call, and dividing these up into parties, I detailed half as guards, while the others were employed in collecting together the ammunition and arms of those who had fallen, packing them on the camels and depositing them in the little village, which, standing on a small sandy plain, afforded us a fairly clear field of view; then, collecting a quantity of thorn-bushes, we constructed a *zariba* as quickly as possible, fearing that at any moment the enemy might return. This done, our next thought was for the wounded; those only slightly hurt had already crawled to the *zariba*, and the severely wounded we now carried in, and did what was possible to alleviate their sufferings.

As far as the eye could reach, the ground was strewn with dead bodies, and what numbers too lay in the forest out of view! Curiously enough, this disaster had taken place on the actual spot where, years before, Adam Tarbush, the *vizir* of Sultan Hussein, had suffered a similar defeat and lost his life.

Now came the terribly sad duty of calling the roll. Of my fourteen infantry officers, ten had fallen, and one was wounded. The Gellaba chiefs, Sheikh Khidr, Mangel Medani, Hassan Wad Sattarat, and Suleiman Wad Fatah had been killed, as well as Fiki Ahmed, Hassib, and Shekelub. Of the thirteen artillerymen, one only remained alive. The Greek Alexander, too, who had previously been wounded at Deain, and who had not yet recovered, had been killed. Sorrowfully we collected the dead, to pay them the last honours. Amongst a heap of bodies we found Sharaf ed Din, stabbed to the heart. In the soft damp ground we hurriedly dug rough graves, and officers and chiefs we buried in twos and threes,—a terribly sad task.

As for the poor wounded, there was little we could do for them. Those only slightly hurt were already dressing their own wounds; but for the severe cases, we had no means of dressing them, and a few comforting words was all the small help we could give them. It was indeed painful to see such suffering, and feel how utterly incapable one was of alleviating it. Catching sight of one of my boys, who was carrying my satchel with a few bandages in it, I took it from him and began dressing one or two cases, when it suddenly occurred to me that I had not seen my other boy, Morgan Hosan, who was leading one of my horses. He was a fine, intelligent young fellow, scarcely sixteen years old, honest, quiet, and brave.

"Isa," said I to the boy carrying the satchel, "where is Morgan, who was leading my horse Mubarak (on which were my note-books and sketches in the saddle-bags); he is an active fellow, and perhaps mounted the horse, and has managed to escape." Sad and broken-hearted, poor Isa shook his head, and, his eyes filling with tears, he handed me a bit of my horse's bridle. "What is this?" I asked.

"Master," said he, "I did not want to make you more sorry than you are. I found him not far from here, lying on the ground with a spear-wound in his chest. When he saw me he smiled and whispered, 'I knew you would come and look for me. Say goodbye to my master, and tell him I was not a coward. I did not let go his horse, and it was only when I fell down stabbed in the chest that they cut the bridle to which I clung, and took him; show my master the bit of the bridle that is still in my hand, and tell him that Morgan was faithful. Take the knife out of my pocket,—it belongs to my master; give it to him, and

FIGHT BETWEEN THE RIZIGHAT AND EGYPTIAN TROOPS.

say many *salams* to him from me.'" Isa, his voice choked with sobbing, handed me the knife, and I, too, now quite broke down. Poor Morgan, so young and so true! Poor master, to have lost so faithful a servant and so true a friend!

"Tell me, Isa, what was the end?" I said.

"He was thirsty," he replied, "and I took his head in my hands, and in a few seconds he was dead. I then got up and left him; I had other things to do, and there was no time to cry."

Ordering the *zariba* to be strengthened, and trenches to be dug inside, I then had the drums beaten, bugles blown, and some rifle shots fired, so that any who might still be fleeing, or stopped by the swampy ground slightly wounded, might know that a place of refuge was at hand. During the day, a considerable number came in, and, calling over the roll in the evening, I found we mustered in all nine hundred men, including regulars and Bazingers,—a sad and broken remnant out of a force of eighty-five hundred men, but still something for which to be thankful. Of our horsemen and cavalry, thirty only were left,—the enemy had probably captured a large number, and some had perhaps escaped and returned to Dara or to their own homes; but of arms and ammunition of those who had fallen we had abundance.

At sunset the Rizighat Arabs returned from the pursuit, and, to their astonishment, found us in an entrenched position, ready to fight them. Madibbo now sent forward his Bazingers to attack us; but after a short struggle we drove them back, and darkness coming on, all firing ceased. Whilst sitting talking to my officers, Sheikhs Abder Rasul, Muslim Wad Kabbashi, and Sultan Begu approached, and asked whether it would not be better to retreat from our present position under cover of night, as after our heavy defeat and losses we had no chance now against the enemy. "Well," said I, "you wish to retreat during the night; but what will you do with all our wounded comrades and brothers? Do you want to leave them to the tender mercies of our enemies?"

Shamefaced, they were silent and did not reply. "No," said I, "your proposal is not a good one; I have been talking over the matter with my officers, and we have resolved to remain where we are for a few days. We have now nothing to fear but hunger; the wounded and tired camels can be killed for food for the soldiers. Besides, we can exist somehow or other for a few days. We shall most certainly be attacked, as we have already been, but we shall equally surely drive off the enemy. In this way the men will regain confidence after the terrible shock we have all suffered. I know the Rizighat; they will not stay here and watch us. I feel confident we shall settle accounts with Madibbo, his Bazingers, and Sheikh Jango, who fled once before to the Bahr el Ghazal. Our wounded comrades will have time to recover their strength a little; those only suffering slightly will be able to march in a few days, and the others we can mount on our horses. I think my proposal is a much better one than yours."

Whilst I had been talking I had overheard Sultan Abakr making remarks of approval, and by the time I had finished all had agreed to stay.

Speaking generally to all present, I said to them, "Can any of you understand how it was we were defeated today?"

"No," they all answered.

"Well, I will tell you," I replied. "This evening I saw amongst the wounded the assistant of Hassan Wad Sattarat, commander of the rear guard. He said, 'Sharaf ed Din did not carry out your instructions to relieve the rear guard, as on the previous days; the regulars were annoyed, and joined their companies without permission, and no fresh men were sent in their places. At the same time the friendly Arabs joined the flank guards, and when we were attacked, Hassan Wad Sattarat had at his disposal only about two hundred and fifty Bazingers armed with old percussion-guns.' Sharaf ed Din has paid for his negligence with his life, and we have all suffered as well. It is too late for recrimination now; let us think of something else. Go and cheer up your men; get some sleep, so that you may be fit for what tomorrow may bring. But you, Said Agha Fula, as you are wounded, will probably not be able to sleep; so we will put an *angareb* for you to lie down on at the gate of the *zariba*, and, should any one attempt to go out without my permission, you have my orders to shoot him."

Now that I was alone, I had time to think over the situation. It was very probable we should succeed in retiring on Dara, we had over eight hundred rifles and guns. But I bitterly deplored the losses; all my best officers and advisers were killed, and I dreaded lest the news of our disaster should reach Dara before I could communicate, as, in the event of this, the effect might be most serious both on the garrison and amongst the inhabitants. I therefore woke up my clerk and ordered him to write two short notes,—one to Zogal, and the other to the commandant, Adjutant-Major Mohammed Farag, informing them that, in spite of heavy losses, we were well, and that we hoped to return to Dara in about a fortnight; but should fugitives come in and spread false and alarming news about our situation, they were to be arrested and kept under guard till I returned.

I myself wrote a few lines to Gottfried Rott, describing the situation, and informing him that I hoped to return to Dara before long with the remainder of the troops; that he must not be down-hearted, but should do his utmost to keep up the spirits of all. I enclosed also a note to my mother, brothers, and sisters, bidding them farewell, as it was impossible to foresee what would be the end of all this trouble. In case I should fall, I begged Rott to send these on to my dear ones at home.

Taking the letters in my hand, I now went to Abdulla Om Dramo, Sheikh of the Messeria Arabs, who resided near Dara, and, waking him up, I said, "Where is your brother Salama?"

"There he is," said he, pointing to the man lying beside him, and waking him up also.

"Salama," said I, "you can render me a great service, which will also be of much advantage to yourself. You see these letters, you must take them to Dara and hand them over to the European Rott, whom you have often seen with me; I shall give you my own horse, which you always say is such a good one, for this mission. You must leave at once, and when you get near the line of the enemy encircling us, ride sharply through, for they are all asleep, and you will have disappeared in the dark before they can get their horses ready; once through their lines you will be safe, and in two days you should be in Dara. As a reward, I, will give you my black mare, which is in my stable."

Whilst I was talking, Salama had tightened up the cloth round his chest and loins, and merely said, "Where are the letters?" I gave them to him, and, taking them, he said, "Please God and with the help of the Almighty I shall take these letters to their destination. But I prefer to ride my own horse; he may not be so swift as yours, but he is quite strong enough to take me home on his back. I know my horse, and he knows me. Mutual acquaintances are always an advantage on such expeditions." Whilst he was girthing up his saddle, I scribbled a line to Rott, telling him to give the bearer of these letters my black mare, and, handing it to him, I told him what I had written; then, leading his horse to the gate, we came to Said Agha Fula, who was lying restlessly and in pain on his *angareb*: he was wounded in the right leg and left arm. I told him about Salama's mission, and he then ordered the gate to be opened. In a moment Salama had mounted, and, holding in his right hand his long spear, and in his left his bundle of small spears, he started off.

"I commit you to God's keeping," I cried.

"I trust in God," was his reply. Going slowly at first, he approached the lines cautiously; then I heard the rapid clatter of hoofs, in a few minutes one or two rifle-shots rang out in the still night, then all was as silent again as death.

"May God go with him!" we all ejaculated, and then re-entered the *zariba*. Exhausted nature now claimed me, and, utterly tired out, I was soon fast asleep.

When I woke up at early dawn I found the men already at work strengthening the breastworks, and, as I had anticipated, the enemy renewed their attack at sunrise. For some time a very brisk fire was kept up on both sides; but, owing to our dominating position the Arabs were at length forced to retire, after suffering considerable loss. On our side there were a few killed and wounded; amongst the former being Ali Wad Hegaz, a Jaali, and one of the best and bravest of his tribe. As it was our intention to remain here four or five days, the men busied themselves in strengthening the *zariba*, and we also buried the bodies of friends and foes in the immediate vicinity, as already the air was contaminated with the fetid smell of decaying corpses.

Amongst my men were two Bazingers whom on a former occasion I had employed to carry messages to my friend Lupton, who had succeeded Gessi as Governor-General of Bahr el Ghazal. It now occurred to me that it would be advisable to let him know the situation in Darfur, and ask him, should he be not otherwise occupied, to make an expedition against the Rizighat and Habbania Arabs, who in the wet season took their cattle into his province. I had ascertained that trouble had broken out in the Bahr el Ghazal as well, from a wounded Rizighat slave-hunter who had fallen into our hands; and he had told me that the Janghé tribe had revolted. Sheikh Janghé had attached Telgauna and sacked it; but having been subsequently defeated, he had joined Madibbo, and had been present with two hundred men in yesterday's action.

However, I had no doubt that Lupton was better off than I was; and, provided the government officials were loyal, I knew he had nothing to fear, for the tribes were too disunited to join in common action against the government. Besides, the religious factor, which was the bond of union amongst the northern tribes, did not enter into the Bahr el Ghazal situation, where the majority of the Black tribes were pagans.

In the Bahr el Ghazal the most important tribes, who are principally negroes and negroids, are the Janghé, Farogé, Kâra, Runga, Fertit, Kraitsh, Baya, Tega, Banda, Niam Niam, Bongo, Mombuttu, etc.; all these were entirely distinct from one another, having their kings or rulers, and there were continual feuds between them. It was this fact which enabled the Nile Arabs to enter the country with comparative ease, as Zubeir Pasha had done; it was a very simple operation to collect a number of the inhabitants, train them to the use of fire-arms, and utilise their services to invade a neighbouring tribe. These savage chiefs were too ignorant to understand that by combining in their opposition to foreign intrusion they would probably have been able to preserve their own integrity; but it is contrary to the traditions of these tribes to be ruled by any but their own chiefs, unless it be by Arabs or Europeans; and this fact accounts for the ease with which the slave-hunters pursued their nefarious traffic, almost unopposed, throughout the length and breadth of this vast province, which is peopled by the most warlike races in the Sudan, and who are capable of making excellent soldiers.

To Lupton, therefore, I decided to write, requesting him to advance against the Arabs on the Bahr el Ghazal frontier,—an operation which would certainly weaken the latter, or at least prevent them from entering Darfur. These few lines I concealed in a dry pumpkin gourd, and despatched by the hands of the two Bazingers.

We passed five days in the *zariba*, attacked once, if not twice, every day. During the action fought on the third day Koreina Nur, the commander of Madibbo's gun-bearers, and the bravest and boldest of his Arabs, was killed; and henceforth the enemy's attacks diminished greatly in vigour.

But now we had a new enemy to contend against,—famine. Almost everything eatable in the camp had been consumed; the camel meat, which had amply sufficed for the men, was now finished; there was not a grain of *dhurra* left; my officers and I had lived for some time on some old crusts of *dhurra* bread, which we had cooked with the leaves of a plant called *kawal*, and stirred up into a sort of tasteless porridge. We had no prospect of being relieved, to stay longer where we were was impossible, and already we were weakened by want of food; I therefore assembled the entire force,—consisting of nine hundred men, almost all of whom were armed with rifles and guns, except a few Arabs, who, being ignorant of fire-arms, prepared to trust to their lances,—and, addressing them in a few words, I told them that the blood of their dead officers and chiefs cried to them for vengeance; that their wives and children anxiously awaited their return, but that it was impossible to reach them without enduring troubles with patience, and facing difficulties with courage and endurance; and I closed my harangue by saying that those in whose hearts was fear had left us in the day of battle, but those now before me had bravely stood their ground against overwhelming odds, and that I had no doubt they would do so again, and that God would crown our efforts by victory.

A shout, and the shaking of rifles and guns over their heads, which is their usual method of signifying their obedience and courage, was their reply; and I then dismissed them, with orders to prepare to march the following day. I now took out the hammers from the percussion guns belonging to the killed, which lay heaped up in the middle of the zariba, and threw them into a rain pool; but of the stocks I made a bonfire. The filled shells for the gun I threw into the water, and as much ammunition as possible was distributed amongst the soldiers, each man carrying from sixteen to eighteen dozen rounds; but all the percussion gun ammunition I was obliged to destroy, in case it should fall into the hands of the enemy; the lead in the cartridges was removed, and some of the very severely wounded having just died, I placed it in the open graves, over which we laid the bodies of our poor comrades, as guardians of our precious metal.

It was on a Saturday, the seventh day after our disaster, and just after sunrise, that we marched out of the *zariba*, and, forming up in square with flank and rear guards, we began our retreat. The only two camels remaining drew the gun in the middle of the square, and I sent out two Arab horsemen as far as possible on each side to scout. We had one hundred and sixty wounded inside the square, and as many of them as could march did so; but the most severe cases we mounted on the few remaining horses, each horse carrying two or three men. I myself was prepared to walk; but, at the urgent request of my officers, I mounted, so as to obtain a better view over the country. We all knew that when we had marched some distance from the *zariba* we should most certainly be attacked; I therefore had the gun loaded, and we resolved to sell our lives dearly. We well understood the Arab mode of fighting, and were confident that if we succeeded in driving back the first two or three attacks, we should not be further molested. It was decided the line of direction should be northeast, as the ground was more open; but we were ignorant of the whereabouts of the rain-pools, as our guides were either killed or had deserted.

Before we had been on the march an hour, we were attacked in the rear by horsemen, and I knew the decisive moment had come. Halting instantly, I called in the flank guards closer to the square, and, accompanied by my own escort of fifty men, proceeded to the rear guard, distant about two hundred yards. The gun was run out to the rear face of the square, and several of the slightly wounded held the cartridges and shell ready to reload without delay. Before the enemy's footmen were in sight we could hear the sound of their advance; and when they did appear, a few well-directed volleys from the rear guard had the effect of slightly checking them; but, encouraged by those coming up behind, they rushed towards us, waving their great lances in their right hands, and carrying in their left bundles of small throwing spears.

They succeeded in coming so close that several of our men were wounded by thrown spears; but our fire created havoc amongst their ranks, and the gun played on them freely from the square. Their spearmen now gave way to Madibbo's and Jangho's Bazingers, and a very brisk fire was maintained on both sides; but, getting reinforcements from the square, we succeeded, after twenty minutes' hard struggle, in driving back the attack. On the first shots being fired, I had at once jumped off my horse, which is always understood in the Sudan to mean that, abandoning his chance of flight in case of a reverse, the commander has determined to conquer or die with his troops; and now that the action was over, the men came round me, and we had a great mutual hand-shaking over this, our first success.

Whilst we had been engaged in combating the attack on the rear, the left flank guard had also become engaged, and, though the enemy had been driven off, nevertheless it had suffered somewhat, and my best remaining officer, Zeidan Agha, was dangerously wounded. He was a Nubian by birth, and during the Darfur campaign had shown conspicuous gallantry in recapturing, at the head of only twelve men, a gun which had been taken by the enemy. For this service he had been promoted to the rank of an officer; and now he lay with a bullet through his right lung. I asked him how he was, and, giving me his hand, he murmured, "Now that we have conquered, we are all right;" and, pressing my hand, in a few minutes he was dead. Besides him we had lost twenty men killed, and several wounded. Our dead we buried roughly, as there was no time to dig graves; but we covered them sufficiently to avoid the reproach that we had left our dead unburied, and then continued our march with the same precautions, but with considerably increased confidence.

About three o'clock another attack on the rear was signalled; but this time it was not pressed home, and we drove off the enemy without suffering any loss ourselves. We now halted and formed a zariba, momentarily expecting another attack. But, to our surprise, we passed the night undisturbed, and the next morning at sunrise, having finished all our water, we resumed our march. Again we were subjected to an attack; but on this occasion it was even weaker than that of the previous afternoon, and was driven off without any trouble. We continued our march till midday, without finding any water; but got a little rest under the shady trees, and found a quantity of "*fayo*," a sort of native radish and very juicy. Three small leaves springing from the ground denote its presence, and it was sucked with avidity by our parched troops, and in some measure assuaged our thirst; but still it was absolutely necessary to find water.

After a short halt we pushed on again, and by good fortune accidentally came across a Rizighat shepherd, driving before him a flock of sheep. In an instant the men had seized the sheep, while the unfortunate shepherd, taken completely by surprise, did not attempt to escape, and would certainly have been killed, had I not rushed forward and prevented the men from harming him. I now had all the sheep driven inside the square; and meanwhile, my boys, having tied the Arab's hands behind his back, brought him before me. But before interrogating him, I gave orders for the sheep, of which there were over two hundred, to be distributed amongst the famished men, to every five men one sheep, and we kept a few for ourselves. What a godsend to us was this food!

Turning now to the Arab, I told him that his life would be spared if he would guide us to a rain pool; and that if he proved faithful I should give him a good reward, and let him go to his own home. He agreed, but said that there were only a few small pools in this neighbourhood, and that if we went on some distance further, and then halted, he would guarantee to bring us to the "*fula el beida*" (the white rain-pool) early the next morning, where there was sufficient water to last us for months. I was somewhat suspicious of him, and, therefore, ordered a non-commissioned officer and eight men to keep guard over him, and not to allow him to go far from me. We then resumed the march, halted at sunset, and made our *zariba* as usual.

We came across a few pools, but they were quite insufficient; and as we were still suffering considerably from thirst, I started on again at earliest dawn, having passed a miserable and sleepless night. About midday the guide pointed out some large trees, under which he said the pool lay. Halting, therefore, at once, I ordered the gun to be dismounted and loaded, and all preparations made to resist. It seemed to me very probable that the enemy, knowing that we should be suffering from thirst, would be in concealment somewhere near the water, and would charge us as we were approaching. I now called on the men to strictly obey all orders, and on no account to become undisciplined. But as soon as the water came in view, the poor thirsty troops could contain themselves no longer, and rushed pell-mell towards it.

I managed to restrain the forty men I had as escort, and there were about the same number with the rear guard; and although I sounded the "assembly" again and again, the men were now completely out of hand, plunging up to their waists in the water, in their frenzy of delight. But, as I had anticipated, the enemy were concealed behind the trees—fortunately, at some distance off—and, seeing our disorder, they now made a general attack from all sides. Galloping to the front, followed by the escort, we opened fire; while Mohammed Suleiman did the same as regards the rear. Our demoralised men, seeing the situation, at once fell in, and after some heavy firing we drove off the enemy, losing in this *mêlée* only one horse. We now selected a suitable position near the water, and set to work to make a *zariba*; and that finished, the men killed their sheep, fires were lighted, and in an hour they were enjoying the first solid meal they had had for many a day. As we were all sadly in need of a rest, I decided to remain in this position till the following day.

That evening a report came in from the outposts that a man was seen waving a piece of white calico and asking to be allowed to see me. I did not wish him to enter the *zariba* and see all our wounded; I therefore went out, and found that he was one of Madibbo's slaves, bearing a letter for me from his master. In this letter Madibbo called on me to surrender and hand over my arms. He further wrote that the *Mahdi* was now encamped before El Obeid, which he expected to capture shortly. He promised to treat me with all respect, and to send me, under safe escort, to the *Mahdi*. I now ordered this letter to be read aloud to the men, who greeted it with jeers, and asked the slave if his master was mad; to which the terror-stricken man replied that he did not really know.

I then turned to him seriously, and, speaking loud enough for all to hear, I said, "Tell Madibbo it was God's will we should have suffered losses, but we are not defeated. We are wandering about in his country, and if he does not like us to do so, he must accept the situation, as he has neither the power nor the courage to stop us. If he is really an adherent of the *Mahdi*, and desires to enjoy the pleasures of Paradise promised him, then let him come here tomorrow morning. We shall wait for him, and for his sake we shall not march tomorrow."

Most of the men had now gathered round us, and were listening to this speech and laughing; and when I bade the messenger goodbye, some of the wits begged him to give Madibbo their compliments, and tell him they hoped soon to have the pleasure of his personal acquaintance. The men were now in the highest spirits; they really did wish to make Madibbo's acquaintance, and wipe out, if possible, the defeat they had suffered at Om Waragat.

That evening I presented our guide with a piece of red cloth, a pair of silver bangles, and a few dollars, which I borrowed from the surviving merchants, and he quitted the *zariba* full of gratitude. At the same time I told him that should he come to Dara I would repay him the value of his sheep.

The next morning we ascertained in various ways that Madibbo was not far off, and after our boasting it behoved us to be very cautious. However, we were not attacked. Some of the men outside the *zariba* were amusing themselves by making small caps of twisted palm-leaves, like those worn by some of the Arabs we had killed, when a Rizighat horseman, who had evidently lost his way, came galloping towards us, thinking we were Madibbo's people. My men at once stopped him, and, making him dismount, brought him before me. Suddenly realising his mistake, he cried out, "*Allahu Akbar! ana kataltu nafsi*" (God is most great! I have killed myself). However, I consoled him, and handed him over to Mohammed Suleiman to be watched, and gave his horse to Mohammed Khalil, who had lost his in yesterday's action. That night I sent in a letter, by a runner to Dara, informing Zogal and Gottfried Rott that we were all well, and hoped soon to be with them.

The next morning I gave orders to march, and sent for the Arab who had come in yesterday, to speak to him about the road, but was told that some of the men, infuriated at the death of their comrades, had split open his head with an axe. Mohammed Suleiman denied all knowledge of the perpetrators of this crime, and knowing in what condition my men were, I thought it better to let this incident of brutality pass. During this day's march, as if to bid us farewell, we were once more attacked, but the enemy was again driven off. We picked up a wounded Arab, who told us that Mohammed Abu Salama and several Habbania Sheikhs were still with Madibbo, but that Sheikh Jango, owing to the heavy losses he had suffered at Om Waragat, had returned to the Bahr el Ghazal. I had no doubt the man would be picked up by his own friends, so I left him, and that evening reached a place some distance southeast of Deain. On the following day we reached Bir Dilwei, and thence we continued our march without interruption to Dara.

On the road letters reached me saying that Salama, whom I had sent off from Om Waragat, had arrived safely; they reported rumours that the Mima intended to revolt; and Rott, in a letter of which the handwriting was scarcely legible, told me that he had been taken ill the previous Saturday, and was very anxious to see me. I also received a report from Omar Wad Darho, stating that he had heard El Obeid was besieged, and that he did not think the Homr Arabs would dare to attack Om Shanga again, after their constant defeats. The reports of the Mudir of El Fasher were in general satisfactory, except as regards the Mima Arabs. News from Kebkebia and Kulkul was also good.

At length we reached Dara, and our entry was by no means a cheerful one. Many, of course, were happy to see their husbands, fathers, and brothers again; but how many more wept and wailed for their dead, lying on the distant battle-field!

It behoved me now to look after my own bruises. In the various fights I had been wounded three times. A bullet had shattered the ring-finger of my right hand, which had to be amputated almost to the root; the fingers on either side were also damaged. Another bullet had struck me in the upper part of my leg, and, flattening against the bone, made it protrude. A thrown lance had also struck me in the right knee. In spite of these wounds, I had been able to go through the campaign without much suffering; but I felt weak and overdone, and was very glad of a few days' rest.

I found poor Gottfried Rott very seriously ill. He wanted to move to Fasher for change of air; and having again heard from Said Bey Guma that it was impossible to get camels to send the remainder of the ammunition for which I had asked, I now hired all the camels I could in Dara,—the property of officers, officials, and merchants, about fifty in all,—and sent them under escort of one hundred regulars to El Fasher, ordering Said Bey to load them up with ammunition, send them back without delay, and with them as many other beasts of burden as he could procure. I wrote also to Adam Amer, the commandant, ordering him to send me a reinforcement of two hundred men (one hundred regulars and one hundred Bazingers) from Kebkebia direct to Dara. With this caravan I sent Gottfried Rott in charge of an officer, who was ordered to take him to my house in El Fasher, and at the same time I wrote to a Greek merchant named Dimitri Zigada, and asked him to do all he could for the patient.

The news from Kordofan being very contradictory,—though at the same time the general tenor was unsatisfactory,—I set to work to try and procure some reliable information. I therefore sent Khaled Wad Imam and Mohammed Wad Asi—the latter a most faithful man—to that province, with instructions either to send me news with the least possible delay, or return with it themselves. Khaled Wad Imam had been brought up with Zogal, and although they were not related to each other, they were generally looked upon as brothers. My reason for sending him with Asi was that he should protect him in El Obeid, and the plan succeeded admirably; for Khaled was naturally anxious to do nothing which would jeopardise Zogal, who, of course, remained with me at Dara. At the same time I cautioned Asi to remain on as friendly terms as possible with Khaled, and to try and find out if Zogal was in communication with the *Mahdi*, and, under any circumstances, to return to me as quickly as possible.

The day after my return to Dara, I sent orders to Omar Wad Darho to go back at once with all his men to El Fasher, leaving one of his officers, El Ata Wad Melek Usul, of the Shaigia royal blood, as commander of the newly recruited horsemen at Om Shanga. I also learnt that Abo Bey el Bartawi, the official in charge of the Toweisha district, was in communication with the Mima, and was inclined to revolt,—a rumour which was subsequently confirmed, as he refused to obey my summons to him to come to Dara, and he did not explain his reasons for not doing so.

In twelve days the caravan returned from El Fasher with the fifty camels, a hundred boxes of Remington ammunition, and ten *kantars* of lead. Said Bey made the usual excuses that he could hire no camels from the *employés*, and Adam Amer wrote that, owing to the disturbed aspect of affairs in the Fasher district, it was impossible to send me the reinforcements I had ordered.

I now thoroughly understood the situation. The officers were undoubtedly hostile to me. They had talked amongst themselves, and had spread rumours all through the country that Ahmed Pasha Arabi had turned his master, the Khedive, out of Egypt, because he was friendly to Christians, and admitted them into his service; that Arabi was now master of the country, and had turned out all who were not Egyptians, such as Turks and Circassians, and had confiscated their property, which had been turned over to the government. They had further declared that I had been discharged from my position, but that, owing to the roads being cut, the authority for my dismissal had not come to hand.

Of course the more sensible people placed no credence in these idle tales; but there was no doubt my authority was distinctly impaired, and this state of things was taken full advantage of by those who bore me a grudge. Hitherto there had been no overt act of disobedience to my orders; but excuses were being continually made, as there was evident inclination not to comply with them. However, such was the situation, and I had to put up with it and be as cheerful as I could under the circumstances. I was reminded of the Arab proverb, "*El kalb yenbah wa el gamal mashi*" (The dog barks, whilst the camel *unheeding* passes by); in other words, I thought it better to take no notice of all this cackling.

Beshari Bey Wad Bekir, head-*sheikh* of the Beni Helba Arabs, whom I had summoned to Dara, pleaded sickness; but anxious not to break off entirely with me, he sent me two horses and thirty oxen, which he begged me to accept as a token of submission, adding that as soon as the state of his health permitted he would certainly come. I gave the horses to the officers who had lost theirs in battle, and the thirty oxen I gave to the men.

By the same post which brought me news of Omar Wad Darho's arrival at El Fasher I heard of poor Gottfried Rott's death. In spite of most careful nursing and attention, he gradually sank, and was buried at El Fasher, beside Dr. Pfund and Friedrich Rosset, who had died there some years before.

The Mima were now in a state of open revolt. They had killed one of the government mounted postmen, and had turned out their own Sultan Daud, who was peaceably inclined to government, and replaced him by another. I therefore sent instructions to Omar Wad Darho to proceed with two hundred regulars and two hundred horsemen into their country, to chastise them; and at the same time I decided to operate against the Khawabir, who were acting in conjunction with the Mima. Darho started off, and had a successful little campaign, defeating the Mima at Fafa and Woda, whilst I proceeded, with a hundred and fifty regulars and fifty horsemen, *via* Shieria, to Bir Om Lawai, where the Khawabir, apprised of my approach, were waiting to attack me. After a short fight they were defeated and dispersed, and we captured a considerable number of sheep and oxen.

When these operations were over, I instructed Darho to leave a sufficiently strong force at Fasher, and to join me at Bir Om Lawai with the remainder of his men. In a few days he arrived, and gave me a full account of all his doings, and further details of the *Mahdi's* successes in Kordofan, which to me were excessively disquieting. Abo Bey having now openly joined in the Mima revolt, I decided to send Omar Agha with a sufficiently strong force to Toweisha, with instructions to destroy his residence, distant two days, whilst I despatched Omar Wad Darho and his men to again worry the Khawabir, who had retired to their sand-hills. He, however, met with no very signal success. The Khawabir country, except at Bir Om Lawai, is a sandy tract, destitute of trees and vegetation; but the rain, which lies for some months in the depressions of the ground, enables the Arabs to live here; and when it dries up they drink the contents of the water-melons, which grow in abundance near the pools, and which, when pressed, yield a somewhat sour but pleasant-tasting juice.

On the evening in which I was writing out Darho's instructions for his expedition against the Khawabir, a certain Abderrahman Wad Sherif came and urgently begged to speak to me. He was a well-known Dara merchant, and had previously travelled to Khartum. He began by saying that as I had always treated him with kindness, he thought it his duty to inform me that El Obeid had capitulated, adding that the early news of this sad event might enable me to take the measures I considered necessary. This was a terrible blow; but I thanked him for his melancholy news, and he then described to me in detail what had taken place. He was present at the time of the surrender and had left three days afterwards to visit his family in Dara; but hearing at Toweisha that I was at Bir Om Lawai, he had come straight to me, as he was most anxious that this news should reach me first through a friend.

As I knew it was useless to try and keep this secret, I summoned Darho and Suleiman Basyuni, and told them what I had heard, and we talked over the steps which we should now take. It was very evident that this news would prove an immense incentive to those hostilely inclined to the government, and there was no doubt my presence in Dara was an urgent necessity. As the Mima and Khawabir had been chastised, the next thing in order of importance was to send an expedition to Toweisha, and on the following day I wrote to Said Bey Guma that Om Shanga should be evacuated, and that the garrison, merchants, and any who wished should withdraw to El Fasher. I explained that as El Obeid had fallen, it was more than probable the Arabs would now turn on Om Shanga, and if invested, it would be quite impossible to send relief; and that, under any circumstances, it was imperative that the principal fighting forces in the province should be concentrated at Fasher. I also ordered him to establish a strong post at Fafa and Woda, in the Mima country, in order to keep open communication between Fasher and Dara. Omar Wad Darho and his men I instructed to return forthwith to El Fasher, adding that any booty taken from the Mima should be distributed amongst his men and the Fasher garrison, whilst that taken from the Khawabir should go to the Dara troops. On the following day we separated,—Darho to Fasher, and I back to Dara.

In a few days the news of the fall of El Obeid had spread far and wide, and the effect on the Arab tribes became immediately apparent: meetings were held in all parts of the country, and it was decided almost unanimously to rise against the government.

The day I arrived at Dara, I ordered all the *dhurra* I could find to be bought up; we had a considerable amount now in store, but more would certainly be advantageous. Sheikh Afifi now sent me news that his tribe had revolted and had joined the Rizighat, but he himself, true to his promise, was leaving his own country with his family and relatives and was coming to me *via* Dar Helba, and that he had sent his brother Ali with a message to Beshari Bey Wad Bekir, the head-*sheikh* of the Beni Helba, with whom solemn oaths had been exchanged, agreeing to his safe conduct through his country, and therefore he hoped to be with me in a few days.

I was awaiting his arrival when the sad news came that he had been killed. In him I lost my most faithful Arab *sheikh*. It transpired that the Beni Helba, who had been ordered by their *sheikh* to let him through, wanted to take from him his numerous sheep and oxen, and, having refused, a fight had ensued; he had performed prodigies of valour, but had been slain by some spearmen concealed amongst the trees, when in pursuit of the mounted Arabs, whom he had twice successfully driven off.

Mohammed Wad Asi, whom I had sent with Khaled Wad Imam, now returned from Kordofan, and gave me the fullest particulars regarding the situation there. He brought me the good news that government was collecting a large force in Khartum for the re-conquest of Kordofan, but that no doubt a considerable time must elapse before the expedition could start. I told him to spread this news in all directions, and then inquired as to Zogal's relations with the *Mahdi*. He replied that in spite of the most careful investigation, he could not ascertain definitely if any direct correspondence took place between them, but he had no doubt that Zogal received verbal messages from the *Mahdi*, brought by itinerant merchants; he however shared my views, that Zogal, being a man of position and education, must be well aware of the actual motives of the revolt, and would not be likely to embark on any foolish undertaking.

No doubt the capitulation of El Obeid had greatly weakened our position, and with the whole of Kordofan in the hands of the enemy, it behoved us to act with the greatest caution and circumspection. Wad Asi's news about the expedition preparing in Khartum would probably have the effect on the mahdi of making him keep his forces together so as to offer a united resistance; it was not, therefore, likely he would turn to us just at present. We must give all our attention to the revolt of the Arab tribes, who, now thoroughly inflamed by the news of the capitulation of El Obeid, and stirred up by fanatical proclamations, were ready to proceed to all extremities. As the operations of the intended expedition to Kordofan would not probably be finished till the winter, it was imperative that we should try and hold out by some means till then.

In spite of the formation of the military post at Fafa and Woda, the Bir Om Lawai Khawabir Arabs had again collected, and, joined by a number of Mima who had been irritated by the roads to their country being cut, and stimulated by the fall of El Obeid, were now stirring up the entire country between Fasher and Dara, whilst the troops at Fafa were not in sufficient force to attack them. I therefore decided on another expedition against them, as I was resolved to show them that the fall of El Obeid had not discouraged us. Selecting two hundred and fifty old soldiers well inured to war, I had them trained in bayonet-exercise for a few days preparatory to my departure, the date of which I kept strictly secret.

Taking with me all the horses I could muster at the time, some seventy in number, and instructing Wad Asi to keep me informed of events in Dara during my absence, I advanced rapidly; and in two days reached the neighbourhood of Bir Om Lawai, where both the Mima and Khawabir were collected. We took with us only our arms and ammunition, as our intention was to attack them, and then return. The instant, therefore, the enemy came in view I gave the order to "fix bayonets," and, in spite of the Bazingers and their guns, after a sharp fight of twenty minutes we drove them off and dispersed them. A few of the Mima Arabs had got amongst my men, but had all been bayoneted. I now ordered the horsemen to take up behind them the regulars and pursue, and do their utmost to discover where the water-melons were stored, as they would undoubtedly make for them to quench their thirst.

This order was well carried out, the water-melons were destroyed, and a number of women and children captured; whilst the tribesmen were scattered over the country in search of water, and many died of thirst. The next day the enemy's camp was burnt, and the women and children, who would otherwise have perished, I ordered to be brought to Bir Om Lawai, which I now attacked. The enemy here made a most determined defence, and I lost sixteen men killed, and twenty wounded. This loss brought home the fact to me that I had very few good regulars left, whilst the enemy, even if defeated, were daily increasing in number.

The women and children brought from Bir Om Lawai I handed over to Muslem Wad Kabbashi with directions that he should take them to Hilla Shieria, and thence to their homes at Fafa and Woda. The trees at Bir Om Lawai I ordered to be cut down and thrown into the wells, which I then filled up with earth, and returned to Dara.

Being the solitary European in a foreign country, and in the midst of an intriguing and unfriendly population, I had to resort to all sorts of means to discover the plots and designs of those by whom I was surrounded; and sometimes by money, or by gifts distributed in secret, I was able to learn beforehand what was likely to occur, and take measures accordingly. Through the help of my servants I utilised the services of some of the profligate women of the town, who, as was the custom of the country, prepared the native beer, or *marissa*, which is consumed in large quantities by the lower classes in the brothels. These houses were the rendezvous for every description of loafer, grumbler, and tattler who wished to let his tongue wag without restraint, under the influence of drink.

My servants had told me that during these drinking-bouts they frequently talked of the great religious rising of the *Mahdi*, for which, it may be readily imagined, those present had not much sympathy. It was, however, generally agreed that the government, having placed so many Christians and unbelievers in high positions, in which they were employed in combating this religious reformer, the result must be bad. The soldiers who frequented these houses of ill-fame often remarked, I was told, that although they liked me, they attributed the losses we had suffered in action to the fact of my being a Christian. I was perfectly well aware that these views were not the outcome of the brain of the Black soldier, who, as a rule, cares little about religion, but were instigated by those who were doing their utmost to upset and nullify my authority and make me unpopular with the men.

Now, on my return from Bir Om Lawai still more serious news awaited me. My servants told me that in one of the brothels belonging to a woman in my secret pay, daily meetings were held, in which the soldiers discussed the project of wholesale desertion. On inquiry I found that the principal instigators of these seditious meetings were non-commissioned officers and men of the Fur tribe, who were reported to be tired of this constant fighting, and who declared that the days of Turkish authority were numbered. Their plan was to desert to Sultan Dud Benga, the successor of Sultan Harun, who resided on the western slopes of Jebel Marra.

As the Fur section was the most numerous and powerful in the battalion, the matter was a most serious one; I therefore sent for the battalion commander, Adjutant-Major Mohammed Effendi Farag, and told him what I had heard. He appeared greatly surprised, and assured me he knew nothing of the matter, and that he should not fail to unearth the plot and bring the ringleaders to justice. I ordered him to maintain the strictest secrecy, and do nothing which would raise the slightest suspicion. Whilst he was with me I sent for my servant and handed him a bag full of money, telling him to take it to the woman and instruct her to invite the various persons concerned to her house the next day, and give them an exceptionally good entertainment at her own expense; at the same time I told my servant to induce her to let him hide somewhere in the house where he could overhear what was said; and that if she could carry out these directions to my satisfaction I should reward her handsomely. Soon after, my servant returned, telling me he had arranged everything.

The day following the entertainment I again sent for the adjutant-major, and was now able to communicate to him the names of six of the ringleaders, whom I ordered him to instantly arrest; moreover I was able to give him the details of the design and the actual date of its intended execution. In half an hour he returned with the six prisoners, whose hands were tied behind their backs. They comprised one sergeant, three corporals, and two lance-corporals,—all of the Fur tribe. They were accompanied by a crowd of *kavasses* and spectators, whom I sent off; and then, in the presence of their commanding officer, I asked them what instigated them to revolt against the government. They absolutely denied having any such intention, and assured me of their innocence.

"But," said I, "I know perfectly well you have been holding meetings in the house of your compatriot Khadiga. I gave you plenty of time to come to reason, but you grew daily more rebellious. Yesterday you were all with Khadiga, drinking *marissa*, and you agreed that the day after to-morrow you would execute your plan. Your object was to join with your friends in the third, fourth, and fifth companies, take your arms, open the western gate of the fort, and desert to Sultan Abdullahi, and, if necessary, to have recourse to force to carry out your design. Did you not assert yesterday, Sergeant Mohammed, that you had almost two hundred men at your disposal? You see now I know everything, and it is useless to deny it."

They listened in silence; they knew they had been discovered, and now they freely confessed and asked for my pardon. "That is out of my hands," I replied. "Go now with your commandant and confess openly that you are guilty in the presence of the other officers of the battalion; the law shall then decide." I then instructed the commandant to assemble a court-martial, and to arrange that all the non-commissioned officers should be present whilst the evidence was being taken; but at the same time I warned him to let it be understood by all (as I was afraid that some of the men might desert through fear) that other men implicated in the case should not be punished, as I held the non-commissioned officers alone responsible.

The same afternoon the proceedings of the case, with the full confessions, were brought to me, but without the sentence. I therefore returned them to the court to give sentence, and soon afterwards the commandant returned. The court had sentenced them to death, but recommended them to mercy. In my opinion an example was absolutely necessary, and though it was pain and grief to me, I confirmed the sentence of death, which was ordered to be carried out at once.

The regulars and irregulars were marched to an open space outside the *zariba*; six graves were dug, and the condemned men, who showed no signs of fear, after saying two *rakas* (short prayers), were led to the brinks of the graves, and there shot dead by the six detachments. I spoke to the assembled men, warning them that any one again found guilty of mutinous or seditious conduct would undoubtedly suffer the same penalty, and I sincerely trusted this would be the first and last case of the kind that should ever be brought to my notice. I hoped we should all be better friends in the future, and that times would improve. I then ordered the garrison to march back to the fort.

I was upset and sad. I thought of the number of good men lost in our fights, and now I was forced to take the most extreme measures to maintain discipline. On all sides intriguers were doing their utmost to impair my authority, quite ignoring the fact that should they succeed they would be no better off,—indeed, times were to come when they would be only too glad to obey the orders of the European they now so detested. That evening I sent for Mohammed Effendi Farag, and questioned him about the day's proceedings, and whether the men had been impressed by the execution; remarking at the same time that the soldiers must thoroughly understand their non-commissioned officers fully deserved the punishment they received, and moreover that it was an act of great leniency on my part not to take action against the other men implicated in the plot.

"Now, Farag Effendi," said I, "I want you to be thoroughly true and straightforward with me. I know that you are friendly-minded towards me, otherwise I should not certainly have asked you to come and speak with me alone. Tell me, how am I regarded personally by the men and the officers, excepting, of course, those who are selfishly seeking their own interests?"

"Although not accustomed to such severe discipline," he answered, "they are fond of you, and you are beloved by the men because you pay them regularly, which was not formerly the case. Besides, they much appreciate your custom of distributing the plunder amongst them. But this year we have had very heavy losses, and the men are getting tired of continual fighting."

"But," said I, "we have to fight. I do not go out on expeditions to make conquests or gain honour and glory; personally, I would much prefer rest and peace."

"Of course I quite understand that," said Farag Effendi, "still, these losses, which might have been avoided, have greatly affected the men. One man has lost his father; another his brother; many have lost friends and relatives; and if this goes on they will become disinclined to fight."

"I also quite understand that," I replied. "Although I have not lost a father or brother, still I have lost friends; and I risk my precious life equally with my officers and men. I am always with them, and am just as liable to be struck by bullets and spears as they are."

"They are well aware of that," he answered, "and you should give them credit for their obedience to foreigners, with whom they are always ready to risk their lives."

"Certainly I am a foreigner and a European," I said; "and I have no reason to make a secret of it, or be ashamed of it. Is this what they object to? Now, tell me truly?"

Mohammed Farag was one of my best-educated officers. He had studied in various schools in Cairo, but had been taken as a conscript; he was one of those rare men who acknowledge others' merits, and was always ready to learn from those he thought better educated than himself. He was neither fanatical nor religious, but he was a grumbler, and rather hot-tempered. These were, I think, his only bad qualities, and they had led him to commit some crime, for which he had been banished to the Sudan.

When I now called upon him to tell me the truth he threw up his head and looked straight at me and said, "Well, you wish me to tell you the truth, then here it is: they do not object to you on account of your nationality, but on account of your faith." At last I had drawn out of him what I was so anxious to know.

"Why on account of my faith?" I asked. "During all these years that I have been in Darfur they knew that I was a Christian, and yet no one ever said a word to me."

"Ah!" said he, "the times were very different then, and much better; but now that this rascally Dongolawi has made a cloak of religion, he has adherents everywhere who purposely incite the people so as to attain their own evil ends. The idea has got about in the battalion (I do not know who started it) that in this religious war you will never be able to gain a victory, and that in every battle you fight you will suffer great losses, till at length you yourself will be killed. You can perfectly understand how an ignorant soldier would credit all this, and how he would impute it to the fact of your being a Christian. Our men are far too stupid to realise that our losses are due to the vastly superior strength of the rebels, and that as we have no chance of being relieved, so we must go on suffering defeat."

"Suppose that I now turned Mohammedan," said I, "would my men believe in me and hope for victory? and would that give them more confidence in me?"

"Of course the men would believe you," said he,—"at least the majority of them; have you not taken every opportunity of showing respect to our religion, and even caused it to be respected by others? They will trust you implicitly; but will you change your faith from conviction?" he asked, smiling.

"Mohammed Effendi," said I, "you are an intelligent and well-educated man; here conviction has nothing to do with the case. In this life one has often to do things which are contrary to one's persuasions, either by compulsion or from some other cause. I shall be quite content if the soldiers believe me and abandon their silly superstitions. Whether others believe me or not, is a matter of indifference to me. I thank you most sincerely; keep our conversation entirely to yourself. Goodnight!"

Mohammed Effendi Farag now left, and after a few minutes' deliberation I resolved to present myself to the troops the following morning as a Mohammedan. I was perfectly well aware that in taking this step I should be placing myself in a curious position, which could not fail to be condemned by some. However, I made up my mind to do it, knowing that I should thereby cut the ground from under the feet of these intriguers, and should have a better chance of preserving the province with which the government had intrusted me. In my early youth my religious ideas were somewhat lax; but at the same time I believed myself to be by conviction as well as by education a good Christian, though I was always inclined to let people take their own way to salvation. The simple fact was that I had not been sent to the Sudan as a missionary, but as an official of the Egyptian Government.

At sunrise the next morning, I sent for the adjutant-major, and ordered him to have all the troops paraded and to wait for me; I then sent word to Zogal to summon before me the *kadi*, Ahmed Wad Beshir, and the chief merchant, Mohammed Ahmed. When they came I talked to them on general matters, and then told them to come on parade with me inside the fort, only a few hundred paces from my door. Taking command of the parade, I ordered the troops to form square, and, mounted on horseback, I then entered it, accompanied by the officers, attendants, and officials.

"Soldiers!" said I, "we have passed through many hard times together; the presence of danger shows what a man is made of. You have fought and endured bravely, and I am certain you will continue to do so. We fight for our master the *khedive*, the ruler of this country, and for our lives. I have shared with you your joys and your sorrows. Where danger was to be faced I was there with you, and that shall ever be my place. Although I am your chief, my life at such times is of no more value than yours."

"*Allah yetawel umrak! Allah yekhallik!*" (May God give you long life! May God preserve you!) shouted most of the men.

I then continued, "I hear that I am considered a foreigner and an unbeliever. You also all belong to different tribes; my birthplace is far away, it is true, but I am not a foreigner. I am not an unbeliever; I am as much a believer as you. *Ashhadu inna la ilaha illallah wa inna Mohammed rasul Allah!*" (I bear witness that there is no God but God, and Mohammed is His Prophet). On my uttering these words the soldiers raised their rifles, shook their lances, and shouted out congratulations to me, whilst the officers and officials advanced and shook hands with me. When order was restored, I told them that I should openly attend prayers with them, and, ordering the men to re-form, Farag Effendi gave the "present arms," and the men then marched off to their quarters.

When everything was over, I invited Zogal Bey, my former companion, and the officers to remain and partake of food and coffee with me; they then bade me goodbye, assuring me of their delight, fidelity, and obedience. They made as if they credited me with my convictions, and I gave them equally to understand that I believed in the reality of their feelings and sentiments (though I well knew how little they were really worth). When they left I told Farag Effendi to select twenty of the best oxen from our stock and distribute them amongst the men as "*karama*" (sacrificial offerings), as well as one ox for each officer, at my own expense.

The effect on the men of the step I had now taken was much greater than I expected; there was no longer any reluctance to be sent on expeditions, although our enemies were increasing daily in number and strength.

It will be remembered that I had sent Gabralla and Ahmed Katong some time before to Sirga and Arebu—a country which had been desolated by war and was peopled by the ignorant Fur tribe—with instructions to collect a force of his own people in these districts, and uphold the government authority there. Instead of doing so, however, he had sold them as slaves to the Gellabas after a peculiar method of his own. Despatching messengers to the Gellabas with orders to come to him at once under pain of punishment, he then insisted on each of them marrying three or four women, and instructed the latter to depart with their new husbands, accompanied by their brothers and sisters.

Many of the former husbands having been killed in the wars, it happened that most of the women thus disposed of were widows; but should any of them happen to have husbands, the latter Gabralla threw into chains and compelled them to work in the fields. For each human being thus made over to the Gellabas he received a small sum of money. When these extraordinary proceedings had been brought to my notice, I had ordered the roads to be watched, and it was not long before a batch of newly married women and their relatives was seized; I had sent for Gabralla and put him in chains, and about twenty months later I had released him on bail; but shortly afterwards he had disappeared, together with his guarantor, and had joined the Beni Helba, who, after the murder of Afifi, had actively joined in the revolt.

Next to the Rizighat, the Beni Helba was the most powerful tribe in Darfur, and they soon began worrying the Tagu and Messeria Arabs, who had up to now remained faithful, and lived in the neighbourhood of Dara. I therefore resolved to attack them, but before doing so sent a message to Beshari Bey Wad Bekir, warning him that he must make no more incursions. Although my letter remained unanswered, it seemed that my threatening attitude had had some effect, for the neighbouring tribes were not further molested.

Merchants whom I paid to send me news from Kordofan informed me that reinforcements were daily arriving at Khartum from Cairo, and that the government was hurrying on preparations for the despatch of the expedition, under European officers, to retake Kordofan; whilst the entire population without exception had joined the *Mahdi*, and were determined to offer a powerful resistance.

In Darfur all the southern tribes were now in open revolt; but thanks to our military posts and to the fact that the northern tribes had been in contact with Egypt, from which they had derived considerable benefit through the caravan routes, they had hitherto shown no hostility. Of course it had been for long impossible to gather taxes in any part of the country; I had, therefore, paid the troops out of our reserve stores.

The *Mahdi's* continual victories were at last beginning to tell openly on Zogal Bey, and I noticed a distinct change in his conduct, though he still appeared loyal and submissive. It was abundantly clear to me that in his heart he wished all success to his cousin, the *Mahdi*, because he knew that, in that eventuality, he would be one of the first to reap tangible benefits. He was a man much liked by the officials under him; fairly well educated for a Sudanese, he was ever ready to do a favour when his own pocket was not thereby touched, and he got the character of being liberal. He was very wealthy, and kept up an enormous household in great state. He kept an open table, and his popularity amongst the officials was, I think, in a large measure due to the fact that, as acting governor, he had freely pardoned past offences, and took no steps to prevent them enriching themselves in all sorts of illicit ways.

Through his influence, most of his relatives had secured good positions and become wealthy. He was, therefore, a man with whom I had to reckon somewhat circumspectly. His popularity, coupled with the fact that he generally concurred in and executed my orders, rendered an open split with him undesirable, and would have certainly led to a diminution of my authority; I was therefore inclined to let him alone for the present. "*Ebed en nar an el kotn wa enta terta*h" (Keep fire away from cotton, and you will be at ease), as the Arabs say, seemed to me to thoroughly apply in this case, and to that principle I adhered.

Summoning Farag Effendi, Wad Asi, and Kadi el Beshir, all of whom were loyal to government, and prayed from their hearts for its success, I communicated my plans to them, in the strictest secrecy, and obtained their full concurrence. When they had left me I summoned Zogal, and now conversed with him quite alone. "Zogal," I began, "you and I are perfectly alone here, and God is our witness. For years we have eaten bread and salt together, and although from the day I arrived I have been your superior, our relations with each other have been rather those of a friendly than of an official nature. I now ask you to do two things for me,—trust me and render me a service."

"Well, *Mudir umum*" (Governor-General), he replied, "you are my superior; tell me what you want and I shall obey."

"Your cousin the *Mahdi*," said I, "has now conquered Kordofan, El Obeid has fallen, and the entire population has joined him. The country between us and government is in his hands. His extraordinary success has inclined your heart to him; have you forgotten all the favours you have reaped from government? Are you unmindful of the distinction bestowed upon you by the *khedive*, in the shape of a decoration and rank obtained for you through the good offices of the government? Have you forgotten the duties required of you from your position? Speak, is it not so?"

"It is so," replied Zogal, quickly; "the *Mahdi* is my cousin, and I cannot deny that our blood-relationship has inclined me to him. Still, hitherto I have faithfully performed my duties, and I trust I shall continue to do so in the future."

"Speaking generally," I replied, "you have performed your duties well; but I am told you are in communication with the *Mahdi*; why should you hide this from me?"

"I do not communicate directly," replied Zogal, quickly; "but merchants coming from Kordofan give me verbal messages from him, and I have sworn to the bearers of these messages that I would not tell you; that is why I kept it secret. But I assure you that they only referred to news from Kordofan, and no attempt has been made to win me to his cause."

"Well, let it be," said I, "I do not want you to justify yourself; but, tell me, what have you heard about this expedition which the government is preparing to send to retake Kordofan?"

"I have heard," replied he, "that a large expedition has arrived at Khartum, and that they are going to try and reconquer the country."

"Not only will they try, but they will effect the reconquest of the country," I answered. "Now, Zogal, you are a man of sense and intelligence: it must be perfectly clear to you that, if compelled by circumstances, I am still sufficiently powerful to make you harmless; but I do not think this would be an advantageous step to take, and it would pain me deeply to take action against a man like yourself, who has served the government loyally for many years, and has always befriended me. I will therefore discharge you for the present, and you may now go to Kordofan with my full consent. Religious movements, such as that now going on have a certain amount of glamour from a distance, and induce sympathy; but when examined more closely, they are neither so seductive nor so alarming. I shall intrust you with letters to the government which I want you to send secretly to Khartum, and which will inform them of the nature of your mission.

"As the expedition will probably start for Kordofan next month, I want you to do your utmost to prevent the *Mahdi* sending a force into Darfur or despatching proclamations to the tribes inciting them to revolt. If you can arrange this, it will be of advantage both to him and to you. Should the expedition succeed, I will take all responsibility for your conduct on my shoulders, and you need have no fear; but if the *Mahdi* is successful,—which God forbid,—then we shall be entirely cut off from all hope of relief, and will probably be compelled to submit, in which case it shall be of advantage to him to have the country handed over in fairly good condition. As a guarantee for the loyal conduct of your undertaking, I shall keep your wives, children, and households in the fort here. The *Mahdi* will respect this, and for your sake will not run the risk of endangering their lives."

"I shall carry out your instructions," said Zogal, "and prove to you that I am loyal. Are you going to write a letter to the *Mahdi*?"

"No," I replied, "because I do not want to have any dealings with him. I know perfectly well that you will repeat the whole of this conversation to him. Your cousin is very cunning, and, privately, will give me credit for having spoken the truth, and he will, no doubt, make as much capital as he can out of your mission; but as long as you hold loyally to your promise, I shall take every care of your family, and although you are nominally discharged, I shall continue to issue your pay in full; but should you fail to keep to the conditions of this arrangement, the guarantee will no longer hold good. I should like you to start as soon as possible, and in three days I shall expect you to be ready; I think that should be sufficient time."

"I would prefer to stay here with my own people," said Zogal; "but as you wish me to perform this mission, and to put my loyalty to the test, I shall carry it out, but with a sorrowful heart."

Sending now for Farag Effendi, Wad Asi, and the *kadi*, in Zogal's presence I told them of the arrangement we had made; they showed much apparent surprise and excitement, and summoned Zogal to swear a solemn oath of loyalty. He swore on the *Koran* by the oath of divorce[1] that he would adhere truly and faithfully to the agreement made between us.

I now wrote the necessary letters to the government, giving a brief account of the situation in Darfur; and three days later, Zogal, accompanied by three servants, left Dara for El Obeid, *via* Toweisha. It was well known he was a relative of the *Mahdi*; he had therefore nothing to fear, and I subsequently learnt he was received everywhere with open arms.

I now set to work to build fresh batteries at the angles of the fort, and collected all the corn I could find; but this short period of tranquillity did not last long. Beshari Bey Wad Bekir, chief of the Beni Helba Arabs, instigated by his father-in-law, Sheikh Taher et Tegawi, planned a raid on Dara. In spite of my threatening letter, he had attacked the Tagu and Messeria Arabs, killing a number of them,

---

1. One of the most solemn forms of administering an oath is for the person taking the oath to say, "I impose upon myself divorcement."

and capturing many women and children. In consequence, I placed two hundred and fifty regulars and one hundred Bazingers under the command of Mattar, one of Zogal's relatives,—but I could only take twenty-five horses, as most of them had been attacked by some sort of disease,—and with this force I quitted Dara.

After three days' march we arrived at Amaké, where I was attacked by the Beni Helba, under Beshari Bey, with whom was my old friend Gabralla; they were in considerable force, but had few fire-arms, and we succeeded in beating them off and dispersing them without much difficulty. The next day they attacked us again at Kalambasi,—a march of a day and a half from Amaké; but here again we put them to flight with equal ease. Our insignificant losses on both occasions were ascribed by my men to the efficacy of my Friday prayers with them, and not to the small number of fire-arms possessed by our enemies. We now advanced on Hashaba which was the head-*sheikh's* village, turned him out, and then offered to conclude peace with him.

In reply to my letter, one of Beshari Bey's relatives, named Fiki Nurein, arrived, asking my terms. I demanded two hundred horses and two thousand oxen. He returned to his people, and came back to me the following day, saying that they were prepared to conclude peace, but thought my terms very hard; and as I was anxious to settle matters without delay, I agreed to accept half the original demand, on condition that they absolutely refrained from further aggression, and agreed to send back the women and children captured from the friendly tribes. I now returned to Dara; but Fiki Nurein arrived two days later, and said that, to the great regret of Beshari Bey, his Arabs had rejected the terms of peace, though he himself was perfectly prepared to accept them.

This change of front had been brought about by Sheikh Tegawi's daughter, who had called her husband a coward for making peace, and therefore, in honour bound, he was obliged to continue fighting. Fiki Nurein told me he had been commissioned by Beshari Bey to offer me his best thanks for having sent him some barley cakes covered with sugar, when I had been obliged to turn him out of his house. It happened that just before starting on my last expedition, Zogal's wife had sent me some exactly similar cakes, which I had handed over to my servants; as they were still untouched, I gave them to Fiki Nurein to take to Beshari Bey with my compliments, and he left with a sorrowful heart, feeling convinced that in the next fight he must be defeated.

I now left for Hashaba, and proceeded thence to Guru, about half a day's march further on. On the way, the twelve mounted scouts in advance were suddenly attacked by Beshari Bey alone, who broke through their line, wounded one of them slightly, and then, turning to the left, he drew his horse up between the scouts and my main body, at the edge of the forest and about eight hundred yards from us. Advancing some three hundred paces closer, I recognised him, but purposely did not shoot; instead, I sent one of my boys, unarmed, to him, saying, "Isa, give my compliments to Beshari Bey, and tell him that if he wants to show his wife how brave he is, he should set about it in a different way; if he repeats this manoeuvre he will certainly be killed." The road was fairly open, with trees only here and there; and as we marched on I could see my servant standing for a few seconds before Beshari Bey, and then returning towards us; on reaching us, he said, "Beshari Bey sends you his compliments; he says he has no wish to live any longer, and seeks death." Deluded man, he soon found it!

Arriving at Guru, we constructed a *zariba*, and the owner of the village, which was close by, now came forward and asked us for peace and protection, which was of course given him. He was a Gellaba named Ahmed Wad Serug, who had settled here many years before. He now told me that Beshari's nephew Rahmatalla had, since yesterday, been seeking an opportunity to come in and ask for pardon, but had been afraid to do so, and was concealed in the forest close by. I told Ahmed to go out and offer him pardon and peace and bring him in. That evening at sunset he arrived, bare-headed and barefooted, and made the most profuse promises of fidelity, saying he would do his utmost to induce his tribe to stop fighting. He admitted that the majority of the Arabs were not anxious to prolong the war, but were continually incited by Sheikh Tegawi.

Nothing happened the next day, but that evening Rahmatalla brought in two Arabs with the news that Sheikh Beshari had collected all the available horse and spear men, and intended attacking us in the morning. Mohammed Bey Tia and Sultan Abakr el Begawi had just joined me with forty horsemen; I had now, therefore, at my disposal some seventy irregular cavalry. My *zariba* lay close to the wells in an open spot with a good view in all directions. At sunrise the following morning I saw the first signs of the enemy at the edge of the forest to the south. Feeling sure that Beshari's ill-considered dash would make him attack the *zariba*, I ordered the troops to move out about three hundred paces, whilst I posted the cavalry on the flank and sent forward about twenty horsemen to try and decoy the Arabs out of the wood. The latter had barely started when I saw two mounted Arabs dashing at them full speed, with lances lowered; they were Beshari Bey and his attendant. Before he reached my men his horse stumbled and fell; and while his companion was holding his horse to enable him to mount, my horsemen seized the occasion to attack him, and, a thrown spear striking him full in the eye, he fell, whilst his attendant was struck by a spear in the back and killed.

Meanwhile I had galloped up to the spot, and there I found Beshari Bey lying dead: my men had twice plunged a huge spear into his body. His son Abo, who had dashed out to his aid, was also wounded, but succeeded in escaping, though two other *sheikhs* who had accompanied him—Shartia Habiballa and Et Tom—were killed. Seizing their horses, I now called out to the regulars to advance; and on their arrival I ordered each of the horsemen to take up an infantryman behind him and pursue the Arabs, who I felt sure would not attempt to stand after the death of their leaders. After a gallop of about two miles we came up with the flying Arabs, and, ordering the regulars to dismount and fire, I turned the horsemen against the mounted Beni Helbas. No quarter was given, as my men were determined to avenge the death of Sheikh Afifi, who had been killed near here.

After a few hours the rout was complete, and we now returned to the *zariba*. On our way back we stumbled across Beshari's body, beside which sadly sat his nephew, Rahmatalla. My officers at once asked to be allowed to cut off his head and send it to Dara; but out of respect to his nephew, who had pleaded yesterday for peace, I prevented them from doing this, giving over the body to him, with a piece of calico in which to enshroud it, and I myself attended the burial of my old friend who had fought against us,—contrary to his own convictions,—and who, seeking death, had now found it. In this engagement we lost two killed and several wounded, amongst whom was the faithful Salama, who had taken my letter from Om Waragat to Dara, and who was ever foremost in pursuit.

The following day I sent spies to Roro, Sheikh Tegawi's village, and hearing he was there, I resolved to surprise him that night. I arrived in the early morning, but found the nest empty,—my bird had flown: he had evidently got wind of my coming; my men, however, seized all the portable things they could find in his house, and then set it and the village on fire.

I now returned to Guzu. The disease of *filaria medenensis* (guinea-worm) had broken out in the upper part of my leg and in both feet, and caused me such excruciating pain that I could scarcely remain in the saddle. Having crushed the Beni Helbas, it was useless for me to remain out any longer; I therefore handed over the command to Mohammed Bey Tia, and told him to take every occasion to chastise the Arabs, but on no account to penetrate into the Taaisha country. The latter had previously written to me expressing loyalty to the government, and, curious to relate, this tribe, to which Khalifa Abdullahi belonged, was one of the few in the whole of the Egyptian Sudan which, in spite of tribes revolting all around them, remained neutral. I now wrote to them that should the Beni Helba attempt to take refuge in their country, they might seize their flocks and herds, and I should not ask them to give them back. Accompanied by ten men, I now returned to Dara.

Up to the present, Fasher had been left undisturbed, and hitherto the tribes in the neighbourhood had not shown any open signs of hostility; but the chief of the station at Om Shanga had refused to attend to my order to return to Dara, having been bribed by the merchants to remain, and had been attacked by the Arabs; he had succeeded, however, in repulsing them, though the road was still cut, and one of my faithful *sheikhs*, Hassan Bey Om Haj, had passed over to the enemy.

About a fortnight later, Mohammed Bey Tia returned to Dara with a large amount of plunder: exclusive of the quantities he had distributed on his own account, he brought with him no less than three thousand oxen and a few horses. The latter I made over to the men, and also divided between them and the loyal Arabs a thousand oxen; another thousand I handed over to Farag Effendi to keep with the general reserve; and the remaining thousand I exchanged for corn and cotton stuffs.

In spite, however, of our success against the Beni Helba, our situation was anything but satisfactory. All eyes were directed to the *Mahdi*, in Kordofan; he had representatives and agents everywhere, who were inciting the people to revolt. In the province of Dara, besides the Taaisha, Messeria, and Tagu Arabs, those in the districts of Bringel and Shieria were also quiet; but I ascribed this fact to the proximity of the fort, for they were well aware that should they revolt, they would be in the greatest danger.

Chapter 8

Hicks Pasha's Expedition

After the capture of El Obeid the *Mahdi* turned all his attention to increasing his power. His adherents on the river kept him very fully informed of all that passed. He was aware that Abdel Kader had applied to Cairo for reinforcements, which had arrived, and he did not doubt the government would do all in its power to reconquer its lost provinces; that was his reason for so constantly preaching the *Jehad*, and reminding his followers that a great war was impending, in which they would be victorious.

Giegler Pasha had been successful at Duem in November, 1882, and at the end of January, 1883, Abdel Kader Pasha had scored a signal success at Maatuk. But the *Mahdi* paid little attention to these defeats; he was principally concerned with the news that an expedition was being prepared in Khartum, under European officers, for the reconquest of Kordofan.

Meanwhile Mohammed Pasha Said thought it his duty to draw up a report justifying the surrender of El Obeid, which he intended to send to Khartum. He exposed the courage and endurance of the garrison who had been at length obliged to capitulate, after having been more than decimated by famine and disease, and he explained that they were still thoroughly loyal, and longed for the success of the government arms. This document was signed and sealed by all the officers, Said Pasha and Ali Bey Sherif heading the list, and also by Ahmed Bey Dafalla and Mohammed Yasin; it was then given to an Arab, who was promised a large reward if he took it to Khartum.

Amongst the officers who signed was a certain Yusef Mansur, formerly police officer at El Obeid, but who had been dismissed by Gordon, sent to Khartum, and afterwards allowed to return to El Obeid, where he had settled. Fearing that the report might be intercepted, and that he might suffer with the others, he, to show his fidelity and submission to the *Mahdi*, fell at Khalifa Abdullahi's feet, confessed everything, and earnestly entreated for pardon, which was granted. On his way home he met another officer, named Mohammed Bey Skander, whom he also urged to seek the *khalifa's* pardon; and the latter, although he cursed his friend for his cowardice, thought that now the secret was out he had better save himself, so he, too, begged the *khalifa's* forgiveness.

The Arab letter-carrier was intercepted and thrown into chains, and of course the occasion was taken advantage of to spread far and wide the story that the *Mahdi* had discovered this plot by direct inspiration from the Prophet. This gave him a ready pretext to make away with his enemies. All those who signed the document were seized, and, after consultation between the *Mahdi* and his *khalifas*, it was decided they should be banished. Said Pasha was sent to Aluba, where he was handed over to the tender mercies of Ismail Delendok; Ali Bey Sherif was sent to Nawai, Sheikh of the Hawazma; while Ahmed Bey Dafalla and Yasin were sent to Madibbo at Shakka. Of the other officers, some were exiled to the Nuba mountains, and others to Dar Homr. Yusef Mansur and Mohammed Bey Skander were the only officers allowed to remain at El Obeid, and the former, in order to mark his fidelity to the cause, was made commandant of the *Mahdi's* artillery.

Soon afterwards, in accordance with his orders, Said Pasha was killed with axes, and Ali Bey Sherif was beheaded, while Abdullahi, who had, on the day after Ahmed Bey Dafalla's departure, taken his wife as his concubine, despatched one of his relatives, Yunes Wad ed Dekeim, to Shakka with orders to have both Dafalla and Yasin executed in the presence of Madibbo. Such was the end of the four men who had so bravely defended El Obeid, and in truth they deserved a better fate!

It was about this time that Fiki Minna, of the powerful Gowama Arabs, having quarrelled with Abdullahi, thought to make himself independent; but the *Mahdi*, knowing how serious would be a split, did not hesitate to send a large force against him under Abu Anga, Abdulla Wad Nur and Abderrahman Wad en Nejumi. Fiki Minna was surprised, seized, and instantly executed, and the *Mahdi* lost no time in at once despatching proclamations ordering the tribes to leave their districts and join him. To these assembled multitudes he now preached more fervently than ever, urging them to renounce the pleasures of this life, and think only of the life to come. *"Ana akhreb ed dunya wa ammer el akhera*" (I destroy this world, and I construct the world to come), was his endless theme.

To those who were obedient he promised pleasures in Paradise beyond all the heart could conceive; but the disobedient he threatened with condign punishment and hell-fire. Circulars written in this sense were despatched far and wide, and the *emirs* were enjoined to allow only those to remain in their districts whose services were absolutely necessary for the cultivation of the lands, but that all others must forthwith immigrate to him and range themselves under his banners.

Men, women, and children now flocked in hundreds of thousands to El Obeid to see this holy man and catch even a word of his inspired doctrine; and the ignorant multitudes saw in his face and person what they believed to be truly "a man sent from God."

Dressed only in a *jibba* and *sirual* (drawers), with a belt of *gus*, or straw, round his waist, and wearing a Mecca *takia* (skull-cap), round which was bound a muslin turban, he stood with all humility before his followers, preaching of love to God and the cause, and of the necessity of renouncing the vanities of this world. But once in his house it was quite another matter; here he lived in a state of grandeur and luxury, and became a slave to those passions for food and women to which the Sudanese are so addicted. Should any women, young girls, and slaves be captured, they were brought before him, and all the prettiest and the best found a home in his *harem*; whilst the maid-servants, who were versed in all the arts of the most approved Sudan cooking, were relegated to his kitchen.

After the siege of El Obeid he considered whom he should appoint as his fourth *khalifa*, and decided that Mohammed es Sennusi, the most influential religious *sheikh* in North Africa, should be nominated; he therefore despatched Taher Wad Ishak, of the Zaghawa tribe, with a letter to him to that effect; but Sennusi treated the offer with scorn, and left the letter unanswered.

The *Mahdi* now set to work to regulate his government. His administration was based on very simple lines. First of all he established the Beit el Mal, or treasury, over which he placed his faithful friend Ahmed Wad Suleiman. In this treasury were deposited the tithes (*ushr*) and the *fitra* and *zeka* (alms for the poor, two and a half *per cent*) on all booty taken in war as well as confiscated property, and fines for theft, drinking, and smoking. There was no system to regulate the revenue and expenditure. Ahmed Wad Suleiman was, therefore, free to give what he liked to whom he pleased.

Jurisdiction was placed in the hands of the *kadi*, who was called by the *Mahdi* "Kadi el Islam," and several assistants. Ahmed Wad Ali, who had formerly been *kadi* at Shakka under me, and who had been one of the foremost in the storming of El Obeid, was the first to hold this high position. Of course the *Mahdi* and his *khalifas* reserved to themselves the right to punish all crime—more especially anything connected with doubt or suspicion as to the Divine nature of the *Mahdi*—with death. As such judgments were in entire opposition to the *sharia* (or Moslem religious law) as taught, the *Mahdi* strictly forbade the study of theology, and ordered all books of this description to be burnt; the *Koran* alone being allowed to be read, though even this he did not permit to be openly expounded.

Communication between the *Mahdi* and the inhabitants of the Gezira, who now looked upon themselves as his most devoted adherents, was of course frequent and detailed. He learnt of Abdel Kader's departure for Kawa and Sennar with a large force in February. That town had been besieged by Ahmed el Makashef; but the *pasha* inflicted a defeat on him at Meshra ed Dai, and had raised the siege. Saleh Bey had pursued the rebels as far as Jebel Sekhedi, and had driven them into the waterless plain between that place and Kawa, where numbers perished from thirst. This district is still called by the local people, "*Tibki wa teskut*" (You cry and are silent).

These defeats, however, in no way diminished the *Mahdi's* popularity; they relieved the situation for the soldiers and officials, it is true, but they only put off the evil day which was surely to come. Had attention been paid to Abdel Kader Pasha's advice, the whole situation in the Sudan might have been changed. He was against the despatch of a large expedition to reconquer Kordofan, but recommended the reinforcements coming from Cairo should be garrisoned in strong defensive positions along the White Nile, and that for the time being the rebels should be left to themselves. The military forces at his disposal were quite sufficient to stamp out the revolt in the Gezira (Island) between the Blue and White Niles, and to check the advance of the Mahdists from the west.

Had this plan been adopted, and the rebels been left to themselves, it is more than probable the complete absence of any regulated system of administration would have soon resulted in discord breaking out, and gradually, at a later period, government would have been able to recover the ground it had lost. I certainly could not have preserved authority in Darfur until that time; but even if that province were lost, it would undoubtedly have been the lesser of two evils. However, those at the head of the government in Cairo thought otherwise. The edict went forth that the prestige of the government was to be restored at all costs, and this was to be effected by an army despatched under the English General Hicks, assisted by other European officers; Abel Kader Pasha was recalled, and relieved by Ala ed Din Pasha, formerly Governor-General of the Eastern Sudan. All these facts were known almost at once to the *Mahdi*, and he took good account of them.

Meanwhile Zogal had arrived at El Obeid, where he had received an enthusiastic reception; one hundred guns were ordered to be fired in his honour, and it was reported far and wide that Darfur had surrendered to the ever-victorious *Mahdi*. Zogal's return to Darfur was considered quite a sufficient guarantee for the preservation of the province as a possession of the new ruler; consequently no force was despatched, and the *Mahdi* now directed all all his attention to events on the Nile.

General Hicks shortly after his arrival proceeded with a portion of his force to Kawa, inflicted a defeat on the rebels at Marabia (29 April, 1883), and killed Ahmed el Makashef.

Amongst the various emissaries despatched to different parts of the country was Osman Digna, the former Suakin slave-dealer, who was enjoined to raise the *Jehad* in the neighbourhood of his own town. The *Mahdi* showed much astuteness in selecting this man, who subsequently became so celebrated; and he rightly judged that a local revolt in the Eastern Sudan would in all probability seriously embarrass the Khartum Government, and delay, or perhaps put off altogether, the expedition about to be sent to Kordofan.

The details of the various encounters between this redoubtable *emir* and the government troops are too well known to require more than a mere passing reference here; suffice it to say that the operations in the eastern districts, although successful to the Mahdists, did not have the effect of causing the government to alter their intention in regard to the Kordofan expedition, and early in September, 1883, the ill-fated Hicks left Khartum for Duem, on the White Nile, where he joined Ala ed Din Pasha, who had been instructed to accompany the expedition.

Surely the situation in Kordofan must have been misunderstood by the Cairo authorities if they imagined that, by the despatch of this expedition, they would succeed in overturning the *Mahdi*, who was then supreme ruler of these western districts in which every man was his most devoted adherent. Did they not realise that the annihilation of Rashed, Shellali, and Lutfi, as well as the fall of Bara, El Obeid, and a host of other towns had placed the *Mahdi* in possession of a far larger number of rifles than those disposed of amongst Hicks's force of ten thousand men? Were they not aware that these rifles were now in the hands of men who thoroughly understood how to use them,—men who had been owners of Bazingers, who were elephant and ostrich hunters, and had now at their command contingents of reliable fighting material?

Besides, were there not now enrolled under the *Mahdi's* banners thousands of regulars and irregulars who had been formerly in the government service? Did they imagine for a moment that all these men, when the chance came, intended to desert and join Hicks? No; they seemed to realise nothing of this, and, on completely wrong presumptions, they risked the lives of thousands. Surely there were those amongst the government advisers who had sufficient knowledge of the Sudan to realise how fully the negro proverb applied in this matter: "*Illi beyakhud ummi hua abuya*" (He who marries my mother is my father). The *Mahdi* had conquered the country, and had thus metaphorically married their mother; him, therefore, they had fully accepted as their lord and master. What do those people care about good actions and kindnesses previously done to them? I do not, of course, deny that to this general rule there are not exceptions; yet unquestionably my remarks, severe as they are, apply to the majority.

Ten thousand men in square formation, with six thousand camels in their midst, were to march through districts overgrown with vegetation and grass taller than a man's height; at most they could not see more than two hundred or three hundred yards to their front, in the little open patches where the sparse population had cultivated small clearings. They must be ready at any moment for the attack of an enemy far more numerous and as well armed as themselves, besides being infinitely better fighters, and who to this day pride themselves on their bravery and headlong dash. Along almost the entire route by which the army was to march there were scarcely any wells, though plenty of stagnant rain-pools; and when they had drunk up the water in them, what were they then to do?

Had they adopted the northern road, *via* Gebra and Bara, they would at least have had the advantage of open ground and a good supply of water at certain places, which, if insufficient, could, with modern appliances, have been made amply sufficient for the whole force. At the same time the support of the powerful Kababish tribe against the Mahdists would have been assured, and the enormous train accompanying the force could thus have been greatly diminished.

Six thousand camels, huddled together in the centre of a square, presented a perfect forest of heads and necks; it was impossible for a bullet fired by one of the enemy from behind a tree to altogether miss this gigantic target: if it failed to strike in front, it would most certainly have its billet in the centre or rear. Then again an advance might have been made by detachments, and the great baggage-train left under strong guard at either Duem or Shatt, the men merely advancing in light marching order, clearing the road north, south, and west, and establishing a military post whenever they had subdued a district. Of course this plan would have taken some time—perhaps a year—to execute; but there was no hurry. Then internal dissensions were rife,— Hicks and his European officers on the one side; Ala ed Din Pasha, his officials, and most of the Egyptian officers on the other.

And were not the troops composed mostly of the disbanded rabble of Arabi Pasha's army, which had just been defeated by the British? General Hicks no doubt fully understood matters; and, replying to a question put to him by one of his friends at Duem as to what he thought of the situation, he replied quietly, "I am like Jesus Christ in the midst of the Jews." Still, he marched off; perhaps he thought that if he refused to advance, his honour might be impugned.

Slowly moved the great mass of men and animals onward; the few inhabitants who lived in this part of the country had long since fled. Now and then in the far distance Arabs were seen watching the advance, and then disappearing from view. On one occasion Hicks, looking through his glasses, observed some horsemen amongst the trees; halting the square, he ordered a division of irregular cavalry to advance and attack them. A few minutes later they returned in hopeless confusion; they had lost some killed and many wounded, and reported they had been attacked by a greatly superior force. Hicks then despatched Colonel Farquhar with half a battalion of regulars to examine the spot where the skirmish had taken place. He reported that he found six cavalrymen lying dead, shot in the back; they had been completely stripped, but nothing was to be seen of the "powerful enemy;" there were the hoof-marks of at most ten horses, and no doubt by these the cavalry division had been put to flight.

The following day three horsemen again appeared in sight, when Colonel Farquhar, accompanied only by his servants, galloped at them, killing two, and bringing in the third a prisoner. I was told of both these episodes by the survivors of the expedition, and they related how the huge square crawled forward like a tortoise. Under the circumstances it was impossible to send out the camels to graze; they had to eat anything they could pick up in the square, and that was very little; of course they died in quantities. They used to eat even the straw pads of their saddles, and consequently the hard wood came down on their haunches and galled them till they became in a truly pitiable condition; still they dragged along, carrying not only their own loads, but those of their broken-down companions in misery.

No doubt Colonel Farquhar, Baron Seckendorff, Major Herlth, the other European, and some of the principal Egyptian officers did all they could to help General Hicks in this critical situation, but the bulk of the army appeared to be utterly regardless of the impending catastrophe. Poor Vizetelly made his sketches, and O'Donovan wrote his diary; but who was to send them home to those who were so anxiously awaiting them?

No sooner did the *Mahdi* learn that the expedition had started than he again sent proclamations to all the tribes, summoning them instantly to the *Jehad*, with the usual promises of reward to those who obeyed, and of punishment to those who hung back. Quitting El Obeid himself, he encamped under an enormous Adansonia tree near the town, and there he awaited the approach of the Egyptians; his *khalifas* and *emirs* followed his example, and soon a gigantic camp of *tukuls* (straw huts) was formed. Reviews were held daily, war-drums beaten, guns fired, and men and horses trained in all sorts of exercises, in preparation for the great battle. The Emirs Haggi Mohammed Abu Girga, Omar Wad Elias Pasha, and Abdel Halim Mussaid had already been sent to Duem to watch the enemy's advance and cut their communications; but they were strictly forbidden to attack the main body of the army. Before leaving, the real condition of the advancing force was known, and they begged the *Mahdi's* permission to attack it, but it was refused.

Shortly before the expedition reached Rahad, Gustav Klootz, a German non-commissioned officer, formerly Baron Seckendorff's, and latterly Mr. O'Donovan's, servant, foreseeing the almost certain annihilation of the force, deserted, with the intention of joining the *Mahdi*. Ignorant of the country, he wandered about, and the next morning was found by a small party of Mahdists, who were about to kill him; but he endeavoured to make them understand, in his broken

Arabic, that he wanted to be taken to the *Mahdi*, and, after robbing him of all he possessed, he was sent under escort to El Obeid, three days distant. Although clothed only as a servant, thousands of people crowded round to see this English general who had come to ask for terms of peace. He was brought before the *Mahdi*, and, through the other Europeans present, was questioned about the state of the expedition. Gustav did not hesitate to say that it could not be worse, and that neither courage nor harmony existed amongst its ranks. Naturally this news greatly pleased the *Mahdi*; but Gustav added that the army would not submit without a fight, and that in all probability it would be annihilated. Immensely cheered by this information, the *Mahdi* now summoned Gustav to be converted to Islam, in which he of course readily acquiesced, and he was then handed over for further care to Osman Wad el Haj Khaled.

So confident of victory had the *Mahdi* become after Gustav's statement that he had hundreds of summonses written out and distributed along the road, calling on Hicks and his officers to surrender. Of course they were left unanswered; but at the same time they had their effect on many who were concerned about their own safety. Others, on the contrary, used these papers in a manner which so irritated the *Mahdi* that for long he visited his wrath on the unfortunate survivors who had dared to put to such contemptuous uses documents in which divinely inspired words were written.

Prior to his departure from Duem, Hicks had been informed by the government that he would be joined *en route* by six thousand men from Jebel Tagalla, as well as some hundreds of Habbania Arabs; and he daily expected to meet these, and thus revive the flagging courage of his demoralised men. But he waited in vain,—not a man came to him, nor did he ascertain a word of news. On quitting Rahad he advanced to Aluba in Dar Ghodayat, in the hope of obtaining an abundant supply of water there; and on the 3rd November he reached Kashgeil, some thirty miles southeast of El Obeid.

Meanwhile the *Mahdi* had worked up his fanatical followers to a pitch of the wildest enthusiasm, and had told them the Prophet had announced to him that on the day of battle they would be accompanied by twenty thousand angels, who would attack the unbelievers. On 1st of November he quitted El Obeid for Birket, where his followers, uniting with the force previously despatched to watch the square, now worried the tired and thirsty Egyptians incessantly. On the 3rd November Abu Anga and his Black Jehadia, concealed in

A Dervish Emir.

the thick forest and broken ground, poured a continuous fire on the square, which was forced to halt and *zariba*; and here human beings and animals, huddled together, offered a target which none could fail to hit. Every moment a weary man, horse, camel, or mule would fall to the bullet of an invisible enemy; and for hours this decimation continued, whilst the wretched troops suffered agonies from thirst, and were unable to move in any direction. It was not till the afternoon that the enemy drew off just out of rifle range, and from this position kept careful watch on the square, as a cat would play with a mouse.

Their losses had been insignificant; one or two *emirs*, amongst them the son of Elias Pasha, had fallen,—and no wonder! his fanaticism had induced him to dash up almost alone to within a yard of the *zariba*. How terrible must have been the feelings of poor Hicks! Instead of water, his wretched men received a hail of lead,—yet only a mile off there was a large pool of rain water; but none in that doomed square knew the country, and even had they known, it was now too late to reach it. Abu Anga and his men, under cover of darkness, crept close up to the *zariba*, and all night long poured an incessant fire into this seething mass of men and animals. Utterly demoralised, poor Hicks's troops moaned, "*Masr fein, ya Sitti Zenab dilwakti waktek!*" (Where is Egypt! Oh, our Lady Zenab, now is your time to help us!) while the hardy Blacks, lying flat on the ground within a few yards of the zariba, unharmed by the shower of bullets which passed overhead, would answer back "*Di el Mahdi el muntazer*" (This is the expected *Mahdi*).

The next morning (4th November), Hicks continued the advance, leaving behind him a heap of dead and dying and a few guns, the teams of which had been killed; but ere he had proceeded a mile, he was attacked by at least one hundred thousand wild fanatics concealed amongst the trees. In a moment the square was broken, and a wholesale massacre took place. The European officers, with a few Turkish cavalry, alone attempted to make a stand under the wide-spreading branches of a large *Adansonia* tree; but, attacked on all sides, they were eventually killed almost to a man. The heads of Baron Seckendorff (who wore a full, light-coloured beard) and General Hicks were cut off and sent to the *Mahdi*, who at once summoned Klootz (now known as Mustafa) to identify them; but this seemed hardly necessary, as it was well known they had been killed.

With the exception of two or three hundred who had escaped death by hiding themselves under the heaps of dead bodies, the entire force had been annihilated. Little mercy was shown; a few of the survivors were pardoned, but the majority of them were subsequently executed. Ahmed ed Dalia, the *Mahdi's* executioner, told me that he and Yakub, Khalifa Abdullahi's brother, with a few hundred horsemen, came across a party of about one hundred Egyptians who showed fight. Through Dalia, Yakub sent them a message that their lives would be spared if they gave up their arms; but no sooner had they done so than he and his men, calling them unfaithful dogs, charged, and killed everyone.

One Egyptian owed his life entirely to his presence of mind; becoming separated from the rest, he fled, but was followed by some Gellabas, who caught him up. "Do not kill me, O friends of the *Mahdi*," he cried, "I know an art which will make you all wealthy men." Their cupidity now aroused, they spared him, and promised to do him no harm if he would tell them his secret. "Certainly I shall do so," he answered. "You have spared my life, you deserve to know my secret; but I am too exhausted to tell you now, take me before your master the *Mahdi*, whom I long to behold; let me seek his pardon, and then I shall have rest and be able to make myself useful to you." Taking him in their midst, they brought him before the *Mahdi*, to whom they explained he was a man who had long since been convinced of his Divine mission, but had not succeeded in coming to him before; he was pardoned, and swore to become henceforth his most devoted adherent.

No sooner was he dismissed from the presence of the *Mahdi*, than his captors surrounded him, and insisted on knowing his secret. Sitting on the ground, he now said quite simply, "I used to be a cook, and know how to make very good sausages." Irritated and insulted to a degree, the men would now have killed him; but he at once made his way to the *Mahdi*, told him what had occurred, and begged for his protection. The *Mahdi* laughingly called his would-be persecutors his compatriots, and ordered them to take every care of their fellow-countryman.

After this immense victory, the *Mahdi* and his *khalifas* now returned with their troops to Birket, literally drunk with success.

Several *emirs* and their men had been left on the battlefield to collect the plunder and bring it to the Beit el Mal. The thousands upon thousands of dead bodies which lay piled up in heaps, were divested of every stitch of clothing. Sometime later the note-books of Colonel Farquhar and Mr. O'Donovan were sent to me. I read all they contained most carefully, and terribly sad reading it was! They

The Death of Hicks Pasha.

both wrote much about the discord that existed, and of the quarrel between General Hicks and Ala ed Din Pasha. Farquhar attacked his chief somewhat severely for his military mistakes. Both had foreseen what had now occurred, and Farquhar reproached him bitterly for having ever started with a force whose condition and *morale* were such as to warrant certain disaster.

The European officers got little assistance; apparently one of the few Egyptian officers who helped them was a certain Abbas Bey. One passage in Colonel Farquhar's diary I well remember; he wrote, "I spoke to Mr. O'Donovan today, and asked him where he thought we should be eight days hence? 'In Kingdom-Come,' was his reply." O'Donovan's journal was also written in much the same strain; he was greatly annoyed about Klootz's flight, and quoted it as an instance of the general feeling existing in the force. "What must be the condition of an army," he remarked, "when even a European servant deserts to the enemy?" In another passage he wrote, "I make my notes and write my reports, but who is going to take them home?"

Some fifteen days afterwards, when all the plunder had been deposited in the Beit el Mal, the *Mahdi* returned to El Obeid. Besides the guns, machine-guns, and rifles, a considerable sum of money had been found; but quantities of loot were carried off by the Arabs, in spite of the barbarous punishments for theft enacted by Ahmed Wad Suleiman: it was no uncommon thing for a thief to have both his right hand and left foot cut off. The cunning blacks had secreted quantities of arms and ammunition in the forests and in their own camps, which at a later period proved very useful to them.

Nothing could have exceeded the savage grandeur of the *Mahdi's* triumphal entry into El Obeid after the battle. As he passed along, the people threw themselves on the ground and literally worshipped him. There is not the slightest doubt that by his victory at Shekan, the *Mahdi* had now the entire Sudan at his feet. From the Nile to the Red Sea, from Kordofan to the frontiers of Wadai, all looked to this holy man who had performed such wonders, and they eagerly awaited his next move. Those who had been already convinced of his divine mission were now of course more than ever his ardent supporters, and spread his fame far and wide; those who had doubted, doubted no longer; and the few who in their hearts understood the imposture, decided amongst themselves that if government was not strong enough to send a force sufficient to uphold its authority even in the Nile districts, they must, against their own convictions, side with the stronger.

Several Europeans and some Egyptians living in the large cities and towns now realised the seriousness of the situation, and lost no time in making the best of their way out of the doomed country, or at any rate despatched north as much as they could of their portable property, well knowing that it was impossible to stay any longer in the Sudan, across which the *Mahdi's* hands now stretched from east to west.

CHAPTER 9

The Fall of Darfur

By this time I had recovered from my disease (*filaria medenensis*), and felt strong enough to undertake another expedition; but the number of my trusted followers had sadly diminished, and our stock of rifle ammunition was getting very low. Said Bey Guma still affirmed that it was impossible for him to send me any from Fasher, owing to the fact that the Zayedia and Maheria Arabs had begun to show signs of defection, and had been raiding cattle in the neighbourhood of the town, which they had refused to restore.

All my hopes were now centred in the success of the Hicks expedition. Fortunately at that time I knew nothing of the route they had chosen, nor of the demoralised condition of the force. For almost a year I had received no news direct from Khartum, and latterly, in order to keep up the spirits of the men, I had to have recourse to stratagem, by asserting that I had received news of great victories for the government forces. These scraps of news I of course concocted myself, and wrote out in the form of messages, which when received were read out with great *éclat* before the assembled troops, and were greeted by the salute of guns and general rejoicings.

As a matter of fact, about this time I did receive a little slip of paper from Ala ed Din Pasha, informing me that His Highness the Khedive had officially appointed me commandant of the troops in Darfur, and that it was the intention of the Government to send a strong force to chastise the rebels and re-establish authority. I despatched copies of this note to Fasher and Kebkebia, with orders that it should be read publicly and salutes fired. I gave the bearer of the letter a public reception, and loaded him with presents; he announced that when he left Khartum the expedition was being prepared, and described the force as certain to be victorious. Those who really knew, hesitated to credit the glowing accounts of the appearance of the troops; but at the same time their hearts were full of glad expectation.

A few days later, Khaled Wad Imam, whom I had sent to Kordofan to collect news, returned, and gave me a verbal message from Zogal, as the latter thought it inadvisable to write; he sent me his best regards, and confirmed the news just received as to the intention of the government to despatch an expedition against the *Mahdi*. Khaled, however, told me privately that many refugees had reached El Obeid from Khartum, and had reported that several vultures had been seen hovering over the troops when they were out practising manoeuvres; and that this was a most unlucky omen for their success. He then proceeded to give me a detailed account of the *Mahdi* and his doings, and after a time I had little doubt that at heart he had become one of his adherents; but I took good care not to let him see what I had discovered, and thanked him for his loyalty and good service; at the same time I gave secret instructions that he should be carefully watched.

A few days afterwards a man was intercepted wandering off to Shakka, bearing a letter from Khaled to Madibbo, in which he told him to be prepared to meet him shortly, in order to aid him in his enterprise. I was also informed by my servants, who were friendly with Zogal's household, and to whom I gave money, in order to give the latter presents, that Khaled was really Zogal's secret and confidential agent, and was always at his house in the fort, where he made himself completely at his ease; that he had privately warned Zogal's wives to be ready to fly with him, as the people in Dara were soon to endure hard times; but that the women had refused to obey the summons, and had made a great commotion.

I now ordered Khaled to be seized and brought before me, he admitted he had received Zogal's orders to take his wives away to some safe refuge beyond my jurisdiction, and his two special ones he had ordered to be brought to him in Kordofan. It was on this account he had written to Madibbo.

It was now abundantly clear to me that Zogal, influenced by his relative's enormous successes, had definitely decided to join him, and had thus broken the solemn agreement between him and myself. I now sent for Zogal's brother, Fiki Nur, and some of his relatives, and in the presence of the *kadi*, the commandant and officers, I openly explained the situation, telling them that their relative was now disloyal to government and had broken his promise, and that therefore I considered they were all of his opinion and in consequence quite untrustworthy. Of course they denied it; but I had them all arrested, placed Khaled in chains, and had his and Zogal's property confiscated and removed to the Beit el Mal, while that of the other persons arrested was sequestrated.

Sending the *kadi* to Zogal's house, I told him to inform the women that they should stay where they were, and I should have them cared for as before; his Bazingers, however, I incorporated with the government forces. Amongst those arrested was Zogal's son-in-law, Idris, who, being of a different tribe, I proposed releasing; but he refused, and said he preferred to go to prison with his relatives. Before being marched off, he asked to be allowed to speak to me privately, and then told me that, according to the custom of the country, it would be most dishonourable for him not to go to prison with the rest of the family, but he wished to assure me of his absolute loyalty. He then informed me that Zogal, before his departure, had secretly assembled the three officers whom I imagined to be most loyal to me, and they had sworn to him that should he send them news that Mohammed Ahmed was really the *Mahdi*, they would all join him. I thanked him for this most important information, the truth of which I had little reason to doubt, and at his own request I allowed him to go to prison with the rest.

My difficulties were now increasing daily, one might almost say hourly. Zogal's disloyalty did not disturb me very much, as I had long suspected it; but I was greatly put about by the unsatisfactory news of the state of the expeditionary force. Zogal was, I knew, an astute man; had the news from Khartum been really disquieting to the *Mahdi*, I felt sure that he would have stayed at El Obeid, according to our arrangement, to watch events; but now he had intentionally broken faith with me. Could it be that he had been befooled by the *Mahdi's* doctrines and preaching? I wish I could have thought this possible, but I knew him too well. He was, so to speak, playing his cards, with the absolute conviction that he would win; and so he did.

Madibbo now collected a force of horsemen and Bazingers, and advanced to Karshu, a day's journey south of Dara, where he desolated the country and derided the Beni Helba for their timidity. Taking fifty horsemen and one hundred and fifty regulars, I marched out from Dara at night and surprised Madibbo at sunrise. He was completely unprepared for this sudden attack, and barely escaped with his life on a horse which he mounted barebacked; but his entire camp fell into my hands, and we captured his well-known copper drums. Unfortunately Mohammed Bey Tia, one of my best and most faithful officers, and who was ever to the front in pursuit, was shot dead by some Bazingers hidden behind the trees; I had also a few men killed and several wounded. But although we had scored a success, we could not be said to have inflicted a heavy defeat on our enemies; we had brushed them off as one drives flies off meat, only to let them settle again.

A few days after my return to Dara news arrived that the Mima Arabs had attacked the military post on the road to Fasher, the garrison of which had been reduced by Said Bey Guma to thirty men, all of whom had been killed. Said Bey informed me that he had despatched three hundred and fifty regulars and four hundred horsemen under Omar Wad Darho to chastise them and re-occupy the post; but the messenger who brought this letter, and who had the greatest difficulty in reaching me, reported that the Arabs were collected in considerable force, and were ready to attack the expedition on its arrival.

A few days later, the faithful Muslem Wad Kabbashi, Sheikh of Hilla Shieria, brought me the mournful news of the complete overthrow of Darho and his men. It appeared that Darho had advanced against the Mima at Woda, where they had been joined by the Khawabir, Birket, and Manasera Arabs. He had begun the attack with his horsemen, who, driven back, retired in headlong flight on the infantry square, followed by an overwhelming number of Arabs; the regulars, firing alike on friend and foe, were scattered by this living avalanche, and twelve only had escaped the slaughter, while of the four hundred horsemen, one hundred and eighty were saved; the gun, arms, and ammunition were all lost, and the road between Fasher and Dara was now completely cut.

It was of immediate necessity to communicate with Fasher; but I had the greatest difficulty in procuring messengers to take a letter to Said Bey Guma, ordering him—if he had not already done so—to at once make all preparations for defence, buy up all the available corn in the town, and, if possible, carry out my previous instructions to withdraw the Om Shanga garrison.

About a month previous to this event I had proposed to my officers to abandon Dara and retire on Fasher; but my suggestion had been unanimously vetoed. The question had of course two sides to it, and as I clung ardently to the hope that the expedition from Khartum would succeed in relieving us, I did not force the project. Should the Egyptian army defeat the *Mahdi*, then the whole of Darfur would be saved; if, on the other hand, it should fail, then how could we at Fasher stand against the whole Sudan? My ammunition was running very low, and

I was puzzled as to how to replenish my waning stock. I had sufficient powder and shells, but lead was my difficulty. However, I refilled the empty Remington cases, by melting down the bullets for the percussion guns and muskets, of which a small quantity still remained, and I also made copper bullets out of the supply of that metal which was in store from the mines of Hofret en Nahas, and which I augmented by buying up the bracelets and anklets of the Black women who much affected copper ornaments.

Muslem Wad Kabbashi now brought in news that Abo Bey, at the head of some Mima and Khawabir Arabs, was encamped near Shieria. I was unfortunately at this time suffering from fever, and was too weak to sit on a horse; but I could think of no one to whom I could intrust a large command, and therefore decided to send Kuku Agha, a brave Sudanese, with only eighty men to attack Abo Bey, then only eight hours distant from Dara. Muslem Wad Kabbashi offered his services as guide, and they left that evening at sunset with our best wishes for their success. The following evening Wad Kabbashi returned wounded, accompanied by only ten men.

"Where are Kuku Agha and the soldiers?" said I, in a state of considerable agitation.

"Scattered or killed," he calmly answered. "But do not distress yourself, several are following after me; I left in all haste to bring you the news."

"But how did it occur? Tell me," I said.

He now seated himself on the edge of my carpet, so as not to soil it with his blood, and began: "We marched all night with only one short halt; but Abo Bey, who had been largely reinforced the previous day, got news of our coming, and, ordering his camp-fires to be lighted, he went into ambush on our line of march. Towards dawn he attacked us suddenly, when we were quite unprepared. In the dark I became separated from Kuku Agha, who was making for some rising ground to the north, whilst I began retiring to the south, with a few soldiers who had collected around me. Alternately fighting and retiring, I at last reached here, and I hope that Kuku Agha is following with the remainder of the men."

Two days passed in anxious expectancy; only four men came in, and there was now no doubt that the rest had perished.

Omar Wad Darho's defeat, followed by this last disaster now greatly encouraged the rebels; and those who had been previously held back by fear, joined *en masse*. Muslem Wad Kabbashi brought his family into Dara, saying he preferred to conquer or die with us. Hassan Wad Saad Nur, whose pardon, it will be remembered, I had procured in Khartum, and whom I had brought with me on my own guarantee to Dara, to whom I had given a house just outside the fort, and, when his horse died of disease, I had given him another, and who, being a native of the place, I had intrusted with procuring news, now sadly disappointed me. Unmindful of all the benefits I had bestowed on him, under the pretence of visiting a relative he mounted the horse I had given him, and rode straight to El Obeid, where he became one of the *Mahdi's* faithful followers.

Madibbo, enraged at the loss of his precious war-drums, which in the Sudan counts as a disgraceful defeat, now collected all his Arabs, and sent word to his neighbours to join him in laying siege to Dara. For a long time past, communication with Khartum had become impossible, the Mahdists were fully on the alert, and any men I attempted to send with letters were invariably intercepted. On one occasion, when fighting against the Beni Helba Arabs, I managed to send a letter to Egypt by a caravan marching along the Arbaïn road to Assiut. But now the various methods of concealment which I had successfully employed, such as fixing letters between the soles of shoes or sandals, soldering them into the inside of ablution water-bottles, or placing them in hollow spear staves, had all been discovered.

One morning, whilst inspecting the fort, I noticed some soldiers giving a donkey medical treatment. It was lame in the foreleg; and, having thrown it on the ground, they proceeded to make an incision in the shoulder, in which they placed a small piece of wood, so as to tighten the skin, across which they made several transverse slits, and then, taking out the stick, poured in powdered *natron*. The idea at once struck me that I might conceal a letter in this way under the skin. I therefore procured a good-sized donkey, and, in the privacy of my own house, I repeated the operation I had just seen performed, inserting in the first cut a small note describing the situation, which I enclosed in a goat's bladder. The entire size of the communication in its cover did not exceed that of a postage stamp. I then sewed up the wound with silk thread, and the donkey walked without the smallest difficulty.

The man to whom I intrusted this mission subsequently told me that he had delivered the packet to Ala ed Din Pasha at Shatt a day or two before the expedition started for El Obeid, and the latter had told the messenger a reply was unnecessary, but that he should accompany the force to El Obeid, whence he would despatch him to me with a letter.

The various tribes, obedient to Madibbo's summons, had now collected a day's march from Dara. Abdullahi Om Dramo, Sheikh of the Messeria Arabs, alarmed that he should lose his property, had unwillingly joined Madibbo, and it was through him I received this information. Ismail Wad Barnu and Bakr el Begawi had also come to Dara with their families for protection, and had constructed a small zariba for themselves about six hundred yards from the fort, which the rebels had attempted one night to attack, but had been driven off, with the assistance of some soldiers. I was now, however, in a sorry plight as regards ammunition. The total in charge of the men and in the magazines amounted to twelve packets per rifle; and if I had attempted to risk a fight, at least half would have been at once expended. Relief I knew was still far off, and the question was how to hold out till then with this slender quantity of cartridges.

In order to gain time, I now had recourse to the following stratagem. Taking aside Om Dramo, whom I knew to be loyal to me, I told him to go to the rebels, and as it were on his own initiative, and without my knowledge, suggest to them they should propose an armistice. The same evening Om Dramo returned, and informed me that the enemy were in great strength, that the *Mahdi* had summoned them to the *Jehad*, and they called upon me to surrender. I told him to return to them and say that I was prepared to capitulate; but I would not agree to my life or that of my soldiers being intrusted to the hands of Arabs against whom I had been continuously fighting for more than a year. I said, however, that should the *Mahdi* despatch a special delegate to me, I was ready to make the necessary conditions of peace. Om Dramo left me with the promise that he would do his utmost to induce them to accept my proposition, and I also agreed that should a parley be necessary, I was prepared to meet them under the large *Adansonia* tree, a few hundred yards from the fort. Some hours later Om Dramo returned radiant, and told me that the Arab chiefs, who had now been appointed *emirs*, fully concurred in my proposal, and were ready to meet me under the tree; Madibbo had alone dissented, and urged the siege to be continued until I should be forced to surrender.

I arranged for the meeting to take place at sunrise the following morning, and made a solemn oath to Om Dramo that should we not arrive at an understanding, the lives of all the *emirs* would be perfectly safe, and they should be allowed to return unmolested; as an equivalent I demanded that the *emirs* should come to the meeting quite alone.

Early the next morning my faithful intermediary arrived, and told me the chiefs had come; I therefore at once went out, accompanied only by my two servants. The *kadi* and Farag Effendi begged to be allowed to go with me; but I thought it would give the Arabs greater confidence if I went alone. I therefore told them to wait in one of the batteries about four hundred yards from the tree.

On arrival at the rendezvous, Om Dramo brought forward his friends Abo Bey, of the Berti tribe, Mohammed Bey Abu Salama, of the Maalia, Helu Wad Gona, of the Beni Helba, and Hamed Wad Nuer, of the Habbania. All of them shook hands with me cordially, and we took our seats just as if nothing had happened between us. I now ordered my boys to hand round dates, not alone with the object of showing them hospitality, but also I wished them to know that I still indulged in these luxuries, in spite of the hard times. I then inquired for Madibbo, and they replied that he had refused to come to the meeting, but perhaps if we arrived at some definite arrangement, he might join the majority. I explained that I was ready to submit to the *Mahdi*, but I had no intention of surrendering myself and my people to the Arab tribes.

"Tell me now," said I, well knowing how jealous they were of each other, "to which of you should I hand over my arms and my horses?" They replied that they were just as before; that is to say, each one head of his own tribe, independent of the other, but at the same time all fighting in the common cause of the *Mahdi*. After a long palaver, it was at last agreed that I should send a letter to the *Mahdi*, announcing my submission, by the hands of one of my own people, who should be accompanied by two of their delegates. All should proceed together to El Obeid. On Abo Bey's suggestion, hostilities at Om Shanga were to cease, and it was further agreed that the delegate sent by me should be either a Turk or an Egyptian.

I suggested a certain Mohammed el Gretli, who was well known to them. He had formerly been a *kavass*, and later a leader of twenty-five horsemen; he had a light complexion, long fair moustache, and had also been employed as tax-collector; in him the Arabs concluded they had secured an influential man. Pending the *Mahdi's* reply, it was agreed there should be an armistice, during which the various tribes should retire to their districts, and all hostilities should cease, while the ground in front of the fort should be utilised as before as the market-place, in which all business transactions could be conducted without let or hindrance. By this arrangement I hoped to gain time to gather a considerable supply of corn, cattle, etc. We both solemnly swore on the *Koran* to each adhere faithfully to our respective pledges, and then separated, to meet again at two o'clock to read the letter to the *Mahdi* and despatch it forthwith.

When I returned, the *kadi* and Farag Effendi were greatly pleased with the agreement; and, directing Gretli to be ready to start, I proceeded to write two letters, one to the *Mahdi*, and the other to the garrison of Om Shanga.

At the appointed time we again met under the tree; but Madibbo was still absent, and on inquiry I was told that he entirely disagreed with the arrangement, and charged me with merely attempting to delude and cheat them. All the other *emirs*, however, declared they were perfectly ready to adhere to the conditions to which we had sworn, and that if Madibbo did not care to join, he was free to stay away. My letter to the *Mahdi* ran as follows:—

> In the name of the Most Merciful God. From the slave of his God, Abdel Kader Salatin (Slatin) to Sayed Mohammed el *Mahdi*. May God protect him and confound his enemies! Amen! For a long time I have been defending the province which the Government confided to my care, but God's will cannot be fought against. I therefore hereby declare that I submit to it (God's will) and to you, under the condition that you send one of your relatives, with the necessary authority to rule this country, and to whom I shall hand it over. I demand a pledge from you that all men, women, and children within the fort shall be spared. Everything else I leave to your generosity.

My letter to the Om Shanga garrison, demanded by Abo Bey, ran thus:—

> To the Commander of the Garrison at Om Shanga:
> Circumstances have compelled me to write to the *Mahdi* regarding the surrender of Darfur, under certain conditions. Abo Bey, who takes this letter to you, will raise the siege; and you are hereby instructed to cease from all hostilities. I forbid you, in my capacity as commandant of the troops, to hand over to the enemy any war material, except in my presence.
> (Signed)   Governor-General of Darfur
> and Commandant of the Troops,
> Slatin.

Abo Bey objected to this last sentence; but when I explained to him that the main point was that I submitted to the *Mahdi* only, he was satisfied. Before Gretli left, I told him to point out to the *Mahdi* that the surrender of Darfur before the impending battle was fought would probably bring upon him a number of difficulties from which, at such a time, he would prefer to be free, and I also warned him to tell Zogal. As a last request, Abo Bey and Mohammed Abu Salama asked me to liberate Zogal's relations from prison; but this I told them the *Mahdi's* deputy alone could do. Our palaver having ended to the complete satisfaction of all parties, the meeting broke up, and we separated.

Gretli now proceeded to the *emir's* camp; at sunset we heard the beating of the war-drums announcing his departure, and soon afterwards the besiegers quitted the neighbourhood of Dara. I sent spies to see if Madibbo was still staying behind; but they returned, and reported that he had gone with the rest. It appeared that he had only decided to go at the last moment.

Communication with Fasher was still interrupted; but sometime afterwards I received a letter from Said Bey Guma to the effect that although the tribes were in revolt, they had not attacked the town, but had prevented all communications with the outside world.

The days which now passed were for me full of anxious expectancy. I knew that by this time Hicks's force must have almost reached El Obeid, and that the decisive battle, on the result of which hung all our hopes and fears, was about to be fought. I used to frequent the market and chat with the people on all the topics of the day. Everyone was aware that a large army was advancing on El Obeid, but none yet knew how it was progressing.

At length, towards the end of November, to my unutterable grief, rumours began to circulate that the army had been defeated, and although they sounded suspiciously near the truth, still we could not absolutely credit them; but a day or two later, definite news was received that the expedition had been annihilated. Gloom settled down on us all. After so many hardships and such constant trouble to at length fall into the hands of the enemy, without the smallest chance of escape! Yet could it be possible the news was grossly exaggerated? A flicker of hope still remained, only to disappear finally when information was received that Zogal had arrived at Om Shanga, and that the garrison had surrendered to him as Mudir Umum el Gharb (Governor-General of the West), appointed by the *Mahdi*.

On the 20th of December, 1883, Mohammed el Gretli arrived at the gate of the fort dressed in a *jibba*, and was brought in to me. He related to me in full detail the heart-rending news of the complete overthrow of the expedition, of which he himself had been a witness; he also brought me a letter from Zogal, calling on me to surrender; and to prove the disaster which had overtaken the Egyptians, he sent me several of the principal officers' commissions, a number of reports on the situation, and the journals of Colonel Farquhar and Mr. O'Donovan. At the same time Gretli informed me that Om Shanga had surrendered, and that Zogal was staying in Bringel; with him were Abderrahman Wad Ahmed Sharfi and Said Abd es Samad, both relatives of the *Mahdi*, besides the Emirs, Omar Wad Elias Pasha, Gabr Wad et Tayeb, Hassan Wad en Nejumi, and several others, accompanied by their *rayas* (flags).

To keep this news secret was quite out of the question; I therefore summoned the Kadi and the leading merchants, and directed Gretli to repeat to them what he had just told me. This over, I sent for the officers in whom I trusted, and told them to talk over the matter between themselves, and come to a decision without my interference, as I should reserve to myself the right of accepting or rejecting their proposals as I thought best.

That evening Farag Effendi and Ali Effendi Tobgi, the commandant of the artillery, told me that the officers had decided to surrender to the *Mahdi* but not to Zogal Bey. They stated their reasons for coming to this decision very simply: everyone, from the highest to the lowest, was now absolutely convinced that we had not the smallest chance of relief; the total force of regulars in Dara amounted to five hundred and ten men, of whom a large number were quite useless; the spirit of the troops was such as to render all idea of eventual success quite out of the question; the ammunition was scarcely sufficient to last out one fight if we were attacked or if we took the offensive. Both the officers pointed out that I should never succeed in getting the men to fight any longer; they had made up their minds to surrender, and they urged that there was now no other course open. I told them I would carefully consider the matter, and would give them an answer the following morning.

That night I did not close my eyes. To think that after all the dangers and difficulties through which we had passed, there was no other course now open but to submit! And after that what was to be our fate?

I reviewed the situation from beginning to end during those sleepless hours. For four years I had struggled alone to uphold the government's authority in the province which had been intrusted to my care,—first against the local revolts, which I had suppressed; and latterly against the great fanatical movement which had attacked the very roots of my administration, and whose canker-worm had spread into the branches, till at length the leaves withering one by one, the tree was all but dead.

In short, this strange fanaticism had thoroughly taken possession of my officers and men; they had openly held out against it as long as it was possible for me to dangle before their eyes the prospect of an immediate reassertion of government authority, through the anticipated success of the Egyptian expedition under Hicks, and the consequent advantages which would accrue to one and all of those who had loyally served the government. By every means in my power I had striven to prove to my officers and men that the government must eventually succeed; but at length the crash had come, and all prospect of relief was absolutely and entirely gone. I had struggled against intrigues from within and without, with what success the reader can judge. With the small amount of ammunition that remained, I might have made a vain struggle for a few hours; but would my officers and men have obeyed my orders? They had no wish and no heart to fight; they knew as well as I did the futility of it; and why should I call on them to sacrifice themselves, and perhaps their wives and children, to a cause to which they were no longer attached?

Looking at the matter entirely from a general point of view, I had no doubt in my own mind that capitulation was not only the right course, but was practically inevitable. Having arrived at this conclusion, I had now to turn to the personal aspect; and the solution of this problem was to me beset with the greatest difficulties. As an officer, the idea of surrender to such an enemy was repulsive in the extreme. I had no fear of my own life; I had risked it sufficiently during the past four years to effectually dispose of any notion that my surrender was occasioned by any want of personal courage,—on that point I felt sure that, if spared, I could without the smallest difficulty vindicate my action to my military superiors; but the very word "surrender" was repellent to me, and doubly so when I thought over the consequences which must follow to me—a European and a Christian—alone amongst thousands and thousands of fanatical Sudanese and others, the meanest among whom would consider himself superior to me.

It is true I had nominally adopted the religion of the country; but this I had done merely as a means of stifling the injurious opinions which I knew existed in the minds of officers and men, that the cause of my defeat lay in my being a Christian. My ruse had succeeded to a greater extent than I had expected, but the proceeding had been a distasteful one to me. I had no pretensions to holding very strict religious views on the expediency or otherwise of the step I had taken; nevertheless, at heart I was, I believe, as good a Christian as the majority of young men of my acquaintance, and that being so, a continuance of the life of religious deception I was then living was by no means a prospect which I appreciated.

Moreover, I was well aware that my surrender would place me absolutely and entirely in the hands of this mock-religious reformer, and that not only should I have to show myself to be a Moslem in the ordinary sense of the term, but to carry out the *rôle* surrender would entail on me, I must be prepared to pursue this religious deception to its fullest extent,—I must become a devotee, and henceforth I must show myself heart and soul a *Mahdist*!

Can anyone imagine that this was a pleasing prospect? Nevertheless, I confess that the religious considerations involved in the step I contemplated—although they weighed with me to no small extent—did not occupy my mind so fully as the considerations in regard to my duty. Generally speaking, I felt it to be my duty to surrender, and make no further sacrifice of life in a cause which could not now, by any possibility, succeed. There was no particular reason, however, why I should voluntarily submit to the indignities and practical slavery which must follow on my personal surrender; to be accessory to my own death occurred to me more than once, but my nature revolted against this thought. I was young, my life during the past four years had been one of anxious responsibility, but of stirring adventure as well, and I had no particular desire to bring it to a close, even with the dark prospect in front of me. God in His mercy had spared me almost miraculously in this constant fighting, and perhaps He would still spare me to be of use to the government I had tried to serve most loyally.

These were the thoughts which were uppermost in my mind when the dark hours of anxious meditation gave place to the first streaks of the dawn of perhaps the most memorable day of my life. Yes, I concluded, there is nothing for it now but submission; I must become, so to speak, the slave of those whom I have governed, I must be obedient to those who in every respect are my inferiors, and I must, above all, be patient: if by a careful practice of these I should succeed in saving my life and eventually recovering my liberty, no doubt the experience which I should gain would be valuable to the government in whose service I still was.

With this determination and resolution I rose, and dressed for the last time for many a long year in the uniform, the honour of which I had done my utmost to uphold, now to be discarded for the *Mahdist* garb, in which I was to play an entirely new part in life; but beneath it would beat a heart as truly loyal as ever to government, and filled with a determination that, come what might, if it were God's will I should be eventually restored to liberty, the strange experiences which it would now be my fate to undergo might be turned to useful account. It was now to be a case of my wits against those of my new masters,—who would win? I did not quail from the contest, though I should have had no little excuse for doing so, could I have scanned the future, and seen before me the long years of servitude, and the double life which I should be compelled to lead, in order to carry through the resolution at which I had now arrived.

The next morning, the two officers arrived; I showed them Zogal's letter, calling on me to surrender peacefully, and to meet him on the 23rd of December at Hilla Shieria, where he would personally hand me the *Mahdi's* letter; he further wrote that, in accordance with his present instructions, my life and those of all the men, women, and children in the fort should be spared, and we should be afforded all protection.

Whilst we were talking over the matter, the orderly officer reported that Abder Rasul Agha, with all the Bazingers, as well as the chief merchant with his family, had deserted the town during the night, with the evident intention of joining the enemy.

This was the last straw. It was absolutely clear to me that further resistance was impossible. I therefore sent for my clerk and dictated to him a letter to Zogal, giving in my submission and that of the garrison, and agreeing to meet him at Hilla Shieria on the 23rd of December; this I handed to Gretli, with instructions to take it to Zogal, who was now to be called Sayed Mohammed Ibn Khaled.

The following day, in the afternoon, I assembled all the officers, and told them that, as further resistance was not possible, I had concurred in their proposals; that I was leaving Dara that evening in order to meet Zogal the next day at Hilla Shieria, and that I would take the *kadi* with me, but would leave the officers to look after the garrison during my absence. In a few words, which seemed to stick in my throat, I thanked them for their loyalty, their readiness to sacrifice their lives in the service of the government, and their adherence to me; then, warmly shaking each of them by the hand, and taking a general leave of the civil officials, I departed.

At midnight, accompanied by my *kavasses*, Kadi Wad el Beshir, Sultan Abakr el Begawi, Ismail Wad Barnu, and Muslem Wad Kabbashi, who remained faithful to the last, I quitted Dara. During my service in Darfur I had had many disagreeable experiences, but this journey was quite the hardest. Not a word passed. We were all fully occupied with our miserable thoughts. At sunset we made a short halt, but the food put before us by the servants remained untouched. Our appetites had gone, so we rode on. As we approached Hilla Shieria, I sent an orderly ahead to see if Zogal had arrived, and he soon returned, stating he had been there since yesterday, and was waiting for me. In a few moments we reached the spot where he was standing, and, jumping off my horse, I advanced to salute him; he pressed me to his heart, and assured me of his entire friendliness, begged me to be seated, and then handed me the *Mahdi's* letter. It merely stated that he had appointed Sayed Mohammed Khaled as Emir of the West, had granted me pardon, that he had commissioned his nephew to treat me with the respect to which my rank entitled me, and to act with leniency and forbearance to all those who were formerly government officials.

After I had finished reading the letter, Zogal informed me that it was entirely owing to his good offices on my behalf that the *Mahdi* had pardoned me, and that he would, of course, do his utmost to help me. I thanked him for his kind sympathy. The *emirs* were then introduced to me: Elias, Tayeb, and Hassan Nejumi I had met before. After partaking of food, Zogal discussed his intended journey to Dara; whilst we were talking, one of my officers, Mohammed Agha Suleiman, arrived, and, without taking the smallest notice of me, went up and greeted Zogal most effusively; I at once recognised him as one of the three officers whom I had been told were "Black Zogal's" (as he was called) secret agents.

Mohammed Khaled, as I must call him in future, now took me aside, and spoke to me about his relatives and his family. I told him that I had left them all well, and that the former were still in arrest. He at once said he quite concurred in the steps I had taken, which of course were in the interests of self-preservation, and best for us both. We then started off, and encamped the same evening near Dara. Several of the inhabitants and officials came out to greet the new governor, already dressed in their Dervish clothes.

During my absence, Mohammed Khaled had directed Abd es Samad, who was at Bringel with the Dervish troops, to move down towards Dara and occupy the buildings to the south of the town, which had formerly belonged to the Vizir Ahmed Shatta. Joined on his march by most of the country people, he had arrived at the appointed place, had established friendly relations with the townspeople and garrison, and had distributed quantities of the new clothing in presents.

That night I again passed almost without closing my eyes. It was Christmas Eve. I thought of home and of the beautiful Church festival which was being celebrated there, whilst I, alone and defeated, was handing over my men and arms to the enemy. In those still hours—they were the saddest in my life—I passed in review all that had happened. More fortunate by far were those who had fallen on the field of honour!

The next morning, Zogal officially received all those who had come out to pay homage to him, and then ordered them and the troops under Abd es Samad to march past. This over, he dismissed his relatives who had come out to greet him, regretting the discomfort they had suffered under arrest, and he then proceeded to his house outside the fort, having, meanwhile, ordered my men to hand over their arms by companies,—a duty which was performed with very scant regard for our feelings. The fort was now garrisoned by Dervish troops, and this completed his occupation of the country. The inhabitants flocked to him to give their oaths of allegiance to the *Mahdi*, and later in the day the troops were paraded by his order, to go through the same ceremony.

Madibbo, who had joined Abd es Samad at Bringel, and had come to Dara with him, followed me home. We shook hands, and I begged him to be seated; he then began: "You seem to be annoyed with me, and accuse me of having broken faith with you: but now listen to me. I was discharged from my position of head Sheikh by Emiliani, and proceeded to the Bahr el Arab, where the *Mahdi's* summons reached me. I am a good Moslem, and therefore I followed him; I beheld the *Mahdi's* divine nature, and listened to his doctrines; I was also present at the marvellous destruction of Yusef Shellali. I therefore believed in him, and am still a believer. You of course trusted in your strength, and did not wish to submit without fighting. We both fought, each seeking his own advantage: I fought against the government, but not against you personally. God knows, I have never forgotten that you were friendly minded to me, therefore let anger depart from your heart and be a brother to me!"

"I am not at all angry at what you have done," I answered, "you are but one among many: and should I have been annoyed with you, your words have quite reconciled me."

"I thank you," said Madibbo. "May God strengthen you, and as He has protected you hitherto, may He continue to protect you!"

"In truth," I replied, "I put my trust in Him. Still it is hard to have to bear all that has now happened; but I suppose it must be!"

"Not so," he answered; "I am only an Arab, but listen to me. Be obedient and patient; practise this virtue, for it is written, '*Allah ma es saberin*' (God is with the patient). However, I have come to ask you something, and my request is this: If you are really a brother to me, then, in token of our friendship, I wish you to accept my favourite horse. You knew him before; he is the *Sakr ed Dijaj* (the Chicken-hawk)." Before I could reply, he had got up and gone outside, and in a few minutes returned, leading his horse, which was the finest and most handsome animal owned by the tribe; he then handed me the leading-rope.

"I do not wish to insult you," I replied, "by refusing to accept your present, but I do not require it; I shall not want to ride much now."

"Who knows?" said the *sheikh*. "*Illi umru tawil bishuf ketir* (He who lives long sees much). You are still young, and may often ride yet,—if not on this horse, then on another."

"You may be right, Madibbo, but now do you accept from me this token of friendship," said I, pointing to his precious war-drums, which my servants took up and handed to him; these drums, it will be remembered, I had taken in the night attack on Kershu. On the drums I also laid a sword which I had taken down from the wall. "Today," said I, "these are mine, and I can offer them to you; tomorrow they may be another's."

"I thank you, and accept them gladly," said the *sheikh*. "Only a short time ago your men captured my war-drums; but, as the Arabs say, '*Er rigal sharrada urrada*' (A man runs away and comes back again),[1] and I may truly say I have fought many times in my life, and sometimes I have run away, then I have returned and have succeeded." Madibbo now ordered his men to carry off his drums, and departed in great delight. His conversation had affected me considerably. So I was now

---

1. More familiarly, "*He who fights and runs away, lives to fight another day.*"

to be "obedient and patient; for he who lives long sees much."

Mohammed Khaled soon sent for me, and informed me that on his arrival at Shieria he had despatched a letter by one of Wad Darho's relatives to Said Bey Guma, summoning him to surrender, and had at the same time sent a certain Abderrahman as his representative. He now called upon me to write officially to him to hand over Fasher and summon everyone to submit. I replied that the clerks were no longer in my service, and that the document could be made out, should he think it necessary, and I would sign it. The orders to this effect were given, I signed them, and Khaled, addressing the letter to the commander of the Fasher garrison, despatched it at once.

The following morning the new governor began his seizure of the state moneys. The inhabitants of Dara, with the exception of all troops below the rank of officer, and myself, being considered as Ghanima,[2] were ordered out of their houses; they were only permitted to take with them a few necessary cooking utensils and the clothes they wore, and were ordered to collect in front of the police-station near the market, whilst their dwellings were ransacked and the contents carried off to the Beit el Mal which was opened in the Mudiria. As no money or jewellery was found, all those suspected of having any were brought before the *emirs*, who ordered them to instantly produce it; and in carrying out the search disgusting cruelties were perpetrated: they flogged mercilessly, beat them with sticks or tied them by the legs head downwards in wells until the rush of blood to the head rendered them unconscious.

Amongst those who exercised more cruelty than the rest was my old Khartum friend Hassan Wad Saad en Nur, whom I reported, in his presence, to Khaled. Hassan instantly turned to me, saying, "Do you still think you are Governor-General of Darfur and can say what you like?" I replied that he should be careful not to go too far, and reminded him that it was I who secured his release from prison, and that the horse he was then riding was mine. To this he answered impudently, "It was God who released me, and it is God, and not you, who has given me your horse to ride."

Khaled, who heard these remarks, angrily ordered him off, and said to me, "Take no notice of him, his father, Saad en Nur, was the *sultan's* slave, and slave-blood always shows itself."

---

2. According to Mohammed Ibn Taher, "*fai*" is booty taken from a country which submits to Islam without resistance, as distinguished from "*Ghanima*," or plunder. The *Mahdi* adopted the "Ghanima" principle entirely.

As we were now alone, I complained to Khaled of the ill-treatment visited on those who had shown complete submission, and I reminded him of his pledge to protect all men, women, and children. "I am not going to put any one to death," answered he, sharply, "but they have no right to the money they are concealing; it is contrary to the arrangement, and it must be taken from them by force." My experiences were beginning. I went home, and here several of the poor people who had been turned out of their houses came and begged me to give them something. I furnished them with a little corn; but since our troubles began I had received no pay, so had no money to offer them.

The male and female servants of the former officials were now distributed amongst the *Mahdi*sts, but all the good-looking young girls were put aside for the *Mahdi* himself.

Seven days after our surrender Khaled informed me that Said Bey Guma had sent the principal officials to make their submission, and that he himself was in the neighbourhood of the town awaiting further orders; he therefore collected his forces and prepared to march out to meet him. The delegates sent by Said Bey Guma were Omar Wad Darho and some of his officers, Hanafi el Koreishi the grand Kadi, and Ali Bey Khabir. Khaled received them with great satisfaction, and one of the clerks, coming forward, presented the documents relating to the transfer of the government to Abderrahman; in these were included the lists of arms and ammunition in store, the number of guns, etc.

Khaled now took his guests into the town and entertained them with the best of everything, pledging himself to preserve, not only their lives and the lives of all the women and children in Fasher, but also, when all the money and valuables were collected, he promised that half would be returned to the owners. The following day, however, it was rumoured that the Fasher garrison had decided not to surrender after all, and in the evening news arrived that Fiki Abderrahman had been warned to leave the city, which he had done, and that all preparations were being made for defence. Khaled now anxiously inquired of the messengers what had occurred to cause this sudden change in Said Bey's intentions; but they replied it was not the doing of Said Bey, but of some of the officers, who had been told by refugees from Dara that their comrades had been badly treated, and they had, therefore, decided to fight to the end.

Khaled now gave orders that all his people should prepare to advance at once on Fasher, including the entire garrison, with their arms and ammunition, with the exception of the officers, whom he ordered to remain behind and to be carefully watched. He waited, however, two days longer, in the hope that he might get different news; but as the first account was further corroborated by some of Darho's men and Ali Khabir's servant, who came in that evening from Fasher, he set out on 3rd January to lay siege to the town, followed by large numbers of men marching by various roads.

On 7th January he, his *emirs*, and the Dara troops under Mohammed Agha Suleiman, reached Wad Beraj, on the outskirts of the town, where they pitched camp. The next day a letter was written which I was obliged to sign, reminding Said Bey Guma and the officers of the agreement they had made to surrender through Omar Wad Darho, Kadi Hanafi, and others. My—or rather Khaled's—letter remained unanswered; for it was quite understood in Fasher that, being now under Khaled, I had no other course open than to obey his orders. The messenger who took the letter was told to warn all those who complained of ill-treatment to come and state to Khaled what they required; and this becoming known to the Fasher garrison, several who had no desire to fight left the fort, and were accepted in the *Mahdis*t camp. Wad Darho's men, who lived outside the fort, also came over to Khaled immediately, and orders were given to begin the siege forthwith; the operations being intrusted to Darho.

I now asked Khaled to be allowed to talk to him privately, and I told him plainly that this opposition on the part of the Fasher garrison was entirely due to their fear of suffering in the same way as the Dara people. This he quite admitted. I then told him I was very unwilling to fight against those who had formerly been under my rule, and, as he was well aware, the events of the last few days had considerably affected my health; I therefore begged to be allowed to return to Dara. In reply to my request he said that were it not that he liked me, he would most certainly have punished me severely for the words I had just uttered; nevertheless, he would allow me to return to Dara, on condition that I pledged myself to abstain from any acts of hostility; at the same time he showed me some letters which had been addressed to me, but which he had opened.

One of them was a reply to my report sent from the Beni Helba country to Cairo regarding the desert road to Assiut. They had been given to some Magharba Arabs to bring to me, and on their entry into the country they had been arrested by the Saidia Arabs and kept as prisoners, and on Khaled's arrival at El Fasher they had been sent on to him. He allowed me to make notes of their contents. The letters were all of old dates. One was from His Highness the Khedive Tewfik Pasha, expressing his complete satisfaction with the services I had rendered, urging me to continue to fulfil with diligence the duties of my position, and telling me that he was despatching an army under Hicks Pasha to subdue the rebels in Kordofan and restore peace. Another was from H. E. Nubar Pasha, Prime Minister, who also expressed satisfaction with my services, and repeated the information about the Hicks expedition. The third was from Zubeir Pasha, who sent me his kind regards, and asked me to make inquiries about the family of his son Suleiman.

As far as I knew, Suleiman had left only one child, who with his mother I had handed over to the care of Omar Wad Darho with instructions to take an early opportunity to send them to Zubeir's relatives on the Nile. The mother, however, preferred to marry one of Darho's relations, and she was charged with bringing up the child. The feelings which I underwent on reading these letters can be better imagined than described. How we had placed all our hopes on the success of the Hicks expedition, and how rudely had those hopes been dashed to the ground! However, I did my best to master my feelings, and handed the letters back to Khaled, who was contentedly smiling at my agitation. "Your *effendina* [the *khedive*] thought he would defeat the *Mahdi*," said he, "but the 'expected one' has turned the tables on him; there are still harder times in store for these deluded Turks and Egyptians."

I smothered the retort which hung on my lips, and said nothing. "Be obedient and patient" was Madibbo's advice; but how difficult it was to follow it!

I then got up and took leave of Khaled, who lost no opportunity of showing me that he was my superior, and then proceeded to Dara without delay. I was really ill, and on my arrival there kept to my house for some days; but the weeping and wailing of the unfortunate people gave me no rest: they had been robbed of all their means of livelihood, and now eked out a miserable and wretched existence as best they could.

Meanwhile the *Mahdi*sts were besieging Fasher, and had taken up their position on the hill to the east of the fort, from which they were separated by the Khor Tendelti; they had taken possession of all the wells, both near the hill, as well as those in the valley. Said Bey Guma was the actual commandant, though the preliminary success of the garrison was principally due to the energy of the two officers, Said Agha el Fula and Ibrahim Agha et Tagalawi. The former had been wounded with me at Shakka, and I had sent him to his family at Fasher to recover; the latter was an exceptionally brave officer, and had considerable influence with the troops.

As there was no water in the fort, the continuance of the siege depended on the possession of the wells. Said Bey Guma disposed of eight hundred and fifty rifles, which were more than were required for the size of the fort; but Khaled was still better off. Nevertheless, the Fasher garrison succeeded, after a sharp contest, in regaining the wells, and the *Mahdists* were forced to retire to Wadi Baraj; here, however, they were reinforced by a portion of the Kebkebia garrison. Adam Amer had surrendered, and had despatched a large party of Bazingers, under Babakr Wad el Haj, with several regulars to Khaled's support; and with this addition to their strength another attack was made, which resulted in the garrison losing the wells.

Several heroic sorties were made; but after a seven days' siege the garrison was obliged to submit, on the 15th of January, and Khaled, the conqueror, entered the ancient capital of his new kingdom. After the arms had been handed over and the fort occupied, the seizure of property began, as at Dara, and similar, if not worse, cruelties were perpetrated on the luckless inhabitants. Said Bey himself was, comparatively speaking, more fortunate than other commanders; the greater part of his property was confiscated, it is true, but he was not maltreated nor insulted, and for the time being he and his family were banished to Kobbé, where he was given a house, and was thus saved the misery of seeing his comrades and inferiors being tormented.

Amongst the latter was a certain Major Hamada Effendi, who, in spite of every effort to make him confess, persisted in declaring that he had no money. One of his female slaves, however, told his persecutors that he had a quantity of gold and silver, but she did not know where he had concealed it. Consequently he was brought before Khaled, who called him an unbelieving dog. Hamada Effendi, losing control of himself, retorted that he was a wretched Dongolawi; and Khaled, furious at this insult, ordered the unfortunate man to be flogged until he confessed the hiding-place of his treasure. For three days in succession he received a thousand lashes a day, but it was all in vain; had he been a block of wood or stone, he could not have stood this awful flogging more doggedly.

To the repeated questions of his tormentors as to where his money was, he merely answered, "Yes, I have concealed money, but it will remain buried in the ground with me." Khaled now ordered the flogging to be stopped, and the poor mangled man was handed over to the Mima Arabs, who were told to guard him; and even they were struck with the resolution of this officer, from whom no amount of torture could wring a confession. Ibrahim Tegalawi, who had been called a "slave" by one of the *emirs*, deliberately shot dead his own wife, his brother, and then himself; Said Agha Fula also preferred to commit suicide than undergo torture. After these occurrences, Khaled gave orders to stop the flogging, and banished the Egyptian officers to various places in the neighbourhood.

Shortly after the fall of Fasher I received a summons from Khaled to join him, and I arrived there early in February; he gave me Said Bey Guma's house to live in, and told me that I might send to Dara for my horses and servants, but as regards the house furniture, that must be passed into the Beit el Mal as an "act of renunciation." I carried out these instructions, and handed over all the property in my house in Fasher to the treasurer of the Beit el Mal, Gaber Wad et Taib, only retaining such things as were absolutely necessary for daily life. I had heard on my arrival here of Hamada's heroism, and sought out the poor old major, whom I found in a truly terrible state.

The gaping wounds from his shoulders to his knees were mortifying rapidly, and his tormentors used to pour over them daily a strong solution of salt and water well seasoned with Sudan pepper, thus hoping to wring a confession from him during the awful pain which ensued. But it was useless; he absolutely refused to utter a word. In desperation I went to Khaled, told him of the poor man's horrible condition, and begged him to allow me to take him to my own house and treat him there. "He is dishonest," said Khaled; "he has concealed money and has publicly insulted me: for this he must die a miserable death."

"For the sake of our old friendship," said I, "I beg and pray you will forgive him and hand him over to me."

"Well," said he at last, "I will if you will prostrate yourself before me."

In the Sudan this is considered a terrible humiliation. The blood rushed to my face: to save my own life I would never do such a thing; but if by this self-sacrifice I could rescue the poor wretched man from his awful sufferings, I ought surely to do so. For a moment I hesitated; then, with a fearful effort of self-control, I knelt down, and laid my hands on his bare feet. He drew them back, raised me up, and, apparently ashamed of having asked such a sacrifice of me, said, "It is only for your sake that I shall liberate Hamada; but you must promise that, should you find out where his treasure is, you will let me know." I promised to do so, and he then sent a man with me to Hamada.

Calling up my servants I had him carried on an *angareb*, as tenderly as I could, to my house, and washed his wounds, spreading over them fresh butter to deaden the pain. It was quite impossible he could live much longer. I gave him a little soup, and in a low voice he called down all the curses of Heaven on his enemies. He lay in my house four days, and then, calling me to his bedside, he motioned to the servants to leave us; he now whispered, in words which were scarcely audible, "My hour has come. May the Lord reward you for all your kindness to me! I cannot do so, but I will show you that I am grateful. I have buried my money—"

"Stop!" said I. "Are you going to tell me where you have hidden your treasure?"

"Yes," he murmured; "it may be of some use to you."

"No," I answered, "I will not and cannot use it; I secured your release from your tormentors on the one condition that, should I learn where your money was hidden, I should tell Khaled your enemy. You have suffered greatly, and are paying with your life for your determination not to let your treasure fall into your enemy's hands; let it lie unknown in the ground, it will keep silence!"

Whilst I was talking, Hamada held my hand; with a supreme effort he murmured, "I thank you; may you became fortunate without my money! *Allah Karim* (God is merciful!);" then, stretching out his limbs, and raising his forefinger, he slowly muttered, "*La ilaha illallah, Mohammed Rasul Allah*," closed his eyes, and died.

As I gazed at his poor mangled corpse my eyes filled with tears. How much was I still to suffer before it came to my turn to enter into everlasting rest? Calling my servants, I bade them bring in two good men to wash the body, and wrap it in some linen I had procured; meanwhile, I went to Khaled to inform him of his death. "Did he not tell you where his money was buried?" said he, sharply.

"No," said I, "the man was too stubborn to betray his secret."

"Then may God curse him!" said the *emir*, turning to me. "However, as he died in your house, you may bury him; he really deserves to be thrown out like a dog on the dunghill." Quitting him, I went home and buried poor Hamada, with the usual form of prayer, just in front of my house.

Khaled was a very cunning man, excessively strict with the former government officials, and unnecessarily lenient in his transactions with the local population. He filled all important positions by his own relatives, and although he strove by every means in his power to squeeze all he could out of the country, he was specially careful to avoid the risk of incurring popular discontent. He appropriated to himself the greater part of the revenues, and every now and then he sent as presents to the *Mahdi* and his *khalifas* a batch of pretty girls, some good horses, or some exceptionally fine camels, so as to retain his good reputation in the household of his lord and master. He kept up great state, and surrounded himself with an enormous household.

He married Mariam Isa Basi, the sister of the Sultan of Darfur, although she was over fifty years old. This good lady had hundreds of male and female slaves, and kept up her state in true Sudanese fashion. It did not seem to occur to Khaled that any self-abnegation, as required by the *Mahdi* creed, should be demanded of him. Every evening he caused a hundred dishes, plates, and twisted mats, full of every variety of food, to be distributed amongst his followers, who, seated at their ease under the palm-trees, would sing the praises of the *Mahdi*, coupling every now and then his name with that of their benefactor and *emir*, Khaled.

At about this time a long letter, sent from Cairo to me, through the Mudir of Dongola, by the hands of a trusty Arab, arrived. In it I was ordered to concentrate the troops at Fasher, hand over the province to Abd es Shakur bin Abderrahman Shattut, a descendant of the Darfur Sultans, and move with all troops and war *matériel* to Dongola. The king's son in question was, however, still in Dongola, unable to find means to come to Darfur; and I greatly doubt if his arrival would have made the smallest difference in the situation. Concentration at Fasher would have been rendered impossible by the defection of the officers and men; and had I been able to collect sufficient troops ready to obey my orders, and had I been able to march out with them and the war *materiel* unmolested, I could equally well have been able to stay in the country and maintain my position; in which case the Egyptian Government would have had in me a vassal of equivalent, if not greater, fidelity than the powerless Abd es Shakur. Khaled showed me these letters, and also gave me permission to write a few lines to my family at home, which he allowed the Arab who brought the letters to take back; but I do not think my letter ever reached its destination.

During all this time I remained quietly at my house, awaiting the instructions of the *Mahdi* as to my movements. About the middle of May, Khaled informed me that, owing to scarcity of water, the *Mahdi* had quitted El Obeid and marched to Rahad, that he wished to know me personally, and that, therefore, I should make preparations to start at once.

News now reached us of the fall of Bahr el Ghazal, under Lupton Bey, and of the despatch of the Emir Karamalla, as Mahdist Governor of the Province. This Karamalla had formerly lived with his brother Kerkesawi, who was commander of Lupton's Bazingers, and on the outbreak of the revolt had proceeded with his brother's permission to El Obeid, where he had been well received by the *Mahdi*. Appointed *emir*, he was sent back, and was immediately joined by all the Bazingers and most of Lupton's officials, including finally his sub-governor, Arbab ez Zubeir, who had hitherto served the government most loyally. Thus deserted by all his people, Lupton had no other course open than to capitulate, which he did, without fighting, on 28th April 1884. Had it not been for the defection of his own men and officials, Lupton, by a judicious management of the Negro tribes, could have held his province against all comers for years; but deserted by all, and by them sold over to the *Mahdi*sts, he could not do otherwise than surrender.

Khaled wished Said Bey Guma to accompany me as well; he was still living at Kobbé, and, in spite of his intrigues against me, I agreed to the proposal; also a certain Greek merchant named Dimitri Zigada asked to accompany me, and Khaled gave him permission to do so. This man had been long resident in Darfur, and had been a meat contractor for the troops at Fasher and Kebkebia. Previous to my capitulation, he had presented to me claims for £8,000 for meat supplied, which I had granted, and my signature to that effect he sewed into his clothes.

Procuring the necessary camels, and confining ourselves to as few servants as possible, as at that time of the year water was very scarce along the road, we prepared for the journey.

Hearing that I could sell horses at a good price in Kordofan, I took four of mine with me, hoping in this way to obtain sufficient money to cover our daily expenses. At Khaled's express wish, I gave him the bay pony which Gordon had presented to me. Said Bey had now arrived from Kobbé, bringing with him only one wife; the remainder and his seven children he had, to his great regret, been obliged to leave behind him. About the middle of June, Zigada and I quitted Fasher, heartily glad to leave the place where we had suffered so many hardships and bitter experiences. Khaled supplied us with an escort of ten men under Fiki Shakir, of the Berti tribe, and no doubt the latter was instructed to keep a careful watch over us. In bidding him goodbye, I thanked Khaled for his friendship, and begged him to be kind to the few remaining male and female servants I had left behind me.

Our route lay through Toweisha *via* Woda and Fafa; on the way we were constantly exposed to the inquisitive importunity of the country people, and had to submit to many an insulting remark regarding our present situation, which they invariably said was much better than we deserved. To save our horses, we marched slow, and on the fifth day reached Toweisha, where, being our guide's native place, we stayed a few days; during this time he treated us as his guests, and did all he could to make us comfortable. On leaving, I gave his little daughters a few ivory bracelets, which are much prized in Darfur, and which I had brought with me in lieu of money; I also obtained a few dollars, which I gave to our host in order to secure his friendship.

He told me confidentially that Khaled had particularly instructed him to note carefully all we said to each other on the journey, and, should we make disparaging remarks about the *Mahdi* and his doings, he was at once to let Khalifa Abdullahi know; he asked me to tell my companions this, so that they might take heed not to allow any ill-advised expressions to drop which might be made fatal use of by those evilly-disposed to us. I thanked him heartily for this confidence, and we took special pains to say nothing of a compromising nature during the rest of the journey.

Passing through Dar Homr, we were subjected to the insulting curiosity of the Messeria Arabs, and, continuing our journey towards El Obeid, we procured water from the Baobab reservoir-trees, for which we had to pay heavily, and at length reached that city. The *Mahdi* had left here as governor a most dissolute old relative of his named Sayed Mahmud; we found him sitting on the ground in hot dispute with some merchants. I told him who I was, and he had already been warned of our approach; but he took not the slightest notice of us, keeping us standing for some minutes.

Eventually, he gave us a discourteous greeting, and sent one of his men to take us to a house which was to serve as our lodging. An hour later, they brought us a sheep, and a sack of corn as food for the camels and horses, and directed us to attend public prayers. Dimitri Zigada pretended to be ill; but Said Bey and I went and stayed in the open court of the mosque from noon till sunset; during the whole of this time, Sayed Mahmud and his staff instructed the congregation on the beauties and high importance of the *Mahdi's* doctrine, and, turning to us, urged us to serve him honestly and faithfully, or we should suffer unheard-of punishments in this world, and hell-fire in the world to come. At last, pleading fatigue after our long journey, we were allowed to withdraw; and Mahmud directed us to proceed the next day to Rahad, where the *Mahdi* was now encamped.

CHAPTER 10

The Siege and Fall of Khartum

After the destruction of Hicks Pasha's expedition, the *Mahdi* well knew that the whole Sudan was at his feet; to take possession of it was merely a question of time. His first step was the despatch of his cousin Khaled to Darfur, where he knew no resistance was possible. Through the influence of Karamalla, he was able to acquire possession of the Bahr el Ghazal, the *employés* having merely transferred their allegiance from the Khedive to the *Mahdi*. Already Mek Adam of Tagalla had submitted, and had come to El Obeid with his family. *Mahdi*sm had seized a firm hold of the Eastern Sudan, and found a ready home amongst the brave Arabs of those regions; Egyptian troops had been annihilated at Sinkat and Tamanib; General Baker's disaster at Teb had given the tribes great confidence; and Mustafa Hadal was besieging Kassala. In the Gezira, between the Blue and White Niles, the *Mahdi's* brother-in-law, Wad el Basir of the Halawin tribe, had scored successes against the government; and such was briefly the condition of the country when Gordon reached Berber, on 11th February 1884.

The Egyptian Government, in accord with the British Government, thought that by the despatch of Gordon, who had special knowledge of the Sudan, the agitation would be stopped; but neither these governments, nor Gordon himself, seemed to realise how serious the situation really was. Did they imagine for a moment that Gordon, who had had occasion to show considerable personal bravery, who had gained a name for charity and benevolence amongst the lower classes of the Darfur population, and had suppressed a number of revolts in the Equatorial Negro lands, was capable of checking the blazing flames of fanaticism? The Jaalin between Berber and Khartum, and throughout the Gezira, had become restive and dissatisfied; and was the personal influence of Gordon going to pacify them?

On the contrary, these same tribes had every reason to remember with little satisfaction the name of the governor-general who had issued the ejection edict against the Gellabas of the southern districts, during the Suleiman Zubeir war against the Arabs. In the events which followed on this drastic measure, and which I have described elsewhere, many of these people had lost fathers, brothers, and sons, and had been reduced to beggary; were they likely to forgive Gordon this?

On the 18th February he reached Khartum, and received a warm welcome from the officials and inhabitants. Those who were in immediate contact with him, and anticipating for themselves much personal benefit, were convinced that the government would never leave a man like Gordon in the lurch. Almost his first step was to issue a proclamation appointing the *Mahdi* Sultan of Kordofan, permitting the slave-trade, and proposing to enter into relations with him; in his letter he also asked for the release of the prisoners, and sent the *Mahdi* some very fine clothes. Gordon's letter would have been all very well if he had had a force at his back with which to march into Kordofan; but the *Mahdi* had been told that he had arrived at Khartum with merely a small body-guard. Naturally he thought it an extraordinary proceeding for Gordon to give him what he had already taken by force of arms, and which it was most improbable any troops at Gordon's disposal could have wrenched from him; and it was in this frame of mind that the *Mahdi* couched his reply advising Gordon to surrender and save his life.

Meanwhile, the immense crowds which had collected round El Obeid began to exhaust the water supply; and, to reduce the pressure, the *Mahdi* despatched Abu Anga, with a large force, against Jebel Daïr, where the Nuba tribes were offering a stubborn resistance to his rule.

In all these matters, Khalifa Abdullahi was the *Mahdi's* principal adviser, and, consequently, he was detested by the immediate relatives of the Prophet, who did all in their power to frustrate his designs, and intrigue against him. He was, however, well aware that the *Mahdi* could not get on without him; he therefore retaliated by complaining against these intrigues, and asked the *Mahdi* to take an occasion to openly acknowledge his services. This led to the issue of a proclamation which, to this day, is referred to whenever any exceptionally severe measure or important change is contemplated by his successor. It runs as follows:—

A Proclamation

From Mohammed el Mahdi to all his Followers.

In the name of God, etc., Know ye, O my followers, that the representative of the righteous (Abu Bakr), and the *emir* of the *Mahdi* army, referred to in the Prophet's vision, is Es Sayed Abdullahi Ibn es Sayed Hamadalla. He is of me, and I am of him. Behave with all reverence to him, as you do to me; submit to him as you submit to me, and believe in him as you believe in me; rely on all he says, and never question any of his proceedings. All that he does is by order of the Prophet, or by my permission. He is my agent in carrying out the will of the Prophet. If God and His Prophet desire to do anything, we must submit to their will; and if any one shows the slightest disinclination, he is not a believer, and has no faith in God. The Khalifa Abdullahi is the representative of the righteous. You are well aware of the love of God and His apostle for the righteous; therefore, you can readily understand the honourable position which should be held by His representative. He is guarded by the "*Khudr*," and is strengthened by God and His Prophet. If any one of you speak or think ill of him, you will suffer destruction, and will lose this world and the world to come.

Know, therefore, that all his sayings and actions must never be questioned; for he has been given wisdom and a right judgment in all things. If he sentence any of you to death, or confiscate your property, it is for your good; therefore do not disobey him. The Prophet says that, in next degree to the Prophet, Abu Bakr was the greatest living man under the sun, and also the most righteous. The Khalifa Abdullahi is his representative; and, by order of the Prophet, he is my *khalifa*. All those who believe in God and in me must also believe in him; and, should any one notice anything apparently wrong in him, they should attribute it to a mystery which they cannot understand, and that, therefore, it must be right. Let those who are present tell those who are absent, so that all may submit to him, and attribute to him no wrong. Beware of doing any harm to the friends of God; for God and His Prophet curse those that behave or think badly of His friends.

The Khalifa Abdullahi is the commander of the faithful, and is my *khalifa* and agent in all religious matters. Therefore, I leave off as I have begun,—"Believe in him; obey his orders; never doubt what he says, but give all your confidence to him, and trust him in all your affairs." And may God be with you all. Amen.

As the water was daily becoming more scarce, the *Mahdi* resolved to move his entire camp to Rahad, about one day's journey from El Obeid; and, about the middle of April, the transfer of this immense mass of men, women, and children to the new position was completed. He had left his old relative, Sayed Mahmud, at El Obeid with very strict orders that any persons found remaining in the town, without his permission, were to be sent to Rahad by force; and he sent further reinforcements to Jebel Dair, which was only a day's march distant, and where the plucky Nubas were defending themselves most gallantly.

The camp at Rahad soon became a perfect sea of straw huts, or *tokuls*, stretching as far as the eye could reach; and, all day long, the *Mahdi* occupied himself in his religious duties, preaching and praying incessantly. Mohammed Abu Girga, he nominated Emir of the Gezira, and despatched him, with a considerable following, to the Nile, with instructions to head the revolt in these districts, and besiege Khartum.

Such was the state of affairs when, towards sunset, Said Bey Guma, Dimitri Zigada, and I approached Rahad. We stopped for the night at some huts on the outskirts; and it was not long before a considerable number of people became aware of our arrival, and we received several visits from those who were anxious to know the situation in Darfur when we had left. At sunrise, having donned our new *jibbas*, we took leave of our hosts, and proceeded towards the camp where we were expected in two hours time; my servants, who knew something of tailoring, had made me a *jibba* with broad black patches sewn on with such evenness and regularity that, at a short distance, I must have looked exactly like a lady in a fancy bathing costume, whilst Said Bey and Zigada wore party-coloured patches which gave them the appearance of harlequins.

I now sent on one of my servants to apprise the much-feared *khalifa* of our approach; but, as he delayed returning, we rode on along the broad road leading to the market-place. As we approached, we heard the dismal sound of the *ombeÿa*, which was the signal that the *khalifa* had gone out on his horse. By chance, I came across a Darfuri who, when I asked him what the *ombeÿa* was being sounded for, replied, "Very probably Khalifa Abdullahi is giving orders for some one's head to be cut off, and this is a summons to the people to witness the execution."

Had I been superstitious, I should certainly have taken this as a bad omen,—an execution the moment I entered the camp! However, we rode on, and soon came in sight of a large open place where we saw my servant and another man hastening towards us. "Stay where you are," cried he, "and come no further; the *khalifa*, with his escort, has gone out to meet you; he thought you were still outside the camp." We halted while the other man returned to let the *khalifa* know we had arrived. A few minutes later, we saw hundreds of horsemen surrounded by numbers of armed footmen approaching us, and marching to the sound of the *ombeÿa*. At the farther end of the open space was the *khalifa* himself; he had halted, and several horsemen, ranging up to his right and left, stood awaiting his instructions. He now ordered them to begin their horse exercise, which consisted of batches of four men abreast, with poised lances, galloping at full speed towards some point, then suddenly pulling up, turning round and galloping back again; this useless sort of drill continued until men and horses became utterly exhausted.

Sometimes I was the objective of their charge, and, as they galloped up, they shook their spears close to my face, shouting, "*Fi shan Allah wa Rasulahu*" (For God and His Prophet), and then galloped back again. After repeating this operation for upwards of half an hour, one of the *khalifa's* servants at length approached me on foot, and told me that the *khalifa* wished me also to gallop towards him. I did so, shook my lance in his face, shouted, "*Fi shan Allah wa Rasulahu!*" and then returned to my place. He now sent word to me to ride behind him, and in a few minutes we reached his quarters. He was assisted to dismount by a special attendant, the remainder keeping at a respectful distance; and he disappeared behind the fence. In a few moments, he sent out a message to us to come in; and we were conducted to a spot fenced off from the rest of the enclosure, which is designated the *rekuba*; it was merely a small, square apartment with straw walls and a thatch roof. In it were several *angarebs* and palm-mats; we were told to seat ourselves on these, and were served with a mixture of honey and water in a pumpkin gourd, and some dates. Having partaken of this, we patiently awaited the appearance of our hospitable host and master. He soon came in, and we at once rose; seizing my hand, he pressed me to his heart, saying, "God be praised, we are at last united! How do you feel after your long and tiring journey?"

"Yes, indeed," I replied, "God be praised for having granted me to live to see this day! When I beheld your countenance, my fatigue at once left me!" I well knew that, to win his favour, I must flatter him as much as possible; he now gave his hand to Said Bey and Dimitri to kiss, and asked how they were. I scrutinised him very carefully; he had a light-brown complexion, a sympathetic Arab face, on which the marks of small-pox were still traceable, an aquiline nose, a well-shaped mouth, slight moustache, and a fringe of hair on his cheeks, but rather thicker on his chin; he was about middle height, neither thin nor stout, was wearing a *jibba* covered with small square patches of different colours, and a Mecca *takia*, or skull cap, round which was bound a cotton turban; he generally spoke with a smile, and showed a row of glistening white teeth.

Having greeted us, he told us to be seated; and we at once sat on the palm-mats on the ground, whilst he sat cross-legged on an *angareb*. Once more he inquired after our health, and expressed his great delight that we had at last reached the *Mahdi*. On a sign to one of his servants, a dish of *asida*, and another of meat, were laid before us, and, sitting beside us, he told us to help ourselves; he himself ate heartily, seeming to thoroughly enjoy his food, and, during the meal, he asked several questions.

"Why," said he, smiling, "did you not wait for me outside the camp, instead of entering without permission? You know you are not supposed to enter a friend's house without his permission."

"Pardon," said I, "my servant kept us waiting so long, and none of us thought you would take the trouble to come out and meet us; then, as we reached the entrance of the camp, we heard the beating of war-drums and the sound of your *ombeÿa*, and, when we inquired what that meant, we were told that you had ridden out to witness the execution of a criminal; we therefore intended following the sound of your *ombeÿa*, when your order reached us."

"Am I then known as a tyrant amongst the people," said he, "that the sound of my *ombeÿa* should always mean the death of some one?"

"No, indeed, sir," said I, "you are generally known to be strict, but just."

"Yes, I am strict," he replied; "but this must be so, and you will understand the reasons as you prolong your stay with me."

One of the *khalifa's* slaves now entered, and said that several people were waiting outside, and sought his permission to greet me. The *khalifa* at once asked if I was not too fatigued after my journey; and when

I said no, he allowed them to come in. The first to enter was Ahmed Wad Ali (the Kadi el Islam), who was formerly one of my government officials, but had deserted from Shakka; then followed Abderrahman ben Naga, who had come with the Hicks expedition, in the course of which he had lost an eye, and had been wounded in several places, but had been rescued by some of his slaves who were with the Mahdists; Ahmed Wad Suleiman, the Treasurer of the Beit el Mal, Sayed Abdel Kader, the *Mahdi's* uncle, Sayed Abdel Karim, and several others followed.

All of them kissed the *khalifa's* hand with deep reverence, and, after asking his permission, greeted me. The usual complimentary speeches passed between us; and, after reciprocal congratulations that we had lived to see the glorious time of the *Mahdi*, they withdrew; Abderrahman alone gave me a wink with his one eye as he said goodbye, from which I knew he had something to say to me, so I walked forward a few steps with him, and, in a low quick tone, he muttered: "Be very careful; hold your tongue, and trust no one." I took his warning to heart.

The *khalifa* then departed, recommending us to take some rest, as he would present us to the *Mahdi* at noon-day prayers. We now inquired about our servants, and were told that they had been taken in and given food. Once alone, and convinced that there were no eavesdroppers near, we spoke of our excellent reception, and I warned the others to be most careful about what they said. Dimitri Zigada was now getting quite pleased with himself, and began searching about in his pockets for a piece of tobacco to chew; he produced some from under his *jibba*, and at once put it in his mouth. I begged him to be careful, as such practices were entirely forbidden by the *Mahdi*; he replied by saying he intended asking the *khalifa* to allow him to go and live with his compatriots, of whom there were a considerable number in camp. "I am only a common merchant," said he, "and have lost all my money; the *khalifa* won't take any further notice of me; but you will have to keep a sharp lookout yourselves, for you are former government officials and military men, so he will watch you very carefully."

About two o'clock in the afternoon a message reached us from the *khalifa*, to perform our ablutions, and prepare to go to the *mesjed* (place of worship); a few minutes later he arrived himself, and told us to follow him. He was on foot, as the mosque, which was close to the *Mahdi's* hut, was only about three hundred yards off. On arrival, we found the place crowded with devotees, ranged in closely packed lines; and, when the *khalifa* entered, they made way for him with great respect. A sheepskin was spread on the ground for us, and he directed us to take our places beside him. The *Mahdi's* quarters, consisting of several large straw huts fenced off by a thorn *zariba*, were situated at the southwest end of the mosque. A gigantic tree afforded shade to a number of the worshippers, but those beyond had no protection from the burning sun. A few paces from the front line, and to the right, lay a small hut which was reserved for those with whom the *Mahdi* wished to converse in private.

The *khalifa* now rose and entered this hut, probably to inform his master of our arrival; for, in a few moments, he returned, again seated himself beside me, and almost immediately the *Mahdi* himself came out. The *khalifa* at once arose, and with him Said Bey, Dimitri, and I, who were just behind him, whilst the others quietly remained in their places. The *Mahdi* being the Imam, or leader of prayers, his sheepskin was spread out in front; and he then stepped towards us. I had advanced slightly, and he greeted me with "*Salam aleikum*," which we at once returned by "*Aleikum es salam*." He then presented his hand for me to kiss, which I did several times, and Said Bey and Dimitri followed my example. Motioning us to be seated, he welcomed us, and, turning to me, said, "Are you satisfied?"

"Indeed I am," I replied, readily; "on coming so near to you I am most happy."

"God bless you and your brethren!" (meaning Said Bey and Dimitri) said he; "when news reached us of your battles against my followers, I used to pray to God for your conversion. God and His Prophet have heard my prayers, and as you have faithfully served your former master for perishable money, so now you should serve me; for he who serves me, and hears my words, serves God and His religion, and shall have happiness in this world and joy in the world to come."

We of course all made professions of fidelity; and as I had been previously warned to ask him to give me the "*beia*," or oath of allegiance, I now besought this honour. Calling us up beside him, he bade us kneel on the edge of his sheepskin, and, placing our hands in his, he told us to repeat after him as follows:—

Bism Illahi er Rahman er Rahim, bayana Allaha wa Rasulahu wa bayanaka ala tauhid Illahi, wala nushrek billahi shayan, wala nasrek, wala nazni, wala nati bi buhtan, wala nasak fil maruf, bayanaka ala *tark ed dunya wal akhera, wala naferru min el jeha*d.

In the name of God the most compassionate and merciful, in the name of the unity of God, we pay God, His Prophet, and you our allegiance; (we swear) that we shall not associate anything else with God, that we shall not steal, nor commit adultery, nor lead any one into deception, nor disobey you in your goodness; we swear to renounce this world and (look only) to the world to come, and that we shall not flee from the religious war.

This over, we kissed his hand, and were now enrolled amongst his most devoted adherents; but at the same time we were liable to suffer their punishments. The *muazzen* (prayer caller) now gave the first signal to begin prayers, and we repeated the usual *formulæ* after the *Mahdi*. When they were over, all those present raised their hands to Heaven, and besought God to grant victory to the faithful. The *Mahdi* now began his sermon. An immense circle was formed around him, and he spoke of the vanity and nothingness of this life, urging all to renounce the world, and to think only of their religious duties, and of the *Jehad*; he painted, in most glowing terms, the delights of Paradise, and the heavenly joys which awaited those who paid heed to his doctrine. Every now and then he was interrupted by the shouts of some fanatic in an ecstasy; and, indeed, I am convinced every one present, except ourselves, really believed in him.

The *khalifa*, having something to do, had left the mosque, but had ordered his *mulazemia* (bodyguard), who remained, to tell us to stay with the *Mahdi* till sunset. I had now a good opportunity of making a careful survey of Mohammed Ahmed; he was a tall, broad-shouldered man of light-brown colour, and powerfully built; he had a large head and sparkling black eyes; he wore a black beard, and had the usual three slits on each cheek; his nose and mouth were well shaped, and he had the habit of always smiling, showing his white teeth and exposing the V-shaped aperture between the two front ones which is always considered a sign of good luck in the Sudan, and is known as *"falja."*

This was one of the principal causes which made the *Mahdi* so popular with the fair sex, by whom he was dubbed *"Abu falja"* (the man with the separated teeth). He wore a short quilted *jibba*, beautifully washed, and perfumed with sandal-wood, musk, and *attar* of roses; this perfume was celebrated amongst his disciples as Rihet el *Mahdi* (the odour of the *Mahdi*), and was supposed to equal, if not surpass, that of the dwellers in Paradise.

We remained exactly on the same spot, with our legs tucked away behind, until the time for evening prayers came. Meanwhile the *Mahdi* had frequently gone to and fro between his house and the mosque; and, prayers over, I begged leave to depart, as the *khalifa* had told me to return to him at that hour. He gave me permission, and took the opportunity of saying that I must adhere closely to the *khalifa*, and devote myself entirely to his service. Of course I promised to obey him to the letter, and Dimitri, Said Bey, and I, covering the *Mahdi's* hand with kisses, quitted the mosque. My legs were so cramped by the posture in which I had been sitting for hours together that I could scarcely walk; but, in spite of the pain, I was obliged to keep as cheerful a face as possible in the *Mahdi's* presence. Said Bey was more used to it, and did not seem to suffer so much; but poor Dimitri limped behind, muttering Greek in an undertone, which I have no doubt conveyed the most frightful imprecations,—at any rate I can vouch that they were not songs of praise of the *Mahdi*. A *mulazem* returned with us to the *khalifa's* house, where he was waiting for us to sit down to supper with him.

He told us that since he had seen us in the morning, Sheikh Hamed en Nil of the Arakin Arabs, and one of the principal Sheikhs of the Gezira, had arrived, and that his relatives had begged him to ride out and meet him; but he refused, as he preferred spending the evening with us. We of course thanked him profusely for his goodwill and kindness; and we were loud in the praises of the *Mahdi*, which evidently much pleased the *khalifa*. He now left us to attend evening prayers, and, on his return, talked to us about Darfur; he also mentioned that Hussein Khalifa, formerly Mudir of Berber, was expected within the next few days. So it was true Berber had fallen; we had heard rumours to this effect, on the Darfur frontier, but met no one whom we could ask confidentially about it. The town must have fallen through the Jaalin; and now communication with Egypt must be entirely cut off. This was terribly bad news. I anxiously looked out for Hussein Khalifa's arrival; he would be able to give us all the facts.

The *khalifa* now left us for the night; and, utterly tired out, we stretched out our weary limbs on the *angarebs*, and gave ourselves up to our own thoughts. There were of course no lights; but in the dark I heard Dimitri's mouth at work, and I had no doubt the man was again chewing tobacco. Once more I spoke seriously to him, and warned him that he would fare badly if discovered; to which he sleepily replied, that his little stock of tobacco was now done, and that the bit in his mouth was positively his very last piece.

Early the next day, after morning prayers, the *khalifa* again came to see us, and asked how we were getting on. Soon after Sheikh Hamed en Nil's relatives arrived, and begged the *khalifa* to allow them to present their *sheikh* to him; he was admitted into his presence as a penitent, his neck in a sheba, his head sprinkled with ashes, and a sheepskin bound about his loins. On entering, he knelt down, saying, "*El afu ya sidi!*" (Pardon, sire!). Standing up, the *khalifa* directed one of his servants to remove the *sheba*, and take the ashes off his head, and then told him to put on his clothes, which were being carried for him. This done, he asked him to be seated; and the *sheikh*, repeatedly begging pardon, expressed his deep regret that his visit to the *Mahdi* had been so long delayed. The *khalifa* pardoned him, and promised to present him to the *Mahdi* in the afternoon, when he also would, in all probability, forgive him. "Master," said Hamed en Nil, "since you have pardoned me, I am now happy, and at ease. I consider that your forgiveness is the same as the *Mahdi's*; for you are of him, and he is of you," and saying these words, he kissed the *khalifa's* hand (he had cleverly repeated the words in the proclamation already referred to).

After partaking of a breakfast of *asida* and milk, we separated; the blowing of the *ombeÿa*, and the beating of drums, announced that the *khalifa* was about to ride; and horses were at once saddled. Directing my servants to get two horses ready,—one for myself and the other for Said Bey,—we mounted and soon caught up the *khalifa*, who had gone on ahead. He was riding for pleasure round the camp, accompanied by some twenty footmen; on his right walked an enormous Black of the Dinka tribe, and on his left, a very tall Arab named Abu Tsheka, whose duty it was to help the *khalifa* in and out of the saddle.

When he came again to the open space, he directed the horsemen to repeat yesterday's exercises; and, after watching this for some time, we rode on to the end of the camp, where he showed me the remains of an immense *zariba* and small tumbled-in trench, which he told me had been one of Hicks's last halting places before his annihilation, and where he had awaited reinforcements from Tagalla. The trench had been made for his Krupp guns. The sight of this awakened very sad memories; to think of the thousands, who but a short time before had been camped in this great *zariba* having been killed almost to a man, and that this disaster was the cause of my being where I now was!

On our way back, the *khalifa* took me to pay a visit to his brother

Yakub, whose huts were close to his own, the fences being merely separated by a narrow passage. Yakub received me very kindly, and appeared as pleased to see me as Abdullahi had been; he warned me to serve him faithfully, which I of course promised to do. Yakub is a somewhat shorter man than the *khalifa*, broad-shouldered, with a round face deeply pitted with small-pox; he has a small turned-up nose, and slight moustache and beard; he is distinctly more ugly than handsome, but has the art of talking in a curiously sympathetic way.

He, too, like the *Mahdi* and the *khalifa*, smiled continually; and what wonder, when their affairs were progressing so very satisfactorily! Yakub reads and writes, and knows the *Koran* by heart, whilst Abdullahi is comparatively very ignorant. He is some years the *khalifa's* junior, and is his trusted and most powerful adviser. Woe to the unfortunate man who differs in opinion with Yakub, or who is suspected of intriguing against him, he is infallibly lost!

Partaking of some of the dates he offered me, I took leave of him and returned to the *rekuba*, whence, in accordance with the *khalifa's* order, we proceeded to the mosque, and stayed till sunset, as we did the previous day. Again the *Mahdi* preached renunciation, urging his hearers to be ready for the *Jehad*, so as to enter into the future joys of Paradise. Again and again, the faithful devotees, half intoxicated with fanaticism, shouted his praises; whilst we poor wretches, enduring agonies in our cramped position, imprecated in our hearts *Mahdi*, *khalifa*, and his whole crew of base hypocrites.

The next day, the *khalifa* summoned us, and asked if we wished to return to Darfur. I knew the question had only been put to us as a test; and we at once answered with one voice, that we should deeply regret leaving the *Mahdi*. I saw that he anticipated this answer, and, smiling, he commended us for our wise decision. The *khalifa* now, of his own accord, suggested that a longer stay in the *rekuba* was probably distasteful to us; he, therefore, sent Dimitri with a *mulazem* to the house of his future *emir*, who was a Greek, and he also gave instructions to Ahmed Wad Suleiman to issue twenty dollars to him. After he had gone, he turned to Said Bey, saying, "Said Guma, you are an Egyptian, and everyone likes his own compatriots best; we have with us several Egyptians, many of proved fidelity. You are brave and I know I can count on you; you will therefore join the *emir* of all the Egyptians, Hassan Hussein, and he will give you a house, and see to your requirements. I shall also do what is necessary on my side." Said Bey was of course much pleased with the arrangement.

Then, turning to me, he said, "Abdel Kader, you are a stranger here, and have no one else but me. You know well the Arabs of Southern Darfur; therefore, in accordance with the *Mahdi's* orders, you are to remain with me as a *mulazem*."

"That is the very wish of my heart," I answered readily; "I call myself fortunate to be able to serve you, and you can rely on my obedience and fidelity."

"I knew that," said he; "may God protect you and strengthen your faith; you will no doubt be of much use to both the *Mahdi* and myself."

Soon afterwards, the Emir Hassan Hussein came in; the *khalifa* had summoned him, and now recommended to his care Said Guma, who promised he would do all he could for him. He also instructed him to send for Said Bey's family, which had been left behind at Kobbé; and the latter, taking a grateful leave of the *khalifa*, proceeded, in company of a *mulazem*, to Ahmed Wad Suleiman, who had been authorised to supply him with forty dollars and a female slave.

Once more I was alone with the *khalifa*, and again he repeated how gratified he was to have me in his service, and always beside him; at the same time he warned me not to associate with his near relatives, whose jealous feelings might lead to an estrangement between us. He also gave orders for some straw huts to be erected in the *zariba* next his own, belonging to Abu Anga, who was now absent, fighting against the Nubas; meanwhile he said I was to stay in the *rekuba*, and without fail attend the *Mahdi's* noon-day and evening prayers. Thanking him profusely for all these favours, I promised to do my utmost to please him and continue in his good graces.

At supper the same evening, the *khalifa* told me with delight that Hussein *khalifa* had arrived, and was to be presented the next day. Consequently, at noon, the *khalifa* received him with his relatives, in ashes and *sheba*, just as he had received Sheikh Hamed en Nil. Knowing what his feelings were as regards the *Mahdi*sts, I realised it must have been a terrible humiliation for him to come in this way; but some of his old friends who were now in high favour with the *Mahdi*, advised him to do so, and he had consented. The *khalifa* had the *sheba* and ashes removed, pardoned him, and then presented me to him, and asked me to be seated.

Being a *mulazem* of the *khalifa*, I was practically in the position of a sort of servant, and as such I always stood up behind him, and of course did my best to carry out my new *rôle* satisfactorily. Abdullahi began the conversation by inquiring after the health of the late Governor of Berber; and, receiving the usual replies, he then turned to the situation on the river, and Hussein described the whole country between Berber and Fashoda as being entirely with the *Mahdi*, and communication between Egypt and the Sudan quite interrupted, whilst Khartum, which was defended by Gordon, was invested by the Gezira tribes. He naturally coloured the situation in the way which he knew would be most acceptable to the *Mahdi*; and that he was favourably impressing the *khalifa*, was evident from the expressions of satisfaction which escaped the latter as the narrative proceeded. Abdullahi promised that at noon-day prayers he would present Hussein Khalifa to the *Mahdi*, of whose forgiveness he might rest assured; in the meantime he was to rest in the *rekuba*.

The *khalifa*, having something to do, now left us together; but as there were several of his relatives there whom I did not know, we could only talk about our personal concerns, and congratulate each other on our good fortune in becoming followers of the *Mahdi*. At noon, the *khalifa* returned, and took dinner with Hussein Khalifa, I also being invited to partake of the meal. In the course of conversation, the *khalifa* asked, "Did you happen to see Mohammed Sherif, the former Sheikh of the *Mahdi*; you must have passed his house on your way here? Is he still possessed of that evil spirit which urges him to fight against the will of God, and to refuse to acknowledge the *Mahdi* as his lord and master?"

"I spent a night at his house," replied Hussein Khalifa; "he has now repented of his infidelity to God, and it is illness alone that prevents him from coming here. Most of his former followers have joined those besieging Khartum."

"It is better for him to serve the *Mahdi*," said Abdullahi; "now get ready, and I shall present you to him."

Before prayers began, the *khalifa* conducted him, as he had conducted me a few days before, to the mosque, and bade him be seated; but I, being a *mulazem*, now took up my position in the second line. On the *Mahdi* approaching, the *khalifa* and his guest stood up; and the latter, on being presented, craved his pardon for the blindness of heart which had hitherto prevented him from becoming one of his faithful adherents. He was pardoned, and, on taking the oath of allegiance, was enjoined to uphold faithfully the new doctrine, and attend prayers without fail. The *Mahdi*, seeing me in the second line, directed me to come forward and take up my position beside the *khalifa*. "Drink of the river of my words," said he, "and that will be of inestimable benefit to you."

I excused myself by saying that as *mulazem* of the *khalifa* I did not think it my place to stand beside my master, and had therefore joined the second line. I was now praised for this act of self-abnegation; the Mahdi added, however, that in future this should always be my position, "For in the place of worship we are all alike."

After prayers, the *khalifa* disappeared as usual, whilst Hussein Khalifa and I remained in the mosque till sunset. My uncomfortable posture brought more curses than prayers to my lips; but I had to put as good a face as I could on the matter. That evening, we supped with the *khalifa*, and talked on general subjects, being continually warned to be honest and sincere. To my great delight, Hussein Khalifa was directed to spend that night in the *rekuba*; but his relatives were allowed to go home. The *khalifa* had left us, and the servants had retired, so we were quite alone, and took this long-looked-for occasion to greet each other most heartily, and to mutually bemoan the sad fate which brought us together to this wretched position.

"Hussein Pasha," said I, "I trust you and yours may rest assured of my silence. Tell me what is the present condition of Khartum, and what are the population doing?" "Alas!" he replied, "it is exactly as I have already described it to the *khalifa*. Gordon's reading at Metemmeh of the proclamation abandoning the Sudan, upset the situation entirely, and was indirectly the cause of the fall of Berber. No doubt, it would have been lost later on; but this action of Gordon's greatly precipitated it. At Berber, I stopped him from taking this fatal step; and I cannot think what induced him to disregard my advice almost immediately afterwards." We talked so long about the situation and the various events that Hussein Pasha, who was old and tired, fell asleep; but this conversation had banished all sleep from my eyes.

So this is to be the end, I thought, of all Gordon's efforts to settle the country; and is all the blood and treasure expended in past years to go for nothing? Now the government wanted to abandon this great country which, though hitherto it had not proved a financial benefit to Egypt, was a land of great prospects, and could at least produce thousands of splendid black recruits with whom to fill the ranks of its army. So the government was to leave this country to its own people, and yet to remain on friendly terms with it; it was to withdraw the garrisons and war *matériel*, and to establish a form of local government, when a form of such government had already sprung into existence by the most violent of means,—namely, by the wholesale overturning of every vestige of the authority which it was to replace, and the massacre or capture of almost every individual representative of the ousted ruling power.

To carry out this plan, they had sent Gordon in the hope that his personal influence with the people, and their regard for him,—which he was inclined to estimate somewhat highly,—would enable him to succeed in this herculean task. Gordon, it is true, was popular with some of the Western and Equatorial tribes, whom he had won over by his munificence and his benevolent nature. During his stay in these districts, he had constantly travelled about; and his noted courage and fearlessness in action had won him the sympathy of those tribes whose greatest pride it is to possess such qualities. Yes, there is no doubt he had been popular with the Western Arabs: but they had now a *Mahdi* whom they adored; they had almost forgotten Gordon. The Sudanese, it must be remembered, are not Europeans; they are Arabs and blacks, and are little given over to sentimental feelings. But, in this particular case of the reading of the proclamation, the people concerned were river tribes; and, of all others, the Jaalin were perhaps the most hostile to Gordon, for they had not forgotten the eviction of the Gellabas.

The mere fact that Gordon had come to Khartum without a force at his back, proved to these people that he depended on his personal influence to carry out his task; but, to those who understood the situation, it was abundantly clear that personal influence at this stage was as a drop in the ocean. Then what could have induced him to read that fatal notice, proclaiming far and wide that the government intended to abandon the Sudan? At Hussein Pasha's advice, he had not read it at Berber; but at Metemmeh, he had proclaimed it before all the people. Had Gordon never been informed of the *Mahdi's* proclamations, sent to all the tribes after the fall of El Obeid? Was he not aware that these proclamations enjoined all the people to unite in a religious war against the government authority, and that those who disobeyed the summons, and were found giving assistance to the hated Turk, were guilty of betraying the faith, and as such would not only lose their money and property, but their wives and children would become the slaves of the *Mahdi* and his followers?

Gordon's idea was to obtain the assistance of these tribes, in order to facilitate the withdrawal of the garrisons; and he would have come to terms with them to effect this object: but how could he expect them to help him, when, in the words of that fatal proclamation, it was decreed they were to be abandoned to their fate, and what would, in this eventuality, have been their fate? Could they have opposed the *Mahdi*, his forty thousand rifles, and his hosts of wild fanatics panting for blood and plunder? No, indeed, these tribes were sensible enough to understand that assistance given to Gordon to retreat, meant the annihilation of themselves and the enslavement of their families; why should they commit this self-sacrifice? How could Gordon's personal influence avail him for an instant against the personal interests of every man, woman, and child in the now abandoned Sudan?

If, for political or other reasons, it was impossible for the government to maintain the Sudan, or to reconquer it by degrees, it was an equally useless step to have sent Gordon there to sacrifice him. It did not require a person of any special military capacity to remove the garrisons and war *matériel* by the steamers to Berber, under pretext of relieving that town, and thus the whole or a considerable portion of the Sudan garrisons might have been successfully withdrawn, though it would have been necessary to do this without delay, and it could not have been feasible after the fall of Berber; but Berber, it must be remembered, did not fall till the 19th of May,—three months after Gordon's arrival in Khartum. However, under any circumstances, the reading of that fatal proclamation precipitated matters to an alarming extent; the intention of the government was openly declared to the Sudanese, and they naturally, from that moment, looked to their own immediate interests, which were now directly opposed to those of the Government so hopelessly overturned by their victorious compatriot the *Mahdi*.

How could Gordon's qualities of personal bravery and energy, great as they undoubtedly were, arrest the progress of events after that most grave political error?

Perplexed and worried with such thoughts as these, I was tossing about on my *angareb*, whilst Hussein Khalifa was snoring. There was no small advantage in being a fatalist; but as yet I was too European to have arrived at this stage, though gradually I learnt to look at such matters with more equanimity, and my experiences in the Sudan have undoubtedly taught me to practise that great virtue—patience.

The next morning, the *khalifa* honoured us with a visit, and asked me why my eyes were so red; I answered that, owing to a severe attack of fever, I had passed a sleepless night, on which he advised me to take care of myself and not to go into the sun; and he also excused me from attending the *Mahdi's* prayers. However, when prayer-time came, I performed them under the shade of the *rekuba*, and in the sight of the servants; as it was my object to appear to them as devout as possible, well-knowing they would report my every action to their master. The following day my huts were ready, and, with the *khalifa's* permission, I entered into occupation. Hussein Khalifa had already been allowed to live with one of his relatives; and he made a point of going through all five prayers daily, in order to secure the good-will of the *Mahdi* and *khalifa*, hoping in this way to obtain their leave to go back to his own country. I decided to remain as near the *khalifa* as possible, and to only go occasionally to the *Mahdi* when he recommended me to do so.

A few days afterwards, a rumour was spread through the camp that Abu Girga had been attacked by Gordon, and had been wounded; his forces, which were then investing Khartum, were reported to have been repulsed, and the siege raised. This news filled my heart with delight, though openly, I was obliged to appear quite unconcerned.

Saleh Wad el Mek now arrived in the camp; he had been obliged to submit at Fedasi, and had been sent on by Abu Girga. He received the pardon of the *khalifa* and *Mahdi*, and confirmed the above news; he also privately gave me much interesting information about Gordon. That evening, the *khalifa* summoned me to supper with him; and no sooner had we set to work to tear the huge piece of meat before us, than he asked, "Have you heard the news today about Hajji Mohammed Abu Girga?"

"No," I replied, hypocritically, "I did not leave your door the whole day, and have met no one."

"Gordon," continued the *khalifa*, "made a sudden attack on Hajji Mohammed from both the river and the land, when the Blue Nile was in flood; and he has built structures on the steamers which stop the bullets of our faithful Ansar. The unbeliever is a cunning man; but he will reap God's punishment. Hajji Mohammed's men, who have suffered, have been obliged to retire before superior force. Gordon is now rejoicing in his victory; but he is deceived. God will grant victory only to those who believe in Him; and, in a few days, God's vengeance will fall upon him suddenly. Hajji Mohammed is not man enough to conquer the country; the *Mahdi* is therefore sending Abderrahman Wad en Nejumi to besiege Khartum."

"I hope," said I, "that Hajji Mohammed has not suffered serious loss?" meaning in my heart exactly the reverse.

"Battles cannot be fought without loss," said the *khalifa*, with some truth; "but I have not heard the full details yet." He was anything but affable today. Gordon's victory had thoroughly upset him; and he evidently anticipated that the effect would be serious. When I returned to my hut, I sent my servant to ask Saleh Wad el Mek if he could come and see me secretly; he was only a few huts off, and arrived some minutes afterwards. I told him the *khalifa's* corroboration of the news; but he had already heard it from his relatives; and we continued talking over past and present till a late hour. This victory had raised my spirits enormously, and I found myself chatting quite hopefully of the future; but Saleh looked on the success as only temporary, and his reasons for this view were, I felt, fully justifiable.

He explained that, very soon after Gordon's arrival at Khartum, the effect of the fatal proclamation began to be felt, and his difficulties increased. The Jaalin had begun to collect, and had chosen as their chief, Haj Ali Wad Saad, who soon had at his disposal a considerable force; but, for personal reasons, he was secretly inclined to the government, and therefore delayed actually fighting as long as possible. The consuls of the various nationalities at Khartum, seeing the situation getting worse, had applied to Gordon to send them to Berber; but it was doubtful if it would have been safe to let them go, and, at Gordon's suggestion, they decided to remain. The inhabitants of Khartum had themselves begun to look with mistrust on Gordon; for they realised, from the proclamation of which they had heard, that Gordon had only come to withdraw the garrison, though, later on, they thoroughly understood that Gordon himself had come to conquer with them or to die.

The Sheikh El Obeid, one of the great religious *sheikhs* of the Sudan, had collected together his followers at Halfaya to besiege Khartum. Gordon had sent troops under Hassan Pasha and Said Pasha Hussein, who had been formerly Governor of Shakka, to drive the rebels out of their position; and, watching the operations through a telescope from the top of the palace, he had seen his trusted officers endeavouring to make over his troops to the enemy, whilst they themselves were retreating to Khartum. He had tried these traitorous officers by general court-martial, and had had them shot. In spite of this disaster, he had succeeded in relieving the Shaigias, who were loyal to government, and had brought them, under their commander Sanjak Abdel Hamid Wad Mohammed, to Khartum.

Saleh Wad el Mek, himself invested by the rebels at Fedasi, had begged Gordon to relieve him; but it was impossible to do so, and he had been obliged to surrender with one thousand four hundred irregulars and cavalry, with all their arms. In consequence of this success, Hajji Mohammed Abu Girga had collected all the inhabitants of the Gezira to besiege Khartum. Whilst these events were happening in the neighbourhood of that town, the *Mahdi's* former teacher, Sheikh Mohammed el Kheir (formerly Mohammed ed Diker), had come to the river, and had been appointed by his early pupil Emir of Berber; he had placed all the tribes in the province under his orders, and the latter, collecting adherents from his own tribe, the Jaalin, and reinforced by the Barabra, Bisharia, and other Arabs, had laid siege to Berber, which had fallen in a few days.

The province of Dongola had hitherto held out, owing principally to its crafty *mudir*, Mustafa Bey Yawer, who had twice written to the *Mahdi*, offering him his submission; but the latter, fearing to trust one of the hated Turks, had sent his relative, Sayed Mahmud Ali, to join the Shaigia Emir Sheikh el Heddai, who had already headed a disturbance in the province, to take possession. But Mustafa Bey, secretly learning that he was not acceptable, had fallen suddenly on Heddai at Debba, and, encouraged by the presence of a British officer[1] in his province, had followed up this success by inflicting a crushing defeat on the Mahdists at Korti, in which both the Emirs Mahmud and Heddai were killed.

At Sennar, matters were not so satisfactory; it was closely invested, but had large reserve supplies of corn. Communication with the outside was, however, completely stopped, though Nur Bey, the brave commander, had made a successful sortie which had driven off the rebels to some distance, and enabled the town to breathe again.

Appeals now reached the *Mahdi*, from all parts, to come down to the river; but he was in no particular hurry, for he knew that the country was securely in his hands, and that it would require a large Egyptian or foreign army to re-conquer it from him. Every Friday, he held a review of his troops, at which he himself was always present. His force was divided into three portions, each under the command of a *khalifa*, though, in addition, Khalifa Abdullahi was entitled "*Reis el Gesh*" (Commander-in-chief of the Army). His own special division was known as the *Raya ez Zarga*, or blue flag, and his brother Yakub represented him as its commander. The *Raya el Khadra,* or green flag, was under the command of the Khalifa Ali Wad Helu; while the red flag, the *Raya el Ashraf* (flag of the nobles), was placed under Khalifa Mohammed Sherif. Under each principal flag were grouped the flags

---
1. Major Kitchener, now Sir Herbert Kitchener, the Sirdar of the Egyptian Army.

of the various *emirs*.

When the reviews took place, the *emirs* of the *Raya ez Zarga* deployed into line with their banners facing east; those of the green flag were drawn up opposite to them, facing west; and, connecting these two lines, and facing north, were the *emirs* and flags of the Ashraf. The numbers of the *Mahdi's* followers being now enormous, an immense square was thus formed, open on one side; and the *Mahdi* and his staff, advancing to the centre, would receive the salute, and would then ride along the lines, welcoming his faithful adherents with the words, "*Allah yebarek fikum!*" (May God bless you!)

During these Friday reviews, called *Arda* or *Tarr*, extraordinary occurrences were said to take place. One would assert that he saw the Prophet riding beside the *Mahdi*, and talking with him; others would say they heard voices from Heaven, shouting blessings on the *Ansar*, and promises of victory. They would even affirm that a passing cloud was formed by angels' wings in order to give shade and refreshment to the faithful.

About three days after the news had been received of Abu Girga's defeat, an Italian named Joseph Cuzzi arrived at Rahad from Khartum; he had been residing in Berber at the time of its fall, having been left behind by A. Marquet, the agent of Debourg and Company, to wind up some of their affairs. Mohammed el Kheir had sent him, as a prisoner, to Abu Girga, and he had despatched him with a letter to Gordon; but the latter had refused to see him, and had sent him back to the enemy's post, on the east bank of the Blue Nile, opposite Khartum. The *Mahdi* now sent Cuzzi back in company with a Greek named George Calamatino, with letters to Gordon summoning him to submit. By the hands of this Greek, I also sent secretly a few lines to Gordon Pasha. The Greek was permitted to enter the lines; but Cuzzi was kept at a place some distance off, as, on the first occasion on which he had come, he was reported by the officers to have personally summoned them to surrender.

When the fast of *Ramadan* was over, Abu Anga and his entire fighting force were recalled from Jebel Daïr; and the *Mahdi* then publicly announced that the Prophet had directed him to proceed to Khartum and lay siege to it. Every *emir* was enjoined to collect his men, and order them to prepare for the march; whilst any who remained behind were declared lawful prey, and liable to total confiscation of all they possessed. However, there was no hanging back on the part of the people, whose fanaticism knew no bounds, and who were well aware that treasure and plunder generally fell to the share of the faithful followers. The consequence was that the *Mahdi's* summons brought about a wholesale immigration of the entire population, such as had never before been seen in the Sudan.

We left Rahad on 22nd August, the *Mahdist* forces marching by three separate roads: the northern one, *via* Khursi, Helba, and Tura el Hadra, was selected by the camel-owning tribes; the central road, *via* Tayara, Sherkéla, Shatt, and Duem, was taken by the *Mahdi, khalifas*, and the majority of the *emirs*; whilst the Baggaras and cattle-owning tribes adopted the southern route, which was well supplied with water, owing to the frequent rain pools which served as drinking places for the cattle. I, of course, in my capacity as *mulazem* of the Khalifa, followed my master; but, as a rule, when halted in camp, I used to send my horses and servants to Saleh Wad el Mek, who had joined the *Mahdi's* suite. The *khalifa*, however, for some unknown reason, had a particular aversion to him, and ordered me in the future to remain with my servants near him, and charged his cousin, Osman Wad Adam, to look after me. Nevertheless, every now and then, I used to see Saleh Wad el Mek, who was kept informed of all that was happening in the Nile districts.

Just before arriving at Sherkéla, strange rumours were spread about that an Egyptian who was a Christian had arrived at El Obeid, and was now on his way to overtake the *Mahdi*. Some believed him to be the Emperor of France; others affirmed that he was closely related to the Queen of England. However, there was no doubt a European was coming, and I was naturally most anxious to know who he could be. That evening, the *khalifa* told me a Frenchman had arrived at El Obeid, and that he had sent orders for him to be brought to the *Mahdi*. "Do you belong to the French race?" said he to me, "or are there different tribes in your country, as there are here with us in the Sudan?"—he had not, of course, the slightest knowledge of Europe and the European nations, and I enlightened him as far as I thought necessary.

"But what should a Frenchman want with us, that he should come all that long distance?" asked the *khalifa*, inquiringly; "possibly God has converted him, and has led him to the right way."

"Perhaps," said I, "he is seeking your and the *Mahdi's* friendship."

The *khalifa* looked at me incredulously, and said curtly, "We shall see."

At length, we reached Sherkéla; and, scarcely had we halted, when my master sent for me, and said, "Abdel Kader, the French traveller has arrived; I have now ordered him to be brought before me. You had better wait and listen to what he has to say; I may want you—" Almost immediately afterwards, Hussein Pasha came in, and he too had evidently been summoned by the *khalifa*. After waiting some little time longer, a *mulazem* announced that the stranger was waiting outside the hut; and he was at once admitted. He was a tall, young-looking man, about thirty years of age, I should say, and his face was much bronzed by the sun; he had a fair beard and moustache, and wore a *jibba* and turban. He greeted the *Khalifa* with "*Salam aleikum;*" and the latter, who did not rise from his *angareb*, merely motioned him to be seated. "Why have you come here; and what do you want from us?" were the *khalifa's* first words to him; he replied, in such broken Arabic that it was difficult to understand, that he was a Frenchman, and had come from France.

"Speak in your own language with Abdel Kader," interrupted the *khalifa*, "and he will explain to me what you want."

The stranger now turned and looked at me distrustfully, saying, in English, "Good day, sir."

"Do you speak French?" said I, "my name is Slatin. Stick to business entirely now, and, later on, we can speak privately."

"What are you talking about together," muttered the *khalifa*, in an annoyed tone, "I wish to know what he wants."

"I only told him my name," said I, "and urged him to speak openly to you, as both you and the *Mahdi* are men to whom God has granted the power to read the thoughts of others."

Hussein Khalifa, who was sitting beside me, now broke in, "That is true, indeed! May God prolong the *khalifa's* life;" and then, turning to me, he said, "you did well to call this stranger's attention to the fact."

The *khalifa*, appeased and flattered, now said, "Well, try and find out the truth."

"My name is Olivier Pain," said the stranger, whom I had now told to talk in French, "and I am a Frenchman. Since I was quite a boy I was interested in the Sudan, and sympathised with its people; it is not only I, but all my compatriots, who feel the same. In Europe there are nations with whom we are at feud; one of these is the English nation which has now settled in Egypt, and one of whose generals, Gordon, is now commanding in Khartum. I have therefore come to offer you my assistance, and that of my nation."

"What assistance?" interrupted the *khalifa*, to whom I was translating word for word Olivier Pain's statement.

"I can only offer you advice," said Pain; "but my nation, which is anxious to gain your friendship, is ready to help you practically with arms and money, under certain conditions."

"Are you a Mohammedan?" asked the *khalifa*, as if he had not heard what he had said.

"Yes, certainly," said he; "I have been of this faith for a long time, and at El Obeid I openly acknowledged it."

"Well," said the *khalifa*, "you and Hussein can stay here with the Frenchman, whilst I will go and let the *Mahdi* know, and I shall then come back to you."

When the *khalifa* had gone, I shook hands with Olivier Pain, and introduced him to Hussein *khalifa*; but I confess to feeling considerably prejudiced against him by his offer to assist our enemies. However, I urged him to be most careful, and to say that he had been induced to come here rather out of love for religion than for political motives. Even Hussein Pasha, who was evidently very much annoyed, said in Arabic to me, "Is that what you call politics,—to offer money and arms to people whose only object is to kill others, rob them of their property, and enslave their wives and daughters? Yet if one of us, no matter how poor he may be, buys a Black slave who is really little better than an animal, except that he can till the ground, you call it wicked and cruel, and punish us most severely."

"*Malaish!*" (Never mind!) said I, "he who lives long sees much."

We were now occupied with our own thoughts, whilst waiting for the *khalifa's* return; and at length he arrived, ordered us to make our ablutions and prepare to attend the *Mahdi's* prayers. Having done so, the *khalifa* leading, we went to the place of worship, where there was an immense concourse of people who, having heard of Olivier Pain's arrival, were indulging in the wildest speculations about him. After we had taken our places, Pain was directed to the second row, and the *Mahdi* now arrived. He was dressed in his speckless and beautifully perfumed *jibba*; his turban was more carefully folded than usual, and his eyes were well painted with antimony, which gave them a more fiery expression.

He had evidently done his utmost to appear to the greatest possible advantage. No doubt he was pleased and flattered that a man should have come from so far to offer him assistance. He now sat himself down on his prayer-carpet, and, calling up Olivier Pain before him, greeted him with a very beaming smile, but did not shake hands with him, and, using me as an interpreter, asked him to explain why he had come here.

Pain reiterated the same story as before, which the *Mahdi* told me to repeat in a sufficiently loud voice for everyone to hear; and, when I had finished, he said, in an equally loud tone, "I have heard your intentions, and have understood them; but I do not count on human support, I rely on God and His Prophet. Your nation are unbelievers, and I shall never ally myself with them. With God's help, I shall defeat my enemies through my brave Ansar, and the hosts of angels sent to me by the Prophet." Shouts of acclamation from thousands upon thousands of throats greeted this speech; and, when order had been restored, the *Mahdi* said to Pain, "You affirm that you love our faith, and acknowledge that it is the true one; are you a Mohammedan?"

"Certainly," answered he, repeating the creed, "*La ilaha illallah, Mohammed Rasul Allah,*" in a loud voice. The *Mahdi* after this gave him his hand to kiss, but did not administer the oath of allegiance.

We now took up our positions in the ranks of the faithful, and repeated prayers with the *Mahdi*; and, that over, the Divine Master gave us one of his usual sermons on salvation and renunciation. We then departed with the *khalifa*, who directed me to take Olivier Pain to my tent, and there await further instructions.

Once alone with Pain in my tent, I could talk to him without fear of interruption. I had the strongest aversion to his mission; but I pitied the man who, if he thought to succeed in such an enterprise in this country, was the victim of so absurd a delusion. I again greeted him heartily, saying, "Now, my dear Mr. Olivier Pain, we shall be quite undisturbed for a few minutes; let us speak frankly. Although I do not agree with your mission, I assure you, on my word as an officer, I will do all in my power to secure your personal safety. I have now been for years an exile from the civilised world; tell me something about outside affairs."

"I trust you thoroughly," he replied; "I know you well by name, and have often heard of you, and I thank my good fortune which has brought me to you. There is a great deal to tell you; but for the present I will confine myself to Egypt, which must interest us most."

"Tell me then," said I, "all about the revolt of Ahmed Arabi Pasha, about the massacres, about the intervention of the powers, and about England, which has just occupied Egypt."

"I," said he, "am working for the '*Indépendence*' with Rochefort, of whom you must have heard. England and France are politically antagonistic; and we do what we can to put as many difficulties as possible in England's way. I have not come here as a representative of my nation, but as a private individual with, however, the knowledge and concurrence of my nation. The English authorities, discovering my intentions, issued a warrant of arrest against me, and I was sent back from Wadi Halfa; but on my way down the river at Esna I agreed secretly with some Alighat Arabs to bring me here by the road running west of Dongola, through El Kaab, to El Obeid. Today the *Mahdi* has received me most kindly, and I hope for the best."

"Do you think that your proposal will be accepted?" said I.

"Should my proposal be refused," he answered, "I still hope the *Mahdi* will be induced to enter into friendly relations with France; for the present that will be quite sufficient, and, as I have come here of my own free will, I trust the *Mahdi* will not make my return impossible."

"That is very questionable," said I; "but have you left a family at home?"

"Oh, yes," answered Pain, "I have left my wife and two children in Paris; I often think of them, and hope to see them soon again. But tell me, sir, frankly, why should I be detained?"

"My dear sir," I replied, "as far as I know these people, I do not think you need at present have any fear for your own safety; but when and how you are going to get away from them, it is beyond my power to say. What I sincerely hope is, that your proposals, which may be advantageous to the enemy,—and I admit these *Mahdists* are my most bitter enemies,—will not be accepted, and I also hope they will allow you to return unmolested to your wife and children, who must be anxiously awaiting you."

Meanwhile I had told my servants to get us something to eat; and I had sent for Gustav Klootz, O'Donovan's former servant, to share our meal with us. We had scarcely begun, when two of the *khalifa's mulazemin* entered, and told Olivier Pain to follow them. He was much taken aback at being called off alone, and, in a whisper, commended himself to me. It also struck me as curious, for Pain's Arabic was quite unintelligible. I was talking about this to Mustafa (Klootz), when I also received a summons, and, on entering the *khalifa's* hut, I found him quite alone; he motioned to me to be seated, and I sat on the ground beside him.

"Abdel Kader," said he, confidentially, "I look on you as one of us; tell me what do you think of this Frenchman?"

"I believe he is sincere and means well," said I; "but he did not know the *Mahdi* nor you; he did not understand that you trusted only in God, and sought no support from other powers, and that this is the cause of your continual victories, because God is with those who put their trust in Him!"

"You heard the *Mahdi's* words," continued the *khalifa*, "when he said to the Frenchman that he wished to have nothing to do with unbelievers, and that he could defeat his enemies without their help?"

"Most certainly I did," I replied; "and therefore the man is useless here, and may as well return to his nation, and tell them about the victories of the *Mahdi* and his commander-in-chief, the *khalifa*."

"Perhaps later," said the *khalifa*; "for the present, I have ordered him to stay with Zeki Tummal, who will take all care of him, and attend to his wants."

"But it will be very difficult for him to make himself understood in Arabic," I pleaded; "he is by no means a good Arabic scholar yet."

"He has been able to get here without an interpreter," answered the *khalifa*; "however, you have my permission to visit him." He then talked about other things, and showed me the horses Zogal had sent him from Darfur, some of which I knew very well. After leaving my master, I went in search of Pain, whom I found sitting under the shade of a very battered old tent, his head resting on his hands, and evidently in deep thought; when he saw me, he at once rose, saying, "I don't know what to think about it all. I have been ordered to stay here; my baggage has been brought, and I am told that a certain Zeki has been ordered to look after me. Why don't they let me stay with you?"

"It is the *Mahdi's* nature; and the *khalifa* is even worse in working his will in contrariety to every human being under the sun. You are going through a course of what they call 'putting one to the test in patience, submission, and faith,'" said I, by way of sympathy; "but you need have no fear. The *khalifa* suspects us both, and is anxious to keep us apart, so that we should not criticise his actions. Here comes Zeki Tummal. He was with me in many a fight; I will strongly commend you to him." I had now advanced to meet Zeki, who shook hands with me, and asked how I was. "My friend," said I to him, "this is a stranger and your guest. I recommend him to your kind care; be forbearing with him for old acquaintance sake."

"I shall let him want for nothing as far as it is in my power to do so," he replied; and then, more slowly, he said, "but the *khalifa* has told me not to let him have any intercourse with others, and I therefore beg you will come here only very occasionally."

"These orders do not apply to me," said I; "just this moment I left our master's hut, and he has given me special permission to visit your guest. So again I beg you to treat this poor man with all consideration."

I then returned to Pain and tried to cheer him up, telling him that the *khalifa* had given orders he was not to be allowed to see other people; but this, I said, was no disadvantage, for they would probably have used the occasion to intrigue against him, and so put him in danger. As regards myself, however, I said I would come to see him as often as possible.

The next morning, the *khalifa's* great war-drum, called "*El Mansura*" (the victorious), was beaten; this was the signal for the march to begin again, and off we started. We generally marched from early morning till noon only, and thus our progress was not rapid. When we halted at midday, I went to look for Pain, and found him sitting under his tent as before; he appeared in good health, but complained about the bad food. Zeki, who was present whilst we were speaking, said that he had twice sent him some *asida*, but he would not touch it. I explained that he was not, of course, accustomed to native food yet, and that therefore I proposed getting my servant to prepare some food specially for him; and, returning at once, I ordered him to make some soup and boil some rice, and take it to Olivier Pain.

That evening the *khalifa* asked me if I had seen him. I told him I had; but that, as he was not accustomed yet to native food, I had ordered my servant to prepare something else. I explained that if he were forced to eat the native food he might get ill; and that therefore, with his permission, I proposed sending him, every now and then, something special. The *khalifa* assented. "But," said he, "you eat of our food; it would therefore be better he should get used to it as soon as possible. By-the-bye where is Mustafa? I have not seen him since we left Rahad?"

"He is staying with me, and helps my servants to look after the horses and camels," said I.

"Then send for him," said the *khalifa*. I did so; and in a few minutes he entered and stood before us. "Where have you been? I have not seen you for weeks," said the *khalifa*, angrily. "Have you forgotten that I am your master?"

"With your permission I went to Abdel Kader, whom I help in his work. You do not care for me now, and have left me alone," replied Klootz, in an annoyed tone.

"Then I will take good care of you in the future," cried the *khalifa*, still more angrily; and, calling in a *mulazem*, he ordered him to take Mustafa to his clerk, Ben Naga, who should put him in chains. Mustafa, without uttering a word, followed his guard.

"Mustafa and you," continued the *khalifa*, "have servants enough; and you can quite well do without him. I took him for myself; but he left me without any cause. I then ordered that he should serve my brother Yakub; but he complained and left him too; and now that he is with you, he thinks he can dispense with us altogether."

"Pardon him," said I, "he is merciful who forgives. Let him stay with your brother; perhaps he will improve."

"He must remain a few days in chains," he answered, "so that he may know I am his master; he is not the same as you, who come every day to my door;" this he evidently said to quiet me, as he thought I was getting annoyed. He then ordered supper to be brought in; and I ate more than usual, so that he should not imagine I was doing anything contrary to his orders. He talked very little during the meal, and seemed out of spirits. After supper he made an attempt to say something kind; but I felt that his words belied him. We then separated, and, as I returned to my tent, I thought over the situation.

I had resolved to remain on as good terms as I could with the *khalifa*, until the hour of my deliverance should come; but his imperious character, want of consideration, and immense self-conceit made my task a most difficult one. I had daily before my eyes the examples of several *mulazemin* whom he had thrown into chains, flogged, and deprived of their property (known as "*tegrid*") on the slightest provocation. He judged very quickly, being actuated entirely by his feelings at the moment, and loved to show that he was master. I will now give an example of the sort of man I had to deal with.

Abu Anga, the commander of the black troops (*Jehadia*), and his brother, Fadl Maula, who was his assistant, were both sons of a liberated slave who had borne them to one of the *khalifa's* relatives. Fadl Maula had a great friend and adviser in Ahmed Wad Yunes of the Shaigia tribe, and these two presented themselves before the *khalifa* one day, when Fadl Maula asked his master's permission for Yunes to marry a certain girl, and give him his blessing. It happened, however, that the *khalifa* was in a bad humour, and wished to show his authority; so he immediately ordered the girl's father to be brought before him, and asked him, in the presence of the others, if he wished to give his daughter in marriage to Yunes; and, on the man answering in the affirmative, the *khalifa* said, "I have decided, and consider it to the girl's advantage that she should marry Fadl Maula. Have you any objection?"

Of course the girl's father had to assent, and, without a moment's hesitation, the *khalifa*, turning to his attendants, ordered them to read the marriage "Fatha," or form of prayer and blessing on marriage. This was done, and dates were partaken of. The *khalifa* then dismissed all those present, and Fadl Maula departed one wife to the good, whilst Yunes was one hope the poorer; but what the girl said about the new arrangement, I cannot tell.

With a master of this character, one had to be very careful.

After five days' march, we reached Shatt, where most of the wells were filled up, and had to be reopened, and several straw huts erected; for the *Mahdi* had decided to halt here for some days. During the march, I frequently visited Pain, who daily grew more and more disheartened about the situation. He knew very little Arabic, and was not permitted to talk to anyone but the slaves charged with looking after him. In a few days, the object of his mission had vanished from his mind, and he thought now only of his wife and children. I urged him to look more hopefully on the future, and not to give way to depressing thoughts which would only make him more miserable. The *khalifa* seemed to have almost forgotten his existence, and scarcely ever asked for him.

The day after our arrival at Shatt, the *Mahdi's* former Sheikh, Mohammed Sherif, who had been expected for so long, at length arrived. He also had been forced by his friends, and by fear, to come to the *Mahdi* as a penitent; but the latter received him most honourably, and himself led him to the tents he had specially pitched for him, and also presented him with two exceptionally pretty Abyssinian girls, horses, etc. By this generous treatment, the *Mahdi* attracted to himself almost all Mohammed Sherif's secret adherents.

In the course of time, the *khalifa* forgave Mustafa, allowed him to live with his clerk Ben Naga, and permitted him to talk to me.

Just at the time we left Sherkéla, news arrived that Gordon's troops had suffered a severe reverse; and now in Shatt we received the detailed accounts of the overthrow of Mohammed Ali Pasha at Om Debban by the Sheikh El Obeid.

It appeared that when Gordon had defeated the Halfaya rebels at Buri, he despatched Mohammed Ali with two thousand men to disperse the Mahdists collected at Om Debban, the village of the Sheikh

El Obeid. Mohammed Ali's career had been very rapid: at his own request he had left me in Darfur with the rank of adjutant-major; Gordon had promoted him to major; and, during the siege, he had risen to the rank of colonel, and soon afterwards to that of general. The force which he commanded against the Sheikh El Obeid was composed mostly of irregulars, and he was accompanied by crowds of women and slaves seeking for plunder. When on the march between El Eilafun and Om Debban, he was attacked suddenly rom all sides, and his force was almost entirely annihilated; only a few escaped to bring the sad news to Khartum, where the grief was intense, and to Gordon it must have indeed been a terrible blow.

This success had encouraged the rebels to press the siege more closely; and now, reinforced as they were by Wad en Nejumi and his hosts, Gordon found himself not strong enough to make a successful attack on the *Mahdists*.

From Shatt we now advanced to Duem, where the *Mahdi* held an enormous review; and, pointing to the Nile, he said, "God has created this river; He will give you its waters to drink, and you shall become the possessors of all the lands along its banks." This speech was greeted with shouts of joy by these wild fanatics, who at once believed that the wonderful land of Egypt was to be their prey.

From Duem we proceeded to Tura el Hadra, where we spent the Feast of Great Bairam; Olivier Pain was suffering from fever, and was growing more and more depressed. "I have tried many ventures in my life," said he, "without thinking much beforehand of the consequences; but my coming here was a fatal mistake. It would have been very much better for me if the English had succeeded in preventing me from carrying out my design." I did my best to comfort him, but he only shook his head.

At the Feast of Bairam, the *Mahdi* repeated prayers in an unusually loud voice; and when he read the *Khutba*, he wept long and bitterly. We unbelievers well knew that this weeping was hypocrisy, and boded no good; but it had the desired effect on the fanatical crowds who had flocked to his banners from the river tribes, and who were roused by this touching sermon to the highest pitch of enthusiasm.

After a halt of two days, we again moved on, creeping forward like a great tortoise, so swelled were we by the thousands upon thousands who were now joining daily from every part of the Sudan. Poor Olivier had grown considerably worse; his fever had turned to typhus. He begged me to induce the *Mahdi* to let him have some money, as he was so pestered by the begging appeals of his attendants. I went to him, and explained Pain's condition; and the *Mahdi* at once sent to the Beit el Mal for £5, and wished the sick man a speedy recovery. I had also told the *khalifa* of Pain's serious illness, and that the *Mahdi* had given him £5; but he blamed me for having asked for it without his permission, adding, "If he dies here, he is a happy man. God in His goodness and omnipotence has converted him from an unbeliever to a believer."

Early in the morning, at the end of the first week in October, I was sent for by Pain, and found him so weak that he could not stand up. For two days he had not touched the food I had sent him; and, placing his hand in mine, he said, "My last hour has come; I thank you for your great kindness and care of me. The last favour I have to ask of you is this: when you escape from the hands of these barbarous people, and you happen to go to Paris, tell my unfortunate wife and children my dying thoughts were for them."

As he said these words, tears rolled down the poor man's hollow and sunken cheeks. Again I tried to comfort him, saying that it was too soon to give up hope; and as the war-drum was beating for the advance, I had to hurry away and leave him. It was the last time I saw him alive. I left behind with him one of my servants named "Atrun" (Natron), and during the march I told the *khalifa* of Pain's condition, urging him to leave the poor man behind at some village where he might have a few days' rest; he told me to remind him of it that evening. The evening came, but no sick man arrived; Atrun came alone.

"Where is Yusef?" (this was Pain's Mohammedan name), said I, for the boy seemed much agitated.

"My master is dead," he answered; "and that is the reason we are so late."

"Dead!" said I.

"Yes, dead and buried," replied Atrun.

"Tell me at once what has happened," I asked.

"My master Yusef was so weak," said he, "that he could not ride; but we had to go on marching. Every now and then he lost consciousness; then he would come to again and talk words we could not understand. So we tied an *angareb* on to the saddle, and laid him on it; but he was too weak to hold on, and he fell down suddenly and very heavily. After this he did not come to again, and he was soon dead; so we wrapped him up in his *farda* (cotton shawl), and buried him, and all his effects were taken to Zeki by his slaves."

Olivier Pain was undoubtedly very seriously ill; but the fall was probably the immediate cause of his sudden death. Poor man! with what a high sounding mission he had come; and now this was the end of it all! I immediately went to the *khalifa*, and reported his death to him. "He is a happy man," was his curt remark; he then despatched a *mulazem* to warn Zeki to have all his effects carefully kept, and he sent me to the *Mahdi* to apprise him of his end. The latter took it to heart much more than the *khalifa*, said several sympathetic words, and repeated the prayers for the dead.

After three days, we reached the neighbourhood of Khartum, and halted at a place about one day's journey from the city. On our way, we had seen Gordon's steamers in the distance; they had come up evidently to watch our movements, and had returned again without firing.

It was evening, and we had just finished pitching camp, when a *mulazem* of the *Mahdi* arrived, and directed me to follow him; I went at once, and found him sitting with Abdel Kader Wad Om Mariam, formerly Kadi of Kalakla, and a man who exercised a great influence on the people of the White Nile. Hussein Khalifa was also there; and I formed the fourth of the party.

"I have sent for you," said the *Mahdi*, "to tell you to write to Gordon to save himself from certain defeat. Tell him that I am the true *Mahdi*, and that he ought to surrender with his garrison, and thus save himself and his soul. Tell him also, that if he refuses to obey, we shall every one of us fight against him. Say that you yourself will fight against him with your own hands. Say that victory will be ours, and that you merely tell him this in order to avoid useless bloodshed."

I remained silent till Hussein Khalifa called on me to answer. "O *Mahdi*!" said I, "listen, I beg of you, to my words. I will be honest and faithful; and I pray you to forgive me, if what I say is not pleasing to you. If I write to Gordon that you are the true *Mahdi*, he will not believe me; and if I threaten to fight against him with my own hands, he will not be afraid of that. Now as you desire, under any circumstances, to avoid shedding blood, I shall simply summon him to surrender. I shall say that he is not strong enough to attempt to fight against you who are ever-victorious, as he has no hope of help from outside; and, finally, I shall say that I will be the intermediary between you and him."

"I accept your sincere proposal," said the *Mahdi*; "go now and write the letters, and tomorrow they shall be despatched to Gordon."

I now returned to my quarters. My tent, owing to the difficulties of transport, had been torn to shreds, and I had made a present of the rags to someone; I had in place of it stretched some strips of cloth on sticks, and thus provided a slight shade for myself during the daytime, whilst at night I slept in the open. Searching about for a lantern, I wrote the letters seated on an *angareb* under the open sky. First I wrote a few lines to Gordon in French, explaining that I was writing to him fully in German because, my French Dictionary having been burnt by the *Mahdists*, who thought it was a Prayer Book, I did not feel capable of expressing myself as I wished in that language. I said that I hoped I should soon have an opportunity of joining him; and I prayed God that he might be successful. I also mentioned that some of the Shaigias who had recently joined the *Mahdi* did so to save their wives and children, and not because they entertained any feelings of hostility towards Gordon.

I then wrote a long letter to him in German, saying that I had learnt through George Calamatino that he was annoyed at my capitulation, and that therefore I took the liberty of placing the facts of the case before him, begging him to form his opinion accordingly. I began by recalling my campaigns against Sultan Harun and Dud Benga, and explaining how, on the outbreak of the *Mahdi* revolt, the few officers left, believing that Arabi Pasha had succeeded in driving the Europeans out of the country, had spread reports that my recent defeats lay in the fact that I was a Christian; how I had stifled the injurious effects of these intrigues by giving out that I was a Mohammedan; and how I had, by this means, been subsequently successful until the annihilation of Hicks' army had cut off all hope of relief.

I told him how my constant fights had reduced my available force to some seven hundred men; that my stock of ammunition was well-nigh exhausted; that both officers and men desired capitulation: and what therefore could I do—a European and alone—but submit. I told him how this surrender had been one of the hardest acts of my life; but that as an Austrian officer I felt that I had not acted in a dishonourable manner. I then went on to say that by obedient and submissive behaviour I had in some measure gained the confidence of the *Mahdi* and the *khalifa*, and had obtained their permission to write to him, on the pretext that I was asking him to surrender; but that, instead, I availed myself of this opportunity to offer him my services in order to assure him that I was ready to conquer, or die with him, if God willed, an honourable death.

Should he agree to be an accessory to my escape to Khartum, I begged him to write me a few lines in French to that effect; but, in order to carry through the ruse, I suggested that he should also write me a few lines in Arabic, asking me to obtain the *Mahdi's* permission to come to Omdurman, in order to discuss with him the conditions of surrender. I went on to tell him that Saleh Bey and several of the *sheikhs* wished to express their loyalty and devotion to him; but that, under the circumstances, it was impossible for them to come to him, as, by so doing, they would necessarily sacrifice their wives and children.

I now wrote a third letter, in German, to Consul Hansal, asking him to do his utmost to arrange that I should re-enter Khartum, as, being thoroughly cognisant of the *Mahdi's* plans, intentions, strength, etc., I believed I could be of great service to General Gordon; but, at the same time, as rumours had been in circulation in the *Mahdi's* camp that, if relief should not soon come, Gordon intended to surrender the town, and as at that time I was quite ignorant of Gordon's prospects of relief, I begged Consul Hansal to inform me of this, as, in the event of the town being surrendered subsequent to my having entered Khartum, I should naturally be the *Mahdi's* lawful victim on which to vent all his anger at my escape and my efforts to aid his enemies.

It seemed to me that it was quite reasonable on my part to seek some such assurance. At the same time, rumours being current in the camp that the Khartum garrison were much out of heart and wished to surrender, I strongly urged Hansal in my letter not to feel discouraged, pointing out that the *Mahdi's* forces were not so numerous as he imagined, and that it only required energy and perseverance on the part of the Egyptian troops to be eventually successful, and I urged that they should wait at least six weeks, or two months, longer before submitting, so as to give the relief expedition a chance of saving them.[2]

I also told him there was a rumour in camp that the small steamer which had been sent to Dongola had been wrecked at Wadi Gamr; but that I was not at present in a position to say whether it was true or not.

Early the next morning, the 15th October, I took these letters

---

2. On my return to Cairo in 1895, I learnt that the full text of the letters to which I have referred, had reached the British authorities, and had been published in General Gordon's *Journal*

to the *Mahdi* and he told me to send them by one of my boys to Omdurman. I at once went and fetched Morgan Fur, a boy of about fifteen years of age, and handed him the letters in the *Mahdi's* presence; and the latter ordered Wad Suleiman to give him a donkey and some money. Before sending him off, I gave him the most strict injunctions to speak to no one in Khartum except to Gordon Pasha and Consul Hansal, and to assure them that I wished to come to them.

At midday, some horsemen arrived from Berber, confirming the news of the wreck of the steamer, and of the murder of Colonel Stewart, and those with him. The men brought with them all the papers and documents found on board; and I was ordered by the *khalifa* to examine those written in European languages in Ahmed Wad Suleiman's office. Amongst them, I found several private letters from people in Khartum, as well as official documents and records. The most important of these was, of course, the military report describing the daily occurrences in Khartum; it was unsigned, but I had no doubt it was General Gordon's. A portion only of the correspondence, etc., was shown to me; and before I had had time to peruse it fully, I was again summoned before the *Mahdi*, who asked me what the contents were. I replied, that most of them were private letters, and that there was a military report, which I did not understand.

Unfortunately amongst the captured correspondence were numbers of Arabic letters and reports, from which the *Mahdi* and the *khalifa* were able to thoroughly grasp the situation in Khartum. There was also a half-ciphered Arabic telegram from General Gordon to His Highness the Khedive, which Abdel Halim Effendi, formerly head clerk in Kordofan, was able to decipher. Amongst the consular reports, I found a notice of the death in Khartum of my old friend Ernst Marno, who had succumbed to fever.

The *Mahdi* now discussed, in my presence, what papers should be sent to Gordon, in order to convince him that the steamer had been wrecked, and Colonel Stewart and the others killed, thinking that this would force Gordon to surrender. I pointed out that the only document likely to convince Gordon, was his military report, which I suggested should be returned; and, after a long discussion, it was decided to send it.

The crowds accompanying the *Mahdi* were now complaining greatly of the want of corn and *dhurra*; the price of an *ardeb* had risen to eighteen *medjidie* dollars, which were then equivalent to about nine pounds sterling. This extraordinary rate of exchange had been brought about by the scarcity of dollars, in consequence of which the treasurer had ordered the money captured at Berber—some £70,000 to £80,000 in gold—to be sent to the *Mahdi's* camp; and this had been distributed. At times, a sovereign valued even as little as a dollar and a half. Though *dhurra* was so expensive, the prices of sheep and cattle were unusually low,—a good ox or cow could be purchased for a dollar and a half or two dollars, and a calf for half a dollar.

This arose from the fact that an immense number of cattle-owning Arabs had immigrated with the *Mahdi* from the west, and had brought their flocks and herds with them to the river; here the pasturage was quite insufficient for such quantities of animals. The *Mahdi* had therefore preached a sermon to the herdsmen, to the effect that tending flocks and herds, at the present time, was a useless occupation, and that all their attention should now be centred on fighting the religious war; consequently these ignorant people followed his advice, and sold their cattle at these absurdly low rates.

The next evening, my boy Morgan returned from his mission, but brought no reply. When I inquired how this was, he said, he had reached Omdurman fort, had delivered his letters, and, after waiting for a short time, the commandant had told him to return, as there was no answer. I at once took the boy to the *Mahdi*, to whom he repeated what had occurred; and afterwards I went and informed the *khalifa*. That same evening, the *Mahdi* again summoned me, and ordered me to write another letter, which he said Gordon would be sure to answer, when he heard of the loss of the steamer. I at once expressed myself ready to carry out his wishes; and he directed that my boy Morgan should again act as messenger.

Once more I betook myself to my *angareb*, and, by the flickering light of an old lantern, scribbled another letter, reporting the loss of the steamer, the death of Stewart, and repeating much of what I had said in my first letters, adding that if, in his opinion, I had done anything contrary to the honour of an officer, and if that had hindered him from writing to me, I begged he would give me a chance of defending myself, and thus give himself an opportunity of coming to a correct judgment.

Early the next morning, I went again with Morgan to the *Mahdi*; the latter ordered Ahmed Wad Suleiman to supply him with a donkey, and, taking my letter, he went off, returning the following morning with a reply from Consul Hansal, written in German, with an Arabic translation; it ran as follows:—

Dear Friend Slatin Bey,—Your letters have been duly received, and I request you will come to Tabia Ragheb Bey (Omdurman Fort). I wish to speak to you about the steps to be taken for our rescue; you may then return unmolested to your friend.

Yours very truly,

(Signed)   Hansal.

This letter puzzled me somewhat; I could not be sure if it was written with the object merely of deceiving the *Mahdi*, in which case the Arabic was amply sufficient for the purpose; but I thought he might have written more clearly in German, though perhaps he conceived there might have been someone else with the *Mahdi* who understood that language, and I might have been thereby endangered. Then, taking the letter literally, he seemed to hint at joining us himself,—indeed we had already heard rumours that he, becoming alarmed at the probable fall of the town, wished to submit with the other Austrian subjects to the *Mahdi*; but it was of course quite impossible to say if he meant this or not. Then again, as regards my joining Gordon in Khartum, could he really mean that the latter had refused to listen to my request, or was his expression that I "may then return unmolested to my friend" merely meant as a blind to the *Mahdi*?—I confess I was utterly perplexed; my suspense, however, was not of long duration.

I at once took the letter to the *Mahdi*, and explained to him that the Arabic text exactly corresponded with the German original. When he had finished reading it, he asked me if I wished to go, and I replied that I was ready to comply with his orders, and that my services were always at his disposal.

"I am rather afraid," said he, "that if you go to Omdurman to speak to your consul, Gordon may arrest or kill you. Why did he not write to you himself, if he thinks well of you?"

"I do not know why he is so silent," said I; "perhaps it is contrary to his orders to enter into communication with us; however, when I meet Hansal I may be able to arrange matters. You say you are afraid Gordon might arrest me; but I am not, and even if he did I am quite sure you could release me; but as to his killing me, that is altogether out of the question."

"Well," said the *Mahdi*, "get yourself ready to go, and I will let you know."

On my way to the *Mahdi's* hut, I had heard of Lupton Bey's arrival from Bahr el Ghazal; and now, on my way back, I went in search of him, and found him outside the *khalifa's* door waiting to be received. Although it was against rules to speak to any one before he had received the *Mahdi's* pardon, I could not resist greeting him heartily, and, in a few words, told him about the letters; and he said he earnestly hoped I might be allowed to go to Khartum. He told me he had left his servants and the rest of his people at some hours' distance, and he asked me to obtain the *khalifa's* permission for them to come in. A few minutes afterwards, he was summoned before the *khalifa*, obtained his pardon, was told that he might go and bring in his people, and that he would be presented to the *Mahdi* on his return.

Meanwhile, I went back to my quarters, and lay on my *angareb* impatiently awaiting my orders to be allowed to go to Omdurman; or had the *Mahdi*, perhaps, changed his mind, and decided not to let me go? At length, one of my boys came and told me that a *mulazem* of the *khalifa's* wished to see me, and, getting up, he told me to follow him to Yakub's camp, where his master was waiting for me. Without a moment's delay, I bound my turban round my head, put on my *hizam* (belt), and followed. At Yakub's camp, we were told that the *khalifa* had gone on to Abu Anga's *zariba*, where he was waiting for us. I was beginning to get suspicious; all this wandering about at night was very unusual.

I knew how deceitful these people were, and I was therefore prepared for any eventuality. Arrived at Abu Anga's *zariba*, we were admitted by the sentry. It was an immense enclosure filled with little shelters made of strips of cotton fixed on poles, and separated from each other by small *dhurra*-stalk fences. We were directed to one of these shelters, and there, by the dim light of a lantern, I saw Yakub, Abu Anga, Fadl el Maula, Zeki Tummal, and Hajji Zubeir seated round in a circle talking earnestly; behind them stood several armed men; but no trace was to be seen of the *khalifa* who, I had been told, had sent for me. I was now almost certain in my own mind that foul play was intended. The *mulazem* advanced and spoke to Yakub, and I was then summoned to enter, and to place myself between Hajji Zubeir and Fadl el Maula, while opposite to me sat Abu Anga.

"Abdel Kader," began Abu Anga, "you have promised to be faithful to the *Mahdi*; and it is your duty to keep your word; it is also your duty to obey orders, even should you suffer thereby. Is not this so?"

"Certainly," said I, "and you, Abu Anga, if you give me any orders from the *Mahdi* or the *khalifa*, you will see that I know how to obey them."

"I received orders to make you a prisoner; but I do not know the reason," said he; and, as he spoke, Hajji Zubeir snatched away my sword, which, as was customary, I had laid across my knees whilst speaking, and, handing it to Zeki Tummal, he seized my right arm with both hands.

"I did not come here to fight," said I to Hajji Zubeir; "why should you seize my arm; but you, Abu Anga, of course you must do as you are bidden."

What I had often inflicted on others, I was now about to undergo myself. Abu Anga then stood up, and also Hajji Zubeir and myself, when the latter let go my arm.

"Go to that tent," said Abu Anga, pointing to a shelter which, in the dark, I could scarcely see, "and you, Hajji Zubeir and the rest, go with him."

Accompanied by my gaoler, and some eight others, I went to the tent, where I was directed to sit on the ground, and chains were now brought out. Two large iron rings, bound together by a thick iron bar, were slipped over my feet, and then hammered close; an iron ring was placed round my neck, and to this was attached a long iron chain with the links so arranged that I had the greatest difficulty in moving my head. I endured all this in perfect silence; Hajji Zubeir then left, and I was told, by the two soldiers who were guarding me, to lie down on the palm-mat close by.

Left to myself, I had now time to collect my thoughts; and, first of all, I bitterly regretted not having attempted to escape on my horse to Khartum; but who could tell if Gordon would have received me? Now, in accordance with the *Mahdi's* orders, I was out of harm's way; but what was to be my fate? Was it to be that of Mohammed Pasha Said and Ali Bey Sherif? I was not in the habit of worrying about my personal concerns, and making life miserable. What had Madibbo told me, "Be obedient and patient; for he who lives long sees much." I had been obedient; it was now my turn to practise patience; and as for a long life, that was entirely in God's hands.

About an hour later, during which, as may be imagined, I had not slept, I saw several *mulazemin* approaching, carrying lanterns, and, as they neared the tent, I made out Khalifa Abdullahi walking in the middle. I stood up and waited for him.

"Abdel Kader," said he, when he saw me standing in front of him, "are you submitting with resignation to your fate?"

"Since my childhood," I replied quietly, "I have been accustomed to be obedient; now I must be obedient whether I like it or no."

"Your friendship with Saleh Wad el Mek," said he, "and your correspondence with Gordon, have cast suspicion on you, and we doubt if your heart is still inclined to us; that is the reason I have ordered you to be forcibly directed in the right way."

"I made no secret of my friendship with Saleh Wad el Mek," said I; "he is a friend of mine, and I believe he is loyal to you. As regards my correspondence with Gordon, the *Mahdi* ordered me to write the letters."

"Did he also order you to write what you did?" interrupted the *khalifa*.

"I think I wrote what the *Mahdi* required," I replied; "and no one knows the contents except myself and the person who received the letters. All I require, sire, is justice; and I beg that you will pay no heed to lying intriguers."

I was again alone, and tried to sleep, but was too excited. All sorts of strange thoughts and ideas coursed through my brain; the iron round my feet and neck too pained me considerably, and I could get no rest. I scarcely got a wink of sleep that night; and, at sunrise, Abu Anga came, followed by servants carrying some dishes of food. Seating himself beside me on the palm-mat, the food was placed before us; it was quite a feast, composed of meal, chickens, rice and milk, honey, roast meat and *asida*. But when I told him I had absolutely no appetite, he said, "I think, Abdel Kader, you are afraid; and that is why you do not eat."

"No," I replied, "it is not fear, but want of appetite. However, to please you, I will try and eat something;" and I managed to swallow a few mouthfuls, whilst Abu Anga did all he could to show that I was his honoured guest.

"The *khalifa*," said he, "was rather disappointed yesterday, when he saw you were not humbled; and remarked you were strong-headed, and that, he supposed, was the reason you were not afraid."

"How could I throw myself at his feet," said I, "and crave his pardon for a crime I never committed? I am in his hands, and he can do as he likes with me."

"Tomorrow, we shall advance," said Abu Anga, "and draw nearer to Khartum; we shall press the siege more closely, and then make a sudden attack. I shall ask the *khalifa* to let you stay with me; that will be less hard for you than going to the common prison."

I thanked him for his kindness, and he then left.

All that day, I was quite alone, but went through my prayers most carefully in the sight of the bystanders, holding in my hand the rosary which all good Mohammedans carry; but in reality I was repeating over and over again the *Lord's Prayer*. In the far distance, near Abu Anga's tent, I caught sight of my servants and horses and the little baggage I had. One of my boys also came and told me he had been ordered to attach himself to Abu Anga.

Early the next morning, the great war-drum sounded the advance; tents were struck, baggage packed and loaded on camels, and the whole camp was in movement. The weight of iron on my feet prevented me from walking, so they brought me a donkey; the long neck-chain— the number of figure-of-eight links of which I had amused myself in counting, and which amounted to eighty-three, each about a span long—I wrapped round and round my body, and in this iron casing I was lifted on to the donkey, and held in position by a man on each side, otherwise my weight would have made me overbalance and fall. On the march, several of my old friends passed, but dared do nothing but pity me in silence. We halted on some rising ground in the afternoon, and from here I could see the palm-trees in Khartum; how I longed, as one of its garrison, to join in its defence!

The order was now given to make a temporary camp in this position, under Khalifa Abdullahi, whilst the principal *emirs* went forward to select the site for a permanent camp. By this time, the pangs of hunger had seized me, and I longed for some of the food which Abu Anga had offered me yesterday; but the latter was now with the *khalifa*, and had evidently forgotten all about us. However, the wife of one of my guards found him out, and brought him some stale *dhurra*-bread, which he shared with me. Next morning, we were again ordered to advance, and halted about an hour further on, at the spot selected for the main camp. As Abu Anga had promised, it was now arranged that I should definitely remain under his charge; a tattered old tent was pitched for me, and around it, close to the tent ropes, a thorn *zariba* was made. I was put in here, and the entrance, which was guarded by soldiers, was blocked by a large thorn-bush.

The *Mahdi* now ordered the siege to be vigorously pressed; that evening several *emirs* were sent over to the east bank of the White Nile to reinforce Wad en Nejumi and Abu Girga; and all the local people were summoned to join in the investment. Abu Anga and Fadl el Maula were told off to besiege Omdurman fort, which was situated about five hundred yards from the river, on the west bank, and was defended by Faragalla Pasha,—a Sudanese officer who, in the space of one year, had been promoted from the rank of captain to that of general officer, by Gordon. Abu Anga succeeded in establishing himself between the fort and the river; and, by digging deep trenches, he obtained sufficient shelter to hold this advanced position in spite of the heavy fire from both the fort and the steamers; one of the latter he succeeded in sinking by shells fired from a gun he had placed in position; but the crew managed to escape to Khartum.[3]

During the siege, I was quite neglected; my guards were changed every day, and my welfare entirely depended on their treatment of me. If they happened to be slaves who had been captured, I was most carefully watched, and permitted to have no intercourse with any one; but if they happened to be old soldiers who knew me, I was not so closely restrained, and they often did me little services, though they prevented me from speaking to an one. My food was of the very worst description; and, Abu Anga being always occupied in the siege, I was left to the tender mercies of his wives, to whom he had given orders to feed me.

On one occasion, one of my former soldiers happened to be on guard over me, and I sent him with a message to Abu Anga's chief wife, complaining that I had been kept without food for two days; and I got back the answer, "Well, does Abdel Kader think we are going to fatten him up here, whilst his uncle, Gordon Pasha, does nothing but fire shells all day at our master, whose life is always in danger through his fault? If he had made his uncle submit, he would not now be in chains." From her own standpoint, the woman's views were perfectly justifiable.

Occasionally, some of the Greeks were allowed to come and see me, and they used to tell me the news.

On the day we arrived here, poor Lupton Bey was also thrown into chains, as he was suspected of attempting to join Gordon; besides, when his effects were searched, a document was found, signed by all the officers of his regular troops, stating that he had been forced to surrender his province. His wife and little daughter of five years old were sent to live at the Beit el Mal. The former had been brought up as a black servant girl in the house of Rosset, formerly German Consul at Khartum, and, on his being appointed Governor of Darfur, she had accompanied him there; on his death at El Fasher, she went with Lupton to Equatoria and Bahr el Ghazal. By the Khalifa's orders, all Lupton's property was confiscated; but he allowed his wife and child

---

3. The steamer *Husseinyeh*.

the services of a black female slave to help them in their daily work.

One day, George Calamatino brought me the news that the English army, under Lord Wolseley, was advancing slowly, and had reached Dongola; but they had delayed too long in Upper Egypt, and now that Khartum was in the greatest danger, their advanced guard was no further south than Dongola: under these circumstances, when could their main body arrive?

Sometime after the proclamation of the abandonment of the Sudan had been made known, Gordon had given the Khartum people to understand that an English army was coming up to relieve them; and he had thus inspired the garrison and inhabitants with hope and courage. They had been, so to speak, given a new lease of life, and all eyes were anxiously turned to the north, from whence the expected help was to come. Would it come in time?—that was the question.

These days passed in my tattered tent were full of hopes and fears. It was not that I was concerned about my own safety, but I could not help anticipating coming events with the greatest anxiety; how would it all end, and what was to be my future?

Poor Lupton, in company with some Dervishes, was forced to work a gun which had been placed in position opposite Tuti Island. He had been promised that, in recompense for this work, the condition of his wife and child would be improved, and they would be given better means of subsistence.

Abdalla Wad Ibrahim also came to me, and said it was the *Mahdi's* earnest wish that I should take charge of a gun; and, if I worked it faithfully, he would give me my liberty. I replied that I was too ill and weak to work laden with these chains; and, besides, I had no idea how guns were worked; and that therefore it was impossible for me to buy my liberty at this price.

"Perhaps," said Wad Ibrahim, "you are unwilling to fire on Gordon, who is said to be your uncle, and that is your reason for making these excuses?"

"I have neither uncle nor any other relatives in Khartum," said I; "and my shells alone would certainly not force Khartum to surrender; however, my present state of health will not admit of my undertaking this work."

Abdalla rose and left me; and, a few hours later, some of the *khalifa's mulazemin* came and forged on to my ankles another set of iron rings and a bar,—to humble me I suppose; but as the weight I already bore prevented me from standing upright, and I was obliged to remain lying down day and night, an iron more or less did not make much difference.

The next few days passed without anything noteworthy occurring. Occasionally I heard the crack of the rifles and the booming of the guns of besieger and besieged; but the Greeks were not allowed to come and see me now, and I was in complete ignorance of what was going on.

One night about four hours after sunset, when blessed sleep, which makes one forget all one's troubles, was gradually stealing over me, I was suddenly roused by the sentry, and ordered to get up at once; as I did so, I saw one of the *khalifa's mulazemin*, who announced that his master was just coming; and, as he spoke, I saw men approaching carrying lanterns. What could the *khalifa* want of me at such an hour? I asked myself in great perplexity.

"Abdel Kader," said he, in a kindly tone, as he approached, "sit down;" and, his servants having stretched out his sheepskin, he sat on it beside me. "I have here," he continued, "a piece of paper; and I want you to tell me what is written on it, and so prove to me your fidelity."

"Certainly, if I can do so," said I, taking the paper. It was about half the size of a cigarette paper, and there was plain writing in black ink on both sides of it. I at once recognised Gordon's handwriting and signature; I held the paper close to the lantern, and saw the following words written in French:—

> I have about 10,000 men; can hold Khartum at the outside till the end of January. Elias Pasha wrote to me; he was forced to do so. He is old and incapable; I forgive him. Try Hajji Mohammed Abu Girga, or sing another song.   Gordon.

There was nothing to show for whom it was intended. I was certain there was no one in the camp who knew French, and that was the reason the *khalifa* had come to me.

"Now, then," said the *khalifa*, impatiently, "have you made out what it means?"

"The note is from Gordon," said I, "and it is written with his own hand, in French cipher language, which I cannot understand."

"What do you say?" said the *khalifa*, now evidently much agitated; "explain yourself better."

"There are some words written here the sense of which I cannot make out," said I; "every word has its own special meaning, and can only be understood by these accustomed to the use of ciphers; if you ask any of the old officials, they will confirm what I say."

"I was told that the names of Elias Pasha and Hajji Mohammed Abu Girga are mentioned; is this so?" roared the *khalifa*, now thoroughly angry.

"The man who said that told you the truth, and I also can read their names; but it is impossible for me to understand the reference. Perhaps the man who told you their names were there can make out the rest of the letter," said I, somewhat ironically; "besides I can also make out 10,000 in figures; but whether it means soldiers, or something else, it is quite impossible for me to say."

He now seized the paper from my hand, and stood up.

"Pardon me," said I, "I would with pleasure have proved my fidelity to you, and have thus regained your gracious favour; but it is out of my power. I think your clerks understand about ciphers better than I do."

"Even if I do not know what this paper contains," said the *khalifa*, "still Gordon shall fall, and Khartum will be ours;" and then he departed, leaving me alone with my guards.

Gordon had said in his little note that he could hold Khartum at the outside till the end of January; we were now nearly at the end of December. Could the rescuing army possibly arrive in time? But why should I worry myself with such thoughts? Here am I in chains, and utterly useless to any one, and nothing I can do can change the course of things.

The next morning, I had a visit from a Greek, now called Abdullahi, who had been appointed Emir of the Muslimania (Christians who had become Moslems.) Without letting him know that the *khalifa* had come to me the previous night, I asked him what was the news, and whether anything was known of the English expedition. He told me that the advanced guard had reached Debbeh, and was about to advance to Metemmeh; that the *Mahdi* knew all about this, and had ordered all the Barabra and Jaalin to collect at Metemmeh under Mohammed el Kheir, and await the enemy.

He told me that the siege was drawn more closely round Khartum, and that, the previous day, the garrison had attempted to make a sortie, but had been forced back; that Sanjak Mohammed Kafr Jod, the brother of the imprisoned Saleh Wad el Mek, had been killed, that his head had been cut off and sent to the *khalifa*, who had ordered it to be thrown at the feet of Saleh, who was gazing at the ground. Recognising instantly his brother's head, but without the slightest change of countenance, Saleh said, "*Di gizahu, di kismathu*" (This is his punishment, this is his fate); then, turning to the *saier* (commander of the prison), he said to him, "Did you mean by this to startle me, or inspire me with fear?" What nerves and self-control the man must have had!

The next day, one of my guards told me that Mohammed Khaled had sent reinforcements of men and some ammunition from Darfur to the *Mahdi*; also that some of the Emirs of Khalifa Ali Wad Helu's flag had received orders to leave for Metemmeh, under the command of his brother, Musa Wad Helu. No doubt there was something in the wind.

It was now the beginning of January, and Gordon had said he could hold out till the end of the month; so the decisive moment was drawing closer and closer.

During the next few days, there was very heavy firing between the Dervishes and Omdurman fort. Faragalla Pasha was doing his utmost; and, in spite of the small number of his men, he attempted a sortie, but was driven back. The supplies in the fort were finished, and negotiations were now going on for its surrender. Faragalla had signalled to Gordon for instructions; but the latter, being unable to support him, had told him to capitulate. The entire garrison received the *Mahdi's* pardon. The men had nothing but the clothes in which they stood, and their wives and children were all in Khartum. As they marched out, the *Mahdi*sts marched in, but were almost immediately driven out again by the artillery fire from Khartum; in the fort itself there were two breech-loading guns, but their range did not extend as far as the town. The surrender took place on 15th January, 1885.

Although Omdurman had now fallen, the *Mahdi* did not send any reinforcements to the besiegers south and east of Khartum; he well knew that the number of his followers collected there was quite sufficient for the purpose. Both he and the garrison of Khartum now looked, with the most intense anxiety, towards the north from whence the final decision must be awaited.

Gordon Pasha had sent five steamers to Metemmeh some time ago, under Khashm el Mus and Abdel Hamid Wad Mohammed, in order to await the arrival of the English, and bring some of them, with the necessary supplies, to Khartum as soon as possible. No doubt he was expecting their arrival with the greatest anxiety. He had staked everything on this; and no one knew what had become of them.

At the beginning of the month, Gordon had allowed several of the families to leave Khartum. Up to that time, he could not bear to forcibly drive them out of the town; and, in consequence, he had been obliged to make a daily distribution of hundreds of *okes* of biscuit and *dhurra* amongst these destitute people; and for that he had, no doubt, God's reward, but he thereby ruined himself and his valuable men. Everyone was crying out for bread, and the stores were almost empty! He now did all he could to induce the people to leave the town. Had he only done so two or three months earlier, there would have been ample supplies to last the troops a long time; but Gordon, thinking that help was coming so soon to him, to the troops, and to the inhabitants, did not provide for possible detentions. Did he think that it was out of the question for an English expedition to be delayed?

Six days after the fall of Omdurman, loud weeping and wailing filled our camp; since I had left Darfur I had not heard anything like it. The *Mahdi's* doctrine forbade the display of sorrow and grief for those who died, or were killed, because they had entered into the joys of Paradise. Something very unusual must therefore have happened to make the people dare to transgress the *Mahdi's* regulations. My guards, who were old soldiers, were so curious to know the cause that they left me to make inquiries, and, in a few minutes, brought back the startling news, that the English advanced guard had met the combined force of Barabra, Jaalin, Degheim, and Kenana, under Musa Wad Helu at Abu Teleh (Abu Klea), and had utterly defeated them; thousands had fallen, and the few who had survived had returned, many of them wounded. The Degheim and Kenana had been almost annihilated; Musa Wad Helu, and most of the *emirs*, had fallen.

What news!—my heart was literally thumping with joyous excitement. After all these long years, a crowning victory at last! The *Mahdi* and Khalifa at once gave orders that all this noise should cease; but for hours the weeping and wailing of the women continued. Instructions were now given to Nur Angara to start off with troops towards Metemmeh; but what good would this do, even if he had had the will, which he had not, what could he do with a few troops when thousands and thousands of wild fanatics had failed? Within the next two or three days, came the news of other defeats at Abu Kru and Kubba (Gubat), and of the erection of a fort on the Nile close to Metemmeh. The *Mahdi* and his principal *emirs* now held a consultation.

All the wonderful victories they had gained up to the present were at stake; for those besieging Khartum were terrified and had retired. It was now the question of a few days only, and the *Mahdi* was done.

They must risk everything. Consequently, orders were sent out to the besiegers to collect and make all preparations. Why did the long expected steamers with the English troops not come? Did their commanders not know Khartum, and the lives of all in it, were hanging by a thread? In vain did I, and thousands of others, wait for the shrill whistle of the steamer, and for the booming of the guns announcing that the English had arrived, and were passing the entrenchments made by the Dervishes to oppose them. Yes, in vain! The delay was inexplicable; what could it mean? Had new difficulties arisen?

It was now Sunday, the 25th of January,—a day I shall never forget as long as I live. That evening, when it was dark, the *Mahdi* and his *khalifas* crossed over in a boat to where their warriors were all collected ready for the fight. It was known during the day that Khartum would be attacked the next morning; and the *Mahdi* had now gone to brace up his followers for the fray by preaching to them the glories of *Jehad*, and urging them to fight till death. Pray Heaven Gordon may have got the news, and made his preparations to resist in time!

On this occasion, the *Mahdi* and his *khalifas* had most strictly enjoined their followers to restrain their feelings, and receive the last injunctions in silence, instead of with the usual shouts and acclamations, which might awaken the suspicions of the exhausted and hungry garrison. His solemn harangue over, the *Mahdi* recrossed, and returned to the camp at dawn, leaving with the storming party only Khalifa Sherif, who had begged to be allowed to join in the holy battle.

That night was for me the most excitingly anxious one in my life. If only the attack were repulsed, Khartum would be saved; otherwise, all would be lost. Utterly exhausted, I was just dropping off to sleep at early dawn, when I was startled by the deafening discharge of thousands of rifles and guns; this lasted for a few minutes, then only occasional rifle-shots were heard, and now all was quiet again. It was scarcely light, and I could barely distinguish objects. Could this possibly be the great attack on Khartum? A wild discharge of fire-arms and cannon, and in a few minutes complete stillness?

The sun was now rising red over the horizon; what would this day bring forth? Excited and agitated, I awaited the result with intense impatience. Soon shouts of rejoicing and victory were heard in the distance; and my guards ran off to find out the news. In a few minutes, they were back again, excitedly relating how Khartum had been taken by storm, and was now in the hands of the Mahdists. Was it possible the news was false? I crawled out of my tent, and scanned the camp; a great crowd had collected before the quarters of the *Mahdi* and *khalifa*, which were not far off; then there was a movement in the direction of my tent; and I could see plainly they were coming towards me. In front, marched three black soldiers; one named Shatta, formerly belonging to Ahmed Bey Dafalla's slave bodyguard, carried in his hands a bloody cloth in which something was wrapped up, and behind him followed a crowd of people weeping. The slaves had now approached my tent, and stood before me with insulting gestures; Shatta undid the cloth and showed me the head of General Gordon!

The blood rushed to my head, and my heart seemed to stop beating; but, with a tremendous effort of self-control, I gazed silently at this ghastly spectacle. His blue eyes were half-opened; the mouth was perfectly natural; the hair of his head, and his short whiskers, were almost quite white.

"Is not this the head of your uncle the unbeliever?" said Shatta, holding the head up before me.

"What of it?" said I, quietly. "A brave soldier who fell at his post; happy is he to have fallen; his sufferings are over."

"Ha, ha!" said Shatta, "so you still praise the unbeliever; but you will soon see the result;" and, leaving me, he went off to the *Mahdi*, bearing his terrible token of victory; behind him followed the crowd, still weeping.

I re-entered my tent. I was now utterly broken-hearted: Khartum fallen, and Gordon dead! And this was the end of the brave soldier who had fallen at his post,—the end of a man whose courage and utter disregard of fear were remarkable, and whose personal characteristics had given him a celebrity in the world which was quite exceptional.

Of what use was the English Army now? How fatal had been the delay at Metemmeh! The English advanced guard had reached Gubat on the Nile, on the 20th of January, at 10 a. m.; on the 21st, Gordon's four steamers had arrived. Then why did they not send some Englishmen on board, no matter how few, and despatch them instantly to Khartum? If they could only have been seen in the town, the garrison would have taken fresh hope, and would have fought tooth and nail against the enemy; whilst the inhabitants, who had lost all confidence in Gordon's promises, would have joined most heartily in resisting the Dervish attack, knowing that the relief expedition was now certain to reach them. Gordon, of course, had done his utmost to hold the town: he had announced that an English Army was coming; he had made a

Bringing Gordon's Head to Slatin.

paper currency; had distributed decorations and honours almost daily, in order to keep up the hearts of the garrison; and, as the position had become more desperate, he had made almost superhuman efforts to induce the troops to hold out; but despair had taken possession of them. What was the use of all these decorations now; what good were all their ranks and honours? And as for the paper money, perhaps there were one or two still hopeful people who would buy a pound note for a couple of *piastres*,[4] on the chance that, by some stroke of luck, the government might yet be victorious; but gradually even these slender hopes disappeared.

Gordon's promises were no longer credited; if but one steamer with a few English officers had reached the town, to bring the news that they had won a victory, and had reached the Nile, the troops and inhabitants would have doubted no longer, and they would have been convinced that Gordon's words were true. An English officer would at once have noticed that part of the lines which had been damaged by the overflow of the White Nile, and could have ordered its repair. But what could Gordon do single-handed, and without the assistance of any European officers; it was impossible for him to look to everything, nor had he the means of seeing that his orders were carried out to his satisfaction. How was it possible for a commander who could not give his troops food, to expect these starving men to carry out with precision and energy the instructions he issued?

On the unfortunate night of the 25th of January, Gordon was told that the Mahdists had decided to make an attack; and he had issued his orders accordingly. Perhaps he himself doubted if they would attack so early in the morning. At the time the *Mahdi* was crossing the river, Gordon, to stimulate his followers, had made a display of fireworks in the town; various coloured rockets were fired, and the band played, with the object of reviving the flagging spirits of the famished garrison. The display was over, the music had ceased, and Khartum was asleep, whilst the enemy crept cautiously and silently forward to the attack. They knew all the weak and strong points of the lines of defence; they knew also that the regulars were stationed at the strong points, and that the broken-down parapet and tumbled-in ditch near the White Nile were weakly defended by the feeble inhabitants.

This particular part of the lines was sadly out of repair; it had never been actually completed, and, when damaged by the water, no steps had been taken to re-make it. Every day the Nile became lower, and

---

4. One Egyptian *piastre* = 2½ d.

every day exposed a broader strip of undefended wet mud, which the hungry and hopeless people merely made a show of defending. It was opposite to this open space that, at early dawn, the bulk of the attacking force had collected, whilst the other portion of the *Mahdist* army faced the main position. At a given signal, the attack began. Those holding the White Nile flank, after firing a few shots, fled precipitately; and, while the troops were occupied in repelling the storming parties in their immediate front, thousands and thousands of wild Arabs, dashing through the mud and water which was only up to their knees, poured into the town, and, to their dismay, the defenders on the lines found themselves attacked from the rear.

Very slight resistance was made, and most of the troops laid down their arms. Numbers of the Egyptians were massacred; but, of the Blacks, few were killed, whilst the enemy's losses within the lines did not exceed eighty to one hundred men. Soon afterwards, the gates were opened by the Dervishes, and the troops were permitted to march out to the *Mahdist* camp.

Once the line of the White Nile was crossed, the great mass of the enemy rushed towards the town. "*Lil Saraya! lil Kenisa!*" (To the Palace! to the Church!) was the cry; for it was here they expected to find the treasure and Gordon, who had so long defended the city against them, and had up to that day defied all their efforts. Amongst the leaders in the attack on the Palace were the followers of Makin Wad en Nur, who was afterwards killed at the battle of Toski, and belonged to the Arakin tribe; Makin's brother Abdalla Wad en Nur, their beloved leader, had been killed during the siege, and they were now seeking to avenge his death. Many of Abu Girga's men were also forward in the rush to the Palace; they wanted to wipe out the defeat they had suffered when Gordon had driven them out of Burri.

The palace servants who lived in the basement were instantly massacred; and Gordon himself, standing on the top of the steps leading to the divan, awaited the approach of the Arabs. Taking no notice of his question, "Where is your master the *Mahdi?*" the first man up the steps plunged his huge spear into his body; he fell forward on his face, without uttering a word. His murderers dragged him down the steps to the palace entrance; and here his head was cut off, and at once sent over to the *Mahdi* at Omdurman, whilst his body was left to the mercy of those wild fanatics. Thousands of these inhuman creatures pressed forward merely to stain their swords and spears with his blood; and soon all that remained was a heap of mangled flesh. For a long time, stains of blood marked the spot where this atrocity took place; and the steps, from top to bottom, for weeks bore the same sad traces, until they were at last washed off when the *khalifa* decided to make the Palace an abode for his former and his future wives.

When Gordon's head was brought to the *Mahdi*, he remarked he would have been better pleased had they taken him alive; for it was his intention to convert him, and then hand him over to the English Government in exchange for Ahmed Arabi Pasha, as he had hoped that the latter would have been of assistance to him in helping him to conquer Egypt. My own opinion, however, is that this regret on the part of the *Mahdi* was merely assumed; for had he expressed any wish that Gordon's life should be spared, no one would have dared to disobey his orders.

Gordon had done his utmost to save the lives of the Europeans who were with him. Colonel Stewart, with some of the Consuls and many of the Europeans, he had allowed to go to Dongola; but unfortunately the incapable and disaffected crew of their steamer, the *Abbas*, had run her on to a rock in the cataracts, and had thus given up him and his companions to the treacherous death which had been prepared for them. On the pretext that the Greeks were good men on boats, Gordon had offered them a steamer, on which it was arranged they should make a visit of inspection on the White Nile, thus intending to give them an opportunity to escape south to join Emin Pasha; but they had refused to accept.

Being much concerned as to their safety, Gordon now made another proposal: he ordered all roads leading towards the Blue Nile to be placed out of bounds after ten o'clock at night; and he charged the Greeks with watching them, so that they might have a chance of escaping to a steamer moored close by, in which it was arranged they should escape; but, owing to a disagreement between themselves as to the details of the plan, it fell through. I have little doubt in my own mind that these Greeks did not really wish to leave the town. In their own homes and in Egypt most of them had been very poor, and had held merely subordinate positions; but here in the Sudan many had made their fortunes, and were therefore by no means anxious to quit a country from which they had reaped so great advantages.

Gordon seemed anxious about the safety of everyone but himself. Why did he neglect to make a redoubt, or keep within the fortifications, the central point of which might well have been the Palace? From a military point of view I think this is a fair criticism; but probably Gordon did not do so, lest he should be suspected of being concerned for his own safety; and it was probably a similar idea which influenced him in his decision not to have a strong guard at the Palace. He might well have employed a company of soldiers for this purpose; and who would have thought of questioning the advantage of protecting himself? With a guard of this strength, he could easily have reached the steamer *Ismaïlia*, which was lying close to the palace, scarcely three hundred yards from the gate.

Fagarli, the captain, saw the enemy rushing to the palace. In vain he waited for Gordon; and it was only when the latter was killed, and he saw the Dervishes making for his boat, that he steamed off into mid-stream, and moved backwards and forwards along the front of the town until he received a message from the *Mahdi* offering him pardon. As his wife and family and some of his crew were in the city, he accepted the offer and landed; but how sadly had he been deluded. Rushing to his home, he found his son—a boy of ten years old—lying dead on the doorstep, whilst his wife, in her agony, had thrown herself on her child's body, and lay pierced with several lances.

The cruelties and atrocities perpetrated in the terrible massacre which followed Gordon's death are beyond description. Male and female slaves, and young, good-looking women of the free tribes, alone were spared; and if some others succeeded in escaping, they had only to thank a lucky chance which saved them from the merciless bloodshed of that awful day. Not a few resolved to put an end to their own lives; amongst these was Mohammed Pasha Hussein, the head of the Finance, who, standing beside the dead bodies of his only daughter and her husband, was urged by some friends to fly with them, and let them save him; but he refused. They tried to take him by force; but, in a loud voice, he heaped curses on the *Mahdi* and his followers, and some fanatics passing by soon despatched him. Several people were killed by their former servants and slaves, who, having previously joined the enemy, now acted as guides to the wild hordes thirsting for blood, plunder, and rapine.

Fathalla Gehami, a wealthy Syrian (whose wife was the daughter of the wholesale French dealer Contarini, and to whom, on her father's death some years ago, I had given a lodging with her little child in my house), had buried all his money in a corner of his house, with the assistance of his servant, a Dongola boy whom he had brought up from quite a child. None but he, his wife Lisa, and his boy knew the secret hiding-place; and when the situation became so serious in the town, he called up the lad and, in his wife's presence, said to him, "Mohammed, I have taken care of you since you were quite a child, and I trust you; you know where the money is hidden. Our condition is gradually growing worse. You have relatives with the *Mahdi*; you can go to them, and if the government is victorious you can return to me without fear of punishment. But should the *Mahdi* conquer, then you can repay me for my kindness to you."

Obedient to his master's wishes, the boy left the town, and, on the morning of the attack, he, with some of his relatives, rushed to his employer's house. "Open, open!" he shouted at the top of his voice; "I am your child, your servant Mohammed." Fathalla Gehami joyfully opened the great iron gate which had been so strengthened and barred that it defied entry; and in an instant his faithless servant had plunged his spear into his body. Dashing with his friends over his master's prostrate form, he made for the hiding-place of the money, and instantly seized it; on his way out of the house, he rushed at Fathalla's wife, who had seen the whole proceedings of this ungrateful young bloodhound, and would have killed her too, but she threw herself on the body of her husband, who was in his death-agony; and Mohammed's friends with difficulty drew him off before he had time to plunge his knife into the poor woman who had been his kind protectress for so many years.

The Greek Consul Leontides was called out of his house by a crowd of fanatics who had been worked up into a state of excitement by a man who owed him money; and, on his appearance, he was instantly killed. Consul Hansal was murdered by one of his own *kavasses*, who afterwards tied his hands together, dragged the body out of the house, poured spirits over it, heaped on it all the tobacco he could find, set it on fire, and, when it was reduced to cinders, threw the remains into the river. Butros Bulos, a clerk in the finance office, was perhaps the only man who came well out of that awful day. He lived in a detached house, and had collected round him his relatives; for some time they defended themselves most successfully against all comers, and killed a number of them. When summoned at last to surrender, he said he would only do so if he were promised the *Mahdi's* pardon, and a guarantee that he should not be separated from his family; as it was impossible to turn him out without bringing up guns to bombard the house, Khalifa Sherif gave him the pardon he required, which, curiously enough, was subsequently ratified by the *Mahdi*.

The Shaigia post on Tuti Island surrendered after Khartum had fallen; and the garrison were brought across to Omdurman in boats.

One could fill a volume with the details of the terrible atrocities committed on that memorable day; yet I doubt if the fate of the survivors was very much better. When all the houses were occupied, the search for treasure began, and no excuse or denial was accepted; whoever was suspected of having concealed money (and the majority of the inhabitants had done so) was tortured until the secret was disclosed, or until he succeeded in convincing his tormentors that he had nothing. There was no sparing of the lash; the unfortunate people were flogged until their flesh hung down in shreds from their bodies. Another torture was to tie men up by their thumbs to a beam, and leave them dangling in the air till they became unconscious; or two small pliant slips of bamboo were tied horizontally to their temples, and the two ends, before and behind, being joined together and twisted as tightly as possible, were struck with vibrating sticks which produced agony inexpressible.

Even women of an advanced age were tormented in this way; and the most sensitive parts of their bodies were subjected to a species of torture which it is impossible for me to describe here. Suffice it to say that the most appalling methods were resorted to in order to discover hidden treasure. Young women and girls only were exempted from these abominable tortures, for no other reason than that such atrocities might interfere in some manner with the object for which they had been reserved. All such were put aside for the *harem* of the *Mahdi*, who, on the actual day of the conquest, made his selections, and turned over the rejected ones to his *khalifas* and principal *emirs*. This picking and choosing continued for weeks together, until the households of these libidinous and inhuman scoundrels were stocked to overflowing with all the unfortunate youth and beauty of the fallen city.

The next day, a general amnesty was given to all, with the exception of the Shaigia, who were still considered outlaws; but, in spite of this, murders and atrocities continued for many days subsequent to the fall of Khartum.

The Emir Abu Girga made every effort to discover the hiding-place of the sons of Saleh Wad el Mek; but for three days he was unsuccessful. They were at last found, brought before him, and instantly beheaded. It behoved also all Egyptians to look to themselves during these days of massacre; for, if met alone by these fanatics, they were mercilessly slaughtered. A merchant was making inquiries one day about the bazaar prices in Omdurman, and asked what were at present the cheapest articles and the greatest drug in the market; the man questioned, being evidently a wag, answered: "The yellow-skinned Egyptian, the Shaigia, and the dog," which, being considered an impure animal, was always killed when found. This saying obtained great notoriety amongst the Dervishes, and gives a very fair idea of the estimation in which they held the former ruling class.

The plunder taken in Khartum was carried off to the Beit el Mal; but of course large quantities were made away with. The principal houses were distributed amongst the *emirs*; and, on the day after the town fell, the *Mahdi* and Khalifa Abdullahi crossed over from Omdurman in the steamer *Ismailia* to view the scene of their bloody victory and massacre; without a sign of pity or regret, they occupied the houses selected for them, and, addressing their followers, described the disaster which had overtaken Khartum as the just judgment of Heaven on the godless inhabitants of the city, who had repeatedly rejected the *Mahdi's* summons to them to surrender and become his faithful followers in the true religion.

The first few days were spent in the wildest debauchery and excesses; and it was not until the *Mahdi* and his followers had to some extent satiated their vicious passions, that they turned their attention to the dangers which threatened them from without. To oppose the English expedition, the renowned Emir Abderrahman Wad Nejumi was ordered to collect a large force and proceed forthwith to Metemmeh, to drive out the *infidels*, who were known to have reached the Nile near this town.

On Wednesday morning, two days after Khartum had fallen, at about eleven o'clock, the thunder of guns and the sharp crack of rifles were heard in the direction of the north end of Tuti Island; and soon two steamers came in view,—these were the *Telahawia* and *Bordein*, carrying Sir Charles Wilson and some English officers and men who had come up to assist General Gordon. Sanjak Kashm el Mus and Abdel Hamid Mohammed, whom Gordon had despatched in command of the Shaigias, were also on board; they had already heard of Gordon's death, and of the cruel fate which had overtaken the town and its inhabitants. Although those on the steamer had little doubt of the accuracy of the sad news, they wished to see with their own eyes, and reached a point midway between Tuti Island and the left bank of the White Nile; here they were heavily fired on by the Dervishes from an entrenched position, situated northeast of Omdurman Fort, and having seen Khartum in the distance, and been convinced, they turned about and steamed away.

I subsequently heard from some of the crew of these steamers, that both they and the Englishmen on board were deeply affected by the fall of the city; they now knew that the entire Sudan was in the *Mahdi's* hands. It was the talk on board, they said, that the English expedition had only come up to save Gordon; and, now that he was killed, the object of the expedition had failed, and they naturally concluded that it would retire to Dongola, and that they would be called upon to accompany it. Consequently the chief pilot of the *Telahawia* and the captain Abdel Hamid agreed together to run the steamer on to a rock, and then escape during the night. This plan was successfully carried out; and the steamer stuck so hard and fast that the cargo had to be at once transferred to the *Bordein*.

During the confusion, these two conspirators escaped; and, through the intermediary of their friends, they succeeded in securing the *Mahdi's* pardon, and returned subsequently to Khartum. Here they were well received and publicly commended by the *Mahdi* for having inflicted loss on their enemies, the British; Abdel Hamid, in spite of being a hated Shaigia, and a relative of Saleh Wad el Mek, was presented by the *Mahdi* with his own *jibba*, as a mark of honour, and, moreover, several of his female relatives who, after the sack of the town, had been distributed amongst the *emirs*, were given back to him.

Meanwhile, the *Bordein*, on its return journey towards Metemmeh, struck on a sand-bank, and, being heavily laden, could not be floated off. Sir Charles Wilson's position was now very critical; with his small force he could not have attempted to land on the west bank and attack the enemy, which was entrenched at Wad Habeshi, between him and the British camp at Gubat. It is true that the courage of this body of Dervishes had been considerably shaken by the defeat at Abu Klea; but the fall of Khartum, and the knowledge that Wad en Nejumi with a large force was advancing north to their support, now transformed them into a formidable enemy.

A third steamer, the *Safia*, was still at Gubat. Sir Charles Wilson therefore sent an officer downstream in a small boat to ask for help; the appeal was promptly responded to, the *Safia* starting, without delay, to the relief of the *Bordein*. The enemy hearing of this, at once threw up entrenchments to oppose its progress, and, on its approach, poured on the unfortunate steamer a perfect hail of rifle and cannon shot; but those on board, determined to relieve their comrades in distress, fought most bravely until a shot, penetrating the boiler, disabled the steamer and placed it in the greatest danger.

Undismayed, however, the commander set to work, under a heavy fire, to repair the damage; the work was continued during the night, and early the next morning the *Safia* was able to continue her running fight with the Dervishes, eventually succeeding in silencing the guns, and killing the principal *amir*, Ahmed Wad Faid, and a considerable number of subordinate *emirs* and men. The passage was forced; and Sir Charles Wilson and his men relieved.

This daring exploit, which resulted in the rescue of the little band of Englishmen who had ventured to Khartum, also had a very important, though indirect, effect on the subsequent fate of the small British column near Metemmeh. The advance of Nejumi, which, under any circumstances, was not rapid, owing to the difficulty of collecting the men, was still further delayed by the news of the death of Ahmed Wad Faid, and the defeat of the strong body of Dervishes at Wad Habeshi by one steamer.

I was informed that on hearing of the success of the *Safia* (whose able commander I learnt on my return to Egypt was Lord Charles Beresford), Nejumi addressed his men, and pointed out to them, that if the English advanced with the intention of taking the Sudan, they must of course oppose them; but if, on the other hand, they retired towards Dongola, then he and his men would be able to occupy the country they had abandoned without the risk of further fighting. And it was this latter course which he eventually took. Delaying his advance, he reached Metemmeh only after the British had retired from Gubat; and, although he pursued them as far as Abu Klea, he hesitated somewhat to attack unless quite assured of success.

It was only when the *Mahdi* learnt of the final retirement of the British advanced guard that he was convinced the Sudan had at last been completely won; and now his delight knew no bounds. He announced the news in the mosque and drew a striking picture of the flight of the unbelievers, embellishing it further by a revelation from the Prophet to the effect that their water-skins had all been pierced, through Divine intervention, and that all those who had taken part in the expedition had died of thirst.

On the fifth day after the fall of Khartum, a small band of soldiers suddenly appeared in my tattered tent; and, placing me, still shackled and bound, on a donkey, they carried me off to the general prison, where they hammered on to my ankles a third and exceptionally heavy iron bar and rings (nicknamed the *Hajji Fatma*); it weighed about eighteen pounds, and was only put on those who were considered exceptionally obstinate or dangerous prisoners. I was quite ignorant of the reasons which caused me to fall still lower in the *khalifa's* disfavour; but I found out later that Gordon, when he had ascertained from my letters to him that the *Mahdist* force advancing on Khartum was not a strong one, that many of the *Mahdi's* adherents were discontented, and that there was considerable scarcity of ammunition, had written to this effect to several of the principal officers on the lines; one of his letters containing this information was discovered in the loot handed over to Ahmed Wad Suleiman in the Beit el Mal, by whom it had been passed to the *Mahdi* and *khalifa*. Thus were their suspicions regarding my behaviour confirmed, and my schemes to escape and join Gordon laid bare.

I was deposited in one corner of the immense *zariba*, where I was ordered to stay, and to hold no converse with anyone without permission, on pain of instant flogging. At sunset, I, a number of slaves who were under sentence for having murdered their masters, and other gentlemen of this description were bound together by a long chain passing round our feet and fastened to the trunk of a tree; and at sunrise the next morning, we were unfastened, and I was sent back to my corner again. I could just see Lupton, in the distance, in another corner of the enclosure. He had been in here for some time, and had become used to it; he had permission to speak to others, but was under strict orders of the *saier*, or gaoler, not, on any account, to speak to me.

On the day that I had been brought to the prison, Saleh Wad el Mek had been discharged; his brother, sons, and almost all his relatives had been killed, and he was now allowed to go and search for the survivors. As regards food, I now fared considerably worse; I had, in this respect, fallen out of the frying pan into the fire. I used to complain of being occasionally hungry; but now I received only uncooked *dhurra*, getting the same share as the slaves, and a very small share it was. Fortunately, the wife of one of my warders, a Darfur woman, took pity upon me, and used to take the corn away, boil it, and bring it back to me; but she was not allowed to bring me any other food, as her husband feared the principal gaoler might find out, and he, in his turn, was afraid of incurring the *khalifa's* displeasure. I lay on the bare ground, with a stone for my pillow, the hardness of which gave me a continual headache; but, one day whilst we were being driven to the river—one hundred and fifty yards distant—to wash, I picked up the lining of a donkey saddle, which the owner had evidently thrown away as old and useless; and, hiding it under my arm, I bore it off in triumph, and that night I slept like a king on his pillow of down.

Gradually, my position improved somewhat. The principal gaoler, who was not really disinclined towards me, allowed me to converse occasionally with the other prisoners, and removed my lightest foot-irons; but the *Hajji Fatma* and her sister still remained, and I cannot say this pair of worthies conduced much to my personal comfort during those long and weary months of imprisonment.

One day, a black woman came in with her child—a nice little girl—to visit her poor husband and the child's father, Lupton. The poor little thing wept bitterly, for, young as she was, she was old enough to understand the miserable plight of her father, who, before they left, sent them to say a few words to me. The poor woman looked at me for a few moments, and then, taking my hand, wept aloud. I remembered I had often seen her before; and, between her sobs, she reminded me that she had come to Khartum as a young girl, and had been brought up in Frederick Rosset's house, where, during my first journey to the Sudan, I had stayed for some weeks. Poor Zenoba! she reminded me of many little incidents which had happened in the old days; and, as she related them, she often broke down, comparing her former happiness with her present misery.

I tried to console her, urging her to keep up hope, and that perhaps everything would end well. "Besides," I said, "it was never intended that human beings should always live well and comfortably." Little Fatma, whom we called Fanny, flung herself into my arms, calling me, *ammi* (my uncle); and it seemed as if her heart told her instinctively that, amongst all this crowd, I was next to her father in her affections. I then begged the poor woman to leave me, as I feared taking advantage of the gaoler's patience.

At this time, there was some difficulty in supplying food to the Black soldiers under Abu Anga, whose number had been further increased by the Khartum garrison. As there was no immediate fear of any movement on the part of the government towards Khartum, it was decided to despatch Abu Anga to Southern Kordofan on a punitive expedition against the Nubas, and to procure slaves and send them to Omdurman. Shortly after the fall of Khartum, the *Mahdi* had moved his camp north; and the fort known as Tabia Ragheb Bey, and the ground in the vicinity, had been told off for Abu Anga's camp. When he was ordered off, and his place taken by his brother, Fadl el

Maula, all my servants, male and female, left with him; and, although the latter were not permitted to visit me, I felt that, with Abu Anga's departure, yet another link was severed.

I now received news of the other servants I had left behind at El Fasher. On my arrival at Rahad, I had told the *khalifa* I had left behind two horses, which were almost the best in Darfur, and which I hinted he might have if he wished; but, it being summer, and as they would probably have suffered from the long and hot journey, I had not brought them with me. Subsequently, I had requested him to give orders that not only the horses, but also my male and female servants who had been left behind, should also be sent on. He consequently had written to Mohammed Khaled to this effect; but, on the day on which I had been made a prisoner, he had written to Sayed Mahmud of El Obeid to seize my people as soon as they came from Darfur, but to send on the two horses. The latter had now arrived in Omdurman; and the soldier who had been in charge came to tell me that the *khalifa* was much pleased with them, having taken one for himself and given the other to his brother Yakub.

A few days later, there was considerable commotion amongst the warders; and the *saier* told me privately that the *khalifa* was coming to visit the prison. I asked him to advise me how I should behave; and he recommended me to answer all questions promptly, on no account to make any complaints, and to remain submissively in my corner. About midday, the *khalifa* arrived, accompanied by his brothers and *mulazemin*, and began to walk round and view these victims of his justice. It seemed that the *saier* had given the same advice to all the prisoners that he had given to me, for they all behaved quietly; some were ordered to have their chains removed, and to be discharged.

At length, the *khalifa* approached my corner, and, with a friendly nod, said, "*Abdel Kader, enta tayeb?*" (Abdel Kader, are you well?). To which I replied, "*Ana tayeb, Sidi*" (I am well, sire); and with that he moved on. Yunes Wad Dekeim, the present Emir of Dongola, and a near relative of the *khalifa*, pressed my hand, and whispered, "Keep up your spirits; don't be downhearted; everything will come right."

From that day my condition distinctly improved. Zenoba, the mother of Fanny, was allowed every now and then to send me a little food. I was also allowed to spend the day with a former head-*sheikh* of the Hawara Arabs, who was suspected of having been friendly with the Turks, and had been thrown into chains; as our hatred for the Mahdists was mutual, we spent most of our time in talking about them, and criticising their rules and ordinances. Sheikh Mohammed Wad et Taka, for such was his name, was fed by his elderly wife, who, for his sake, had remained in Omdurman, and used to bring us meals. She may have had some good qualities, but she was a veritable Xantippe who by her sharp tongue made bitter every mouthful her husband swallowed. Carrying a large dish of baked *dhurra*-bread and some *mulakh* (a sort of sauce made with milk and other ingredients), she would place it before us, and then, sitting on the ground beside us, she would begin the battle. "Yes, indeed," she would say, "old women are quite good enough to cook, and do all the hard work; but when men have their freedom, they can do as they like; and then they always turn their eyes to the young and pretty girls."

The *sheikh* had the fortune, or rather the temporary misfortune, of having two young wives as well as this old one; but they stayed in the country with the herds and this fact greatly annoyed the old lady, who exercised her ingenuity in making these sallies against her good man, who, famished by hunger, silently consumed the food she had prepared for him. She frequently related some piquant family details in which her husband's conduct in relation to herself, as compared with his more youthful helpmeets, was invariably open to severe criticism. I used to greatly enjoy these skirmishes, and generally took upon myself the task of mediator, telling her that when she was away, her husband had nothing but good words for her. This used to appease her; and she would affirm that she was doing her utmost to alleviate our condition.

I thoroughly appreciated how valuable she was to me, and how her homely meals lessened my long hours of enforced fasting. All my efforts were therefore directed to pacifying her husband, who, goaded by her sharp tongue, would heap curses on her devoted head. His nature was very changeable: when he was hungry, and saw his old wife coming along carrying his food, no words of praise were sufficient for her; but once satisfied, and stung to the quick by her sarcasm, he would heap insults on her, and some such expressions as, "You who neither fear God nor man, leave me, and let me starve. Some women, as they grow old, instead of becoming more intelligent, gradually get silly; this is the case with you, I think you are possessed of the devil. Get away, and never come near me again; I never want to see you more." Then off she would go; but the next day, when he was famished, he would long to have his old wife back again. Not the least alarmed, she would almost invariably return with her dish full of food; he would be pacified, eat a hearty meal, and then the insults would begin again.

Thus the days slowly passed away. Smallpox had broken out in Omdurman, and every day the disease swept off hundreds,—indeed, whole families disappeared; and I believe that the loss from this disease was greater than that suffered in many battles. Curiously enough, almost all the nomad Arabs were attacked; and several of our own warders went down, and not a few of them died. We prisoners, however, entirely escaped; and, during the whole period of my imprisonment, I do not recollect having seen one of us unfortunates attacked, though most of us were much alarmed. Perhaps God in His mercy thought our punishment already more than we could bear, and spared us a further visitation.

I had now many opportunities of talking to Lupton, who daily grew more and more impatient; indeed, so furious was he at times, that I used to get alarmed, for he would complain most bitterly, and in a loud tone, of our miserable treatment. I did all in my power to pacify him; but the wretched life we were living had affected him to such a degree that I seriously feared for his health. Through constantly speaking to him, I succeeded to some extent in quieting him; but, although scarcely thirty years of age, the hair of his head and beard had, during our imprisonment, grown almost white.

Nature, however, had treated me more kindly. I submitted to my fate with a better grace; and the thoroughly practical lesson I had received from my old friend Madibbo, entirely suited my character. I was still young; and, except for occasional slight ailments, I was endowed with a strong and healthy constitution. My fate was a cruel one it is true; but I felt I could gather from it many a useful experience. I kept on hoping against hope, that, sooner or later, I should return to the civilised world, though, when I thought over my chances of escape, the time seemed very far away.

In order to occupy the prisoners, the *saier* employed them in building a square house for their own habitation; they were therefore ordered to fetch stones which were found near the river; and Lupton and I were the only prisoners who were permitted to pass the day without work. Every now and then, however, we used to accompany them to the place where they got the stones; but my heavy ankle-irons, and my long neck-chain, impeded my progress so much when walking, that I preferred to act as the architect of the building, which now rapidly advanced towards completion. The walls were very thick, and about thirty feet square, and, in the centre, a pillar was erected which served as a support to the crossbeams.

This house was intended for the incarceration of the most dangerous prisoners; and the wood required for the roofing was brought from the now ruined houses of Khartum.

It was about this time that an old friend of mine named Esh Sheikh, a relative of Ismail Wad Shaggar el Kheiri, and who was in the *Mahdi's* favour, informed me confidentially that both the *Mahdi* and the *khalifa* were friendly-minded towards myself and Lupton, and that in a few days we should probably be liberated. He added that should the *khalifa* speak to me, I should not humble myself very much, but merely be careful not to oppose anything he said; then, recommending me to God, he went away. I instantly went off to share this good news with Lupton, who at that time happened to be in one of his most dangerous moods; but I begged him to believe that it was true, and to do nothing which might compromise matters.

A few days later, it was rumoured that the *khalifa* was coming. I had carefully prepared my speech, and Lupton had done the same; but it was more than likely he would speak to me first. At length the critical moment came: the *khalifa*, entering the prisoners' yard, instead of, as was his usual custom, sending for the prisoners one by one, ordered an *angareb* to be brought and placed in the shade; he then directed all the prisoners to be led out, and to sit down before him in a semi-circle. He spoke to several, set a few free who had been imprisoned by his own personal orders, and promised others, who complained against the sentences pronounced by the *kadi*, to inquire into their cases; of Lupton and myself, however, he appeared to have taken no notice. Lupton glanced at me, and shook his head; but I put my finger to my lips to warn him against doing anything foolish.

"Have I anything else to do?" asked the *khalifa* of the *saier* who was standing behind his *angareb*.

"Sire! I am at your service," replied the head gaoler; and the *khalifa* sat down again. He now turned his eyes on me, and repeated the same words he had used on the previous occasion. "Abdel Kader," said he, "are you well?"

"Sire," said I, "if you will allow me to speak, I shall tell you of my condition." He was then sitting at his ease, and he gave me the required permission.

"Master," I began, "I belong to a foreign tribe; I came to you seeking protection, and you gave it to me. It is natural for man to err, and to sin against God and against each other. I have sinned; but I now repent, and regret all my misdeeds. I repent before God and His Prophet. Behold me in irons before you! See! I am naked and hungry; and I lie here patiently on the bare ground waiting for the time to come when I may receive pardon. Master, should you think it well to let me continue in this sad plight, then I pray God for strength to enable me to bear His will; but now I beg of you to give me my freedom."

I had studied this speech very carefully, and had delivered it as effectively as I could; and I saw that it had made a favourable impression on the *khalifa*. Turning then to Lupton, he said, "And you, Abdullahi?" "I can add nothing to what Abdel Kader has said," replied Lupton. "Pardon me, and grant me liberty."

The *khalifa* now turned to me, and said, "Well, from the day you came from Darfur, I have done everything I possibly could for you; but your heart has been far from us: you wanted to join Gordon the *infidel*, and fight against us. As you are a foreigner, I spared your life; otherwise you would not be alive now. However, if your repentance is real and true, I will pardon both you and Abdullahi. *Saier*, take off their irons."

We were then removed by the warders, who, after long and hard work, and by making use of ropes, at last succeeded in opening my foot-irons. We were then again brought before the *khalifa*, who was patiently sitting on his *angareb* waiting for us. He ordered the *saier* to bring the *Koran*, which he laid on a *furwa* (sheepskin), and called on us to swear eternal allegiance to him. Placing our hands on the *Koran*, we swore to serve him honestly in the future. He then rose and directed us to follow him; and we, almost beside ourselves with delight at our release after this long imprisonment, joyfully followed in his footsteps.

My friend the Sheikh of the Hawara was also liberated at the same time. The *khalifa*, having been assisted on to his donkey by his servants, ordered us to walk by his side; but we could scarcely keep up with him, for our eight months' imprisonment in chains had so cramped our legs and feet that we found we had lost the habit of stepping out. When we reached his house, he directed us to wait in a *rekuba* in one of the outside enclosures, and left us. He returned again a few minutes later, and, seating himself beside us, warned us most seriously to adhere to all his orders. He then went on to say that he had received letters from the commander of the army in Egypt, stating that he had seized and imprisoned all the *Mahdi's* relatives in Dongola, and that he demanded in exchange all the captives who had formerly been

Christians.

"We have decided to reply," said he, "that you are now all Mohammedans, that you are one with us, and that you are not willing to be exchanged for people who, though the relatives of the *Mahdi*, are far from us in thought and deed; and that they can do as they like with their captives; or," added he, "perhaps you would like to go back to the Christians?" With these words he ended his speech.

Lupton and I assured him that we should never leave him of our own free-will; that all the pleasures of the world would never tear us from his side; and that it was only by being constantly in his presence that we learnt to act in such a way as would lead to our salvation. Thoroughly taken in by our mendacity, he promised to present us to the *Mahdi*, who had arranged to come to the *khalifa's* house that afternoon, and then he left us.

The *rekuba* being in one of the outer enclosures, into which people were admitted, several friends who had heard of our release came to congratulate us, amongst them Dimitri Zigada, but this time without his usual quid of tobacco. My friend Esh Sheikh also came; and when I told him that we were to be presented to the *Mahdi*, he again gave me the benefit of his good advice, and instructed me how to behave when the momentous occasion arrived. It was almost evening when the *khalifa* came; and, directing us to follow him, he led us to an inner enclosure, where we saw the *Mahdi* sitting on an *angareb*. He had become so stout that I scarcely knew him.

Kneeling down, we repeatedly kissed the hand he held out to us. He now assured us that his only wish was for our good, that when men are placed in chains, it exercises a lasting and beneficial influence on them; by this he meant to say that when a man is timid, this punishment makes him avoid committing offences in the future. He then turned the conversation to his relatives who had been captured by the British, and about the exchange they had proposed, but which he had refused, adding, with a hypocritical smile, "I love you better than my own brethren; and therefore I refused to exchange."

In reply, I assured him of our love and sincerity to him, saying, "Sire, the man who does not love you more than himself, how can his love proceed truly from his heart." (This was a paraphrase of the Prophet's own words which my friend the *sheikh* had suggested I should repeat.)

"Say that again," said the *Mahdi*; and, turning to the *khalifa*, he said, "Listen." When I repeated the words, he took my hand in his and said,

"You have spoken the truth; love me more than yourself." Summoning Lupton as well, he took his hand, and made us repeat the oath of allegiance, saying, that as we had proved unfaithful to our first oath, it must be renewed. This over, the *khalifa* signed to us to retire; and, again kissing the *Mahdi's* hand, we thanked him for his beneficence, and returned to our *rekuba* to await his further instructions.

It was some time before the *khalifa* returned; and when he did, he permitted Lupton, without further ado, to join his family, who were still located in a tent in the Beit el Mal, and, sending with him a *mulazem* to show the way, assured him that he would take every care of him. I was now alone with the *khalifa*. "And you," said he, "where do you wish to go; have you any one to take care of you?" And I felt him gazing at me, whilst I cast my eyes to the ground, knowing that was what he wished me to do. "Besides God and yourself," I replied, "I have no one, sire; deal with me as you think best for my future."

"I had hoped and expected this answer from you," said the *khalifa*; "from this day you may consider yourself a member of my household. I shall care for you, and shall never allow you to want for anything; and you will have the benefit of being brought up under my eye, on condition that, from this day forth, you absolutely sever your connection with all your former friends and acquaintances, and associate only with my relatives and servants; you must, moreover, obey implicitly every order you receive from me. During the day, your duty will be to stay with the *mulazemin* employed on my personal service at the door of my house; and at night, when I retire, you will be permitted to go to the house which I shall assign to you. When I go out, you must always accompany me: if I ride, you must walk beside me, until the time comes when, should I see fit, I will provide you with an animal to ride. Do you agree to these conditions, and do you promise to put them into full effect?"

"Master," I replied, "I agree with pleasure to your conditions. In me, you will find a willing and obedient servant; and I hope I may have strength to enter upon my new duties."

"God will strengthen you," he replied, "and bring you to all good." He then rose, and added, "Sleep here tonight; may God protect you till I see you again tomorrow."

I was now quite alone. So I had gone from one prison to another! I fully grasped the *khalifa's* intentions: he had no real wish for my services, for he had not the slightest confidence in me; nor did he wish to utilise me against the government and against the civilised world. He merely wanted to keep me always under control; probably it flattered his vanity to know he could point to me, his slave, once a high official of the government, who had commanded his own tribe, which was now the foundation on which his power rested, and show them and the other western tribes that I was now his humble servant. Nevertheless, said I to myself, I shall take good care not to displease him, or give him a chance of putting his evil purposes into effect. I thoroughly understood my master; his smiles and friendly looks were not worth a jot, indeed one day he had told me as much himself. "Abdel Kader," he had said to me in the course of conversation, "a man who wants to command must neither betray his purpose by gesture, nor by his countenance; otherwise his enemies or his subjects will discover some means of frustrating his designs."

The next morning, he came to me, and, summoning his brother Yakub, he directed him to show me some spot in the neighbourhood where I might build my huts, adding that it must be as near his house as possible. As, however, most of the vacant spots in the vicinity had been already occupied by the *khalifa's* relatives, a piece of ground, about six hundred yards from the *khalifa's* house, and not far from Yakub's residence, was given to me.

The *khalifa* now summoned his secretary, and showed me a document addressed to the commander of the English army, to the effect, that all the European prisoners had, of their own free-will, become Mohammedans, and that they had no wish to return to their countries. This document he desired me to sign.

All my servants, horses, and baggage had been taken off by Abu Anga, with the exception of an old lame Nubawi who, when he heard of my release, came to see me from Fadl el Maula's house. I at once informed the *khalifa*, and obtained permission to take this man back into my service. I also spoke to him about Abu Anga and my servants; and he asked if the effects were going to be returned to me,—a strange question indeed! When one's possessions have been seized by violence and carried off, are they likely to be given back? I replied much in the same style, that I was sure, that as now I belonged to his household, I could well do without these little trifles, and that I thought it quite unnecessary for him to write to his field-marshal about so trivial a matter. What was I to do with horses, when I was not allowed to ride them? Had not my education with the *khalifa* begun by being forced to walk barefoot!

All the same, I was really very anxious to have my old servants back again, though I did not actually require their services very much; but I knew, that had I attempted to claim them, I should only have aroused the *khalifa's* opposition. The latter was, therefore, greatly pleased with my reply, and began chatting to me about Abu Anga. He then asked me, abruptly, "Are you not a Mohammedan; where then did you leave your wives?" This was, indeed, an ugly question. "Master," said I, "I have only one, and I left her in Darfur; and I am told that she was arrested with all my other servants by Said Mahmud, and is now in the Beit el Mal at El Obeid."

"Is your wife of your own race?" asked the *khalifa*, inquiringly. "No," I replied, "she is a Darfurian; and her parents and relatives were killed in the battle with Sultan Harun. She and several others had been captured by my men; and I gave most of them to my servants and soldiers to marry. This orphan alone was left; and she is now my wife."

"Have you any children?" asked he; and, when I replied in the negative, he said, "A man without offspring is like a thorn-tree without fruit; as you now belong to my household, I shall give you some wives, so that you may live happily."

I thanked him for his kindness, but begged that he would postpone his present until I had at least erected my huts; because, I remarked, this exceptional mark of his favour must not be exposed to the public gaze. To recompense me for my property which had been taken by Abu Anga, the *khalifa* instructed Fadl el Maula to hand over the effects of the unfortunate Olivier Pain, which were at once sent to me. They consisted of an old *jibba*, a well-worn Arab cloak, and a Koran printed in the French language. Fadl el Maula had sent word to me that, during the time which had elapsed, his other effects had been lost. At the same time, the *khalifa* directed that the money which had been taken from me when I was imprisoned, and had been deposited in the Beit el Mal, should be returned to me. It amounted to £40, a few sequins, and a few gold nose-rings which I had collected as curios; all these were handed back to me by Ahmed Wad Suleiman.

I was now able to set to work to build my huts; but whilst they were being put up I lived in the *khalifa's* house. I entrusted my old servant Saadalla, the Nubawi, who was the most competent of all my attendants, with the construction of my residence, which was to consist for the present of three huts and a fence. I myself, from early morning till late at night, was always in attendance at the door of my master. Whenever he went for a short walk or a long ride, I was always obliged to accompany him, barefooted. During the first few days, as my feet got cut and bruised, he allowed me to have some light Arabic sandals made, which, though they gave me some protection against the stones, were so hard and rough that they rubbed off all the skin.

Occasionally, the *khalifa* used to call me in to eat with him, and frequently sent for what was over of his own food to be consumed by the principal *mulazemin*, of whom I was now reckoned as one. When he retired at night, I was at liberty to return to my huts; and there, stretching my weary limbs on an *angareb*, I slept till early dawn, when I was again obliged to await the *khalifa* at his door, and accompany him to morning prayers.

Meanwhile, the *khalifa* had been informed that my huts were erected, and, returning home late one night, my old servant Saadalla informed me that a female slave, closely muffled up, had been brought to my house, and was now installed within. Directing Saadalla to light a lantern and show the way, I followed, and found the poor thing huddled up on a palm-mat. When I spoke to her about her past life, she answered, in a deep voice which did not presage well for the future, that she was a Nubawi, and had formerly belonged to an Arab tribe in Southern Kordofan, but had been captured, and sent to the Beit el Mal, from whence she had just been despatched to me by Ahmed Wad Suleiman. Whilst speaking, she removed her scented white drapery from her head, as slaves always do when talking to their masters, and exposed her bare shoulders and part of her bosom.

I signed to Saadalla to bring the light nearer; and then I had to summon all my presence of mind so as not to be terrified and fall off my *angareb*. Out of her ugly black face, peered two little eyes; a great flat nose, below which were two enormous blubber-shaped lips which, when she laughed, were in danger of coming in contact with her ears, completed one of the most unpleasant physiognomies I had ever beheld. Her head was joined to her enormously fat body by a bull-dog-like neck; and this creature had the audacity to call herself Maryam (Mary). I at once directed Saadalla to remove his compatriot to another hut, and give her an *angareb*.

So this was the *khalifa's* first gift to me: he had not given me a horse, a donkey, or even a little money, which would have been of some use to me, but had presented me with a female slave, for whom, even had she been fair, he knew well I should not have cared, as, let alone her disagreeable presence, her food and dress were items of expense which I by no means relished. When he saw me the next day, after morning prayers, he asked me if Ahmed Wad Suleiman had satisfactorily carried out his wishes. I replied, "Yes; your order was most promptly carried out," and then gave him an exact description of my new acquisition. The *khalifa* was furious with Ahmed Wad Suleiman, who, he asserted, not only did not comply with his order, but had made him unfaithful to the *Mahdi's* ordinances. My candour in describing exactly the class of slave given me, reacted somewhat unpleasantly on my head; for, the following evening, a young and somewhat less ugly girl, selected by the *khalifa* himself, was sent to me, and her also I handed over to the tender mercies of the faithful Saadalla.

The *Mahdi*, his *khalifas*, and their relatives, having now no longer any fear from external enemies, began to build houses suitable to their new positions and requirements. The numbers of young women and girls who had been seized and distributed on the fall of Khartum were now hurried off into the seclusion of these new residences; and their masters, no longer disturbed by the jealous and envious looks of their friends, were able to enjoy their pleasures undisturbed.

Naturally, the *Mahdi*, the *khalifas*, and, more especially, the relatives of the former were most anxious that it should not be known that the greater part of the loot taken in Khartum was in their own hands; it was a striking contradiction of the doctrine of the Divine master, who forever preached renunciation and abandonment of the pleasures of life. They set to work to enlarge their habitations and enclosures, anticipating that they would fill them still further with the rich spoil which was expected from the provinces that still remained to be conquered.

But the *Mahdi* fell suddenly ill; for a few days he did not appear at the mosque for prayers. No particular attention, however, was paid to his absence at first, for he had asserted, over and over again, that the Prophet had revealed to him that he should conquer Mecca, Medina, and Jerusalem, and, after a long and glorious life, should expire at Kufa. But the *Mahdi* was attacked by no ordinary indisposition: the fatal typhus fever had fallen upon him; and, six days after he had sickened, his relatives in attendance began to despair of saving his life. My master, the *khalifa*, was, of course, watching with the most intense interest the outcome of the disease, and did not leave the *Mahdi's* bedside day or night, whilst I and the other members of the body-guard aimlessly waited for our master at his door.

On the evening of the sixth day, the multitudes collected before the *Mahdi's* house, and in the mosque, were commanded to join together in prayer for the recovery of the Divine patient, who was now in the greatest danger; and this was the first occasion on which the malignant disease from which the *Mahdi* was suffering was announced to the public. On the morning of the seventh day, he was reported to be worse; and there was now little doubt that he was dying. In the early stages, he had been treated by his wives and by Sudanese quacks with the usual domestic remedies; and it was only at the last moment that Hassan Zeki, one of the detested Egyptians, formerly medical officer of the Khartum hospital, who, by a lucky chance, had been saved on the day of the attack, was called in.

Asked to prescribe, he affirmed that the complaint had now reached such a stage that it was not advisable to use any medicines, and that the only hope lay in the resistance of his powerful constitution, which, with God's help, might drive out this terribly malignant disease. Hassan Zeki, indisposed as he was to render any assistance, was perfectly well aware that the *Mahdi* was now beyond the reach of medicines; he also knew that if he had prescribed, and the *Mahdi* had subsequently died, he would undoubtedly have been credited with the cause of his death, and his life would have been in the greatest danger. From all these considerations, he therefore wisely refrained from interference.

The disease had now reached its crisis. By the *Mahdi's angareb* stood the three *khalifas*, his near relations, Ahmed Wad Suleiman, Mohammed Wad Beshir (one of the principal *employés* of the Beit el Mal in charge of the *Mahdi's* household), Osman Wad Ahmed, Said el Mekki (formerly one of the most renowned religious Sheikhs of Kordofan), and a few of his principal and most faithful adherents, to whom special permission had been granted to enter the sick-room. From time to time, he lost consciousness; and, feeling that his end was drawing near, he said, in a low voice, to those around him, "Khalifa Abdullahi Khalifat es Sadik has been appointed by the Prophet as my successor. He is of me and I am of him; as you have obeyed me and have carried out my orders, so should you deal with him. May God have mercy upon me!" Then gathering up all his strength, with one final effort, he repeated a few times the Mohammedan creed (*La Illaha illallah, Mohammed Rasul Allah*), crossed his hands over his chest, stretched out his limbs, and passed away.

Around the body, which was not yet cold, the late *Mahdi's* adherents swore fidelity to Khalifa Abdullahi, Said el Mekki being the first to take the *khalifa's* hand, own his allegiance, and praise his name. His example was immediately followed by the two *khalifas* and the remainder of those assembled. It was impossible to keep the *Mahdi's* death secret; and the crowds waiting outside were informed about it: but, at the same time, strict injunctions were given that no weeping and lamentation should be made; and it was further announced that the *khalifa* (successor) of the *Mahdi* should demand the oath of allegiance from the entire populace.

The *Mahdi's* principal wife, named Sittina Aisha Um el Muminin (Our Lady Aisha, Mother of the Believers), who lay huddled up and closely veiled in a corner, and who had been a witness of the death of her master and husband, now arose and proceeded to the *Mahdi's* house, bearing to the other wives the sad news of his death. Her office was to comfort them, and prevent them from making loud lamentation. Most of these good women rejoiced secretly in their hearts at the death of their husband and master, who had brought such terrible distress upon the land, and whom, even before he had fully enjoyed the fruits of his success, Almighty God had summoned to appear before the Supreme Seat of Judgment.

In spite of the strict and oft-repeated injunctions against loud lamentation, weeping and wailing arose from almost every house on the death of the Mahdi el Muntazer, who, it was reported, had voluntarily departed from his earthly abode to God, his master whom he longed to see.

Some of those now present began to wash the body, and then wrap it in several linen cloths; whilst others dug the grave in the room in which he had died, and which, after two hour's hard work, was finished. The three *khalifas*, together with Ahmed Wad Suleiman and Wad Beshir, now placed the body in the grave, built it over with bricks, and then filled it up with earth, on which they poured water. This over, lifting up their hands, they recited the prayers for the dead; then, leaving the room, they proceeded to pacify the impatient crowd awaiting the news without.

We *mulazemin* were the first to be summoned before the new ruler, who, henceforth, was called *Khalifat el Mahdi* (successor of the *Mahdi*); and he gave us the oath of allegiance, directing us at the same time to move the *Mahdi's* pulpit to the entrance door of the mosque, and to inform the populace that he was about to appear before them. Informed that this had been completed, he left his late master's grave, and, for the first time, ascended the pulpit as ruler. He was in a state of intense excitement. Great tears rolled down his cheeks as, with a trembling voice, he began to address the multitude:

Friends of the *Mahdi*, God's will cannot be changed. The *Mahdi* has left us, and has entered into heaven, where everlasting joys await him. It is for us to obey his precepts, and to support one another, just as the stones and walls of a house go to make a building. The good things of this life are not lasting. Seize, therefore, with both hands the good fortune which is yours, of having been the friends and adherents of the *Mahdi*, and never deviate in the slightest degree from the path which he has shown you. You are the friends of the *Mahdi*, and I am his *khalifa*. Swear that you will be faithful to me.

This short address over all those present now repeated the well-known oath of allegiance; but the *khalifa* altered the first sentence of it as follows: "*Bayana Allah wa Rasulahu wa Mahdina wa bayanaka ala tauhidillahi,* etc."

As only a certain number could take the oath of allegiance at one time, those who had finished made way for others; and the crowd was so enormous that many were in danger of being trodden to death. The ceremony went on till nightfall. The *khalifa* had now long since ceased weeping, and was rejoiced to see the crowds who thronged to him to swear him eternal allegiance. From continual talking, he had become quite exhausted; and, descending from the pulpit, he took a draught of water to moisten his parched throat. But the thought that he was now the assured ruler of the enormous masses before him seemed to keep him up; and it was only when darkness actually supervened that some of his principal men urged him to desist, and leave the pulpit.

Before doing so, however, he summoned all the *emirs* of the Black Flag, and called upon them to take a special oath of allegiance, admonishing them to adhere faithfully to him and to his brother Yakub, and calling their attention to the fact that, being strangers and foreigners, they should endeavour to live in harmony with each other as long as they were in the valley of the Nile, for they would require union in order to successfully oppose the intrigues of the local inhabitants; and once again he impressed upon them the all-important necessity of adhering most strictly to the doctrines of the *Mahdi*. By this time it was past midnight; but it was out of the question to think of going home. Utterly exhausted, I lay on the ground and heard the passers-by loud in their praises of the late *Mahdi*, and assuring each other of their firm resolve to support his successor in carrying out their late master's precepts.

Now what had the *Mahdi* done, and wherein lay his power to revive a religion which had become so debased? What was the nature of his teachings? He had preached renunciation; he had inveighed against earthly vanities and pleasures; he had broken down both social and official ranks; he had made rich and poor alike; he had selected as clothing a *jibba*, which became the universal dress of his adherents. As a regenerator of religion, he had united the four distinct Moslem sects: the Malaki, the Shafai, the Hanafi, and the Hambali, which differ from each other only in minor details,—such as the method of performing ablution, the method of standing or kneeling down in prayers, the manner of conducting marriage ceremonies; and, by astutely making certain much needed reforms, he had succeeded in combining these four great divisions.

He had made a collection of certain specially selected verses from the *Koran*, which he called the *Rateb*, and which he enjoined should be recited by the entire congregation after morning and afternoon prayers,—a ceremony which lasted at least forty minutes. He had facilitated the method of performing prayer ablutions, and had strictly forbidden the drinking bouts which were an invariable accompaniment of marriage ceremonies in the Sudan; he had reduced the amount of the "*Mahr*" (the present usually given by the bridegroom to the bride) to ten dollars and two dresses for unmarried girls, and to five dollars and two dresses for widows. Whoever sought for more or gave more was considered to have performed an act of disobedience, and was punished by deprivation of all property. A simple meal of dates and milk took the place of the costly marriage feast. By these innovations, the *Mahdi* had sought to facilitate the ceremony of matrimony, and had strictly enjoined on parents and guardians to see that their daughters and wards were married early.

At the same time, he had forbidden dancing and playing, which he classified as "earthly pleasures;" and those found disobeying this order were punished by flogging and confiscation of all property. The use of bad language was punished with eighty lashes for every insulting word used, and seven days' imprisonment. The use of intoxicating drinks, such as *marissa* or date wine, and smoking were most strictly prohibited. Offences of this description were punishable by flogging, eight days' imprisonment, and confiscation of goods. A thief suffered the severance of his right hand; and should he be convicted of a second offence, he lost his left foot also. As it was the general custom amongst the male population of the Sudan, and especially amongst the nomad

Arabs, to let their hair grow, the *Mahdi* had directed that henceforth all heads should be shaved. Wailing for the dead and feasts for the dead were punishable by deprivation of property.

In order, however, that the strength of his army should not be decreased and endangered by desertion, owing to the severe mode of life he had prescribed, and fearful that his doctrines which were considered unorthodox should be made known in the various foreign countries by which he was surrounded, he practically made a cordon round the countries he had already conquered, and absolutely prohibited passage of persons through these districts for the purpose of performing a pilgrimage to Mecca. Should anyone cast the slightest doubt on the Divine nature of his mission, or should there be the slightest hesitation to comply with his orders, on the evidence of two witnesses, the delinquent was invariably punished by the loss of the right hand and left foot. On some occasions, witnesses were dispensed with,—a revelation from the Prophet was even more efficacious in proving the guilt of the offender.

As, however, most of these dispositions and ordinances were entirely at variance with the Moslem law, he therefore issued most strict injunctions that the study of theology and all public commentaries thereon should cease, and ordered, moreover, that any books or manuscripts dealing with these subjects should be instantly burnt or thrown into the river.

Such were the teachings of the expected *Mahdi*; and he had left no stone unturned to carry into the fullest effect the ordinances he had made. Openly, he showed himself a most strict observer of his own teachings; but, within their houses, he, his *khalifas*, and their relatives entered into the wildest excesses, drunkenness, riotous living, and debauchery of every sort, and they satisfied to their fullest extent the vicious passions which are so prevalent amongst the Sudanese.

CHAPTER 11

Early Rule of Khalifa Abdullahi

From the date of the *Mahdi's* departure from Rahad, up to the time of his death, nothing of importance had happened in the various provinces of the Sudan which could be calculated to change the course of events.

Mohammed Khaled had settled in El Fasher, and had despatched his Emirs in various directions. Instead of meeting with resistance, they were received everywhere with open arms by the deluded inhabitants, who vied with one another in their anxiety to become subjects of the *Mahdi*. The western districts of Dar Gimr, Massalit, and Dar Tama, as far as the frontier of Wadai, all sent in their submission, and a number of valuable presents; Saleh Donkusa too, and his friends the Bedeyat, also anxious not to expose themselves to new dangers, sent in a deputation conveying their salutations and gifts. Mohammed Khaled had also sent one of his friends, a merchant named Hajji Karar, from Kobbé, with presents to Sultan Yusef, of Wadai. On his arrival, Sultan Yusef had received him kindly, and had sent him back to Khaled with a present of several horses and female slaves, and with the assurance that he might consider him an adherent of the *Mahdi*, whose rules and ordinances he was at all times ready to obey.

Abdullahi Dudbenga, on the other hand, Sultan Harun's successor in Jebel Marra, paid no heed to the summons calling him to El Fasher; he had a personal quarrel with Khaled, and had no desire to put himself within his reach. However, finally, when he received an ultimatum to either come at once, or to risk a war, he submitted and came in; but a few days later fled, fearing that he was about to be placed in chains, and his money and property confiscated. Instead, however, of returning to the Jebel Marra, he proceeded to Omdurman, where he was well received by Khalifa Abdullahi, who gave orders that his family and effects should be brought from Darfur to Omdurman. Meanwhile, Khaled, furious at his flight, had him pursued as far as the Kordofan frontier, and ordered that all villages which gave refuge to the fugitive should become the property of the government, and that the village *sheikhs* should be shot. He also despatched Omar Wad Darho with a considerable force to Jebel Marra, with instructions to announce to the inhabitants that, having hitherto failed to make their submission, or to give presents, they should in consequence be considered "*Ghanima*" (booty).

Omar Wad Darho, anticipating quantities of loot, proceeded to his destination; whilst Khaled thought the present occasion a fitting one to send some of his best horses and his fairest women to the *Mahdi* and his *khalifas*. Darho met with little resistance in Jebel Marra. The villagers fled to the hills; but, having procured good guides, he pursued them into the most inaccessible places, and succeeded in putting numbers of them to the sword. Their women and children he divided up amongst his men, selecting and sending to Khaled all the best. His men, however, unused to this continual hill marching, became exhausted, and his horses were, for the most part, without shoes; nevertheless he succeeded in collecting a quantity of loot, and returned to El Fasher on the actual day that the terrible and unexpected news of the *Mahdi's* death had arrived there.

Darho, anticipating important changes owing to this untoward event, did not hesitate to take advantage of the situation; and, proceeding forthwith to Kobbé, he declared himself independent, stating he would no longer serve under Khaled's orders; indeed, he made preparations to fight him, and make himself eventually ruler of Darfur. He went so far as to propose to the *emirs* who had accompanied him to Jebel Marra, that he would divide amongst them the lands of Darfur; but the latter, deeming Darho's action ill-considered, argued that they were not likely to get more from him than they did from Khaled. They therefore urged him to desist, declaring that in the event of his refusal, they would make full report of the circumstances to Khaled. Darho's party daily diminished in numbers; and it was not long before he recognised the rashness of his act.

Meanwhile, Khaled, alarmed by Darho's pluck and resolution, determined to entrap his old friend by stratagem: he despatched his acquaintance Ali Bey Khabir to him with a message to the effect that he solemnly swore to do Darho no harm, should he return, and that he would at once forget the matter which, after all, would never have happened had it not been for the perfectly comprehensible excitement occasioned by the *Mahdi's* sudden death. In order, however, to satisfy public opinion, he enjoined that Darho should come to El Fasher as a penitent, and publicly acknowledge his error, promising that henceforth he would faithfully serve the *Mahdi's* successor.

Ali Khabir succeeded in convincing Darho of Khaled's sincerity. At this time the hostile party consisted only of a few soldiers, the Shaigia, and some local tribesmen, and was quite incapable of any sustained resistance; accompanied therefore by these, he proceeded to El Fasher, and, before entering the town, they placed iron chains about their necks, and followed Khabir to the meeting place designated by Khaled. On their way, they were insulted by the populace, who had collected in crowds to jeer at them; Darho was infuriated, and, on reaching Khaled's presence, cried out that had he had any notion he was to be received in this insulting manner, he would never have come.

Khaled, seizing on Darho's words as a pretext, instantly ordered him and his officers to be arrested and thrown into chains; Darho, now losing all control of himself, insulted Khaled in the most open manner, and, in consequence, they were hurried off to the prison, their numbers being increased by three former officials, *viz.*, Ibrahim Seian and Hassan Sharkassi, both Egyptian officers, and Yakub Ramzi, chief clerk of the Court of Justice, who were accused of having been in secret correspondence with Darho. These latter, pleading that they had been former government officials, and had not now sufficient to live upon, admitted that they had written a letter to Darho, though only regarding the death of the *Mahdi*; but it was affirmed that they had instigated him to revolt. In spite of their undoubted innocence, Khaled ordered them, as well as Darho and his friends, to be shot dead at sunrise the following morning; but this sentence was not allowed to be publicly known.

Khabir Ali, however, learning what was intended, rushed to Khaled's house, and endeavoured to dissuade him from his purpose; but this was not till the following morning, and on his way he stumbled across the bodies of his decapitated friends. Raising his voice, he declared before the bystanders that, had he thought for a moment such measures would have been taken, nothing would have induced him to act as a mediator; and he deplored most bitterly the death of his old friends who had been slain in so treacherous a manner.

Abu Anga was now in Kordofan. This province had submitted entirely to the *Mahdi*, with the exception of the southern mountainous regions, the inhabitants of which were looked upon as slaves who had objected to pay tribute, and who were consequently ordered to emigrate to Omdurman. As they had refused to comply with these demands, Abu Anga had been despatched south, with injunctions not only to enforce their subjection, but also to quarter his enormous force of Jehadia on them, and to procure plenty of slaves. After losing a considerable number of men, and a quantity of ammunition, he succeeded in carrying out these orders to some extent; but a large proportion of the inhabitants still continued to defend themselves most bravely in their mountain fastnesses, and remained independent. Thus, with the exception of this small proportion of the natives, the entire Western Sudan, from the banks of the White Nile to the frontiers of Wadai, acknowledged the sway of the *Mahdi*.

In the eastern districts, however, the Governors of Sennar and Kassala continued to defend their posts. Whilst Khartum was being besieged, steamers had been sent under Subhi Pasha to Sennar, and, after replenishing the posts, had returned to the capital. But when the local tribes had been summoned by the *Mahdi* to join in the holy war, they, collecting under their head-*sheikh*, Merdi Abu Rof of the Gehéna tribe, laid siege to the town. Surrounded for several months, the brave but famishing garrison at length made a sortie, drove off the besiegers, and captured in their camp a quantity of stores and grain which lasted them for some time.

The *Mahdi*, believing that the local tribes were somewhat lukewarm in their efforts, reinforced them by his cousin Abdel Kerim, with a considerable force from Khartum. The latter, learning that the garrison was now suffering severely from famine, determined to take the town by storm; but he was forced back, and the garrison, making a counter attack, drove him out of his position. In spite of this victory, however, the condition of Sennar became hopeless; constant fighting, famine, and the impossibility of relief began to tell at last.

Meanwhile, Kassala had been closely besieged; and, although the garrison had made several successful sorties, they had gained no really decisive victory, and had not been able to replenish their store of provisions.

The Egyptian Government, learning the critical situation of the garrisons in the Eastern Sudan, now appealed to King John of Abyssinia to co-operate in relieving the posts of Gallabat, Gira, Senhit, and Kassala, and bring their garrisons to Massawa. The Governor of Kassala, however, declared that as the garrison of the town was composed for the most part of local people, he could not induce them to leave the country. The *Mahdi* now sent Idris Wad Abder Rahim and El Hussein Wad Sahra with reinforcements to hasten the fall of the town. Meanwhile, King John had succeeded in relieving the garrisons of Senhit, Gira, and Gallabat, and removing them to Massawa; thus all the Arab tribes lying within the Suakin-Berber-Kassala triangle became fanatical adherents of the *Mahdi*. Osman Digna had already been appointed *emir* of this district; whilst Mohammed Kheir was ordered to proceed from Berber with instructions to occupy Dongola with the Jaalin and Barabra, after the retirement of the British army.

Such was briefly the situation in the Sudan when Khalifa Abdullahi became its ruler. It was not, therefore, without reason that he summoned the western Arab tribes to unite together, and seriously called their attention to the fact that they were strangers and foreigners in the Nile valley. It can be readily understood that the Aulad-Belad, or local population, more especially the Barabra, Jaalin, and the inhabitants of the Gezira, did not appreciate the advent of the *khalifa* and his western Arabs, from whom they entirely differed in ideas and character; they saw with dread the new ruler seizing the reins of government, and relying entirely for the execution of his orders on his western compatriots.

One of the *khalifa's* first steps was to expel from his position Ahmed Wad Suleiman, whom he detested, and whom he knew to have given a large share of the booty to the *ashraf* (*Mahdi's* relatives), who looked on him with no friendly eye. The unfortunate Ahmed was ordered to give an account of the funds which had passed through his hands during the previous year; Abdullahi well knew that the *Mahdi* had trusted Ahmed entirely, and had never called on him to keep full and accurate accounts, because the money he issued was almost invariably given under the *Mahdi's* verbal orders, and he held no receipts. It was, of course, impossible for Ahmed to produce the account; and his expulsion from the Beit el Mal, and the confiscation of his property, and that of several of his assistants, was looked upon by the populace as an act of justice. The *khalifa* appointed in his place Ibrahim Wad Adlan, who was of the Kawahla tribe located on the Blue Nile, but had spent many years of his life as a merchant in Kordofan, and was in favour with the *khalifa*.

Adlan was now ordered to open ledgers showing the revenue and expenditure, and to keep his books in such a manner that at any moment, on the demand of the *khalifa*, he should be able to give an exact statement of the financial situation. He also ordered him to keep a careful list of those to whom money was issued, or who were in receipt of pensions.

Almost simultaneously with the death of the *Mahdi*, came the news of the failure of the attack on Sennar, and of the repulse of Abdel Kerim. The *khalifa*, therefore, at once despatched Abderrahman en Nejumi to take supreme command; and, in August, 1885, the garrison surrendered to that redoubtable warrior. As usual, the fall of the town was the signal for a series of brutal atrocities and cruelties. A number of the inhabitants were sent to the *khalifa*, amongst them, all the good-looking young girls, and the daughters of the former government officials, of whom the *khalifa* kept some for himself, and distributed the remainder amongst his *emirs*.

Abdullahi entertained a particular aversion for the *Mahdi's* cousin Abdel Kerim, and he now summoned him and his followers to Omdurman. Abdel Kerim, being Khalifa Sherif's assistant, had taken with him when he went to Sennar the Black soldiers of Sherif's flag; it was rumoured at the time, that he had said that, if supported by his own adherents, as well as by those of Khalifa Sherif, he would be sufficiently powerful to force Khalifa Abdullahi to hand over his authority to Sherif, who, being a relative of the *Mahdi*, and a *khalifa*, had every right to succeed. It was not known if Abdel Kerim was really serious in his intentions, or if these were mere idle tales; but Abdullahi prepared himself, and all his relatives, and directed his brother Yakub to hold his men in readiness when Abdel Kerim came.

On the same day that he arrived in Khartum, his men were ordered to be transferred to Omdurman, and he himself received instructions to parade for the *khalifa's* inspection. Accordingly, on the following day, at the head of six hundred men, he took up his position by the flag; and Abdullahi arrived accompanied by the force prepared by his brother, and by several thousands of others. He heartily greeted Abdel Kerim and his troops, praised them for their courage in the siege of Sennar, and then dismissed them. On his return to his house, he ordered the two *khalifas* and all the *Mahdi's* relatives to come to his residence immediately after evening prayers.

At sunset, we *mulazemin* were ordered to hold ourselves in readiness to introduce the expected visitors to the *khalifa*. On their arrival, they were taken to the inner part of the house, and directed to seat themselves on the ground; the two *khalifas* only were given sheepskins to sit upon, while Abdullahi seated himself on a small *angareb*. From his elevated position, the *khalifa* now ordered his secretary to read the document which had been written by the late *Mahdi* in his favour. This done, he informed the assembled people that Abdel Kerim was unfaithful. The latter of course denied it; nevertheless, he was found guilty, and Khalifa Ali Wad Helu seized the occasion to declare, in the most vehement terms, that he was a most faithful adherent of the *Mahdi*, and Khalifa Abdullahi's slave.

He based this declaration on the contents of the statement just read, and on the *Mahdi's* last words as he lay on his death-bed. Abdullahi, not wishing to appear too much concerned about Abdel Kerim's conduct, gave him a full pardon, but ordered that his black soldiers should be at once handed over. Khalifa Sherif and his relatives were obliged to accept this condition; and Ali Wad Helu, on a wink from Abdullahi, suggested that they should all renew the oath of allegiance. The proposal was accepted; the Holy *Koran* was brought in; and those present, placing their hands on the sacred volume, swore that it was their duty to hand over to the *khalifa* all their black soldiers and arms. By way of encouragement, Khalifa Ali was the first to swear, and in this respect aided and abetted his master at a critical moment to no inconsiderable extent. Khalifa Sherif and his relatives, however, swore very unwillingly; and, after Abdullahi himself had administered the oath, they were permitted to leave. This was the *khalifa's* first blow to his antagonists; and he thus crippled their power, and reduced them to a harmless position.

Now Mohammed Khaled alone was left; and, being one of the *Mahdi's* near relatives, he had for long been a thorn in Abdullahi's side.

That evening, I happened to be alone with the *khalifa*, and he talked over the events of the day, remarking that, "A regent cannot share authority;" by this he inferred that the action of the two other *khalifas* had placed him in the position of an absolute ruler.

On the following morning, Abdel Kerim and Ahmed Wad Suleiman, representing Khalifa Sherif, handed over all their Black soldiers, arms, and ammunition to the *khalifa's* brother Yakub, who received them in the open space in front of his house. Khalifa Ali also made over the soldiers in his charge; and the united force of Blacks was now placed under the command of Abu Anga's brother, Fadl el Maula, who, in order to exercise control, took up his residence temporarily in the barracks. Not content with these measures, Abdullahi now sent for the war-drums in charge of the other *khalifas*; and they were at once handed over, without further ado, to his deputy. Still not satisfied, he ordered the flags, which hitherto were always planted in front of the residences of the respective *khalifas*, to be collected and placed all together in front of Yakub's residence.

The previous day he had, by kind words, won over Khalifa Ali to his side; and now the latter was the first to plant his flags in their new positions. Khalifa Sherif was powerless to do anything; all his Black soldiers, his flags, and his war-drums, which are always known as signs of authority in the Sudan, were safely deposited in Yakub's hands; and the populace were not slow to recognise that Abdullahi meant to be the one and only ruler, and was resolved to have his commands obeyed.

Whilst all these important matters were transpiring in the capital, the news arrived that Kassala had surrendered, and that Osman Digna was fighting against the Abyssinians under the leadership of Ras Alula. Although the Abyssinians had been victorious, and had driven Digna back to Kassala, they did not pursue him, but returned to their own country.

Osman Digna now accused the former governor, Ahmed Bey Effat, of having incited the Abyssinians to take up arms against him, and of having been in communication with them. There were no grounds for this suspicion; but, nevertheless, he and six former officials of Kassala had their hands tied behind their backs like criminals, and were shot dead.

Idris Wad Ibrahim, who, it will be remembered, had been despatched to Kassala, was now ordered to return to Omdurman with all his men, ammunition, loot, and women that he had captured, and to leave the country in the hands of Osman Digna.

Abdullahi fully realised that his action in regard to the other Khalifas would naturally rouse the ire of the *Mahdi's* relatives, with whom he was already on bad terms; but this was a matter of little concern to him. He was determined, by all the means in his power, and, if necessary, by recourse to violence, to enforce his commands, whatever they might be. But, on the other hand, he did not wish to entirely alienate public opinion, nor to give grounds to the numerous *Mahdi*sts, who, owing to their love for the *Mahdi*, entertained a certain affection for his relatives, for bringing against him accusations of injustice or hostility; he therefore presented them with numbers of female slaves, and to Khalifa Sherif he gave some very fine horses and mules, and distributed quantities of slaves amongst his retainers.

He took good care to make these gifts widely known; and the populace, in their turn, praised him for his magnanimity, and went so far as to extol his justice and liberality in songs. Still bent on improving his position, he despatched his relative and my friend, Yunes Wad ed Dekeim, and his cousin Osman Wad Adam to Kordofan, and, in order to remove from Omdurman the Black troops he had taken away from the *khalifas*, he despatched them also to the west. Yunes was instructed to bring into subjection the Gimeh tribe, which was both rich and strong, but which had shown some lukewarmness in obeying the *khalifa's* summons to immigrate to Omdurman. Osman Wad Adam was ordered to join Abu Anga, and await further instructions.

To both, however, he gave strict injunctions to collect as many male and female slaves as possible, and instruct the former in the use of fire-arms. Previous to the arrival of Yunes in Gimeh, the head-*sheikh*, Asaker Wad Abu Kalam, had already been summoned to Omdurman, and had been imprisoned there; but his cousin, unwilling to submit to the rule of Yunes, had, while endeavouring to escape, been overtaken and killed, while his tribe was now deprived of the greater part of its property, and forced to proceed to Omdurman. Yunes, having crossed the river at Goz Abu Guma, had established a settlement there, and now returned to the *khalifa* for further orders. He had already despatched thousands of cattle to Khartum, and, in consequence, received a very warm welcome. The *khalifa* now instructed him to remove the tribe to Wad el Abbas, opposite Sennar, where he would send him further orders. Yunes had a considerable attachment for me, and asked the *khalifa's* permission to take me with him, in order to assist in the transport arrangements, as the Gimeh people were peculiarly unmanageable. At first, the *khalifa* refused the request, but eventually acceded to Yunes's pressing demand.

I had already taken possession of my new quarters the previous month, and my servant, with his three wives, who had been detained at El Obeid when on his way from Darfur, was now brought here by the *khalifa's* orders. Three other male servants and their wives also arrived; but as they did not appear anxious to remain in my service, I handed them over to Fadl el Maula, who, in accordance with the *khalifa's* orders, took them into the ranks. My household now consisted of four male servants with their wives; and I asked the *khalifa's* permission to take three of them with me to Sennar.

"There is no necessity for you to take any of your servants with you," said the *khalifa*. "Leave them here, and I will see that they are looked after; while Yunes will be responsible for your comfort during the journey. I hope you will justify my confidence in you. Carry out the orders of Yunes, and you will regain my regard; go now to him, and tell him that I permit you to accompany him on his journey."

Yunes, delighted at the *khalifa's* permission, said that he would do all he could to make my journey pleasant, and talked so quickly and incessantly that I scarcely understood half of what he said. I was delighted at the thought of leaving Omdurman, and being away from the tyrant whom I was obliged to serve day and night; I secretly cherished a hope that during the journey I might find some occasion to escape from the hands of my tormentors.

One of the *mulazemin* now summoned me again to the *khalifa's* presence. "Did you inform Yunes," said he, "that you are going to accompany him?" and when I replied in the affirmative, he ordered me to sit down, and again began to give me the benefit of his advice. "I urge you," said he, "to serve me faithfully; I look upon you as my son and my heart is inclined toward you. God's holy word, the *Koran*, promises rewards to the faithful, but threatens the traitor with the Divine wrath. Yunes is your well-wisher, and will attend to what you may say to him. Should he attempt to undertake anything which is not likely to lead to his advantage, you should warn him, for he is your master; but I have told him that I look upon you as my son, and he will take heed of what you say."

"I will always endeavour," said I, "to act in accordance with your instructions; but Yunes is my master, and will naturally do what he thinks right. Do not therefore attribute ill-will to me; and I beg you will not make me responsible for anything which may happen contrary to your wishes."

"You are only in a position to offer an opinion," said he; "but you have no power to act. Should he pay heed to you, well and good; if not, it will be his own lookout if matters go wrong." He then turned the conversation to affairs in Darfur, and told me that he had written some time ago to Mahmud Sherif to return with all available troops to Kordofan, leaving in Darfur a commander who, in his opinion, would be equal to the position. He had replied that amongst his relatives there was no one capable of representing their interests; and he recommended the selection of someone who could not only see after the public affairs of the province, but also his private business as well.

In reply, the *khalifa* had assured him of his favour, urged him not to listen to intriguers, but to come as soon as possible to Kordofan, and thence to Omdurman. The last news he had received was to the effect that Mahmud was on the point of coming with all his forces, and that he was already on the road. "Do you think," said the *khalifa*, "that he will comply implicitly with my orders, and will come? You know him better than the others."

"Undoubtedly he will come," I replied; "for he does not dare to act contrary to your instructions."

"I hope that this is so," replied he; "a timid subject is always more easy to rule than one who is not afraid to act disobediently."

The conversation had already lasted some time; and I was about to ask permission to retire, when he beckoned to one of his eunuchs who was standing close by, and whispered a few words in his ear. I knew my master well, and had a foreboding of ill.

"I have already instructed you," said he, "to leave behind all the members of your household; for, having only just arrived from a long journey, they must be fatigued, and I do not wish to expose them further. Yunes will give you a servant; but I am giving you a wife, so that, in case of indisposition or illness, you may have someone to attend on you. She is pretty, and not plain like the one Ahmed Wad Suleiman sent you," he said with a smile; and now beckoning to the woman who had just entered, to come nearer, the latter approached and threw off her veil. I glanced at her, and, in spite of her dark colour, she really was very pretty. "She was my wife," added the *khalifa*; "she is very good, and patient; but I have so many, I therefore gave her her freedom; but you may now call her your own."

I was much embarrassed, and all the time had been casting over in my mind how I could refuse this gift without offending the giver.

"Sir, allow me to speak candidly," said I.

"Certainly," said he, "here you are at home. Speak!"

"I am at home where I need fear nothing," I began, hastily; "this woman was your wife, and has in consequence a right to be treated with consideration for your sake; this of course is an easy matter. But, sire, how can I, your servant, take your own wife for myself? Moreover, you said yourself that you look upon me as your son." Having said this, I dropped my head, and fixed my eyes on the ground, continuing, "I cannot accept this gift;" and then I awaited his answer with anxiety.

"Your words are good, and I pardon you," said he, signing to the woman, who was standing near us, to withdraw. "Almas!" said he, to the eunuch, "bring my white *jibba!*" and when the servant brought it, he handed it to me, saying, "Take this *jibba*, which I have often worn myself, and which was specially blessed by the *Mahdi* for me.[1] Hundreds and thousands of people will envy you this; guard it carefully, for it will bring you blessings."

I was delighted with this present, and fervently kissed his hand, which he extended to me; but inwardly I rejoiced to be rid of the woman, who would have been a useless encumbrance to me, besides an additional expense; and I thought the *jibba* an excellent exchange. I then begged leave to withdraw, and carried off with me my valuable present.

Yunes had fixed his departure for that day; but, before leaving, I was summoned once more to the *khalifa*, who, in the presence of Yunes, again reminded me to be faithful and submissive.

That evening, we left Omdurman on board the steamer *Bordein*, which had been floated off the place where it had gone aground; and, on the second day, we reached Goz Abu Guma. In accordance with the *khalifa's* instructions, we were to hurry on the Gimeh people to Wad el Abbas as quickly as possible; and we called on the Beni Hussein tribe to supply us with camels to carry the water-skins. Yunes was specially kind and considerate to me; he gave me one of his horses and three female slaves, and instructed two old soldiers to wait on me as servants. His total force numbered ten thousand combatants, of whom seven thousand belonged to the Gimeh tribe, who were encumbered with a mass of women and children.

I distributed the camels and water-skins amongst them; and we now prepared for the journey. Our road led through Sekedi Moya, across a plain which, as I remarked before, had been named Tibki Teskut (You weep and are silent); and as I crossed it, I recalled all the bloodshed and fighting which had taken place in the Sudan. In the houses which lay close to the track, we saw innumerable skeletons of the rebels who had been driven away from the wells by Saleh, and had succumbed to thirst.

On the third day, we reached the banks of the Blue Nile, and saw Sennar in the distance; the *khalifa* had issued strict orders that we should on no account proceed to this city, which was now lying half ruined, and which, as it had held out until after the *Mahdi's* death, the *khalifa* said, would bring us no luck. We found several boats in readiness, and in them crossed the Blue Nile, which is here about four hundred yards broad; but this operation took us several days. Just north

---

1. Unfortunately, the *jibba* was too big and long for me, consequently I was unable to wear it at the time of my escape.

of Wad el Abbas, there is a strip of high sandy ground; and this was selected as the position of the camp, because the land in the vicinity is low-lying, and unfit for habitation during the rainy season. All my thoughts were now bent on flight; but, as most of the people entirely sympathised with the *khalifa's* government, it required the greatest care on my part to select any one in whom to place confidence. Very soon after our arrival at Wad el Abbas, I received a letter from the *khalifa*, which ran as follows:—

> In the name of God, the All-bountiful and Merciful, from the noble Sayed Abdullahi Ibn Sayed Mahmud, by the grace of God, Khalifat el *Mahdi*, on whom be peace, to our brother in God, Abdel Kader Saladin.
>
> After this greeting of peace, this is to inform you that I have not received any letter from you since your departure; but I hope that, by the grace of God, you are in good health. You know my instructions, and you have drunk from the river of my eloquence; I have urged you to remain faithful, and I know that you will uphold your promise.
>
> This day, I received a letter from one of the *Mahdi's* friends, who tells me that your wife, coming from the land of the unbelievers, has reached Korosko, and is at this moment endeavouring to bribe people to induce them to fly with you, in order to bring you to her; and I have been told that you know all about this. I therefore again urge you to adhere steadfastly to the faith of the Prophet, and to perform with honesty the duties upon which you have entered; but I wish to add that no doubt has entered into my heart of your fidelity. I only wish you peace, and I greet you.

At the same time, a letter arrived for Yunes to the effect—so his secretary told me in confidence—that news had come from Berber, and that a very strict watch was to be kept over me. Under these circumstances, I could not conceive why the *khalifa* had written to me. Yunes did not tell me that he had received these instructions, and, outwardly, was more friendly than ever with me; but I was guarded very closely both by day and night, and when, a few days later, some hundreds of the Gimeh Arabs were, in accordance with the *khalifa's* orders, embarked on a steamer to proceed to Omdurman, Yunes instructed me to return with them in order, he said, to give the *khalifa* a verbal account of the situation. I perfectly understood what was meant, and realised that he wished to avoid the responsibility of having me with him.

When all the people were embarked, I went to say goodbye to Yunes, who gave me orders to inform the *khalifa* on a number of points. I said that when this duty was over, I presumed I should return to him, to which he replied, "Perhaps you wish to remain with our master the *khalifa*, or possibly he may require your presence in Omdurman. Had I better send the horse I gave you after you, or shall I keep it here?" I assured him that I looked upon the horse as his, and not mine; for I was well aware that once back in Omdurman, I should again have to walk barefoot.

As a token of his friendship, Yunes gave me a hundred hides, and a letter of recommendation to the *khalifa*. The second day after leaving Wad el Abbas, I reached Omdurman, handed over the Gimeh under my charge to Yakub, and was then received by the *khalifa*. He affected great surprise at seeing me, saying that he thought I should have some difficulty in leaving Yunes even for an hour. These were of course mere empty words; for I knew perfectly well that this was a plan arranged between them to get me back without my suspecting it. Meanwhile, he gave me permission to go and visit my household, after which I was to return to him for further orders.

In the evening, we were once more alone, and he began to talk of the letter which had come from Berber. I assured him that if the letter had really come, it must have been written with an intention to do me harm, or that there was some mistake; and, in proof of this, I told him that I had never been married, and that, in consequence, there could be no pining wife to come and look for me. Should any one, however, come to Omdurman and try to induce me to fly, my first step would be at once to inform the *khalifa*. He assured me that he did not believe the rumour, and then asked me if I preferred to stay with him or return to Yunes.

Guessing his intention, I told him that nothing in the world would induce me to leave him again, and that I considered the time spent with him as the happiest in my life. Although pleased at my flattering words, he took occasion to remind me, in a very serious tone of voice, to be faithful and true, and to have nothing whatever to do with people other than his own household; and he then ordered me to take my place as usual before the gate.

On withdrawing from his presence, and thinking the matter over, I had no doubt now that his suspicions against me had not only taken root, but had begun to grow.

At this time the force in El Obeid included about two hundred Blacks, mostly old soldiers, whose numbers had been increased by the arrival of a portion of the former garrison of Dara. Many of them were inhabitants of Jebel Daïr, who were in constant enmity with the Mahdists, and who had been captured by them and utilised as slaves to build their huts. Indignant at this treatment, they resolved to regain freedom by force. Fadl el Maula Bekhit, one of my servants who had been detained in El Obeid, and Beshir, a former lieutenant, were the ringleaders of this conspiracy; and it is always a wonder to me that the Mahdists did not succeed in discovering the plot. Sayed Mahmud, it will be remembered, had been summoned to Omdurman; and the mutineers now thought the favourable moment had arrived to put their plans into execution.

Suddenly, at midday, the inhabitants of El Obeid were startled by the firing of rifles; the soldiers had seized the isolated building which was used as a storehouse for the arms and ammunition, and were firing on the Dervishes, who had attacked them in this position. The latter were driven back; and the former then succeeded in collecting their wives and children. The Dervishes, having only a few fire-arms, had retreated to the government buildings, and had barricaded the doors. The soldiers, encouraged by their success, now attempted to take these buildings by storm; but were forced to retire. In this attack, Abder Rahman el Borusi, formerly one of my best and bravest subalterns, was killed; while the Dervishes lost Abdel Hashmi, Sayed Mahmud's representative, who was greatly detested by the soldiers on account of his overbearing ways.

If the soldiers had only had a good leader, El Obeid would certainly have fallen into their hands; but, under the circumstances, they had no special desire to take this post, and were merely bent on regaining their freedom. That night they spent in the powder magazine, where they were joined by quantities of male and female slaves, who took this opportunity to run away from their masters. Early the next morning, the inhabitants and the Dervishes attempted an attack on the soldiers, but were utterly defeated, and lost a large number in killed and wounded. The soldiers, longing for freedom, now left El Obeid, and marched in a southerly direction towards the Nuba mountains; but, before leaving, they plundered a number of houses, and, seizing the women they found there, made them their slaves.

The Dervishes now attempted to pursue them; but the soldiers, elated by their freedom, again utterly routed them. Unfortunately, the *emir* of the soldiers, a certain Wad Abdulla, a native of Wad Medina, and who had also been one of my officers at Dara, knew of the plot, but did not join in time, fearing it might fail; he was now seized by the Gellabas, and, in spite of his innocence, was beheaded.

The news of this mutiny was at once sent to Sayed Mahmud in Omdurman; and the *khalifa*, no longer requiring his services there, permitted him to return to El Obeid, with instructions to come back as soon as possible to Omdurman with his family, and with all the other relatives of the late *Mahdi*, but forbade him to pursue the mutineers. When, however, he arrived at El Obeid, moved either by feelings of revenge, or thinking perhaps that by killing the mutineers he should obtain favour, he disregarded the *khalifa's* orders, and, collecting all the able-bodied inhabitants of the town and neighbourhood, advanced against the soldiers. The latter had taken up a strong position in the Golfan and Naima hills, and had established there a sort of military republic, nominating as their chief Beshir, who was formerly a sergeant. He gave careful instructions that the ammunition was not to be wasted; and he forbade the mention of the name of the *Mahdi* under pain of punishment. They acknowledged the Khedive as their master, and swore in his name; and the neighbourhood supplied them with abundant food.

Sayed Mahmud, on his arrival at El Obeid, had despatched secret agents to assure the mutineers that he loved them as his own children, and that he would give them a full and free pardon should they submit to him. The soldiers jeeringly replied, that he should first of all convince himself of their affection for him. Thereupon, Mahmud resolved to storm the mountain, and, carrying his own banner at the head of his troops, he was shot dead while leading the assault. Several of his adherents who attempted to recover his body met with a like fate, whilst the remainder of his following dispersed, and fled in all directions, pursued by the Nuba mountaineers, who inflicted heavy loss on them.

Hamdan Abu Anga, who at this time was only a few days distant from the scene of operations, at once reported this occurrence to the *khalifa*, and asked to be allowed to punish the victorious mutineers; but he was instructed to take no further action, as his master had more important duties for him to perform; he had now to deal with Mohammed Khaled.

In Omdurman, however, the *khalifa* declared publicly, that Sayed

Mahmud had been justly punished by God for his disobedience; and that instead of coming to him as ordered, he had sought fame and revenge, in attacking the rebels contrary to his wishes.

For some time back, Khaled had received letters from the *khalifa*, asking him to come to Omdurman, and offering him a high position and honours. The latter had made all preparations for his departure, and was on the point of starting, when the news came of the action taken by the *khalifa* in regard to Khalifa Sherif, and the relatives of the late *Mahdi*. Khaled now received further letters from Abdullahi, telling him how the action of these relatives had forced him to take this unfortunate step; he begged him, in consequence, to come with all speed, as he had no doubt that his practical common sense would assist him in bringing about a reconciliation with all parties. Khaled, believing in these assurances, and anxious to be of assistance to his relative, hastened his journey and camped at Bara. He had under his command a very considerable force, which was augmented by a large number of the local population of Darfur who had been unwillingly compelled to immigrate. He had at his disposal upwards of a thousand cavalry, and three thousand rifles, whilst his followers could not have numbered less than twenty thousand persons.

Previous, however, to Khaled's arrival, Abu Anga, who had with him over five thousand rifles, had received secret instructions to move to Bara, and now advanced thither by forced marches. At sunrise one morning, Khaled found his camp completely encircled by Abu Anga's troops, who were prepared to carry out his instructions, should the slightest opposition be made. Abu Anga now summoned Khaled to appear before him; and the order was at once obeyed. On his arrival the *khalifa's* instructions were handed to him, which were to the effect that, as a token of his submission and fidelity, he should at once make over to Abu Anga all his soldiers and cavalry, as the latter was considered commander-in-chief of the army; Khaled complied with this order without demur, and, being detained by Abu Anga, who obliged him to give the necessary instructions, in a short time the whole of the Darfur troops were placed under the command of subordinates nominated by Abu Anga. This over, Abu Anga now summoned all the *emirs* who accompanied him from Darfur, and read out to them a very flattering document from the *khalifa*, in which they were given the option of remaining with him, or returning to Omdurman.

Khaled and his relatives, however, were arrested; their property confiscated; and all the treasure accumulated in the Beit el Mal was taken possession of by Abu Anga. Said Bey Guma, who, for a considerable time, had acted as chief of Abu Anga's artillery, also reaped considerable benefit from this episode, by obtaining permission to reannex all his slaves, wives, and property which had been confiscated in Darfur, and which Khaled had brought along with him.

Khaled himself was placed in irons, and sent to El Obeid; where he had leisure to think over the *khalifa's* letter, and to recognise that there is a wide difference between making a promise, and carrying that promise into effect.

The *khalifa*, however, was completely satisfied with the result of his plan. Once more he had inflicted a crushing blow on his opponents, who had counted greatly on Khaled's return, but who now saw Abu Anga's army augmented by the very men they had thought to utilise for their own purposes. Abu Anga's force now numbered several thousands; he soon acquired an influence over the Darfur *emirs* and their subjects, whom he considered his compatriots, and several of them proceeded to Omdurman, where they were received by the *khalifa* with the highest honours. Thus were the fears of the inhabitants of the Nile valley increased, owing to the growing prestige and power acquired by the western Arabs; and they realised that for them a reign of despotic tyranny was approaching.

Abu Anga now received instructions to attack and destroy the rebels in the Golfan mountains, who, after the death of Mahmud, considered themselves masters of the situation, and began to treat the inhabitants of the district tyrannically, the result being that internal dissensions arose amongst the various tribes, and they began to scatter and return to their own homes. On the approach of Abu Anga, my old servant with his wife, feeling that he could not count on success, went over to him, saying he was tired of fighting, and was ready to submit to such punishment as his crime merited, all he begged was permission to defend himself.

He represented that he had been my servant in Darfur, and that he, with several others, had been forcibly prevented by Mahmud from continuing his journey, that owing to the constant insults he had received, he had become angry and disgusted, had joined the mutineers, and had taken an active part in the fighting; but that now he had come to beg forgiveness, and ask permission to join me, or suffer the punishment to which he was justly entitled. Abu Anga, whose father had been a slave, and who always had compassion on his own tribesmen, and detested the Gellabas (a name which the western Arabs used generally for all inhabitants of the Nile valley), knew perfectly well that the soldiers had been driven into revolt by the unjust treatment they had received, and, consequently, generously pardoned my servant for the sake, he said, of his old friendship for me, and to do me honour in my position as mulazem of the Khalifa. He thereupon gave him a letter to me, announcing that he had great pleasure in returning to me my old servant, and that he rejoiced we were again united.

Beshir, who had refused the offer of submission, was attacked by Abu Anga's troops the following day, and, after making a magnificent stand, was killed, together with Fadl el Maula, and several soldiers who had remained true to him to the end. On the night previous to this action, several of his men had deserted secretly, and had hidden themselves in various parts of the country; but one after the other they were forced to surrender and accept the pardon offered them. Abu Anga himself, however, took advantage of his success only in so far as to requisition the inhabitants to supply his army with food, and to acquire male and female slaves; whilst he left his cousin Osman Wad Adam as his representative in El Obeid. An order now arrived that the latter should take over the command of Darfur, where Sultan Yusef, a son of Sultan Ibrahim, who had been killed in Zubeir's time, was in revolt.

I ascertained, from a merchant who had recently arrived from Kordofan, that my friend Joseph Ohrwalder had quitted El Obeid, and would shortly arrive in Omdurman. Although I knew that I should have considerable difficulty in meeting him, I rejoiced to think that one of my old countrymen would be near me. I sat at my master's gate, ready at all times to obey his orders. Occasionally, I was spoken to kindly, and commanded to dine with him; at other times, without rhyme or reason as far as I knew, I was taken no notice of for days, receiving from my master only the blackest and most disdainful looks; but this was due to the extraordinary changeability of his character, and I knew I must put up with it. I suppose this was part of my education. To my comrades, I showed myself absolutely callous to everything that happened in the country, so that they should have no reason to increase the distrust felt by the *khalifa*, who, I knew, frequently inquired as to my conduct.

As a matter of fact, however, I watched all the occurrences as closely as my position would allow, and endeavoured to impress them on my mind; for I was, of course, prohibited from writing a single line. The *khalifa* contributed very little towards the support of my household, and only occasionally gave orders for me to be supplied with a few *ardebs* of *dhurra*, or a sheep, or a cow.

Ibrahim Adlan, whom I had known in the time of the government, used to send me monthly from ten to twenty dollars; and a few of the officials and merchants who were in better circumstances than myself, used secretly to send me small sums of money. Thus, though by no means well off, I did not lack the absolute necessaries of life, and only occasionally felt the actual pinch of want; anyhow I was better off than my friend Lupton, whom the *khalifa* had promised to assist, but paid absolutely no attention to his wants. Lupton, it is true, enjoyed a certain amount of freedom: he was allowed to wander about in Omdurman, and to talk to the people; nor was he obliged to attend the five prayers daily at the mosque; but, in spite of this, life to him was full of trouble and sorrow.

I begged Ibrahim Adlan to interest himself in Lupton, and to give a kind thought to him occasionally, by helping him with small sums of money; but this was not sufficient to keep him, and, though ignorant of any trade, he had perforce to earn a livelihood by mending old arms. Having been an officer in the English merchant service, I thought he might know something about machinery. Meeting him one day in the mosque, he complained bitterly of his wretched position; and I suggested to him that if he could secure an appointment in the Khartum dock-yard, it might improve his condition. He jumped at the idea; and I promised that I would do my best to help him.

A few days later, it happened that the *khalifa* was in a good temper, and showed a friendly disposition towards me, as Abu Anga had sent him a present of a young horse, some money, and some of Khaled's slaves. I was commanded to dine with him; and, in the course of conversation, succeeded in turning the subject to the steamers and their machinery, which, up to that day, had been an absolute mystery to him.

"The steamers," said I, "require competent men to look after them and repair damages. As most of the workmen in the dock-yard were killed during the siege of Khartum, I suppose you have had some difficulty in replacing them?"

"But what is to be done?" said the *khalifa*. "These steamers are of the greatest value to me; and I must do all I can to preserve them."

"Abdullahi Lupton," said I, "was formerly engineer on a steamer; if he received a good monthly salary from the Beit el Mal, I believe he would be really useful for this work."

"Then will you speak to him," said he, apparently much pleased; "if he undertook this work of his own free-will and accord, without being forced into it, I believe he would be of some use in these matters, of which, I admit, I know absolutely nothing. I will order Ibrahim Adlan to pay him well."

"I do not even know his whereabouts," said I. "I have not seen him for a long time; but I will make inquiries. I feel confident that he will be only too glad to serve you."

The following day, I sent for Lupton, told him of the conversation, but begged him to do as little as he possibly could for our enemies.

He assured me that the steamers, of the machinery of which he had only a superficial knowledge, would, under his charge, grow worse instead of better, and that it was only his unfortunate circumstances which obliged him to accept the position. The *khalifa* had also spoken to Ibrahim Adlan; and that evening, Lupton sent me word that he was now appointed an *employé* in the arsenal, with pay at the rate of forty dollars a month, which would be just sufficient to save him from absolute want. The *khalifa* took this occasion to dismiss from the arsenal a certain Sayed Taher, an uncle of the *Mahdi*, by whom he had been appointed director. He had been formerly a carpenter in Kordofan, was excessively ignorant, but excelled in every description of dishonesty, and freely sold iron and other material; he was replaced by an Egyptian who had been born in London, and was of such a timorous nature that he did not dare to be dishonest.

The *khalifa* now found that the Kababish, who inhabited the northern portion of Kordofan as far as Dongola, and whose herds pastured down to Omdurman, were not sufficiently submissive for his purpose; he therefore gave instructions to Ibrahim Adlan to confiscate everything they had, under the pretext that they had been frequently ordered to undertake a pilgrimage, and that they had refused to comply. Ibrahim Adlan accordingly sent off a a party, who confiscated the Kababish flocks.

This tribe used to do all the carrying trade of gum from Kordofan, and possessed considerable sums of money, which, in accordance with the usual Arab custom, they buried in some out-of-the-way place in the desert known only to themselves; they were now maltreated and tortured in order to make them disgorge, with the result that large amounts reached the Beit el Mal. The tribe as a whole submitted without much fighting; but Saleh Bey, the head-*sheikh*, and a brother of Sheikh et Tom, who had been beheaded by the *Mahdi*, collected his nearest relatives, and, together with them, proceeded to the wells of Om Badr, where nobody dared to follow them.

The *khalifa* thereupon despatched two well-known Sheikhs, Wad Nubawi of the Beni Jerrar and Wad Atir of the Maalia, to ask him to come to Omdurman, not only promising him full pardon, but also his nomination as Emir of the Kababish. Saleh Bey listened quietly to the proposition, and, to the astonishment of the messengers, took some tobacco, which is detested by the Mahdists, and, putting it into his mouth, said, "I have well understood what you have said; the *khalifa* forgives me entirely, and desires me to come to Omdurman. Supposing now that on my arrival the Prophet should appear to the Khalifa—for we all know that the *khalifa* acts altogether on the inspirations of the Prophet—and instructs him not to forgive me; what then?"

The messengers were not able to answer this question, and, each having received a present of a camel, returned to the *khalifa* and related exactly what had occurred. Several of the Kababish who had been deprived of their property, now deserted to Sheikh Saleh at Om Badr; and, in a very short time, although not a very powerful enemy, he was sufficiently so to prove of considerable annoyance to the *khalifa*.

In Omdurman, the Kababish camels and sheep were sold by auction in the Beit el Mal, and the price of meat fell considerably in consequence, but the price of grain rose in proportion: the reason of this being that Yunes permitted his men in the Gezira to do just as they liked. These districts were the granary of Omdurman; and Yunes, having introduced into them thousands of the Gimeh tribe, with their wives and children, who had been deprived of all they possessed, these now organised themselves into bands of brigands who not only seized all the grain they could lay their hands on, but terrorised the inhabitants who cultivated the land. Thus the store of grain diminished daily; whilst the army of Yunes, to his great delight, grew in numbers, being augmented by runaway slaves and a large supply of independent individuals.

It was the *khalifa's* intention to weaken the power of the Gezira people, who belonged, for the most part, to Khalifa Sherif's party; but now the paucity of grain somewhat alarmed him, and he therefore sent orders to Yunes to return to Omdurman with his entire force. In accordance with these instructions, this great mass of people swept towards Omdurman, seizing everything they could lay their hands on; and Yunes entered the capital, as it were, at the head of a conquering army laden with loot of every description. He was ordered to take up a position towards the south end of the city, near the forts; and to this day the place is known as Dem Yunes.

Shortly after his arrival, it was rumoured in Omdurman that the Abyssinians intended attacking Gallabat. It was said that a certain Hajji Ali Wad Salem, of the Kawahla, who resided in Gallabat, and who had formerly had some trading transactions with the Abyssinians, was travelling in their country, had been made an *emir* of a portion of his tribe, had invaded Abyssinian territory, and had destroyed the Church of Gabta.

A certain Takruri named Saleh Shanga, who had resided at Gallabat, and had held a position of some importance under government, had quitted that town on its evacuation by the Egyptian troops, and had settled down in Abyssinia; but his cousin Ahmed Wad Arbab had been made Dervish Emir of the district. Ras Adal, Governor of the province of Amhara, now called on Arbab to deliver up Hajji Ali, who had been disturbing the peace; and as this demand was refused, he had collected a considerable force, and had invaded Gallabat. Meanwhile, Arbab, who had received warning of Ras Adal's approach, now collected his followers, amounting to some six thousand men, and awaited his arrival outside the town.

The rush of the Abyssinian force, which was ten times as strong as that of Arbab, was terrible: in a few minutes, the *Mahdi's* forces were completely surrounded; Arbab himself killed, and almost all his troops massacred, only a very few escaping. The Abyssinians mutilated the bodies of all, except that of Arbab, which, out of consideration for Saleh Shanga, was untouched. The Dervishes had stored their spare ammunition in an isolated house, and had placed it in charge of an Egyptian, who, being called upon after the battle to surrender, refused to do so; and on the Abyssinians attempting to storm it, he blew it up, thus destroying himself and his enemies. The wives and children of those who had been killed, were now carried off into captivity by the Abyssinians. Gallabat itself was burnt to the ground; and, for a long time, its site was little else than a great open cemetery, the abode of nothing save hyenas.

When the news of the destruction of Wad Arbab's army reached the *khalifa*, he sent a letter to King John requesting him to release the captive wives and children in exchange for a sum of money which he asked him to fix; but, at the same time, he ordered Yunes to quit Omdurman with his entire force, and proceed to Gallabat, where he was to await further orders. On the departure of the army of Yunes, the *khalifa* himself, with a number of his followers, crossed to the west in a steamer, and, after staying with them three days, he gave the warriors his parting blessing, and then returned to Omdurman.

Some time since, Gustav Klootz, who had failed to make a living in Omdurman, had disappeared, and I thought he must have escaped out of the country; but I now learnt, from some merchants who had just arrived from Gedaref, that he had reached that place, but had succumbed to the fatigues of the journey, and had died just before the Abyssinian invasion.

Nejumi and Abu Girga were now ordered, the former to Dongola, and the latter to Kassala, with instructions to occupy the country with their troops, whilst Osman Digna was appointed ruler of the Arab tribes between Kassala and Suakin. The *khalifa*, however, in order to keep himself fully informed of the actions and intentions of Nejumi and Abu Girga, who, with their men, originally belonged to the Nile valley, and did not, in consequence, possess his entire confidence, nominated two of his own relatives, Mussaid Wad Gaidum and Osman Wad Ali, as his representatives, with instructions that they should on all occasions be consulted. In this manner, not only did Mussaid and Ali obtain a certain amount of control, but the arrangement also tended to give them a species of authority amongst the Nile Arabs.

Thus, gradually, he extended his power over the entire Sudan, by lessening the authority of the local inhabitants, and placing his own relatives and tribesmen in positions of importance. He and his *emirs* enlarged their households almost daily, and their luxurious mode of life required the expenditure of considerable sums of money; it was therefore necessary to acquire a thorough hold over the revenues of the country. The number of his personal followers, and especially his armed *mulazemin*, increased rapidly, and it was necessary to arrange for their maintenance. Money was required for them, as well as for those who were secretly hostile to him, and whom he wished to gain over to his side without an open rupture.

Ibrahim Adlan was now called upon to regulate the finances. The revenues consisted of *fitra* (poll-tax), which every living man was obliged to pay at the end of the great fast of Ramadan; its payment was usually made in grain,—approximately eight *rotls*,—but it might also be paid in cash. No one was exempt from this obligation; and parents were compelled to pay not only for their children under age, but even for their newly-born babes. Another source of income was the *zeka* (or two-and-a-half-*per-cent* "alms for the poor") which was paid in grain, cattle, or money in accordance with the Moslem Law. The officials appointed to gather this tax were nominated by Yakub and Ibrahim; and it was presented by them to the *khalifa*. They were obliged to keep a strict account of all receipts, which they had to render to the Beit et Mal, supported by vouchers.

An attempt was also made to regulate the expenditure, that is to say, Ibrahim Adlan was forbidden to pay away money as he thought proper. Of course, certain persons,—such as the *kadi*, his clerks, the chiefs of the *mulazemin*, etc.,—whose services were absolutely necessary to the *khalifa*, were granted certain specified sums, which were paid monthly, but which were so small that they were scarcely sufficient to provide for the bare necessaries of life; for instance, the chief *kadi*, who bore the title of Kadi Islam, received only forty dollars a month; the *khalifa's* secretary, thirty; and so on. Khalifa Sherif and his relatives received a certain sum in accordance with the *khalifa's* special orders; but Khalifa Ali Wad Helu, owing to his submission and obedience, was in the *khalifa's* favour, and obtained a somewhat larger amount. The principal share, however, of the Sudan revenue was absorbed by the *khalifa* and his relatives; and he and his brother Yakub utilised it in satisfying the demands of the western tribes, whose adherence to his cause was most necessary, and who, having left their own country, were occasionally in considerable straits.

Another means of increasing the revenue was by the hiring out of ferries along the whole extent of the river; and Ibrahim Adlan also started a soap-boiling establishment, which was made a government monopoly. One day, the *khalifa*, riding through the city, entered a district which he did not usually visit, and there his olfactory nerves were greeted with an odour which he well knew; he at once ordered search to be made to discover from whence it came, and, in a few minutes, a poor half-naked individual was brought before him, holding in his hand a stewpan in which he had been attempting to boil soap. The *khalifa* at once gave orders that he should be thrown into prison, and his property, consisting of a stewpan and an *angareb*, should be confiscated.

An immense stock of silver trinkets, captured in the various campaigns, lay stored up in the Beit el Mal; and quantities of these had been sold for much below their value and had been secretly taken, from time to time, by dealers to Egypt. In order to put a stop to this, the *khalifa* now decided to make his own coinage. After the fall of Khartum, Ahmed Wad Suleiman had attempted to coin silver dollars and gold guineas; but, on the *Mahdi's* express wish, he had abandoned it. Ibrahim Adlan, however, now began to strike half, quarter, and whole dollars; and it was arranged that the new dollar, which weighed eight *drachms*, should consist of six *drachms* of silver and two of copper, but should have the same value as the *Medjidi* dollar. The merchants, however, refused to accept these; and, as a punishment, the *khalifa* confiscated their goods and closed their shops.

This brought them to reason; and, on agreeing to accept them at their whole value, their property was restored; but they were warned that, if they made any further difficulties, they would be punished by the loss of the right hand and left foot. The natural outcome of these arbitrary measures was an immediate rise of prices to compensate for the difference in value between the new and old dollars; of course, all the *khalifa* knew was that the dollar had been accepted, and with that he was satisfied.

Another source of income realised by Ibrahim Adlan was the organisation of the sale of slaves; it was now arranged that slaves of both sexes should be sold at a certain specified place near the Beit el Mal. The vendor was obliged to make out a bill, endorsed by the Beit el Mal, admitting that the object of negotiation was absolutely and entirely the property of the purchaser; and for this bill a tax was levied.

The Beit el Mal was now arranged in the most comfortable manner possible; it was removed from the vicinity of the mosque, and located in a large walled enclosure near the river. Adlan had special buildings erected for his own clerk, for counting-houses, and for drug-stores where the old medicines which had escaped destruction in the sack of Khartum, were now deposited; he also erected large grain stores. In fact, Ibrahim Adlan was ambitious enough to endeavour to make his position rank next to that of the *khalifa* in importance; and, while doing all he could to remain in his good graces, he did not forget that the latter was also to a large extent in the hands of the Kadis, or religious judges, of whom the chief was Ahmed Wad Ali, Kadi of Islam.

All lawsuits and quarrels of a public or private nature, as well as *government* litigation, were brought before the Court of Kadis to be decided; and, in accordance with the *khalifa's* instructions, they were supposed to execute judgment as laid down in the Sheria Mohammedia (Religious Law), the *Manshur el Mahdi* (Instructions of the *Mahdi*), and *El Ishara* (Signs and commands of the *khalifa*). The natural result of this was, that, instead of upholding the law, they became the prime abusers of it. It frequently happened that the "instructions" of the *Mahdi* differed entirely with the religious law; and then, besides this, the "signs and commands" of the *khalifa* had also to be observed,—that is to say, each case was judged in accordance with the *khalifa's* wishes; and it invariably happened that judgment was given in favour of the *Mahdi* or *khalifa*, even in private quarrels in which, in order to obtain some personal advantage, the *Khalifa* frequently and most unjustifiably interfered.

In the Kadi el Islam, the *khalifa* had a most faithful servant, ever ready to obey his master's wishes to the letter, no matter how grossly the law was misapplied. Human life was of no account; and the *kadi* and his colleagues would, without the smallest hesitation, give a judgment utterly opposed to right and truth, and which would have the most direful consequence on perfectly innocent persons. In order to qualify the grossest miscarriages of justice, he would publicly announce from his pulpit, that he himself would be perfectly prepared to submit to this jurisdiction, and that should any one consider himself in the smallest degree oppressed by the judgment just given, he had only to appeal to the Court of Kadis.

On one occasion, a dweller on the White Nile, who had been recently, and very unjustly, dismissed from his position as *emir*, believing in the genuineness of the *khalifa's* statement, summoned him to appear before the *kadis*. He complied with the summons, and entered the mosque where the judges were sitting in an attitude of complete submission; and, the news having got about that the *khalifa* had been invited to appear before a Court of Justice, an immense crowd collected to hear the proceedings. The plaintiff, Abdel Minem, stated that he had been wronged by the *khalifa*, having been dismissed by him from his position as *emir*, which he had held during the whole period of the *Mahdi's* rule, and that he was popular with his own tribe, who did not wish him removed.

The *khalifa*, having dismissed him because he suspected him of leanings to the party of Khalifa Sherif, defended himself by saying that he had summoned him on several occasions, in order to give him some important instructions, but that he was never to be found either in his house or in a place of worship, which was a proof that he was neglectful in matters of religion, and that it was on this account he had dismissed him. Without the slightest hesitation, the court gave judgment in favour of the *khalifa*; and the plaintiff was flogged until he bled, carried off to prison, and, on his way there, was almost lynched by the mob.

The whole country, however, rang with the praises of the Khalifat el *Mahdi* and representative of the Prophet, who, so great was his sense of justice, did not fear to appear in the court, side by side with his own subjects, and submissively await the judgment of the *kadis*. But in order to delude the public with the idea that he was of a most kind and forgiving nature, he released his antagonist the following day, and presented him with a new *jibba* and a wife.

CHAPTER 12

Events in Various Parts of the Sudan

Mohammed Khaled had left Sultan Yusef, the son of Sultan Ibrahim, and the legitimate successor, as chief Emir of Darfur. He was quite a young man, and endeavoured to strengthen his position by soliciting the good-will of Abu Anga and his assistant, Osman Wad Adam, who then resided at El Obeid. Every now and then he sent them quantities of horses and slaves; and they, in their turn, sent what they thought advisable to the *khalifa*. Khaled, on leaving Darfur, had taken with him almost all the Mahdists who were inhabitants of the Nile valley; Yusef, therefore, found himself governing the land of his forefathers principally by means of his own subjects; and the latter, in their turn, assuming that his government would be mild, fully appreciated the change.

Shortly after the *Mahdi's* death, the *khalifa* had sent messengers to Karamalla, in the Bahr el Ghazal, instructing him to leave the country, and come, with all his troops, to Shakka. Karamalla, after Lupton had surrendered the country, had taken possession of the province, and had proceeded to Suda, and forced the mutinous Sultan Zemio to quit his residence, which he had fortified under the directions of Dr. Junker. Zemio had barely escaped with his life, and, taking with him some of his wives, had left most of his treasures of ivory in Karamalla's hands. After this success, Karamalla had moved in a southeasterly direction into the Equatorial Provinces, which were then under the rule of Emin Pasha, and was just approaching the Nile, when he received the orders to turn back.

Had it not been that he had the full support of his own countrymen, Karamalla could not have obeyed the *khalifa's* command; for it was an operation of great difficulty to induce the Bazingers to leave their own homes and go to Shakka. However, after the evacuation of the Bahr el Ghazal, several of the Gellabas had hurried from Darfur and Kordofan to join Karamalla, and procure ivory and slaves for themselves. In consequence, the riverain element, consisting principally of Jaalin and Danagla, represented a considerable portion of the force, and it was impossible for the Bazingers to refuse to return. Thus, partly of his own free-will, and partly from stress of circumstances, Karamalla returned, bringing with him an immense number of female slaves, whom he had kidnapped from the districts through which he passed. In spite of all his precautions, several of his Bazingers managed to escape on the march with their arms; but he had still at his disposal over three thousand rifles on his arrival at Shakka, where he sold his enormous quantities of male and female slaves to the dealers, who paid him in ready money.

Like a sensible man, he sent some of the money and the pick of the slaves, by his brother Suleiman, to the *khalifa*; and the latter, much pleased with his present, ordered him to remain at Shakka. Both Abu Anga, and Osman Wad Adam also came in for a fair share of the spoil.

At Shakka, however, Karamalla conducted himself as if he were ruler of the whole country, and perpetrated every description of tyranny and extortion. Madibbo, the *emir* and ruler of this part of these districts, reproached him bitterly; but Karamalla, who had seized a number of horses and slaves from the Rizighat Arabs, told him to mind his own business. Several of the malcontents now rallied round Madibbo, and this was exactly what Karamalla wanted. He sought an excuse for a quarrel; and when Madibbo, who had been ordered to appear before him, refused to obey the summons, he proceeded against him as a rebel. A fight took place; Madibbo was defeated, and fled towards Darfur; while Karamalla followed him up through Dara as far as the neighbourhood of El Fasher, and had thus an opportunity of seeing for himself the richness of the country.

He now requested Sultan Yusef to follow up and capture Madibbo; whilst he himself returned to Dara, where he settled down, much to the annoyance and disgust of Sultan Yusef's officials. Madibbo was captured by Zaguna at about two days' distance from Fasher, and was handed over to Sultan Yusef; and the latter sent him, under escort, to Abu Anga in Kordofan, and at the same time took occasion to complain of Karamalla's conduct. The latter, however, had written direct to the *khalifa* in Omdurman, informing him that the Furs were trying to revive the dynasty, and that Sultan Yusef was only a Mahdist in outward appearance. Abu Anga had also forwarded the letters he had received from Sultan Yusef; and now the *khalifa* had to choose between Karamalla and Yusef; but, with his usual astuteness, he did neither.

Abdullahi rightly concluded that Yusef, being the direct descendant of the old dynasty, would, if permitted to remain, endeavour to strengthen his own position to such an extent that he might eventually struggle to regain his independence. On the other hand, Karamalla, being a Dongolawi, and a relative of the *Mahdi*, was undoubtedly a partisan of Khalifa Sherif; moreover, most of the Bazingers belonged either to the Danagla or Jaalin, and it was not to the interest of the *khalifa* to strengthen either of these parties, although they were at present openly disposed towards him.

He therefore wrote to Sultan Yusef that he was lord of the country, that he did not entertain the slightest doubt as to his fidelity, and many similar phrases; but instead of instructing Karamalla to quit Dara, he sent orders for Abu Anga to officially occupy the district. Yusef, imagining that the *khalifa* had fully confirmed him in his position, and finding that Karamalla was now in occupation of Hillet Shieria and Toweisha, as well as Dara, determined to drive him out of the country; an army was collected. His chief, Magdum Said Bros, attacked the posts of Shieria and Toweisha, which were completely destroyed; and Karamalla, after suffering very heavy losses, was forced to retire on Shakka. In this engagement, Karamalla lost most of his best fighting Sheikhs, amongst them Hassan Abu Taher, Ali Mohammed, and others—all Danagla—who had fought under Yusef Shellali and Gessi Pasha in the Bahr el Ghazal; but the *khalifa* had so many enemies the less.

Madibbo was brought to Kordofan, and handed over to Abu Anga, who had an old account to settle with him. When serving under Suleiman Wad Zubeir, he fell, on one occasion, into the hands of Madibbo, who was very hostile to him, and forced him to carry a huge box of ammunition on his head during several days' march, and, when he complained about it, mercilessly flogged and abused him. When Madibbo was brought before Abu Anga, he had little hope of his life; but he determined to try and obtain justice, affirming that he had not fought against the *Mahdi*, but had been forced to take up arms by Karamalla. But of what use were all his excuses and proofs of innocence, or his fidelity?—the only answer he received from Abu Anga was: "And yet I will kill you."

Madibbo, now convinced of the uselessness of his pleading, resigned himself to his fate, and, despairing of his life, said, "It is not you who will kill me, but God. I have not asked for mercy, but for justice; however, a slave like you can never become noble. The traces of the lashes of my whip, which may still be seen on your back, were well deserved. In whatever form death may come upon me, it will always find me calm and a man. I am Madibbo, and the tribes know me."

Abu Anga ordered him to be sent back to prison, but forbore to have him flogged; and, the following morning, he had him executed in front of his whole army. Madibbo was true to his word. Standing in an open space, with a chain round his neck, he sneered at the soldiers who galloped up to him shaking their lances over his head. When told to kneel down to receive the death-blow, he called on the people who stood round to report faithfully after his death how he had borne himself; a moment afterwards all was over. Thus ended Madibbo, one of the ablest Arab *sheikhs* in the Sudan.

When his head was brought into Omdurman, there was general mourning amongst the Rizighat Arabs, who had years before quitted their country as pilgrims. Even the *khalifa* himself regretted his death; but as the deed had been done, he would not blame his greatest *emir*. He therefore concealed his indignation; but to me he remarked that had Abu Anga not killed him, Madibbo might have done him many a valuable service.

Yunes was now apparently quite happy. He had gone from Abu Haraz to Gedaref and Gallabat, where he had settled down; and, as his authority was an extended one, and the people over whom he ruled were turbulent, he asked the *khalifa's* permission to undertake a campaign against the Abyssinians, and Abdullahi, having received no answer from King John to his peaceful letters, gave his consent. His troops, under Arabi Dafalla, now attacked the villages along the frontier, destroyed several of them, killing the men and carrying off their wives and children as captives. By the rapidity of their movements, committing wholesale robberies one day, and making murderous raids twenty miles distant the next, they had become a perfect scourge to the Abyssinians; but, in spite of all this, the latter still continued their commercial relations with Yunes, who, by his amicable treatment of them in Gallabat, had induced them to come in larger numbers to sell the produce of their country, such as coffee, honey, wax, tomatoes, ostriches, etc., as well as horses, mules, and slaves.

The market-place lay just beyond the town; and when one day an exceptionally large caravan of merchants, consisting of Gebertas

(Abyssinian Moslems) and Makada (Abyssinian Christians) arrived at Gallabat, the rapacity of Yunes could not be controlled, and, on the pretext that they had come as spies of Ras Adal, he threw them into chains, and seized all their goods. They were then sent under escort to Omdurman, where the ignorant mob imagined them to be the spoil of a great victory; while the *khalifa*, ever ready to increase his and his people's prestige, publicly dubbed Yunes "*Afrit el Mushrikin*" (The Devil of the Polytheists), and *Mismar ed Din* (The Nail of the Faith). Yunes had been careful to send him all the prettiest of the Abyssinian girls taken in the various raids, as well as a number of horses and mules; thus, greedy of more victories, he decided to unite the army of Yunes and Abu Anga, and attack King John, who, by not answering his letters, had mortally offended him. In the meantime Yunes was instructed to remain strictly on the defensive.

Abu Anga now received instructions to despatch fifteen hundred of his men, all armed with Remington rifles, to Osman Wad Adam, who had been appointed Emir of Kordofan and Darfur; but he himself was ordered to come to Omdurman with the remainder of his troops.

Latterly, Sheikh Saleh el Kabbashi had been left undisturbed at the wells of Om Badr; but, knowing that he would be attacked sooner or later, he despatched to Wadi Halfa fifty of his most faithful slaves with letters begging the support of the Egyptian Government; and the faithful Saleh's agent obtained two hundred Remington rifles, forty boxes of ammunition, £200 in cash, and some beautifully embossed revolvers.

At this time, there resided at Assuan a German merchant named Charles Neufeld, who had previously made the acquaintance of Dafalla Egail, a brother of Elias Pasha who had recently escaped from the Sudan; from him he learnt that in Northern Kordofan there was a large quantity of gum which the merchants had been unable to dispose of, in consequence of the rebellion, and which could easily be brought to Wadi Halfa with the assistance of Sheikh Saleh. Enticed by this pleasant prospect of making money, and filled with a love of adventure, he resolved to join Saleh's people, in order to travel with them to their *sheikh*. He had apparently no difficulty in obtaining permission from the government to proceed on his journey, promising that he would send detailed accounts of the situation in the Sudan; and, early in April, 1887, he left Wadi Halfa with the caravan.

Nejumi, who had full information of the departure of the caravan, now had all the roads carefully watched; and, to add to their misfortunes, their guide lost his way, and the caravan suffered considerably from thirst. When, at length, they approached some wells near El Kab, they found them in possession of a party of Dervishes who were on the lookout for them. A fight ensued in which Saleh's people, exhausted and thirsty, were utterly defeated; most of them were killed by rifle fire, and the remainder, Neufeld amongst them, were captured.

At the beginning of the action, Neufeld had seized a rifle, and, with his Abyssinian female attendant, had taken up a position a short distance from the caravan; and here, on some rising ground, he had determined to sell his life dearly; but he was not attacked. When the fighting was over, they offered him pardon, which he accepted, and was then taken off to Nejumi in Dongola. The latter had all the captives beheaded, with the exception of Neufeld, who was spared in order that he might be sent to Omdurman. I had heard privately that an European captive was about to arrive; and, consequently, I was not surprised when, one day in May, 1887, I saw a crowd of people approaching the *khalifa's* house, and, in their midst, under escort, rode an European on a camel. It was generally rumoured that he was the Pasha of Wadi Halfa.

At that period, the buildings in Omdurman were not very far advanced, and between the wall of the *khalifa's* house and the wall of the mosque was a large *rekuba* built of straw, which served as a house for the *mulazemin*; and into this Neufeld, after dismounting, was ushered. I held aloof, as I well understood the nature of my master and his spies; and I pretended to be quite indifferent to what was going on. The *khalifa*, on Neufeld's arrival, had sent for the two *khalifas* and the *kadis*, Taher el Magzub, the Emir Bekhit, and Nur Angara, who had just arrived in Omdurman from Kordofan, where he had been fighting under Abu Anga; Yakub had also been summoned. As they entered, I whispered to Nur Angara, "Do your utmost to save the man."

To my delight, the *khalifa* now summoned me, and ordered me to sit with his advisers. He informed us that the man had been brought in as an English spy; and he instructed Sheik el Taher Magzub to question him. I at once asked to be allowed to speak to him in European language; and, the request being granted, I went with Taher into the *rekuba*.

When my name was mentioned, Neufeld shook my hand with great delight. I at once drew his attention to the fact that he must address himself to Sheikh Taher, who was the principal personage to judge him, and that he should behave as submissively as possible. He spoke Arabic very well; and his extreme readiness to talk made a bad impression on those present, who ordered me to take him before the *khalifa*, their general opinion being, "He is a spy, and should be killed." Once in the presence of the *khalifa*, the latter said to me, "And what is your opinion?"

"All I know is," I replied, "that he is a German, and, consequently, belongs to a nation which takes no interest in Egypt." I could see the *khalifa* watching me very carefully as he handed me some papers, and ordered me to look through them: they included a list of medicines written in German, and a letter to Neufeld in English, regarding news received in the Sudan; also a long letter from General Stephenson, in which he was granted permission to proceed to the Sudan with the caravan, and, at the same time, requested to give the fullest accounts of the state of affairs in the country. I translated this letter, but omitted the general's request for information.

"Sire," I said, "this letter shows that he has asked permission of the government to make this journey, and that he is a merchant, as he told Sheikh Taher." Again the *khalifa* looked suspiciously at me, and then ordered us to withdraw and await his further commands outside the house. An immense crowd had by this time collected near the *rekuba* to see the English Pasha; and, in a few moments, some of the black *mulazemin* whom the *khalifa* had summoned, came out, and, having tied his wrists together, ordered Neufeld to leave the *rekuba*. The *kadi*, Nur Angara, and I had climbed up on a heap of bricks, and from this position could see exactly what was going on. Neufeld, who evidently thought his last hour had come, raised his eyes to heaven, and knelt down, without having received any order to do so, and was at once ordered to get up.

Meanwhile, a man arrived, carrying an *ombeÿa*, and began to make its melancholy notes resound over Neufeld's head; I was delighted to see that this did not appear to disturb him in the least; his poor servant, in her devotion to her master, now rushed out of the *rekuba*, and begged to be killed with him; but she was at once driven back. The *kadi* and I quite realised that the *khalifa* was playing with Neufeld, just as a cat plays with a mouse; and, as sentence had not yet been given, I endeavoured to signal to him; but he did not appear to quite understand me. In a few moments, we were again summoned before the *khalifa*.

"Then you are for having the man killed?" said the *khalifa* to Sheikh Taher, who replied in the affirmative. "And you?" he said, turning to

Nur Angara, who, in a few brief words, recalled Neufeld's bravery, and begged to have him pardoned. "And now, Abdel Kader, what have you to say?" he said, turning to me.

"Sire," I replied, "the man deserves to be killed, and any other ruler but yourself would have had him killed; but, of your magnanimity and mercy, you will spare him; for he says he has turned Mohammedan, and your mercy will strengthen his faith."

Kadi Ahmed was also for pardoning him; and now the *khalifa*, who, I saw from the first moment, had no intention of killing Neufeld, ordered his fetters to be removed, and that he should be taken back to the *rekuba*; but, that afternoon, he said to the *kadi*, "Let him be shown to the crowd beneath the scaffold, and then imprison him till further orders; and as for you," he said, turning to me, "you will have no more intercourse with him." We now all withdrew, but took occasion to tell Neufeld that, although he had been pardoned, he was to be shown to the populace that afternoon under the scaffold. The *kadi* carried out his instructions; and, to the delight of the mob, Neufeld's head was placed in the noose by the *saier*.

The following day, the *khalifa* summoned me before him, and informed me that Nejumi had reported that Neufeld had been induced by the government to go and join Sheikh Saleh el Kabbashi, and assist him in fighting the Mahdists. I explained that this could not possibly be true, and that Neufeld's papers were all in order. Moreover, I said that the government would never have taken upon itself to do such a thing. For the time being, I think he credited my explanation; but he revenged himself by showing the most marked mistrust and contempt for me for some time.

A few days afterwards, the *khalifa* held a great review; and Neufeld, whose feet were in irons, was mounted on a camel, and taken to see it. The *khalifa* asked him what he thought of his troops; and he replied that, although they were very numerous, they were not well trained, and that the discipline in the Egyptian Army was much better. The *khalifa*, who did not appreciate candid speaking, at once had him sent back to prison.

Osman Wad Adam, who had received the *khalifa's* orders either to capture or kill Saleh Kabbashi, now sent an expedition under Fadlalla Aglan; and Greger, Sheikh of the Hamada Arabs, was given to him as a guide. The latter was well known to be Saleh's mortal enemy. The Kababish had quitted the wells of the Hamada, and had moved eastward into the desert, in order to await the arrival of the caravan sent to Wadi Halfa; and now, when the disaster which had overtaken it became known, several of the tribesmen whom Saleh had collected dispersed, and many returned to Omdurman. Saleh, now deprived of all hope of assistance from his own countrymen, was no longer able to make any determined opposition. He therefore fled, with his family and near relatives, but was overtaken at a well and killed. On the approach of his enemies, he bowed to his destiny; and, seated on a sheepskin which had been spread on the ground for him by his slaves, he patiently awaited death. His enemy, Greger, jumping off his horse, approached him, and blew out his brains with his pistol. Thus ended the last of the Sheikhs faithful to government.

About the middle of June, news arrived that Abu Anga had reached the Nile at Tura el Hadra with an army of between nine and ten thousand men, all armed with rifles, and about an equal number of cavalry. It was expected that he would be at Omdurman about the end of the month. The *khalifa* used frequently to ride out to the lines near Tabia Regeb Bey, and employ himself pointing out the limits which the camp should occupy; and, on these occasions, I used to accompany him on foot. During one of these excursions, I cut my foot when walking by the *khalifa's* side, and could scarcely proceed. Seeing me limping, and my foot bleeding profusely, he dismounted at Fadl el Maula's house, and called me up before him, praised me for my perseverance, and gave me the horse which Fadl el Maula himself had presented to him, telling me that in any future rides I could mount it, and, as usual, remain near him.

Towards the end of June, Abu Anga arrived, and, when about two hours distant from Omdurman, pitched his camp. That night, the *khalifa* received him alone in his house, no witnesses being present. The conference lasted till long past midnight; and then Abu Anga returned to his camp. At dawn the next morning, the beating of war-drums and the sound of the *ombeÿa* proclaimed that the *khalifa* intended to be present on the entry of Abu Anga's army into Omdurman. Just after sunrise, he rode out, accompanied by all his *emirs* and an immense crowd, to the parade ground, at the east end of which a tent had been pitched. Khalifa Abdullahi, the other *khalifas*, and the *kadis* now entered this tent; and, soon after, the approach of Abu Anga and his army was heralded by the sound of trumpets and drums.

The entire force passed the *khalifa* twice in review; and he was delighted with the immense number of the troops. Summoning the *emirs* before him, he called down God's blessing on their heads, and then ordered them to take their troops to the allotted camping ground. Now followed a period of the wildest debauchery, in which his soldiers and subjects squandered the booty taken in Kordofan at weddings and banquets; in so doing, they deviated widely from the stringent orders of the *Mahdi* in such matters; but this did not seem to displease the *khalifa*.

Abu Anga himself, who had brought considerable sums of money, as well as quantities of male and female slaves, for his master and his brother Yakub, now distributed presents freely amongst his friends and acquaintances. He sent me my old servant and his wife; but he did not return my other servants, horses, and effects which had been taken from me during my imprisonment.

A few weeks afterwards, the *khalifa* celebrated the Feast of Bairam on the largest scale I have ever seen. Hundreds of thousands of the faithful repeated prayers with the *khalifa* on the parade ground; and he then returned in state to his house, under the thunder of guns and the wildest acclamations of his subjects, who crowded through the streets in such numbers that several were killed and trampled underfoot by the horses.

The Emir Merdi Abu Rof, of the Gehéna tribe, now received instructions to come with all his tribe and cattle to Omdurman; but, having refused to obey the summons, it was decided that he should be punished, and made an example to others. A large portion of Abu Anga's army, under the orders of Zeki Tummal, Abdalla Wad Ibrahim, and Ismail Delendok, was ordered to march against them and destroy them. The Gehéna tribe, generally called by the Arabs the Abu Rof, and celebrated for their thoroughbred horses and camels, were also known to possess very fine male and female slaves. The well known proverb, "*Gehéna el Ol—Ashra fi Sol*" (There are ten Gehéna children to every man), faithfully represented the tribe.

In the fighting which ensued, their *emirs*, Merdi Abu Rof and Mohammed Wad Melek, fell, as well as their former Sheikh, and the greater part of the tribe was annihilated. The finest of the young women and children captured were selected and sent as presents to the *khalifa*; but the remainder were brought to Omdurman, where they eked out a miserable existence by becoming water-carriers, or makers of straw mats. Their great herds of cattle went for almost nothing in the bazaars; and the price of an ox or a camel, which formerly varied between forty and sixty dollars, fell to two or three dollars.

After the destruction of this tribe, Abu Anga received orders to proceed from Omdurman to Gallabat, and take the command of the troops there. Collecting the forces from the southern districts at Abu Haraz, he proceeded to his destination, and arrived just in time to save Yunes.

One of Yunes's postmen had asserted that he was Saidna Isa (Jesus Christ), and obtained a numerous following; many really believed in him, whilst others were extremely dissatisfied with Yunes, who had become so mercenary that he began to rob even his own people. Eleven of the principal *emirs*, amongst them the keeper of the ammunition stores, now sided with Isa, and made a plot to assassinate Yunes; the day for carrying it into execution had been actually arranged, when Abu Anga suddenly arrived. His generous nature had given him many friends; and, in a few days, he was fully informed of the whole affair, and instantly arrested the conspirators. Yunes, utterly ignorant that any plot was hatching, complained to Abu Anga about the arrest of his *emirs*, and asked for an explanation of his proceedings. "Because they intended to murder you," was Abu Anga's simple reply. When the assassins were brought before the *kadi*, they did not deny their intentions; and their leader declared most firmly that he was Jesus Christ, and that, in a short time, this fact would be revealed to the world.

Abu Anga now despatched a special messenger to Omdurman for orders; and the *khalifa*, greatly alarmed, wished to keep the whole matter secret. He summoned Yakub and Kadi Ahmed to consult with him; and it was agreed that all the conspirators should be executed. I heard all about the matter from Mohammed Wad esh Shertier, who had been forbidden the *khalifa's* house, and had orders to leave the same day for Gallabat. The following day, however, the *khalifa* changed his mind, having realised that of the eleven *emirs*, ten belonged to the powerful western tribes; and not only would their loss to him be considerable, but he feared their relatives and friends might turn against him.

He therefore sent camel-men, in hot haste, with a reprieve, and with orders that the prisoners should be brought to Omdurman under escort. The camel-men, however, failed to overtake Shertier who had had two days' start; and they arrived in Gallabat to find the eleven bodies hanging on the scaffold; all had died faithful to their Jesus Christ. Yunes, being a relative of the *khalifa*, only submitted to Abu Anga owing to his superior force, but always looked upon him as his slave, though, as a matter of fact, he was infinitely braver and more courageous. Yunes now reproached him for having been precipitate,

AN ABYSSINIAN SCOUT.

and from this episode arose an estrangement between the two men, which ended in Yunes being recalled to Omdurman, where he was commanded to perform his devotions daily in the front row in the mosque.

Abu Anga now collected all his forces, in order to revenge the defeat of Wad Arbab. He had at his disposal the largest force which had ever been collected by Khalifa Abdullahi: according to the rolls brought in, he had upwards of fifteen thousand rifles, forty-five thousand spearmen, and eight hundred cavalry; and quitting Gallabat with this force, he marched through the Mintik (pass) towards Ras Adal. Up to this day, I have failed to understand why the Abyssinians did not attack their enemy whilst crossing the narrow passes and deep valleys, in which it would have been most difficult to use fire-arms with effect; if they had not succeeded in checking the advance in this manner, they would have at least inflicted very heavy losses on the Dervishes. I can only conceive that the Abyssinians made certain of their ultimate success, and purposely enticed their enemies far into the country, with the object of cutting off their retreat, and utterly annihilating them. Fighting began on the plain of Debra Sin. Ras Adal had about two thousand rifles, and had taken up a position threatening Abu Anga's left; but the latter had sufficient time to clear the hills, and arrange his troops in battle array.

Attacked over and over again by the Abyssinians, the Dervishes drove them off with frightful loss; and Abu Anga, taking the offensive, succeeded in gaining a complete victory. So sure were the Abyssinians of gaining the day, that they had taken up a position in front of a river; and now many of them, in their flight, were drowned while attempting to cross it. For a short time, the Abyssinian cavalry was to some extent successful; but, after suffering considerable loss, they fled with Ras Adal. The entire Abyssinian camp, consisting of quantities of tents, fell into the hands of Abu Anga, who captured Ras Adal's wife and grown-up daughter, and in this victory practically conquered the whole of the Amhara Province.

He advanced without delay on Gondar, where he expected to find great treasures, but was disappointed; for, with the exception of some goods belonging to the Geberta, and some large stores of coffee, honey, and wax, which were of no value to him, as he had no means of transport, he got practically nothing. In the large and lofty stone building said to have been erected by the Portuguese, they found one poor old Coptic priest, who was thrown out of the highest storey into the street below. Staying here only one day, Abu Anga ordered the town to be fired, and, on his way back, attacked and looted villages right and left, killing the men and seizing the women and children as captives; the Geberta, and some little boys alone, were spared and carried off as booty. In this manner thousands of Abyssinian women and girls were driven in front of the army, urged on by the lash. On arrival at Gallabat, a fifth of the loot was sent to the *khalifa*, and several hundred women were despatched to the Beit el Mal in Omdurman, where they were sold to the highest bidders. The road between Gallabat and Abu Haraz was strewn with corpses, and amongst them the daughter and young son of Ras Adal.

Abu Anga, in accordance with the *khalifa's* instructions, now began to put Gallabat into a state of defence; for, in spite of the success just gained, they knew that the Abyssinians would seek revenge. But he did not long survive his victory; although only fifty-two years of age, he suffered from constant illness, and was always trying to cure himself. He had grown immensely stout, owing to the good living in which he indulged, which contrasted greatly with what he had been formerly accustomed to; he suffered much from indigestion, and used to treat himself with a poisonous root which came from Dar Fertit.

One day, however, he took an overdose, and in the morning was found dead in his bed. In him, the *khalifa* lost his best *emir*, who, though by descent a slave, had, through his liberality and kindness, gained the affection of all who knew him, as well as the esteem and regard of his subjects, who admired his personal courage and sense of justice. He was mourned by his entire force,—by Arabs as well as by blacks,—who recognised in him a strict though just master, and one who, though he punished very severely any offences against his orders, was ever ready to help those in need. He was buried in his red-brick house; and many of his servants and slaves worshipped him as a saint.

At the same time that Abu Anga had left Omdurman for Gallabat, Osman Wad Adam had received instructions to move with his whole force towards Shakka and Darfur. At this time, a garrison was not required in Kordofan: for Sheikh Saleh had been killed, and the land of the Gimeh was deserted; the Gowama had been ordered to immigrate to Omdurman; and the resistance of the southern mountains had been broken down by Abu Anga. Karamalla, after having been driven back to Shakka, had persistently demanded tribute from the Rizighat Arabs, who, however, recognising that he was not all-powerful, rose as one man in mutiny against him, and with such success that at length both

Kerkesawi and Karamalla, who were in want of ammunition, were practically besieged at Shakka and Injileila.

They now begged the *Khalifa's* help; and though the latter had originally intended not to assist them, he was by no means anxious to lose all his armed slaves. This was the reason for Osman Wad Adam's despatch to Shakka. On arrival, he wrote letters to the Rizighat, who were fighting rather personally against Karamalla than against the *Mahdist* rule, ordering them to suspend hostilities, and promising that he would give them justice. Fearful of Osman's power, they reluctantly complied; but Karamalla, under the pretext of making peace negotiations, enticed their *sheikh* into his *zariba*, and there executed him. Osman now moved forward by forced marches, not only on account of Karamalla, but in fear of a mutiny on the part of Sultan Yusef, who, for a long time, had sent no consignments of horses and slaves, and was evidently beginning to feel himself sufficiently powerful to overturn the *khalifa's* authority.

Osman's arrival at Shakka relieved Karamalla and his garrison from a very dangerous position; he then assured the Arabs, who were clamouring for justice, that he would settle their case as soon as he had subdued Darfur. His total force, including Karamalla's men, now numbered some five thousand rifles, and with these he marched against Dara. He had previously written to Sultan Yusef, ordering him to join him, and informing him that in the event of his refusal, he would treat him as a rebel. To this summons he received a reply that, as he had joined his sworn enemy, Karamalla, it was impossible to come; at the same time, news reached him that Sultan Yusef was concentrating his forces at Fasher.

On his arrival at Dara, Osman found the place deserted; but, on the following day, he was attacked by Said Mudda, and only succeeded in driving him off after a very closely contested fight. A week later, he was again attacked by the *sultan's* old *vizir*, Hussein Ibrahim, and Rahma Gamo, who had collected Said Mudda's people, and had received reinforcements as well; but these also were forced to retire. Osman now marched on El Fasher. Had Sultan Yusef attacked him with his entire force at Dara, he would in all probability have defeated him, and Darfur would thus have been freed forever; but he had previously divided his army, his *vizirs* were hated, and his own people had lost heart after their recent defeats.

A fight took place near Wad Berag, south of Fasher; and Osman gained an easy victory. Sultan Yusef fled, but was overtaken at Kebkebia and killed; whilst Fasher, in which all his wives and relations had been collected, as well as a quantity of goods belonging to Fezzan and Wadai merchants, also numbers of women and children, fell into Osman's hands. Thus Darfur, which had been practically lost to the *Mahdists*, was retaken by them in the same month (January, 1888), just at the time that Abu Anga had gained his great victory over the Abyssinians. In this short campaign the Darfurians had shown great fidelity to their native ruler; and Osman, fearing to expose himself to continual difficulties by supporting their dynastic sentiments, determined that all males of royal blood should either be put in irons, executed, or sent to Omdurman, where they were placed amongst the *khalifa's mulazemin*, and treated as slaves.

All female members of the royal family were declared to be "*khums*" (a fifth of the booty), and put at the *khalifa's* disposal. Some of these he took into his own *harem*; and the remainder he distributed as "*suria*" (concubines) amongst his followers. He liberated, however, the two old sisters of Sultan Ibrahim, namely, Miriam Isa Basi and Miriam Bakhita; the latter was the wife of Kadi Ali, who was then in Omdurman.

Whilst these momentous events were transpiring in the east and west of the Sudan Empire, the *khalifa* governed the country at Omdurman in a most tyrannical and despotic manner. He mistrusted every one. Numbers of spies were employed by his brother Yakub; and their duty was to tell him of everything that went on in the city. He was kept fully informed of the general temper of the people; and should any persons express doubt about the truth of the *Mahdi's* Divine mission, they were punished with special severity. It happened, one day, that a sailor used some irreverent expression regarding *Mahdism*, and was reported to the *khalifa*. The plaintiff, who was a fanatical Baggari, had, however, no witnesses, those who were present at the time admitting to the *khalifa* that they were too far off to hear what passed; but the latter determined to make an example.

He therefore summoned the *kadi*, and ordered him to force a confession out of the accused. at the same time advising him how to set about it. Two persons were then sent to the prisoner, to apprise him that witnesses had been found; but that if he made a confession of his own free-will, and admitted that he was sorry, before the witnesses had been questioned, the *khalifa* would mitigate his sentence, and would probably pardon him. The poor man failed to see the trap that had been laid for him, made a confession, and begged the *khalifa's* pardon. The confession was taken down in writing, and submitted to Abdullahi, who ordered the sentence—which was execution—to be carried out in accordance with the *Mahdi's* code. The *khalifa*, in giving sentence, said that had the insult been against his own person, he would have forgiven him; but the prisoner, having sinned against the *Mahdi*, he would be committing a crime if he mitigated it in the slightest degree.

That afternoon, the *khalifa* gave orders for the *ombeÿa* to be sounded, while the dull beats of the great *Mansura* (war-drum) boomed through the city, and he himself rode with an immense escort to the parade ground. On his arrival, his sheepskin was spread on the ground; and on this he sat, facing the east, whilst the *kadi* and others stood behind him in a semi-circle. He then ordered the accused to be brought before him. Already his hands had been tied behind his back; but he showed not the slightest signs of fear. When within a hundred paces of the *khalifa*, he was decapitated by Ahmed Dalia, the chief executioner.

Soon after this, a certain *fiki* called Nur en Nebi (The Light of the Prophet), who had collected a considerable number of disciples, preached to them about the necessity for religious zeal, and urged them not to be led away by innovations. Yakub reported this to the *khalifa*, with the result that the *fiki* was at once arrested, and brought before the *kadi*. The necessary witnesses were procured; and the *fiki* openly declared before them that he was a good Mohammedan, but not a follower of the *Mahdi*. By command of the *khalifa*, the judges ordered him to be laden with chains; his hands tied behind his back; and, under the deafening shouts of the mob, he was dragged to the market-place, where he was hanged on the scaffold erected there.

I remember looking at the body, whilst suspended from the gallows, and was struck by the calm and smiling expression on the face of this man who had died for his convictions. Several hundred houses, surrounding the abode of the murdered man, were confiscated; their inmates arrested, bound, and carried off to prison; but, through the intervention of Adlan, they were subsequently liberated. The *khalifa* now issued a proclamation to the effect that all the inhabitants of the city were responsible for the actions of their neighbours; and persons found involved in political or religious intrigues were threatened with the most condign punishment. On mere suspicion, several of the natives of the Nile valley were thrown into chains, and deprived of all they possessed. Thus did he deal with all suspected persons, and at the

A Slave *Dhow* on the Nile.

same time considerably enriched his treasury.

On another occasion, he had a meeting of the *kadis*, and told them, in confidence, that, in his opinion, all vessels on the Nile were really "*ghanima*" (booty); for, as he truthfully remarked, whilst he was in Kordofan, the owners had, in spite of his frequent appeals, invariably refused to assist the *Mahdi's* cause. They had not only failed to attack the government steamers on the river, but had also frequently provided the government stations with grain and wood. Of course the *kadis* fully concurred in his opinion; and, the following morning, they received a letter from Ibrahim Adlan, asking them whether all vessels were not state property. The all-powerful judges replied in the affirmative, supporting their answer by extracts from the *Mahdi's* code, according to which the owners were to be considered *mukhalafin* (obstinate persons).

This pamphlet was read publicly, in the presence of the *khalifa*, who remarked, in conclusion, that those vessels alone were exempt which did not float, or which were not built of the wood of the forests, which were all the property of the state. These vessels, numbering upwards of nine hundred, of from twenty to five hundred *ardebs* carrying capacity, now all passed into the possession of the Beit el Mal; and, as they were almost without exception the property of Jaalin and Danagla, who lived on the river, the means of support of these unfortunate people was entirely gone. The boats were now utilised by Ibrahim Adlan to carry cargoes of grain to the Beit el Mal; or they were hired out annually at a high rate, to persons who were considered worthy of this confidence.

In order to show his veneration for the *Mahdi*, the *khalifa* decided to erect a monument to him, as is the custom in Egypt; but this he did rather to satisfy his own vanity, than out of respect for his late master. A square building was erected, some thirty feet high, and thirty-six feet each way; and the stone for this construction, of which the walls were upwards of six feet thick, had to be brought all the way from Khartum. Above this a hexagonal wall fifteen feet high was built, from which rose a dome forty feet high. On the corners of the main building were four smaller domes. This was called *Kubbet el Mahdi* (*Mahdi's* dome). It was furnished with ten large arched windows, and two doors; and in the hexagonal portion were six skylights. It was whitewashed all over, and surrounded by a trellis-work fence; the windows and doors were made by the workmen in the Khartum arsenal; while directly beneath the dome, and over the *Mahdi's* grave, a wooden sarcophagus was erected, covered with black cloth.

On the sides of the walls, candelabra were hung; while, suspended by a long chain from the centre of the dome, was an immense chandelier taken from the Government Palace in Khartum. The sombre appearance of the inside of the building was relieved by some gaudy painting on the walls. A few yards from the building is a small cistern, built of red bricks cemented together; and this is used by the visitors for their religious ablutions. The plans for this building were devised by an old government official who had been formerly employed as an architect; but, of course, public opinion dutifully attributed the design to the *khalifa*.

The ceremony of laying the foundation-stone of this building was conducted with great unction by the *khalifa*, who "turned the first sod." Accompanied by a crowd of upwards of thirty thousand people, he proceeded to the river bank, where the stones were heaped up, and, lifting one of them on his shoulder, carried it to the spot, his example being followed by every individual person in this vast assemblage; the noise and confusion were perfectly indescribable. Numbers of accidents happened; but those injured thought it fortunate to suffer on such an occasion. The building was not completed till the following year, and entailed a considerable amount of labour, though little expense; and, during its construction, the *khalifa* frequently asserted that angels lent their assistance. An Egyptian, hearing this, and aware that many of his compatriots were masons, was constrained to remark to them, "You are probably the *khalifa's* angels, and require neither food, drink, nor payment." Had the *khalifa* heard this, he would undoubtedly have removed this wag's head.

As usual, I was always in close attendance on the *khalifa*; and, as a token of his goodwill, he presented me with one of the Abyssinian girls sent by Abu Anga. Her mother and brother had been killed before her eyes; and the poor creature had been torn from their bodies, and driven into captivity at the end of the lash. Although not treated as a slave by my people, who did all they could to lighten her sad lot, she never seemed bright or happy; she continually brooded over her losses and her home, until, at length, death released her from her sufferings. Occasionally Father Ohrwalder used to visit me secretly; but, as the *khalifa* did not approve of our meeting, his visits were few and far between. We used to talk of our home, and of our present wretched existence; but we never lost hope that, sooner or later, our captivity would come to an end.

THE MAHDI'S TOMB.

Abu Girga, who commanded at Kassala, was now ordered to proceed to Osman Digna, and assist him in his fighting; leaving Ahmed Wad Ali as his representative at Kassala, he was summoned to Omdurman to report to the *khalifa* on the state of the Arab tribes in the Eastern Sudan. He arrived late one evening, and was at once received in long private audience by the *khalifa*; and, on withdrawing, hurriedly told me that he had given him a letter from my family in Europe. A few minutes later, I was called in, and informed that the Governor of Suakin has sent a letter to Osman Digna, which was supposed to be from my family, and which he had sent on.

In handing me this letter, the *khalifa* ordered me to open it at once, and acquaint him with its contents. I glanced through it hurriedly, and, to my intense grief and sorrow, saw that it was an announcement from my brothers and sisters that my poor mother had died, and that, on her death-bed, she had expressed an earnest hope that we should all be reunited. The *khalifa*, impatient that I took so long to read it, again asked me who had written it, and what were its contents.

"It is from my brothers and sisters," I replied; "and I will translate it to you." I had no reason to conceal its contents; it was merely a few lines from distressed brothers and sisters to their distant brother. I told him how disturbed they were about me; and how they were ready to make any sacrifice in order that I should regain my liberty. When I came to the part about my mother, it required all my self-control; I told him that, owing to my absence, her death was not so peaceful as it might have been, and that during her long illness, her constant prayer to God had been that she might see me again. Her prayer, alas, had not been answered; and now this letter had brought me her last greeting, and her tender hopes for my welfare. My throat felt parched and dry, and had not the *khalifa* suddenly interrupted me, I must have broken down.

"Your mother was not aware that I honour you more than anyone else," said he; "otherwise she certainly would not have been in such trouble about you; but I forbid you to mourn for her. She died as a Christian and an unbeliever in the Prophet and the *Mahdi*, and cannot therefore expect God's mercy."

The blood rushed to my head; and, for a moment, I could say nothing; but gradually regaining my self-control, I continued to read on that my brother Henry was now married, and that Adolf and my sisters were quite well. Finally, they begged me to let them know how I could obtain my liberty, and urged me to write to them. "Write and tell one at least of your brothers to come here," said the *khalifa*, when I had finished the letter. "I would honour him, and he should want for nothing; but I will talk to you about this another time." He then signed to me with his hand; and I withdrew.

My comrades, who had already heard that a letter had arrived for me, were very inquisitive, and asked me all manner of questions; but I answered them only briefly, and, as soon as the *khalifa* had retired to rest, I went home. I flung myself down on my *angareb*, and my servants, much concerned, asked me what was the matter; but I told them to leave me. "Poor mother, then it was I who made your last hours so unhappy!" My brothers and sisters had written her last words:

> I am ready to die; but I should have loved to see and embrace my Rudolf once more. The thought that he is in the hands of his enemies makes my departure from this world very difficult for me.

How well I remembered her words when I left for the Sudan:

> My son, my Rudolf, your restless spirit drives you out into the world! You are going to distant and almost unknown lands. A time, perhaps, will come when you will long for us, and a quiet life.

How true had been her words,—poor mother! How much trouble I must have given her! And then I cried and cried,—not about my position, but for my dear mother, who could never be replaced.

The next morning, the *khalifa* sent for me, and again made me translate the letter to him; and he ordered me to reply at once that I was perfectly happy in my present position. I did as I was told, and wrote a letter praising the *khalifa*, and saying how happy I was to be near him; but I put inverted commas against many words and sentences, and points of exclamation, and wrote at the bottom of the letter that all words and sentences thus marked should be read in exactly the opposite sense.

At the same time, I asked my brothers and sisters to write a letter of thanks to the *khalifa* in Arabic, and to send him a travelling-bag, and to me two hundred pounds, and twelve common watches, suitable for presents; as, on certain seasons of the year, the *emirs* attended the feasts in Omdurman, and would greatly appreciate them. I also asked them to send me a translation of the *Koran* in German, and advised them not to worry for the present; but that I hoped to find some means of being reunited to them. I told them to send the things, through the Austrian Consul-General in Cairo, to the Governor of Suakin, by whom they would be forwarded to Osman Digna. I handed this letter to the *khalifa*, who gave it to some postmen who were going to Osman Digna with instructions to send it to Suakin.

About a month before I received the sad news of my mother's death, I had to deplore the loss of one of my comrades in captivity, Lupton. He had been working in the dock-yard at Khartum until recently; but the feeble state of his health had obliged him to ask to be relieved from this position. He had then returned to Omdurman, and had suffered great want; but, to his relief, Saleh Wad Haj Ali, with whom he was on very friendly terms, returned from Cairo, and brought him some money which he had received from Lupton's family.

Haj Ali naturally tried to make as much money out of the transaction as he could. He had advanced a sum of a hundred dollars to Lupton as a loan, receiving from him, in return, a bill on his brother for two hundred pounds, which had been cashed on his arrival in Cairo; and, returning again to Omdurman, had paid Lupton two hundred dollars, keeping the remainder, about eight hundred dollars, for himself. In spite of this robbery, this small sum delighted poor Lupton, and helped him, for a short period, to stave off the miseries of living like a beggar. He also rejoiced that a medium of communication had been found with his relatives, whereby he eventually hoped to regain his freedom. These hopes, alas, were not to be realised.

He had come home one Tuesday morning from the mosque with me, and was consulting me as to whom he should entrust what remained of his two hundred dollars, so as to obtain small sums when he required them, as it was necessary for him to be most careful not to attract attention to himself by spending large sums, and thus endanger his communication with Egypt. We talked of home and of our present situation; and he seemed more cheerful than usual, but complained of pains in his back, and of a general feeling of indisposition. I left him about midday; and, on the following Tuesday, he sent his servant to me, begging me to go and see him, as he felt very ill.

In reply to my question, the man told me that his master was in a high fever, and had been in bed for three days. I promised to come as quickly as possible, and, that evening, asked the *khalifa's* permission to go and see him. The next morning, having obtained leave to spend that day with the invalid, I at once went to his house, and found him in a dying condition. He was suffering from typhus fever; and already the illness had reached such a stage that he scarcely recognised me, and, in a few broken words, begged me to take care of his daughter. He then said something about his father and mother; but he was almost incoherent, and, at times, became quite unconscious. I understood, however, that he was begging me to be the bearer of his dying messages, should I ever succeed in escaping.

On Wednesday, the 8th May, 1888, he passed away at midday, without having recovered consciousness. We washed him, wrapped him in a shroud, and, according to the usual custom, carried him to the mosque, where the prayers for the dead were recited; and then we buried him in a cemetery near the Beit el Mal. Father Ohrwalder, the majority of the Greek colony, and a number of natives who had learnt to love and respect his noble and unassuming character, were present.

I obtained the *khalifa's* permission to see to his household, and handed over his money to a Greek merchant to take charge of for his daughter Fanny, and thus save her from want. I also succeeded in getting a situation at the arsenal for one of his black boys whom he had educated, and who receives pay up to the present time. Fanny's mother, Zenoba, married, two years later, an Egyptian doctor named Haasan Zeki; and, although I made frequent efforts to send her daughter to Europe to be educated, my plans were always frustrated by the reluctance of mother and daughter to separate. Under such circumstances, it can readily be understood that the girl fell into a thoroughly Sudanese mode of life, adopting their ways and customs, and looking upon herself as a native. Had she gone to Europe,—and she could only have been sent there by force,—the effort to lead a life to which she was utterly unsuited, and away from her Black mother, would have made her miserable.

At this period of my narrative, the *khalifa* was in a peculiarly good humour. After the re-conquest of Darfur, he had given orders that everything should be done to induce the Arab tribes to undertake pilgrimages to Omdurman, and, if necessary, to force them to do so. Osman Wad Adam had sent notice that the *khalifa's* entire tribe,—the Taaisha,—consisting of upwards of twenty-four thousand warriors, with their wives and families, had decided to immigrate to Omdurman, and that several of them had already reached El Fasher. Thus, at length, the ardent wish of his heart—to gather his own tribe and relatives about him, and make them masters of the situation—was accomplished.

Nejumi was now in Dongola with instructions to undertake offensive operations against Egypt; but the final orders to move forward with the main body were frequently postponed. His army, however, was increased, from time to time, by the arrival of *emirs* whom the *khalifa* was anxious to remove from Omdurman; and thus a fairly considerable force was gradually accumulating on the northern frontier of the Mahdist Empire.

Osman Wad ed Dekeim, the brother of Yunes, was now sent to Berber, which had hitherto been administered by a representative of the late Mohammed Kheir, and, reinforced by six hundred cavalry, he took over the reins of government. Thus another district fell under the sway of one of the *khalifa's* own relatives.

CHAPTER 13

The Abyssinian Campaign

It was not, however, to be supposed that the *Mahdist* victories in the east and west would remain entirely undisputed. King John, who had been carrying on a war in the interior, now determined to avenge the attack on Gondar, and therefore resolved to march against Gallabat, and utterly destroy the enemies of his country and religion. On Abu Anga's death, the *khalifa* appointed one of his former subordinates, Zeki Tummal of the Taaisha tribe, to take the command and to complete the fortifications of Gallabat, which had already been begun. During Abu Anga's lifetime, his army had been divided into five parts, under the respective commands of Ahmed Wad Ali, Abdalla Ibrahim, Hamdan (one of Abu Anga's brothers), while Zeki himself commanded some two thousand five hundred *mulazemin*. The force of Yunes still remained under the command of Ibrahim Dafalla.

King John now collected an immense army, and moved towards Gallabat. The Dervishes were in great consternation, and did all they could to strengthen their fortifications. King John's army was divided into two portions: one division was made up of his own tribe, the Tigré, and King Menelek's troops, under the command of Ras Alula; whilst the other portion consisted of the Amhara legions under Ras Barambaras. Arriving almost within range of Gallabat, they pitched their camp, and began the attack the following morning. The lines of Gallabat, which were some fifteen miles in circumference, were defended only at intervals by Zeki's troops; and the Amhara leader, being well informed by spies, made a determined attack on the western side, which was weakly held.

After a short resistance, they succeeded in penetrating; and the remainder of the garrison were in the unpleasant position of having to defend themselves from the outside, whilst, within, the enemy was pillaging the town. Had the Amhara, instead of looting, attacked the garrison from the rear, they would no doubt have succeeded in capturing the position; but they concerned themselves only with pillaging and driving out of the town thousands of women and children. King John, who was in his tent, having received news that the Amhara, whom he had frequently accused of cowardice, had succeeded in entering the lines, whilst his own tribe, the Tigré, had failed, fell into a passion; and, ordering his followers to carry him on his seat—a small gold *angareb* covered with cushions and carpets—he was brought into the midst of the fighting line.

The defenders, noticing a crowd of followers clothed in velvet and gold, directed their fire on them; and when King John had almost reached the defences, he was struck by a bullet, which, breaking his right arm above the elbow, entered his body. The courageous man, declaring that his injury was of no consequence, continued urging on his men, but soon fell back unconscious on his couch, and was carried to the rear by his followers, who had suffered great loss. The news that he was wounded spread amongst his troops like wildfire; and, though on the point of success, they retired. On the evening of the 9th March, 1889, King John expired in his tent. An effort was made to keep his death secret; but the news gradually leaked out, and the Amhara, deserting the camp in the night with all their loot, returned to their homes.

Ras Alula, being the most important of the Tigré chiefs, nominated Hailo Mariam as their temporary ruler; but fearing the possibility of dissensions breaking out amongst his unruly troops, he thought he had better return to his country, and therefore ordered a retreat.

In fear and trembling, the Mahdists awaited the renewal of the Abyssinian attack the next morning; but when the sun rose, they found, to their surprise, that the white tents which had been visible the previous day had disappeared. Zeki Tummal now sent out troops to reconnoitre; and they returned with the joyful news that the Abyssinians had retired. They had also learnt from the wounded that King John was dead. A council was immediately held, and, as the enemy had carried off a number of the Mahdist women and cattle,—amongst them much of the late Abu Anga's property,—it was agreed that they should be pursued.

The Abyssinians had pitched their camp about half a day's journey from Gallabat; already half the army was on the move; and Ras Alula, Hailo Mariam, the temporary Negus, and other chiefs were on the point of breaking up the camp, when they were suddenly attacked by the Dervishes. Hailo Mariam was killed at the tent-door, within which lay King John's body, already partly embalmed, in a wooden coffin. Ras Alula beat a hurried retreat, leaving the camp in the hands of his enemies. The Dervishes captured an immense amount of booty, including horses, mules, arms, tents, coffee, etc.; they did not, however, succeed in re-capturing the women, who had already been carried on ahead. In Hailo Mariam's tent King John's crown was found. It is doubtful whether this was the imperial Abyssinian crown, as it was made of silver gilt; his sword also was taken, as well as a letter to him from Her Majesty the Queen of England.

Neither the attack on Gallabat, nor the Dervish defeat of the rearguard the following day, had by any means broken the Abyssinian army; but, owing to the accidental death of their king, the Dervish victory had been most complete. The country now fell into a state of internecine warfare; there were several aspirants for the throne, and dissensions and quarrels put a stop to combined action. The Italians had been in occupation of Massawa since the beginning of 1885, and had occupied some of the adjacent country. This fact reacted satisfactorily on the Dervish occupation of Gallabat; for they were well aware that the Abyssinians would be fully occupied with their European enemies; and once more they began raiding the Amhara frontier.

Whilst the garrison of Gallabat was in danger of destruction at the hands of King John, Osman Wad Adam was in considerable peril in the west. On the death of Sultan Yusef, his troops raided the country in all directions, and his *emirs* were guilty of the greatest oppression and cruelty. Thousands of women and children were declared to be *ghanima* (booty), and dragged to Fasher by main force. The people were in despair; and the distress and anguish extended to the limits of Dar Tama. Here a youth resided who hailed from Omdurman, and probably belonged to one of the riverain tribes, but had been driven from his own home, and, under the shade of a wide spreading Gemmaiza (wild fig) tree, sat and read the *Koran*.

He had intended proceeding to Bornu and the Fellata country,—as far away as possible from the tyrannical Sudan,—when some of the unfortunate people who had been robbed of all they possessed, came and told him of their misfortunes. A party of Dervishes, they said, had arrived at the neighbouring village, had seized their cattle, and were about to carry them off, together with the women and girls of the village, under the pretext that they had been ordered to undertake a pilgrimage to Fasher, and had not done so. "If you do not wish to fight for your wives and children, for what then will you fight?" asked the young man. "Do you not know that he who falls fighting for his women and children goes straight to Paradise?"

The effect of these words on the people resembled a spark falling into a barrel of gunpowder. Hastening back to their village, they demanded the instant liberation of their families; and when this was refused, they fought for it. The Mahdists were annihilated; and the infuriated villagers mutilated their bodies. Their example was followed by other villages with equal success; and, in a few days, Dar Tama had shaken itself free from its enemies. But who was the originator of this movement which had already been so successful? It was the young man under the Gemmaiza tree, who lived there as a hermit, subsisting only on some dry bread and a little grain. A pilgrimage to see him was at once organised; the people called him Abu Gemmaiza, adored him as a saint, and looked upon him as the liberator of the fatherland.

The Emir Abdel Kader Wad Delil, who was then residing at Kebkebia, and had heard of the massacre of his men, now advanced on Dar Tama, determined to avenge it; but he was defeated, and barely escaped with his life. Khatem Musa, on his way from Fasher, suffered a like fate. Osman Wad Adam, furious at the losses he had sustained, resolved to annihilate his enemies, and, with this object in view, despatched his assistant, Mohammed Wad Bishara, and a large number of his *mulazemin* to Kebkebia, to unite with Wad Delil and Khatem; but scarcely had he arrived, when he was attacked by the hosts of Abu Gemmaiza, who were marching on Fasher.

Defeated with great loss, he fell back on that town. Adam now fully realised the seriousness of the situation, and summoned a council; several of the *emirs* were for evacuating the province at once, when the news suddenly arrived that Abu Gemmaiza was dead. As a matter of fact, to the great good fortune of Fasher, he had been taken seriously ill of small-pox at Kebkebia. The excited multitudes refused either to return or disperse; and, electing his assistant as his successor, they continued their advance on Fasher; but, in spite of their former victories, their belief in their leader's success had waned when he had fallen ill, and when he died, it vanished altogether.

Osman Wad Adam had taken up a position in the south end of the city; and when the rebels advanced to the attack, they were driven back to Rahad Tendelti with fearful loss. Abu Gemmaiza's successor was killed, and his troops, dispersing in all directions, were pursued and slaughtered. The whole country seemed covered with dead bodies; but Fasher and Darfur were saved. There is a curious coincidence in the dates of these momentous occurrences in the East and West Sudan: the previous year, both armies had advanced—the one to Darfur and the other to Abyssinia; both had been attacked by their enemies in their fortifications—the one by King John, and the other by Abu Gemmaiza, in the same month; and both had been unexpectedly successful.

Previous, however, to these occurrences, the *khalifa* had again directed his attention towards Egypt. He had questioned several persons regarding the country; and they had excited in him an avaricious longing for the grand palaces, large gardens, and immense *harems* of white women (he himself had black in abundance). Of course the most suitable man to undertake operations against Egypt was Nejumi. He was an exceptionally brave man, and, when a simple merchant, had travelled a great deal, knew the country well, and, moreover, was an ardent devotee to the cause of Mahdism, to which he had won over great numbers. The greater part of his force consisted of tribesmen of the Nile valley; many had seen Egypt, and had until recently much intercourse with the frontier tribes of Upper Egypt.

Such were the outward and visible reasons which the *khalifa* brought forward when selecting the chief; but, in reality, he was well aware that a campaign against Egypt was a serious undertaking; and, on this account, he was anxious not to involve in it his own relatives, and the western tribes who were his special adherents. Nejumi, therefore, with his Jaalin and Danagla, and a proportion of Baggaras, formed the expedition; but the two former, being followers of the Khalifa Sherif, Abdullahi always looked upon as his secret enemies. Should the campaign be successful,—and he never for a moment doubted the capacity and devotion of its leader,—then so much the better, he would have conquered a new country; but should the Egyptian troops succeed in repelling the invasion, then the remnant of his defeated forces would retire on Dongola, with heavy loss, and would be so far weakened as to be unworthy of further consideration.

He therefore despatched Yunes Wad ed Dekeim as Emir of the Dongola Province, and to hold the country, whilst Nejumi was to receive his orders from Yunes, and proceed with the advanced troops. The Dongola Province, at this period, it must be remembered, was entirely under Baggara domination. Amongst the reinforcements despatched thence were Ahmed Wad Gar en Nebbi and some of the Batahin tribesmen, who came from the country north of the Blue Nile, between the Shukria district and the river. Many of this tribe had been previously despatched to Dongola and Berber; and now the few who were left refused to comply with the *khalifa's* orders, in consequence of which Gar en Nebbi had deserted, and, being pursued, had wounded one of the *khalifa's* men. Abdullahi, indignant at this disregard of his orders, had despatched Abdel Baki, accompanied by Taher Wad el Obeid, to seize by force all the Batahin; the latter now fled in all directions, but, with the exception of a very few, were captured.

During the pursuit Abdel Baki, guided by Wad el Obeid, suffered severely from thirst; and this he imputed to the ill-will of the latter, who, in consequence, was deprived of his position and thrown into chains at Omdurman. Abdel Baki now brought in sixty-seven men of the Batahin, with their wives and children. This tribe was celebrated for its bravery during the government days; and now the *khalifa*, who had already privately given his views on the matter to the judges, ordered them to be summoned before the court. It was unanimously decided that the Batahin were *mukhalefin* (disobedient). "And what is the punishment for disobedience?" asked the *khalifa*. "Death," was the reply of the judges. They were sent back to prison, and the *khalifa* busied himself with carrying the sentence into execution.

In accordance with his orders, three scaffolds were immediately erected in the market-place, and, after midday prayers, the *ombeÿa* was sounded and the great war-drum was beaten, summoning all the *khalifa's* subjects to follow him. Riding to the parade ground, he dismounted and seated himself on a small *angareb*, whilst his followers collected around him, some sitting and some standing. The sixty-seven Batahin were now brought before him, with their hands tied behind their backs, escorted by Abdel Baki's men, whilst their unfortunate wives and children ran after them crying and screaming. The *khalifa* gave instructions that the women and children were to be separated from the men, and, summoning Ahmed ed Dalia, Taher Wad el Jaali, and Hassan Wad Khabir, consulted them in an undertone; the latter then went forward to the Batahin, and instructed the escort and prisoners to follow them to the market-place. After a delay of a quarter of an hour, the *khalifa* got up, and we all walked on behind him. Arrived at the market-place, a terrible scene awaited us.

The unfortunate Batahin had been divided into three parties, one of which had been hanged, a second had been decapitated, and a third had lost their right hands and left feet. The *khalifa* himself stopped in front of the three scaffolds, which were almost broken by the weights of the bodies, whilst close at hand lay a heap of mutilated people, their hands and feet lying scattered on the ground; it was a shocking spectacle. They did not utter a sound, but gazed in front of them, and tried to hide from the eyes of the crowd the terrible sufferings they were enduring. The *khalifa* now summoned Osman Wad Ahmed, one of the *kadis*, who was an intimate friend of Khalifa Ali, and a member of the Batahin tribe; and pointing to the mutilated bodies, he said to Osman, "You may now take what remains of your tribe home with you." The poor man was too shocked and horrified to be able to answer.

After riding round the scaffolds, the *khalifa* proceeded along the street leading to the mosque; and here Ahmed ed Dalia had been continuing his bloody work; twenty-three decapitated bodies lay stretched along the roadside; these unfortunates had calmly met their death, submitting to the inevitable. Several of them, as is the custom amongst the Arabs, had given proof of their courage by uttering a few sentences, such as: "Death is ordained for everyone." "See! today is my holy day." "He who has not seen a brave man die, let him come and look here." Each one of these sixty-seven men had met his death heroically. The *khalifa's* work was done; he was satisfied with it, and rode home. On his arrival there, by way of an act of clemency, he sent one of his orderlies with instructions that the women and children of the murdered men should be set free; he might just as well have distributed them as slaves.

In spite of all these horrors, I was secretly rejoicing, for I had heard that letters from home were on their way; not only were there letters, but I had also been told, confidentially, by some merchants who had come from Berber, that there were two boxes of money for me. I scarcely dared think about it, and to wait patiently was no easy matter. One morning, whilst I was sitting at the door, a camel laden with two boxes was brought up; and the man asked to be taken before the *khalifa*, saying that he had arrived with letters and goods from Osman Digna. The *khalifa*, being apprised of this, ordered the boxes to be sent to the Beit el Mal, and the letters to be given to his clerks. I was wild with impatience; but it was the *khalifa's* pleasure not to summon me till after sunset, and then he handed me the letters.

They were, as I expected, from my brothers and sisters, expressing their great delight at having at last received news direct from me. One letter was written in Arabic, and addressed to the *khalifa*, and contained profuse thanks to him for his kindness to me, recommending

The Execution of the "Batahin."

me to him for further assurances of his good-will, for which they sent many expressions of gratitude. This letter, which had been written by Professor Dahrmund, was composed in such flattering terms that the *khalifa* had it read aloud the same evening in the mosque; and so gratified was he, that he ordered the boxes to be made over to me.

Meanwhile, I translated to him my letters, which contained only private and personal information, and in which my brothers and sisters told me they had sent a travelling-bag for the *khalifa* in token of their devotion to him, begging him to accept this trifling present, which was quite unworthy of his exalted position. He expressed his readiness to accept it, and ordered me to bring it to him the next morning. He then sent two of his people, so that the boxes might be opened in their presence; and, late that night, we went to the Beit el Mal, and there opened them. They contained £200, twelve ordinary watches, some razors and looking-glasses, some newspapers, a German translation of the *Koran*, and the *khalifa's* present. These things were all handed over to me; and, having read my letters once again, I literally devoured the newspapers. News from home!

There were only a few numbers of the "*Neue Freie Presse,*" but quite sufficient to afford me, who had had no news for six years, the pleasure of reading at night-time for months. I gradually got to know them by heart, from the political leader down to the last advertisement, in which an elderly maiden lady advertised that she was anxious to find a kindred spirit with a view to matrimony. Father Ohrwalder came to me secretly by night to borrow the papers, and studied them just as conscientiously as I did,—only I do not suppose that he paid quite so much attention to the last advertisement!

Early the next morning, taking the present with me, I went to the *khalifa*; he told me to open it, and when he saw all the little crystal boxes, silver-topped bottles, brushes, razors, scissors, etc., etc., he was greatly surprised. I had to explain to him their various uses; and he then sent for the *kadis*, who, in duty bound, were obliged to express even greater astonishment than he, though I had no doubt that several of them had seen such things before. Then, without any further delay, he sent for his clerk, and ordered him to write a letter to my brothers and sisters, in which he himself informed them of the honourable position I held in his service; he invited them to come to Omdurman and visit me, and gave them the assurance that they would be free to return.

He also ordered me to write in the same strain; and, although I knew perfectly well that my people would never avail themselves of such an invitation, which was merely a spontaneous outburst of delight, I took good care to warn them fully against thinking of it for an instant. The letters were then returned by the man who had been sent by Osman Digna; and the latter was instructed by letter to forward them. The real reason, however, for the *khalifa's* good-humour lay in the fact that his own tribe, the Taaisha, had arrived in Omdurman. They had marched through Kordofan to the White Nile at Tura el Hadra. The *khalifa* had written to them that they should come to take possession of the countries which the Lord their God had ordained to be theirs; and on their arrival they certainly behaved as if they were sole masters.

They appropriated everything they could lay their hands on: camels, cows, and donkeys were forcibly carried off from their owners; men and women who had the misfortune to cross their path, were robbed of their clothing and jewellery; and the populations of the countries through which they passed bitterly rued the day which had made a western Arab their ruler. For their convenience, the *khalifa* erected immense grain *depôts* all along the roads by which they travelled; and, on their arrival at the river, ships and steamers were ready to transport them to Omdurman. But, before they reached the city, the *khalifa* ordered them to halt on the right bank of the river; and, dividing them into two sections, he had all the men and women freshly clothed at the expense of the Beit el Mal; and they then were brought in detachments, at intervals of two or three days, to Omdurman.

In order to make the populace thoroughly understand that the new masters of the country had arrived, Abdullahi drove out of their houses all the inhabitants of that portion of the city lying between the mosque and Omdurman Fort, and handed it over to the Taaisha as their residence. Other ground was allotted to those who had been forced to give up their houses, and they were promised assistance from the Beit el Mal in order to rebuild; but, of course, this was mere empty form, and resulted in their having to shift entirely for themselves.

In order to facilitate the maintenance of his tribe, and as grain began to rise in price, the *khalifa* issued an order for all grain stored in the houses to be taken to the *meshra el minarata* (grain docks), under pain of confiscation; and, having obtained the services of some of his own myrmidons, he ordered them to sell this grain at the lowest possible rate to the Taaisha; and the money thus obtained he divided amongst the original owners, who, in their turn, were obliged to re-purchase at the high rates from other sources. This wholesale robbery can be better understood, when I explain that the money paid by the Taaisha for ten *ardebs* of grain would scarcely pay for two *ardebs* purchased in the ordinary manner.

When the supply of grain at Omdurman was diminishing, he despatched messengers to the Gezira to confiscate what was still there; and, in this manner, by publicly showing his preference for his own tribe, he completely estranged himself from his former followers. This, however, was a matter of little concern to him, as, by the advent of the Taaisha Arabs, he had acquired a reinforcement of several thousands of warriors.

After the *Mahdi's* death, the *khalifa* had sent four messengers to Cairo with letters addressed to Her Majesty the Queen of England, His Majesty the Sultan, and His Highness the Khedive, in which he summoned them to submit to his rule and to adopt *Mahdism*. The messengers returned from Cairo, where due note had been made of this insolent demand, without any answer; and the *khalifa* was greatly offended. Early in 1889, however, when he had decided to send Nejumi to invade Egypt, he again despatched four messengers to Egypt, conveying his final warning; but these were kept for a time at Assuan, and again sent back without any answer.

The campaigns in the east and west having been successfully concluded, the revolt of Abu Gemmaiza having been suppressed, and King John of Abyssinia having been killed, and his head despatched with others to Omdurman, the *khalifa* now sent it to Yunes at Dongola to be forwarded by him to Wadi Halfa, as a warning, and as a proof of his victory over all those who refused to believe in the *Mahdi*. Having overcome his difficulties, and being strengthened by the arrival of fresh contingents of Arabs, the *khalifa* now considered that the time had come when he might venture an attack on Egypt, and conquer it. Consequently, Nejumi received special instructions to start forthwith, with all under his command; and, avoiding Wadi Halfa, to capture Assuan, and there await further orders.

In addition to his own followers, Nejumi had been reinforced by the Batahin, the Homr, and other Arabs of whom the *khalifa* was anxious to rid himself; and with these he quitted Dongola early in May, 1889. Meanwhile, the Egyptian Government had been kept well informed of the advance of this ill-equipped force, and had taken all precautions; whilst Nejumi, instead of material support, received continual orders from Yunes to hurry on; and it was not till he had arrived within the Egyptian frontier that some reinforcements of Jaalin, under Haj Ali, reached him. At the village of Argin, a portion of his troops, contrary to his orders, had descended from the desert high ground to the river, and, coming in contact with the troops of the Wadi Halfa garrison under Wodehouse Pasha, sustained considerable loss.

Meanwhile, Grenfell Pasha, *sirdar* of the Egyptian Army, having started with a force from Assuan, wrote a letter to Nejumi, in which he pointed out the danger of the situation, and how impossible it was for him to hope to be successful. He therefore summoned him to surrender; but this Nejumi stubbornly refused to do; and a battle ensued at Toski, in which General Grenfell and the Egyptian army utterly annihilated the *Mahdists*. Nejumi and almost all of his *emirs* were killed; thousands were taken prisoners; and only a very few succeeded in escaping back to Dongola.

The *khalifa* had ridden to the Beit el Mal, and was praying on the banks of the Nile, when mounted men arrived in hot haste from Dongola, and handed letters to his secretary, who, for the moment, suppressed the news, and only read it to him when he returned home. The letters described the death of Nejumi and the destruction of his army; and the effect on the *khalifa* was terrible. He had no great confidence, it is true, in the tribes who had gone forward to invade Egypt; but, at the same time, their annihilation was a frightful blow to him. He had hoped that they would either have been victorious, or would have beaten a safe retreat; but now he had lost upwards of sixteen thousand of his men; and he at once thought the government would advance and re-occupy Dongola.

For three days he did not go near his *harem*; and, day and night, I was obliged to stay at his door and pretend to sympathise with him in these occurrences, though secretly I was rejoicing. He at once despatched reinforcements to Yunes; but, at the same time, sent him instructions that, should the government advance, he should not attempt to oppose the army, but was to retreat with his entire force to Sannum, in Dar Shaigia.

But disasters never come singly: grain rose daily in price. No rain had fallen the previous year, and the crops in consequence had been very bad; the parties who had been sent to the Gezira had orders to procure grain by force at the rate fixed by the *khalifa*. Of course those who had any at once hid it and denied having anything; but in truth there was really very little in the land. Famine first broke out in the Province of Berber, which was entirely dependent on the Gezira for supplies; and here Osman Wad ed Dekeim was obliged to disperse his men and horses throughout various parts of the country.

The irrigation of this province is carried on by water-wheels at intervals along the river banks; and even in prosperous times the supply of grain is scarcely sufficient to meet the wants of the local inhabitants; there was therefore now considerable difficulty in maintaining all Osman's people as well. Several of the inhabitants wandered to Omdurman, which was already over-populated; and here the situation became most critical: the price of grain rose at first to forty dollars, and subsequently to sixty dollars, the *ardeb*. The rich could purchase grain; but the poor died wholesale.

Those were terrible months at the close of 1889; the people had become so thin that they scarcely resembled human beings,—they were veritably but skin and bone. These poor wretches would eat anything, no matter how disgusting,—skins of animals which had long since dried and become decayed, were roasted and eaten; the strips of leather which form the *angareb* (native bedstead) were cut off, boiled, and made into soup. Those who had any strength left went out and robbed; like hawks they pounced down on the bakers and butchers, and cared nothing for the blows of the *kurbash*, which invariably fell on their attenuated backs.

On one occasion, I remember seeing a man who had seized a piece of tallow, and had crammed it into his mouth before its owner could stop him. The latter jumped at his throat, closed his hands round it, and pressed it till the man's eyes protruded; but he kept his mouth tightly closed until he fell down insensible. In the market-places, the incessant cry was heard of "*Gayekum! Gayekum!*" (He is coming to you!), which meant that famished creatures were stealthily creeping round the places where the women had their few articles for sale, to protect which they were frequently obliged to lie upon them, and defend them with their hands and feet. The space between the *khalifa's* and Yakub's houses was generally crowded at night with these wretched people, who cried aloud most piteously for bread. I dreaded going home; for I was generally followed by several of these famished beggars, who often attempted to forcibly enter my house; and at that time I had scarcely enough for my own slender wants, besides having to help my own household and my friends, who had now become wretchedly poor.

One night,—it was full moon,—I was going home at about twelve o'clock, when, near the Beit el Amana (ammunition and arms stores),

I saw something moving on the ground, and went near to see what it was. As I approached, I saw three almost naked women, with their long tangled hair hanging about their shoulders; they were squatting round a quite young donkey, which was lying on the ground, and had probably strayed from its mother, or been stolen by them. They had torn open its body with their teeth, and were devouring its intestines, whilst the poor animal was still breathing. I shuddered at this terrible sight, whilst the poor women, infuriated by hunger, gazed at me like maniacs. The beggars by whom I was followed, now fell upon them, and attempted to wrest from them their prey; and I fled from this uncanny spectacle.

On another occasion, I saw a poor woman who must formerly have been beautiful, but on whose emaciated face the death-struggle was visible, lying on her back in the street, whilst her little baby, scarcely a year old, was vainly trying to get some nourishment from its mother's already cold breasts. Another woman, passing by, took compassion on the little orphan, and carried it off.

One day, a woman of the Jaalin, who are perhaps the most moral tribe in the Sudan, accompanied by her only daughter, a lovely young girl, dragged herself wearily to my house; both were at death's door from starvation, and begged me to help them. I gave them what little I could; and the woman then said, "Take this, my only daughter, as your slave; save her from death by starvation!" and, as she said this, the tears streamed down her poor wan cheeks, whilst in her weak, scarcely audible voice, she continued, "Do not fear that I shall molest you any further; only save her; do not let her perish!"

I gave them all I could spare, and then asked them to leave me, telling them to return when they were in great want; but I never saw them again,—perhaps some charitable person took pity on them. Another woman was actually accused of eating her own child, and was brought to the police station for trial; but of what use was this?—in two days the poor creature died, a raving maniac!

Several sold their own children, both boys and girls, pretending they were their slaves,—this they did not to obtain money, but simply to save their lives; and, when this year of misery was over, some parents bought them back again at even higher prices. The dead lay in the streets in hundreds; and none could be found to bury them. The *khalifa* issued orders that people were responsible for burying those who were found dead near their houses; and that, should they refuse to do so, their property would be confiscated. This had some effect;

FAMINE STRICKEN

but, to save themselves trouble, they used to drag the bodies near their neighbours' houses; and this gave rise to frequent quarrels and brawls. Every day, the waters of the Blue and White Niles swept past Omdurman, carrying along hundreds of bodies of the wretched peasantry who had died along the banks,—a terrible proof of the awful condition of the country.

In Omdurman itself, the majority of those who died belonged rather to the moving population, than to the actual inhabitants of the town; for the latter had managed to secrete a certain amount of grain, and the different tribes invariably assisted each other; but, in other parts of the Sudan, the state of affairs was considerably worse. I think the Jaalin, who are most independent, as well as the proudest tribe in the Sudan, suffered more severely than the rest; several fathers of families, seeing that escape from death was impossible, bricked up the doors of their houses, and, united with their children, patiently awaited death. I have no hesitation in saying that in this way entire villages died out.

The inhabitants of Dongola, though they suffered considerably, were somewhat better off; and for this they had to thank Nejumi, whose departure had considerably reduced the population of the province. Between Abu Haraz, Gedaref, and Gallabat, the situation was worst of all. Zeki Tummal, at the commencement of the famine, had given orders to some of his myrmidons to forcibly collect all the grain in the neighbourhood; and this he stored for his soldiers, thus saving the bulk of his force, with the result that an immense proportion of the local inhabitants died of starvation.

After a time, no one dared to go out into the streets without an escort; for they feared being attacked and eaten up; the inhabitants had become animals,—cannibals! One of the *emirs* of the Homr tribe,—who, in spite of the terrible year, still preserved a fairly healthy appearance,—notwithstanding constant warning, insisted on going to visit a friend after sunset; but he never reached his friend, nor returned to his abode; the next morning, his head was found outside the city, and I presume his body had already been consumed.

The Hassania, Shukria, Aggaliun, Hammada, and other tribes had completely died out; and the once thickly populated country had become a desert waste. Zeki Tummal sent a detachment of his force to the southern districts of the Blue Nile, towards the Tabi, Begreg, Kukeli, Kashankero, and Beni Shangul mountains, the inhabitants of which, although they paid tribute to the *khalifa*, refused to make a pilgrimage or provide warlike contingents. This he had done not so much with the idea of military operations, as to provide some means of maintaining his troops; but the commander, Abder Rasul, succeeded in capturing a number of slaves, as well as a quantity of money.

The situation in Darfur was little better than that in Gedaref and Gallabat; the western provinces, such as Dar Gimr, Dar Tama, and Massalit, had no need of grain; but not being in complete subjection, they prevented its export to Fasher. Indeed, it seemed as if this famine had come as Heaven's punishment on all districts owning subjection to the *khalifa*, whilst the neighbouring countries, which had had sufficient rest to cultivate their fields, had acquired enough grain for their maintenance. A few Omdurman merchants hired some vessels, and proceeded to Fashoda, where they exchanged beads, copper rods, and money for *dhurra*; the undertaking succeeded, and now crowds of others followed their example, proceeding sometimes as far as the Sobat, whence they imported quantities of grain, thus enriching themselves, and saving their fellow-countrymen from terrible want.

Had the King of Fashoda, who was not then subject to the *khalifa*, forbidden the export, half Omdurman would have perished. At length, the rain fell; the thirsty land was refreshed; the crops sprang up; harvest was near; and the whole country once more rejoiced at the prospect of help and deliverance. But now the atmosphere became obscure with swarms of locusts of an unusual size, and the prospect of a rich harvest vanished; everything, however, was not destroyed by this plague, which, from that date, has become one of annual occurrence. The *khalifa*, anxious for the welfare of his own tribe, now forced the natives to sell the little grain they had collected, at an absurdly low price, to his agents; but small as this was, in comparison with the price he ought to have paid, he determined to still further economise, and, consequently, ordered Ibrahim Adlan to proceed personally to the Gezira, and induce the inhabitants to give up their *dhurra* of their own free-will, and without payment.

Adlan, who thoroughly disapproved of this measure, now left; and his enemies, seizing the occasion of his absence, did all they could to bring about his fall. This able official had, by his thoroughness and sagacity, risen high in the *khalifa's* favour; but ambition induced him to strive for the first place. He frequently made use of his position to upset the plans of others; but, in reality, Abdullahi sought nobody's advice, and discussed state affairs with his brother Yakub only, whose animosity Adlan had incurred, though Yakub was too clever to show it.

As natives go, Adlan's character was good: he did not care to lend himself to evil designs, and, far from oppressing people, was often the means of lightening the burdens of others; he was most liberal and well-disposed to those who were submissive to his will; but he was bitterly hostile to those he suspected of finding fault with his actions, or who endeavoured to obtain appointments and positions without his intervention. Like all Sudanese, he was bent on making money by fair means or foul; and as he was head of the Beit el Mal, through whose hands all the taxes passed, this was not a matter of difficulty. He was suspected, and not without reason, of having made an immense fortune, and of this the *khalifa* was not ignorant; consequently, during his absence, Yakub and several of his confidants informed the *khalifa* that Adlan's influence in the country was almost as great as his own, and that he had frequently spoken disparagingly of his master and his system of government; they even went as far as to say that Adlan had attributed the famine entirely to the *khalifa's* treatment of his own tribe.

Adlan, who was somewhat slow in carrying out the *khalifa's* instructions in the Gezira, and against whom the Taaisha were clamouring bitterly, was recalled by the *khalifa*, who, for the first few days after his arrival, did not show his hand; but when the Taaisha, instigated by Yakub, continued clamouring, the *khalifa* summoned him, and accused him in harsh terms of infidelity and abuse of confidence. Furious at this treatment, and trusting to the confidential nature of his position, Adlan, for a moment, forgot that after all he was merely the *khalifa's* slave, and retorted in equally sharp terms, "You reproach me now," said he,—"I who have served you all these years; and now I do not fear to speak my mind to you. Through preference for your own tribe, and your love of evil-doing, you have estranged the hearts of all those who have hitherto been faithful to you. I have ever been mindful of your interests; but as you now listen to my enemies, and to your brother Yakub, who is ill-disposed towards me, I cannot serve you any longer."

The *khalifa*, alarmed and shocked by such language, which no one had ever dared before to use in his presence, was furious. If Adlan had not had such power in the country, he would never have dared to speak like this; and if he had not accumulated considerable wealth, he would never have risked giving up so lucrative a position. Abdullahi, however, controlled himself, and replied, "I have taken note of what you have said, and will think it over; leave me now, and I will give you an answer tomorrow."

He went out; but ere he had reached the door the *khalifa* had made up his mind. After sunset the next day, the two *khalifas*, all the *kadis*, and Yakub were summoned to a council; and, shortly afterwards, Adlan was called before them. In a few words, similar to those he had used the previous day, the *khalifa* spoke to him about his attitude, adding, "You spoke against Yakub, and said that I had estranged myself from the hearts of my partisans; do you not know that my brother Yakub is my eye and my right hand? It is you who have estranged the hearts of my friends from me; and now you dare to do the same with my brother; but the Almighty God is righteous, and you shall not escape your punishment." He then made a sign to the *mulazemin*, who had been kept in readiness, to seize him and carry him off to prison. Without uttering a word of reproach, with a firm step, and holding his head high in the air, he submitted to his fate, determined that his enemies should not have the satisfaction of seeing him downhearted or afraid.

The *khalifa* at once gave instructions that Adlan's house should be confiscated, and the Beit el Mal property seized. A careful search of the former was ordered; and the *employés* of the latter were instructed to render immediate and complete accounts. In Adlan's pocket was found a piece of paper inscribed all over with mysterious writing, in which the name of the *khalifa* frequently appeared; it had been written with a solution of saffron, which is supposed to possess some secret power; and the unfortunate Adlan was not less superstitious than the majority of the Sudanese.

The paper was declared to be sorcery, which is punishable most severely; Adlan was pronounced to be *mukhalef* (disobedient) in not carrying out his orders, and a traitor, because he had attempted to sow dissension between the *khalifa* and his brother Yakub, and, in the endeavour to effect this, had been guilty of the use of sorcery. The verdict was mutilation, or death, and he was allowed to make his choice; he selected the latter.

With his hands tied across his chest, and to the strains of the melancholy *ombeÿa*, he was led forth to the market-place, accompanied by an immense crowd. Calmly mounting the *angareb* beneath the scaffold, he himself placed his head in the noose, and, refusing to drink the water offered to him, told the hangman to complete his work; the rope was pulled taut, the *angareb* was removed, and there Ibrahim swung like a marble statue, until his soul left his body, the outstretched index finger alone indicating that he died in the true faith of Islam. In spite of the interdiction, wails of sorrow filled the city; but the *khalifa* rejoiced that he had rid himself of so dangerous an enemy, and refrained from punishing this disobedience to his orders. He sent his brother Yakub to the funeral, as if to show to the world that Adlan had merely been punished in accordance with the law, and that the well-known animosity between the two had nothing to do with the matter.

His successor as Emin Beit el Mal was a certain Nur Wad Ibrahim whose grandfather was a Takruri. He did not, therefore, belong to the tribes of the Nile valley, and thus had a greater claim on the *khalifa's* confidence and consideration.

As regards myself, the *khalifa* seemed to grow daily more suspicious. Previous to Ibrahim Adlan's departure for the Gezira, the answer to my letter, which had been sent to my family through Osman Digna, had arrived. It contained only news of a private nature, and expressed the great delight of my family that they had succeeded in at last getting into communication with me. At the same time, they wrote to the *khalifa* in submissive words, expressing their gratitude for the kind and honourable treatment which I received at his hands. They also assured him of their great devotion to him, and thanked him for the high honour he had conferred upon them by inviting them to come to Omdurman; but my brother regretted his inability to accept, as he was at that time a secretary in the office of the High Chamberlain of His Majesty the Emperor of Austria, whilst the other brother was a lawyer and lieutenant in the Artillery Reserve; they were therefore both unable, in virtue of their positions, to undertake so long a journey.

My master had called me up, and, on handing me the letters, had ordered me to translate them to him; then, considering for a few moments, he said to me, "It was my intention to induce one of your brothers to come here and see me; and I did what I had never done before,—wrote a letter to them. As they make excuses and refuse to come, and as they now know that you are well, I forbid you to have any more correspondence with them. Further communications would only make you unhappy. Do you understand what I mean?"

"Certainly," I replied, "your orders shall be obeyed; and I also think that further communication with my relatives is not necessary."

"Where is the Gospel that has been sent to you?" asked he, looking at me fixedly.

"I am a Moslem," I answered, for I was now on my guard; "and I have no Gospel in my house. They sent me a translation of the *Koran*, the Holy Book, which your secretary saw when the box was opened, and which is still in my possession."

"Then bring it to me tomorrow," he said, and signed to me to withdraw.

It was perfectly clear to me that he no longer trusted me; and I knew that after Nejumi's defeat he had several times spoken in this sense to the *kadis*. I had already spent almost all the money I had received in gifts amongst my comrades; and now some of these began to murmur, and were disappointed that the sum was so small; and I knew that they were intriguing against me. Who could have induced him to believe that the *Koran* which had been sent to me was the Gospel? The next day, I gave it to him. The translation was by Ullman. He examined it carefully, and then said: "You say that this is the *Koran*; it is in the language of unbelievers, and perhaps they have made alterations."

"It is a literal translation into my own language," I replied, calmly, "and its object is to make me understand the Holy Book which has come from God, and was made known to mankind by the Prophet, in the Arabic language. If you wish, you can send it to Neufeld, who is in captivity in the prison, and with whom I have no intercourse; and you can ascertain from him if my assertion is correct."

"I do not mistrust you, and I believe what you say," he replied, in a somewhat more amiable tone; "but people have spoken to me about it, and you had better destroy the book." When I had told him that I was perfectly willing to do this, he continued, "Also I wish you to return the present your brothers and sisters sent me; I can make no use of it, and it will be a proof to them that I place no value on worldly possessions."

He now had his secretary summoned, and ordered him to write a letter in my name to my family, to the effect that it was not necessary to correspond anymore; and, after I had signed it, it was sent, together with the travelling-bag, to the Beit el Mal, to be despatched to Suakin. From that day, I was more careful than ever to do nothing to increase the mistrust which I saw had sprung up in Abdullahi's mind. After Adlan's death, however, he thought it necessary to warn me again, and cautioned me most seriously against becoming mixed up in any sort of conspiracy. Assembling all his *mulazemin*, he asserted, in the most forcible language, that I was suspected of being a spy; that he had been told I invariably questioned the camel postmen who arrived, about the situation; that I received visitors in my house at night who were known to be out of favour with him; and that I had gone so far as to inquire in what part of his house his bedroom was situated. "I am afraid," he continued, "that if you do not change your line of conduct, you will follow in the footsteps of my old enemy Adlan."

This was rather a blow to me; but I knew that now, more than ever, I had need of being calm and collected. "Sire!" said I, in a loud voice, "I cannot defend myself against unknown enemies; but I am perfectly innocent of all they have told you. I leave my detractors in the hands of God. For more than six years, in sunshine and rain, I have stood at your door, ever ready to receive and carry out your orders. At your command, I have given up all my old friends, and have no communication with anyone. I have even given up all connection with my relatives, and that without the slightest remonstrance. Such a thing as conspiracy has never even entered my heart. During all these long years, I have never made a complaint. Sire, what have I done? All that I do is not done out of fear of you, but out of love for you; and I cannot do more. Should God still have further trials in store for me, I shall calmly and willingly submit to my fate; but I have full reliance in your sense of justice."

"What have you to say to his words?" he said to the assembled *mulazemin*, after a moment's silence. All, without exception, admitted that they had never noticed anything in my behaviour which could give rise to such a suspicion; my enemies also—and I well knew who they were, and who were responsible for getting me into this dangerous position—were obliged to admit this. "I forgive you," said he; "but avoid for the future giving further cause for complaint," and, holding out his hand for me to kiss, he signed to me to withdraw. He must have felt that he had wronged me; for the next day he summoned me, spoke to me kindly, and warned me against my enemies, who, he said, were as a thorn in my flesh. I professed affection and confidence in him; and he then said, in quite a confidential tone, "Do not make enemies, for you know that *Mahdia* is conducted in accordance with the Moslem law: should you be accused before the *kadi* of treason, and two witnesses make good the accusation, you are lost; for I cannot go against the law to save you."

What an existence in a country where one's very life hung on the evidence of two witnesses! Thanking him for his advice, I promised to follow it, and said I would, of course, do all in my power to deserve his confidence. When I returned home at midnight, tired and worn out by this constant strain, my devoted Saadalla informed me, to my great annoyance, that, only a few minutes before, one of the *khalifa's* eunuchs had brought a closely-veiled female, who was now in my house.

I ought to have been greatly pleased about this, for it was a proof that the *khalifa* had forgiven me; but my first thought was, how to rid myself of this present without creating suspicion. Saadalla and I now entered the house; and, to my horror, I found that underneath the veil was an Egyptian who had been born at Khartum, and who was, consequently, from a Sudanese point of view, a lady of a comparatively fair complexion. She was seated on the carpet; and, after we had exchanged greetings, she replied to my query as to her nationality with such rapidity of speech that I, who spoke Arabic fairly well, had the greatest difficulty in following the romantic history of her life.

She was the daughter, she said, of an Egyptian officer who, I afterwards learnt, had only been a private soldier, and who had fallen in the fight against the Shilluks, under Yusef Bey. As this had taken place upwards of twenty years before, I could, without any great effort of calculation, estimate fairly accurately that this good lady was well out of her teens; and as she admitted that her first husband had been killed during the capture of Khartum, that her mother was an Abyssinian who had been educated in Khartum, and was still alive, and that she had an enormous number of relatives, I really believe that, had my head not been clean-shaven, my hair would veritably have stood on end. This far-travelled and widely-experienced lady informed me that she had been one of the many hundreds of Abu Anga's wives, and I had now been chosen as the happy successor of this old slave.

After his death, she had been captured, with several of her rivals, by the Abyssinians, when King John attacked Gallabat, but had been subsequently liberated by Zeki Tummal; and she knew so many details of all the fights in this neighbourhood, that, had my memory been only capable of retaining them, they would have now been of great interest to my readers. A short time ago, the *khalifa* had ordered Abu Anga's remaining widows to be brought to Omdurman, for distribution amongst his followers; she then went on to say that the *khalifa* himself had specially selected her as my wife, and she added, in a subdued tone, that she rejoiced to have fallen into the hands of a fellow-countryman.

I explained to her that I was not an Egyptian, but an European. As, however, my skin was somewhat tanned, and the circumstances in which I lived gave her a pretext for claiming me as a compatriot, I was obliged to say that I would provide as far as possible for her maintenance and comfort; and, as the night was well advanced, I bade her follow my servant Saadalla, who would make arrangements for her.

Such were the *khalifa's* presents: instead of allocating a small sum of money from the Beit el Mal, by means of which I could have procured for myself a few comforts, he kept on sending me wives, who were not only a source of considerable expense to me, but also a cause of much anxiety and worry, inasmuch as I was continually struggling to free myself from their unwelcome presence. The next morning, the *khalifa* laughingly asked me if I had received his present, and if I liked it. With the lesson of two days ago still fresh in my mind, I assured him that I was only too happy to receive this fresh proof of his affection, and that, please God, I should always live in the enjoyment of his favour. When I returned to my house before midday prayer, I found it full of females, who, notwithstanding the remonstrances of Saadalla, and jeering at his wrath, had entered by main force, and now introduced themselves to me as the nearest relatives of Fatma el Beida (The White Fatma), as the *khalifa's* present was called.

A decrepid old Abyssinian lady introduced herself as my future mother-in-law; from her loquacity, I should instantly have recognised her as the mother of Fatma el Beida; and I could not help wondering how so small and fragile a body could contain so noisy and voluble a tongue. She assured me of her pleasure that her daughter had been confided to my care, adding that she was convinced that I would accord to her her rightful position in my household. Here was I, the slave of a tyrant, and obliged to submit to the most wretched of circumstances; and now she talked to me of the position due to her daughter! I assured her that I would of course treat her daughter well; and, apologising that my time was so fully occupied, I fled. Before leaving, however, I ordered Saadalla to entertain them as well as he could, according to the custom of the country, and then to turn them all out, neck and crop, and, if necessary, to call the other servants to his assistance.

A few days afterwards, the *khalifa* again inquired about Fatma; and as I knew that he was most anxious that I should lead as quiet and secluded a life as possible, I told him that, for the present, I had no objection to her person; but as her numerous relatives might possibly come in contact with people whose acquaintance neither he, my master, nor I should consider desirable, and that as in my efforts to prevent this I frequently came into collision with both sides, it was naturally my earnest wish to prevent such disturbances. And I then went on to say that, should she not submit to my arrangements, I proposed surrendering Fatma entirely to her relatives; and with this proposition the *khalifa* appeared perfectly satisfied.

There was, however, no truth in this statement, for since Saadalla had entertained and turned out his visitors I had seen no one; fearing to betray my intentions to the *khalifa*, I waited some time longer, and then sent Fatma el Beida to her mother, whose whereabouts Saadalla had at length discovered, and I instructed the lady to stay with her mother until I should send for her. A few days afterwards, I sent a few clothes to mother and daughter, and a small sum of money, with a message that she was free, and no longer under any obligations to me. Of course I told the *khalifa* what I had done, reiterating that I was most anxious to have nothing to do with people who were strangers to him and to me; and in this he saw an additional proof of my anxiety to obey his orders. About a month later, the mother came to see me, and asked my permission to marry her daughter to one of her relatives. I agreed to this proposition with the greatest alacrity; and I left Fatma el Beida the mother of a happy family in Omdurman.

Chapter 14

Mahdist Occupation of the Southern Provinces

Karamalla, from whom Osman Wad Adam had taken away all his Bazingers and female slaves, and who was now in a state of poverty in Omdurman, had, whilst Emir of the Bahr el Ghazal Province, advanced to the vicinity of the White Nile, and had worried Emin Pasha. Fortunately for the latter, Karamalla had been recalled; and the Bahr el Ghazal Province having been abandoned, no news had been received from Equatoria for a long time, and those merchants who were engaged in the grain trade brought little information from any of the countries south of Fashoda. The *khalifa*, who was always turning over in his mind how he could increase his revenue, had heard of the richness of these countries in ivory and slaves, and, in consequence, had decided to organise an expedition to attack and take possession of them; but, as the undertaking was a risky one and success doubtful, he hesitated to involve in it his relatives or his tribe; he therefore nominated Omar Saleh, who had been educated amongst the Taaisha tribe, as chief of the expedition, which was composed for the most part of tribes of the Nile valley,—Jaalin and Danagla.

Three steamers were now manned, as well as eight sailing-vessels filled with cargo, consisting principally of Manchester goods, beads, etc.; and Omar Saleh was given a force of some rifles and five hundred spearmen. The *khalifa* sent letters to Emin Pasha, including one which I was obliged to sign, in which I called upon him to surrender; George Stambuli, who had formerly been Emin Pasha's private agent in Khartum, was also obliged to write a letter. At this time, the Shilluks were in considerable force; and as they did not owe allegiance to the *khalifa*, Omar Saleh was instructed to pass by Fashoda as quickly as possible, and only to defend himself in case of attack.

The expedition quitted Omdurman in July, 1890, passed Fashoda without difficulty; and after that Omar had no further opportunity of reporting on his position. It was not till a year had elapsed, and the *khalifa* was beginning to get uneasy, and was considering how he could procure information, that a steamer arrived with some ivory and a quantity of slaves, the captain of which gave a full account of the progress and position of the expedition. The Egyptian garrison of Reggaf had surrendered, and some of the officers of that place had been sent to Duffilé, with orders to seize Emin Pasha, whose soldiers had mutinied, and hand him over to Omar Saleh. After the departure of the party from Reggaf, a rumour had been circulated amongst the Mahdists that they had been deceived by the officers, and that it was the intention of the latter, on their arrival at Duffilé, to join with the garrison of that place and attack Omar Saleh; he therefore seized the officers and men who had remained behind, threw them into chains, and distributed their property and slaves amongst his followers.

The officers who had gone to Duffilé had really intended to capture Emin, who had in the meantime left with Stanley; and, hearing of what had happened to their wives and property, they now collected the soldiers who, on Emin's departure had created a sort of military republic, and with them marched towards Reggaf. The Mahdists, getting information of this, met them on the road; and a fight ensued, in which Omar Saleh was victorious. The officers were killed; but most of the men succeeded in beating a retreat towards Duffilé followed by the Mahdists, who attacked the position, but were driven off and forced to retire.

In spite of this victory, great dissensions prevailed amongst the men; and, eventually, they dispersed in bands throughout the province, in order to gain their own livelihood. The *khalifa*, rejoicing at Omar Saleh's success, and his cupidity excited by the exaggerated accounts of Wad Badai, who had arrived on the steamer, now gave instructions for another expedition to be equipped, with which he despatched Hassib Wad Ahmed and Elias Wad Kanuna, and took advantage of the occasion to rid himself of many characters which were obnoxious to him. From that date, Reggaf became a colony for the deportation of convicts, and of persons whose presence in Omdurman was considered dangerous to the state.

Several persons who had been accused of theft, and incarcerated in the *Saier*, were handed over to Wad Kanuna, who, at the same time, had all persons suspected of leading an immoral life seized, thrown into chains, and sent up to Reggaf; the opportunity was made the most of by several of the *emirs* and other influential people to rid themselves of any persons whom they thought dangerous or disagreeable to them.

The two chiefs also took advantage of the occasion to visit all the villages on the river bank between Omdurman and Kawa, and ruthlessly seize the people, under the pretext that they belonged to this category, and had been sentenced by the *khalifa* to transportation; they could only regain their freedom by the payment of a considerable sum of money to the two *emirs*, who continued their depredations until they reached the Shilluk and Dinka country, the inhabitants of which they feared too much to attempt such outrages on them.

From merchants who had gone to Fashoda in the years 1889 and 1890 to obtain grain, we had heard a good deal about the people who lived in these countries. The districts in close proximity to the river were mostly inhabited by the Shilluks and Dinkas, who, untrammelled by the despotic tyranny of the *khalifa*, lived a quiet and undisturbed life in the midst of their families. They were ruled over by a descendant of the *mek* (king) of the old Shilluk royal family, who had certain restrictive rights over his subjects, and, with his own interest always to the fore, permitted commercial relations with the Mahdists, avoiding at the same time any actual allegiance to the *khalifa*, to whom he did not pay tribute.

Wad Badai, who had had sufficient opportunities of seeing the wealth of the country between Fashoda and Reggaf, now gave it as his opinion that the *khalifa* would considerably profit by its acquisition. At this time, Zeki Tummal was at Gallabat with his army, which, owing to famine, had considerably decreased in numbers, though he had done his best to maintain it at the expense of the local population; he had, moreover, made constant raids on the Amhara country. But now the condition of the district had become so poor that he had great difficulties in finding sufficient supplies for his men, with whom he was unusually strict, punishing them most rigorously for the most trivial offences; and on this account he was not only unpopular amongst them, but also amongst his *emirs*.

He now received instructions from the *khalifa* to proceed to the Shilluk country; and, marching to Kawa, where he embarked, he went direct to Fashoda. The King of the Shilluks, being under the impression that Zeki's steamers were on their way to Reggaf, was much surprised when the *emir* suddenly landed; the *mek* fled, was pursued, captured, and, having refused to disclose the hiding-place of the money he had received in exchange for the grain, was promptly executed.

The Shilluks, however, who are the finest and bravest of the Sudanese black tribes, collected both north and south of Fashoda, and defended their liberty and their homes with magnificent courage and resolution; but Zeki's men, used to constant fighting, and armed with Remington rifles, were almost invariably victorious. It was not, however, until after many bloody fights, in which the Shilluks, armed only with their lances, frequently broke the squares and inflicted considerable loss on the soldiers, that they had at last to admit they were beaten. They dispersed, with their families, throughout the country, but were pursued in all directions by Zeki, who captured large numbers of them. The men he invariably put to the sword; but the women, young girls, and children were embarked on the steamers, and despatched to Omdurman.

Here the *khalifa* ordered the young boys to be taken charge of by his *mulazemin*, by whom they were to be brought up, whilst most of the girls he kept for himself, or distributed amongst his followers and special adherents. The remainder were sent to the Beit el Mal, where they were publicly sold; but thousands of these poor creatures succumbed to fatigue, want, and the change of climate. Unused to life in this squalid city, these wild blacks were huddled together in wretched quarters, and eventually found homes amongst the poorest class of the population. It was no uncommon occurrence for a girl to be sold as a slave at the rate of from eight to twenty dollars (Omdurman currency).

When Zeki left Gallabat, the Emir Ahmed Wad Ali took his place, and his brother Hamed Wad Ali was nominated Emir of Kassala. Avaricious to a degree, he mercilessly robbed the people of their property and cattle, with the result that the eastern Arab tribes, such as the Hadendoa, Halenga, Beni Amer, etc., who had really captured Kassala for the *Mahdi*, now revolted, and, wandering eastwards in the direction of Massawa, placed themselves under the protection of the Italians. Thus it was that this once thickly populated country became almost denuded of inhabitants. Amongst others, the once powerful Shukria tribe, which had suffered terribly during the famine year, was now almost extinct; whilst the fertile district of Kassala was almost completely deserted, and the garrison there had the greatest difficulty in maintaining itself.

The *khalifa*, alarmed at the progress of the Italians from Massawa, now looked upon Kassala as the mainstay of his authority in these districts. He was furious with his cousin, Hamed Wad Ali, whom he accused of having ruined the country, and recalled him to Omdurman, where he was ordered to attend prayers in the mosque five times daily; and he replaced him at Kassala by Abu Girga, who had hitherto been with Osman Digna.

Osman Digna, who had been made responsible for the government of the Eastern Sudan, had been successful in subjugating most of the Arab tribes; and, through them, he had for several years been a menace to Suakin. He had had several engagements with the government troops; and, on one occasion, Sir Herbert Kitchener, the present *sirdar* of the Egyptian Army, had been severely wounded whilst making an attack on his camp at Handub. Eventually, the government sent an expedition which drove him out of the position he had taken up to besiege Suakin; and he now made his headquarters at Tokar, where he remained for some years, making constant incursions in the vicinity of Suakin, and harrying the friendly tribes of which the Amarar was the principal; but, tired of this constant fighting, and irritated by Osman's undue severity, the local tribes began to desert the cause, and not a few of them became actually hostile to the *khalifa's* authority.

Informed of this state of things Abdullahi, more anxious to defend his newly acquired realm than to occupy himself in propagating the Mahdist doctrine, instructed Osman Digna not to go too far, and sent Mohammed Wad Khaled to him with this message. The latter, after the confiscation of his property at Bara, had been kept for more than a year in chains in Kordofan; he had then been brought to Omdurman, had received the *khalifa's* pardon, and had received back a small portion of his property. For years, he had said his prayers daily in the mosque under the *khalifa's* eye, and had apparently broken off all relations with his relatives, whom he accused of unfairness and ingratitude; but, as usual, his astuteness had not failed him: he was well aware of the *khalifa's* hostility to all the *Mahdi's* relatives, and that was the reason he so studiously avoided all contact with them; hence his nomination as the *khalifa's* personal representative with Osman Digna.

In this mission he was most successful; and, having completed it, he was instructed to proceed to Abu Hamed, and report on the general condition of the Ababda tribes, who were subject to the Egyptian Government, but who were at the same time in close relationship with the Mahdist tribes of the Berber Province. Khaled's mission, however, did not have any lasting effect on Osman Digna; for, a few weeks after his departure, the Egyptian troops, under Holled Smith Pasha, attacked Tokar, and utterly routed Osman, who fled to the Atbara. The *khalifa*, who had been informed by Osman that he was about to be attacked, awaited the result with the greatest anxiety; but he openly declared to his followers that he had not the slightest doubt that victory was insured; when, therefore, the news came of Osman's utter defeat and flight, he was greatly upset. Councils of war were at once held, for it was feared the government troops would advance towards Kassala and Berber, both of which places were only weakly held; consequently, instructions were issued to the commanders of these places that, should the troops advance, they should fall back on Metemmeh, where it was his intention to make a fortified camp.

Great, however, was his relief when he received news that the government had contented itself with the recapture of Tokar. The loss of this district was undoubtedly a very heavy blow to him, and left open to the tribes friendly to the government the roads leading to both Kassala and Berber. A few months later, Osman Digna, who had taken up a position on the high ground south of Berber, with the remnant of his force, suffered greatly from want of food, and was obliged to disperse his men over the country; he therefore received orders to proceed to Berber with his *emirs*, and, having obtained new clothing, he and the newly nominated Emir of Berber, Zeki Osman, were summoned to Omdurman.

Here he was received in a friendly manner by the *khalifa*, who, convinced of his fidelity and trustworthiness, consoled him about his defeat, and, after treating him honourably for a few weeks, sent him back with some horses, camels, and women to the Atbara, where he was instructed to make a camp and agricultural settlement, and collect his scattered forces.

At this time, only Eastern Darfur remained subject to Osman Wad Adam. The country had been almost depopulated by famine, and this *emir* now decided to advance against Dar Tama and Massalit; but, on the frontier, he encountered such severe opposition that he began to think the undertaking too dangerous. He was attacked in his *zariba* by the natives, who, armed only with small spears, forced their way in; and he had to thank his Remington rifles and the *sheikhs* who were with him, for a dearly earned victory; had he been attacked on the line of march, he would almost certainly have been annihilated. His heavy losses considerably delayed his march; and, ere he could obtain reinforcements, a severe epidemic of typhoid fever broke out amongst his men, and he was forced to retire; falling ill himself on the march, he died two days after his arrival at Fasher.

His loss was a great blow to the *khalifa*, who looked on his young cousin (he was barely twenty years of age) as a courageous leader who paid careful attention to the wants of his men, and had done much to increase the strength and number of the Mahdist forces; he invariably sent to the *khalifa* the fair share of the booty, and disinterestedly divided the remainder amongst his people, keeping only for himself what sufficed for his immediate wants. He was a magnificent rider, was most popular with every one, and avoided leading an effeminate and enervating existence, for long after his death he was looked upon as a fine example of a bold and courageous Arab.

He was succeeded in the command of Darfur by another of the *khalifa's* youthful relatives, Mahmud Wad Ahmed, who was a great contrast to his predecessor: he thought only of enriching himself; his sole pleasure consisted in leading a life of debauchery with women of evil repute, dancers, and singers, and he took a special delight in all their unseemly ways. A mutiny soon broke out amongst his men, which was suppressed with the utmost severity, and resulted in a considerable weakening of his forces.

Yunes, who, since his despatch to Dongola, had always been considered Nejumi's superior, now attached to his councils Arabi Wad Dafalla and Mussaid; but, as each one was bent entirely on enriching himself as rapidly as possible, differences soon broke out, for the country was quite unable to sustain the strain of overburdened taxation. Mussaid and Arabi complained to the *khalifa* that Yunes allowed his *emirs* to govern the country entirely according to their own ideas, with the result that prices were continually rising; and, in consequence of this report, he was recalled from Dongola.

This province being adjacent to the Egyptian frontier, large numbers of the inhabitants had emigrated to Egypt; and, as the Egyptian garrison at Wadi Haifa was being constantly reinforced, the *khalifa*, dreading an attack, insisted on a more lenient treatment of the people. He therefore appointed Khaled as Yunes's successor, as he was convinced that his character and capabilities exactly suited him for this post, and instructed him that he should tax the people in accordance with the number of the *sakias* (water-wheels) and date-palms; but not being entirely without suspicion of Khaled's behaviour, he ordered a detachment of his own men, armed with rifles, to be placed under

Arabi Wad Dafalla, whilst the spearmen of his own tribe were made over to Mussaid.

The natural outcome of these arrangements was renewed dissension. Khaled, anxious to increase the revenue of the country without augmenting taxation, began filling up vacant posts with men of his own choice, whilst Arabi and Mussaid did their utmost to nominate their own relatives and friends; failing to arrange matters with Khaled, they now began to make the most exorbitant demands, with which he could not possibly comply, and, from dissensions, they came to insults, and very nearly to blows, the two parties being actually drawn up facing each other with arms in their hands. Khaled's party was composed principally of inhabitants of the Nile valley,—Jaalin and Danagla,—whilst that of Arabi and Mussaid was composed of Jehadia and western Arabs.

Message after message was despatched to the *khalifa* by both sides, whilst actual conflict was prevented by intermediaries and peacefully disposed persons. Abdullahi immediately sent Yunes to take the place of Arabi and Mussaid, who were recalled; and, immediately after they had arrived, he sent instructions to Khaled to appear before him in Omdurman, to be present, he said, at the punishment of Arabi and Mussaid; but no sooner had he reached the capital than he was arraigned in court with his antagonists. The judges consisted of the *khalifa* as President, and a number of *kadis* and devoted *Emirs* as members; Khaled was accused of having spoken disparagingly of his master and relatives, by saying that they had been the cause of the ruin of the country. The *khalifa's* brother Yakub was as usual at the bottom of this intrigue, and there is no doubt the *khalifa* himself regretted having given Khaled so influential a position; he therefore gladly seized this opportunity of getting rid of him.

During the proceedings a letter arrived from Yunes (who had beforehand received Yakub's private instructions) to the effect that whilst the parties were mediating, Khaled had clandestinely concealed six boxes of ammunition, which he intended to send to his relatives in Omdurman. Before the arraignment, the *khalifa* had privately arranged the verdict, and of course no one dared to take the part of the accused; he was found guilty, sentenced to imprisonment for an indefinite period, and was hurried off to the *Saier*, where he was kept in solitary confinement.

Curiously enough, an explanation of the *khalifa's* action appeared in an Arabic newspaper published in Cairo, in which an extract from the Italian paper *La Riforma* had been published to the effect that Khaled had been in communication with the Egyptian Government for the surrender of the province with which he had been entrusted. In consequence of this, the *khalifa* again assembled the judges, showed them the newspaper as a proof of Khaled's treachery; and he was at once condemned to be executed. The *khalifa*, however, declared that he was most anxious not to cause the death of one of the *Mahdi's* relatives and a descendant of the Prophet, he therefore commuted the sentence to imprisonment for life.

His magnanimity on this occasion was of course praised on all sides, whilst he himself rejoiced that he had for ever ridden himself of the only one of the *Mahdi's* relatives of whose knowledge and astuteness he was justly in considerable awe. He now used Khaled's treachery as a handle by which to irritate the Ashraf in general; and lost no opportunity of doing all he could to weaken their cause, and reduce them to a position of impotence, with the result that an insurrection eventually broke out in Omdurman, which ended in the complete success of the plans which Abdullahi had long since prepared.

Chapter 15

Dissension and Discord

The Khalifa Mohammed Sherif, in conjunction with two of the *Mahdi's* sons, who were scarcely twenty years of age, and many of his relatives, now agreed amongst themselves to shake off the hated yoke of Khalifa Abdullahi and seize the reins of government. They secretly elaborated their plans in Omdurman, and gradually took into their confidence several of their friends and fellow-tribesmen. They also despatched letters to the Danagla living in the Gezira, whom they invited to come to Omdurman and join them; but one of the Jaalin *emirs* betrayed them. He had been bound over by an oath to tell only his brother or best friends; and he at once informed the *khalifa*, saying that he considered him his best friend. Apprised of the conspiracy, Abdullahi at once made counter arrangements; but the Ashraf, warned by their spies of the *khalifa's* secret orders and doings, realised that their plot had been discovered, and immediately collected in that part of the town just north of the *khalifa's* house, prepared for the fray.

All the Ashraf and Danagla in Omdurman assembled in the houses in the vicinity of the *Mahdi's* tomb; and the sailors and most of the boats' crews joined them, saying that they were ready to fight and conquer for the sake of the religion which the *khalifa* had abused. The arms which had been secretly hidden were now brought out and distributed. They numbered scarcely a hundred Remington rifles, a small quantity of ammunition, and a few elephant guns. Ahmed Wad Suleiman behaved like one demented. He declared that he had seen the Prophet and the *Mahdi*, who assured him of the victory of his party; and he urged forward the commencement of hostilities.

Even the *Mahdi's* widows, who, after his death, had been kept strictly locked up in their houses by the *khalifa*, were not allowed to see any one, and were given scarcely sufficient food to keep them alive, longed for the conflict, hoping that their position would be ameliorated. Indeed the Um el Muminin (The Mother of the Believers), the *Mahdi's* principal widow, girded a sword round her waist, with the intention of taking a part in this Holy War. Whilst all this was going on at night, and within scarcely a hundred yards of the *khalifa's* house, he himself was quietly taking his precautions.

It was on a Monday evening, after prayers, that the *khalifa* summoned his special *mulazemin*, and, in a few words, informed us of the intentions of the Ashraf. He instructed us to arm ourselves as best we could, and on no account to quit our posts in front of the gate. Ammunition was served out to the black *mulazemin* Jehadia, and they were ordered to take up positions in the streets leading to the houses of the rebels, and cut off any reinforcements which might attempt to join them.

Upwards of a thousand rifles were distributed amongst the Taaisha Arabs, who were posted in the open space between the *Mahdi's* tomb and the *khalifa's* house, and also along the enclosure of the latter. The Black troops, under the command of Ahmed Fedil, took up a position in the middle of the mosque, and there awaited further orders; and here also were posted the infantry spearmen and cavalry under the command of Yakub. Khalifa Ali, whose people were suspected of sympathising with the rebels, was ordered to occupy the northern portion of the city, and cut off all communication in that direction.

When the sun arose, the mutineers were completely surrounded; and they had now to choose between fighting and surrendering. Before, however, any blows were exchanged, the *khalifa* despatched his *kadi*, accompanied by Sayed Mekki, to Khalifa Sherif and the *Mahdi's* sons, reminding them of their late father's proclamation, and of the words he had spoken before his death. At the same time, he instructed the *kadi* to inquire into their grievances, which he promised to rectify, if it was possible for him to do so. The curt answer to the *khalifa* was that they preferred to fight.

Abdullahi had given strict injunctions to all his *emirs* to abstain, as far as possible, from blows, and only to defend themselves in the event of a sudden attack. He was most anxious to quell the insurrection by conciliatory measures, as he fully realised that, if a fight ensued in which there was little doubt he would be victorious, Omdurman would almost certainly be sacked and ruined. He was well aware that the western Arab tribes would gladly seize the occasion to satisfy their ruling passion for murder and plunder; their one desire would be to obtain all the loot they could, and to this end to spare neither friend nor foe, with the result that, in all probability, they would fight amongst themselves, and then go off to their own country, which they had quitted with considerable reluctance. Once more he sent the *kadi* to the insurgents, who returned with a similar reply.

Personally, I longed for the fight, for I had only my life to lose, and that was in daily peril. I had before me the example of Ibrahim Adlan; and I knew that Abdullahi had no regard for the lives of his best and truest friends. Internal fighting must result in the weakening of my enemies, and that alone would have been a source of satisfaction to me; moreover, in the confusion which must arise, I might find an occasion to regain my liberty, and possibly I might be able to exercise some influence over the former government troops, who I knew were much dissatisfied with their present treatment. Under such abnormal circumstances, it was impossible to frame any distinct plan of action. My desire was that a fight should take place, and that I should make as much capital out of it as I could for my own personal benefit.

Some of the most excited of the mutineers now began firing, and some of those on our side, contrary to orders, replied; but it was by no means a fight,—merely a few stray shots. The insurgents did not seem to know what they wanted; their party was undecided, their weapons were bad and out of repair, and so also was the courage of the Ashraf and their followers. After a short time, the firing ceased, and on our side the total loss was five killed. Again the *Khalifa* sent out a proclamation, which was borne this time by Khalifa Ali Wad Helu, and to this summons the reply was more favourable; they wished to know, they said, the conditions of reconciliation; and they were then told to name their proposals.

The negotiations continued all that day and far into the night. They began again the following day, and, to my great regret, a clear understanding was arrived at, and was agreed to by the *khalifa* under a solemn oath: he promised complete forgiveness to all who had taken part in the insurrection, to give to Khalifa Mohammed Sherif a position worthy of his dignity, and a seat in Council, to allow him to again take possession of the standards which, after Nejumi's death, had been laid aside, and to collect volunteers under them, and promised pecuniary support from the Beit el Mal to the *Mahdi's* relatives, in accordance with Sherif's proposals.

In return for these concessions, the insurgents agreed to give up all their arms, and submit unconditionally to the *khalifa's* orders. The agreement was now ratified, and the terms of peace concluded by the delegates on both sides; but somehow no one seemed in any hurry to execute them. On the following Friday morning, the leaders of the insurgents came themselves before the *khalifa*, and obtained a renewal of the promises he had made, in return for which they gave fresh attestations of loyalty; and, on the same afternoon, Khalifa Sherif and the *Mahdi's* sons approached Abdullahi. Peace was now fully concluded, and the cavalry and infantry, which had been with us day and night since the disturbances began, were permitted to leave the mosque and return to their quarters; but, as the arms had not yet been handed over, the *jehadia* and *mulazemin* were ordered to remain at their posts.

On Sunday afternoon, I had sent one of my servants to the Missionary Father, Joseph Ohrwalder, to inquire after him, and he had found his door closed; I had thoughtlessly made inquiries about him of his neighbours, the Greeks and some of the former merchants who, as my servant told me, had made a most careful search for him, but had been unable to trace him or the missionary sisters who had been with him. It at once flashed through my mind that possibly, during the disturbances, he might have found some trusty persons who had undertaken to effect his escape; and so it eventually transpired. Before evening prayer, the Emir of the Muslemania (Europeans who had been forcibly made to adopt Mohammedanism), and the Syrian George Stambuli anxiously came and asked to be taken before the *khalifa*, as they had something of considerable importance to tell him.

The *khalifa*, fully occupied with matters which he considered of great importance, ordered them to wait at the mosque; and, after night prayers, he asked them what they wanted. With trembling voices, they informed him that Yusef el Gasis (Joseph the Priest) was missing since yesterday, also the women who were with him. Very much annoyed, the *khalifa* at once summoned Nur el Gereifawi, the Emin Beit el Mal, and Mohammed Wahbi, the Prefect of the Police, and commanded them to do all in their power to overtake the fugitives and bring them back to Omdurman, dead or alive. It was fortunate for the poor Greeks that the *khalifa* was so much occupied with other matters or he would—as Ohrwalder had lived amongst them—have arrested many and confiscated their property.

Luckily, however, on the day of the outbreak, all the camels had been sent into the districts in order to bring in the troops; and Gereifawi and Wahbi could only procure three camels for the pursuit of Ohrwalder, who knew that the success of his flight depended on its rapidity. From the depth of my heart I hoped he might succeed. He had suffered a great deal, and had borne it with Christian fortitude and patience. I now felt completely deserted; he was the only man with whom I was intellectually on a par, and with whom I could—though very rarely—talk a few words in my mother tongue.

The following day, I was summoned before the *khalifa*, who angrily reproached me for Ohrwalder's flight. "He is one of your own race, and is in communication with you; why did you not draw my attention to its possibility, so that I might have taken precautions? I am positive you knew of his intention to escape," said he.

"Sire, pardon me!" said I; "how could I know of his intention to escape, and how could I tell you that he had done so? Since the outbreak of the revolt attempted by your God-forsaken enemies, and which, thanks to the Almighty, you have now defeated by your wisdom, I have not moved day or night from my post. Had I known that he was a traitor, I should have at once told you of it."

To this he angrily replied, "No doubt your consul arranged for him to be taken away from here."

Amongst the last letters which I had received, was one written in Arabic from the Austro-Hungarian Consul-General, Von Rosty, to the *khalifa*, in which he thanked him for the kind treatment of the members of the former Catholic Mission, and, at the same time, asked his permission to send them a messenger, for whom he begged a free pass, as they were under Austrian protection, and as His Majesty the Emperor had a special regard for them. The *khalifa* had shown me the letter, which he had left unanswered; but from that day he had looked upon the members of the mission as my compatriots, and was now convinced that they had been assisted to escape by the aid of the consul-general. I now remarked to the khalifa that possibly merchants belonging to the frontier tribes, and who often came to Omdurman, might have taken advantage of the disturbances in order to help Ohrwalder and the sisters to escape, so as to obtain some pecuniary reward for themselves. Abdullahi, who was still much pre-occupied with the revolt, came round to my opinion; and, after admonishing me to remain perfectly loyal, he dismissed me.

In spite of the reluctance of the Ashraf to surrender their arms, they were gradually obliged to give them all up; and, having achieved this much, the *khalifa* now set to work to mature his scheme of revenge. Twenty days perhaps had passed since the beginning of the outbreak, but we were still kept in constant readiness, watching day and night over our master. He now summoned the two *khalifas*, the *kadis*, and the chiefs of the Ashraf and Danagla to a meeting. He reproached the latter severely, saying, that in spite of his previous pardon, they had shown great reluctance in obeying his orders, they seldom attended prayers, and were scarcely ever present at the Friday morning parades; he also had the *Mahdi's* proclamation read out to them. Then, true to the system adopted by his predecessor, of acting entirely in accordance with prophetic inspiration, he announced to the meeting that the Prophet had appeared to him, and had commanded him to mete out punishment to the disobedient, whom he had mentioned by name. Thirteen persons in all were included in this category: Ahmed Wad Suleiman, whom he detested, headed the list; then followed Shenudi, one of the *khalifa's* secretaries, a Dongolawi who was under suspicion of sympathising with the rebels and giving them information of the *khalifa's* plans.

One by one, as each name was called, the unfortunate wretches had their hands tied behind their backs, were carried off to the prison, and thrown into chains; a few days later, the *khalifa* sent them by boat, under a strong escort, to Fashoda, where Zeki Tummal had them closely confined for eight days in a *zariba* with scarcely any food or water, them only just sufficient to keep them alive; then, in accordance with the secret instructions he had received, he had them beaten to death with freshly cut sticks from thorny trees. The execution took place in front of the whole army, and, before this cruel operation began, their clothing was ruthlessly torn from their emaciated bodies.

Immediately the insurrection was over, the *khalifa* despatched two of his relatives, Ibrahim Wad Melek and Saleh Hamedo,—the former to the Blue and the latter to the White Nile,—to arrest all the followers and relatives of the Ashraf, who, being absent, were not included in the general amnesty. In compliance with these orders, upwards of a thousand men were sent in *shebas* to Omdurman, where they were accused by the *khalifa* of having taken part in the conspiracy. For many days, they were kept in close confinement, huddled together in the prison-yard, and in hourly dread of execution; but at length the *khalifa* pardoned them, on condition that they should share all they possessed with him; and of course the poor wretches had to agree to these conditions.

Orders were issued to carry out the distribution in accordance with the curious arithmetical rules instituted by the *khalifa*, who, of course, received the lion's share; on their return to their villages, they found themselves divested of almost everything they possessed. Those who had been well off were left with a mere pittance; and the poorer members had nothing, whilst they found their daughters had been dishonoured, and their wives abused. Deprived of all their arms, they had to submit to the inevitable; but in their hearts they longed for some opportunity of revenge.

The *khalifa*, after having taken all he required of their property for himself and his brother, distributed the remainder amongst the western Arabs, and of these, the Jubarat section, to which he belonged, was given the largest share. This roused the discontent of the other tribes, to whom the Taaisha had for some considerable time been a constant source of annoyance; not only were they given the preference in almost every case; but they were overbearingly insolent, and whenever complaints were made to the *khalifa* or Yakub, the petitioners were invariably sharply rebuked. During all these disturbances, the natives in the provinces and the various garrisons had remained quiet; and their commanders had received secret instructions to gradually disarm the Danagla, of whose disloyalty there was no longer any doubt.

Abdullahi now turned his attention to the *Mahdi's* two uncles, Mohammed Abdel Kerim and Abdel Kader Wad Sati Ali. He affirmed he had received information that they were indignant about his actions, and had been guilty of instigating others against him; they utterly denied the charge, but were sentenced by Kadi Ali to imprisonment. The *khalifa* ordered them to be put in chains, and sent on to Zeki Tummal, who, as usual, was provided with secret instructions.

Zeki's forces had dispersed all the Shilluk gatherings throughout the country, and destroyed their villages; but, an epidemic of typhus having broken out amongst the men, the *khalifa* ordered him to quit Fashoda and come with his entire army to Omdurman, but, before doing so, to raid the Dinka tribe, who had already made their submission without fighting, seize their cattle and enslave their wives and children. These unsuspecting Blacks were summoned together under the pretext of a great feast; and, when all had assembled, they were massacred almost to a man, and their wives, children, and cattle carried off.

Whilst on this expedition he met, near Gebel Ahmed Agha, the boat conveying the *Mahdi's* uncles; and, having perused the letters from Omdurman, he ordered the prisoners to be landed after sunset. The wretched captives, knowing the fate that was in store for them, besought pardon, but were only jeered at by Zeki Tummal; they were taken inland, and their heads were split open with the small axes which are used in the Sudan for lopping off branches of trees.

Zeki Tummal now returned to Omdurman laden with booty; he brought with him thousands of female slaves, and immense herds of cattle, the sale of which brought in a large sum of ready money. Most of Zeki's *emirs* indignantly complained of his tyranny, and even asserted to the *khalifa* that, if he could obtain sufficient followers, he would not hesitate to make himself independent; but the latter, by making rich presents of female slaves, money, and cattle to the *khalifa* and his brother, succeeded in remaining in their good graces.

Whilst Zeki Tummal was in Omdurman, the *khalifa* carried out a series of manoeuvres between his forces and those quartered in Omdurman, and personally took the command; but as he had absolutely no idea of military science, and as the thirty thousand troops of whom he disposed were entirely without discipline, the manoeuvres resulted in the most hopeless confusion and disorder; and the blame for this invariably fell on my devoted head, for the *khalifa* employed me as a sort of *aide-de-camp*, and when he became inextricably muddled up he hurled abuse at me, and said I had purposely perverted his orders to make mischief. Of course I did not dare remonstrate with him, and quietly continued to carry out his orders. At length he declared the exercises over, ordered Zeki Tummal off to Gallabat, and, as was usually the case, commended me for my services, and presented me with two black young ladies as a proof of his good-will.

Meanwhile, Khalifa Sherif had heard of the murder of his two relatives, and openly protested against this tyrannical proceeding; thus giving Abdullahi an opportunity of taking the revenge for which he had so patiently waited. He declared him to be guilty of disobedience to the instructions which the *Mahdi* had so strictly enforced, and of inattention to the Divine inspiration of the Prophet. He therefore ordered Khalifa Ali and the *kadis* to take him to task for the manner in which he had expressed himself, and to point out to him that the entirely false impression he had of his own rights as *khalifa* had brought about the death of his own relatives and followers.

Promptly assembling all the *kadis* and principal *emirs*, they decided that Khalifa Sherif should be immediately arrested; on the following day, the *mulazemin* being formed up in square on the open space between Abdullahi's house and the *Mahdi's* tomb, they went in a body to him, informed him that he was to be arrested, counselled submission, and advised him to come with them of his own free-will. Too late, he now realised what he had brought upon himself by his careless and ill-considered talking. Going outside, he was received by the *mulazemin* under the command of Arabi Dafalla; when he asked for his shoes, they were refused him; and, on coming out of the mosque, he was driven and pushed along at such a rate that he twice fell to the ground from pure exhaustion, arriving at length at the *Saier* in a deplorable condition. Here six irons were hammered on to his legs, so that he could scarcely move; and a small straw hut was allotted to him as his abode.

Cut off from all intercourse with his fellow-creatures, and with only the bare ground to lie upon, he had ample time to realise that the sacred promises given by a *khalifa* were of no avail when it was a question of upholding his authority, or satisfying his thirst for vengeance. The *Mahdi's* two young sons were sent to their grandfather, Ahmed Sharfi, who was ordered to keep them closely locked up in his house, and allow no one to see them. This Ahmed was an old man, and had made an immense fortune by robbery; fearing to lose it, he was as submissive as a slave to the *khalifa*, and had thus to some extent gained his affection.

Soon after this occurrence, I passed through a period of considerable excitement. Yunes had sent on a man from Dongola to the *khalifa*; he had come from Cairo, and was charged with important information from the government. He was received personally by the *khalifa* in the presence of all the *kadis*. I had a foreboding that the man's arrival was somehow connected with me, and I endeavoured to discover from one of the *kadis*, who was a friend of mine, what had happened; he hurriedly told me that I had nothing to fear, and advised me not to show the slightest interest in the matter, lest I might be suspected. After prayers, the *kadis* and the messenger were again summoned before the *khalifa*, and, to my great relief, I saw the man soon afterwards tied hand and foot and carried off to prison.

My comrades were quarrelling amongst themselves as to the cause of the man's imprisonment; but, mindful of the advice I had received, I was careful to abstain from any interference. The following day, when I had gone to my house for a short time, I was suddenly summoned by the *khalifa*, and found several of the *kadis* with him. In compliance with his orders, I seated myself down with them, and he began to speak.

Turning to the assembly, he informed them that he had continually urged me to be loyal, that he cared for me as a father cared for his son, and that he had steadily refused to believe the numerous accusations which were, from time to time, brought up against me; and then, turning to me, he completed his speech with the Arabic proverb, "*Where there is no fire, there is no smoke,*" adding, "but with you there is a great deal of smoke. The messenger said yesterday that you are a government spy, and that your monthly salary is paid to your representative in Cairo, who forwards it to you here. He affirms that he has seen your signature in the government office in Egypt, and that you assisted Yusef el Gasis to escape; he adds, moreover, that you are pledged to the English, in the event of an attack on Omdurman, to seize the powder and ammunition stores, which they know are situated opposite to your house. We have at once had the man imprisoned, for he formerly escaped from here; what have you to say in your defence?"

"Sire!" I replied, "God is merciful, and you are just. I am no spy: I have never had any communication with the government; and it is absolutely untrue that I receive a salary which is forwarded to me here. My brothers, your *mulazemin,* who go in and out of my house, know that I am often in the greatest want, and it is only my deep respect for you which prevents me from complaining; but if he states that he has seen my signature, then he is guilty of a second lie, for I am certain that he is quite unable to read any European language. I will, if you wish, write on a paper several names, and amongst them my own; if he can discover it, then it will be a proof that he can read our language; but that will not necessarily prove that I am a spy."

"And what else have you against the man?" asked the *khalifa.*

"What service has the man rendered to government," I continued; "that, supposing I am a spy, I should trust this fugitive with my secrets. As far as Yusef el Gasis is concerned, you, my master, well know that he escaped at a time when it was absolutely impossible for me to have any communication with him. I, who am always near you, have no intercourse with people who assist others to fly; and even supposing I had, and that I were a traitor, it would certainly be much more natural that I should have escaped myself. It is quite possible the English may know that my house is opposite to the powder magazine; for the man who, with your kind permission, brought me the letters from my brothers and sisters knew it, and, in all probability, told them about it.

"It is also possible that my relatives with whom, at your express command, I have ceased to have any communication, should make inquiries about my welfare through the government clerks and merchants who sometimes go from here to Cairo, and who probably know the position of my house; but the assertion that, in case of war, I had engaged myself to seize your ammunition stores, is quite ridiculous. As far as I can judge, the government would never dare to attack you, who are the ever victorious and unconquerable *khalifa*, in your own country; and if this well-nigh impossible event should take place, how do I know that I shall be in my present house at that time? Moreover, at such a critical period, my hope and desire is to stand in the front rank of your victorious troops, and there seek an opportunity of proving my loyalty and devotion by shedding my blood in your cause. Sire, I rely upon your justice, which is well known to all; will you sacrifice one who has been for so many years your devoted servant, to the whim of a Dongolawi who is one of your enemies?"

"How do you know that the man who has given evidence against you is a Dongolawi?" asked the *khalifa*, quickly. "Some time ago I saw the man at your gate with Abderrahman Wad en Nejumi esh Shahid ("the martyr," as he was called after his death),[1] and owing to his forwardness and impudence I had to call on your *mulazemin* to remove him by main force; no doubt he now wishes to revenge himself, and at the same time curry favour with you, by casting suspicion on me. You to whom God has given wisdom to govern your subjects, will also judge me righteously and fairly."

"I have summoned you here," said the *khalifa*, after a long pause, "not to judge you, but to show you that, in spite of the frequent attempts to cast suspicion on you, I have in no way withdrawn my confidence in you. Had I believed what the man said, I should not have imprisoned him; no doubt you have enemies here, and there are probably envious people who are jealous of your being near me. But beware! *where there is no fire, there is no smoke.*" He then signed to me to withdraw, and soon afterwards the assembly broke up.

That night I asked one of my comrades whom I knew I could trust, to tell me what the *khalifa* had said after I had left. He told me that Abdullahi admitted the man was a liar, but that there might be some truth in his statement; he had also said I might possibly have enemies in Cairo who were intriguing against me. This had also occurred to me whilst I was speaking, but I did not mention it, as I hesitated to throw down all my cards; now that he had thought of it himself, my silence had stood me in good stead, for I could bring forward this argument in my defence, should some fresh accusation be

---

1. By mere chance I had heard that the man's name was Taib Wad Haj Ali, and that he had once been in Omdurman with Nejumi.

brought against me.

But how long was I to continue in this wretched position? How long was I to keep up this constant strain of always standing on the defensive; how much longer could my present relations with the *khalifa* last? I knew he was only waiting for an opportunity to make me harmless, for he was perfectly well aware that I was at heart his enemy; but in truth I thanked God most fervently that he treated me with greater leniency than he did the rest. How difficult it was to carry out Madibbo's advice; but how true it was that he who lives long sees much!

The following morning, after prayers, as I was on my way home, I was overtaken by Gereifawi, who had succeeded Adlan and was on friendly terms with me. "You are a rare visitor," said I, shaking hands with him; "please God you have good reasons for it!"

"Yes," said he; "but I am come to disturb you. I require your house; and I must ask you to leave it today. I will give you one in place of it which lies to the southeast of the mosque, and in which the *khalifa's* guests are usually housed; it is somewhat smaller than your own, but you have only the road between it and the mosque, and this will thoroughly suit a pious man like you!"

"All right," said I; "but tell me privately who sent you here, the *khalifa* or Yakub?"

"Ah, that is a secret!" said he, laughing; "but after your conversation yesterday with the *khalifa*, you can surely understand the reason; probably," he continued ironically, "our master, out of his great love for you, wishes to have you in close proximity to himself; your house is scarcely two hundred paces from his own. When may I come and take over your old house?"

"I shall have finished moving by the evening," said I; "it will take me some little time to remove the fodder for my horse and mule. Is the house I am to have uninhabited?"

"Of course it is. I have given orders for it to be cleaned, and will now return to make the necessary arrangements; but you had better begin moving at once, and I hope your new house will bring better luck than your old one," said Gereifawi, leaving me.

Undoubtedly this was a very clear case of want of confidence in me on the *khalifa's* part. He was anxious to remove me from the neighbourhood of the ammunition stores and powder magazine, which, in case of war, I was supposed to seize. I now called together my household, and told them to begin moving at once. They cursed the *khalifa* freely, and called down all the punishments of Heaven on his head. Little by little, year by year, they had gone on building. They had dug wells fifty feet deep, had planted lemon and pomegranate trees, which were just about to bear fruit, and had, so to speak, made themselves comfortable. For me, the move was quite immaterial. How I had prayed to leave this house, though not in this way! However, as Gereifawi had said, perhaps the new house would bring me better luck; and I was by no means the only man who had been turned out of his abode at short notice.

The whole portion of the city lying north of the *khalifa's* house had been vacated at a moment's notice by the Ashraf and their relatives; and they had not even been allowed to remove their furniture, nor had they received the smallest compensation. They had been given a patch of stony ground to the west of the town, where they had been ordered to build fresh houses. After all, I was better off than they. Recent events had depressed me considerably, and I saw that the situation was now becoming almost unbearable; but more trouble was in store for me which was to throw completely into the background that of which I now complained.

One of my acquaintances, a Darfur merchant who had frequently travelled backwards and forwards to Egypt, Alexandria, and Syria, and who had gradually understood the various nationalities, realised that I was an Austrian. He had surmised correctly that, although a captive for many years, and shut off from all communication with my own people, I still took an intense interest in all that concerned my native land. He spoke to me in the mosque, told me hurriedly about affairs in Egypt, and then handed me an Egyptian newspaper of old date which, he said, had accidentally come into his hands in Alexandria, and which contained an article about Austrian affairs.

Hurrying home, I opened the paper, and found, to my dismay, the news of the death of our Crown Prince Rudolf. I cannot describe the distress which this news caused me. I had served in his regiment; and I had never given up hope that someday I should return home, and have the pleasure of assuring him that, under all the strange and sad circumstances of my eventful life, I had always endeavoured to uphold the honour of an officer belonging to the Imperial regiment. But what were the trials and troubles of one obscure individual in comparison with this great national calamity,—nothing!

Again and again my mind turned to the grief of our beloved emperor, to whom we Austrians look up as to a father. What must he have felt and suffered!

Here in the midst of this unsympathetic crowd my mind was filled with these sad thoughts; but I did not dare show that I was affected. It required all my self-control to hide from the rude gaze of the Mahdists the expressions of distress which came over my face when I thought of my beloved home; and, in the internal struggle which was going on almost continuously, I sometimes longed for the time when an end should be put to my wretched existence. Today all the old sores had broken out afresh. The man would have done me a far greater service had he kept back the newspaper. It had only brought fresh trouble upon me, and depressed me more than ever.

My comrades at the *khalifa's* door—ignorant of the real cause of my sorrow—advised me to appear as cheerful as possible, and to show no displeasure about my enforced removal to another house, as the *khalifa* was sure to have instructed his spies to watch me carefully, and see how I took his unwelcome order. I therefore tried to look as unconcerned as possible, and, to account for my depression, I pretended to be unwell,—what a life of dissimulation! Fortunately the *khalifa* was busied with other matters. A letter had reached him from Ahmed Wad Ali at Gallabat, complaining of the treatment he received at the hands of his superior, Zeki Tummal; and, a few days afterwards, he arrived, in order to make his complaint personally. He said that in his own name, and in the name of all the other *emirs*, he refused to put up with the continual insults and arbitrary confiscation of property on the part of Zeki, whom he also accused of conspiring to make himself independent.

The *khalifa* knew perfectly well that most of these complaints arose from Zeki's unpopularity with his assistants. He therefore wrote to him to at once refund all the confiscated property, and to accord to his *emirs* the treatment to which their position entitled them. At the same time, he instructed Ahmed Wad Ali to return forthwith to Gallabat, and gave him secret orders to watch closely his chief's movements, and personally report to him.

Abu Girga, who by this time had been recalled from Kassala, and had been replaced there by Mussaid, being a Dongolawi, was considered by the khalifa to be a source of danger in Omdurman. Under the pretext, therefore, of sending reinforcements to Reggaf, he despatched him with two steamers up the White Nile, and, at the same time, Omar Saleh was recalled to give a report of affairs in Equatoria. Abu Girga was nominated *emir* of the whole country, and commander of all the rifle and spear men; but, at the same time, Mukhtar Wad Abaker, one of the khalifa's relatives, was appointed to superintend him.

A few days after the steamers had left, the *khalifa* fell seriously ill with an attack of typhus fever. All Omdurman watched the course of the illness with the most intense anxiety, for his death would have been the signal for a complete change in the administration of the country. Khalifa Ali Wad Helu, who, according to Mahdist law, should be the successor, watched the illness with almost breathless interest; and his followers and tribe showed such deep concern that they fell under the suspicion of wishing to seize the reins of government. The *khalifa's* powerful constitution, however, got the better of the malady; and it seemed as if the wretched inhabitants of the Sudan had not been sufficiently punished, and that God did not yet intend to remove from them this terrible scourge.

After an illness of about three weeks, Abdullahi took the first possible opportunity of appearing before his followers, who greeted him with frantic acclamations,—the outcome, in the majority of cases, of a desire merely to make a noise. Only his own relatives and some of the western Arabs really rejoiced at his recovery. But the *khalifa* had no delusions about the imaginary sentiment to which his followers had given vent during his illness. He knew perfectly well that in showing the preference to his own tribe, he had given umbrage to many of the western Arabs, who, being strangers in the land, it was most necessary to retain on his side.

The inhabitants of the Nile valley and of the Gezira, the majority of whom were Jaalin and Danagla, were his enemies; but, disarmed, and their property confiscated, he had made them powerless, and every now and then he sent considerable detachments of them to reinforce Darfur, Gallabat, and Reggaf. He did not hide from himself that Khalifa Ali and his followers were anxious to step into his shoes; but he knew that they would never be foolish enough to attempt to carry out their plans by main force, as the Ashraf had done.

Now that I had my abode close to him, he was more suspicious than ever of me. He continually inquired of my comrades if this strict supervision did not make me indignant, and he did all he could to find fault with my conduct; but, fortunately, the *mulazemin* were on friendly terms with me, and always reported favourably of me. At the same time, they secretly warned me that the *khalifa's* dislike of me was increasing, and that I must be most careful.

One day, in the month of December, 1892, when I had just left the *khalifa's* door to take a short rest, one of the *mulazemin* summoned me to the *khalifa's* presence. I found him in the reception room, surrounded by his *kadis*, and the threats and reprimands which I had received on the occasion of Taib Haj Ali's calumny were still fresh in my mind. I was therefore considerably dismayed when the *khalifa*, without returning my salute, ordered me to take my seat amongst the judges. "Take this thing," said he, after a short pause, and in a very severe tone, "and see what it contains." I at once arose and took in both hands the object he gave me, and then sat down again. It consisted of a brass ring of about four centimetres in diameter, attached to which was a small metal case about the size and shape of a revolver cartridge.

An attempt had been made to open it, and I could plainly see that it contained a paper. This was indeed an anxious moment for me. Could it be a letter from my relations, or from the Egyptian Government; and had the messenger who brought it been captured? Whilst I was engaged in opening the case with the knife which had been given me, I turned over in my mind how I should act, and what I should say; and, as good luck would have it, I had not on this occasion to have recourse to dissimulation. Pulling out two small papers, and opening them, I found inscribed on them, in minute but legible handwriting, in German, French, English, and Russian languages the following:—

> This crane has been bred and brought up on my estate at Ascania Nova, in the Province of Tauride, in South Russia. Whoever catches or kills this bird is requested to communicate with me, and inform me where it occurred.
>
> (Signed) F. R. Falz-Fein.
> September, 1892.

I now raised my head, which hitherto I had kept closely bent down; and the *khalifa* asked, "Well, what do the papers contain?"

"Sire," I replied, "this case must have been fastened to the neck of a bird which has been killed. Its owner, who lives in Europe, has requested that anyone who finds the bird should let him know where it was caught or killed."

"You have spoken the truth," said the *khalifa*, in a somewhat more amiable tone; "the bird was killed by a Shaigi near Dongola, and the cartridge case was found attached to its neck. He took it to the Emir Yunes, whose secretary was unable to decipher the writing of the Christian, and he therefore forwarded it to me. Tell me now what is written on the paper?"

I translated the message, word for word, and, at the *khalifa's* command also tried to describe the geographical position of the country from which the bird had come, and the distance it had travelled before it was killed. "This is one of the many devilries of those unbelievers," he said, at last, "who waste their time in such useless nonsense. A Mohammedan would never have attempted to do such a thing."

He then ordered me to hand over the case to his secretary, and signed to me to withdraw; but I managed to take one more hurried glance at the paper,—Ascania Nova, Tauride, South Russia, I repeated over and over again to imprint it on my memory. The *mulazemin* at the door anxiously awaited my return; and when I came out from the presence of my tyrannical master with a placid countenance, they seemed greatly pleased. On my way to my house, I continued to repeat to myself the name of the writer and his residence, and determined, that should Providence ever grant me my freedom, I should not fail to let him know what had happened to his bird.

In accordance with orders, Mahmud Ahmed now returned to Omdurman with all his available troops (about five thousand) from Darfur, leaving there only sufficient men for the garrison. He pitched his camp at Dem Yunes on the south side of the city.

Once more I underwent a period of considerable trial. The *khalifa* again instituted a series of military manoeuvres for all the troops in Omdurman; and, as usual, they resulted in the wildest confusion. I had to perform the duties of *aide-de-camp,* and invariably had to bear the blame for everything that went wrong; but all things come to an end, and at last Mahmud Ahmed was ordered back to Gallabat, after his troops had renewed their oath of allegiance, in return for which they received some new *jibbas.*

The *khalifa* now turned his attention to the Equatorial regions, where Abu Girga resided as nominal governor, and despatched two steamers with three hundred men, under the command of his relative Arabi Dafalla, to Reggaf with instructions to depose Abu Girga, and throw him into chains. It was abundantly clear that the latter had only been sent to Reggaf to get him out of the way. Dafalla's departure was also taken advantage of to exile Khaled, who had been lying heavily chained in the Saier.

Dafalla was instructed to extend the Mahdist territory as far as possible in all directions, and to send back to Omdurman as many slaves and as much ivory as he could obtain. Whilst the expedition was being got ready, the *khalifa,* under the pretext of giving Zeki Tummal special verbal instructions regarding an intended campaign against the Italians, recalled him to Omdurman. Ahmed Wad Ali had faithfully carried out his secret instructions, which had resulted in the recall of his chief. A few days after the steamers had left, Zeki arrived at Omdurman accompanied by some of the *emirs* whom he looked upon as friendly.

During his absence, he had nominated Ahmed Wad Ali as his representative, and had ordered him to await his return at Gedaref. The *khalifa*, to all outward appearance, received Zeki in the most friendly manner possible; and, a few days after his arrival, in spite of their orders, Ahmed Wad Ali and the other *emirs* arrived at Omdurman, and were frequently received in secret audience by Abdullahi. They brought proofs of Zeki's duplicity and disobedience to the *khalifa's* commands in not restoring the property which he had confiscated; and they showed how he had subverted his instructions by inducing his men to become participators in a conspiracy by which he should become independent. The *khalifa* and his brother Yakub took counsel together, and agreed to make him harmless once and for all. They thought that if they merely removed him from his position, dissensions might arise amongst his men.

On the following morning, therefore, the unsuspecting Zeki, relying on the former services he had rendered, and anticipating merely a reprimand, was enticed into Yakub's house, where he was immediately seized from behind by four men, his sword wrenched from him, and his hands tied behind his back. He had frequently spoken disrespectfully of Yakub and Kadi Ahmed, saying that, in comparison with a brave warrior like himself, they were little better than women, and were only happy in receiving presents and leading comfortable and voluptuous lives. Disarmed and bound, he was now brought, a miserable captive, before his master, who awaited him in an adjoining court.

"Well, my fine hero, where is your courage now?" said Yakub. "You owed your promotion to me," said Kadi Ahmed, who, when Zeki had been nominated to the supreme command, had conveyed the news to him in Gallabat; "and now you have to thank me for your present humiliation. Praise be to God, who has preserved me to this day in order that I may see you standing thus before me."

Livid with rage, and grinding his teeth, Zeki answered, "I have been surprised and betrayed. Were I in an open field, not a hundred men like you would terrify me. I know I am lost; but after my death you will try to find men like me to take my place, and you will not find them." At a signal from Yakub, he was hurried off to the general prison, where his body was covered with as much weight of iron as it could possibly bear. He was then removed to a small detached stone hut, deprived of all communication with others, and not even allowed sufficient bread and water to sustain life, and consequently, after an imprisonment of twenty days, he succumbed to hunger and thirst.

On his arrest, his house was sequestrated, and in it were found fifty thousand *Maria Theresa* and *Medjidi* dollars, and quantities of gold rings and other jewellery looted from the Abyssinians. Some of the Black soldiers who were devoted to him, and had accompanied him from Gallabat, were also thrown into chains and died of starvation.

Ahmed Wad Ali now succeeded Zeki in the supreme command, and at once returned to Gedaref, whither, in the meantime, the entire army had moved from Gallabat. In accordance with the *khalifa's* instructions, he confiscated the whole of his predecessor's property, consisting of horses, camels, cattle, and slaves, which he despatched, together with all his wives (numbering one hundred and sixty-four), and twenty-seven children, to Omdurman. The *khalifa* kept the cattle and slaves for himself, and distributed the childless widows amongst his followers; but he married the mothers to his slaves, so that the children, whose father had been a slave, should be brought up as slaves. Seven of Zeki's brothers and near relatives were cruelly murdered by Ahmed Wad Ali; and one of his sisters was flogged to death on the pretext that she had concealed money.

Wad Ali, now in supreme command, was anxious to refute any idea of timidity, and sought to gain military renown. He obtained the *khalifa's* permission to undertake operations against the Arab tribes living between Kassala and the Red Sea, who were subject to the Italians; but he received distinct orders not to attack any troops quartered in forts. He was allowed to utilise the services of the Kassala garrison under Mussaid Gaidum, and now made all preparations for a campaign. Leaving Gedaref with his army, early in November, 1893, he joined the Kassala troops, and his force numbered in all some four thousand five hundred riflemen, four thousand spearmen, and two hundred and fifty horsemen, and advanced against the eastern Arab tribes,—the Beni Amer, Hadendoa, and others.

The latter, apprised of his intention, drove off their cattle and retired before him; but at Agordat he came up with the Italian troops, who were in an entrenched position. As they were in such small numbers, he resolved, in spite of the *khalifa's* instructions, to attack them; but he was heavily defeated, and himself killed, together with his two principal leaders, Abdalla Wad Ibrahim and Abder Rasul, and a number of *emirs*. The loss in killed and missing was estimated at about two thousand, and these belonged, almost without exception, to the Gedaref force, because Mussaid and the Kassala troops did not come to Ahmed Wad Ali's assistance. Had the Italian troops been in a position to pursue the Mahdists, who were retreating in wild disorder on Kassala, there is little doubt the latter would have been almost entirely annihilated.

The news of the defeat and death of Ahmed Wad Ali caused the greatest consternation in Omdurman, though in public the *khalifa* tried to appear unconcerned. He affirmed that the losses sustained by the Italians were infinitely greater than those suffered by his troops, and that he thanked God, Ahmed Wad Ali and some of his leaders had died the death of martyrs on the field of battle, fighting against the cursed Christians. In reality, however, he spent many sleepless nights; for he feared that the Italians, encouraged by their victory, would be induced to advance on Kassala, and he fully realised that, in view of the panic which prevailed, they would have no difficulty in seizing and occupying it.

It was not till some days had elapsed, and he had received news that the enemy had not quitted its position, that he calmed down somewhat, and began to consider whom he should nominate as Wad Ali's successor. The army of the latter had been dispersed throughout the Gedaref districts; and it was necessary to despatch reinforcements without delay. The inhabitants of Omdurman, however, saw in the defeat of Wad Ali, Heaven's just retribution for the death of Zeki Tummal, who, though he had been guilty of cruelty and oppression, had been the victim of intrigue and false evidence. They were justly enraged against the *khalifa*, who in his vengeance had not been satisfied with Zeki Tummal's murder, but had also massacred his relatives and seized his women and children.

The *khalifa* now nominated his cousin Ahmed Fedil as commander of the Gedaref army, and gave him strict injunctions to remain entirely on the defensive. He proceeded to his post by way of Kassala, in order to collect the scattered troops, who, after the defeat at Agordat, had forced themselves on the villagers, and were harrying the country for food. Once again the *khalifa's* equanimity was upset by a rumour that the Italians now intended advancing on Kassala; but this news was followed soon afterwards by a contradiction, and he became pacified. Indeed, he had publicly announced his intention of avenging Ahmed Wad Ali's defeat, though in reality he had not the slightest idea of doing so; but, in his ignorance, he believed that these false threats would prevent his enemies from assuming the offensive. He also sent small detachments of horse and spear men to Gedaref.

A few months had elapsed since this catastrophe, when one day, just after morning prayers, three men presented themselves at the door of the *khalifa's* house, and urgently demanded to be taken before him. I at once recognised them as Baggara *emirs*, who had been stationed at Kassala, and from the expression of their faces I could see that the news they brought would not be welcome to the *khalifa*. In a few minutes, they were admitted, and soon afterwards a considerable disturbance took place round the *khalifa's* door. Khalifa Ali Wad Helu, Yakub, as well as all the *kadis*, received a sudden summons to attend at a council. The *khalifa's* suspicions had been verified, and Kassala, after a short fight, had been captured by the Italians.

It was impossible to withhold this news from the public. The *ombeija* was sounded, the great war-drums were beaten, the horses were saddled, and the *khalifa*, accompanied by all his *mulazemin* and an immense number of horse and spear men, solemnly rode down to the banks of the Nile. Arrived here, he forced his horse into the river till the water reached its knees; and, drawing out his sword, and pointing towards the east, he shouted out in a loud voice, "*Allahu akbar! Allahu akbar!*" (God is most great!). Each time the cry was taken up by the immense crowd; but the majority were inwardly rejoicing at the *khalifa's* discomfiture. They longed for him to receive fresh humiliation, thinking thereby to lighten the terrible yoke they bore.

After this display, the *khalifa* turned his horse about, came back to the river bank, dismounted, and sat down on his sheepskin. A great crowd now collected round him; and he informed them of the fall of Kassala, declaring that his followers had been taken unawares by enormous numbers of the enemy, just after morning prayers, and had been forced to retire. He stated, however, that all the war material, women, and children had been saved, that the losses had been insignificant, whilst the enemy had suffered so heavily that they now bitterly regretted having taken the town. Even his most devoted adherents well knew that these words were a mere pretext for covering a disgraceful defeat.

Almost immediately after the three *emirs* had arrived in Omdur-

THE KHALIFA INCITING HIS TROOPS TO ATTACK KASSALA.

man, it was known far and wide that the garrison had been surprised, that partly from fear, and partly owing to the unpopularity of Mussaid, they had refused to fight; and, almost without offering any resistance, they had retired towards Goz Regeb. The *khalifa* now realised that his capital was more fully exposed than ever to a successful advance on the part of his enemies; but he had not yet learnt all; and when it eventually came to his ears that his faithful followers, instead of gladly laying down their lives for the cause, had lost the fanatical spirit which had for so many years made them the terror of their enemies, he understood that not only in Kassala had public opinion changed, but that throughout the whole country his popularity had waned.

He now took occasion to announce publicly that Kassala was merely a minor position of no special importance; but that in a short time he meant to retake it, as well as the entire country up to the shores of the Red Sea. He returned home late that evening, and held a council with his brother Yakub and the *kadis*, regarding the precautions which should now be taken. He must have bitterly regretted the absence of his chief *kadi*, Ahmed Wad Ali, who, though he neither sought nor took his advice, had been his faithful friend and servant for the last ten years. As chief judge, he had acquired an immense influence in the country; and, considering the circumstances, he had during that time collected very considerable wealth.

Upwards of a thousand slaves worked on his immense estates. He employed merchants to take the produce, such as India-rubber and ostrich feathers, to Egypt. He possessed immense herds of cattle, and quantities of camels and magnificent horses; but his most coveted possession was his *harem*, in which were collected a large number of lovely women and female slaves. All this had roused the cupidity of Yakub and of the *khalifa's* young son. The former was intensely irritated against Ahmed, as he seldom paid the smallest attention to his opinions or proposals. Even the *khalifa* had become jealous of his influence, and lent a willing ear to Yakub's insinuations that he abused his power, and made use of his position to increase his own wealth.

Under the pretext that Ahmed had acted contrary to the instructions which the *khalifa* had specially laid down, he himself, as President of the Court of Kadis, had sentenced him to perpetual imprisonment. Thus a just retribution had at length fallen on the head of this unscrupulous judge, who had ruthlessly condemned numbers of innocent persons, had robbed them of all they possessed, had turned wives and children into widows and orphans, and had perpetrated every description of injustice. He had been seized by the black soldiers, thrown into prison, and lost all his wealth, whilst the *khalifa*, his son, and his brother Yakub had rifled his *harem* of the best and prettiest women, and distributed the remainder amongst their followers.

The *khalifa* knew perfectly well the difficulties of re-capturing Kassala; but, in order to make a show of doing something, he sent instructions to Osman Digna, who was at Adarama on the Atbara, some three days' march from Berber, to join Mussaid at Goz Regeb with all his available forces. At the same time, he ordered Ahmed Fedil to make a military post of a thousand rifles at El Fasher on the Atbara, about one and a half days' journey from Kassala. He also sent detachments of troops from Omdurman to Asubri on the Atbara, midway between El Fasher and Goz Regeb. He continued to assert most resolutely that he intended shortly to advance on Kassala; but all these arrangements were made entirely with a view to establishing a series of defensive posts along the line of the Atbara, whilst the troops he was constantly collecting were intended to oppose the advance of the enemy towards Omdurman.

In the midst of all this disturbance and excitement, the satisfactory news arrived that a messenger sent by Arabi from Reggaf had arrived at Omdurman from Katena, a town on the White Nile. Two steamers soon followed, bringing cargoes of ivory and slaves; and, in a day or two, four hundred male slaves were marched with great pomp and ceremony through the city, as proof of Dafalla's successes in the Equatorial regions. As a matter of fact, the latter had attacked and defeated a detachment of Emin Pasha's troops who had separated from the main body, and had been living independently, and at their own risk, in a track of country governed by Fadl el Maula, one of Emin's subalterns.

On the *pasha's* departure, this man had entered into communication with the advanced agents of the Congo Free State, and had agreed with them that, if they should assist him to re-occupy the Equatorial Province, he would enter their service. His real intentions, however, were to remain independent, and though nominally a servant of the Congo Free State, to derive from them as much profit as he could for his own personal benefit. Misled by false information, Fadl el Maula had ventured close to the station of Reggaf, which he believed to be only lightly held by the Mahdists; but he discovered his mistake too late. He beat a rapid retreat, but was followed up and overtaken, after several days' march, by Arabi Dafalla, who surprised his camp whilst most of the men were out on a foray.

Fadl el Maula himself was killed, with most of the men in camp, whilst defending their wives and children; and Arabi captured a quantity of loot, all the women and children, and a number of rifles. Amongst the trophies he sent to Omdurman were four Congo Free State flags made of blue bunting, with a five-pointed yellow star in the centre, also two suits of black uniform with buttons, on which the words "*Travail et Progrès*" were engraved. This was the first time I had seen the badge of the Congo Free State, of the existence of which I had heard; but I had no notion of its size or the extent of its boundaries. Several European letters had also been found in Fadl el Maula's camp; but the *khalifa* did not show them to me. He preferred to remain in ignorance of their contents, rather than that I should gain some insight into affairs in those regions.

The brilliance of this last success of his arms was, however, considerably dimmed by the news which came soon afterwards, that Christian agents from the south and west were advancing towards the Equatorial Provinces. Arabi had received information that a force was in Uganda, and that Christian troops were advancing from the western districts of Central Africa; and he appealed for instructions as to how to act. A reinforcement of four hundred men was at once despatched to Reggaf; and orders were sent to him to withdraw all outlying posts, should he be threatened, but under no circumstances to abandon Reggaf.

When the expedition had been sent against Emin Pasha, it was the *khalifa's* intention not to acquire more territory in this direction, but to make a station from which raids could be made on the Black countries, in order to procure ivory and slaves.

After the steamer had left with reinforcements, the *khalifa* again turned his attention to affairs in the east. He ordered all the Jaalin in Omdurman to proceed to Asubri, and nominated Hamed Wad Ali, the brother of Ahmed Wad Ali, to the command of this post. He subsequently despatched thither the Danagla, as well as a number of Arab horsemen to Gedaref; and the camel-owning Arabs were instructed to supply three thousand camels, of which a thousand were incorporated with the mounted corps at Gedaref, whilst the remainder were used to transport grain from Rufaa and Abu Haraz on the Blue Nile to Asubri, which, having been abandoned by its former inhabitants, was now left entirely uncultivated; and in consequence the troops there were suffering great privations. By these measures, the *khalifa* imagined that he had turned the line of the Atbara into a sort of wall, by which he hoped to block the enemy's advance; but it seemed as if he were likely to have no rest this year.

Mahmud Ahmed now reported that Christians had entered the Bahr el Ghazal districts, and were attempting to win over the native tribes, with whom they had already made treaties. They had arrived, he said, at Hofret en Nahas (the copper mines near Kalaka on the southwestern Darfur frontier). This news was of the greatest importance; and the *khalifa* had every reason to feel alarmed and uneasy.

When Egypt governed the Sudan, it was from the Bahr el Ghazal Provinces that they recruited the men for the Sudanese battalions, who had come either of their own free-will or had been forcibly impressed. Owing to the climate and plenteous rainfall, the country is more highly cultivated than any portion of the Nile valley lying between Kowa and Reggaf. Besides, the majority of the tribes who inhabit these districts are, owing to internal dissensions, incapable of uniting, and would thus rather facilitate than retard the advance of any foreign power wishing to make itself master of the province.

For the *khalifa*, however, the possession of this country is of vital importance. Its ruler, he knows, virtually holds the Sudan in his hands. These various Black tribes have no love for the Arab slave-hunters, and would aid any power which would guarantee their protection. The recruitment of four or five thousand local levies, possessing fighting qualities of a high order, would, for such a power, be a matter of no difficulty; and in the space of four or five years an army of from fifteen to twenty thousand men might be raised, by which not only Darfur and Kordofan, but indeed the whole Sudan, could be conquered.

Abdullahi, therefore, was not slow to realise the situation; and he at once gave orders to Mahmud Ahmed to despatch a force from Southern Darfur into these districts, and drive out the strangers who had dared to penetrate the Bahr el Ghazal Province.

In compliance with these instructions, the Emir Khatem Musa, with a considerable force, was sent south from Shakka into the northern Bahr el Ghazal districts, and the Faroghé, Kâra, Bongo, and other frontier tribes with whom the Europeans had made treaties, being left without support, at once submitted to the Mahdists who occupied their countries.

One day, I was summoned before the *khalifa*, who handed to me several documents written in French, which he ordered me to translate. They included two letters from Lieutenant de La Kéthulle to his assistants, containing various orders and instructions. They had been originally in the hands of the Sheikh of Faroghé, who had handed them over to Khatem Musa. In addition to these, the *khalifa* showed me a treaty which had been drawn up between Sultan Hamed Wad Musa of the Faroghé and the representative of the Congo Free State, which was to the effect that,—

> 1. Sultan Hamed Wad Musa, chief of the Faroghé tribe, acknowledged the suzerainty of the Congo Free State, and placed himself under its protection.
> 2. Sultan Hamed Wad Musa bound himself to enter into commercial relations with the Congo Free State, and establish intercourse between it and the Darfur frontier districts, and agreed to give protection to all officials of that State travelling in his country.
> 3. The Congo Free State bound itself to assist Sultan Hamed Wad Musa in all his undertakings, and uphold his authority in the country.

This treaty was signed in August, 1894, by Hamed Wad Musa and the representative of the Congo Free State; and was witnessed by Sultan Zemio and the Sultan of Tiga, the names of the two latter being written in European characters.

I hurriedly translated these papers verbally to the *khalifa*, and was much interested in seeing how, on this occasion, his curiosity got the better of his suspicions; though he did all he could to prevent me from noticing this.

"I did not summon you," he said, "merely to translate these letters, which, after all, are of not the smallest importance to me, though I have instructed Mahmud Ahmed to drive out these Christians, who are only travellers, and in small numbers, from the Bahr el Ghazal Province; but I have also a proposal to make to you. I look upon you as one of us,—as my friend and faithful adherent,—and I have decided to publicly make known this fact by giving to you as a wife one of my cousins,—one of my next of kin. What have you to say to this?"

This offer did not greatly surprise me; for he had several times hinted as much. I was perfectly well aware that his object was not to publicly show appreciation of me, but to have me carefully watched in my own house. He wished to place me under surveillance in order to discover if I had any secret relations with outside countries. Through trusty friends, I had ascertained that he earnestly sought some plausible grounds for making me, as he called it, "harmless;" but in doing so he wished to justify his action before the public, by showing me more consideration as a foreigner than if I had been a native. I knew too well, however, that a man of his unscrupulous determination, who had not spared his best friends, such as Ibrahim Adlan and Kadi Ahmed, would not hesitate to take full advantage of the slightest proof of my disloyalty in order to rid himself of me.

"Sire," I replied, "may God bless you, and give you victory over all your enemies. I feel highly honoured by your magnanimous offer; but hear of me, I pray you, the truth. Your relative is not merely descended from royalty, but from the Prophet himself. She therefore deserves to be treated with every consideration. Unfortunately, I have a very quick temper, and at times have great difficulty in controlling myself. Domestic quarrels would undoubtedly arise, which might be the cause of estrangement between you, my master, and myself. My only desire is to remain in your greatest favour. I pray God this may ever be so; for I dread the occurrence of anything which might cause me to fall into disfavour."

"I have known you now intimately for ten years," said the *khalifa*; "and I have never known you to be thoughtless or quick-tempered. I have often presented you with wives, and they have never complained to me of domestic quarrels. It is true, however, that I have heard you have either made presents of them to your servants, or have given them their liberty. It seems to me that although you pretend to be one of us, you really wish to adhere to the manners and customs of your tribe. (He did not refer to religion, as I suppose he thought that might hurt my feelings.) I mean that you wish to have only one wife."

"Sire," I replied, "you have often honoured me with presents of slaves; but you surely do not wish me to be their slave. If I have married them to my servants, or sent them away, it is because they have been disobedient, or have behaved badly. You have been misinformed, if you think that I wish to adhere to the custom of my country to have only one wife; for I have already three."

"Very well," he said, "I believe you; and so you refuse to marry my cousin?"

"Sire," I replied, "I do not refuse; but I merely inform you of my uncertain temper, so that I may prevent unpleasantness in the future. Indeed, I am highly honoured by your kind offer; and I beg you to try and see if I am worthy of it." He understood perfectly well that what I had said was tantamount to a refusal; and he closed the conversation by making a sign to me to withdraw. This offer had placed me in a most difficult position. I thoroughly understood the *khalifa*. By not joyfully accepting his offer, I had hurt his pride; and now I longed more than ever for liberty. Some months before, I had sent a Sudanese merchant to Cairo, and had begged the Austrian Consul-General to place, through him, the necessary means at my disposal to effect my escape. But how often had I attempted negotiations of this sort through merchants and others, and how often had I been doomed to disappointment and failure.

CHAPTER 16

Miscellaneous Remarks

I will now say a few words regarding the *khalifa's* person and his characteristics.

Sayed Abdullahi Ibn Sayed Mohammed belongs to the Taaisha section of the Baggaras (as all cattle-owning nomad Arabs are called). This section inhabits the country in the southwestern portion of Darfur; and the *khalifa* himself is descended from the Aulad Om Sura of the Jubarat family. I have already referred to Abdullahi's early life, and how he had established a connection with the slave-hunting Arabs, when still quite a youth. He joined the *Mahdi* at the age of thirty-five, and was then a slim and active, though powerfully built man; but latterly he has become very stout, and his lightness of gait has long since disappeared. He is now forty-nine years of age, but looks considerably older; and the hair of his beard is almost white.

At times, the expression of his face is one of charming amiability, but more generally it is one of dark sternness, in which tyranny and unscrupulous resolution are unmistakably visible. He is rash and quick-tempered, acting often without a moment's consideration; and when in this mood, even his own brother dares not approach him. His nature is suspicious to a degree to everyone, his nearest relatives and members of his household included. He admits that loyalty and fidelity are rare qualities, and that those who have to deal with him invariably conceal their real feelings in order to gain their own ends.

He is most susceptible to flattery, and consequently receives an inordinate amount from every one. No one dares to speak to him without referring, in the most fulsome terms, to his wisdom, power, justice, courage, generosity, and truthfulness. He accepts this absurd adulation with the greatest pleasure and satisfaction; but woe to him who in the slightest degree offends his dignity.

The following episode will give the reader a fair idea of his arbitrary nature:—

A certain *kadi* named Ismail Wad Abdel Kader, who had been well educated in Cairo, had gained great favour with the *Mahdi* by having written a laudatory account of his early victories. This had so fully gratified the great religious reformer that he instructed Abdel Kader to continue to chronicle the various important events as they happened, and further instructed his principal *emirs* to forward to him detailed histories of all that occurred within their respective commands. In time, these chronicles grew into an elaborate historical and inflated statement of Mahdist rule in the Sudan; and, after the *Mahdi's* death, the *khalifa*, who had installed Abdel Kader as state chronicler, ordered the continuance of the work.

One day, however, during a pleasure-party, the historian had been overheard to say that present affairs in the Sudan, as compared with those in Egypt, might be described by the following simile: The *khalifa* might be considered as the Khedive Ismail Pasha, whilst, in the same proportion, he, Abdel Kader, might be likened to Ismail Pasha el Mofettish, who had been the viceroy's principal adviser and friend. This thoughtless statement was immediately reported to Abdullahi, who, furious at such a comparison, at once ordered the judges to assemble and make a full inquiry into the matter; and if Abdel Kader had actually made such a statement, he should be at once condemned. To the *kadis*, he argued thus:

"The *Mahdi* is the representative of the Prophet Mohammed, and I am his successor. Who, therefore, in the whole world holds so high a position as I? Who can be nobler than the direct descendant of the Prophet?" The inquiry proved the guilt of Abdel Kader, who, at the *khalifa's* command, was thrown into chains and transported to Reggaf. "What business has he to compare affairs here with those of Egypt?" said the pompous *khalifa*. "If he wishes to compare himself to a *pasha*, then I, the descendant of the Prophet, will never demean myself to be put on a par with the *khedive*,—a mere Turk."

I suppose by these assertions he thought to impress the populace. The stupid man too, in his offended dignity, did not stop here. He at once ordered all the chronicles (of which several copies had been made) to be instantly burnt; but I heard privately that his secretary, who was being frequently referred to by the *khalifa* on the subject of the early events of his reign, secreted one copy for private reference; and if these strange chronicles could only be procured and translated into European languages, they would expose to the civilised world the methods of Mahdism in all its barefaced mendacity.

Abdullahi's pride and confidence in his own powers are indescribable. He firmly believes that he is capable of doing anything and everything; and as he pretends to act under Divine inspiration, he never hesitates to appropriate the merits of others as his own. For example, he stated that the *Mahdi's* tomb, which had been built with immense labour and trouble by the former government architect Ismail, had been designed by himself entirely in accordance with Divinely inspired plans. He ascribed Osman Wad Adam's victory over Abu Gemmaiza, as well as Zeki Turmal's over King John of Abyssinia, to the inspired orders which he pretended he had issued. His character is a strange mixture of malice and cruelty. He delights to annoy and cause disappointment; and he is never happier than when he has brought people to complete destitution by confiscating their property, throwing them into chains, robbing families wholesale, seizing and executing all persons of tribal influence and authority, and reducing entire races to a condition of powerless impotence.

During the *Mahdi's* lifetime, he was entirely responsible for the severity of the proceedings enacted in his name, and for the merciless manner in which he treated his defeated enemies. It was Abdullahi who gave the order for no quarter at the storming of Khartum; and it was he who subsequently authorised the wholesale massacre of the men, women, and children. After the fall of that city, it was he who, for the period of four days, declared the whole Shaigia tribe to be outlaws. When distributing the captured women and children, he was utterly regardless of their feelings. To separate children from their mothers, and to make their re-union practically impossible by scattering them amongst different tribes, was his principal delight.

When Osman Wad Adam sent to Omdurman the sisters of the late Sultan of Darfur, the Princesses Miriam Isa Basi and Miriam Bakhita, he gave them their liberty, but took most of their female relatives into his own harem, and distributed the remainder amongst his followers; and, hearing that some Darfur people who were residing in Omdurman had called on the Princesses, and offered them presents, he had the latter arrested and made over as slaves to his two *emirs*, Hassib and Kanuna, who were on the point of starting for Reggaf. In vain poor Bakhita's blind mother implored to be allowed to accompany her daughter; but she was forcibly prevented by the *khalifa's* special orders, and died a few days later of a broken heart. Her daughter threw herself into the river as the boat started. She was saved, but subsequently died on the journey from fatigue and misery.

Ahmed Gurab, an Egyptian born in Khartum, who had quitted the city as a merchant before the destruction of Hicks Pasha's army, had left behind him his wife, who was a Sudanese, and his daughter. He eventually returned to see them; and, on the day he arrived in Omdurman, he was brought before the *khalifa*, to whom he explained the reasons of his return, and expressed a wish to enter his service. "I accept your offer," said the *khalifa*. "You will at once proceed to Reggaf, and fight in the Holy Cause against the heathen."

In vain the unfortunate man begged and implored to remain with his wife and daughter, or at least to be allowed to see them; but the *khalifa* ordered his *mulazemin* to take him at once on board the steamer, and guard him carefully, and on no account permit him to see his family. With a smile of fiendish delight, he said: "His fellow-passengers are Isa Basi and Bakhita. He may enjoy their society as much as he likes, if their masters will allow him."

Without the smallest rhyme or reason, he has caused the death of thousands of innocent people. He had the right hand and left foot of a certain Omar publicly cut off in the market-place, because he had failed to make lead, which he had said he could do, and for which purpose he had received a small sum of money in advance. During the horrible execution and mutilation of the Batahin, he had been present, and had looked with pleasure on the slaughter of his victims. I have described how his best friends and most faithful servants were victimised through his caprice, and how he had ruthlessly seized for himself their wives and daughters. Then what could be more cruel than his punishment of the Ashraf? No doubt they were guilty of mutiny; but he might have exiled or imprisoned them, instead of killing them with clubs and axes as if they had been dogs; and yet these were the near relatives of his former lord and master, the *Mahdi*.

In all intercourse with him, he demands the most complete humility and submission. Persons entering his presence stand in front of him with their hands crossed over their breasts and their eyes lowered to the ground, awaiting his permission to be seated. In his audience chamber, he is generally seated on an *angareb*, over which a palm-mat is spread, and his sheepskin stretched out on it, whilst he leans against a large roll of cotton cloth which forms a pillow. When those brought before him are allowed to be seated, they take up a position as in prayers, with their eyes fixed on the ground; and in this posture they answer the questions put to them, and dare not move until permission is given them to withdraw.

Even in the mosque, when prayers are over, and he converses on general subjects, those in close proximity to him invariably maintain this attitude. He is most particular that all persons brought before him should keep their eyes downcast, whilst he himself scrutinises them most carefully. Some years ago a Syrian named Mohammed Said, who had the misfortune to have only one eye, happened to be near him when he was delivering a religious lecture, and unintentionally cast his blind eye in the direction of the *khalifa*. The latter at once called me up, and told me to tell the Syrian never to come near him again, and if he did never to dare to look at him. At the same time he told me that everyone should be most careful to guard themselves against the evil eye. "For," said he, "nothing can resist the human eye. Illness and misfortunes are generally caused by the evil eye."

In spite of his tyrannical nature, the *khalifa* shows to greater advantage in his private life. He is devoted to his eldest son Osman, who is now twenty-one years of age, and who has been instructed in all the commentaries of the *Koran* by able Mohammedan teachers; but his father never hesitated to change the teachers as often as his son wished; and when Osman affirmed to his father that he was sufficiently instructed, the latter at once withdrew his teachers. When he reached his seventeenth year, he was married to his cousin, the daughter of his uncle Yakub; and on this occasion the *khalifa* departed from the strict observances as regards marriage enjoined by the *Mahdi*, and arranged a series of banquets extending over a period of eight days, to which almost every inhabitant in Omdurman was invited.

He had a large red brick house built for his son in the space lying opposite to Yakub's residence, and had it furnished with all the comfort available in the Sudan. An attempt was even made to lay out a garden on the stony ground within the enclosure. Shortly afterwards, he gave his son two more of his female relatives in marriage, and innumerable concubines, which he himself selected; but he declared, in the most emphatic manner that he would never permit him to marry a woman from any of the Nile valley tribes. He watches over his son's intercourse with strangers with the greatest jealousy, and considers it a most dangerous proceeding; and when he heard that, in the perversity of youth, his son entirely disregarded his injunctions, and held nightly orgies in his house, he had a new residence built for him within the Omdurman wall close to his own, so as to exercise greater supervision, and handed over his old house to Yakub.

He married his own daughter to the *Mahdi's* son Mohammed, to whom he bore no good will; whilst the latter was anxious to marry one of his own relations, and had no love for the *khalifa's* daughter. Abdullahi, however, as father-in-law, guardian, and master, absolutely forbade him to enter into any such alliance, and tried to insist on his affection for his daughter, with the result that a complete estrangement was brought about between man and wife, ending in a divorce; but the *khalifa* was so annoyed that, out of pure fear, Mohammed had to take her back, and swear entire devotion to her for the rest of his life.

The *khalifa* thought it incumbent on his position to maintain a large establishment; and as this was also entirely in conformity with his own inclinations, he gradually became possessor of a *harem* of over four hundred wives. In accordance with the Mohammedan law, he has four legal wives, who belong to free tribes; but, being a lover of change, he never hesitates to divorce them at will, and take others in their places. The other women of the household consist for the most part of young girls, many of whom belong to tribes which have been forced to accept Mahdism, and whose husbands and fathers fought against him. They are therefore regarded as booty, and have only the rights and claims of concubines, or, in some cases, of slaves.

This large assortment of ladies varies in colour from light brown to the deepest black, and comprises almost every tribe in the Sudan. They are divided into groups of from fifteen to twenty, presided over by a superior; and two or three of these groups are placed under the orders of a free woman, who is generally a concubine specially selected by the *khalifa*. A certain amount of grain and money is granted monthly to these superiors for the maintenance of their charges; and they also receive means to purchase the necessary cosmetics, consisting of various sorts of oils, grease, and scent. The value of their clothing is regulated entirely by the comparative beauty, position, and character of the wearers, and consists for the most part of native-woven cotton cloth with parti-coloured borders, or of bright silk or woollen shawls imported from Egypt.

These are always distributed by the *khalifa* himself or by his chief eunuch. As the wearing of silver jewellery was strictly prohibited by the *Mahdi*, mother-of-pearl buttons and oblong strips of red coral and onyx, threaded together, are worn round the wrists, ankles, and head. The hair is usually worn in innumerable small plaits, which are arranged in all sorts of different ways, and bedaubed with a quantity of oily and greasy scents; and to European olfactory nerves the odour emanating from a Sudanese lady *"en grande toilette"* is repulsive in the extreme.

For the last few years the wives of the upper classes have again taken to wearing gold and silver jewellery; and the *khalifa's* principal women indulge in these luxuries to a greater extent than the rest. The latter live in a series of large detached houses, something like barracks, surrounded by courts encircled with high walls. Special women are maintained to watch over their state of health; and they are obliged to report it to their master, the *khalifa*, from time to time. When he wishes to summon any lady in particular to share his affections, he communicates his desire by means of little boy eunuchs.

Occasionally, he holds an inspection of his entire household, and makes use of such opportunities to rid himself of those of whom he is weary, in order to make room for new attractions. Those disposed of in this way he generally passes on to his near relatives, his special favourites, or his servants. The *harem* courts are carefully guarded by eunuchs and the black *mulazemin*. The women are almost entirely cut off from intercourse with the outer world; and perhaps once a year their female relations are allowed to converse with them for only a short time.

The *khalifa's* principal wife is called Sahra, and belongs to his own tribe. She has shared with him from earliest days all his joys and sorrows, and is the mother of his oldest children Osman and Kadija. During the early years of his reign, he would only eat the simplest food, cooked by her or under her superintendence. It consisted, as a rule, merely of *asida*, roast meat, and chickens; but as his household increased, he began to try the various sorts of cookery known to his new wives, many of whom were acquainted with the Turkish and Egyptian methods; and now, in place of the simple food, he indulges in far more luxurious fare, though to outward appearance he still pretends to lead a life of simplicity and abstinence. These innovations brought about a quarrel between him and his wife Sahra, who pointed out that the new dishes might be bewitched or poisoned, and might end in his death, with the result that he twice sent her letters of separation; but, on the strong representations of his brother Yakub and the other members of the family, he was induced to cancel them.

He has in his service in all some twenty eunuchs, chief of whom is a certain Abdel Gayum, who is also charged with the superintendence of large quantities of land which are cultivated by slaves for the use of the household; and it is his duty to purchase the necessary supplies of grain, and have in readiness the sheep and cattle required for domestic purposes. He also draws from the Beit el Mal the necessary amounts required for the payment of the women and servants of the harem. He has also charge of considerable sums of private money with which the *khalifa* purchases the presents he secretly makes to his *emirs* and other influential persons. To assist him in carrying out his multifarious duties, he has a staff of clerks and servants, who are always eunuchs or slaves, as the *khalifa* will on no account allow any stranger to get an insight into his *harem*.

Abdullahi's dress consists of a *jibba* made of superfine white cotton cloth with a coloured border, loose cotton drawers, and on his head a beautifully made Mecca silk skull-cap, around which a small white turban is wound. Around his body a narrow strip of cotton, about five yards long, called *wassan*, is worn, and a light shawl of the same material is thrown across his shoulders. He formerly wore sandals; but latterly he has taken to wearing soft leather stockings of a light brown colour, and yellow shoes. When walking, he carries a sword in his left hand, and in his right a beautifully worked Hadendoa spear, which he uses as a walking-stick. He is invariably accompanied by twelve or fifteen little boy-slaves as his personal attendants.

Many of these are children of Abyssinian Christians seized by Abu Anga and Zeki Tummal. Their duty is to remain always near him, and act as his messengers to various parts of the town. They usher into his presence all visitors, and must be ready day and night to carry his orders. When they reach the age of seventeen or eighteen, they are drafted into the ranks of the *mulazemin*, and their places taken by others. The *khalifa* thinks that by employing young boys, his secrets are less likely to be betrayed; and in this he is not far wrong, when one considers the extraordinary amount of bribery and corruption which prevails amongst the older classes.

Within the house, into which these young boys are never admitted, he employs young eunuchs, who wait upon him, whilst the more advanced in age of this unfortunate class are relegated to the outer dependencies of the household. Even these juvenile domestics suffer considerable brutality at his hands. The slightest mistakes are punished by flogging, or the offenders are thrown into chains and starved.

Upwards of three years ago, he conceived the idea of augmenting his *mulazemin* by a species of body-guard; and for this purpose he selected a number of Jehadia from Mahmud Ahmed's and Zeki Tummal's armies. In addition to these, he called on the Emirs of the western tribes to provide a number of recruits for his *mulazemin*; but his orders were only partially obeyed. He selected a few of the sons of the best Jaalin families for incorporation in the body-guard; but he rigorously excluded all Danaglas and Egyptians, in whom he has no confidence. In this manner, he created a force of from eleven to twelve thousand men, who, with their wives and children, are all quartered close to his and his son's houses, and within the newly erected wall. This force is subdivided into three corps, under the respective commands of his son Osman, the *khalifa's* young brother Harun Abu Mohammed, who is barely eighteen years of age, and his cousin Ibrahim Khalil, who has been recently replaced by an Abyssinian named Rabeh, who has been brought up in the *khalifa's* household.

Osman, in all matters regarding the *mulazemin*, is looked upon as the *khalifa's* representative. The corps are subdivided again into sections of one hundred men, over each of which an officer called *ras miya* (head of the hundred), who has several assistants, has command. Over every five or six *ras miya* an *emir* presides, who is also provided with an assistant. The Black soldiers, or Jehadia, are incorporated in the subdivisions, not with the free Arabs, but under the special command of the *emirs*, who have therefore under their respective orders two or three hundred Jehadia, and the remainder Arabs. Almost all these are armed with Remington rifles, which, however, are kept in store, and are only issued on special feasts.

The monthly pay of the *mulazemin* consists of half a Dervish dollar, and, every fortnight, one-eighth of an *ardeb* of *dhurra*. The grain is received fairly regularly; but the cash payment is merely a nominal one, and is very seldom issued. The salaries of the *ras miya* and *emirs* are proportionately higher; and they receive frequent gifts of women and slaves from the *khalifa*. The duty of the *mulazemin* and body-guard is to protect the person of the *khalifa*; and all must accompany him when he rides out or holds reviews. Even when making a comparatively small expedition into the town they must proceed with him. They have always to remain in readiness in the open square in front of his house.

Although the *khalifa* has forbidden all Egyptian music, he has collected the former black buglers, two of whom invariably accompany him. The call for a *ras miya* is that of captain; for *emir* that of major; and for commander that of colonel. Abdullahi frequently inspects the *mulazemin* at night, in order to see that they are in occupation of the posts allotted to them; and he pays special attention to the outposts. Owing to this unusually hard service, the *ras miya* and *emirs*, under the pretext of illness, frequently go secretly to their houses, and great discontent prevails amongst them.

The *khalifa's* public duties consist in saying the five prayers daily in the large mosque. At early dawn, he begins with the morning prayers, after which the *Rateb* is read in various groups, as enjoined by the *Mahdi*. This consists of a selection of verses and special prayers from the *Koran*, and occupies about an hour. The *khalifa* then returns, as a rule, to his private apartments, but sometimes walks about in the mosque in order to see for himself whether the inhabitants of Omdurman comply with his orders to attend prayers regularly. He holds midday prayers at about two o'clock, and two hours later follows the Asr, or evening prayer, after which the *Rateb* is repeated.

Prayers are said again at sunset, and, three hours later, night prayers are held. On all these occasions, the *khalifa* attends in his *mihrab* (niche), which has been erected immediately in front of the lines of believers. It is a square-shaped structure, consisting of a series of columns connected by open iron-work, through which he can see all that is going on around him. Immediately behind him are the seats of his son, the *kadis*, and a few persons specially selected by himself. The *mulazemin* take up a position to the right and left, whilst the Black soldiers occupy large open enclosures which are separated from the mosque by a wall. On the right of the *mulazemin* are the places of Yakub, the *emirs*, and most of the western tribes, whilst to the left are some of Yakub's followers, a few of *khalifa* Ali Wad Helu's Arabs, and the Jaalin and Danagla. Behind these, the people are seated in ten or twelve rows, and repeat the prayers in unison after the *khalifa*.

On all occasions there are several thousand persons present; and the *khalifa* is most particular that all the principal *emirs* and influential people should assist him. If he bears any special dislike or ill-will to any persons, he invariably condemns them to regularly attend the five daily prayers in the mosque, under the supervision of people specially selected for this purpose. In making these strict regulations regarding prayers, the *khalifa* is by no means actuated by devotional ideas, but utilises these occasions to keep his followers together under his own personal control.

As several of the people live a considerable distance away from the mosque, they are generally so tired and exhausted, after these frequent journeys to and fro, that they do not collect in the evening in each others' houses,—a practice which the *khalifa* specially abhors, for his object is to destroy, as far as possible, what he is pleased to call "social life;" that is to say, social gatherings, for he is perfectly well aware that his deeds and actions on such occasions are invariably discussed and criticised, and not generally very favourably.

If, for any reason, such as illness, he is prevented from attending prayers, his place is taken by one of his *kadis*, or by a very pious *mulazem* of the Takruri tribe; but on such occasions the substitute Imam is never allowed to occupy the *mihrab*, but stands outside. Khalifa Ali Wad Helu, who, in accordance with the religious law, should, on such occasions, represent the *khalifa*, is scarcely ever permitted to do so.

In the afternoon, or between afternoon and evening prayers, he receives reports, news, and letters, and interviews the *kadis* and *emirs* whose names have been previously submitted to him, as well as any other persons whom he specially wishes to see.

His postal arrangements are very primitive. He keeps up from sixty to eighty riding camels, with a specially selected staff of postmen; and these he despatches to different parts of his empire with orders and instructions. Ibrahim Adlan had suggested to him that he should make special stations for the posts along the various main roads, and establish a more regular and less expensive system; but he utterly refused to entertain the idea, saying that he placed special value on the verbal accounts of the postmen who were despatched direct, and he frequently obtained from them important information concerning the attitude and behaviour of his governors.

The *emirs* of the various districts also have a similar postal system of their own, and despatch camel-men with important information to Omdurman. There is no system of postal communication for private persons, though sometimes the camel-postmen convey letters secretly. The *khalifa* being intensely suspicious of all intercourse with strangers, any communications between his subordinates and the outside must be carried out with the greatest circumspection and secrecy. Utterly ignorant of reading and writing, the *khalifa* orders all letters that arrive to be handed over to his secretaries, Abu el Gasem and Mudasser, who are obliged to explain the contents, and write replies in accordance with his orders. These two individuals lead a wretched life; for they know that he will not forgive the slightest mistake, and should he have the least suspicion of their having revealed any of his secrets, even through carelessness, he would not hesitate to treat them as he treated their comrades Ahmedi and his four brothers, who, having been accused of communicating with the Ashraf, were executed.

He converses principally with his *kadis*, who are, for the most part, willing tools in his hands, and serve to give a veneer of justice to his despotic actions. These myrmidons, submissively seated in a semi-circle on the bare floor, their heads bowed down, listen to his orders, which are generally given in an undertone; and rarely any one of them dares to open his mouth or make a suggestion, no matter how necessary he may think it. In addition to the *kadis*, he occasionally interviews *emirs* and other influential persons, from whom he ascertains the condition of the country and tribes; but he invariably stirs up intrigue, and tries to pit one against the other. He generally consults, immediately after night prayers, with Yakub and some of his near relatives; and these meetings often last till long past midnight. They are usually convened for discussing the ways and means of ridding themselves of persons who are objectionable, or who are in the smallest degree a menace to their authority.

Occasionally, he makes short riding excursions to various parts of the town, or visits his houses in the north or south of Omdurman. The melancholy notes of the *ombeija* and the beating of war-drums announce to the inhabitants that their master is about to appear in public. Horses are at once saddled in the large thatched enclosure immediately behind the mosque. The doors are thrown open, and the *mulazemin* stream out from all directions, and, last of all, follows the *khalifa*, mounted, as a rule, on horseback. A square is immediately formed around him; and the men advance in front of him in detachments, ten or twelve abreast.

Behind them follow the horse and foot men of the town population, while on the *khalifa's* left walks an immensely powerful and well-built Arab named Ahmed Abu Dukheka, who has the honour of lifting his master in and out of the saddle. On his right is a strongly-made young black, who is chief of the slaves in the royal stables. The *khalifa* is immediately preceded by six men, who alternately blow the *ombeija* by his orders. Behind him follow the buglers, who sound the advance or halt, or summon, at his wish, the chiefs of the *mulazemin*. Just behind these follow his small personal attendants, who carry the *Rekwa* (a leather vessel used for religious ablutions), the sheepskin prayer-carpet, and several spears.

Sometimes, either in front or rear, as the case may be, follows the

The Khalifa and Kadis in Council.

musical band, composed of about fifty black slaves, whose instruments comprise antelope-horns, and drums made of the hollow trunks of trees covered with skin. The strange African tunes they play are remarkable rather for the hideously discordant noise they make than for their melody. These rides are generally undertaken after midday prayer; and the *khalifa* returns at sunset. Whilst he is advancing in this solemn state, the *mulazemin* generally indulge in displays of horsemanship. Galloping four abreast, with their spears poised high in the air, they dash up towards him at full speed, drawing up their horses almost on to their haunches. They then slowly retire to repeat the operation.

During the early years of his rule, the *khalifa* was present every Friday on the large parade ground where the ceremony of trooping the colours is performed; but now he attends only four times a year, *viz.*, on the birthday of the Prophet, on the Feast of Miraj, the Feast of Bairam, and the Feast of Kurbam Bairam; on this last date all the troops in the neighbourhood, as well as the Darfur and Gedaref armies, are assembled during peaceful times. On the first day of the Feast of Bairam, the *khalifa* holds prayers on the parade ground, and retires himself within a *zariba* in which a small mud-brick house has been built.

A few special favourites, and a number of *mulazemin*, remain with him; but the rest of the troops and populace range themselves in long lines; and when the prayer is over he mounts a wooden pulpit, and delivers a sermon, which is generally specially prepared for him by his secretaries. This over, a salute of seven guns is fired, and all those who can afford it kill the sacrificial lambs prescribed by the religion; but, owing to the prevailing distress and poverty of the inhabitants, very few of them are in a position to bear this expense, and are obliged to content themselves with a sort of porridge which takes place of a sacrificial dish. During the three following days, a review is held. Long before sunrise, the *emirs*, with their flags and followers, collect and march to their allotted positions on the parade ground, which is an almost perfectly flat sandy plain, with a few stones here and there. The troops are marshalled in long lines in rear of each other, facing east.

Yakub has the principal flag,—an immense piece of black cloth, which is hoisted exactly opposite the *khalifa's zarib*a, and about four hundred yards from it. To the right and left are ranged those of the different *emirs*, while on the north side flies the green flag of the Khalifa Ali Wad Helu, on either side of which are the flags of his *emirs*. On the left flank, the horse and camel-men are drawn up, while on the right flank are ranged the riflemen, consisting partly of Jehadia, and partly of men belonging to the various *emirs*, who are only specially provided with arms for the time being. Immediately after sunrise, the *khalifa* comes out of the *zariba*, and, mounted on his horse, stands surrounded by his *mulazemin* and bodyguard, whilst the entire army passes in review before him, the troops being generally provided with new *jibbas* and turbans in honour of the feast.

Sometimes the *khalifa* mounts on a camel; and, on one occasion, he drove in the carriage of one of the former governors-general which had been captured in Khartum, and which was kept stored away in the Beit el Mal. Two horses were specially trained to draw this vehicle, which the *khalifa* ordered to be driven at a foot pace, as he feared being upset; but, latterly, he has given up this plan, and generally rides on horseback direct from the mosque along the road leading due west towards the black flag, and on reaching it, he solemnly contemplates it for a few moments, and then rides to the *zariba*, at the south front of which a small shelter, consisting of trunks of trees lashed together and covered with palm-mats, has been erected. Here he dismounts and reclines on an *angareb*, surrounded by his *kadis*, whilst the troops file past.

Occasionally, he starts from his own house, and, taking a southern road, marches out of the town, then turns west and rides along the front alignment of his troops, after which the usual march past takes place. At these reviews the horsemen are generally clad in coats of mail, of European or Asiatic origin, whilst on their heads they wear heavy iron helmets and curious cotton caps of various colours and the most grotesque shapes, round which a small turban is wound. The horses are clothed in large padded patchwork quilts, somewhat resembling those worn by the knights of old at tournaments; and one might almost imagine one was gazing at one of those old mediaeval displays. These reviews terminate at the end of the third day; and the troops brought from beyond Omdurman are permitted to return to their respective garrisons.

I propose now to briefly consider the *khalifa's* political intentions and ideas.

As I have already stated, when the *Mahdi* first declared himself, he nominated three *khalifas, viz.*, Abdullahi, Ali Wad Helu, and Mohammed Sherif, who were to succeed him in this order, if they survived. On his death, Abdullahi succeeded as arranged; but, from the moment he took over the reins of government, he did everything in his power to increase his personal ascendancy, and make it hereditary in the family. The mutinous Ashraf, who prided themselves on their relationship to the *Mahdi*, afforded him a welcome pretext for compassing their downfall; and he did not hesitate to possess himself of the Black troops belonging to both his rival *khalifas*. An obscure member of a western tribe, he was a complete stranger in the country; and he knew that he could not reckon on the Jaalin, Danagla, inhabitants of the Gezira, and other Nile valley tribes to support his authority.

He therefore sent secret emissaries to the western Arabs to induce them to make a pilgrimage to the *Mahdi's* tomb, and emigrate to the Nile valley. His agents drew a tempting picture of the magnificent country to which they had been invited, telling them that they were the Lord's chosen people, and that they should go out to possess the land, the inhabitants of which were rich in cattle and slaves, which should be theirs. Tempted by these glowing accounts, many of these tribes emigrated of their own free-will to Omdurman; but as this contingent was not sufficient, the *khalifa* instructed his *emirs* in Darfur and Kordofan to enforce his orders; and, in consequence of this, an immense emigration took place, and continues, on a reduced scale, down to the present day. By this means the *khalifa* has surrounded himself with hordes of strangers who have ousted the rightful owners of the soil, and have made themselves absolute masters of the situation.

All offices and important situations are filled by them, and by his own relatives, the majority belonging to the Taaisha section. Almost the only one of the old *emirs* left is Osman Digna; and the reason for this is that the eastern Arab tribes he governs speak a language which is unknown to the western Arabs. Besides many of these tribes are gradually coming under Egyptian and Italian influence, and the few that are left are merely attached to Osman Digna because he is one of them. Thus the Taaisha tribe has acquired all the power and authority in the land; and they fill their pockets with the waning revenues of the impoverished Sudan.

Years ago, the *emirs* of Dongola and Berber had been instructed by the *khalifa* to weaken the local population as much as possible; and, in consequence, fire-arms and weapons of all descriptions were taken from them, and they were reduced to a condition of complete harmlessness. Moreover, in the actions of Toski and Tokar numbers of Jaalin and Danagla were killed, whilst large contingents of them had been sent to Darfur and Gallabat in the hope that they may be eventually exterminated. In this manner the *khalifa* has secured their countries, and rendered any attempt to oppose his authority almost impossible. The same may be said of the inhabitants of the Gezira, who have also been drafted off into various remote parts of the country, or have been forced to come to Omdurman with their families, where they have endured the greatest hardships and privations.

Moreover, they were called upon to give up more than half their cultivated lands, which were distributed amongst the western Arabs; and all their best fields are now possessed by the *khalifa's* own relatives and favourites. The former owners are often obliged to till the soil for their new masters, who have annexed their servants, slaves, and cattle. Thus the cultivable area of the Gezira, which, in former times, was the most populous and prosperous part of the Sudan, has been reduced by at least a half; and such commotion prevailed in the districts that the *khalifa* was himself obliged to intervene on behalf of the inhabitants, who were ill-treated, tyrannised over, and oppressed to an incredible extent.

As I have before stated, his own tribes are preferred on all occasions. Not only do they hold all the best positions and posts, but the greater part of the money and spoil which passes into the Beit el Mal from the provincial treasuries at Darfur, Gallabat, and Reggaf finds its way into their hands. For their special benefit he has imposed a horse tax, which must be paid in kind; and in this manner he has provided the majority of the Taaisha with chargers. His own section, the Jubarat, of course gets the lion's share of everything.

He never hesitates to make use of every description of intrigue in order to strengthen his own side and weaken the other. For example, on the defeat and death of Nejumi, whose flags belonged to those of Khalifa Sherif, and from whom Abdullahi had withdrawn all power of command over other *emirs*, the remnant of the defeated force was placed under the direction of the Emir Yunes, and, in order to replace those who had been killed he appointed fresh Jaalin and emirs as well as men from Omdurman. These he first placed under the command of their compatriot Bedawi Wad el Ereik; but, instead of sending them to Dongola, they were despatched to Gedaref, and as an unavoidable delay occurred in their departure, he made out that this was a proof of disobedience, and condemned Bedawi, with six of his emirs, to be banished to Reggaf; and in their place he nominated other *emirs*, whom he placed under the direct command of his cousin Hamed Wad Ali.

It is human nature to seek the protection of the most powerful;

and now, instead of being desirous to serve under their own Emirs, the greater number of the so-called opposition party vie with one another in their efforts to be placed under the direct command of the *khalifa* or of Yakub; even the adherents of Ali Wad Helu come under this category. As an instance of this, I will quote the case of Hamed Wad Gar en Nebbi, who was the principal cause of the destruction of the Batahin. He belonged to the Hassanab tribe, which was commanded by Ali Wad Helu. Recognising how matters stood, he wished to place himself and his tribe under Yakub's command; but he was short-sighted enough to tell Khalifa Ali's relatives of his plans. He even went so far as to state in public that on the death of Abdullahi he would be succeeded by his brother Yakub or his son Osman, and that, as they had all the power in their hands, Khalifa Ali could expect nothing, and was, moreover, a weak man without energy.

Several of the bystanders retorted that the *Mahdi* had nominated Khalifa Ali to be Abdullahi's successor, to which he replied that times had changed, that Abdullahi was all-powerful, and that the *Mahdi's* commands were never attended to or taken into consideration. When this interview came to the ears of Khalifa Ali, he charged Gar en Nebbi before the *kadi*; and it was proved beyond a doubt that the latter had actually made these statements. He was consequently convicted of being "irreligious," having doubted the maintenance of the *Mahdi's* doctrines and instructions. Abdullahi could not therefore publicly interfere. Had he done so, he would have revealed his own intentions, which were in reality well known, and would have corroborated Gar en Nebbi's assertions. The judges sentenced him to death; and although Abdullahi did all in his power to induce Ali Wad Helu to grant a reprieve, the latter insisted that the sentence should be carried out; and Gar en Nebbi was publicly executed in the market-place as an unbeliever and a disturber of public tranquillity. All the tribes under the command of Yakub, as well as the *khalifa's* immediate followers, received instructions to show general dissatisfaction with the execution by openly absenting themselves from it.

Whenever it is a question between himself and his opponents, the *khalifa* invariably relies upon his arms, which are far more than sufficient to overcome with ease any attempt to dispute his authority, whether it be in Omdurman itself or in any other part of the country. Within the Sudan, therefore, he is all-powerful; but he is not in a position to offer determined resistance to outside enemies. His leaders are neither capable nor sufficiently instructed to ensure victory. His men are not now loyal enough to fight with that determination which early fanaticism had inspired. They have little or no faith in the cause for which they are supposed to be fighting; and there is little doubt that the *khalifa's* forces could not resist the advance of a foreign power bent on re-occupying the Sudan.

The table on the next page shows approximately the forces at present at the *khalifa's* disposal. Of the forty thousand rifles shown in the table, there are not more than twenty-two thousand Remingtons in good condition. The remainder consist of single and double barrel smoothbores, and other guns of a variety of pattern. Several of the Remington barrels, however, have been cut short with the object of lessening the weight, and with entire disregard to the altered trajectory thus occasioned. Of the sixty-four thousand swords and spear men, at least twenty-five *per cent* are either too old or too young to be considered effective for a campaign. The seventy-five guns comprise six *Krupps* of large calibre, and for which there is only a very small amount of ammunition, eight machine guns of various patterns, and sixty-one brass muzzle-loading guns of various shapes and sizes, the ammunition for which is manufactured principally in Omdurman, and is of a very inferior quality, the range being little over six or seven hundred yards.

Let us now consider for a few moments the present limits of the *khalifa's* influence.

Until a few years ago, Dervish authority extended from near Wadi Halfa in a southeasterly direction towards Abu Hamed, thence eastwards to the Suakin neighbourhood, including Tokar and the Khor Baraka, thence in a southerly direction, including Kassala, Gallabat, and the southeastern slopes of the Beni Shangul and Gulli mountains, and from here it trended in a southwesterly direction towards the White Nile, and included Fashoda, Bohr, and Reggaf. On the west, it extended in a southwesterly direction through the southern Libyan desert, including Selima, the Dongola, Kordofan, and Darfur Provinces, up to the Wadai frontier, and thence southward across the Bahr el Arab through Dar Runga, and included Dar Fertit, the Bahr el Ghazal, and a portion of Equatoria.

The defeat of Nejumi obliged the Mahdists to evacuate the northern portion of the Dongola Province; and their most northerly outpost is now Suarda, some three days' march from Dongola. The Egyptian victories at Tokar and Handub gave back to the local tribes the districts in the immediate neighbourhood of Suakin and Tokar, whilst

Position and Garrisons	Emirs	Armed Strength			Guns	Rifles and Smooth Bores
		Jehadia	Cavalry	Swords, Spearmen		
Omdurman (mulazemin)	Osman Sheikh ed Din	11,000	....	....	..	11,000
"	Yakub	4,000	3,500	45,000	46	4,000
" (in store)		....	....	....	..	6,000
Reggaf	Arabi Wad Dafalla	1,800	....	4,500	3	1,800
Western Sudan:						
El Fasher }						
El Obeid }	Mahmud, etc.	6,000	350	3,500	4	6,000
Shakka, etc. }						
Berber	Zeki Osman	1,600	500	1,300	6	1,600
Abu Hamed	Nur en Nau	400	100	700	4	400
Eastern Sudan:						
Adarama	Osman Digna	450	350	1,000	..	450
Gedaref	Ahmed Fedil	4,500	600	1,000	4	4,500
El Fasher		1,000	200	500	..	1,000
Asubri	Hamed Wad Ali	900	400	1,400	..	900
Gallabat	En Nur	50	....	200	..	50
Dongola	Yunes ed Degheim	2,400	500	5,000	8	2,400
Suarda	Hammuda	250	100	1,000	..	250
Total		34,350	6,600	64,000	75	40,350

the capture of Kassala threw into the hands of the Italians all districts lying east of that town, in consequence of which the river Atbara may now be considered the *khalifa's* eastern frontier. The main force originally stationed at Gallabat under Ahmed Fedil has been moved to Gedaref, and only an insignificant force is maintained at the former station. The chief of the Beni Shangul districts—Tur el Guri—and many of the neighbouring *sheikhs* have declared themselves independent.

In the extreme west, the Massalit, Tama, Beni Hussein, and Gimr tribes, who formerly paid tribute, have now revolted against the Mahdi's government, and until lately were independent. They entered into an offensive and defensive alliance with Sultan Yusef of Wadai; and the *khalifa* was about to despatch an expedition with the object of bringing them into subjection, when the alarming news, to which I have already referred, regarding the appearance of Europeans in the Bahr el Ghazal induced him to alter the destination of Khatem Musa's force to that neighbourhood. After the retirement of the Dervishes, orders were sent to Khatem Musa not to proceed further south until he had received reinforcements from Omdurman.

The Shilluks and Dinkas were, as I have already stated, reduced to subjection by Zeki Tummal, and the route opened to Reggaf, which continues to be the most southerly of the Dervish garrisons; in consequence of the disquieting news of European movements in these districts, the strength of the force there is by no means inconsiderable. The *khalifa's* object in retaining these districts is to replenish his supplies of slaves and ivory; and, under the energetic command of Arabi Wad Dafalla, frequent expeditions are despatched south and west, some of which have collided with the forces of the Congo Free State; but, as I quitted the Sudan before the result of these expeditions was known, I am not in a position to state which side was victorious.

The *khalifa's* revenue and expenditure is worked entirely on the Beit el Mal system.

The following are the principal:—

   Beit el Mal el Umumi (General Treasury).
   Beit el Mal el Mulazemin (the Mulazemin Treasury).
   Beit el Mal Khums el Khalifa (or the Treasury of the *khalifa's* fifth tithes).
   Beit el Mal Warshat el Harbia (Treasury of the War Department).
   Beit el Mal Zabtia es Suk (Treasury of the Bazaar Police).

The following are the sources of revenue of the General Treasury, viz.:—

1. The "*zeka*" and "*fitra*" as laid down in the Moslem Law.
2. Confiscated property.
3. The *ushr* (or tenth) tax paid by merchants and traders on goods.
4. The gum-tax.
5. The boat-tax.
6. Loans from merchants (which are never repaid).
7. The ferry or "*meshra*" tax (*i. e.* the farming out of ferries).
8. The produce of all lands on the east of the Blue Nile and the west of the White Nile, as far south as Karkoj and Fashoda, and as far north as Haggar el Asal.
9. A percentage of the revenues of the principal Beit el Mals.

The following are the main expenses borne by the Treasury:—

1. Transport of troops and supplies to the different provinces.
2. Pay of the troops (Jehadia).
3. Pay of the various officials.
4. Alms.

The revenues of the Mulazemin Treasury come from the Gezira lands; and the main item of expenditure is the pay of the *mulazemin*.

The revenues of the Treasury of the *khalifa's* fifth tithes are:—

1. The greater part of the balance revenues of the Provincial Treasuries.
2. The revenues of all islands, including Tuti Island, and all "Ghenima" lands, including the Halfaya and Kemlin districts, which formerly belonged to His Highness, the *Khedive*.
3. The *ushr* on all goods coming from Berber to Omdurman.
4. All slaves sent from the provinces.
5. Revenues of the majority of steamers and boats.

The expenditure of this Treasury is devoted to the *khalifa's* household.

The War Department Revenues are:—

1. The produce of the Khartum gardens.
2. The revenue of some "*sakias*" (water-wheels) in the vicinity of Khartum.

3. Ivory from Equatoria.

Expenditure:—

1. Dockyard expenses.
2. Beit el Amana (arsenal) expenses.
3. Saltpetre refining.
4. Expenses in connection with the manufacture of arms and ammunition.

Revenue of the Police Treasury:—

1. Confiscated property of drunkards and gamblers.
2. Shop-tax.

Expenditure:—

1. Pay of police officers and men.
2. Expenses connected with Yakub's guest-house.
3. Expenses in connection with the building of the great wall.

It will be readily understood, that the above system produces a considerable revenue for the *khalifa's* private treasury; and I know that a very large sum of money has been hoarded by him, and is stored in ammunition boxes, kept in his house; but I am unable to state, even approximately, what the amount may be. He has also several boxes, made of skins in which are quantities of gold and silver ornaments, collected from all parts.

As I have stated, a show is made of keeping correct accounts; but the system in vogue admits of endless peculation, and any persons having business in the Beit el Mal invariably acquire considerable fortunes. The *khalifa*, however, is aware of this, and makes up for it by wholesale confiscations of property.

When the *Mahdi* first acquired possession of the Sudan, he naturally obtained considerable quantities of gold and silver money; and, with the assistance of Ahmed Wad Suleiman, he began to make his own coinage: he struck gold sovereigns which resembled the Egyptian sovereign; but, as he did not understand the exact amount of alloy which should be mixed with the gold, the weights and values varied considerably, and, as the amount of gold in the Sudan was small, the coining of sovereigns had soon to be suspended. Silver coining was then carried on with some vigour; and the following table, showing the various descriptions of dollars coined during the last ten years, is an interesting indication of the decline of Dervish power and government; for instance, the first dollar coined by the *Mahdi* was made up of seven parts silver and one part copper, whereas, the last dollar, coined by the *khalifa* about a year ago, is composed of two parts silver and five parts copper,—indeed, the present dollar is merely a heavy copper coin covered over with a thin layer of silver.

	Weight in Dirhems.	
	Silver.	Copper.
1. The Mahdi dollar	7	1
2. The first dollar made by Ibrahim Adlan	6	2
3. The second dollar made by Ibrahim Adlan . . .	5	3
4. The first dollar of Nur el Gereifawi (this is known as the Makbul dollar)	4	4
5. The second dollar of Nur el Gereifawi (this is known as the Abu Sidr or Makbul)	3	4
6. The dollar of Suleiman Abdulla (this is known as the Abu Kibs or "crossed-spear" dollar) . . .	2½	4½
7. The first dollar of Abdel Mejid (also called the Makbul)	2½	4½
8. The dollar of Weki Alla	2½	4½
9. The dollar of Omla Gedida (new money)	2	5

Coining money is a lucrative trade; and, at present, the Mint is presided over by two individuals, who pay six thousand dollars a month each, for the privilege. All money issued by them must be accepted as good money. The merchants, of course, object most strongly to these arbitrary measures; but wholesale confiscation of their property, accompanied by flogging and imprisonment, has forced them to realise the futility of attempting to go contrary to the *khalifa's* will. *Maria Theresa* dollars and *Medjidi* dollars were the principal currency when the Egyptian Government occupied the Sudan; and the present rate of exchange is:—

One Maria Theresa dollar = five Omla Gedida dollars.
One Medjidi dollar = eight Omla Gedida dollars.

In consequence of this introduction of base coinage, the prices of certain articles have risen enormously: for instance, blue cotton stuff, which is principally used for women's dresses, and which cost formerly three-quarters of a dollar the piece, has now risen to six dollars, whilst ordinary linen, which was sold at a dollar for twelve yards, has risen to eight dollars for the same amount. Half a pound of sugar costs a dollar, and so on. In fact, all goods which come from Egypt have risen in price, whilst local produce, such as grain and cattle, has proportionately diminished in value: for instance,—

			Dervish Dollars.
A baggage camel	costs from	60 to 80
Riding camel	"	"	200 " 400
Abyssinian horse	"	"	60 " 120
Country bred horse	"	"	200 " 600
Ordinary cow	"	"	100 " 160
A calf	"	"	30 " 50
Milch cow	"	"	100 " 120
A sheep	"	"	5 " 20
An ardeb of dhurra	"	"	6 " 8
An ardeb of wheat	"	"	30 " 40

If the above rates were calculated in the former currency, it will be seen that the price of these articles is less now than it was in the days of the Egyptian Government; and it is evident that this state of things is brought about by bad sales, depression of trade, and general poverty. The unfortunate natives, who, at most, own only a few acres of ground, and a small stock of domestic animals, are obliged to sell them in order to obtain the bare necessaries of life, and pay the oppressive taxes.

CHAPTER 17

Miscellaneous Remarks (Continued)

Throughout the preceding pages, I have frequently referred in general terms to the *khalifa's* system of administering justice. The *kadis*, or judges, are ready tools in the hands of their astute master. They are only permitted to act independently in trivial cases, such as family disputes, questions of property, and the like; but in all matters of importance, they must invariably refer to the *khalifa* for final decision, in giving which the latter invariably consults his own immediate interests; but at the same time his earnest endeavour is to appear before the public to be within the bounds of justice. The judges therefore, have a somewhat difficult task to perform: that is to say, they must invariably carry out the *khalifa's* wishes, and give them the appearance of being legally correct; whereas, in nine cases out of ten, they are entirely contrary to the first elements of justice and right.

The nominal codes of justice are the Moslem religious law and the "Instructions" of the *Mahdi*,—the latter being supposed to regenerate the former, which, through abuse and corruption, had been misapplied and, metaphorically speaking, trodden under foot. The main principle governing the "Instructions" is the necessity for absolute belief in the *Mahdi's* Divine mission,—to doubt this is considered an act of apostasy punishable by death, confiscation of property, or imprisonment for life. The *khalifa's* object being to seize all power, the "Instructions" are applied on every possible occasion; and he generally takes council with Yakub as to the means to be employed to secure his end; and as Yakub is the embodiment of every description of base intrigue and violence, the application of these laws results in the grossest injustice, oppression, and brutality.

The following comprise the Court of Justice of the two principal *kadis*: Hussein Wad Sahra, Jaali; Suleiman Wad el Hejaz, Gehemabi;

Hussein Wad Gisu, Homr; Ahmed Wad Hamdan, Arakini; Osman Wad Ahmed, Batahini; and Abdel Kader Wad Om Mariam, who was formerly Kadi of Kalakla and Prefect of Khartum; also Mohammed Wad el Mufti, who is the judge of petty disputes amongst the *mulazemin*. In addition to these, there are several *kadis* of the western tribes; but they are not permitted to give judgment, and merely give their votes to their higher colleagues.

Hussein Wad Sahra, whom the *khalifa* recently appointed to succeed the Kadi el Islam, Ahmed Wad Ali, completed his studies at the Azhar Mosque in Cairo, and is known as the most learned man in the Sudan. In spite, however, of his erudition, he made the fatal mistake of writing a small pamphlet in favour of the claims of Mohammed Ahmed to be the true *Mahdi*; and, having realised his error, he inwardly became his most bitter antagonist. Having now been summoned by the *khalifa* to fill this important position, he was unwillingly obliged to accept it; his sense of justice has occasionally got the better of his fear, and, in several instances, he has given just judgments contrary to the *khalifa's* wishes; consequently, he is not at present in favour with his master. He still nominally holds the post, but is seldom called to the councils. If fear of his life does not eventually get the upper hand, he will undoubtedly be shortly numbered amongst those who are to be got rid of.

Whenever the grand Council of Kadis assembles, it is always understood that they are about to pronounce some special judgment in accordance with the *khalifa's* wishes, which have been previously communicated to them. As a *kadi's* salary is not large,—from twenty to forty Dervish dollars a month,—it may be readily understood that venality enters largely into the minor judgments with which the *khalifa* does not interfere.

In accordance with the "Instructions," the evidence of witnesses is inviolable: it is not permitted to the accused to protest; and, consequently, it is the judges' prerogative to accept or refuse witnesses at will, and such a system naturally gives them ample opportunities of increasing their incomes.

The Kadi of the Mulazemin has special instructions that any case between one of the body-guard and natives of the country—even if they be the highest in the land—shall invariably be given in favour of the former; and so rigorously is this rule enforced, that it is now never thought worthwhile to enter into a lawsuit with one of the body-guard.

Attached to the Beit el Mal are two *kadis* whose special duty is to keep up connection with the *Mehekema* (Law Courts); they also issue the papers which must be signed when slaves are bought and sold, and on which they collect a small tax. There are also *kadis* in the market, police stations, and at the ferries who are charged with settling disputes and carrying out the duties of the Court of Small Causes.

The following brief notes on the state of religion, education, agriculture, commerce, and slave-trade may be of some interest.

Religion in the Sudan, as far as my experience goes, is governed by the principle that the end justifies the means. Proclamations and pamphlets enjoining strict attention to the performance of religious duties, and urging the abandonment of all earthly pleasures, are despatched to the remotest parts of Africa and Arabia, to Bornu, Dar Fellata, Mecca, and Medina. The *khalifa*, if his health permits it, attends the five daily prayers most regularly; and yet, at heart, no man could be more irreligious. During all the years in which I have been in the closest communication with him, I have never once seen or heard him say a prayer in his own house. Should any religious rite or ceremony interfere in the smallest degree with his wishes or ambitions, it is instantly abolished; but in doing so he is careful that the proposition for its abolition should emanate in the first instance from his *kadis*, who declare it necessary for the "maintenance of the faith;" and the astuteness with which these obsequious myrmidons twist and turn matters in order to suit the *khalifa's* will is deserving of a better cause. Whenever it is quite impossible to create some pretext for the execution of an unusually gross piece of injustice, Divine interposition and inspiration is invariably called to the rescue.

Abdullahi often addresses his followers from the pulpit in the mosque; but as he is entirely ignorant of theology, and knows little or nothing about the rudiments of religion, the scope of his sermons is excessively limited, and consists of a repetition of stereotyped phrases. On first mounting the pulpit, he greets the multitude with the words, "*Salam Aleikum ya ashab el Mahdi!*" (Peace be upon you, O friends of the *Mahdi!*). To this the congregation shout in one voice, "*Aleik es Salam ya Khalifat el Mahdi!*" (Peace be with thee, O *khalifa* of the *Mahdi!*). The *khalifa* then adds, "God bless you! God preserve you! May God lead the *Mahdi's* followers to victory!" and between each sentence the congregation shout, "*Amin*" (Amen).

He then goes on to say, "See, O friends of the *Mahdi*, how evil is the world! Think for how short a time we live in it! Were it not so the

Prophet and his follower, the Mahdi, would still be with us. We shall surely follow them. Prepare, therefore, for your journey to the next world. Do not seek earthly joys; say the five prayers daily. Read the *Mahdi's Rateb*; and be ever ready to fight against the unbelievers. Obey my orders (this sentence he frequently repeats), and the joys of Paradise will be yours. Those who are disobedient, and do not take heed of my words, are lost; for them, as for the unbeliever, eternal damnation and hell fire is prepared. I am the shepherd, and you are the sheep. As you tend your cattle and see that they do not eat what will harm them, so I watch over you and see that you do not get into evil ways. Think always of the Almightiness of God.

"Think of the cow, which is made of flesh and blood and skin and bones; and yet you can obtain sweet white milk from her. Do you not recognise God's power in this?[1] Remain faithful to your vows to the *Mahdi* and to myself. Obey my commands, which will give you peace on earth and joy in the world to come. As the stones of a building go to make the structure complete, so should you support one another. Forgive one another. Love each other as the sons of one mother (and the crowd shouts, "We forgive each other!"). May God bless you! May He lead you to victory! May He ever preserve and keep you! Depart now in peace; but, before we separate, shout in one voice, '*La Illaha ilalaha Mohammed Rasul Allah.*' This will enlighten your hearts and strengthen your faith." The congregation then disperses with loud shouts of "*Amin, la illaha,* etc." All his sermons vary very little from the above.

The repetition of the five prayers, and the reading of the *Koran*, on which no commentaries are permitted to be made, make up the sum total of religion, interspersed now and then with the reading of the *Mahdi's* instructions and the repetition, twice a day, of the *Rateb*. If any person says prayers at home, instead of at the mosque, without just cause or reason, he is adjudged by the *khalifa* as "disobedient;" and such prayers are, he says, not acceptable to God. From his point of view, true religion consists of servile obedience to his commands; and by this means alone can the soul enter into everlasting joys.

He has forbidden pilgrimage to Mecca, having substituted for it pilgrimage to the tomb of the *Mahdi*, who is the Prophet's representative. Although the Sudanese intensely dislike this innovation, they are perforce obliged to accept it; and as it is now impossible for them to

---

1. The *khalifa*, being a Baggari, or cattle-owning Arab, frequently draws similes of this description.

return to the orthodox faith, which they so unwittingly cast aside, they now accept the situation, and carry out their mock religious duties in the most businesslike manner, but without the smallest belief in their efficacy.

Education and religious instruction are practically non-existent. Some boys, and occasionally a few girls, are taught to recite the *Koran* and the *Rateb* in the *mesjids* (religious schools attached to the mosques), of which a few are allowed to be privately kept up. A small percentage of these children, when they have completed their course in the *mesjids*, are sent to the Beit el Mal, where they become apprentices to the old government clerks, and learn a certain amount of business correspondence. The system of theological instruction which obtains in most Moslem countries, but which was never much in vogue in the Sudan, has now ceased to exist altogether.

Cultivation of the land south of Berber is carried on during the rainy season, which in the northern districts begins in July, and in the southern at the end of May, or early in June, and lasts till the end of October; but there are now immense tracts of once fertile soil which, through want of cultivation and depopulation, have become tracts of desert or a tangled wilderness. The staple grain of the Sudan is *dhurra*, and if there is a plentiful rainfall, the supply is generally good; but if there is a scarcity of rain, a famine almost invariably ensues, and the poorer classes of the population undergo terrible privations. On these occasions, they generally have to proceed to Karkoj on the Blue Nile, or some distance up the White Nile, and bring *dhurra* to Omdurman in boats.

From Wadi Haifa to Fashoda on the White Nile, or to Famaka on the Blue Nile, narrow strips of river bank are cultivated by *sakias* (water-wheels) or *shadufs* (hand-buckets); and, in addition to *dhurra*, Turkish maize, beans, lentils, peas, and pumpkins are cultivated. Owners of water-wheels in the vicinity of the larger towns cultivate small quantities of sugar-cane, water-melons, radishes, sweet cucumbers, and various kinds of vegetables, which find a ready market; and when the rainy season is over cotton is planted. The most productive land is, of course, on the islands, which, during high Nile, are often completely submerged; and as the river sinks they are sown almost without labour, and produce excellent crops.

Oranges and lemons are grown in the neighbourhood of Khartum; but they are very small, and contain little juice. A few pomegranates, grapes, and figs are also to be had; but they are all of a very inferior quality. There are, of course, quantities of date-palms, of which the fruit forms one of the principal items of food; but the supply is barely sufficient for the consumption. In the Dar Mahass and Sukkot districts of the Dongola Province the supply of dates is very considerable; and they are brought from thence to various parts of the Sudan, the drying process being carried on principally in the Berber and Robatab districts.

Gum-arabic is collected in the forests of Southern Kordofan, and at one time constituted the principal wealth of this province. It was gathered principally by the Gimeh and Gowama Arabs; but the former have been forced to emigrate, and the latter, through constant tyranny and oppression, have been so reduced that scarcely a sixth remains of their original numbers. In the days of the Egyptian Government, from eight hundred thousand to one million *kantars* of gum-arabic were gathered annually; but at present at most thirty thousand *kantars* are produced, and were it not that one of the former chiefs of the Beit el Mal had represented to the *khalifa* the increase which would accrue to his private treasury by allowing the collection of gum, it is probable the custom of gum picking would have fallen into entire disuse.

The cultivation of tobacco was formerly one of the principal pursuits of the native population; but as smoking is strictly prohibited by the Mahdist code, this product has entirely died out, though occasionally small quantities are smuggled in from the Tagalla and Nuba mountains, and fetch large prices; but any persons guilty of infringing the regulations in this respect suffer very heavy penalties.

The once extensive commerce of the Sudan has now sunk down to comparatively nothing and the roads which were formerly traversed by numberless caravans are now deserted, obliterated by sand, or overgrown with rank vegetation. The principal routes were,—

1. The Arbaïn or forty days' road, from Darfur to Assiut, or from Kordofan through the Bayuda desert to Dongola and Wadi Halfa.
2. From Khartum, *via* Berber, to Assuan, or *via* Abu Hamed, to Korosko.
3. From Khartum, *via* Berber or Kassala, to Suakin.
4. From Gallabat, Gedaref, and Kassala to Massawa.

At present the only roads used by occasional caravans are from Berber to Assuan and Suakin. Shortly after the capture of Khartum, the Sudan merchants imported to Assuan considerable quantities of the captured gold and silver ornaments; and, partly owing to this fact, and partly to the amount of spoil accumulated in the *khalifa's* private treasury, the supply of these metals has become so reduced that Abdullahi has given strict orders to the merchants that they should on no account take with them to Egypt any gold or silver except what was absolutely necessary for the expenses of the journey. This amount was fixed by the Beit el Mal, and had to be taken in old currency, the value of which was inserted in the passport.

As the sadly diminished trade with Egypt began to revive, natural products, which had been the former wealth of the Sudan, were again made the medium of commerce. Gum, ostrich feathers, tamarinds, *senna*-leaves, etc. were collected in the Beit el Mal, as well as ivory, and were sold by auction at local currency rates; but as the majority of these products came from the western districts, which, owing to war, famine, and disease had become almost depopulated, the supply was scanty. In exchange for these, the merchants brought from Egypt Manchester goods, which are greatly in demand in the Sudan. Gum is a monopoly, and the price paid for it varies greatly.

The Beit el Mal purchases at the rate of twenty to thirty dollars (Omla Gedida), and sells to the merchants at the rate of thirty to forty dollars. The purchaser generally receives permission to take it to Egypt, and is taxed at the rate of a dollar a hundred weight at Berber, where the amount is carefully checked with the bill of lading. If he wishes to take it to Suakin or Assuan, he is obliged to pay a tax of a further dollar a hundred weight; but in this case it is a *Maria Theresa* dollar, which is equivalent to five *Omla Gedidas;* and thus already a sixth of the original cost has been added in taxation.

Ostrich-hunting has now become almost impossible, as the Arabs have practically no guns, and it is most difficult to procure any ammunition. An attempt was made to hunt ostriches on horseback; but this also was forbidden by the *khalifa*, and, consequently, very few feathers are brought into the market. The Arabs then tried ostrich-breeding, and caught some young birds; but this again was forbidden on the grounds that it was not allowed by religion, and the plucking of birds was made an offence which was most severely punished. The *khalifa's* object in imposing these absurd strictures was merely to appear in the eyes of the public as a very religious Moslem.

In consequence, ostrich-breeders had no other course but to kill their birds, and for some days Omdurman was flooded with ostrich meat. I have heard that attempts are made by some of the desert Arabs to rear ostriches in a species of cage made of the branches of trees; but the feathers obtained in this way are so few as to make the trade in this commodity almost unappreciable.

Ivory comes from the Equatorial regions in considerable quantities about once a year, and generally finds its way to Suakin; and as these districts appear to be gradually passing out of Mahdist control, it is hardly probable that the amount will increase in future years. Occasionally, a few tusks are brought from the Southern Darfur districts; but unless the Dervishes re-occupy the Bahr el Ghazal in force, their ivory trade stands in danger of dying out altogether.

Goods can only be imported from Egypt by the Assuan and Suakin roads. Formerly, a certain amount of trade was carried on between Suakin and Kassala, and Kassala and Massawa; but since the occupation of the Eastern Sudan by the Italians, it has almost entirely ceased. The goods imported are generally of an inferior quality, and consist mostly of material for women's dresses and men's *jibbas*; but to the inhabitants of the Sudan this is a matter of little consequence, for they much prefer gaudy and tawdry material to the more durable fabrics. Indeed, it would be very difficult, if not impossible, to find purchasers for a better class of goods in the Sudan.

One of the principal imports is scent of every variety, such as sandal-wood oil, cloves, scented seeds, etc., for all of which the Sudanese ladies have a strong predilection. A certain amount of sugar, rice, inferior jams, and dried fruit also find purchasers amongst the more wealthy of the population. The importation of all articles made of iron, brass, tin, copper, etc. has, for some time past, been rigorously prohibited by the Egyptian Government, and now it is almost impossible to obtain a pair of scissors or a razor. Copper cooking-utensils have risen to an enormous price; and most of those which previously existed have been bought up by the arsenal for the manufacture of cartridges. Consequently, food is now cooked almost entirely in earthenware vessels.

The tax of *ushr* (a tenth) is levied on all goods imported to the Sudan. It must be paid in either money or kind, and is frequently taken more than once along the road. All goods on arrival in Omdurman are taken to the Beit el Mal and stamped; and here the *ushr* is again taken. Merchants, therefore, owing to the heavy taxes imposed, in addition to the presents they have to make to the various chiefs, have generally paid half as much again over and above the value of their goods. They are therefore obliged to considerably raise the price; and even then the total profit is by no means a large one. Several of the more wealthy inhabitants of the Sudan have taken to trading with Egypt, not so much with a view to making money, as to spending a few months away from the atmosphere of the *khalifa's* authority. It is by means of trade alone that any of the unfortunate inhabitants of the Sudan can temporarily escape from the hands of that tyrant, whose rule is more detested than ever. Most of the merchants, having their wives, families, and relatives in the Sudan, are obliged eventually to return; and, were it not for these ties, I think that few men who have the chance of leaving the Sudan would ever return.

But if trade in general is in a state of depression, there is one trade to which the advent of the *Mahdi* and *khalifa* has given a great impulse. I refer, of course, to the slave-trade. As, however, the export of slaves to Egypt is strictly prohibited, this trade is confined entirely to the provinces under the khalifa's control. In prohibiting the export of slaves, the *khalifa* acts on the wise principle that he should not increase the power of his adversaries at his own expense. It is, of course, quite impossible for him to absolutely prevent slaves being taken occasionally to Egypt or Arabia; but the slave-caravans which were formerly sent from the Sudan have now almost completely stopped.

A few years ago, (as at time of first publication), quantities of slaves were sent from Abyssinia by Abu Anga, and from Fashoda by Zeki Tummal, as well as from Darfur and the Nuba mountains by Osman Wad Adam, and were generally sold by public auction for the benefit of the Beit el Mal, or the *khalifa's* private treasury. The transport of slaves is carried on with the same execrable and heartless cruelty which characterises their capture. Of the thousands of Abyssinian Christians seized by Abu Anga, the majority were women and children; and under the cruel lash of the whip they were forced to march on foot the whole distance from Abyssinia to Omdurman; wrenched from their families, provided with scarcely enough food to keep body and soul together, barefooted, and almost naked, they were driven through the country like herds of cattle. The greater number of them perished on the road; and those who arrived in Omdurman were in so pitiable a condition that purchasers could scarcely be found for them, whilst numbers were given away for nothing by the *khalifa*.

After the defeat of the Shilluks, Zeki Tummal packed thousands of these wretched creatures into the small barges used for the transport of his troops, and despatched them to Omdurman. Hundreds died from suffocation and overcrowding on the journey; and, on the arrival of the remnant, the *khalifa* appropriated most of the young men as recruits for his bodyguard, whilst the women and young girls were sold by public auction, which lasted several days. Hungry, and in many cases naked, these unfortunate creatures lay huddled together in front of the Beit el Mal. For food, they were given an utterly inadequate quantity of uncooked *dhurra*. Hundreds fell ill; and for these poor wretches it was also impossible to find purchasers. Wearily they dragged their emaciated bodies to the river bank, where they died; and as nobody would take the trouble to bury them, the corpses were pushed into the river and swept away.

But a worse fate than this befell the slaves who had the misfortune to be sent from Darfur along the broad stretches of waterless desert which lie between that province and Omdurman. These miserable creatures were mercilessly driven forward day and night; and it would be impossible for me to describe here the execrable measures adopted by these brutal slave-drivers to force on their prey to their destination. When the poor wretches could go no further, their ears were cut off as a proof to the owner that his property had died on the road. Some of my friends told me that on one occasion they had found an unfortunate woman whose ears had been cut off, but who was still alive. Taking pity on her, they brought her to El Fasher, where she eventually recovered, whilst her ears had been duly exposed in Omdurman as proof of her death.

Latterly, no large caravans of slaves have arrived in Omdurman, because the majority of the slave-producing districts, such as Darfur, have become depopulated, or, in some cases, the tribes, such as the Tama, Massalit, etc., have thrown off allegiance to the *khalifa*. Consignments, however, still come from Reggaf; but, owing to the long and tedious journey, numbers of them perish on the way. As the supplies from Gallabat, Kordofan, and Darfur have considerably diminished, the *khalifa* now allows the *emirs* to sell slaves to the itinerant Gellabas; and the latter are obliged to sign a paper giving a descriptive return of their purchase, and the amount paid. They are permitted to re-sell on the same conditions.

There is of course a daily sale of slaves in Omdurman; but the purchase of male slaves is forbidden, as they are looked upon as the *khalifa's* monopoly, and are generally turned into soldiers. Anyone wishing to dispose of a male slave must send him to the Beit el Mal, where a purely nominal price is paid for him; and he is then, if likely to make a good soldier, recruited for the *mulazemin*, but if unsuitable, he is sent off to work as a labourer in his master's fields. The sale of women and girls is permissible everywhere, with the proviso that a paper must be signed by two witnesses of the sale, one of whom, if possible, should be a *kadi*, certifying that the slave sold is the actual property of the vendor. This system was brought into force because slaves frequently ran away from their masters, were caught and sold by other persons as their own property, and thus theft of slaves was a very common practice in Omdurman. They were frequently enticed into other people's houses, or secretly induced to leave the fields, then thrown into chains and carried off to distant parts of the country, where they were sold at very low rates. In accordance with the Mohammedan Law, slaves cannot be witnesses; and, being well aware of their inferior position, these stolen creatures, as long as they are kindly treated, are not dissatisfied with their lot.

In Omdurman itself, in an open space a short distance to the southeast of the Beit el Mal, stands a house roughly built of mud-bricks, which is known as the Suk er Rekik (slave-market). Under the pretext that I wanted to buy or exchange slaves, I several times received the *khalifa's* permission to visit it, and found ample opportunity for closely observing the conduct of the business. Here professional slave-dealers assemble to offer their wares for sale. Round the walls of the house numbers of women and girls stand or sit. They vary from the decrepit and aged half-clad slaves of the working-class, to the gaily-decked *surya* (concubine); and as the trade is looked upon as a perfectly natural and lawful business, those put up for sale are carefully examined from head to foot, without the least restriction, just as if they were animals. The mouth is opened to see if the teeth are in good condition. The upper part of the body and the back are laid bare; and the arms carefully looked at. They are then told to take a few steps backward or forward in order that their movements and gait may be examined.

A series of questions are put to them to test their knowledge of Arabic. In fact, they have to submit to any examination the intending purchaser may wish to make. *Suryas*, of course, vary considerably in price; but the whole matter is treated by the slaves without the smallest concern. They consider it perfectly natural, and have no notion of being treated otherwise. Only occasionally one can see by the expression of a woman or girl that she feels this close scrutiny; possibly her position with her former master was rather that of a servant than a slave, or she may have been looked upon almost as a member of the family, and may have been brought to this unhappy position by force of circumstances, or through some hateful inhumanity on the part of her former master.

When the intending purchaser has completed his scrutiny, he then refers to the dealer, asks him what he paid for her, or if he has any other better wares for sale. He will probably complain that her face is not pretty enough, that her body is not sufficiently developed, that she does not speak Arabic, and so on, with the object of reducing the price as much as possible; whilst, on the other hand, the owner will do his utmost to show up her good qualities, charms, etc., into the detail of which it is not necessary to enter here. Amongst the various "secret defects" which oblige the dealer to reduce his price are snoring, bad qualities of character, such as thieving, and many others; but when at last the sale has been finally arranged, the paper is drawn out and signed, the money paid, and the slave becomes the property of her new master. Payment is always made in local currency (*Omla Gedi*da dollars), and runs approximately as follows:—

For an aged working slave, fifty to eighty dollars; for a middle aged woman eighty to one hundred and twenty dollars; for young girls between eight and eleven years of age, according to looks, one hundred and ten to one hundred and sixty dollars; and for *suryas* (concubines), according to looks, one hundred and eighty to seven hundred dollars. These rates, of course, vary also according to market value, or special demand for a particular race.

There are practically no industries in the Sudan, as, with the exception of the articles I have already mentioned, there are no exports. Formerly, gold and silver filigree work was sent to Egypt; but, owing to the scarcity of these metals, and to the *Mahdi's* edict against wearing jewellery, this export has altogether ceased. There is a considerable manufacture and trade in long and short spears of various shapes, stirrup-irons, horse and donkey bits, knives for fastening on the arm, as well as agricultural implements. Wooden saddles for horses, camels, and mules, *angarebs*, boxes for carrying clothes, and doors, windows, and shutters of a primitive description are also made. Formerly, boat-building was extensively carried on; but, owing to the *khalifa's* confiscation of all boats on the Nile, it ceased almost entirely, till about a year ago, (1897), when, with the *khalifa's* permission, it recommenced. As, however, all new boats are taxed highly by the Beit el Mal, there is little inducement to the builders to undertake such profitless work.

There is a certain amount of leather-work in red and yellow shoes, sandals, saddles of different sorts, harness, amulets, sword scabbards, and

IN THE SLAVE MARKET, OMDURMAN.

knife sheaths, etc., whilst whips in large quantities are made from the hide of the hippopotamus. There is also a considerable cotton industry. Every woman or girl spins for her own use or for sale; and in every village there are numbers of weavers who work the spun-yarn into a variety of materials. In the Gezira are woven common cotton stuffs,—such as *tobs*, *damur*, and *geny* (names of cloths) in lengths of about ten yards. These are brought to the market in large quantities, and are principally used for the clothing of the commoner classes.

The finest yarns are spun in the province of Berber. Strips of coloured silk are frequently interwoven in the material, which is used principally for turbans and *hazams* (the strips of cotton which are used to bind round the body), as well as coverings of various sorts, and shawls. A certain amount of cotton stuff is made in the Dongola province; but that district is chiefly noted for the manufacture of sailcloth. Materials from Kordofan are noted for their durability rather than for their beauty.

In addition to spinning, the women occupy themselves largely in plaiting mats of various shapes and sizes from the leaves of the *dom* palm, which are sold largely in all parts of the Sudan. The best quality of these mats is made from the narrow strips of the palm leaves, barley straw, and thin pieces of leather. Mats of a similar description are also made for placing under dishes on the dinner-table. The workmanship of some of these is so fine and good that a certain quantity find their way to Egypt, where they are sold as curiosities. The Darfur women are specially clever in making these mats, into which are interwoven various sorts of glass beads, and the result is sometimes extremely pretty.

In the preceding pages, I have endeavoured to give a brief outline of the *khalifa's* life, and the existing state of affairs in the country; but this would not be complete without a few remarks regarding the moral condition of the people. The attempted regeneration of the faith by the *Mahdi*, who disregarded the former religious teaching and customs, has resulted in a deterioration of morals, which, even at the best of times, were very lax in the Sudan. Partly from fear of the *khalifa*, and partly for their own personal interests and advantage, the people have made religion a mere profession; and this has now become their second nature, and has brought with it a condition of immorality which is almost indescribable.

The majority of the inhabitants, unhappy and discontented with the existing state of affairs, and fearing that their personal freedom may become even more restricted than it is, seem to have determined to enjoy their life as much as their means will allow, and to lose no time about it. As there is practically no social life or spiritual intercourse, they seem to have resolved to make up for this want by indulging their passion for women to an abnormal extent. Their object is to obtain as many of these in marriage as possible, as well as concubines; and the *Mahdi's* tenets allow them the fullest scope in this direction. For instance, the expenses in connection with marriage have been greatly diminished.

The dowry for a girl has been reduced from ten to five dollars; and for a widow, five dollars, a common dress, a pair of shoes or sandals, and a few scents. Should a man desire to marry a girl, her father or guardian must consent, unless there are some very cogent reasons for not doing so. Under any circumstances, they are held responsible that their daughters or wards become wives as soon as they reach a convenient age. The acquisition, therefore, of four wives—which is the number authorised by the *Koran*—has become a very simple matter, and in most cases is considered merely a means of acquiring a small amount of personal property.

Moreover, a large proportion of the women are quite agreeable to this arrangement, and enter into matrimony either with the object of obtaining some clothes and a little money, or temporarily changing their mode of life, being well aware that, in accordance with the law, they can dissolve marriage ties without difficulty. If a woman seeks a divorce, she retains her dowry, unless the separation rises from aversion to her husband, in which case the dowry is returned if the man wishes it. I know many men who, in the space of ten years, have been married forty or fifty times at least; and there are also many women who, during the same period, have had fifteen or twenty husbands, and in their case the law enjoins that between each divorce they must wait three months at least.

As a rule, concubines, of whom a man may legally have as many as he likes, lead a most immoral life. They rarely live in the same house as their master, unless they have children by him, in which case they cannot be sold; but in the majority of cases they are bought with the object of being retained merely for a very short time, and subsequently sold again at a profit. This constant changing of hands leads to great moral deterioration. Their youth and beauty quickly fade; and, as a rule, they age prematurely, and then enter upon a life of hardship and moral degradation which it is almost impossible to conceive.

It is a common practice for merchants to make pecuniary profit out of the immorality of their slaves. They buy young girls, permit them to enjoy a certain amount of freedom by seeking a shelter and livelihood in the manner which suits them best; and for this privilege they refund to their masters a percentage of their gains.

The greatest vice exists amongst the slaves of the *mulazemin*. The latter entice women to their quarters, where they remain a short time with them as their wives; but the freest interchange takes place between them. The *khalifa* does not seem to think it worthwhile to check this immorality, as he imagines that by allowing them to please themselves, his own slaves will become more attached to him, and will not wish to leave him. It may be readily conceived that the result of this moral laxity has led to the prevalence of the worst sort of disease, which has taken such a hold of all classes of the population, both free and slaves, that were it not for the warm and dry climate, the ravages would be terrible. As it is, the general state of health is very unsatisfactory, and is considerably aggravated by the complete absence of medicines necessary to check the malady.

A certain number of people also indulge in unnatural love: and at first the *khalifa* made some attempt to check this by banishment to Reggaf; but latterly he has given up doing so. He has come to the conclusion that it is much easier to rule by despotism and tyranny, a degraded nation than one which possesses a high standard of morality. For this reason, he both hates and fears the Jaalin, who inhabit the Nile banks between Hagger el Asal and Berber, because they are almost the only Arabs in the Sudan who maintain a well-regulated family life, and hold morality in high esteem as a necessary condition for a healthy and contented existence.

The widows of the *Mahdi* are forcibly prevented from leading a corrupt life; as, immediately after his master's death, the *khalifa*, in honour of his memory, confined these women in houses surrounded by high walls, in the immediate vicinity of his tomb, where they are strictly guarded by eunuchs. Much against their will, not only the wives and concubines, but also many of the young girls,—most of whom were daughters of former government officials, and who were taken into the harem when quite young, in order to become his future wives,—have been thus forcibly deprived of the possibility of re-marrying, and are so closely guarded that they are only permitted to see their female relatives once a year. They are supplied merely with the bare necessaries of life, and long for their freedom. Let us hope that before very long it may come!

In spite of his despotism, the *khalifa* is in considerable fear of his life. He ruthlessly evicted all the local inhabitants of those portions of the town in the immediate neighbourhood of his own residence; and their places have been taken by his enormous body-guard, whose numbers he daily seeks to increase. These he has surrounded by an immense wall, within which he and his relatives live, while all persons of whom he is in the slightest degree suspicious are forced to reside without the enclosure. Within, however, all is not peace and contentment. The constant duties he imposes on his body-guard have produced a feeling of irritation. They grumble at the small pay they receive, and do not appreciate the restrictions imposed on their social life.

Thousands of these who belong to the free Arab tribes are prevented from having any intercourse whatever with their relations. They are scarcely ever permitted to quit the enclosure; and their smallest offences are punished with appalling severity. Abdullahi is surrounded day and night by his own specially appointed guard, and by numbers of faithful servants; and no persons—not even his nearest relatives—are permitted to approach him with arms in their hands. Should anyone be commanded to see the *khalifa*, his sword and knife, which he invariably wears, are taken from him, and he is generally searched before being admitted to the audience-chamber. This general mistrust has added to his unpopularity; and, even amongst his most devoted adherents, remarks are frequently let fall in an undertone, commenting on his despotism and his personal fears.

In spite, however, of all this undue severity, the *khalifa* has not succeeded in keeping his own tribe in hand. On their first arrival in the Nile valley, they indulged in wholesale raids on the local population, seizing their grain, ravishing their women, and carrying off their children. Indeed affairs became so serious that the *khalifa* was obliged to issue an order that no Taaisha Arab would be permitted to leave the town without special permission; but his instructions were practically ignored, and lawlessness is even more rife than before. The conduct of these Arabs is unbearable. They openly boast that their relationship with the *khalifa* has made them masters of the country, and that they intend to assert themselves. They have seized all the best pastures for their cattle and horses; and they live on the fat of the land,—a state of affairs which has caused considerable jealousy amongst the other western tribes, who view the Taaisha with no very friendly feelings.

Of all this the *khalifa* is well aware; but I do not think he realises how unpopular he really is, and his constant effort is to retain the sympathy of his *emirs* by frequently sending them secretly by night presents of money and slaves. The latter do not hesitate to accept these gifts, which they know have been unfairly gained; and their opinion of the *khalifa*, instead of being improved, remains as it was before. He imagined that the learned and educated element of the population—which is exceedingly small—was on his side, because he allowed Kadi Hussein to give lectures in the mosque afternoon and evening prayers on the subject of the Moslem rights of inheritance. As all such reunions were forbidden by the *Mahdi*, some of the *ulema* (learned men) were stupid enough to think that this new departure was a sign of progress.

The *khalifa* himself attended these lectures; and, noticing one day that some of the *ulema*, in order to rest themselves, sat cross-legged instead of in a submissive attitude of prayer, he openly reprimanded them, and declared in a loud voice that all persons, whether learned or ignorant, must in his presence pay him the respect due to him. A few days later, Kadi Hussein inadvertently quoted in his lecture a chapter to the effect that learning was a high virtue, and that kings and princes should realise this, and accept the advice of learned men. The *khalifa*, who is utterly ignorant of reading and writing, got up and left the mosque in a rage; and, a few days later, he issued an order that the meetings should be discontinued for the future. Kadi Hussein immediately fell in favour, and soon afterwards had the further misfortune to disagree with the *khalifa* on a question respecting slaves.

The latter had called upon the *kadis* for an opinion as to whether all male and female slaves who might have taken refuge with the *mulazemin*, and were not claimed by their rightful owners within twenty days, should not become the actual property of their new masters; but as no persons living outside the wall are under any circumstances permitted to enter the enclosure, it stands to reason that masters of runaway slaves have no possibility of searching the quarters of the *mulazemin*. On these grounds the *kadi* suggested that runaway slaves should be publicly exposed in the market-place for a short time, and that if no one appeared to claim them within a specified period, they should then become the property of the Beit el Mal. As the *khalifa* had previously given private instructions to his *mulazemin* to retain all slaves belonging to the Nile valley tribes, and to return only those who belonged to the western Arabs, the *kadi's* proposition did not at all suit him, whilst the other *kadis*, to whom he had referred the matter, concurred with him against Kadi Hussein. The friends of the latter now trembled for his life; but the *khalifa* allowed it to pass for the moment, and is only waiting for some other opportunity to involve him more deeply in what he is pleased to term "an act of disobedience."

The *khalifa* has not moved out of Omdurman for upwards of ten years. Here he has centralised all power, stored up all ammunition, and gathered under his personal surveillance all those whom he suspects, obliging them to say the five prayers daily in his presence, and listen to his sermons. He has declared Omdurman to be the sacred city of the *Mahdi*. It is strange to think that ten years ago this great town was merely a little village lying opposite to Khartum, and inhabited by a few brigands. It was not for some time after the fall of Khartum that the *Mahdi* decided to settle there. Mimosa-trees filled up the space now occupied by the mosque and the residences of the three *khalifas*.

Abdullahi took as his own property all ground lying south of the mosque, whilst that on the north side was divided between Khalifa Sherif and Khalifa Ali Wad Helu. During his lifetime, the *Mahdi* had declared that Omdurman was merely a temporary camp, as the Prophet had revealed to him that he should depart this life in Syria, after conquering Egypt and Arabia; but his early death had shattered all his plans and the hopes of his followers.

From north to south, the new city covers a length of about six English miles. The southern extremity lies almost exactly opposite the southwest end of Khartum. At first, everyone wanted to live as near the river banks as possible, in order to facilitate the drawing of water, consequently the breadth of the city is considerably less than its length; and it is in no place over three miles in width. At first, it consisted of thousands and thousands of straw huts; and the mosque was originally an oblong enclosure surrounded by a mud wall four hundred and sixty yards long and three hundred and fifty yards broad; but this has now been replaced by one made of burnt brick, and then whitewashed over.

After this, the *khalifa* began building brick houses for himself and his brother, then for his relatives, whilst the *emirs* and most of the wealthy people followed his example. I have already described the construction of the *Mahdi's* tomb; but before I left Omdurman much of the whitewash had been knocked off by the weather, which spoilt its general appearance. Above the apex of the dome are three hollow brass balls, one above the other, connected together by a lance, the head of which forms the top ornament of the structure. I have often heard people say that the *khalifa* erected this spear to show that he is perfectly prepared to declare war against the heavens if his wishes are not carried out.

Occasionally Abdullahi shuts himself up for hours in this mausoleum, probably with the object of obtaining some special inspiration; but since the execution of the *Mahdi's* relatives, his visits are much less frequent; and it is generally supposed he dreads to be alone with the body of his dead master, whose tenets and influence he has, not in words but in deeds, so persistently overturned. Every Friday, the large doors in the surrounding enclosure are opened to admit the pilgrims; and as every Mahdist is ordered to attend on these days to repeat the prayers for the dead, thousands are to be seen in the various attitudes of prayer, beseeching the protection of the Almighty through the intermediary of the Saint (?) who lies buried there; but I doubt not that many fervent prayers ascend to the throne of God for relief from the terrible oppression and tyranny of his despotic successor.

South of the tomb, and adjoining the great mosque, lies the enormous enclosure of the *khalifa*. It consists of a high wall built of red bricks, which is subdivided into several smaller courts, all of which are in communication with each other; and nearest to the mosque are his own private apartments, to the east of which are those of his wives, the stables, store-houses, quarters of the eunuchs, etc., etc. In the centre of the eastern face of the mosque is a large wooden door (the other entrances to the mosque have no doors) through which admission is obtained to the *khalifa's* private apartments and reception chambers. On entering the main gate, one passes through a sort of porch, leading into a small court, in which are two rooms, one side of each of which is left completely open; and it is here that the *khalifa* receives his guests.

A door leads out of this court into the private apartments; and the youthful attendants are the only persons allowed to enter. The various houses within the enclosure are constructed in the shape of large detached halls, on one or both sides of which are verandahs. On the roof of one of these buildings a second story has been added, on all four sides of which are windows, from which a complete view of the town can be obtained.

The reception chambers are furnished with the greatest simplicity. An *angareb*, over which a palm-mat is spread, is the only article of furniture; but his interior apartments are provided with all the luxuries it is possible to procure in the Sudan. Brass and iron bedsteads with mosquito curtains,—the spoil of Khartum,—carpets, silk-covered cushions, door and window curtains of every variety of colour and texture, are the principal articles of furniture, while the verandahs are provided with the universal *angareb* and palm-mat. Compared with the *khalifa's* early mode of life, these articles constitute the most extreme luxuries.

To the east of the *khalifa's* enclosure lies the house of his son, which is furnished much in the same style as that of his father, but with even greater luxury. Several large brass chandeliers from Khartum are suspended from the ceilings; and there is an immense garden made from earth transported from the banks of the Nile, and in which hundreds of slaves are employed daily. The latter are justly irritated with the great love of show which is the distinguishing characteristic of their young master, whilst they themselves are provided with scarcely enough food for their maintenance.

The *khalifa* and his son spend much of their time in building and furnishing new apartments, and in making their lives as pleasant and comfortable as possible. Yakub follows their example; and every day numbers of workmen are to be seen streaming towards these two houses, carrying beams, stone, mortar, and other requisite building-material. Khalifa Ali Wad Helu's house is very much smaller, and is furnished with great simplicity.

In addition to his principal residence, Abdullahi possesses houses in the northern and southern districts of the city; but they are built and furnished on much simpler lines, and are merely used by him as rest-houses when he despatches troops on expeditions from the capital, or goes out to inspect freshly arrived detachments from the provinces. He seldom stays in these houses more than a day or two at a time. He has also built a house near the river, and close to the old government fort, the ditches of which have now been filled in. He generally goes to this house when steamers are about to start for Reggaf, in order that he may personally superintend embarkations.

The Beit el Amana, or arsenal, is separated from Yakub's house by a broad open space. It consists of a large building enclosed by stone walls, and here are stored the guns, rifles, ammunition, and other warlike material, as well as the five carriages belonging to the governor-generals and to the Catholic Mission. At intervals of every few paces sentries are posted in small sentry boxes; and they are charged to allow no unauthorised persons to enter the building. Just north of the arsenal lies a building in which are stored the flags of all the Emirs residing in Omdurman; and beside it is a semi-circular building about twenty feet high, provided with stairs, where the *khalifa's* war-drums are kept. A little further to the east is the cartridge and small-arms manufactory.

On the north side of the city, and close to the river, is the Beit el Mal, which is an enormous walled-in enclosure subdivided into a variety of courts in which are stored goods coming from all parts of the Sudan and from Egypt, as well as grain stores and slave courts. A little to the south of the Beit el Mal lies the public slave-market, and, in close proximity, the Beit el Mal of the Mulazemin has been erected.

The town of Omdurman is built for the most part on fairly level ground, but here and there are a few small hills. The soil consists mostly of hard red clay, and is very stony, with occasional patches of sand. For his own convenience, the *khalifa* has driven large straight roads through various parts of the town; and to make way for these numbers of houses were levelled, but no compensation was given to their owners. A glance at the rough plan attached to the end of the book will give the reader an approximate idea of the extent and general situation of the town and principal buildings, and its relative position with reference to Khartum, which is now a complete ruin, the dock-yard alone being kept up, and communication between it and Omdurman maintained by a submarine cable worked by some of the former Government telegraph officials.

Outside the large unfinished wall built along the road leading to the Beit el Mal are a number of shops belonging to the various trades, all of which are kept quite distinct,—such as carpenters, barbers, tailors, butchers, etc., etc. The *Mehekemet es Suk* (market police) are charged with maintaining order in the town; and the gallows erected in various parts of the city are a very evident indication of the system of government of the country.

The population of the city is located entirely according to tribes. The western Arabs live for the most part in the southern quarters, whilst the northern portion has been allotted to the Nile valley people; and in addition to the market police, the various sections of the populace are obliged to supply a number of watchmen for the preservation of public security in their respective quarters, and they must report any disturbances to the night patrols.

With the exception of the few broad roads which the *khalifa* has made for his own convenience, the only communications between the various quarters consist of numbers of narrow winding lanes; and in these all the filth of the city is collected. Their wretched condition, and the smells which emanate from these pestilential by-paths are beyond description. Dead horses, camels, donkeys, and goats block the way; and the foulest refuse lies scattered about. Before certain feast-days, the *khalifa* issues orders that the city is to be cleaned; but, beyond sweeping all these carcases and refuse into corners, nothing further is done; and when the rainy season begins the fetid air exhaling from these decaying rubbish heaps generally produces some fatal epidemic, which sweeps off the inhabitants by hundreds.

Formerly, there were cemeteries within the city; but now all the dead must be buried in the desert north of the parade ground.

Fever and dysentery are the prevailing maladies in Omdurman, and between the months of November and March an almost continuous epidemic of typhus fever rages.

Of late years numbers of new wells have been made. Those north of the mosque give good water; but those in the southern quarters of the city are mostly brackish. They vary in depth from thirty to ninety feet, and are generally dug by the prisoners under the direction of the *saier*.

"*He has been taken to the Saier*," is an expression one frequently hears; and it means that some wretched creature has been carried off to the prison. The mere mention of this word awakens feelings of horror and dread in the minds of all who hear it. The prison is situated in the southeastern quarter of the city, near the river, and is surrounded by a high wall. A gate, strongly guarded day and night by armed Blacks, gives access to an inner court, in which several small mud and stone huts have been erected. During the daytime, the unhappy prisoners, most of them heavily chained and manacled, lie about in the shade of the buildings. Complete silence prevails, broken only by the clanking of the chains, the hoarse orders of the hard-hearted warders, or the cries of some poor wretch who is being mercilessly flogged. Some of the prisoners who may have specially incurred the *khalifa's* displeasure, are loaded with heavier chains and manacles than the rest, and are interned in the small huts and debarred from all intercourse with their fellow-prisoners. They generally receive only sufficient nourishment to keep them alive.

Ordinary prisoners receive no regular supply of food; but their relatives are allowed to provide for them. It often happens that long before a meal reaches the person for whom it is intended, a very large portion of it has been consumed by the rapacious and unscrupulous

Coming from Market, Omdurman.

warders; and sometimes the prisoner gets nothing whatever. At night, the wretched creatures are driven like sheep into the stone huts, which are not provided with windows, and are consequently quite unventilated. Regardless of prayers and entreaties, they are pushed pell-mell into these living graves, which are generally so tightly packed that it is quite impossible to lie down.

The weaker are trampled down by the stronger; and not infrequently the warder opens the door in the morning to find that some of his victims have succumbed to suffocation and ill-usage in these horrible cells. It is a painful sight to see scores of half-suffocated individuals pouring out of these dens, bathed in perspiration, and utterly exhausted by the turmoil of the long and sleepless night. Once emerged, they sink down, more dead than alive, under the shade of the walls, and spend the remainder of the day in trying to recover from the effects of the previous night, and gain sufficient strength to undergo the horrors of that which is to follow.

One would think that death was preferable to such an existence. Still these unfortunates cling to life, and pray to God to relieve them from their sufferings. In spite of the prison being invariably overcrowded, and notwithstanding the horrors of prison life, I do not ever remember having heard of a case of suicide amongst the unfortunate inmates.

Charles Neufeld has spent some years in the *Saier*, often ill, subject to the greatest privations, and merely kept alive by the occasional supplies which reached him through the black servant he brought with him from Egypt, and who, in turn, was assisted by the other Europeans in Omdurman. He managed to survive, though heavily chained by the neck, and wearing two large irons round his feet. On one occasion, he refused to spend the night in one of the stone huts, which he aptly described as "the last station on the way to Hell," and for this act of disobedience he was severely flogged; but he bore it without a murmur, until his tormentors—amazed at his powers of endurance—cried out, "Why do you not complain? Why do you not ask for mercy?" "That is for others to do, not for me," was the strong-hearted reply which gained for him the respect of even his gaolers.

After enduring three years of imprisonment, his irons were lightened; and, with only a chain joining his ankles, he was removed to Khartum, where he was ordered to refine saltpetre for the manufacture of gunpowder, under the superintendence of Wad Hamednalla. Here his condition was much improved; and he received a small monthly remuneration for his work, which sufficed to provide him with the bare necessaries of life. As the saltpetre refinery adjoins the old church of the mission, the latter has thus been saved from destruction.

After his daily hard work is over, Neufeld is allowed to rest in the mission gardens; and here, no doubt, his thoughts often revert to his family at home, and he must in his heart curse the evil day which induced him to quit Egypt, and thoughtlessly venture into the clutches of the *khalifa*. For him fate has indeed been cruel; and most fervently do I hope that ere long he may be reunited with his relatives, who have not abandoned all hope of seeing him again. In Europe, there is no lack of friends who are ready to do all in their power to help him; but it rests with God alone to release this poor captive from his misery.

It makes my heart ache to think of all the horrors that have been enacted in that dreadful prison. There was the sad case of poor Sheikh Khalil, who had been despatched from Cairo with letters to the *khalifa*, informing him of the number and names of the prisoners who had been captured at the battle of Toski, all of whom, he was assured, were being well cared for, and would eventually be set free; and he was requested to hand over to the *sheikh* the sword and medals of General Gordon, which, it was assumed, were in his possession. Khalil's companion, Beshara, was sent back with the letters unanswered, whilst the unfortunate emissary, who was an Egyptian by birth, was thrown into chains, under the pretext that he had been sent as a spy. Ill-treated and deprived of nourishment, he became so weak that he could not rise from the ground. His tormentors even refused him water to drink; and at last death came to him as a happy release from his sufferings.

Malech, a Jewish merchant of Tunis, who had come to Kassala with Abu Girga's permission, was seized by the *khalifa's* orders, and brought to Omdurman, where he remains in captivity in the Saier to this day, (as at time of first publication). He is as thin as a skeleton, and is driven almost to despair. He is kept alive by the efforts of his own community, who have been forced to become Moslems, and who succeed in providing him with small quantities of food.

Two Ababda Arabs, arrested on suspicion of carrying letters to Europeans in Omdurman, were seized and imprisoned, and died soon after of starvation. The alarm in the European colony was great; but fortunately it transpired that the letters were for a Copt from his relations in Cairo.

The great *sheikh* of the Gimeh tribe, Asakr Abu Kalam, who had shown such friendship and hospitality to the *khalifa* and his father in early days, was ruthlessly seized and thrown into chains, because it came to the *khalifa's* ears that he had spoken disparagingly of the present condition of the Sudan, and had expressed regret at having taken up arms against the government. He was eventually exiled to Reggaf, whilst his wife, who was a well-known beauty in the Sudan, was torn from the arms of her husband at the hour of his departure, and carried off to the *khalifa's harem*.

The well-known *emir*, Zeki Tummal, on being seized, was thrown into a small stone building the shape of a coffin, the door of which was built up. He was given no food whatever; but a small amount of water was handed to him through an aperture in the wall. For twenty-three days, he suffered all the horrors of starvation; but no sound or complaint was heard to issue from that living grave. Too proud to beg, and well aware of the futility of doing so, he lingered on till the twenty-fourth day, when death carried him out of reach of his tormentors.

The *saier* and his warders watched, through the aperture, the death agonies of the wretched man; and when at length he had ceased to struggle, they hurried off to give their lord and master the joyful news. That night Zeki's body was removed to the western quarter of the city, and there buried amongst a heap of old ruins, with his back turned towards Mecca.[1] The *khalifa*, not content with having tormented him in life, thought thus to deprive him of peace in the world to come.

I have already described how the *khalifa* disposed of his most trusted adherent, the Kadi Ahmed. On reaching the *Saier*, he was thrown into the hut in which Zeki had been interned; and, a few days after, he was visited, at the command of the *khalifa*, by two other *kadis*, who asked where he had hidden his money. "Tell your master, the *khalifa*," said he, "that I have settled my account with this world; and I know of no place where gold or silver can be found." To their further inquiries he remained perfectly silent; and the two myrmidons returned, crestfallen, to their master. This happened only a few days before I quitted Omdurman. Since my return to Egypt, I have ascertained that he died shortly afterwards, under similar circumstances to those of Zeki.

One could fill a volume with descriptions of the horrors and cruelties enacted in the terrible *Saier*; but it is useless to weary the reader with further accounts of the atrocities committed by order of that merciless tyrant, the *khalifa*.

---

1. All true Moslems are buried facing Mecca.

Chapter 18

Plans for Escape

In keeping me constantly close to his person, the *khalifa* had a twofold object. He knew that I was the only remaining high Egyptian official who had a thorough knowledge of the Sudan, had traversed almost the entire country, and was complete master of the language. Utterly ignorant of the political situation, he imagined that if I succeeded in escaping, I should induce the Egyptian Government, or some European power, to enter the Sudan; and he well knew that in that case I should form a link between it and the principal tribal chiefs who were disaffected to him, and longed for the return of a settled form of government. On the other hand, it flattered his vanity to have practically as his slave the man who had formerly governed the whole of the great province of Darfur, including his own country and tribe.

He never attempted to conceal his feelings in this respect, and frequently said to the western Arabs, "See, this is the man who was formerly our master, and under whose arbitrary rule we suffered. Now he is my servant, and must obey my commands at all times. See, this is the man who formerly indulged in the pleasures and vices of the world, and now he has to wear an unwashed *jibba* and walk barefooted. God indeed is merciful and gracious!" He paid much less attention to the other European captives, who gained a small livelihood by working at various trades in a quarter near the market-place, where they had built their own huts, and were left almost undisturbed by the other inhabitants of the city. Father Ohrwalder lived by weaving. Father Rosignoli and Beppo Rognotto (a former Mission brother) kept a cookshop in the market-place, and the Sisters lived with them until—with the exception of Sister Theresa Grigolini—they succeeded in escaping.

Then there is Giuseppe Cuzzi, one of A. Marquet's former clerks, and a number of Greeks, Syrian Christians, and Copts,—in all some forty-five men who have married either Christians born in the country or Egyptians. The entire colony is termed the Muslimania[1] quarter, and they have elected from amongst themselves an Emir, under whose orders they agree to live, and who is responsible to the *khalifa* for every member of the colony. The present *emir* is a certain Greek called Nicola, whose Arabic name is Abdullahi. No one is on any account allowed to quit Omdurman; and they are obliged to guarantee each other. Consequently when Father Rosignoli escaped, his companion Beppo was thrown into prison, and was in chains when I left the town.

After Father Ohrwalder's flight a much stricter surveillance was exercised over all these unfortunates. A place has been allotted to them in the northeastern portion of the mosque, where they have to attend prayers daily; but not being under special control, they take it in turns to be present, so that, in case of inquiry, the colony shall always be represented. Their huts are built adjoining each other, and in this way they can communicate without difficulty, and thus derive some alleviation of their sad lot by mutual sympathy; but their children are obliged to live in the various *tekias* (religious rest-houses), where they are taught the *Koran*.

I have already described my own surroundings and mode of life; and it now remains for me to add that I was only permitted to converse with a few of the body-guard who were, like myself, either under surveillance or specially employed as spies by the *khalifa* to watch and report our every action and word. I was seldom permitted to enter the town; and I was strictly forbidden to make any visits.

The *khalifa* is very fond of watches and clocks; and one of my many duties was to wind them up, and generally look after them. I availed myself of this privilege to occasionally visit an Armenian watchmaker named Artin, on the pretext that a clock or watch required repair. His house was situated near the market-place; and here I used to arrange meetings with some of the people I particularly wished to see. I never confided in Artin, and those who came to the shop invariably made some small purchases; and in doing so we succeeded in exchanging, as it were quite casually, a few words.

Most of my time was spent at the *khalifa's* gate reading the *Koran*. I was not permitted to write, as Abdullahi thought it unnecessary for me to practise an art of which he himself was ignorant. I invariably ac-

---

1. The term "*Muslimani*" is generally given to the descendants of "unbelievers;" is an opprobrious epithet, and is applied by the Mahdists to all so-called renegades.

companied my master to the mosque, or when he appeared in public, and on these occasions my duties were somewhat those of an *aide-de-camp*. Being in receipt of no salary, my food was of the simplest, and consisted generally of *asida*, various sorts of sauces, and occasionally a little meat purchased in the market.

Abdullahi knew perfectly that I longed for freedom; and, in spite of all my efforts to conceal it, I could not overcome his very rational suspicion of me. By constant gifts of slaves, by offers of marriage with his family, and various other expedients, he did all he could to make ties which he thought would hold me down; but my continued refusal of these very questionable benefits only confirmed his suspicions that I intended to escape on the first possible occasion. After the fall of Khartum, my family had done all in their power to obtain news of me; but fortunately they realised how careful they must be. Herr Von Gsiller, the Austro-Hungarian Consul-General in Egypt, spared no pains to get news of me, and his efforts were heartily seconded by the officers attached to the Egyptian army, and other officials.

It was at his suggestion that my relatives had communicated with me through the Governor of Suakin, in 1888; and I have described in the preceding pages how I was eventually forbidden by the *khalifa* to hold any further intercourse with the outside world. Already my relations with the *khalifa* had become much strained, owing to these events; and they became much more so when a letter reached the *khalifa* from Herr Von Rosty (who had succeeded Herr Von Gsiller), asking his permission to send a priest to minister to the members of the Mission, who, he stated were Austrian subjects. At the same time, he had written to me asking for information on the present situation in the Sudan. The *khalifa*, of course, took no notice of Herr Von Rosty's letter, and accused me of duplicity and disloyalty, because I had previously informed him that the members of the mission, with the exception of Father Ohrwalder, were Italians.

I had deliberately done this, as I feared that Abdullahi, in one of his sudden outbursts of passion against me, might vent his rage on those whom he believed to be my compatriots, and whom I was anxious to save; but now this letter, stating directly the contrary, was a heavy blow. It was quite beyond the *khalifa's* capacity to understand that members of various nationalities could be, for the purpose of the Mission, under Austrian protection; and for a long time he incessantly upbraided me for having deceived him.

My family had placed a considerable sum of money at the disposal of the Austrian Consul-General, with the object of assisting me; and they, through the kind intervention of the various *sirdars* of the Egyptian army, and of Major Wingate, the Director of Military Intelligence, succeeded in sending me occasional sums by the hands of trustworthy Arabs. Of course I invariably received considerably smaller sums than those which had been originally confided to them, though I was obliged to give receipts for the full amounts. However, I was truly thankful for what I received; and by the system which was established I was enabled to send my relatives scraps of information about myself and my affairs. I was obliged to exercise the most extreme caution in spending the money thus received, lest suspicion should be aroused; and therefore I continued to live as simply as possible, and expended all I could spare in cementing my various friendships.

My friends in Cairo had fully realised that, after I had been prevented from holding any communication with the outside, it was quite impossible for them to secure my release from the *khalifa's* hands by ordinary methods. They therefore spared no efforts to afford me the means of affecting my escape should an opportunity occur. From the earliest days of my captivity, I had realised that my only hope of freedom lay in flight; and although the rise and development of this great movement interested me considerably,—especially as I had exceptional means of watching it,—I never for an instant abandoned the idea of succeeding in my object, though I little dreamt that twelve long years of hardship, misery, and humiliation must elapse before it could be accomplished.

For years, I did not confide my secret to a soul; but eventually I told Ibrahim Adlan of my intentions; and he promised to assist me to the best of his ability. Unfortunately, the *khalifa* executed him soon afterwards; and in him I lost a true and kind friend and protector. On his death, I confided my secret to two influential individuals on whose silence I could rely; and though I knew that partly owing to their liking for me, and partly owing to their hatred of the *khalifa*, they would have willingly assisted me in the accomplishment of my object, our negotiations came to nothing. The money required would, I knew, be forthcoming; but they dreaded that after my escape their names might be eventually divulged; and as they were tied by their families to live in the Sudan, they knew that, in the event of discovery, the *khalifa* would wreak his vengeance on their defenceless wives and children.

Meanwhile, my family had not been idle; and no sacrifice was too great for their love. Living in Vienna, ignorant of the real state of affairs in the Sudan, and not aware of how they could best help me, they trustfully continued to place considerable sums of money at the disposal of the Austrian Agency in Cairo, the representative of which received instructions from the Minister of Foreign Affairs to utilise it to the best of his ability. His Excellency Baron Heidler von Egeregg—now Ambassador and Minister Plenipotentiary, and who has been for some years Consul-General in Cairo—took a personal interest in my affairs, and did everything in his power to facilitate my escape.

But it is only possible to secure the services of reliable persons through the intermediary of government officials; and with this object in view, he enlisted the sympathies, first of Colonel Schaeffer Bey, and subsequently of Major Wingate, who had on several previous occasions endeavoured to assist me; and it is to his and to Baron Heidler's incessant efforts that I owe my freedom. Without their intervention, it would not have been possible to procure reliable Arabs to bring me occasional sums of money; and I owe to them my heartiest thanks for their frequent attempts to effect my rescue; and although, with the exception of the last, they all failed, the arrangements were such that the *khalifa* and his myrmidons never had the slightest suspicion of them.

Early in February, 1892, the former chief of the Dongola camel postmen, Babakr Abu Sebiba, arrived in Omdurman from Egypt. He was an Ababda Arab; and when brought before the *khalifa*, he asserted that he had escaped from Assuan, that he sought the *khalifa's* pardon, and begged to be allowed to settle down in Berber. As he had letters of introduction to the Emir of Berber, Zeki Osman, permission was accorded to him; and when going out at the door of the mosque, he nudged me, and whispered, "I have come for you; arrange for an interview."

"Tomorrow after evening prayers, here in the mosque," was my reply; and he then disappeared. Although I had not given up hope of escape, I never dared to be very sanguine; for I had had much experience of these Arabs and Sudanese, and knew that often their words go for nought, and their promises are more frequently broken than kept. I therefore spent the following day much as usual, though I could not help wondering what would be the upshot of the interview.

After evening prayers, and when all the people had left the mosque, Babakr passed the door at which I had seen him the previous day.

Cautiously I followed him; and together we entered the thatched portion of the building, which was in deep shade. Out of sight, and out of hearing, Babakr now handed me a small tin box, which, from the smell, seemed to contain coffee, saying, "This box has a double bottom. Open and read the papers enclosed in it; and I shall be here again tomorrow at the same hour." Concealing the box under my *jibba*, I returned to my place, and, as chance fell out, was summoned that evening to sup with the *khalifa*. Imagine my feelings: for the box was sufficiently large to be seen under my clothes; and here was I seated opposite my master with his lynx eyes fixed on me. Fortunately he was rather tired, and only talked on general subjects; though he did not fail to caution me to be loyal, or he would punish me unmercifully. Of course I assured him of my fidelity and affection for him; and, after having partaken of a little meat and *dhurra*, I feigned sudden illness, and obtained permission to withdraw. Hurrying home with all speed, I lit my little oil lamp, tore open the box with my knife, and there found a small piece of paper, on which the following words were written in French:

Babakr Wad Abu Sebiba is a trustworthy man.
    (Signed.)   Schaeffer, Colonel.

On the other side of the paper were a few lines from the Austrian Agency confirming this. The writers had wisely omitted my name, fearing that it might fall into the hands of enemies; and now I had to exercise more patience until the following evening.

As agreed, I met Babakr as before; and he briefly informed me that he had come to arrange my escape, and that, having seen me, he would return to Berber to complete his preparations. As the Emir Zeki Osman had been ordered to come to Omdurman in July for the manœuvres, he proposed to accompany him, in order to carry out his object. I assured him that I was ready at any time to make the attempt; and, after imploring him to do all in his power to help me, we parted. He returned, as arranged, in July with Zeki Osman; and, in a secret meeting, he told me that, in order to disarm suspicion, he had got married in Berber; that he had brought four camels with him, but that he had not yet arranged about our crossing the river.

Should I, however, decide to risk flight, he would guide me through the Bayuda desert and by El Kaab (west of Dongola) to Wadi Halfa; but I knew that the camels could not possibly perform such a journey in the height of summer. I soon saw that the man wanted to spend a few more months in the Sudan, probably with his newly acquired bride; and so we agreed to postpone the attempt till the month of December, when the long nights would be more favourable to the enterprise. Months passed and I heard from secret sources that Babakr was still at Berber. December went by, and the year 1893 had begun. Still no sign of my friend.

At length he returned in July, and told me that the messenger whom I had despatched to Cairo asking for £100 had been delayed on the road; and that as he had arrived there at a time of year when the journey would have been impossible, the authorities had refused to supply him with the funds. He added, however, that he had brought two camels, and that if I would risk flight, he would try to procure a third. I saw that the man had been making inquiries, and had ascertained that at most it would only be possible for me to obtain a few hours' start, which would not be sufficient to insure success; besides he knew that it was out of the question starting in July.

When, therefore, I proposed again postponing flight till the beginning of the winter, he readily acquiesced merely for form's sake. His constant visits to Omdurman had aroused the *khalifa's* suspicions; and one of the *kadis* notified him that he must attend the mosque five times daily, and should not leave Omdurman without the *khalifa's* permission. Alarmed probably at the turn affairs had taken, he escaped and returned to Egypt. Three days after he had left, his absence was discovered. On his arrival in Cairo, as I subsequently learnt, he informed those who had sent him that he had frequently come to Omdurman; but that I had persistently refused to risk flight with him. Baron Heidler and Major Wingate, however, realised that the man's statement was untrue; and sometime later I had an opportunity of informing them, through a trusty agent, of the man's behaviour.

These gentlemen subsequently made an agreement with a merchant named Musa Wad Abderrahman, promising him £1000 if he succeeded in effecting my escape, while at the same time he was furnished with what was necessary for the undertaking. In the winter I received information of this fresh enterprise; but it was not till June, 1894, that one of Musa's relatives, named Ahmed, told me that some Arabs had been secured who would arrive in a few days, and would attempt to fly with me. He also told me that a station had been prepared in the desert, where a change of camels would be in readiness, and that, in spite of the great heat, there was every prospect of the success of the undertaking.

On 1st July, Ahmed warned me that the camels had arrived, and that I should be ready to start the next night. That evening, I told my servants that one of my friends was dangerously ill, and that I had obtained the *khalifa's* permission to visit him, that I would probably stay the night, and that, therefore, they need not be uneasy if I did not return. That night, when my master had retired to rest, accompanied by Ahmed, I quitted the mosque; and, with bare feet and armed only with a sword, we hurried along the road leading towards the parade ground, and then turned off in a northeasterly direction.

The night was dark. During the day the first showers announcing the beginning of the rainy season had fallen; and, as we crossed the cemetery, I put my foot into an old grave, which had been washed out by the rain, and my foot got twisted in the bones of the skeleton on which I had stepped. It seemed as if the dead as well as the living were conspiring to throw difficulties in my path; but, in spite of the pain, I struggled on, and reached Khor Shambat. We crossed to the other side, where it was arranged the camels would await us. We searched up and down the banks. Ahmed even called out in a low tone; but not a sign of them was to be seen. The night was cool; but our efforts had bathed us in perspiration, and, after wandering to and fro for hours, in our vain search, we were at length obliged to give up and retrace our steps.

What could have happened to our men? Could they have been noticed by some Dervishes who had perhaps arrested them on suspicion? Full of doubts and fears, we reached our homes in safety. I had parted from Ahmed on the parade ground; and I had begged him to let me know in the evening what had happened. At the same time, I repeated that I was prepared to renew the attempt at any time. The dawn was just breaking as I reached the threshold of my hut, which I had quitted a few hours before, as I thought for the last time, and my feelings can be better imagined than described I had scarcely been back more than a few minutes, when one of my fellow *mulazemin*, named Abdel Kerim, arrived with a message from the *khalifa* to inquire the reason of my absence from morning prayers. I replied that I had been ill; and indeed my wretched appearance almost warranted such an assertion.

In vain I waited that evening for news from Ahmed; but I did not learn from him till two days afterwards, that the Arabs had reconsidered the matter, and had come to the conclusion that the risk of recapture was too great, and had returned to their homes instead of coming to the place of rendezvous. So we had completely failed, and considered ourselves lucky to have returned unnoticed from our midnight ramble.

Again I informed my Cairo friends of what had happened. They were unsparing in their efforts, and had now the valuable aid of Father Ohrwalder, who, when in Vienna, had visited my family, and had obtained from them some ether pills, which are very strengthening on a journey, and ward off sleep. They had been prepared by Professor Ottokar Chiari, and had reached me safely. They were in a small bottle which I had buried carefully in the ground.

I now made a confidant of Abderrahman Wad Harun, whom I despatched to Cairo with a message to Baron Heidler to place at his disposal the requisite means for my escape. Again an agreement was made between this merchant and the Austrian Agency, with the concurrence of Major Wingate, and the assistance of Milhem Shakkur Bey and Naum Effendi Shukeir of the Intelligence Department. If successful, Abderrahman was to receive £1000; and he was also given the necessary outfit and £200 in advance.

Meanwhile, Major Wingate, who had been despatched to Suakin as acting governor, fearing another failure, made a similar agreement with a local Arab named Osheikh Karrar, who, it was arranged, should attempt my rescue *via* Tokar or Kassala. One day, a Suakin merchant in Omdurman handed me a small slip of paper, on which was written,—

> We are sending you Osheikh Karrar, who will hand you some needles, by which you will recognise him. He is a faithful and brave man. You can trust him. Kind regards from Wingate.
> (Signed.)   Ohrwalder.

Soon afterwards I heard from one of Abderrahman Wad Harun's relatives that the latter had arrived at Berber from Cairo, and was making preparations for my escape; but in order to avoid being suspected, he had decided not to come to Omdurman, and in this I fully concurred.

The 1st of January, 1895, had dawned. How many weary years of deprivation and humiliation I had spent in closest proximity to my tyrannical master! And would this year come and go like the rest, leaving me still in his clutches? No. I felt sure that the time was at length approaching when my friends would be able to break asunder the bonds which held me down, and that I should once more see my relatives, fatherland, and the friends of my youth.

One evening, about the middle of January, a man I had never seen before passed me in the street, and made a sign to me to follow him;

and as I brushed up against him, he whispered, "I am the man with the needles." Joyfully I led him in the dark to a little niche in the outside wall of my hut, and begged him to tell me his plans quickly. He first presented me with three needles and a small slip of paper, and then, to my dismay, told me that at present flight was impossible. "I came," said he, "with the full intention of taking you to Kassala; but now that military posts have been formed at El Fasher, Asubri, and Goz Regeb on the Atbara, which are in constant communication with each other, flight in this direction is not possible."

He added further that one of his camels had died, and that he had lost money, owing to bad trade; and, in consequence, he had not sufficient means to arrange for the escape. He therefore begged that I would give him a letter to Major Wingate, asking for a further sum of money, and promising to return again in two months. I felt sure that the man did not really mean to risk his life for me; and, as he informed me he wished to leave without delay, I told him to meet me the following evening at the mosque. We then separated; and I returned once more to my post at the *khalifa's* door. The note from Suakin contained a few lines of recommendation from Father Ohrwalder, to which I wrote a reply, briefly describing what had taken place; and the next night when we met, I handed to Osheikh the letter, which he hurriedly thrust into his pocket, hoping that it would be the means of obtaining more money.

Bitterly disappointed, I was returning disconsolately to my house, when I suddenly came across Mohammed, the cousin of my friend Abderrahman. As if by mere chance I found him walking at my side; and, in a whisper, he said to me, "We are ready. The camels are bought; the guides are engaged. The time arranged for your escape is during the moon's last quarter next month. Be ready!" and without another word he left me.

This time I felt convinced that I was not to be doomed to disappointment. Towards the end of January, Hussein Wad Mohammed, who had also been engaged by Baron Heidler and Major Wingate, arrived in Omdurman, and secretly told me that he was ready to help me to escape. He begged me to let my friends in Cairo know what I had decided to do, and said that one of his brothers, who was about to proceed to Egypt, would be the bearer of the letter. As I was bound to Abderrahman, I decided to wait and see if his efforts would succeed, and, should they fail, I decided I would try Hussein; but I merely told the latter that at present I was not well enough to attempt so long a journey, and that at the end of February I would let him definitely my decision.

At the same time, I gave him a letter to my friends telling them that I intended to attempt escape with the assistance of Abderrahman; and, in case of failure, from which I prayed the Almighty to preserve me, I would seek the help of Hussein. I was now in some alarm that, so many people being in the secret, the *khalifa* might suspect something. Had he obtained the slightest clue to what was going on, I should have certainly paid for it with my life.

On Sunday, the 17th of February, Mohammed, in a few hurried words, told me that the camels would arrive the next day, that they would rest two days, and that the attempt would be made on the night of the 20th. He said that on Tuesday evening he would communicate with me by a sign by which I should know that everything was ready; and that I should then do all in my power to arrange that we should have as long a start as possible.

At last Tuesday night arrived, and I found Mohammed waiting for me at the door of the mosque. In a hurried whisper he told me that all was ready; and, after arranging a rendezvous for the following night, when the *khalifa* had retired to rest, we separated.

I confess that I passed the greater part of that night in a state of fevered excitement. Would this attempt also fail like the others? Would some unforeseen event frustrate this effort too? These thoughts kept me awake and restless; and it was not till towards morning that sleep, which was so necessary to keep up my strength during the journey, came at length, and I had two or three hours of sound repose.

The next morning, when before the *khalifa's* door, I feigned sickness, and asked the chief of the *mulazemin* for permission to absent myself from morning prayers, as I proposed taking a dose of *senna* tea and tamarind, and remaining quietly at home the following day. The necessary permission was accorded, and Abdel Kerim promised to make my excuses to the *khalifa* should he inquire for me. I felt sure that my master, when he knew that I was not present, would, under the pretext of solicitude for my health, send to my house to see if I was really there; but I could think of no other way of accounting for my absence.

Before sunset, I assembled my servants, and, after making them promise to keep secret what I was about to say, I told them that the brother of the man who had brought me letters, money, and watches from my relatives seven years before, had arrived with a further consignment, and that, as he had come entirely without the *khalifa's* knowledge, I had decided to keep his arrival secret. I told them that I intended visiting him that night, as I wished to arrange with him without delay, and let him return at once. My good domestics, of course, believed the story implicitly; and I knew the thought that they would share some of the good things which were supposed to have come, would make them keep the secret.

In continuation of my imaginary scheme, I ordered my servant Ahmed to meet me the next day at sunrise at the north end of the city, near the Fur quarter, with my mule. I told him not to be impatient if I happened to be late, as the business in hand was important, and might take some time to arrange; but that on no account was he to leave the rendezvous, as I intended to give him the money I received to take home. I impressed upon the others the necessity of maintaining perfect silence, as I ran a great risk of being discovered. Should any of the *mulazemin* ask for me, I told them to reply that I had been very unwell during the night, and had ridden off, accompanied by my servant Ahmed, to seek advice of some man whose whereabouts they did not know, but that they supposed he was someone who could cure illness.

To make my story appear more real, I gave my servants to understand that I should receive a considerable sum of money the next day, and, in anticipation, I presented them with several dollars apiece. My object in making these arrangements was to secure a few hours' delay before the hue and cry that I had escaped should be raised. My servant Ahmed would probably wait for some hours with the mule, while those in the household would anxiously expect my return with the money. I naturally concluded that, should the *khalifa* send to inquire for me, the reply which my servants were to give, would avert suspicion for a time; and then it would take more time for them to find Ahmed, and his story of the arrival of the supposed messenger would still further perplex them.

Of course they must eventually find out the deception; but to me every moment's delay in sending out search parties was of the utmost importance. After afternoon prayers, I once more returned to my house, again impressed on all my servants the immense importance of keeping the secret, and with repeated promises of reward, I stepped across the threshold, praying fervently to God that I might never set foot within my hut again.

CHAPTER 19

My Flight

It was three hours after sunset. We had offered the evening prayer with the *khalifa*, and he had withdrawn to his apartment. Another hour passed without interruption. My lord and master had retired to rest. I rose, took the *farwa* (the rug on which we pray) and the *farda* (a light woollen cloth for protection against the cold) on my shoulders, and went across the mosque to the road that leads north. I heard a low cough, the signal of Mohammed, the intermediary in my escape, and I stood still. He had brought a donkey. I mounted, and was off. The night was dark. The cold, northerly wind had driven the people into their huts and houses. Without meeting a soul we reached the end of the town where a small ruined house stands obliquely to the road, from which a man led out a saddled camel. "This is your guide. His name is Zeki Belal," said Mohammed. "He will guide you to the riding camels that are waiting concealed in the desert. Make haste. A happy journey, and God protect you."

The man sprang into the saddle, and I got up and sat behind him. After about an hour's ride, we arrived at the spot where the camels were hidden among some low trees. All was ready, and I mounted the animal assigned to me.

"Zeki," said I, "did Mohammed give you the medicine?"

"No; what medicine?"

"They call them ether pills. They keep off sleep and strengthen you on the journey."

He laughed. "Sleep!" said he. "Have no fear on that account. Fear is the child of good folk, and will keep sleep from our eyes, and God in his mercy will fortify us." The man was right enough. We rode in a northerly direction. The *halfa* grass and the mimosa-trees, which in places grew rather close together, prevented the camels from making rapid progress in the darkness. At sunrise we reached Wadi Bishara, a valley extending here to a breadth of about three miles, which is sown in the rainy season with millet by the Jaalin tribes who live along the Nile.

With daylight I was now able to see my guides. Zeki Belal was a young fellow, with his beard still downy; Hamed Ibn Hussein, a man in the prime of life.

"Of what race are you?"

"We are from the Gilif mountains, master; and if God will, you will be satisfied with us."

"How long a start have we got from our enemies? When will they miss you?" the elder one asked me.

"They will look for me after the morning prayer; but before all doubt is over as to my escape, and before the men and the beasts are found with which to pursue me, some time must elapse. We may at least reckon on twelve or fourteen hours' start."

"That is not very much," answered Hamed. "But if the animals are up to their work, we shall have left a good bit of ground behind us."

"Don't you know our animals? Have they not been tried?" I asked.

"No. Two of them are stallions of the Anafi breed, and the third a Bisharin mare, bought expressly for your flight from friends," was the answer. "We must hope the best of them."

We drove the creatures at their swiftest pace. The country in these parts was flat, broken now and then by solitary shrubs, with here and there small stony hillocks. We rode without stopping until near midday, when suddenly my guide called out,—

"Halt! Let the camels kneel down at once. Be quick!"

I stopped. The camels knelt.

"Why?"

"I see camels a long way off and two led horses, and fear we have been seen."

I loaded my Remington to be prepared for any issue. "But if we have been seen," I said, "it is better to ride quietly on. Our making the animals lie down will excite their suspicion. In what direction are they going?"

"You are right," said Hamed Ibn Hussein. "They are marching northwest."

We rose and changed our line of march to the northeast, and were almost confident that we had passed unobserved when, to our despair,

SLATIN PASHA FLYING FROM OMDURMAN.

we perceived one of the party, which was about two thousand metres away from us, jump on his horse and gallop swiftly towards us.

"Hamed," said I, "I will go slowly on with Zeki. Do you stop the man, and answer his questions, and in any case prevent him from seeing me close. You have the money on you?"

"Good; but march slowly!"

I rode on quietly with Zeki, hiding my face with my *farda*, so as not to be recognised as a white man.

"Hamed is greeting the man, and has made his camel kneel," said Zeki, looking back. After about twenty minutes, we saw the man remount his horse, and Hamed urging his camel on to rejoin us.

"You must thank God for our safety," he cried, as he came up. "The man is a friend of mine, Mukhal, a *sheikh*, on his way to Dongola with camels to bring dates to Omdurman. He asked me where I was going with the 'white Egyptian.' The man has the eyes of a hawk."

"And what did you answer?"

"I adjured him as my friend to keep our secret, and gave him twenty *Maria Theresa* dollars. We Arabs are all a little avaricious. The man swore a sacred oath to me to hold his tongue if he happened to fall in with our pursuers; and his people are too far off to tell black from white. Urge the camels on; we have lost time."

At sunset, we passed the hills of Hobegi, and camped nearly an hour later in the open country about a day's journey west of the Nile, so as to give our exhausted animals some rest. We had been riding twenty-one hours without stopping, had eaten nothing all day, and only once drunk water. In spite of fatigue we ate bread and dates with a good appetite.

"We will feed our beasts and then get on," said my guide. "You are not tired?"

"No," I replied. "In Europe we say time is money. Here one might say time is life. Make haste."

But to our despair the beasts refused the food which was placed before them. Hamed made a little fire, took a piece of burning wood and a little resin, which he laid on the wood, then walked round the camels muttering some words which I could not understand.

"What are you doing?" I asked him, with some surprise.

"I fear the *fikis* of the *khalifa* have bewitched our camels, and am trying the Arab's antidote."

"For my part," I replied, "I fear that they are second-rate market camels, or are sick. Let us give them a little more rest. Perhaps they will pick up."

As, after another half-hour's rest, the beasts still refused food, and longer delay was out of the question, we tightened up the saddle-girths again and mounted. The tired animals refused to trot, would only walk at a good pace, and as the sun rose we found ourselves on the high ground to the northwest of Metemmeh. The diminishing strength of our mounts filled us with anxiety, and it became clear to us that they would never hold out till the spot, about a day's journey north of Berber, on the edge of the desert, where we were to change camels. Towards afternoon, we let the exhausted animals rest in the shade of a tree, and agreed to make for the Gilif range, distant a good day's journey to the northwest, where I should remain concealed in the uninhabited hills until my guides could succeed in securing other mounts.

About sunset we struck camp. The animals had so far recovered that they could walk at a good pace, and we reached, in the early morning, the foot of the Gilif mountain, which at this spot is quite uninhabited. We dismounted, driving our camels before us after an extremely difficult march of about three hours in a valley hemmed in by sheer rocks.

My guides, Zeki Ibn Belal, as well as Hamed Ibn Hussein, both belong to the Kababish tribe. The Gilif mountain is their own country; and they were familiar with every path. We unsaddled the camels, and concealed the saddles among the boulders.

"We have come into our own country; and she will protect her son," said Hamed Hussein. "Have no fear; as long as we live you need have no misgiving. Remain quietly concealed here. A little way off there is a cleft in the rocks containing water. I will water the animals there. Zeki will bring you a water-skin full. I will also hide the beasts elsewhere, that our halting-place may not be betrayed by the vultures circling above. Wait for me here; and we will see what our next step must be."

I was alone and somewhat depressed. I had hoped to make a straight dash for the Egyptian frontier, and to out-distance my pursuers by speed; and now a crowd of unexpected obstacles was gathering round me. About two hours later, Zeki arrived with the water-skin on his shoulders.

"Taste the water of my native land," he cried. "See how fresh and pure it is. Take confidence. God, if He will, will bring our enterprise to a happy end."

I drank a deep draught. It was delicious indeed.

"I am full of confidence," I said to Zeki; "but a little put out by the delay."

"*Malaish kullu shai bi iradet Illahi* (It matters not. All happens as God ordains), and perhaps this delay has its good side too. Let us wait for Hamed Hussein."

Soon after midday Hamed came. We ate our frugal meal of bread and dates, and while doing so arranged that Zeki should ride to the friends who were privy to my escape, a brief two days' journey, and fetch new animals.

"I will ride the Bisharin mare," said Zeki. "She is strong, and has not yet got to the end of her tether. This is Saturday evening. I shall ride all night and tomorrow, Sunday. Monday morning early, please God, I shall reach our friends. We must allow one to two days there; because, it may be, no animals will be ready. But, Thursday or Friday, I should get here with fresh camels if no misfortune happens to me."

"It is better to put it a little later," I answered. "We will wait for you here till Saturday. If you arrive sooner, all the better; but remember that our life is in your hand. Above all, be cautious in bringing the animals, that you arouse no suspicion."

"Trust in our good fortune and my good-will," and he grasped my hand in farewell.

"God protect you, and bring you back right soon."

He tied a few dates up in a cloth as provision for the journey, and took the saddle on his shoulders. Hamed described the spot accurately to him where he would find the mare. As he turned, he enjoined us to be careful not to be seen; and in a few moments he was lost to sight. We cleared the ground which was to serve as our night's resting-place, of stones, and were in the best of spirits as to our success.

"I have a proposal to make to you," said Hamed to me after a long interval. "A relation of mine, Ibrahim Masa, is *sheikh* of this district, and has his house at the foot of the hill, about four hours' distance from here. Now though, as I hope, no one has seen us, still it would be better to warn him of our arrival, so that he may be prepared for any eventuality. I will describe our situation to him without mentioning your name. As my kinsman, he is bound to give us asylum, and would warn us in time of pursuit, if it should be that our track is followed to the base of the hills, though indeed this is scarcely to be feared. If you agree, I will go during the night, so as to see him without being observed by other people, and will be back with you early in the morning."

"The plan is good; but take twenty more dollars with you, and offer them as a small contribution to his house, and, as you have said, do not mention my name."

Hamed left me at sunset; and I was alone with my thoughts. I thought of my housefolk and companions, to whom, in spite of the difference of race and of many unattractive qualities, I had grown accustomed in the long course of years, and whom I had just left behind me in the hands of the enemy. I thought of the dear ones I was now on my way to meet, of my sisters, my friends and well-wishers. If only my adventures have a successful issue! Exhausted with fatigue, I fell asleep on my hard bed. I woke while the dawn was gray, and shortly afterwards heard the sound of approaching footsteps. I knew it must be my guide.

"All goes well," said he as he came up. "The *sheikh*, my kinsman, greets his unknown guest, and bids God protect you. Fortify yourself with patience. For the present, we have nothing else to do."

He sat down between two blocks of stone, from which his dark skin was hardly distinguishable, and kept watch. I sat a short distance below in the shade of a little tree which struggled for existence among the rocks; and we talked in low tones of the present and the former condition of the country. It was past midday when I suddenly heard behind the noise of footsteps, and, turning round, I saw, to my disgust, a man about one hundred and fifty yards off, climbing the slope opposite me, trying to draw the end of his *farda*, which was twisted round his loins, over his head. Judging from the direction he had come from, he must have seen us.

"In any case it is a fellow-countryman," said Hamed, who had heard the sound, and had perceived him. "Anyhow it will be better that I should overtake him and speak with him. Or do you not agree?"

"Certainly, make haste, and if necessary, give him a small present," I answered.

My companion left his seat, and followed the man at a swift pace. He had now reached the crest of the hill and passed out of my sight. A few minutes later, I saw them both approaching me with smiling faces.

"We are in luck," Hamed cried from a distance. "He is one of my numerous relations. Our mothers are children of two sisters."

The man came up to me and offered his hand in greeting.

"The peace of God be with you. From me you run no danger," he said as he sat down on the stone at my side.

I gave him a few dates, and bade him taste our travelling fare. "Who are you?"

"They call me Ali Wad Feid," he replied; "and, to be honest with you, my intentions were not well disposed to you. I was changing my pasture ground, and arrived a few days ago with my flocks at the foot of those hills which you see from here to the south. I went to the cleft in the rocks to see if there were much water there, because we might need it, although we also get drinking-water in the plain. There I found traces of a camel, and followed them up. When, in the distance, I saw the white skin of your feet which were sticking out of your hiding-place, I realised that a stranger was concealed here, and tried to get away again unobserved, so that," said he, smiling, "I might return again with a few comrades by night, and make your further journey easier by removing your superfluous luggage. I thank God that my cousin here caught me up. By night I should not, perhaps, have recognised him."

"Ali Wad Feid," said my guide, who had listened in silence, "I will tell you a little story. Listen! Many years ago, when I was a little fellow, in the days when the Turks ruled in the land, my father was *sheikh* of these mountains, which then were thickly peopled. One night there came a man, a fugitive, who sought asylum with my father. He was closely pursued by government troops, under suspicion of being a highway brigand who had murdered some merchants. His women fell into the hands of his pursuers; but he himself sought and found protection with my father, who kept him in concealment. A long while after, my father went to the seat of government at Berber, and by money and fair words succeeded in obtaining pardon for the man, against whom there existed no definite proofs of guilt. He went bail for him, and set free his women, who were in prison. That man's name was Feid ——"

"And he was my father," interrupted Ali, whose face had grown grave during his narrative. "I was born later, and heard the story from my dead mother, on whom God have mercy. My brother, let me give you good tidings. What your father did for mine, his son will do for your father's son. In peace or in peril I am with you. But, follow me, and I will show you a better hiding-place."

We went some two thousand yards back round the hill towards the south, and reached a sort of little grotto formed of rock slabs, large

SLATIN IN HIDING IN THE HILLS.

enough to hold two men.

"When evening comes bring your baggage here, although there is nothing to fear, since the hills are uninhabited; but under the cover of darkness you can choose some other spot in the neighbourhood to sleep in. It is impossible to be quite sure that someone may not have perceived you, and have the intention which I confessed to have had, of returning after dark. I have lost time, and my road is a long one. I will go, pick up what news I can, and return tomorrow when it is dark, announcing my presence by a low whistle. Farewell till then!"

As Ali Wad Feid had advised us, we selected a place to sleep in, and early in the morning, before the sun rose, retired again to our cave. Throughout the day Hamed Hussein kept watch from a high point of vantage, like a sentry on a tower, and only came to me when driven in by hunger. Our bread came to an end this day, and we had only dates to eat.

In the evening, two hours maybe after sunset, we heard a low whistle. It was Ali Wad Feid, who, faithful to his promise, had come to visit us. He brought some milk in a small vessel of gazelle-skin (the skin of young gazelles is tanned by the Arabs, and now much used for carrying milk in), and had rolled up some bread (millet cakes) in his *farda*.

"I pretended to my wife that I was going to visit the caravan folk, and show them hospitality," he said, after greeting us. "I cannot trust her with the truth, she is such a chatterbox."

"A feminine quality which many married men complain about in our country at home," I remarked with a smile, delighted at the prospect of such a grateful meal.

"I made inquiries at the well," he continued, "and heard of nothing to cause you uneasiness. Eat and drink your fill. I have every confidence in your good luck."

After we had done honour to his good fare, I begged him to return so as not to awake suspicion with his own folk by remaining out unduly long, and whispered to Hamed to give him a present of five dollars before he went.

"Do not return," I said to him in taking leave. "Your comings and goings may excite suspicion among your people, and your footsteps may perhaps leave traces on the ground which would betray our hiding-place to others, unless, of course, you hear any really disquieting news. Farewell. I thank you for your loyal friendship."

Hamed Hussein accompanied his kinsman some little way.

"Ali would not take the money," he said, when he returned. "I had to press him very hard; and it was only the fear of offending you which induced him at last to accept it."

We once more selected our couches, and rested undisturbed till the morning, when we returned to the cave, or rather I did, for my companion had to go back to his post as watchman. This day went by equally without event, but how slowly the time seemed to pass! The hours grew to days, and thoughts succeeded thoughts in weary sequence. My patience was severely tried, but there was no help for it, and nothing to do but to bear it.

As our water supply threatened to fall short, Hamed Hussein went with the skin to the cleft in the rocks. At the same time, he intended to look up the camels, which had been hobbled, and were getting what food they could from trees and bushes.

"I shall return in about four hours. Meanwhile, remain quiet in the cave," he said to me, "and should any one appear,—which God forbid!—it could only be one of my own countrymen, for no stranger gets so far as this, detain him, and tell him that Hamed Wad Sheikh Hussein is coming in a little while. But do not yourself enter into any negotiation, and above all do not spill blood."

"I will follow your counsel whatever happens," I replied; "but I trust you will find me here undisturbed when you return."

My guide returned with the water-skin full even before the time he had indicated.

"I found the camels somewhat recovered, at any rate in appearance," he said, with evident satisfaction. "Give me a few dates. I am hungry, and must return to my watch tower."

The rest of the day passed slowly, but without episode. At night we betook ourselves to our sleeping-place, talked for a while in a low voice, and prayed that our patience might not be put to too hard a trial.

On Thursday morning, Hamed had gone as usual to his post of observation; and it must have been about midday when I suddenly saw him climb down from his seat I clutched my rifle.

"What is the matter?"

"I see a man running in the direction of our former hiding-place. It must mean news. Remain here till I come back."

I sat down and waited for what seemed an eternity. Then I rose with caution to have a look out, and saw, a long way off, two people approaching me. My eyes could make out Hamed, and with him was Zeki Belal. As I stepped from my hiding-place, he perceived me, and ran up.

"God give you greeting, master. Here is good news for you," said he, shaking my hand. "I have arrived with two fresh camels, and have hidden them some way behind. I will be off and fetch them." And he hurried back again.

About an hour later, he arrived with the new animals.

"You have been quick," I cried with delight. "Now tell your story."

"It was Saturday evening when I left you," he replied. "I rode all night and all day. My Bisharin mare went splendidly over the ground, which was tolerably level, and on Monday morning I reached our friends. They sent immediately for the beasts you now see, which were at a considerable distance. They came in early on Tuesday. I started at midday. I rode slowly so as not to wear them out, and now we can start at once. And, oh, I had almost forgotten to tell you that your friends, after discussing it with me, went off to the camp on the edge of the desert, to warn their people there to be ready. I promised we would reach the tryst on Friday, or at latest on Saturday after sunset."

"Did you bring bread?" I asked the youth, who was talking away in high spirits. "We have got nothing but dates to eat."

"Good heavens! I forgot that in my haste."

"No matter," I replied, seeing him look rather crestfallen. "Even without dates we could hold out for this short ride."

"Zeki," said Hamed, "saddle the light-coloured camel, go with our friend and brother to the hollow rock, and give the camels water. Wait for me there. I will take the other saddle and follow with my own camel, which has recovered sufficiently to stand this comparatively short march. But it will be better," he added, turning to me, "that you should not go right up to the spring, but remain hidden in some suitable spot near till we fetch you. One never can be too sure. There are so many thirsty folk in the wide world."

I went with Zeki, leading one of the camels, towards the cleft where the water was, and hid myself in a place my guide suggested, among the boulders of rock.

About two hours before sunset, Hamed and Zeki came with the three camels that had just been watered, and the skins all filled. We mounted and rode east northeast across hills, which at times were very steep to climb, till, as darkness gathered round us, we arrived in the plain without having been observed.

Throughout the night, we rode without a halt at a slow trot or a walk, and at daybreak Hamed calculated we had left half the road behind us.

"This is the most critical day of our journey," said my guide. "We come into the neighbourhood of the river, and cross pasture grounds of the river tribes. God grant we reach our destination unobserved."

The aspect of the country does not change. The veldt, as one may call it, is covered with a thin mat of grass, with here and there clumps of half-dried mimosa bushes. The ground is sandy, and at times covered with stones. We rode on without stopping, and ate our frugal meal, which consisted of nothing but dates, as we rode. When the sun was at the zenith, we saw in the distance a flock of sheep with its shepherds. We turned a little aside from our straight course, and Zeki rode off to them to ask for news; but when he rejoined us he said he had learned nothing of interest. Though we came upon constant tracks of camels, donkeys, sheep, eta, in the soil, our eyes detected nothing which caused us concern, and the country had become quite flat again.

"Do you see the broad, gray band in front crossing from south to northwest?" Hamed asked me. "That is the great caravan track which leads from Berber to Wadi Gammer and Dar Shaigia. If we pass that without being seen, we have nothing more to fear, for between this and the river there is only stony ground, without a vestige of vegetation, and quite uninhabited. But now you must follow my directions closely. Let the camels advance at a slow pace, and each some five hundred paces from the next till we reach the big track. When we get there we will turn into the road and proceed for a few minutes in the direction of Berber. Then we will leave it again, and march in an easterly direction. Do you see that stone hillock about three miles away? There we will join again. This is the only way to put any one who may be pursuing us off our track."

We did as he had instructed us, crossed the caravan road, which is at most times tolerably frequented, without seeing a trace of anyone, and met again at the spot indicated.

"And now urge the animals on. Don't spare them. Let them do us their last service," said Hamed, with a merry laugh. "All has gone well."

Since I left Omdurman I had not seen a laugh upon his face, and I knew that on this side of the river we had nothing more to fear.

So on we went, driving the weary camels forward with the stick without much mercy, till, leaving a range of hills on our right, we reached the Kerraba.

The Kerraba is a plateau with a sandy soil. The surface is covered with black stones, ranging from the size of a man's fist to that of his head, packed closely together. Single blocks of rock are seen at a certain distance one from another. The animals could scarcely make any progress over the rolling level. It was a break-neck march. Towards evening, we saw the Nile in the far, far distance, like a silver streak across the landscape. Climbing down from the plateau in the darkness we reached a valley lying between stony hills. We halted and took the saddles off. The river was about two hours' march away.

"Our mission is near its end," said Hamed and Zeki, as they sat on the ground munching dates. "Stay here with the animals. We will go to a spot we know near the river; and there we shall find your friends, who will escort you on."

I was left alone, looking forward in the highest spirits to the future. Already in imagination I saw my own people, saw my fatherland. I awoke after midnight. No one had come, and I began to feel somewhat concerned at the delay, for if they did not soon return I could not cross the river that night. It was not till some two hours before dawn that I heard footsteps. It was Hamed.

"What news?" I asked impatiently.

"None!" was the despairing answer. "We could not find your friends at the place indicated. I returned because you cannot remain here after daybreak. You are too near human habitations, and exposed to the risk of being seen. I left Zeki behind to look for your people. Take the water-skin on your shoulders and some dates. I am too exhausted to carry anything. We must go back on to the Kerraba. There you must stay till the day is over, hidden among the stones."

I did as I was bidden, and reached the plateau in about an hour. After we had marched a little further in the darkness, Hamed stood still.

"Stop here," he said. "Make a ring of stones as camel-herds do in winter to protect themselves from the cold, and lie down between them. You know how to do it. You are just as much an Arab as one of us. In the evening, I will come again to fetch you. I go back to the camels. The people of these parts know me, and I have nothing to fear. If they ask me any questions I shall say I have come from Dar Shaigia to look up some people who are settled here. Luckily, I have some relations here also." He went back. I stood upon the rolling plain alone—abandoned.

I piled the stones on top of one another to a height of about half a metre, leaving just room enough between for myself, my water-skin, and my gun. Morning began to grow gray, and I crept into my hiding-place. The ground beneath was sandy. I dug it up with a flat, pointed stone, and heaped up sufficient between the piles of slabs to prevent my being seen from without. I flung myself on my back in weariness, and stretched out my limbs. Again reflection came and thoughts thronged past. I looked back again to the past, and pictured to myself the *khalifa's* anger at my flight.

My imagination sped once more towards my dear ones. I longed to be united to them again, and, unanticipated, almost insuperable obstacles seemed to be springing up round me. What change has come over me? Where is my motto of *"Never despair?"* However desperate the circumstances in which I may have found myself, I have never lost courage, never abandoned confidence in my ultimate good fortune. Today a sense of fear is pressing on me. Perhaps it is that I am already lying in what will be my grave. But that is, after all, the end of every man. Be his days long or short, he can go no other way. And yet to die in a strange land forsaken! God, up there in heaven, have mercy on me, have mercy on a miserable man who, if he has sinned, has surely bitterly atoned for his transgressions. God have mercy on me! Let me see my friends and dear ones, my fatherland again!

Then I grew calm once more. After all, I thought, in spite of a few little delays, affairs are not so bad. Tonight, I shall cross the river. Tomorrow, I reach the desert. In two or three days, I shall be beyond the reach of danger, and fly towards those I crave to see. I smiled once more, and grew full of confidence and hope. The sun was burning hot. I had brought my *farda*, and held it up over me to keep my face in the shade, waiting in patience for what would follow.

A little after midday, I heard a low whistle, and raised myself to look out over the stones. It was Hamed, who approached me smiling.

"Good news," he cried. "We have found your people."

A sense of joy possessed me as I caught his words, and my lucky star was once more in the ascendant. When he came up to me, he sat down outside the stones.

"You may make yourself more comfortable," he said. "I have kept a good lookout all round. You have nothing to fear. Zeki found your people before daybreak, and just now one of them came over to us to find out where we were. They are ready. In the evening, they will come to fetch you. But you will have to take great care, for your flight is known in this part of the country. Come with me now, or, better still, wait till darkness comes on. I am going now. Can you find the way alone, or shall I come back for you?"

"It is not necessary for you to go over the ground again. I know the place, and will join you in the evening."

The sun had disappeared from the horizon when, with gun and water-skin slung upon my back, I left the spot which had cost me such bitter hours of reflection. When I reached my companions, I found myself in the presence of two men who were strangers to me.

They greeted me, saying, "We are sent by your friend Ahmed Wad Abdalla, and are of the Gihemab tribe. We will take you down to the river. He himself will cross the stream with you. On the other side, the camels are waiting ready to take you across the desert. Take leave of your guides. Their task is done."

I shook my old friends by the hand, and thanked them with words which came from the heart for their devotion. "Farewell, and may we meet again in better times of peace."

We saddled two camels and left the third to my former guides. I mounted, and one of the new-comers got up behind me.

"What is your name?" I asked him.

"They call me Mohammed, sir, and my companion's name is Ishaak."

"Do you go with me across the desert?"

"No, there are others told off for that. Let the camel walk slowly; and it will be better to cover your face in spite of the darkness. Orders came from Berber three days ago to have all the roads closely watched; and the ferries have been put under observation. Still, in our country, you have nothing to fear."

After proceeding for about two hours in an east northeast direction, we approached the river. We could hear the groaning of the water-wheel, the cries and laughter of the slaves and their women at work. As we came up to a small clump of bushes, Mohammed, who was riding behind me, sprang down and said, "Make the camel kneel down, slowly—gently, that he may not grunt, and so attract attention."

They knelt down without a sound.

Bidding me remain there till they returned with Ahmed, they disappeared into the darkness. I waited about an hour, and then saw four men approaching. The tallest of them came up and embraced me. Pressing me to his breast, he said in a low voice,—

"God be praised. Welcome to the land of my fathers. I am your brother Ahmed Ibn Abdalla, of the tribe of Gihemab. Believe my words, you are saved. Mohammed, Ishaak, take the saddles off the camels quietly. Make no noise. Ride a good way on along the stream. Blow the water-skins full of air, and tie them round the camels' necks. Then cross the river at different spots, and tomorrow await my orders near the stones of the 'Fighting Bull.' Meantime, do you follow me," he said, turning to me.

He himself, with the fourth man, took the saddles on their backs, and I followed. A few minutes later, we reached the shore of the sacred Nile, and found, in a little hollow washed out by the current, a tiny boat constructed by my friends themselves, scarcely large enough to hold us. We climbed down the steep bank, got into the boat, and pushed off. It took us more than an hour to cross the stream. When we reached the far side, the other man, who had remained in the little boat, guided it back into the river, and bored a hole in the bottom, swimming to the land while the boat sank in the stream, and with it disappeared all traces of our crossing. We marched for about half an hour, and then Ahmed Abdalla bade me wait there while he went away, to return soon after with a dish of milk and bread.

"Eat and drink," said he, "and have no more fears as to the success of your flight, for I swear to you by God and the Prophet you are saved. I had intended that you should start tonight; but the hour is already too late. It will be better that you should wait till tomorrow evening. Besides, tomorrow is the day when your camels should be watered. As we are here too near to human habitations, my nephew, Ibrahim Ali, will conduct you to a place some distance off which is difficult of access. Wait for me there. I will bring you an animal to ride, or do you feel strong enough to go on foot?"

"I am strong, and can walk," I replied. "Where is Ibrahim Ali?"

"He is here; and he will be your guide through the desert."

It was a black night. Ibrahim went first with an empty water-skin in his hand along the caravan track leading beside the river to Abu Hamed, and I followed. After proceeding about three English miles, he went down to the river, filled the skin half full, and then changed the direction, turning inland. The march was very difficult. The big stones with which the hills were covered hindered one's progress. I was dead beat, and staggered about to right and left like a drunken man. At last we halted by a hollow in the ground.

"This is the spot which my uncle indicated," said Ibrahim, who had kept silence up till now. "Remain quietly here without misgiving.

Tomorrow evening, I shall bring the camels, and we will start. Here is water and bread. I will return now to make my preparations."

Once more I was alone. Once more I was exposed for a long day to the scorching sun; but now it was easy for me to bear, for I was near to the goal I had longed for so wildly. At last the sun disappeared from the horizon; and, after waiting about an hour more, I heard the sound of hoofs moving quickly over the stones. I rose, and recognised Ahmed Abdalla, accompanied by two men on donkeys.

Springing off in haste, he pressed me warmly to his breast. "God be thanked that you are safe! These two men," pointing to his companions, "are my brothers, and have come with me to wish you luck."

I pressed their hands in greeting, and, turning to Ahmed, said, "But I do not understand you—your tremendous spirits—"

"Of course not," he replied, "for you do not know the great danger you have escaped. Listen! Three days ago, the Emir of Berber, Zeki Osman, learned, we know not how, that the Egyptian garrison at Murrat had received important reinforcements, and intended to attack the Mahdist station at Abu Hamed. Zeki Osman is sending reinforcements, and today at noon sixty horsemen and about three hundred foot soldiers passed our dwellings. You know these wild bands who call themselves Ansar (defenders of the faith). We had killed a sheep, and were busy preparing a portion for you to take with you on the road, when they suddenly came upon us by surprise. They consumed what was intended for your provision, and then scattered in search of loot. We were in terrible anxiety on your account, fearing one of these wild fellows might find his way to your hiding-place. Now they have marched on. The curse of God go with them! Thanks be to Him, who has protected you!"

And I also humbly thanked my Creator, who had saved me from this great and unexpected danger. As I learned later, the cmmander-in-chief of the Egyptian army, General Kitchener Pasha, had come to Wadi Haifa to conduct the usual manoeuvres. Captain Machell Bey marched with the Twelfth Sudanese Battalion and two hundred of the Camel Corps from Wadi Haifa to Korosko by Murrat, and this accounted for the rumour of a strengthening of the garrison at Murrat, and the contemplated attack on Abu Hamed.

"The camels will be a little late," said Ahmed, continuing. "I sent them hastily away into the interior when the Dervishes came in, for fear they might press them into service to carry their ammunition or other baggage. If, however, you feel inclined to rest in patience till tomorrow, we should be able to procure fresh provisions."

"No. I want at all hazards to start at once, and want of provisions will not alter my resolve," I replied. "I trust the camels will come soon."

It was towards midnight when they brought in the three animals. Ahmed Abdalla presented my two guides to me. "Ibrahim Ali, the son of my brother, and Yakub Hassan, also a near relative of mine. They will conduct you to Sheikh Hamed Fedai, the head of the Amrab Arabs, who are subject to the Egyptian Government. He will assist you in getting on to Assuan."

We filled the water-skins and took our leave.

"Forgive the failure of provision for your journey," said Ahmed Ibn Abdalla. "It is not my fault. You have meal and dates, enough to keep hunger off, though there are no luxuries."

We rode three hours and a half east northeast before the sun rose, and as the dawn grew gray found ourselves east of Wadi el Homar (the Vale of Asses), which, though called after the wild asses which inhabit it, is in a great measure devoid of vegetation. As we proceeded, the country assumed the genuine characteristics of the desert,—wide stretches of sand, with here and there, at long intervals, ridges of hills, but never a tree or trace of grass. After riding for two days, almost without a halt, we reached the hills of Nuranai, formerly occupied by the Bisharin Arabs. The valley, running in a northeasterly direction for the most part, between ridges with very steep walls, grows mimosa-trees along either side, and in one lateral valley are trees which take their name from the hills.

Ibrahim Ali got off and took an observation from the heights, and, finding that the valley was quite unoccupied, we entered it, hastily watered our camels, and partially filled our water-skins.

The well lies in a hollow some twenty-five yards across, and some eighteen feet deep, dug out with a sharp decline towards the centre. Down this sloping plane there are slabs of rock and stones, serving as steps, by which one descends to the water-hole in the middle. As wells are always places where people are apt to collect, we left the spot and rested in the plain, after crossing the hills of Nuranai in about three hours.

There was a great difference between my former and my present guides. The first were brave, devoted fellows, ready even to sacrifice their lives for me, whereas these new ones were just the contrary. They grumbled at the service which it seems their relative Ahmed Abdalla had forced upon them, and were forever complaining of want of sleep and hunger, and at the danger of the enterprise, the reward for which would go to others. Through their carelessness they had dropped my sandals and tinder-box on the road; and the loss of the former was destined to cause me much trouble later on.

The next day, a Thursday, we reached the groves of Abu Hamed an hour before noon, and though the tribes who at present live in these parts are hostile to the Mahdists, I preferred to remain hidden. Ibrahim Ali and Yakub Hassan had been ordered by Ahmed Abdalla to guide me to Sheikh Hamed Fadai; but this did not suit their views.

They came to me in the afternoon and represented to me the risk they would incur if their people missed them for many days. Since it was certain everything would come to the *khalifa's* ears which was calculated to throw light on the question of who had helped me in my flight, and since their tribe was already under suspicion of being friendly to the Egyptian Government, there was danger not only for them but also for my friend Ahmed Abdalla. In conclusion, they begged to be allowed to go and look for a man who was well known to them both, and living in these parts, who would conduct me further. I saw that their reluctance would prove of more harm than service to me as I proceeded further, and agreed to their proposal, almost with alacrity, so distasteful had both my guides become to me, and bade them settle the matter as quickly as possible according to the best of their powers.

It was not yet sunset when they brought back the man in question. He was an Amrab Arab named Hamed Garhosh, and considerably the wrong side of fifty in years.

"Every man looks to his own advantage and profit," he said curtly to me after the greeting. "Your guides, whom I know well, wish me to show you the way from here to Assuan. I am ready to do so, but what shall I earn by the job?"

"On the day of my arrival, I will pay you there one hundred and twenty *Maria Theresa* dollars, and in addition a present, which I shall calculate according to the manner in which your duties are accomplished."

"I accept," said he, giving me his hand. "God and the Prophet are my witnesses, that I trust you. I know your race. A white man does not lie. I will bring you to your own folk, across untrodden mountain ways, known only to the fowls of the air. Be ready. After the sun is down we start."

I selected the strongest of the three camels for the remainder of my journey, took two water-skins, the greater part of the dates, and a portion of *dhurra* for my provision. As the darkness closed in Hamed Garhosh arrived.

His son had gone away on the only camel which he possessed, to the country of Robatab near the river, to fetch grain, and he was therefore obliged to perform his functions as guide on foot. Since the road was most of it mountainous, however, and the camel could only go at a foot's pace, he would not be any the worse off on that account. It was merely a question of good-will and stout legs. I took leave of Ibrahim and Yakub with few words; and, there was no doubt about it, we were mutually glad to part company.

After a march of more than two days, crossing for the most part bare ridges and stony hills, we reached, on Sunday morning, a small well, nearly dried up, called "Shof el Ain;" and though presumably it was not likely to be visited by any one, I waited for my guide, as he desired, at a spot an hour's distance from it.

Our food consisted of dates and bread which we baked ourselves. That is to say, an apology for bread, for I am convinced, though my guide prided himself particularly on his talent, that the stuff which he produced would give our European bakers a proper sense of disgust, both on account of its appearance and its taste. To prepare it, my guide piled together a lot of stones about the size of pigeon's eggs, and laid dry wood on top of them. Then he kneaded dhurra mixed with water in a wooden vessel, and lighted his pile of fuel with flint and tinder. When the wood had burned out, he removed the embers from the glowing stones, poured his dough over them, and then replaced the embers on the top of that again.

A few minutes after he rescued his work of art from its fiery grave, beat it severely with a stick, to remove the superfluous ashes and stones which stuck to it, and served it up. This abortive production we ate, if not quite with pleasure, at any rate with hearty appetite, and realised the truth of the proverb. After resting a little while, we left the neighbourhood of the fountain, and, in a few hours, reached the first slopes of the Etbai mountains.

These mountains (El Etbai), stretching between the Red Sea and the Nile, are inhabited in the southern portion by Bisharin and Amrab Arabs, and in the north by the Ababda tribe. Between lofty black cliffs, absolutely bare of vegetation, rising in sheer perpendicular, stretch broad valleys well wooded, which the camel-breeders of these tribes pasture in. We traversed a well-nigh impassable road, moving on without resting, impelled by my desire to see my own folk and to finish the weary journey as quickly as possible. Though we had nothing more to fear, for we were by now out of the power of the Mahdists and on Egyptian territory, my guide insisted on the importance of not being seen. He was afraid of being recognised by the people, who have commercial relations with the Sudan. Since his home lay on the border, and he was often obliged for various reasons to go to Berber, the knowledge that he had served me in my flight might be fraught with most serious consequences for him.

But with him the spirit was willing though the flesh was weak. Being already advanced in years, the want of proper food and the overtaxing march had their effect on his health. In addition to this, he felt the cold, which was often severe, so much that he fell ill, although I had made over to him my *jibba*, and had nothing myself upon my body but the *farda* and *hezam* (a strip of woollen cloth to wind round the body, eight to nine yards in length). In order to get on I made over the camel to him for the last four days, and walked behind him with my bare feet over the stones; for my former guides had lost my sandals, and this was therefore for me, from the physical point of view, the hardest part of my journey.

Even our camel seemed to be going to leave us in the lurch. He had got a raw place on his off fore-foot, and had besides injured it so severely with a pointed stone that the unfortunate beast could hardly walk on it. I was obliged to sacrifice one of my hezamin, with which, by binding it in quadruple fold, I made a kind of shoe for him, which had, however, to be renewed every twenty-four hours. I had seen this done by camel-herds in Darfur, though they use leather for the purpose, and the old experience now stood me in good stead.

At last, on Saturday, the 16th of March, in the morning at sunrise, descending from the heights, I saw the river Nile and the town of Assuan along its shore. I cannot describe the feelings of joy which possessed me. My woes were at an end; saved from the hands of fanatical barbarians, my eyes beheld for the first time the dwellings of civilised people, in a country governed with law and justice by its ruler. My heart went out to my Creator in thankfulness for His protection and His guiding hand.

I was received in the most friendly manner at their quarters by the English officers in His Highness the Khedive's service, and the Egyptian officers, who only just then learned the surprising news of my arrival; and each vied with the other to do all that was in his power to help me to forget the miseries I had gone through.

The commanding officer and governor of the frontier, who happened to have arrived almost at the same moment in Assuan, Colonel Hunter Pasha, as well as his officers, Majors Jackson, Sidney, and Machell Bey, with Bimbashi Watson, and others whose names I cannot at this moment call to mind, generously placed their wardrobes at my disposal; and I availed myself of their kindness for what was strictly indispensable. Before, however, I changed my clothes, my excellent friend Watson, who is a capital artist, asked leave to make a sketch of me, a request to which I was delighted to accede.

As to my guide, Hamed Garhosh, with the assistance of a former acquaintance, Butros Bey Serkis, who is now British Vice-Consul in Assuan, I at once paid him the one hundred and twenty *Maria Theresa* dollars. He also received from me a present of money, clothes, and arms, while over and above this Hunter Pasha presented him with a gift of £10 as a token of joy at my safe arrival; and so, having suddenly become a "man of means," he took a touching farewell of me and departed.

A short time afterwards, telegrams of congratulation arrived. The first was from Major Lewis Bey on behalf of himself and the garrison of Wadi Halfa. The second, from the chief of the Austrian Diplomatic Agency in Egypt, Baron Heidler von Egeregg, who has been so indefatigable on my behalf. Then from my devoted friend, Major Wingate Bey. Baron Victor Herring and his sons, who were travelling on the Nile, were the first of my own countrymen to greet me.

As it happened that the postal steamer was starting that afternoon, I was recommended to avail myself of it to continue my journey. Escorted by all the officers, to the tune of the Austrian national hymn (played by the band of the Sudanese battalion), which it brought the tears into my eyes to hear, I went on board the steamer, amid the hurrahs of a number of tourists of all nations assembled on the bank.

I was deeply moved. Though I have ever tried to live up to my standard of honour in whatever circumstances I have been placed, which, indeed, any officer in a similar position would surely do, I had done nothing to prepare me for, still less to deserve, this public expression of sympathy, and it made me feel very humble.

I travelled in company with Machell Bey, who commands the Twelfth Sudanese Battalion, and whose march during the manoeuvres from Wadi Halfa by Murrat to Korosko had been the cause of

A Camel Corps Scout, Wadi Halfa.

my provisions being eaten up, and of the short commons I had to put up with in the desert. I took a terrible vengeance. He had to submit unconditionally to all my whims in food and drink, and endured his martyrdom with extraordinary good-nature and soldierly fortitude.

When I arrived on Sunday evening in Luxor, I was again the object of a lively demonstration of sympathy from the European travellers, and here received, through Baron Heidler, a telegram from my dear sisters, and from my native city of Vienna. Sisters and native city! How sweet the words sound!

On Monday, at five in the afternoon, we reached Girga, the southernmost station on the Egyptian State railway, and proceeded to Cairo, which I reached at six in the morning, on Tuesday, the 19th of March. In spite of this early hour, Baron Heidler von Egeregg, with his staff, and the Austrian Consul, Dr. Carl Ritter von Goracuchi, had come to the station to meet me; and there, too, was my dear friend Wingate Bey, to whom I can never sufficiently show my gratitude in word or deed. The *Times* correspondent was also there; and Father Rosignoli, with a number of others, and, of course, a photographer taking snapshots.

We drove to the Austrian diplomatic agency, where I was for a long time the guest of the warm-hearted Baron Heidler, who had worked so hard for my freedom, and whose actions were prompted, not only by a desire to do his duty as a representative of the government, but who was actuated by a deep sympathy for the sufferings of a fellow-creature held down in miserable bondage.

On arrival, I found my rooms adorned with the flags of my dear fatherland, and decked with roses and flowers, whilst above the door was written, "A hearty welcome home." On the same day, I received telegrams of congratulations from my family, friends, fellow-students, and from several newspapers. I also met with a hearty welcome from His Royal Highness, Duke Wilhelm of Würtemberg, and His Serene Highness, General Prince Louis Esterhazy, both of whom had been in the Bosnian campaign when I had served there with my regiment, and who greatly honoured me by their expressions of genuine sympathy with me in the hardships I had undergone, and in the joy I now experienced at having escaped at last from the tyrannical thraldom of the *khalifa*.

I was received in audience, soon after my arrival, by His Highness the Khedive of Egypt, who conferred upon me the title of Pasha. I had entered the Sudan sixteen years before as a first lieutenant of the

Austrian army, and, whilst Governor of Darfur, had been granted the Egyptian military grade of lieutenant-colonel, and now, on my return, I was promoted to the rank of colonel, and posted to the Egyptian Intelligence Department.

A few days after my arrival, when seated on the balcony of the Agency, and looking down on the garden all fresh with the verdure of spring, I espied a tame heron stalking across the flower-beds. Instantly I thought of Falz-Fein of Ascania Nova, in Tauride, South Russia, and I hurried to my room, and then and there wrote to him a full account of the crane which he had released in 1892, and which had been killed in Dar Shaigia. It was the greatest pleasure to feel myself in a position to give the former owner of the bird an accurate account of what had happened; and, soon afterwards, I received a reply from Mr. Falz-Fein, who possesses a large estate in the Crimea, thanking me warmly for my letter, and inviting me to pay him a visit, which, unfortunately, the numerous calls on my time have hitherto prevented me from accepting.

A series of official and private calls, numerous invitations, and other social duties so occupied my time that some weeks elapsed before I could undertake any serious work. My first duty was, of course, to submit a detailed official report to my military superiors; and it was not till some time later, that I began to describe the story of my life during the last sixteen years.

My old friend and comrade in captivity, Father Ohrwalder, who is now a missionary at Suakin, took an early opportunity of coming to Cairo to welcome me. Our meeting was indeed a happy one, and I rejoiced to be able to thank him personally for all the assistance he had given in arranging for my escape.

The contrast between my past and present life, the influence of fresh impressions, the many changes I see around me, sometimes make my head feel heavy,—heavy, as though I had just woke up from an evil dream,—twelve years' captivity, a long dream indeed!

It was long before my excitement subsided, but gradually I began to settle down and collect my thoughts. Now again in the midst of civilised society, once more a man among men, my thoughts often turn back to the fanatical barbarians with whom I had to live so long, to my perils and sufferings amongst them, to my unfortunate companions still in captivity, and to the enslaved nations of those remote territories. My thanks are due to God, whose protecting hand has led me safely through all the dangers behind me.

Chapter 20

Conclusion

After more than sixteen years in Africa, including twelve years of captivity, during which I was cut off from all communication with the civilised world, I have at length had the good fortune to return to Europe. How Africa has changed within this period! Regions in the exploration of which Livingstone, Speke, Grant, Baker, Stanley, Cameron, Brazza, Junker, Schweinfurth, Holub, Lenz, and hundreds of others risked their lives, are now accessible to civilisation. In most of these, in which the explorer had formerly to encounter the greatest dangers, there are now military posts and stations to afford security and facilitate the trade which is constantly becoming more active. From the east, Italy, England, Germany, from the west, the Congo State, France, and England, are daily enlarging their spheres of influence, and are now on the point of joining hands in Central Africa.

Wild tribes, who in their modes of life are nearer to beast than to man, are beginning to know new wants, beginning to understand that there are beings mentally superior to themselves, and who, through the appliances of modern civilisation, are unconquerable even in foreign lands. The more northerly of the still independent Mohammedan States—Wadai, Bornu, and the Fellata Kingdoms—will doubtless sooner or later be compelled to conclude alliances with some of the advancing powers, perceiving that only in this way their hereditary rule can be secured.

In the middle of Africa, between the lands just mentioned and the powers advancing from east, south, and west, lies the former Egyptian Sudan, now under the rule of the Khalifa Abdullahi, the despotic head of the Mahdists. No European can venture to cross the limits of this land, cut off from civilisation, extending in the south along the Nile to Reggaf, and east to west from Kassala to near Wadai; death, or lifelong captivity, would be his lot. Yet it is only within the short period of ten years that the land has been subjected to these miserable conditions. For more than seventy years, since the time of Mohammed Ali, it remained under the rule of Egypt, and was open to civilisation. In the chief towns were found Egyptian and European merchants. In Khartum itself, the foreign powers had their representatives. Travellers of all nations could pass through the land unharmed, and found protection and help through their aid. Telegraphs and a regular postal service facilitated intercourse with the most distant countries. Mohammedan mosques, Christian churches, and mission schools looked after the religious and moral education of the young. The land was inhabited by the most diverse tribes, many of which lived in hostility with one another, but were compelled by the strength of the government to keep the peace.

Discontent, no doubt, prevailed in the land; and in the preceding pages I have shown how the avarice and misgovernment of the officials brought about a condition of affairs which rendered the country ripe for revolt. I have endeavoured to explain how Mohammed Ahmed took advantage of the mood of the people, and, well knowing that only a religious factor could unite the hostile tribes, he maintained that he was the *Mahdi* sent by God to deliver the country from foreign yoke, and to regenerate religion, thus bringing into existence that element of fanaticism which throws such a lurid glow over those dark episodes with which the history of the past twelve years of the Sudan has been so replete. Without fanaticism, the revolt could never have been successful, while with it one is brought face to face with a condition of warfare and religious enthusiasm, to find a parallel to which one must go back to mediaeval history and even further.

In the preceding account of my life and adventures, in the vortex itself of this mighty religious movement, I have endeavoured to briefly trace, step by step, the principal causes which have led to the present situation,—changed greatly, it is true, from the time in which the *Mahdi* and his successor were in the zenith of their power, but nevertheless a situation requiring careful handling and a thorough knowledge of details, in order that those concerned may be enabled to grasp accurately the conditions necessary to restore to civilisation this vast expanse of country which has now fallen into an almost indescribable state of moral and religious decadence.

In the Sudan, we have before us a terrible example of a nascent and somewhat crude civilisation suddenly shattered by wild, ignorant, and almost savage tribes who have built over the scattered remnants a form of government based, to some extent, on the lines they found existing, but from which they have eradicated almost every symbol of right, justice, and morality, and for which they have substituted a rule of injustice, ruthless barbarity, and immorality. Nor can I recall any other instance in modern times of a country in which a semblance of civilisation has existed for upwards of half a century, falling back into a state so little removed from absolute barbarism.

But let us consider for a moment what is this new power which has suddenly grown up, and which seems to the European world to block so completely all their civilising efforts, which have during recent years made such startling strides in almost every other part of the vast continent of Africa.

I have endeavoured to show how, on the *Mahdi's* first rise to power, the entire country was with him heart and soul. How, on his death, real fanaticism gradually waned, and gave place to a temporary power wielded, under the cloak of religion, with reckless severity by the *khalifa* and his western Arabs, who, taking the place of the Egyptian garrisons they had destroyed, ruled the unfortunate populations with a rod of iron, and with such oppression and tyranny as to make them long for a return to any form of government which would give them rest and peace.

It is needless for me to recapitulate the horrors and cruelties which have been enacted by the *khalifa* and his followers in order to maintain their position of ascendancy; but it will be sufficient for my purpose to recall here that at least seventy-five *per cent* of the total population has succumbed to war, famine, and disease, while of the remainder the majority are little better than slaves; and that terrible scourge, the slave-trade with all its attendant horrors, is rampant in the land, and includes amongst its victims numbers of Abyssinian Christians, Syrians, Copts, and Egyptians.

The extent of country now governed by the *khalifa* is little altered, it is true, from that occupied originally by the Egyptian Government, but with what a difference! Prosperous districts with a teeming population have been reduced to desert wastes. The great plains over which the western Arabs roamed are deserted, and their places taken by wild animals, while the homesteads of the Nile dwellers are now occupied by those nomad tribes who have driven out the rightful owners of the soil, or enslaved them to till the land for the benefit of their new masters. Deprived of the means of self-defence, reduced by oppression and tyranny to a condition of hopelessness of relief from their foreign task-masters, their powers of resistance crippled, the comparatively small river populations which are left are little better than slaves.

What can they do of themselves against their despotic rulers? It is folly to imagine that the country can right itself by internal revolt. The helping hand must come from without; and the local populations must realise that the first step to re-establish government authority having been taken, there will be no drawing back. They must be convinced that the *khalifa's* power is doomed, and that the bright era of civilisation is assuredly returning. Then, and not till then, will they heartily throw in their lot with the advancing forces, and lend their aid in breaking down the power of the now waning Mahdist Empire. Let it not, however, be supposed that, although I describe this power as declining, it is likely of itself to become extinct within a comparatively short period.

A careful perusal of the last few chapters will, I think, make it clear to all that the means taken by the *khalifa* to render his position secure against his internal enemies has been most thoroughly effective, and, assuming that his authority is not threatened by external influences, I see no cause why, as long as he is alive, he should not maintain his ascendancy. With his death, it is more than probable some internal revulsion will take place, which might, under certain circumstances, displace the dynasty he has attempted to found, but which would not necessarily bring that unfortunate country much nearer to civilising influences than it is at present. Considered, therefore, from this point of view, the necessary palliative still lies in the introduction of external aid.

The above hypothesis does not, however, entirely meet the conditions of the case. Those who wish to study the present situation in the Sudan must not think of that country as it was in the days of Ismail Pasha, when the civilising influence was represented by the Egyptian Government, and when the various countries lying immediately beyond the Egyptian sphere were barbarous or Pagan states, in which Europeans were almost unknown, and the Arab slave-hunter had barely penetrated; that condition has been little else than reversed. The Mahdist authority, as I have already shown, is at once intolerably obstructive and dangerously insecure. The once comparatively civilised Sudan is now occupied by a barbaric power hostile to both European and Ottoman influence. It blocks the way from the central plateaus along the Nile valley to the Mediterranean; it seals up districts which were at one time fairly tranquil, and open to the influences of commerce and civilisation, while the various countries by which it is bordered are now being gradually opened up. Intercourse between them and the outside world is becoming easier; trade is pushing obstacles out of the way; risk to life is lessened by the protective action of European governments; and the savage races by which they are peopled, are beginning to learn the folly of fighting against the resources of civilisation.

To turn from generalisation to details, what do we find to be the present situation? On the east, Egyptian influence is slowly—very slowly—recovering its lost ground in the vicinity of Suakin and Tokar. To the southeast, the Italians have captured Kassala, and have forced the Mahdists to take up a strong line of defence on the west bank of the Atbara River. Further south, the Abyssinians show no present intention of altering the relations which have previously existed between them and the Dervishes. In the mountainous districts of Fazoglu and the Blue Nile, the inhabitants have thrown off allegiance to the *khalifa*. Far away to the south, at the sources of the Nile, British influence is beginning to make itself felt in those regions where Speke, Grant, Baker, and others gained imperishable renown by their magnificent explorations, and by their efforts against slavery and the slave-trade,—regions which will ere long be connected with the coast by a railway which will open up not only the country it traverses, but will also give an exit to the trade of Southern Equatoria and the adjacent countries.

Next to these British possessions comes the Congo Free State, which within the last few years has made such gigantic strides in bringing under its influence large tracts of country, not only in the vicinity of the Mbomu and Ubangi, but in many districts of the Bahr el Ghazal Province and in Equatoria, almost to within striking distance of the Dervish advanced post at Reggaf in the Nile valley, while behind them, in the Haute Ubangi, or even in juxtaposition with them, the enterprising French pioneers are striving to give effect to their colonial dreams, which have of late years been so fully realised in various parts of Africa. Still further to the northwest, the *khalifa's* authority in those districts is menaced by hostile tribesmen who may, sooner or later, become subject to the guidance of European influence penetrating from the west and north of Africa; and, on the extreme north, lies the Egyptian power, which Abdullahi is gradually learning to dread, as being that most likely to be the first to interfere with the uncertain tenure of his empire.

Such, then, is briefly the present defensive and offensive position of the Mahdist Sudan. All-powerful within his dominions, but threatened from all sides from without, there is little doubt that before the onward march of civilising forces the whole empire of the *khalifa* must crumble and collapse,—and what then? Will Egypt once more become the actual possessor of the country of which she was the legitimate owner? Will all those civilising powers who are marching forward unselfishly realise that should they establish themselves on the banks of the navigable Nile, they must not attempt to cut off or minimise the life-giving water supply of Egypt by introducing skilled irrigation within the territories they may have acquired? Will they unselfishly abandon the advantages which they may have secured through the expenditure of blood and treasure, in order that the legitimate rights of Egypt may not be interfered with?

All these questions enter into the domain of practical and current politics, with which it is not my province to deal. I am merely in the position of expressing my views on the importance and value of the Sudan to Egypt; and on this subject I hold a strong opinion. The reasons which first prompted Mohammed Ali, three quarters of a century ago, to take possession of the Sudan, still hold good. As the Nile is the life of Egypt, so every effort must be made to preserve the Nile valley from intrusion. Any advance, therefore, of civilising influences towards that gigantic waterway must naturally be viewed with alarm by those authorities who are fully alive to the danger which would arise by the creation, on the banks of the river, of colonies whose personal interests would predominate over their regard for the preservation and advancement of Egyptian welfare and prosperity.

Here and there, in the preceding pages, I have referred to the immense importance of the Bahr el Ghazal; and it is perhaps not out of place here to recapitulate once again the peculiar position which this province holds in regard to the remainder of the Sudan. It is a most fertile district, extending over an enormous area, watered by a labyrinth of streams, and covered with mountains and forests in which elephants abound, while the low valleys are subject to inundations. The soil is exceptionally good, producing quantities of cotton and India-rubber. There are cattle in abundance; and I estimate the population at between five and six millions. They are capable of making excellent soldiers. Moreover, the continual feuds between the various tribes prevent any combination of the inhabitants as a whole; hence the ease with which foreigners can obtain an ascendancy in the province, and create an efficient local army.

The port of the Bahr el Ghazal was Meshra er Rek. To this place steamers periodically ascended from Khartum, but were often stopped by the floating vegetation which from time to time blocks the passage of the Upper Nile. Just south of Fashoda, the river emerges from what may have been the bed of an ancient lake. Into this wide marsh trickle a great number of winding streams which are often completely blocked by the suds; and through these dense barriers travellers must at times cut their way with swords and axes. Sir Samuel Baker's expedition, 1870-1874, was delayed a year from this cause.

The geographical and strategical position of the province, therefore, with reference to the rest of the Sudan, renders its possession of the greatest importance. The presence of foreigners, unconcerned in the preservation of Egyptian interests, having at their command the vast resources of this great country, which are estimated at a much higher value in both men and materials than those of any portion of the Nile valley, would place them in such a predominating position as to endanger any occupation by Egypt of her lost provinces.

In the preceding pages, I have described all I know of the movements of Europeans in these districts; and it is possible an attempt in force on their part to reach the Nile *via* Meshra er Rek, or the Bahr el Homr, or Bahr el Arab, might meet with some opposition from the Mahdists, but if well-conducted it would, in all probability, result in their losing their province.

If, therefore, the *khalifa* were to learn that the "Whites" in the Bahr el Ghazal were in greater force than his present information leads him to suppose, he might engage in a campaign against them; and in this case he would be obliged to send reinforcements from Omdurman,—a matter of some difficulty, as the drain on his resources caused by the maintenance of large forces at the threatened points on the Atbara opposite Kassala, and in the Dongola province, is considerable.

Reverting to the Dervish situation in Darfur and Kordofan, it should be noted that the present force of the Emir Mahmud amounts to some thousands of rifle and spear men, scattered in garrisons at El Fasher, Shakka, and El Obeid. Mahmud himself resides at El Fasher with the bulk of this force, and is constantly at war with the Dar Gimr, Massalit, Tama, Beni Hussein, Hotir, and other tribes of the Kebkebia and Kulkul districts. Recently, one of Mahmud's lieutenants, Fadlalla, was killed, and his force of six hundred men heavily defeated in a contest with these revolted tribes; and, just at the time I left Omdurman, permission had been given to Mahmud to send out a punitive expedition from El Fasher, which appears to have been partially successful. These tribes, although nominally independent, owe a certain allegiance to the Wadai Sultanate. It is, therefore, erroneous to suppose that they are acting under the direction of Rabeh Zubeir, whose hostility to Wadai is well known, and whose authority does not extend so far to the east, and now appears to be centred in the districts lying south and southwest of Lake Tchad.

Such, then, was the state of affairs in these southern and western districts when I left the Sudan; and, since my arrival in the midst of civilisation, I have frequently seen many strange and conflicting reports in the press as to the situation in these distant regions, and although concurring with the view that the onward march of civilising forces must eventually cause the collapse of the Mahdist Empire, I feel that my unique position in the centre of Dervish authority entitles me to give a word of warning to the country whose interests I endeavoured for long years to uphold, and whose eventual welfare and prosperity, in a recovered Egyptian Sudan, I earnestly long to see.

I would merely impress upon her the fact that time and tide wait for no man; that whilst she is contemplating with longing eyes the recovery of her lost provinces, there is always the possibility that they may fall into the hands of others who may prove more difficult to dislodge than the *khalifa*, and who, by bringing engineering skill on the life-giving waters of Egypt, may endanger its very existence, and who would—though it is undoubtedly the lesser of two evils—deprive that country of the rich blessings of trade and commerce which, under a beneficent administration in the Sudan, would give wealth and prosperity both to the parent Egypt and her recovered Nile provinces.

With these few words of friendly advice to the country to whose services I rejoice to have returned after twelve long years of captivity, I now end this narrative. But ere I close, I will relate yet one more incident which, were I superstitious, I would consider presaged well for the recovery of what has been lost. In December, 1883, when force of circumstances obliged me to surrender to the *Mahdi*, the sword of Austrian pattern which I had received on entering the Austrian army, and on which I had had my name engraved in Arabic characters, was taken from me.

In August, 1895, when I came to London to attend the Geographical Congress, it was returned to me by Mr. John Cook, Sen., of the firm of Thomas Cook & Son, at his office in Ludgate Circus. It appears that Mr. John Cook had, in 1890, purchased this sword from a native of Luxor, on the banks of the Nile, his attention having been attracted by the Arabic inscription on the blade, from which my friend, Major Wingate, whom he met shortly afterwards, was able to decipher my name. It is, I think, likely the *Mahdi* had presented my sword to one of his followers who had taken part in the invasion of Egypt by Nejumi, in 1889; and when that redoubtable *emir* was overthrown by General Sir Francis Grenfell on the field of Toski, it is probable that the wearer of my sword fell too, and the long-lost weapon was taken from the field by a villager, from whom Mr. Cook purchased it. To have lost my much-prized first sword in the wilds of Darfur, and to find it again in the heart of London, is almost more than a coincidence.

During the last sixteen years, I have led a life of strange vicissitudes; and I have endeavoured to narrate as simply as I could my unique experiences, in the hope that my story may not only prove of interest to those who have shown sympathy with the hard fate of the European captives in the Sudan, but with the most earnest desire that these my experiences may prove of some value when the time for action may arise, and when, if God wills, my services may be utilised in helping to abolish the rule of my tyrannical master and lifelong enemy, the Khalifa Abdullahi, and re-establish in that country the government authority I struggled with some measure of success, but alas vainly, to uphold.

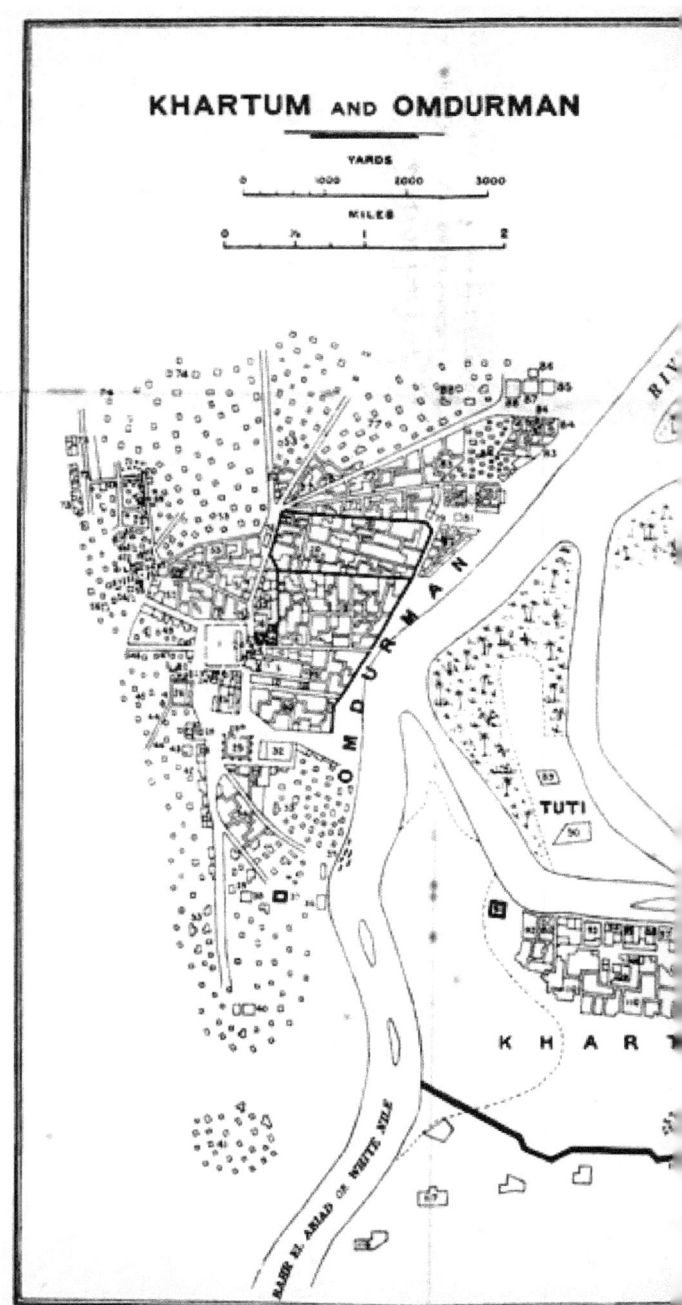

Khartum and Omdurman

OMDURMAN.

1. The Mosque
2. Mihrab
3. Kubbet el Mahdi (Mahdi's tomb)
4. The tin Mosque
5. Khalifa's enclosure
6. Khalifa's special court
7. Khalifa's Palace
8. Khalifa's Harem
9. Khalifa's kuran school
10. Houses of Khalifa's Mulazemin (body guards)
11. House of Mahdi's son
12. Khalifa's stables
13. Khalifa's stores
14. Mahdi's Harem
15. House of Mahdi's family
16. Khalifa Ali Wad Helu's house
17. Houses of Khalifa Ali Wad Helu's Mulazemin & relations
18. House of Khalifa's son (Osman)
19. Great stone wall of Omdurman
20. Mud wall of Omdurman
21. House of the Khalifa's relations
22. Slatin's new house
23. Houses of Kadis
24.
25. Yakub's old house
26. Yakub's new house
27. Houses of Yakub's kateb
28. Slatin's old house
29. Beit el Amana
30a. Flag & drum stores
30. Other houses of Khalifa's relations
31. Prison
32. Arms Factory
33. Quarters of the Western people
34. Quarters of Borgo & Takarna people
35. Mashra (Ferry)
36. Khalifa's house on the Nile
37. Old fort of Omdurman
38. House of the commandant of Jehadia
39. Quarters of the Black Jehadia
40. Khalifa's house in Dem Yunes
41. Hillet village of the Fetihab Arabs
42. Quarters of Bornu, Fellata & Gowama people
43. House of Nur Angara
44. Quarters of Homr Arabs
45. Quarters of Kababish and other camel-owning Arabs
46. Quarters of Hamar Arabs
47. Quarters of Habbania Arabs
48. Quarters of Rizighat Arabs
49. Quarters of Kanana Arabs
50. House of Abdulla Wad Ahmed
51. Quarters of Degheim Arabs
52. Quarters of White Nile tribes
53. Quarters of Jaalin Arabs
54. Carpenters' shops
55. Market courts of justice
56. Scaffolds
57. Salt Market
58. Linen & cloth market
59. Barbers' shops
60. Tailors' shops
61. Vegetable market
62. Butchers' shops
63. Forage market
64. Grain & date market
65. Grain & date stores
66. Wood market
67. Women's market
68. European cook shops
69. The Muslimania quarter
70. Old house of Father Ohrwalder
71. Cemetry
72. Houses of Ahmed Sharfi & family of Khalifa Sherif
73. Quarters of Kunuz Barabra
74. Quarters of the Danagla
75. Quarters of the Beni Jarrar Arabs
76. Tombs of the Martyrs
77. Quarters of different tribes
78. Tombs of the Mahdi's family & relations
79. Powder factory
80. Beit el Mal
81. Slave market
82. Commissariat stores of the Mulazemin & Katebs
83. Quarters of the Fur tribes
84. Quarters of the Egyptians (Ibrahim Pasha Fauzi, Said Bey Guma, Yusef Efendi Mansur & others)
85. Khalifa's Hejra house
86. Khalifa Ali Wad Hulu's Hejra house
87. The Hejra Mosque
88. Quarters of the Wad el Besir & Hellawin Arabs

TUTI ISLAND.

89. Powder Magazine
90. Tuti village

KHARTUM.

91. Mukran fort
92. Gardens
93. Church
94. Sanitary Department
95. Post and Finance offices
96. Austrian Consulate
97. Government House (Hekemdaria)
98. Governor's palace (Saraya)
99. Grain stores
100. Arsenal
101. Barracks
102. Hospital
103. Fort Burri
104. Small arms, ammunition stores
105. Artillery ammunition stores
106. Cartridge factory
107. A place of worship
108. French Consulate
109. Italian Consulate
110. Houses of the natives
111. Bab el Messallamia
112. Fort Kalakla
113. The Eastern palace (Saraya)
114. North Fort

115. Khojali
116. Burri
117. Kalakla
118. Shagaret Mobbi Bey
119. Halfaya

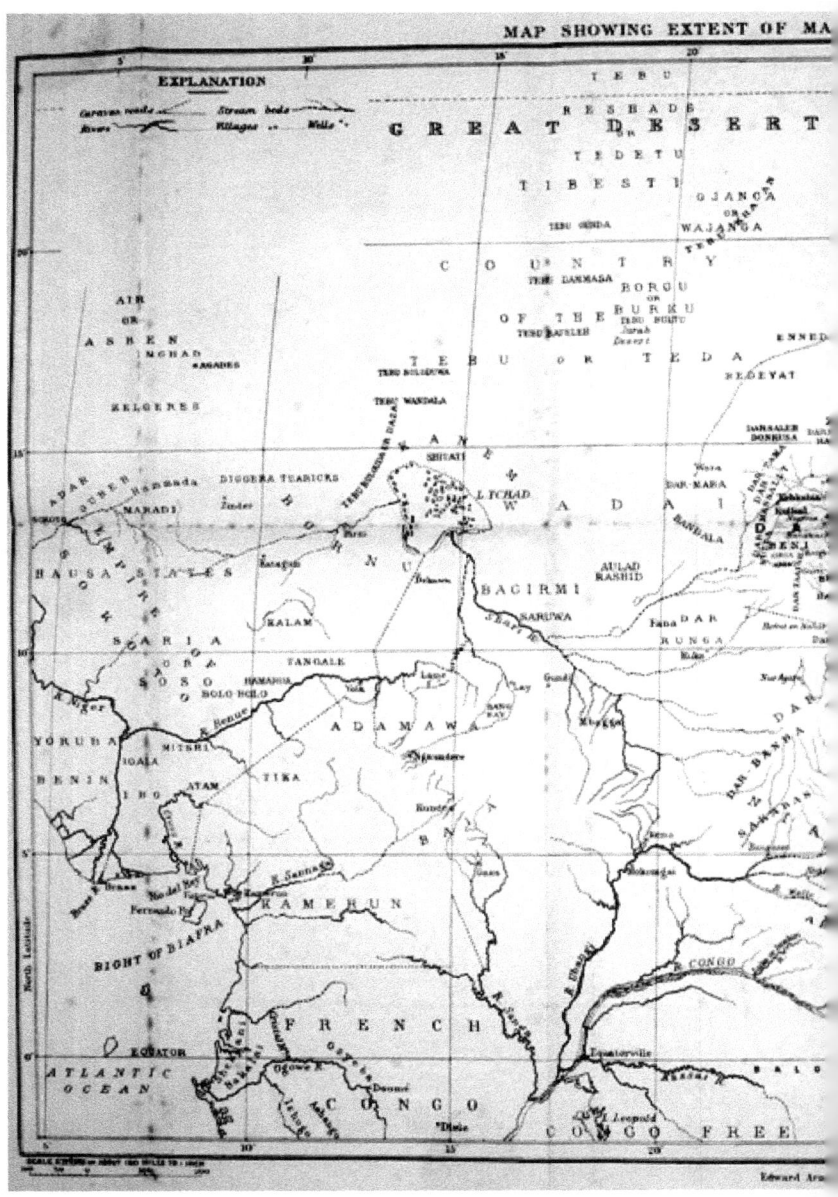

Map Showing Extent of

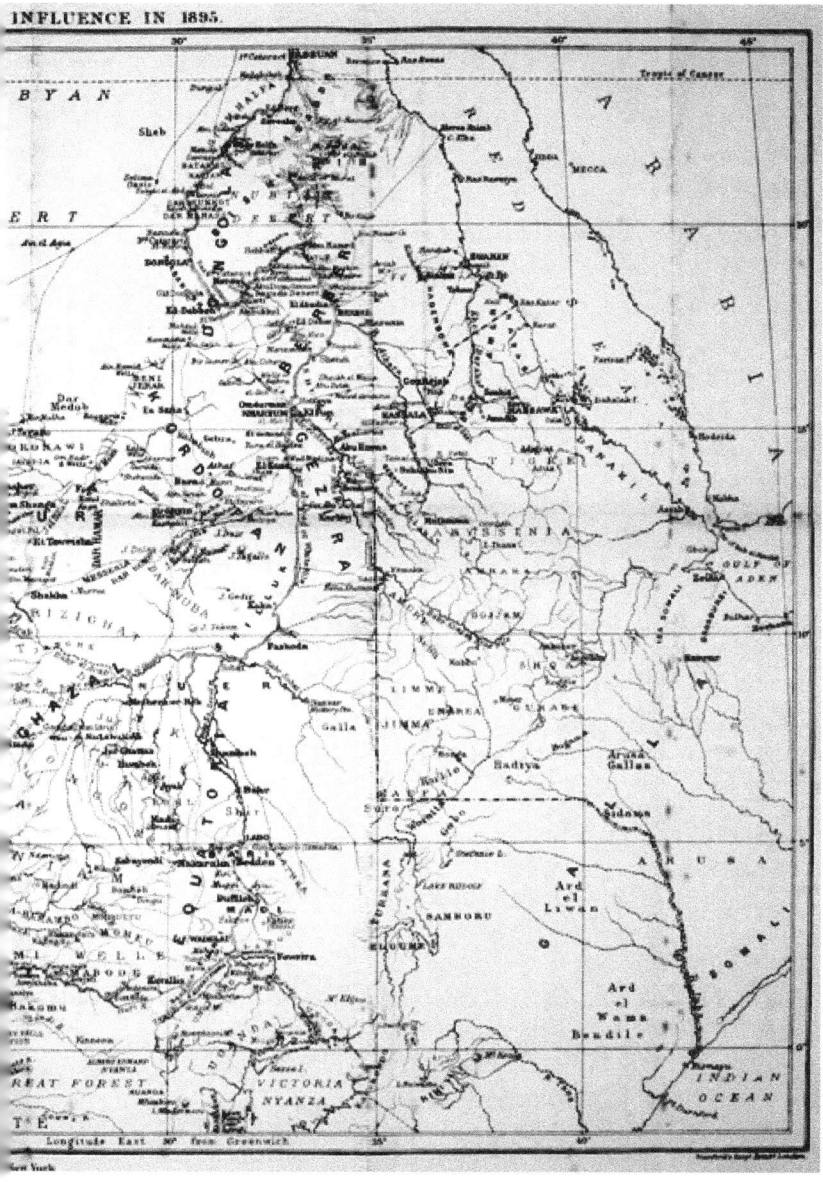

Mahdist Influence in 1895

ALSO FROM LEONAUR
AVAILABLE IN SOFTCOVER OR HARDCOVER WITH DUST JACKET

AT THEM WITH THE BAYONET by *Donald F. Featherstone*—The first Anglo-Sikh War 1845-1846.

STEPHEN CRANE'S BATTLES by *Stephen Crane*—Nine Decisive Battles Recounted by the Author of 'The Red Badge of Courage'.

THE GURKHA WAR by *H. T. Prinsep*—The Anglo-Nepalese Conflict in North East India 1814-1816.

FIRE & BLOOD by *G. R. Gleig*—The burning of Washington & the battle of New Orleans, 1814, through the eyes of a young British soldier.

SOUND ADVANCE! by *Joseph Anderson*—Experiences of an officer of HM 50th regiment in Australia, Burma & the Gwalior war.

THE CAMPAIGN OF THE INDUS by *Thomas Holdsworth*—Experiences of a British Officer of the 2nd (Queen's Royal) Regiment in the Campaign to Place Shah Shuja on the Throne of Afghanistan 1838 - 1840.

WITH THE MADRAS EUROPEAN REGIMENT IN BURMA by *John Butler*—The Experiences of an Officer of the Honourable East India Company's Army During the First Anglo-Burmese War 1824 - 1826.

IN ZULULAND WITH THE BRITISH ARMY by *Charles L. Norris-Newman*—The Anglo-Zulu war of 1879 through the first-hand experiences of a special correspondent.

BESIEGED IN LUCKNOW by *Martin Richard Gubbins*—The first Anglo-Sikh War 1845-1846.

A TIGER ON HORSEBACK by *L. March Phillips*—The Experiences of a Trooper & Officer of Rimington's Guides - The Tigers - during the Anglo-Boer war 1899 - 1902.

SEPOYS, SIEGE & STORM by *Charles John Griffiths*—The Experiences of a young officer of H.M.'s 61st Regiment at Ferozepore, Delhi ridge and at the fall of Delhi during the Indian mutiny 1857.

CAMPAIGNING IN ZULULAND by *W. E. Montague*—Experiences on campaign during the Zulu war of 1879 with the 94th Regiment.

THE STORY OF THE GUIDES by *G.J. Younghusband*—The Exploits of the Soldiers of the famous Indian Army Regiment from the northwest frontier 1847 - 1900.

AVAILABLE ONLINE AT **www.leonaur.com**
AND FROM ALL GOOD BOOK STORES

www.ingramcontent.com/pod-product-compliance
Lightning Source LLC
Chambersburg PA
CBHW030359100426
42812CB00028B/2772/J